ASSET PRICING FOR DYNAMIC ECONOMIES

This introduction to general equilibrium modeling takes an integrated approach to the analysis of macroeconomics and finance. It provides students, practitioners, and policymakers with an easily accessible set of tools that can be used to analyze a wide range of economic phenomena.

Key features:

- Provides a consistent framework for understanding dynamic economic models.
- Introduces key concepts in finance in a discrete time setting.
- Develops a simple recursive approach for analyzing a variety of problems in a dynamic, stochastic environment.
- Sequentially builds up the analysis of consumption, production, and investment models to study their implications for allocations and asset prices.
- Reviews business cycle analysis and the business cycle implications of monetary and international models.
- Covers latest research on asset pricing in overlapping generations models and on models with borrowing constraints and transaction costs.
- Includes end-of-chapter exercises allowing readers to monitor their understanding of each topic.

Online resources available at www.cambridge.org/altug_labadie

SUMRU ALTUG is Professor of Economics at Koç University, Istanbul, and Research Fellow on the International Macroeconomics Programme at the Centre for Economic Policy Research (CEPR), London.

PAMELA LABADIE is Professor of Economics at George Washington University, Washington DC.

ASSET PRICING FOR DYNAMIC ECONOMIES

SUMRU ALTUG AND PAMELA LABADIE

CAMBRIDGE
UNIVERSITY PRESS

CAMBRIDGE
UNIVERSITY PRESS

University Printing House, Cambridge CB2 8BS, United Kingdom

One Liberty Plaza, 20th Floor, New York, NY 10006, USA

477 Williamstown Road, Port Melbourne, VIC 3207, Australia

314-321, 3rd Floor, Plot 3, Splendor Forum, Jasola District Centre, New Delhi - 110025, India

79 Anson Road, #06-04/06, Singapore 079906

Cambridge University Press is part of the University of Cambridge.

It furthers the University's mission by disseminating knowledge in the pursuit of education, learning and research at the highest international levels of excellence.

www.cambridge.org
Information on this title: www.cambridge.org/9780521699143

First published 2008

A catalogue record for this publication is available from the British Library

Library of Congress Cataloging in Publication data
Altug, Sumru.
Asset pricing for dynamic economics / Sumru Altug and Pamela Labadie.
p. cm.
ISBN 978-0-521-87585-1
1. Capital assets pricing model. I. Labadie, Pamela, 1953– II. Title.
HG4636.A448 2008
332.6–dc22
2008024826

ISBN 978-0-521-87585-1 Hardback
ISBN 978-0-521-69914-3 Paperback

Contents

List of figures

List of tables

Preface

The starting point for any analysis in finance involves assigning a current price to a future stream of uncertain payoffs. This is the basic notion behind any asset-pricing model. Take, for example, the price of a share to a competitive firm. Since the share entitles the owner to claims for the future profits of the firm, a central problem is to assign a value to these future profits. Take another asset – a house. This provides housing services in all states of nature and at all dates. Consequently, the value of the house today must reflect the value of these future services. Other examples include the pricing of durable goods or investment projects based on their future expected marginal products. One approach to monetary economics also follows this basic principle – if money as an asset has value in equilibrium (in the absence of any legal restrictions), then this value must reflect the stream of services provided by this asset.

Our approach is to derive pricing relationships for different assets by specifying the economic environment at the outset. One of the earliest examples of this approach is Merton [342]. However, Merton does not relate the technological sources of uncertainty to the equilibrium prices of the risky assets. Alternatively, he assumes a given stochastic process for the returns of different types of assets and then prices them given assumptions about consumer preferences. Consequently, the supply side is not explicitly considered by Merton. The asset-pricing model of Lucas [317] is fully general equilibrium but it is an endowment economy, so that consumption and investment decisions are trivial. Brock [76] develops an asset-pricing model with both the demand and supply side fully specified and links it up to Ross's [369] arbitrage pricing model.

In this book, we will start from an explicit economic environment and deduce the implications for asset prices, and the form of the asset-pricing function from the equilibrium in these environments. To study the problem of asset pricing, we could also follow another approach: we could take a very general and abstract approach, viewing asset pricing as the valuation of a future stream of uncertain payoffs from the asset according to a general pricing function. Given a minimal set of assumptions about the set of payoffs, we could try to characterize the properties of this abstract pricing function. This is the approach taken by Ross [371],

Harrison and Kreps [240], Chamberlain and Rothschild [100], amongst others. One general point to note about the relationship between the two approaches to asset pricing is that the former abstract approach acquires economic content when interpreted in terms of the equilibrium approach. In fact, the benchmark payoff in the pricing function used to price streams of uncertain payoffs turns out to be the intertemporal marginal rate of substitution function for consumption. Depending on the nature of heterogeneity among consumers, the existence of complete contingent claims markets, and the role of money for acquiring consumption goods, the form of this intertemporal marginal rate of substitution function changes.

The purpose of this book is to provide an integrated treatment of a variety of dynamic equilibrium frameworks and to examine their empirical implications. The book is organized in four main parts. In Part I, we present material that constitutes the basis for much thinking in dynamic macroeconomics and finance. We begin by describing a simple version of the Arrow-Debreu contingent claims model, which is one of the building blocks of asset pricing. We also present the basics of arbitrage and asset valuation, expected utility analysis, CAPM and APT, and consumption/savings decisions under uncertainty. In Part II, we present a more fully developed set of results for dynamic economies under uncertainty using a recursive approach. In this part, we describe a pure exchange, representative consumer economy as well as economies with production. This framework allows us to derive the form of the asset-valuation function and to examine such issues as the effects of taxation on asset returns, the optimal financial structure of a firm, and the role of uncertainty in determining asset pricing and equilibrium allocations. Part III is devoted to cash-in-advance models, which allow us to examine the effects of inflation and exchange rate risk. Part IV presents material at a slightly more advanced level. In this part, we examine questions related to market incompleteness and the effects of frictions such as transactions costs. We consider the effects of borrowing constraints on equilibrium allocations and prices in a model with consumer heterogeneity and idiosyncratic risk. The stochastic overlapping generations model has been suggested as a convenient framework for analyzing issues related to "bubbles" in asset prices and the determinants of savings decisions with intergenerational heterogeneity among consumers. We examine a variety of issues using the stochastic overlapping generations framework. In many recent empirical applications of dynamic models, numerical solution methods have been combined with simulation or estimation procedures to assess quantitatively the importance of alternative model features. In this book, we also describe how numerical dynamic programming methods and other numerical methods can be used for solving and simulating a variety of dynamic economic problems.

There are many excellent texts in macroeconomics and finance that also cover material that is presented in this text. Cochrane's [109] text is an excellent reference that covers all of the standard issues in finance, updated using the modern approach to asset pricing. The texts by Darell Duffie [159, 161] also present the modern general equilibrium approach to finance but they are more technical in nature and help to serve as useful references, especially for advanced graduate students. The texts by Ingersoll [261], Huang and Litzenberger [256], Jarrow [263], Copeland and Weston [127], Hull [259], amongst others, present many of the standard issues of finance at differing levels of abstraction. They are recommended for students who (i) either lack a more traditional knowledge of finance and financial markets, or (ii) wish to obtain more detailed knowledge of some of the issues that we cover in this book. There is also some overlap between the topics we consider in this book and other texts dealing with dynamic general equilibrium modeling or macroeconomics such as Sargent [384] or Ljungqvist and Sargent [325].

A unifying feature of our discussion is that many of the dynamic equilibrium models that we consider can be formulated as dynamic programming problems and solved using a contraction mapping approach. Rather than introduce explicit measure-theoretic considerations for analyzing dynamic stochastic models, we describe uncertainty in terms of Markov uncertainty in a discrete-time setting. In Chapter 6, we provide a review of some results from functional analysis that we use in later chapters. For a review of basic results from functional analysis, we refer the reader to Kreyszig [290] and Naylor and Sell [351], and to Papoulis [356] for a review of probability theory and stochastic processes.

We have provided a set of detailed exercises at the end of each chapter and their solutions as a separate file. These exercises are intended to introduce some new topics at the same time that they allow the student to apply the methods described earlier. We developed this book from our teaching of finance, graduate financial economics and macroeconomics at the University of York, Duke University, the University of Minnesota, the University of Wisconsin, and Columbia University. It reflects our desire to provide a unified treatment of material that we could not find in one place. For teaching purposes, this text can be used as the basis for a graduate macroeconomics or financial economics course. We hope that this text will also prove useful to students and practitioners in the fields of macroeconomics, finance, applied general equilibrium modeling, and structural econometrics.

Paul Soderlind gave many useful comments that helped to improve the current version of this text. We have also received helpful comments from various colleagues for the first edition of the text, including Erdem Başci, Thomas Cooley, Scott Freeman, Christian Gilles, Jeremy Greenwood, Steve LeRoy, Bruce Smith, Allan Stockman, the participants of the International Workshop at the University of Rochester, and of a series of seminars at Bilkent University in Ankara, Turkey. We thank Zhenyu Wang for many helpful comments and the numerical calculations. Finally, we are grateful to Irem Demirci and Muharrem Yeşilırmak from Koç University for reading through the chapters and providing editorial comments, for writing exercises and solutions to various chapters, and assisting with other aspects of the production of this manuscript.

PART I

Basic concepts

CHAPTER 1

Complete contingent claims

In competitive asset markets, consumers make intertemporal choices in an uncertain environment. Their attitudes toward risk, production opportunities, and the nature of trades that they can enter into determine equilibrium quantities and the prices of assets that are traded. The intertemporal choice problem of a consumer in an uncertain environment yields restrictions for the behavior of individual consumption over time as well as determining the form of the asset-pricing function used to price random payoffs.

We begin by describing the simplest setup in which consumer choices are made and asset prices are determined, namely, a complete contingent claims equilibrium for a pure endowment economy. In such an equilibrium, a consumer can trade claims to contracts with payoffs that depend on the state of the world, for all possible states. As a precursor of the material to follow, we discuss the relationship of the complete contingent claims equilibrium to security market equilibrium and describe its implications for asset pricing.

The complete contingent claims equilibrium can also be used to derive restrictions for the behavior of consumption allocations. In this context, we discuss the relationship between the contingent claims equilibrium and Pareto optimality, and show the existence of a "representative consumer" that can be constructed by exploiting the Pareto optimality of the contingent claims equilibrium. Some conclusions follow.

1.1. A ONE-PERIOD MODEL

We initially consider economies with one date and a finite number of states. To understand the nature of the trades that take place in a complete contingent claims equilibrium, imagine that all agents get together at time 0 to write contracts that pay off contingent on some state occurring next period. The realization of the states is not known at the time the contracts are written, although agents know the probabilities and the set of all possible states. Once the contracts are signed, the realization of the state is observed by all agents, and the relevant state-dependent trade is carried out.

We assume the following setup:

- There is a set of I consumers, $\{1, 2, \ldots, I\}$
- Each consumer associates the probability π_s^i to state s occurring, where $0 < \pi_s^i < 1$ and

$$\sum_{s=1}^{S} \pi_s^i = 1.$$

- There are M commodities.
- The notation $c_{s,m}^i$ denotes the consumption of agent i in state s of commodity m.
- A consumption vector for agent i is

$$c^i \equiv \{c_{1,1}^i, \ldots, c_{S,1}^i, c_{1,2}^i, \ldots, c_{S,2}^i, \ldots c_{1,M}^i, \ldots, c_{S,M}^i\},$$

which is a vector of length $S \times M$. Consumption is always non-negative and real so that $c_{s,m}^i \in \Re_+$. The *commodity space* is $\Re_+^{SM}$. The commodity space is the space over which consumption choices are made. When there is a finite number of states (or dates) and a finite number of commodities at each state (or date), we say that the commodity space is finite-dimensional.
- The endowment of agent i is a vector of length $S \times M$,

$$\omega^i = \{\omega_{1,1}^i, \ldots, \omega_{S,M}\}$$

The utility of consumer i is a function $u_i : \Re_+^{SM} \to \Re$,

$$u_i(c^i) = \sum_{s=1}^{S} \pi_s^i U_i(c_{s,1}^i, \ldots, c_{s,M}^i) \tag{1.1}$$

Notice that we assume that utility is additive across states, which is the expected utility assumption.

Here are some definitions.

- An allocation is a vector $(c^1, \ldots, c^I)$.
- An allocation is *feasible* if

$$\sum_{i=1}^{I} [c_{s,m}^i - \omega_{s,m}^i] \leq 0 \tag{1.2}$$

for $s = 1, \ldots, S$ and $m = 1, \ldots, M$. This holds for each commodity and for each state.
- An allocation $(c^1, \ldots, c^I)$ is *Pareto optimal* if there is no other feasible allocation $(\hat{c}^1, \ldots, \hat{c}^I)$ such that

$$u_i(\hat{c}^i) \geq u_i(c^i) \quad \text{for all } i \tag{1.3}$$

and

$$u_i(\hat{c}^i) > u_i(c^i) \quad \text{for some } i. \tag{1.4}$$

1.1.1. Contingent claims equilibrium

Imagine now that agents trade contingent claims – which are agreements of the form that, if state s occurs, agent i will transfer a certain amount of his endowment of good m to agent j. Since there are S states and M commodities in each state, a total of $S \times M$ contingent claims will be traded in this economy. For each state and commodity, let $p_{s,m}$ denote the price of a claim to a unit of consumption of the mth commodity to be delivered contingent on the s'th state occurring. The set of prices $p \in \Re_+^{SM}$ is a *price system*. The price function p assigns a cost to any consumption c^i and a value to any endowment ω^i; in our application $p : \Re_+^{SM} \to \Re_+$ has an inner product representation:

$$p \cdot c \equiv \sum_{s=1}^{S} \sum_{m=1}^{M} p_{s,m} c_{s,m} = \sum_{s=1}^{S} \left(p_{s,1} c_{s,1} + \cdots + p_{s,M} c_{s,M}\right).^{1}$$

The markets for contingent claims open before the true state of the world is revealed. Afterwards, deliveries of the different commodities are made according to the contracts negotiated before the state is realized and then consumption occurs.

A *complete contingent claims equilibrium* (CCE) is a non-zero price function p on $\Re_+^{SM}$ and a feasible allocation $(c^1, \ldots, c^I)$ such that c^i solves

$$\max_{c^i} u_i(c^i)$$

subject to

$$p \cdot c^i \leq p \cdot \omega^i \tag{1.5}$$

for all i. The complete contingent claims equilibrium allows us to specify a competitive equilibrium under uncertainty by assuming that prices exist for consumption in each possible state of the world.

We can state the following results.

- The First Welfare Theorem: A complete contingent claims equilibrium is Pareto optimal.
- The Second Welfare Theorem: A Pareto optimal allocation can be supported as an equilibrium.

To prove the First Welfare Theorem, suppose $(c^1, c^2, \ldots, c^I, p)$ is an equilibrium which is not Pareto optimal. Then there exists an allocation

[1] Notice that $p \cdot (\alpha x + \beta y) = \alpha(p \cdot x) + \beta(p \cdot y)$ for any $\alpha, \beta \in \Re$ and $x, y \in \Re^{SM}$ so that the price function is *linear*.

$(\hat{c}^1, \hat{c}^2, \ldots, \hat{c}^I)$ and a non-zero price vector $\hat{p}$ such that $u_i(\hat{c}^i) \geq u^i(c^i)$ for all i and $u_j(\hat{c}^j) > u^j(c^j)$ for some j. Since the utility function is strictly increasing and continuous on $\Re_+^{SM}$, then it can be easily proved that $p \cdot \hat{c}^i \geq p \cdot c^i$ for all i with strict inequality for agent j. This implies

$$p \cdot \sum_{i=1}^{I} \hat{c}^i > p \cdot \sum_{i=1}^{I} \omega^i,$$

which contradicts the feasibility of $(\hat{c}^1, \hat{c}^2, \ldots, \hat{c}^I)$.

The existence of equilibrium and the welfare theorems are discussed by Debreu [142], who provides an introduction to competitive equilibrium when the commodity space is finite-dimensional. Early proofs of the existence of a competitive equilibrium are by Arrow and Debreu [33] and McKenzie [338]. Duffie [159, 161] provides a textbook treatment.

1.1.2. *Computing the equilibrium*

What is the problem of a consumer in a contingent claims equilibrium? Let $c_s^i = (c_{s,1}^i, \ldots, c_{s,M}^i)'$. The problem in Equation (1.5) can be written as

$$\max_{\{c_s^i\}_{s=1}^S} \sum_{s=1}^{S} \pi_s^i U_i(c_s^i)$$

subject to

$$\sum_{s=1}^{S} \sum_{m=1}^{M} p_{s,m}[\omega_{s,m}^i - c_{s,m}^i] \geq 0.$$

Thus, consumer i chooses a vector of length $S \times M$ to maximize his utility subject to a budget constraint.

To analyze the consumer's problem, we make the following assumption on the utility function $U_i(c)$.

Assumption 1.1 *Let $U_i : \Re_+^{S\times M} \to \Re$ be concave, increasing, and twice continuously differentiable and*

$$\lim_{c\to 0} U_i'(c) = +\infty, \quad \lim_{c\to\infty} U_i'(c) = 0.$$

By the Kuhn–Tucker Theorem, there exists a positive Lagrange multiplier λ_i such that c^i solves the consumer's problem:

$$\max_{c^i \in \Re_+^{SM}} u_i(c^i) + \lambda_i(p \cdot \omega^i - p \cdot c^i).$$

We can write this equivalently as:

$$\max_{c^i \in \Re_+^{SM}} \sum_{s=1}^{S} \pi_s^i U_i(c_s^i) + \lambda_i \left[\sum_{s=1}^{S} \sum_{m=1}^{M} p_{s,m}\omega_{s,m}^i - p_{s,m}c_{s,m}^i \right].$$

Notice that the λ_i for $i = 1, \ldots, I$ are not state dependent. The first-order condition is

$$0 = \pi_s^i \left(\frac{\partial U_i(c^i)}{\partial c_{s,m}^i} \right) - \lambda_i p_{s,m} \quad \text{for each } s, m \text{ and } i.$$

This can be written as

$$\frac{\pi_s^i (\partial U_i(c^i)/\partial c_{s,m}^i)}{\lambda_i} = p_{s,m} \quad \text{for each } s,\ m \text{ and } i. \tag{1.6}$$

To illustrate the solution procedure, assure that the utility function U_i is separable across states s and across commodities m.

Define the functions

$$g_i(x) = (U_i')^{-1}(x).$$

These exist since marginal utility is strictly decreasing. Hence, given $\lambda_i p_{s,m}/\pi_s^i$, we can use the Implicit Function Theorem to show there is a solution

$$c_{s,m}^i = g_i(\lambda_i p_{s,m}/\pi_s^i) \tag{1.7}$$

for $s = 1, \ldots, S$, $m = 1, \ldots, M$, and $i = 1, \ldots, I$. The functions $g_i(\cdot)$ are known as the *Frisch demands*, and they express consumption allocations in terms of the product of the individual-specific Lagrange multipliers and the probability-weighted contingent claims prices.

How do we solve for the competitive equilibrium? Now go back to the initial budget constraint and substitute the solution for $c_{s,m}^i$. This yields

$$\sum_{s=1}^{S} \sum_{m=1}^{M} p_{s,m}[\omega_{s,m}^i - g_i(\lambda_i p_{s,m}/\pi_s^i)] = 0. \tag{1.8}$$

For each i, this is an equation in the unknown λ_i, given the price system. Notice that the left side is strictly increasing in λ_i. Hence, by the Implicit Function Theorem, there exists the solutions $\lambda_i^\star = h_i(p)$ for $i = 1, \ldots, I$. Given the solution for λ_i as a function of the prices p, the market-clearing conditions can be used to solve for the prices as:

$$\sum_{i=1}^{I} g_i(h_i(p)p_{s,m}/\pi_s^i) = \sum_{i=1}^{I} \omega_{s,m}^i, \quad s = 1, \ldots, S, m = 1, \ldots, M. \tag{1.9}$$

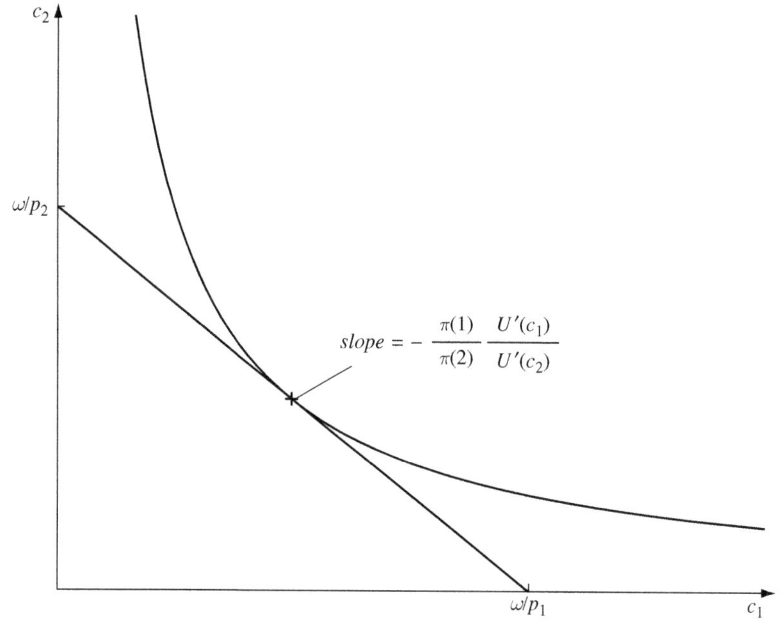

Figure 1.1. The consumer's optimum in an economy with two states

Example 1.1 Suppose that consumer i has preferences given by

$$U_i(c^i) = \frac{(c^i)^{1-\gamma} - 1}{1-\gamma} \quad \gamma \geq 0, \quad \gamma \neq 1. \tag{1.10}$$

Also specialize to the case of two states, two consumers, and one commodity per state, $S = 2$, $I = 2$ and $M = 1$, and assume that $\pi_s^i = \pi_s$.

The first-order conditions in (1.6) are now given by:

$$\pi_s U'(c_s^i) = \lambda_i p_s, \quad s = 1, 2, i = 1, 2. \tag{1.11}$$

Taking the ratios of these conditions across the two states,

$$\frac{\pi_2}{\pi_1}\frac{U'(c_2^i)}{U'(c_1^i)} = \frac{p_2}{p_1}, \quad i = 1, 2. \tag{1.12}$$

Figure 1.1 depicts the consumer's optimum.

Under the preferences given above, $U'(c) = c^{-\gamma}$ and $g_i(x) = x^{-\frac{1}{\gamma}}$. We can substitute for the utility function to evaluate the four first-order conditions in Equation (1.11) as:

$$c_s^i = (\lambda_i p_s/\pi_s)^{-\frac{1}{\gamma}}, \quad s = 1, 2, i = 1, 2. \tag{1.13}$$

Notice that there are four unknowns – $\lambda_1, \lambda_2, p_1, p_2$ – and four equations – the budget constraints for consumers $i = 1, 2$ and the market-clearing conditions for states $s = 1, 2$. Normalize the price of consumption in state 1 as $p_1 = 1$. We can substitute the solutions for c_s^i from (1.13) into the individual-specific budget constraints in (1.8) as:

$$\sum_{s=1}^{2} p_s[\omega_s^i - (\lambda_i p_s/\pi_s)^{-\frac{1}{\gamma}}] = 0, \quad i = 1, 2. \tag{1.14}$$

These equations yield the solution for λ_i as

$$\lambda_i = \left\{ \frac{\pi_1^{\frac{1}{\gamma}} + p_2^{\frac{\gamma-1}{\gamma}} (1 - \pi_1)^{\frac{1}{\gamma}}}{\omega_1^i + p_2 \omega_2^i} \right\}^{\gamma}, \quad i = 1, 2. \tag{1.15}$$

We can substitute these conditions into the market-clearing conditions in (1.14) to solve for the relative price of consumption in state 2, p_2.

Following this approach, the market-clearing conditions for states 1 and 2 with the solutions for c_s^i substituted in are given by

$$(\lambda_1/\pi_1)^{-\frac{1}{\gamma}} + (\lambda_2/\pi_1)^{-\frac{1}{\gamma}} = \omega_1,$$

$$(\lambda_1 p_2/(1 - \pi_1))^{-\frac{1}{\gamma}} + (\lambda_2 p_2/(1 - \pi_1))^{-\frac{1}{\gamma}} = \omega_2,$$

where $\omega_s = \omega_s^1 + \omega_s^2$. Now substitute for λ_1 and λ_2 using (1.15). Taking the ratio of the two market-clearing conditions yields the solution for the equilibrium price as

$$p_2 = \left(\frac{1 - \pi_1}{\pi_1}\right)\left(\frac{\omega_1}{\omega_2}\right)^{\gamma}, \tag{1.16}$$

where $\omega_s = \omega_s^1 + \omega_s^2$ for $s = 1, 2$. This says that the price of consumption in state 2 relative to consumption in state 1 is a function of the ratio of the probabilities and endowments across the two states. This price also depends on consumers' willingness to substitute consumption across states described by the parameter γ. Notice that p_2 is inversely related to the probability of state 1 and the endowment in state 2. If either π_1 is high or ω_2 is large, then there will be less demand for goods delivered contingent on state 2 occurring, and p_2 will be small.

- If the aggregate endowment varies across states but the probability of state 1 equals the probability of state 2, then

$$p_2 = \left(\frac{\omega_1}{\omega_2}\right)^{\gamma}, \tag{1.17}$$

  which varies monotonically with the ratio of the total endowment in each state. If $\gamma = 0$ so that consumers are indifferent between consumption in each state, then $p_2 = 1$. For values of $\gamma > 0$, p_2 decreases (increases) with γ for $\omega_1 < \omega_2$ ($\omega_1 > \omega_2$). In other words, as consumers become less willing to substitute consumption across states, the relative price of consumption across states 1 and 2 adjusts to make their demands consistent with the total endowment in each state.

- If the aggregate endowment is equal across states, $\omega_1 = \omega_2$, then

$$p_2 = \frac{1 - \pi_1}{\pi_1}. \tag{1.18}$$

Thus, the contingent claims price just equals the ratio of the probability of the two states, and it is independent of consumer preferences.[2]

We can also solve for the consumption allocations in each state by substituting for λ^i and p_2 from (1.15) and (1.16) into the Frisch demands in (1.13). However, a simpler approach is to consider the conditions in (1.12). Under the assumption for preferences, these simplify as:

$$c_1^i = \left[\frac{1 - \pi_1}{\pi_1} \frac{1}{p_2}\right]^{-\frac{1}{\gamma}} c_2^i. \tag{1.19}$$

If we substitute the expression for c_1^i obtained from equation (1.19) into the budget constraint, we obtain the solutions for c_1^i and c_2^i as

$$c_1^i = \frac{\left[(1 - \pi_1)/(\pi_1 p_2)\right]^{-\frac{1}{\gamma}} (\omega_1^i + p_2 \omega_2^i)}{\left[(1 - \pi_1)/(\pi_1 p_2)\right]^{-\frac{1}{\gamma}} + p_2}, \tag{1.20}$$

$$c_2^i = \frac{\omega_1^i + p_2 \omega_2^i}{\left[(1 - \pi_1)/(\pi_1 p_2)\right]^{-\frac{1}{\gamma}} + p_2}. \tag{1.21}$$

Notice that even if the aggregate endowment is equal across states, individual consumers' allocations will depend on the value of their endowments in states 1 and 2.

- Perfectly negatively correlated endowments across consumers.

$$\omega_1^1 = 0 \quad \omega_2^1 = 1$$
$$\omega_1^2 = 1 \quad \omega_2^2 = 0.$$

In this case, the total endowment does not vary across states so that the only uncertainty is individual-specific. Since the aggregate endowment equals one in each state, the relative price is $p_2 = (1 - \pi_1)/\pi_1$, as argued earlier. Using (1.20–1.21), we have that $c_s^1 = 1 - \pi_1$

[2] This result depends, however, on assuming that consumers have identical preferences. If consumers have different utility functions, then the equilibrium price will depend not only on the aggregate endowment in each state but also on how this endowment is split between individuals 1 and 2. In this case, p_2 will vary with γ even if the aggregate endowment is equal across states. See Exercise 2.

and $c_s^2 = \pi_1$. If the probability of state 1 is low, the individual who receives endowment in state 1 also receives low consumption in each state. Suppose $\pi_1 = 0.5$. Then the equilibrium price in each state is $p_1 = p_2 = 1$ and $c_s^i = 0.5$ for $i = 1, 2$ and $s = 1, 2$ so that consumption allocations are identical across consumers for all states.

- Positively correlated endowments across consumers.

$$\omega_1^1 = 0.5 \qquad \omega_2^1 = 1$$

$$\omega_1^2 = 1 \qquad \omega_2^2 = 2.$$

Notice that the ratio of the aggregate endowment in states 1 versus 2 equals 1/2, that is, $\omega_1/\omega_2 = 1/2$. It is straightforward to show that $c_s^2 = 2c_s^1$, that is, the second consumer always consumes twice as much as the first regardless of the probabilities of the states. Furthermore, this result does not depend on the parameter γ. The impact of changes in the endowment in this case is merely to adjust the relative price of consumption in state 2.

1.1.3. Pareto optimal allocations

In this section, we show the equivalence between the competitive equilibrium and Pareto optimal allocations. In later chapters, we describe how this equivalence can be exploited to characterize competitive equilibrium in a variety of settings.

Assume that U_i are strictly increasing and concave for all i. The social planner assigns weights $\eta_i \in \Re_+$ to each consumer i and chooses allocations $c^i \in \Re_+^{SM}$ for $i = 1, \ldots, I$ to maximize the weighted sum of individual utilities subject to a set of resource constraints for each state s and each commodity m:

$$\max_{c^1,\ldots,c^I} \sum_{i=1}^{I} \eta_i \sum_{s=1}^{S} \pi_s^i U_i(c_s^i) \quad \text{s.t.} \quad \sum_{i=1}^{I} c^i = \sum_{i=1}^{I} \omega^i. \tag{1.22}$$

First, notice that a feasible allocation that is Pareto optimal solves the problem in Equation (1.22) with a set of positive weights $\eta \in \Re_+^I$ and $c^1 + \cdots + c^I = \omega$. This follows as an application of the Separating Hyperplane Theorem. (See Exercise 1.) Second, notice that if $(c^1, \ldots, c^I)$ solves the problem in Equation (1.22), then it is Pareto optimal.

Let $\mu_{s,m}$ denote the Lagrange multiplier for the resource constraint in each state and for each commodity. The first-order conditions for this problem are

$$\eta_i \pi_s^i \left(\frac{\partial U_i}{\partial c_{s,m}^i} \right) = \mu_{s,m} \quad \text{for each } s, m \text{ and } i. \tag{1.23}$$

Suppose we set

$$\eta_i = \frac{1}{\lambda_i}, \quad i = 1, \ldots, I, \tag{1.24}$$

and

$$p_{s,m} = \mu_{s,m}, \quad s = 1, \ldots, S, \quad m = 1, \ldots, M, \tag{1.25}$$

where λ_i are the agent-specific Lagrange multipliers and $p_{s,m}$ are the contingent claims prices. Under these assumptions, the first-order conditions above are identical to those for a complete contingent claims equilibrium. (See the conditions in Equation (1.6).) Since the allocations achieved under the contingent claims equilibrium and the social planning problem both satisfy the resource constraints, they must be equal.

1.2. SECURITY MARKET EQUILIBRIUM

In actual asset markets, we observe individuals trading in securities that are claims to random payoffs denominated in units of account, not in commodities. We now describe how to formulate an equilibrium with such securities.

1.2.1. *Definition*

The primitives for a security market equilibrium are as follows:

- There are N securities.
- Each security n has the payoffs (denominated in the unit of account, say dollars) $x_{n,s}$ for $s = 1, \ldots, S$.
- We define X as the $N \times S$ matrix of payoffs and $q = (q_1, \ldots, q_N)^T$ in $\Re_+^N$ denotes the vector of security prices.
- Securities are sold before the state s is realized so that their prices are independent of the realized state.
- After the security markets close, agents trade in spot markets for the M commodities.
- Let $\bar{p}_{s,m}$ denote the unit price of the m'th commodity in state s and define $\bar{p}_s$ in $\Re_+^M$ as the vector of spot prices in state s.

A *portfolio* is a vector $\theta^i \equiv (\theta_1^i, \ldots, \theta_N^i)$ in $\Re^N$ which has the market value $\theta \cdot q$ and the $S \times 1$ payoff vector $X^T\theta$ showing the payoff on the portfolio in each state s. Some of the elements of θ may be negative. When the total expenditure or portfolio weight on a security is negative ($\theta_k < 0$), we say that security k has been sold short. If the portfolio weights are required to satisfy $\theta_n \geq 0$ for $n = 1, \ldots, N$, then we say that short selling is ruled out. In the security market equilibrium, we will not rule out short sales on any of the securities.

The i'th agent chooses a portfolio $\theta^i \equiv (\theta^i_1, \ldots, \theta^i_N)$ in $\Re^N$ of securities to purchase and a consumption vector c^i in $\Re^{SM}_+$. Given the security and spot prices $(q, \bar{p})$, the i'th agent solves the problem

$$\max_{c^i, \theta^i} u_i(c^i) = \sum_{s=1}^{S} \pi^i_s U_i(c^i_s)$$

subject to

$$\theta^i \cdot q \leq 0, \tag{1.26}$$

$$\bar{p}_s \cdot c^i_s \leq \bar{p}_s \cdot \omega^i_s + \theta^i \cdot x_s, \quad s = 1, \ldots, S, \tag{1.27}$$

where $\theta^i \cdot x_s$ is the dollar payoff on the portfolio in state s and c^i_s in $\Re^M_+$ is the consumption vector in state s.

Notice that the consumer faces a separate budget constraint for each state of the world. The consumer's wealth in each realized state s is given by his endowment ω^i_s in that state plus the payoff on his portfolio of assets. Unlike the complete contingent claims equilibrium, the consumer cannot purchase claims to consumption for each possible state subject to a single budget constraint that constrains the value of his consumption to be less than the value of his endowment across all possible states. Instead, his feasible consumption in state s is constrained by his realized wealth at that state. Notice also that the consumer's utility does not depend on consumption in period 0. Hence, without loss of generality, the value of his endowment at date 0 is also taken as zero. This means that purchases of some securities are financed by sales of others. This is known as a *self-financing* portfolio.

We define a *security market equilibrium* (SME) as a collection

$$((\theta^1, c^1), \ldots, (\theta^I, c^I), (q, \bar{p}))$$

such that (i) given prices $(q, \bar{p})$, the allocation (θ^i, c^i) solves the problem for agent i; and (ii) markets clear:

$$\sum_{i=1}^{I} \theta^i_n = 0, \quad n = 1, \ldots, N, \tag{1.28}$$

$$\sum_{i=1}^{I} (c^i_{s,m} - \omega^i_{s,m}) = 0, \quad s = 1, \ldots, S, m = 1, \ldots, M. \tag{1.29}$$

Note also that the securities are in net zero supply in the economy. We could instead assume that securities are in net positive supply and that consumers have initial holdings of the securities denoted $\bar{\theta}_n^i$ for $n = 1, \ldots, N$. In this case, consumers choose security holdings to satisfy

$$q \cdot \theta^i \leq q \cdot \bar{\theta}^i$$

and the securities market-clearing condition becomes

$$\sum_{i=1}^{I} \theta^i = \sum_{i=1}^{I} \bar{\theta}^i.$$

For simplicity let the number of commodities in each state equal one, $M = 1$, and normalize the spot price of consumption in each state as $\bar{p}_s = 1$. For the SME, each consumer solves the problem

$$\max_{c^i, \theta^i} \sum_{s=1}^{S} \pi_s U(c_s^i)$$

subject to

$$\sum_{n=1}^{N} \theta_n^i q_n \leq 0,$$

$$c_s^i \leq \omega_s^i + \sum_{n=1}^{N} \theta_n^i x_{n,s}, \quad s = 1, \ldots, S.$$

Let λ_s^i denote the state- and individual-specific multiplier on the goods market constraint and μ^i denote the multiplier on the security market constraint. The FOCs with respect to c_s^i and θ_n^i are as follows:

$$\pi_s U'(c_s^i) = \lambda_s^i,$$

$$\mu^i q_n = \sum_{s=1}^{S} \lambda_s^i x_{n,s}, \quad n = 1, \ldots, N,$$

for $s = 1, \ldots, S$, $i = 1, \ldots, I$.

Market clearing requires that

$$\sum_{i=1}^{I} \theta_n^i = 0, \quad n = 1, \ldots, N \tag{1.30}$$

$$\sum_{i=1}^{I} c_s^i = \sum_{i=1}^{I} \omega_s^i, \quad s = 1, \ldots, S. \tag{1.31}$$

To solve for the allocations and the security price in the SME, substitute for λ_s^i in the first-order conditions with respect to θ_n^i as

$$\mu^i q_n = \sum_{s=1}^{S} \pi_s U'(c_s^i) x_{n,s}, \quad n = 1, \ldots, N. \tag{1.32}$$

By the goods market clearing condition, $c_s^i = \omega - \sum_{j=1,\, j\neq i}^{I} c_s^j$ where $\omega = \omega_s^i + \sum_{j=1,\, j\neq i}^{I} \omega_s^j$. Now substitute for c_s^j using the goods market budget constraints

$$q_n = \sum_{s=1}^{S} \frac{\pi_s U'(\omega_s^i - \sum_{j=1,\, j\neq i}^{I} \sum_{n=1}^{N} \theta_n^j x_{n,s}) x_{n,s}}{\mu^i},$$

for $n = 1, \ldots, N, i = 1, \ldots, I$. Given μ^i and q_n, these are $N + I$ equations in the $N + I$ unknowns – θ_n^i for $n = 1, \ldots, N, i = 1, \ldots, I$. Observe that the right-side of each of these expressions is strictly increasing in θ_n^i. Hence, by the Implicit Function Theorem, there exists a solution denoted $\theta_n^i = g_n^i(\mu, q)$ where $\mu \equiv (\mu^1, \ldots, \mu^I)'$ and $q \equiv (q_1, \ldots, q_N)'$. Given this solution, we can use the security market budget constraints to solve for μ_i as a function of the unknown security prices q as $\mu^i = h_i(q)$:

$$\sum_{n=1}^{N} \theta_n^i q_n = \sum_{n=1}^{N} g_n^i(\mu, q) q_n = 0, \quad i = 1, \ldots, I. \tag{1.33}$$

Finally, we can use the security market-clearing conditions to solve for q_n

$$\sum_{i=1}^{I} \theta_n^i = \sum_{i=1}^{I} g_n^i(h(q), q) = 0, \quad n = 1, \ldots, N, \tag{1.34}$$

where $h(q) \equiv (h_1(q), \ldots, h_I(q))'$.[3] The consumption allocations can be found by evaluating the goods market budget constraints at the optimal values of θ_n^i. Recall that the contingent claims prices in the CCE are defined for each state. By contrast, the security price in the SME in determined *before* the state is revealed and, hence, is expressed as an expectation of its future payoffs.

We can make this point more explicitly by re-writing the price of security n as

$$\begin{aligned} q_n &= \sum_{s=1}^{S} \frac{\pi_s U'(c^i)}{\mu^i} x_{n,s} \\ &= E\left[\frac{U'(c^i)}{\mu^i} x_n\right], \end{aligned} \tag{1.35}$$

[3] The existence of solutions for μ^i and q based on Equations (1.33) and (1.34) can also be shown as an application of the Implicit Function Theorem.

where the expectation is evaluated with respect to the probabilities π_s. This expression shows that the price of security n is derived as the expected discounted value of its payoffs, the discounting being done by the weighted marginal utilities for each consumer i. In the next section, we provide an alternative representation of the security price that is independent of i.

1.2.2. *Attaining a CCE by an SME*

In the complete contingent claims equilibrium, consumers choose allocations subject to a single budget constraint. In the security market equilibrium, they must choose consumption in each state subject to a budget constraint for that state. This suggests that the consumption allocation in a security market equilibrium may differ from the allocation in a complete contingent claims equilibrium. In a singularly important result, Arrow [31] has shown that if the number of securities equals the number of states, then the allocation in a complete contingent claims equilibrium can be attained in a security market equilibrium.

Denote the allocation and prices in a complete contingent commodity markets equilibrium by $(c^1, \ldots, c^I, p)$. Suppose that $N = S$ and that the columns of the payoff X are linearly independent. Then without loss of generality we can define the dividend or payoff vector as

$$x_{n,s} = \begin{cases} 1 & \text{if } s = n \\ 0 & \text{otherwise,} \end{cases} \tag{1.36}$$

for $s = 1, \ldots, S$ and $n = 1, \ldots, S$. Define the price of the sth security such that

$$q_s \bar{p}_{s,m} = p_{s,m} \quad \forall s, m. \tag{1.37}$$

Then notice that the consumer confronted with these prices has the same range of alternatives that are available under the contingent claims equilibrium. Define the portfolio weights so that the number of units of the s'th security that is held by consumer i is equated to the cost of the net consumption choice by i in state s:

$$\theta_s^i = \bar{p}_s \cdot (c_s^i - \omega_s^i). \tag{1.38}$$

If the prices and allocations defined in this manner constitute a security market equilibrium, then (θ^i, c^i) must be feasible for consumer i in the security market equilibrium. Thus,

$$\theta^i \cdot q = \sum_{s=1}^{S}\sum_{m=1}^{M}\left(\frac{p_{s,m}}{\bar{p}_{s,m}}\right)\bar{p}_{s,m}(c^i_{s,m} - \omega^i_{s,m})$$

$$= \sum_{s=1}^{S}\sum_{m=1}^{M} p_{s,m}(c^i_{s,m} - \omega^i_{s,m}) \leq 0,$$

since $(c^1, \ldots, c^I, p)$ constitutes a contingent claims equilibrium. Likewise,

$$\bar{p}_s \cdot c^i_s = \bar{p}_s \cdot \omega^i_s + \theta^i_s = \bar{p}_s \cdot \omega^i_s + \theta^i \cdot x_s \quad \text{for } s = 1, \ldots, S$$

since $x_{n,s} = 1$ only if $s = n$. Hence, given the prices $(q, \bar{p})$, (θ^i, c^i) satisfy consumers' budget constraints in the security market equilibrium.

To show that (θ^i, c^i) solves the consumer's problem, assume that $(\phi^i, \hat{c}^i)$ also satisfies the budget constraints and $u_i(\hat{c}^i) > u_i(c^i)$. Since c^i is optimal for consumer i in the complete contingent claims equilibrium, we have that $p \cdot \hat{c}^i > p \cdot c^i$; otherwise c^i would not have been chosen. If $(\phi^i, \hat{c}^i)$ satisfies the consumer's budget constraints, then $\phi^i_s = \phi^i \cdot x_s \geq \bar{p}_s \cdot (\hat{c}^i_s - \omega^i_s)$ and $\phi^i \cdot q \geq \sum_{s=1}^{S} p_s \cdot (\hat{c}^i_s - \omega^i_s)$ since $q_s \bar{p}_{s,m} = p_{s,m}$. But $p \cdot \hat{c}^i > p \cdot c^i$ implies that $\phi^i \cdot q > 0$ which contradicts Equation (1.26). Spot markets clear because $(c^1, \ldots, c^I)$ is feasible. Security markets clear since

$$\sum_{i=1}^{I} \theta^i_s = \sum_{i=1}^{I} \bar{p}_s \cdot (c^i_s - \omega^i_s)$$

$$= \bar{p}_s \cdot \sum_{i=1}^{I} (c^i_s - \omega^i_s) = 0, \quad s = 1, \ldots, S$$

since $(c^1, \ldots, c^I)$ is feasible for the contingent claims equilibrium.

Example 1.2 Now consider the problem of supporting the CCE in Example 1.1 with a security market equilibrium (SME). For simplicity, consider the case with perfectly negatively correlated endowments. To support the consumption allocations, notice that we assumed $x_{n,s} = 1$, if $n = s$; zero otherwise. This simplifies the first-order conditions with respect to θ^i_n as

$$\mu^i q_s = \lambda^i_s, \quad s = 1, 2.$$

Thus we can re-write the first-order conditions in the SME as

$$\frac{\pi_s (c^i_s)^{-\gamma}}{\mu^i} = q_s, \quad s = 1, 2. \tag{1.39}$$

If we combine the two sets of FOCs under these assumptions, then we can write c^i_1 in terms of c^i_2 such that

$$c^i_1 = \left[\frac{q_1}{q_2}\frac{1 - \pi_1}{\pi_1}\right]^{-\frac{1}{\gamma}} c^i_2. \tag{1.40}$$

Suppose that $q_s = p_s$ for $s = 1, 2$. Then equation (1.40) is identical to equation (1.19). Hence, provided the prices in the SME are set so as to replicate the prices in the CCE described in Example 1.1, the consumption allocations in the SME are identical to the allocations in the CCE. To support the consumption allocations for the CCE, we set

$$\theta_1^1 = c_1^1 - 1$$
$$\theta_2^1 = c_2^1,$$

and

$$\theta_1^2 = c_1^2$$
$$\theta_2^2 = c_2^2 - 1.$$

Since the CCE allocations are feasible, the market clearing conditions in the goods market hold. To show that the portfolio shares sum to zero, we note that $c_s^1 = 1 - \pi_1$ and $c_s^2 = \pi_1$ for $s = 1, 2$. Hence,

$$\begin{aligned}\theta_1^1 + \theta_1^2 &= c_1^1 - 1 + c_1^2 \\ &= 1 - \pi_1 - 1 + \pi_1 = 0,\end{aligned}$$

and

$$\begin{aligned}\theta_2^1 + \theta_2^2 &= c_2^1 + c_2^2 - 1 \\ &= 1 - \pi_1 + \pi_1 - 1 = 0.\end{aligned}$$

We can determine the security prices as

$$q_n = p_1 x_{n,1} + p_2 x_{n,2}, \quad n = 1, 2. \tag{1.41}$$

This shows that the security price is a discounted sum of the random payoffs, the discounting being done with the contingent claims prices.

In Section 1.1.2, we showed that the product of the individual-specific Lagrange multipliers and contingent claims price in state s is equal to the probability-weighted marginal utilities of consumption for each consumer in that state:

$$\lambda_i p_s = \pi_s U'(c_s) \ \ \forall s \text{ and } \forall i.$$

When $N = S$, the asset payoffs are normalized so that $x_{n,s} = 1$ is $n = s$ and zero otherwise, and $q_s = p_s$, then the state-specific Lagrange multiplier in the SME equals the product of the individual-specific Lagrange multiplier and the contingent claims price in the CCE:

$$\lambda_s^i = \mu^i q_s = \lambda_i p_s.$$

This can be verified by comparing equations (1.11) with (1.39). Now define

$$m_s \equiv \frac{U'(c_s)}{\lambda_i}.$$

Then the asset pricing equation in (1.41) can be re-written as

$$q_n = \sum_{s=1}^{S} \pi_s m_s x_{n,s} = E[m x_n], \tag{1.42}$$

where the expectation is evaluated under the probabilities π_s. Based on the representation in equation (1.42), the variable m_s is sometimes called the *stochastic discount factor*. This is a random variable whose properties depend on preferences, endowments, and the nature of trades that agents can enter into. The multiplier λ_i (or μ^i) has the interpretation of the marginal value of current consumption or wealth.

Example 1.3 Now suppose that there is only one asset, a risk-free bond that consumers trade in equilibrium. We assume that these are *pure discount bonds* which have a payoff of 1 and which sell for $q \leq 1$. Bonds are in net zero supply in the economy:

$$\sum_{i=1}^{I} \theta^i = 0.$$

Consumer *i*'s problem is now to solve

$$\max_{c^i, \theta^i} \sum_{s=1}^{2} \pi_s U(c_s^i)$$

subject to

$$\theta^i q \leq 0,$$

$$c_s^i \leq \omega_s^i + \theta^i, \quad s = 1, 2.$$

Let λ_s^i and μ^i denote the multipliers on the goods market and security market constraints, respectively. The first-order conditions with respect to c_s^i and θ^i are as follows:

$$\pi_s U'(c_s^i) = \lambda_s^i, \tag{1.43}$$

$$\mu^i q = \lambda_s^i. \tag{1.44}$$

Solving these conditions, we obtain

$$\frac{\pi_s U'(c_s^i)}{\mu^i} = q, \tag{1.45}$$

which is independent of s! That is, when consumers can only trade a risk-free bond, there is no possibility of setting security prices to replicate the CCE.

Recall that we defined each security to have a unit payoff if state $s=n$ occurs and zero otherwise. More generally, a CCE allocation can be attained in an SME with an arbitrary payoff matrix X whose columns are linearly independent. When the columns of X span $\Re^S$, we say that markets are *complete*. With such spanning securities, a security market equilibrium can be converted into a contingent claims equilibrium. We illustrated this fact in Examples 1.1–1.2. Since the complete contingent claims equilibrium allocation is Pareto optimal, the allocation in the security market equilibrium will also be Pareto optimal. In the absence of spanning, markets are *incomplete* and a security market equilibrium may exist but the equilibrium allocation is not necessarily Pareto optimal. This is the situation in Example 1.3. In this case, there is a single security which has a payoff of one in each state. Thus, there is no way to replicate the CCE with an SME by constructing state-contingent securities whose payoffs are one in each state and zero otherwise. There is, however, a simple way to complete this economy. That involves introducing a stock that has different payoffs in each state. In this case, the payoff matrix will involve the payoffs on the risk-free bond and the stock so that its columns will be linearly independent. This is typically the situation considered in the binomial model of securities markets, which we examine in Chapter 2.

1.2.3. *The Pareto optimum and the representative consumer*

In the economies we examined so far, individuals can differ with respect to their beliefs, their tastes, and their initial endowment or wealth. We refer to such differences as *ex ante* heterogeneity. One approach to deriving asset-pricing relations in the presence of population heterogeneity is to construct a so-called "representative" consumer, as suggested by Constantinides [116] and others. The existence of this representative consumer is based on the Pareto optimality of the complete contingent claims equilibrium.

The preferences of the "representative" consumer can be defined as:

$$U_\eta(\omega) \equiv \max_{(c^1,\ldots,c^I)} \sum_{i=1}^{I} \eta_i u_i(c^i)$$

subject to (1.46)

$$c^1 + \cdots + c^I \le \omega^1 + \cdots + \omega^I \equiv \omega. \tag{1.47}$$

Assume that the single-period utility functions depend on consumption and leisure as

$$U_i(c^i, l^i) = \gamma_0^{-1}\delta(z^i)(c^i)^{\gamma_0}(l^i)^{\gamma_1}, \quad \max(\gamma_0, \gamma_1) \leq 1 \tag{1.48}$$

where $\delta(z^i)$ is a household-specific utility index that is a function of a set of exogenous characteristics of the household. Define the marginal utility of consumption for the "representative" consumer in the social planner's problem by:

$$\frac{\partial U_\eta(\omega)}{\partial c_s} = \sum_i \pi_s \eta_i \frac{\partial U_i(c_s^i, l_s^i)}{\partial c_s^i}, \tag{1.49}$$

where η_i is consumer i's weight in the social planning problem and $c_s \equiv (c_s^1, \ldots, c_s^I)'$. Recall that in a complete contingent claims equilibrium, we have that $\pi_s \delta(z_s^i)(c_s^i)^{\gamma_0 - 1}(l_s^i)^{\gamma_1} = \lambda_i p_s$. Hence, we find that

$$\frac{\partial U_\eta(\omega)}{\partial c_s} = \sum_i \pi_s \eta_i \delta(z_s^i)(c_s^i)^{\gamma_0 - 1}(l_s^i)^{\gamma_1} = p_s, \tag{1.50}$$

where $\eta_i = 1/\lambda_i$ as argued in Section 1.1.3. Hence, the marginal utility of consumption for the "representative" consumer is just equal to the contingent claims price in state s

$$\frac{\partial U_\eta(\omega)}{\partial c_s} = p_s, \tag{1.51}$$

where we have normalized $p_0 = 1$. Substituting back into Equation (1.41) shows that security prices can also be written solely as a function of the preferences of the representative consumer.

In the macroeconomics literature, the existence of such a "representative" consumer has been used to justify ignoring heterogeneity throughout the population in a complete markets setting. However, to determine how we can give content to such an approach, we note that the indirect preferences of the "representative" consumer depend on the entire distribution of individual characteristics (as captured by the agent weights η_i), the individual utility functions U_i, and the equilibrium distribution of the consumption allocation. Recall that one of the elements of the consumption vector is leisure, and that the equilibrium allocation may entail corner solutions for the leisure allocation for a subset of the population. Specifically, if $\gamma_1 \neq 0$ or the states in which households participate in the labor market do not coincide exactly or the function $\delta(z_s^i)$ is not constant over time, then individual preferences do not aggregate in terms of the preferences of a "representative" consumer evaluated using aggregate consumption data. If, however, $\gamma_1 = 0$ and the utility index $\delta(z^i)$ is constant over time, then the security price can be expressed as a function of aggregate consumption alone.[4]

These results show that the distribution of exogenous and endogenous forms of heterogeneity throughout the population may matter. In the financial economics literature, Rubinstein [377] has shown that there exist some sets of homogeneity conditions on individual beliefs, preferences, and wealth such that the asset-pricing relations depend on per capita consumption and some composites of individual characteristics.[5] However, these conditions are typically more restrictive than the observed types of heterogeneity in the population, suggesting that the assumption of a "representative consumer" in asset-pricing models may be far from innocuous. We discuss these issues in later chapters.

1.3. CONCLUSIONS

A complete contingent claims equilibrium provides a natural starting point for studying the behavior of allocations and prices in an environment under uncertainty. If there are as many securities as states, we have shown that there exists a security market equilibrium to support the contingent claims equilibrium. The equivalence between a contingent claims equilibrium and Pareto optimum is a result that is also widely exploited to construct a "representative" or composite consumer. These results constitute important benchmarks that we will repeatedly refer to in our subsequent discussion.

1.4. EXERCISES

1. This exercise illustrates the application of the Separating Hyperplane Theorem. We state a version that is applicable in $\Re^n$. Define a *linear functional* F on $\Re^n$ as a function $F : \Re^n \rightarrow \Re$ satisfying

$$F(\alpha x + \beta y) = \alpha F(x) + \beta F(y), \quad x, y \in \Re^n, \quad \alpha, \beta \in \Re.$$

We have the following theorem.

Theorem 1.1 *(Separating Hyperplane Theorem) Suppose A and B are convex, disjoint sets in $\Re^n$. There is some linear functional F such that $F(x) \leq F(y)$ for each x in A and y in B. Moreover, if x is in the interior of A or y is in the interior of B, then $F(x) < F(y)$.*

[4] See Exercise 3.

[5] Earlier results on the specification of preferences that admit exact aggregation to a representative consumer are due to Gorman [209].

For a more general version that is applicable in arbitrary vector spaces, see Luenberger [326, p.133].
Use this result to show that a feasible allocation $(c^1, \ldots, c^I)$ that is Pareto optimal solves the problem in Equation (1.22) with a set of positive weights $\eta \in \Re^I_+$ and $c^1 + \cdots + c^I = \omega$.

Hint: Assume that the utility functions u_i are strictly increasing and concave for all i. Define the set $A = \{a \in \Re^I : a_i = u_i(x^i) - u_i(c^i), x \leq \omega\}$ and $A' = \{a \in \Re^I_+ : a \neq 0\}$. Show that $A \cap A'$ is empty. Show that A is a convex set and that $0 \in A$.

2. Complete Markets and Consumption Inequality[6]
Consider an economy with two consumers. Each consumer lives for two periods. Consumer a has preferences over consumption c_t as:

$$\sum_{t=1}^{2} U^a(c_t^a) = \sum_{t=1}^{2} \frac{(c_t^a)^{1-\gamma} - 1}{1 - \gamma}, \quad \gamma > 1.$$

Consumer b is less risk averse than consumer a and has preferences:

$$\sum_{t=1}^{2} U^b(c_t^b) = \sum_{t=1}^{2} \ln(c_t^b).$$

Each consumer receives the same endowment in each period, denoted ω_t. There is growth in the economy in that $\omega_1 < \omega_2$.
   (a) Find the solution for each consumer's problem.
   (b) Show that if $\gamma > 1$, then $p < \omega_1/\omega_2$, $c_1^a > c_1^b$, and $c_2^a < c_2^b$.
   (c) Conclude that consumption inequality is increasing in period 2, that is,

$$| c_1^a - c_1^b | < | c_2^a - c_2^b |.$$

   What is the intuition for these results?

3. Consider a two-period version of the model under uncertainty with one commodity in which the state is revealed in the second period. Let c_0^i represent units of consumption in the first period and c_s^i represent units of consumption contingent on the state s occurring, $s \in \{1, \ldots, S\}$ in the second period. Suppose preferences satisfy expected utility

$$u_i(c^i) = U_i(c_0^i) + \sum_{s=1}^{S} \pi_s^i V_i(c_s^i), \tag{1.52}$$

where $\pi_s^i > 0$ denotes the probability of state s occurring and U_i and V_i are strictly increasing, strictly concave, and differentiable functions.

[6] For a further discussion of complete markets and consumption inequality, see Deaton and Paxson [140].

(a) Characterize the contingent claims equilibrium allocations and prices.
(b) Characterize the security market equilibrium.
(c) Under which conditions will the SME replicate the CCE?
(d) Suppose preferences in each period are of the form:

$$U(c) = V(c) = \frac{c^{1-\gamma} - 1}{1 - \gamma}, \quad \gamma \geq 0, \quad \gamma \neq 1.$$

Suppose also that the conditions exist under which the SME can be used to replicate the CCE. Show that the asset prices in the security market equilibrium can be expressed in terms of average consumption data defined as

$$\bar{c}_s = \frac{1}{I} \sum_{i=1}^{I} c_s^i.$$

CHAPTER 2

Arbitrage and asset valuation

In the theoretical finance literature, the absence of arbitrage opportunities in securities trading has been exploited by Ross [371], Harrison and Kreps [240], Chamberlain and Rothschild [100], and others to show the existence of a pricing function that is used to value random payoff streams and to characterize its properties. We now illustrate their approach for the simple setup that we have been studying.

As part of the material for this chapter, we define notions of arbitrage. We then establish the equivalence between the absence of arbitrage and the existence of a strictly positive state-price vector that can be used to value random payoffs on any security. We show that in a complete markets setting, such a state-price vector will be unique.

We begin our analysis by examining the implications of the absence of arbitrage for investors' portfolios. We define such concepts as the law of one price and arbitrage opportunities of the first and second kind.

2.1. ABSENCE OF ARBITRAGE: SOME DEFINITIONS

We assume that there is one date, S states, and one commodity in each state. As a consequence, spot commodity prices can be normalized as unity. As before, we assume that there are S states of the world, and N securities where $N \leq S$. Hence, the number of securities may be less than the number of states.

The $N \times S$ matrix of payoffs of the N securities is given by:

$$X = \begin{bmatrix} x_{11} & x_{12} & \cdots & x_{1S} \\ \vdots & \vdots & & \vdots \\ x_{N1} & x_{N2} & \cdots & x_{NS} \end{bmatrix}. \tag{2.1}$$

Recall that θ_n is the units purchased of security n, and q_n is the price of security n.

Example 2.1 Consider an economy with one date and three states. Suppose there are three securities. Security 1 pays 1 in state 1 and zero otherwise.

Security 2 pays 1 in state 2 and zero otherwise. Suppose that the third security is a risk-free bond. What is the payoff matrix?

$$X_1 = \begin{bmatrix} 1 & 0 & 0 \\ 0 & 1 & 0 \\ 1 & 1 & 1 \end{bmatrix}. \tag{2.2}$$

Markets are complete since the rank of X is 3. The reason is that holding the first two securities allows the consumer to obtain consumption contingent on states 1 and 2. To attain consumption contingent on state 3 occurring, consider a portfolio that involves short selling the first two assets and buying the third. This portfolio has a payoff of one contingent on state 3. Hence, by trading in the first two assets and portfolios involving the third, consumers can achieve any pattern of state-contingent consumption.

Now suppose that there are only two states. In this case, one of the securities is a *redundant* security, that is, a security whose payoff structure can be constructed by using the other securities in the market. In this case, the payoff matrix becomes

$$X_2 = \begin{bmatrix} 1 & 0 \\ 0 & 1 \\ 1 & 1 \end{bmatrix}. \tag{2.3}$$

The consumer can attain a consumption of 1 in each state i) by holding one unit each in the first two securities, or (ii) by holding a unit of the risk-free bond. In the first case, the portfolio satisfies $\theta^1 = (1, 1, 0)'$ whereas in the latter case it is given by $\theta^2 = (0, 0, 1)'$. A redundant security is thus a security whose payoffs can be generated by holding a portfolio of the other securities. In this case, holding the first portfolio yields exactly the same payoff as holding the second portfolio.

We can also consider the case with three states and two securities. Suppose, in particular, that only the two risky securities are available. The payoff matrix is

$$X_3 = \begin{bmatrix} 1 & 0 & 0 \\ 0 & 1 & 0 \end{bmatrix}. \tag{2.4}$$

Now there is no way for consumers to trade in securities to obtain consumption in state 3. Hence, markets are incomplete as the number of securities is less than the number of states.

To characterize behavior in securities markets, we need to make further assumptions regarding the price of a portfolio and its payoff. These issues are discussed next.

2.1.1. *The law of one price*

Recall that for any vector of security prices q in $\Re^N$, a portfolio θ has market value $q \cdot \theta$ and payoff $X^T\theta$. We now make some additional assumptions. The first has to do with the notion of a *payoff space*. For the case of complete markets with S states, the payoff space consists of $\Re^S$. In this case, $N = S$ and investors can attain any payoff in $\Re^S$ by forming portfolios based on the S linearly independent columns of X. When markets are incomplete, there are only $N < S$ linearly independent columns of X and the set of payoffs that investors can obtain is $\mathcal{X} \subset \Re^S$. It is also possible to allow investors to trade in securities that are non-linear functions of the basis payoffs such as options. In this case, the payoff space $\mathcal{X}$ becomes infinite dimensional.

We now make two additional assumptions regarding portfolio payoffs and their prices.

Assumption 2.1 *(Free portfolio formation)*

$$X_1^T\theta \in \mathcal{X}, X_2^T\phi \in \mathcal{X} \Rightarrow X_1^T\theta + X_2^T\phi \in \mathcal{X}.$$

This means that if investors can attain the payoff $X_1^T\theta \in \mathcal{X}$ and the payoff $X_2^T\phi \in \mathcal{X}$, then they can also attain the payoff $X_1^T\theta + X_2^T\phi \in \mathcal{X}$. For the case of complete markets, $\mathcal{X} = \Re^S$, implying that the assumption is satisfied. Notice that the assumption is not without content. For example, it rules out short sales constraints, bid-ask spreads, and transactions costs of various types. We discuss the impact of such frictions below.

Assumption 2.2 *(Law of one price)*

$$(a\theta + b\phi) \cdot q = a(\theta \cdot q) + b(\phi \cdot q).$$

This says that the value of the new portfolio $a\theta + b\phi$, where a and b are constants, must equal the value of its parts. Notice that these assumptions rule out arbitrage opportunities of various types. As an example, suppose there are N securities, with the first $N - 1$ assets denoting stocks and the Nth asset a nominally risk-free Treasury bill. Consider two investment strategies. The first involves investing in a portfolio with one unit of the first stock, say IBM stock, while the second involves investing in a portfolio with 100 units of a one-month Treasury bill. Thus, $\theta = (1, 0, \ldots, 0)'$ and $\phi = (0, 0, \ldots, 100)'$, and the value of each portfolio is $\theta \cdot q = q_1$ and $\phi \cdot q = 100q_N$. Assumption 2.1 says an investor cannot make an instantaneous profit by re-bundling the assets in the two portfolios and selling the assets in the new portfolio for a higher price. That is, the value of $(\theta + \phi) \cdot q$ cannot be greater than $\theta \cdot q + \phi \cdot q$.

Assumptions 2.1 and 2.2 also imply that the zero payoff must be available and must have zero price, that is, $0 \in \mathcal{X}$ and $q(0) = 0$. Otherwise, any payoff could be obtained at any price. To see this, suppose that the law of one price does not hold. Then note that the zero payoff can be purchased at any price because any portfolio of the zero payoff is also the zero payoff. If the zero payoff can be purchased at any price, then any payoff can be purchased at any price.

We now consider two examples in which these assumptions may fail. The first involves a case with a bid-ask spread and the second the presence of a short sales constraint.

Example 2.2 Suppose there are two assets. Let q_b be the buying price of asset 1 and q_s be its selling price with $q_b > q_s$. For asset 2, the buying and selling prices are assumed to be equal, q_2. Also consider two portfolios, $\theta = (-1, 1)'$ and $\phi = (1, -1)'$. According to the first portfolio, an investor sells one unit of asset 1 and buys a unit of asset 2, while with portfolio ϕ he does the opposite. The value of the sum of the two portfolios is:

$$\theta \cdot q + \phi \cdot q = -q_s + q_2 + q_b - q_2 = q_b - q_s > 0.$$

By contrast, the combination of the two portfolios is equivalent to owning zero units of each asset

$$(\theta + \phi) \cdot q = 0,$$

since we know that the price of the zero payoff must be zero. Otherwise, any asset could be obtained at any price. Thus, we find that $\theta \cdot q + \phi \cdot q > (\theta + \phi) \cdot q$, implying that the law of one price does not hold.

Example 2.3 Suppose that the investor faces a short sales constraint for asset 1 such that $\theta_1 \geq -5$. Purchases and sales of asset 2 are unrestricted. Consider the two portfolios $\theta = (-5, 4)'$ and $\phi = (-1, 3)'$. The market value of the individual portfolios is:

$$\theta \cdot q + \phi \cdot q = -5q_1 + 4q_2 - q_1 + 3q_2 = -6q_1 + 7q_2.$$

Now consider a new portfolio that is the sum of the individual portfolios, $\theta + \phi$. To impose the short sales constraint, we can express the market value of this portfolio as:

$$\begin{aligned}(\theta + \phi) \cdot q &= \max(\theta_1 + \phi_1, -5)q_1 + (\theta_2 + \phi_2)q_2 \\ &= -5q_1 + 7q_2 \\ &> \theta \cdot q + \phi \cdot q = -6q_1 + 7q_2.\end{aligned}$$

Hence, we find that the law of one price does not hold. In later chapters we discuss the role of frictions such as borrowing constraints and transactions costs in determining equilibrium asset returns, and allocations. Our discussion here shows that in the presence of such frictions, the pricing function does not satisfy the simple linearity that is implied by the law of one price.

Now consider the relationship between the existence of a discount factor used to price payoffs and the law of one price. Suppose an equilibrium exists. Notice that if $S = N$ so that markets are complete, the price of any security n is expressed as the discounted value of its payoffs using the contingent claims prices p_s.

Equivalently, if markets are complete, the price of any payoff can be expressed as the expectation of the payoff times the stochastic discount factor, which is linear since the expectation operator is linear. Hence, the law of one price holds. If markets are not complete, there may not exist a unique discount factor. Nevertheless, the equilibrium pricing function still exhibits the linearity property, which implies that the law of one price holds.

It is also possible to prove the converse of this result, namely, if the law of one price holds, then there is a discount factor that can be used to price payoffs. We have already demonstrated that under Assumption 2.2, the pricing function is linear. The existence of a discount factor based on the law of one price derives from the fact that any linear function on a payoff space $\mathcal{X}$ can be represented as an inner product.[1] In other words, the pricing function that is used to value any payoff $x \in \mathcal{X}$ is a linear function and has the representation $q = E[x^\star x]$ for $x^\star \in \mathcal{X}$. The existence of the discount factor $x^\star$ is guaranteed by means of a projection argument. Following a more general approach described by Hansen and Richard [234], Hansen and Jagannathan [232] consider a payoff space $\mathcal{X}$ that can be expressed in terms of N basis payoffs. Organize the basis payoffs into the vector $x = (x_1, x_2, \ldots, x_N)$ and also their prices. They show that the discount factor $x^\star \in \mathcal{X}$ that satisfies the law of one price has the form

$$x^\star = q' E(xx')^{-1} x, \tag{2.5}$$

where q denotes the price of the basis payoffs under $x^\star$, that is, $q = E[x^\star x]$.

To show this, notice that the payoff space is generated as $\mathcal{X} = \{c'x\}$. The discount factor that we are seeking must be in the payoff space. Hence, $x^\star = c'x$. Define c so that $x^\star = c'x$ prices the basis payoffs. Hence, we require that $q = E(x^\star x) = E(xx'c)$. Hence, $c = E(xx')^{-1} q$ provided the inverse $E(xx')^{-1}$ exists. But this is guaranteed by the law of one price.

[1] Let $\mathcal{X}$ be a linear space. An *inner product* on $\mathcal{X}$ is a mapping that associates to each ordered pair of vectors x, y a scalar denoted (x, y) that satisfies the following properties: (i) $(x + y, z) = (x, z) + (y, z)$ (Additivity); (ii) $(\alpha x, y) = \alpha(x, y)$ (Homogeneity); (iii) $(x, y) = (y, x)$ (Symmetry); (iv) $(x, x) > 0$ for $x \neq 0$ (Positive Definiteness).

To see how this result applies in the case we have considered, suppose that $\mathcal{X}$ is the space of all random variables $\tilde{x}$ with finite variance. That is, if $\mu = E(\tilde{x})$ is finite, then $\sigma^2 = E(|\tilde{x} - \mu|^2)$ is finite. An inner product on $\mathcal{X}$ is given by $(x, y) = E(\tilde{x}\tilde{y})$.

In other words, if the inverse of $E(xx')$ does not exist, there are multiple solutions for c satisfying the relation $c = E(xx')^{-1}q$. Since c defines the price of any payoff through the linear pricing function, this would mean that there are different prices for the same payoff $x \in \mathcal{X}$. But this would violate the law of one price. Hence, the discount factor is defined as in Equation (2.5). The discount factor is a linear combination of x so it is in the payoff space $\mathcal{X}$. By construction it prices the basis payoffs and it also prices any $x \in \mathcal{X}$:

$$E[x^{\star}(x'c)] = E\left[q'E(xx')^{-1}xx'c\right] = q'c.$$

Finally by linearity we have that $q(c'x) = c'q(x)$.

Note, however, that the discount factor is not guaranteed to be strictly positive. For that we need to define stronger forms of the notion of absence of arbitrage.

2.1.2. *Arbitrage opportunities*

Stronger forms of arbitrage opportunities can also be defined. We have two definitions.

An *arbitrage of the first kind* is a portfolio θ in $\Re^N$ with

$$q \cdot \theta \leq 0 \quad \text{and} \quad X^T\theta > 0. \tag{2.6}$$

An *arbitrage of the second kind* is a portfolio θ in $\Re^N$ with

$$q \cdot \theta < 0 \quad \text{and} \quad X^T\theta \geq 0. \tag{2.7}$$

Examples of economies with arbitrage opportunities of the first and second types are as follows:

Example 2.4 Suppose there are three states of the world, $S = 3$, and two securities, $N = 2$. Let the prices of the securities be $q = (1, 1)'$. Let

$$X = \begin{bmatrix} 1 & -1 & 1 \\ 0 & -1 & 1 \end{bmatrix}. \tag{2.8}$$

Notice that for any vector $(\theta_1, \theta_2)'$ where $\theta_1 > 0$, the payoff on the portfolio is given by

$$X^T\theta = \begin{bmatrix} 1 & 0 \\ -1 & -1 \\ 1 & 1 \end{bmatrix} \begin{bmatrix} \theta_1 \\ \theta_2 \end{bmatrix} = \begin{bmatrix} & \theta_1 \\ -\theta_1 & -\theta_2 \\ \theta_1 & +\theta_2 \end{bmatrix}. \tag{2.9}$$

Thus, $X^T\theta \geq 0$ only if $\theta_1 + \theta_2 = 0$, which is just the definition of an arbitrage opportunity of the first type. Hence, choosing $\theta_1 > 0$ and $\theta_1 = -\theta_2$, the initial outlay for the portfolio is zero but it yields positive profits in some state of nature.

Example 2.5 Suppose that there are two states of the world, $S = 2$, and two securities, $N = 2$. Let the matrix of payoffs be equal to:

$$X = \begin{bmatrix} 4 & -4 \\ 1 & -1 \end{bmatrix}. \tag{2.10}$$

Suppose that the vector of total purchases on the two assets is given by $\theta = (1, -4)$. Then

$$X^T\theta = \begin{bmatrix} 4 & 1 \\ -4 & -1 \end{bmatrix} \begin{bmatrix} 1 \\ -4 \end{bmatrix} = \begin{bmatrix} 0 \\ 0 \end{bmatrix}. \tag{2.11}$$

Notice that the payoff on the portfolio is zero in all states of nature. Let the price of security 1 be equal to 1. As long as the price of security 2 is greater than 1/4, the initial outlay is negative. For example, if $q_2 = 1$, then,

$$q \cdot \theta = (1 \;\; 1) \begin{bmatrix} 1 \\ -4 \end{bmatrix} = -3,$$

which means that the investor receives funds to hold the portfolio.

Clearly, the existence of such arbitrage opportunities cannot be consistent with a security market equilibrium in which the utility function of all agents is strictly increasing in consumption. From the definition of the agent's problem in the security market equilibrium, we see that an arbitrage of the first kind implies that a zero endowment yields a non-negative, non-zero consumption allocation. Consider the problem in Section 1.2.1 where the consumer maximizes date 1 utility by choosing a portfolio of assets subject to the budget constraints in (1.26) and (1.27). If

$$q \cdot \theta \leq 0,$$

then

$$\bar{p}_s \cdot c_s \leq \theta \cdot x_s$$

is satisfied with $c_s > 0$ for some s if $X^T\theta > 0$, which is equivalent to $\theta \cdot x_s > 0$ for some s.

Thus, we can show that if utility functions are strictly increasing (so that there is at least one non-satiated consumer), an arbitrage cannot exist in a competitive equilibrium. Recall that in a security market equilibrium, security prices can be expressed as the discounted value of their payoffs, where the discounting is done using a strictly positive discount factor m. Hence, the existence of a competitive equilibrium in which agents' utility functions are strictly increasing implies the existence of a strictly positive stochastic discount factor that can be used to price any payoff. In the next section, we examine the converse statement, namely, the absence of arbitrage implies the existence of a strictly positive state-price vector.

2.2. EXISTENCE OF A STATE-PRICE VECTOR

The proof that there exists a strictly positive price vector that can be used to price the payoffs on any security based solely on the absence of arbitrage arguments is due to Ross [369]. In this section, we provide a simple proof for an economy with a single date and a finite number of states.[2]

Define a *state-price vector* as a vector ψ in $\Re^S_{++}$ with $q = X\psi$. Notice that it is a strictly positive price vector that is used to assign a price to the random payoffs paid by each security n. If a complete contingent claims equilibrium exists, then the state-price vector is defined as the price function p. Clearly, if a state-price vector exists, then there is no arbitrage. We can also prove the converse.

Theorem 2.2 *There is no arbitrage if and only if there is a state-price vector.*

PROOF

Partition the matrix X as

$$X = \begin{bmatrix} X_1 \\ \cdots \\ X_2 \end{bmatrix} \tag{2.12}$$

such that the payoffs of the first N_1 securities are linearly independent with payoff matrix X_1 and the payoffs on the other $N_2 = N - N_1$ securities are linear combinations of the first N_1 securities with payoff matrix X_2. Then there exists an $N_2 \times N_1$ matrix K such that $X_2 = KX_1$. Thus, we can decompose the payoff matrix X as

$$X = (X_1^T, X_1^T K^T)^T.$$

Let q_1 be the price vector associated with the first N_1 securities and q_2 the price vector associated with the other N_2 securities. Then

$$q = (q_1^T, q_2^T)^T.$$

First, we prove that if there is no arbitrage, then there must be a state-price vector $\psi \in \Re^S_{++}$ such that $q_1 = X_1\psi$. Suppose not. We define

$$A \equiv \{X_1\psi : \psi \in \Re^S_{++}\} \tag{2.13}$$

and

$$B \equiv \{\lambda q_1 : \lambda \in \Re_+\}, \tag{2.14}$$

[2] See Kreps [287] for a proof with continuous time and a continuum of states.

then $A \cap B$ is empty. It follows from the Separating Hyperplane Theorem[3] that there exists a non-zero $\theta_1 \in \Re^{N_1}$ such that

$$\lambda \theta_1^T q_1 \leq \theta_1^T X_1 \psi \quad \forall \lambda \in \Re_+, \ \psi \in \Re_{++}^S. \tag{2.15}$$

This implies that $\theta_1^T q_1 \leq 0$ and $\theta_1^T X_1 \geq 0$. Since X_1 has full rank, there is no $\theta_1 \neq 0$ such that $\theta_1^T X_1 = 0$ and thus we must have $\theta_1^T X_1 > 0$. Let $\theta^T = (\theta_1^T, 0)^T$, then

$$\theta^T q = \theta_1^T q_1 \leq 0 \ \text{ and } \ \theta^T X = \theta_1^T X_1 > 0, \tag{2.16}$$

which implies that θ is an arbitrage.

Second, we prove that $q_2 = X_2 \psi$, where ψ was proven to exist in the previous paragraph. Suppose $q_2 \neq X_2 \psi$, then there exists a $\theta_2 \in \Re^{N_2}$ such that $\theta_2^T(q_2 - X_2\psi) < 0$. Let $\theta_1 = -K^T\theta_2$ and $\theta^T = (\theta_1^T, \theta_2^T)$, then

$$\theta^T X = \theta_1^T X_1 + \theta_2^T K X_1 = 0 \ \text{ and } \ \theta^T q = \theta_2^T (q_2 - X_2 \psi) < 0. \tag{2.17}$$

Thus, θ is an arbitrage.

Therefore, we have proved that $q = X\psi$ with $\psi \in \Re_{++}^S$. Finally it is easy to check that if a state-price vector exists, then there is no arbitrage. ∎

This theorem shows the existence of a strictly positive state-price vector ψ.[4] However, it says nothing about uniqueness. If $N = S$ so that markets are complete, then we know that the state-price vector is unique, and satisfies the equation

$$q = X\psi = Xp,$$

where $p = (p_1 \ldots p_S)'$ is the vector of contingent claims prices. Hence, the state-prices ψ_s may be obtained as the (unique) solution to a set of S linear equations in S unknowns. However, if $N < S$, there may be many solutions for ψ satisfying $q = X\psi$. We can interpret the solutions that are strictly positive as state prices for some underlying complete markets economy that is differentiated by the nature of its preferences, probabilities, or endowment process. However, given information only on a set of securities that does not span the random states, we cannot uniquely identify the underlying economy corresponding to the strictly positive state prices. Likewise, when $N < S$, some of the solutions for the state-price vector may not be strictly positive. In the case of solutions for ψ which are not strictly positive, that is, which have some elements that are zero or negative, then we know that there will exist arbitrage of the first or second kind.

[3] See the statement of Exercise 1 in Chapter 1.

[4] An alternative proof of this result relies on Stiemke's Lemma. See LeRoy and Werner [306] or Duffie [161].

In other words, portfolios of securities which have strictly positive payoffs may have zero prices or portfolios with zero payoffs in some states will have negative prices. In general, when $N < S$, depending on the nature of market incompleteness characterizing the underlying economy, the prices attached to payoffs in different states of the world may differ from the state prices in a complete contingent claims equilibrium. In later chapters, we discuss economies with alternative forms of market incompleteness and study the nature of the equilibrium prices and allocations that arise in them.

2.2.1. *Risk-free asset*

Suppose that a risk-free asset exists, say asset 0. Such an asset has the same payoff in all states of the world, i.e. $x_{0,s}$ is independent of s, or $x_{0,s} = x \ \forall s$. Hence, the price of such an asset today is given by

$$p^f = \sum_{s=1}^{S} \psi_s x$$

$$= x \sum_{s=1}^{S} \psi_s. \tag{2.18}$$

Otherwise, there would exist an arbitrage opportunity. For $x = 1$, the price of an asset today that pays off one unit in all states of nature next period is given by

$$p^f = \sum_{s=1}^{S} \psi_s. \tag{2.19}$$

Suppose $p^f > \sum \psi_s$. Then an investor could sell the security at date 0 and receive p^f. At date 1, s/he would deliver 1 regardless of the state s. Since the cost today of delivering 1 next period regardless of the state s is $\sum_s \psi_s$, the investor would make a profit of $p^f - \sum_s \psi_s > 0$. Conversely, if $p^f < \sum_s \psi_s$, investors could make a profit by buying the security at date zero for p^f and obtaining the strictly positive payoff $\sum_s \psi_s - p^f$ irrespective of the state next period. A similar argument implies that the risk-free rate of return r^f is given by

$$r^f = \frac{1}{p^f}$$

$$= \frac{1}{\sum_{s=1}^{S} \psi_s}. \tag{2.20}$$

2.2.2. *Risk-neutral pricing*

Notice that we can use the state-price vector to derive an alternative representation of security prices. Given a state-price vector ψ_s, we can define the *risk-adjusted probability* of state s as

$$\pi_s^\star = \frac{1}{\sum_{s=1}^S \psi_s} \pi_s \left(\frac{\psi_s}{\pi_s} \right)$$
$$= \frac{\psi_s}{\sum_{s=1}^S \psi_s} \tag{2.21}$$

where $\pi_s > 0$ is the probability of state s occurring. The risk-neutral or risk-adjusted probabilities differ from the objective probabilities by incorporating consumers' attitudes toward risk as captured by the state prices. Recall that the state prices show the valuation of consumption in alternative states of nature whereas the objective probabilities show the likelihood of each state occurring. By contrast, the risk-neutral or risk-adjusted probabilities show the probability of each state occurring, adjusted for the riskiness of that state.

We can use the risk-adjusted probabilities to express the price of security n as

$$q_n = \sum_{s=1}^S x_{n,s} \psi_s$$
$$= \frac{1}{r^f} \sum_{s=1}^S r^f \pi_s \left(\frac{\psi_s}{\pi_s} \right) x_{n,s}$$
$$= \frac{1}{r^f} \sum_{s=1}^S \pi_s^\star x_{n,s}. \tag{2.22}$$

Using the definition of the risk-adjusted probabilities, we can write this last relation as

$$q_n = \frac{1}{r^f} E^\star(x_n), \tag{2.23}$$

where the expectation $E^\star(\cdot)$ is taken with respect to the risk-adjusted probabilities $\pi_s^\star$ for $s = 1, \ldots, S$. This asset valuation formula says that security prices are determined as the expected discounted value of future payoffs, with the risk-adjusted probabilities being used to evaluate the expectation of the random payoffs for each security $n = 1, \ldots, N$. In this formula, consumers' attitudes to risk are accounted for using the risk-neutral probabilities so that "pricing" turns into the problem of evaluating random payoffs with these probabilities and discounting by the risk-free rate.

The relation in (2.23) can be interpreted as a *certainty equivalent* approach to asset pricing. In other words, $E^\star(x_n)$ computes the market-adjusted certainty equivalent of the payoff x_n. In general, different underlying economic environments will assign different certainty equivalents to the same risk embodied in the random set of payoffs X. Equivalently, as we have seen in Chapter 1, different preferences, endowment streams, and probability vectors will, in general, imply a different set of state prices, which will lead to different valuations for the same set of security payoffs summarized by $\{x_{n,s}\}_{s=1}^S$. Finally, since the price of the asset is determined as a certainty equivalent, the time discounting is done using the risk-free rate. This type of valuation is known as *risk-neutral valuation*, and it provides a convenient approach for pricing assets without having to specify some underlying structural model of consumption and asset allocation.

Example 2.6 Suppose there are two securities and two states of the economy. Security 1 pays off 2 in state 1 and 1 in state 2 while security 2 pays off 1 in state 1 and 2 in state 2. For simplicity, suppose that the prices are unity for securities 1 and 2, that is, $q_i = 1$ for $i = 1, 2$. The security prices and payoffs satisfy the relation

$$q = X\psi \quad \Leftrightarrow \quad \begin{bmatrix} 1 \\ 1 \end{bmatrix} = \begin{bmatrix} 2 & 1 \\ 1 & 2 \end{bmatrix} \begin{bmatrix} \psi_1 \\ \psi_2 \end{bmatrix}. \tag{2.24}$$

Since the number of securities equals the number of states, we can solve uniquely for the state prices as

$$\psi = \begin{bmatrix} \psi_1 \\ \psi_2 \end{bmatrix} = X^{-1} q = \frac{1}{3} \begin{bmatrix} 2 & -1 \\ -1 & 2 \end{bmatrix} \begin{bmatrix} 1 \\ 1 \end{bmatrix} = \begin{bmatrix} \frac{1}{3} \\ \frac{1}{3} \end{bmatrix}. \tag{2.25}$$

Given the state prices, the risk-adjusted probabilities are defined as

$$\pi_1^\star = \frac{\psi_1}{\sum_s \psi_s} = \frac{1/3}{2/3} = \frac{1}{2} \text{ and } \pi_2^\star = \frac{1}{2}. \tag{2.26}$$

We can also compute the risk-free interest rate for this economy as

$$r^f = \frac{1}{p^f} = \frac{1}{\psi_1 + \psi_2} = \frac{3}{2}, \tag{2.27}$$

which implies that the (net) real interest rate is $r^f - 1 = 1.5 - 1 = 0.5$.

Suppose instead that there are three states of the economy. Assume that security 1 pays off 1 in state 3 while security 2 pays off 2. Now the payoff matrix becomes:

$$X = \begin{bmatrix} 2 & 1 & 1 \\ 1 & 2 & 2 \end{bmatrix}. \tag{2.28}$$

The state prices satisfy the set of equations:

$$1 = 2\psi_1 + \psi_2 + \psi_3 \tag{2.29}$$

$$1 = \psi_1 + 2\psi_2 + 2\psi_3. \tag{2.30}$$

Since the number of states exceeds the number of securities, there exist multiple solutions for the state prices. Solving for $\psi_1 = 1 - 2\psi_2 - 2\psi_3$ from the second equation and substituting the result into the first shows that any set of ψ_2 and ψ_3 that satisfies the relation $3\psi_2 + 3\psi_3 = 1$ is a solution for the state prices. One set of strictly positive state prices that satisfies these conditions is given by $\psi_1 = \frac{1}{3}$, $\psi_2 = \frac{1}{6}$ and $\psi_3 = \frac{1}{6}$. Associated with these prices are the risk-adjusted probabilities:

$$\pi_1^\star = \frac{\psi_1}{\sum_s \psi_s} = \frac{1/3}{4/6} = \frac{1}{2} \tag{2.31}$$

$$\pi_2^\star = \frac{\psi_2}{\sum_s \psi_s} = \frac{1/6}{4/6} = \frac{1}{4} \tag{2.32}$$

$$\pi_3^\star = \frac{\psi_3}{\sum_s \psi_s} = \frac{1/6}{4/6} = \frac{1}{4}. \tag{2.33}$$

The risk-free rate for this economy is given by:

$$r^f = (p^f)^{-1} = \left(\sum_s \psi_s\right)^{-1} = 1.5 \tag{2.34}$$

as before. However, this is not the unique solution. Another set of state prices is obtained by setting $\psi_3 = 0$ and $\psi_1 = \psi_2 = \frac{1}{3}$. However, we know by Theorem 2.2 that such a set of state prices would admit arbitrage.

2.2.3. *The stochastic discount factor*

Returning to the results of the previous chapter, we can use the existence of the state-price vector to give an alternative representation for security prices. For this purpose, define:

$$m_s = \frac{\psi_s}{\pi_s}, \tag{2.35}$$

where π_s is the probability of state s. (Notice that this definition is consistent with the existence of a complete contingent claims equilibrium in which the contingent claims prices are equal to the probability-weighted intertemporal MRS for any consumer i.)

Example 2.7 Consider the economy with two dates and two states in Example 2.6. For the prices and payoff matrix given in Equation (2.24), the state prices are $\psi_1 = \psi_2 = \frac{1}{3}$. Suppose the objective probabilities of state 1 and state 2 are given by $\pi_1 = 0.1$ and $\pi_2 = 0.9$. Then the unique (strictly positive) stochastic discount factor is

$$m_1 = \frac{\psi_1}{\pi_1} = \frac{1/3}{1/10} = \frac{10}{3} \tag{2.36}$$

$$m_2 = \frac{\psi_2}{\pi_2} = \frac{1/3}{9/10} = \frac{10}{27}. \tag{2.37}$$

If the state prices are not uniquely defined, there also exist multiple solutions for the stochastic discount factor and some of them may not be strictly positive.

Using the definition for m_s, we can derive an expression for security prices as

$$\begin{aligned} q_n &= \sum_{s=1}^{S} \psi_s x_{n,s} \\ &= \sum_{s=1}^{S} \pi_s m_s x_{n,s} \\ &= E[m x_n]. \end{aligned} \tag{2.38}$$

Notice that m_s is the ratio of the state price of state s to the probability of state s; hence, it is positive because state prices and probabilities are both positive. As before, we refer to m_s as the stochastic discount factor for state s. We note that if m_s is small, then state s is "cheap" in the sense that investors are unwilling to pay a high price to receive wealth in that state. If we define the risk-neutral probabilities, then the price of the asset is also proportional to the expected value of the random payoffs. However, we note that the existence of the stochastic discount factor as defined in Equation (2.35) does not depend on the existence of any specific asset-pricing model but only on the absence of arbitrage opportunities.

2.3. BINOMIAL SECURITY MARKETS

The concepts that we have developed in this chapter have found application in markets that are assumed to have very simple structure. Following Cox, Ross, and Rubinstein [129], these markets are known as *binomial* security markets. In such markets, the prices or payoffs of securities are assumed to display either "up" or "down" movements.

2.3.1. *An economy with two dates*

Let's begin with an economy with two dates, date 0 and date 1. Suppose that there are two securities. Let one of the securities be a pure discount bond that matures at date 1 and pays 1 at maturity. The price of the bond at date 0 is $q_b(s_0) = r^{-1}$ where $r > 0$. Let the other security be a stock or equity and assume that at each date the equity price can move either "up" or "down." Hence, starting from a strictly positive initial price $q_e(s_0)$, the price of the stock at date 1 is given by

$$q_e(s_1) = \begin{cases} q_e(s_0)u & \text{if } s_1 = u \\ q_e(s_0)d & \text{if } s_1 = d, \end{cases} \tag{2.39}$$

where $u > 1$ and $d < 1$. Notice that the one-period return on the stock is u or d depending on the event that occurs at date 1. For simplicity, let $q_e(s_0) = 1$. Notice that the payoff matrix denoted X at date 1 is given by

$$X = \begin{bmatrix} 1 & 1 \\ u & d \end{bmatrix}.$$

Since $u > d$, this matrix has full rank. Hence, the rank of the payoff matrix equals the number of states, implying that markets are complete. Given $q(s_0) = (q_b(s_0), q_e(s_0))'$, we can solve for the state-prices for the states "up" and "down" as:

$$p(s_1) = \begin{bmatrix} p(s_0, u) \\ p(s_0, d) \end{bmatrix} = X^{-1} \begin{bmatrix} q_b(s_0) \\ q_e(s_0) \end{bmatrix}.$$

Given X, the state prices have a particularly simple form as:

$$p(s_0, u) = \frac{r - d}{r(u - d)} \tag{2.40}$$

$$p(s_0, d) = \frac{u - r}{r(u - d)}. \tag{2.41}$$

Now suppose that we are interested in pricing a non-traded security in this economy. Consider an *option*. This is a security whose payoff depends on the value of an underlying security, say a stock. The option has a maturity date and a strike price, say K. A *call option* is the right to purchase the stock at the maturity date at the strike price. Notice that the investor will exercise the option if the price of the stock rises above the strike price. Otherwise, the option will not be exercised. For the simple two-period economy, the maturity date of the option is date 1, and the payoffs on the option at date 1 satisfy:

$$x_u = q_e(s_0)u - K \quad \text{if } q_e(s_0)u - K > 0$$

$$x_d = 0 \quad \text{if } q_e(s_0)d - K < 0.$$

The issue is to find the current price of the option, $q_o(s_0)$.

Notice that we have solved for the state prices for this model. Since markets are complete, the option is a *redundant* security in the sense that we can achieve the payoffs associated with the option by using our bond and stock. You can think about the option as a portfolio of one stock bought at date 0 and K bonds shorted at date 0, which pays only if the state is "up." Hence, its price at date 0 is just the sum of its date-1 payoffs times the state prices for date 1 events:

$$\begin{aligned} q_o(s_0) &= [q_e(s_0)u - K] \cdot \frac{r-d}{r(u-d)} + 0 \cdot \frac{u-r}{r(u-d)} \\ &= [q_e(s_0)u - K]\frac{r-d}{r(u-d)}. \end{aligned} \tag{2.42}$$

Recall that we can give an alternative representation for the price of the option by making use of the risk-adjusted probabilities defined in Equation (2.21) as:

$$\begin{aligned} \pi^\star &= \frac{p(s_0, u)}{p(s_0, u) + p(s_0, d)} = \frac{r-d}{u-d} \\ 1 - \pi^\star &= \frac{p(s_0, d)}{p(s_0, u) + p(s_0, d)} = \frac{u-r}{u-d}. \end{aligned}$$

Notice that the risk-adjusted probabilities sum to unity:

$$\pi^\star + (1 - \pi^\star) = \frac{r-d}{u-d} + \frac{u-r}{u-d} = \frac{u-d}{u-d} = 1.$$

Given the risk-adjusted or risk-neutral probabilities, we can price a risky asset such as a derivative instrument using *risk-neutral valuation*, whereby the price of the derivative today is determined as the expected discounted value of its future payoffs. The discounting is done by the risk-free rate. Hence, we can equivalently obtain its price at date 0 as:

$$q_o(s_0) = \frac{1}{r}\left[\pi^\star x_u + (1 - \pi^\star)x_d\right],$$

which is the same expression as in Equation (2.42).

Recall that under risk-neutral valuation, the return on *all* assets should equal the risk-free rate of return r. The return on the stock or equity

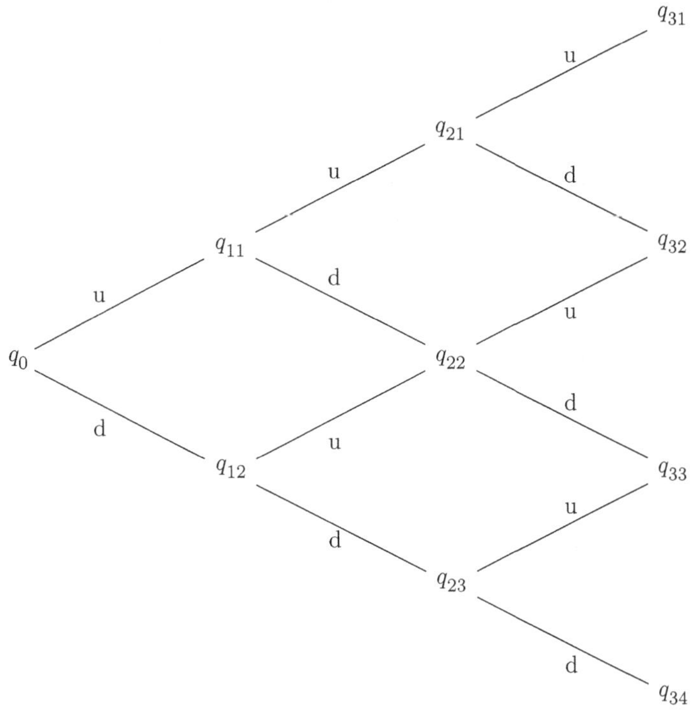

Figure 2.1. Three-period binomial tree

is given by $r_e(s_1) = q_e(s_1)/q_e(s_0)$. Using the risk-neutral probabilities, the expected return of the stock price at date 1 is:

$$\begin{aligned} E^\star[r_e(s_1)] &= \left[\pi^\star u + (1 - \pi^\star)d\right] \\ &= \left[\frac{r-d}{u-d}u + \frac{u-r}{u-d}d\right] \\ &= r, \end{aligned} \tag{2.43}$$

which equals the risk-free rate as claimed.

2.3.2. *A multi-period economy*

Now suppose there are T dates and at each date t there are only two possible states: "up" or "down." Let the variable s_t denote the state at t. Hence, s_t can take on the values "up" or "down." We can define an event at date t as the sequence of "up"s and "down"s that have been realized up to that date, $s^t = (s_0, s_1, \ldots, s_t)'$. Let $\mathcal{S}^t$ denote the set of possible events at t. Figure 2.1 provides a representation of the event s^t in terms of an event tree.

Let us continue to assume that there are two securities that can be traded in this economy, a pure discount bond maturing at date T and a stock whose price can move "up" or "down" in each period. The bond has a payoff of 1 at date T, and its price along the event tree is defined as $q_b(s^t) = r^{-(T-t)}$. Assume that the price of the stock at date 0 is 1, that is, $q_e(s_0) = 1$. Recall that the price of the stock can move either up or down in each period. Hence, starting from its initial price, its price in an event s^t such that the number of "down"s between period 0 and t is n is given by:

$$q_e(s^t) = u^{t-n}d^n, \quad 0 \leq n \leq t.$$

Using the same reasoning the payoff on the stock at the terminal date is just equal to its price at that date and equal to $u^{T-n}d^n$ in the event s^T that the number of "down"s is n.

This type of economy allows us to consider the notion of *dynamically complete* economies.[5] Notice at each date t there are 2^t events s^t depending on the sequence of "up"s and "down"s that has occurred up to that date. In a complete markets setting, agents can trade claims at date 0 to achieve consumption conditional on any event s^t occurring at date t. In Chapter 7, we discuss further economies with multi-period contingent claims such that there exist time-0 prices for consumption contingent on the event s^t occurring at t. In that chapter, we will also consider the equivalence of equilibria with trading at time 0 in a full set of complete contingent claims versus sequential trading in an alternative set of assets.

In this chapter, we consider a related but slightly different issue, namely, under what conditions we can replicate the contingent claims prices at each date t conditional on the history s^t by trading sequentially in a given set of securities. In other words, when can we "complete" a security market by such sequential trades? It turns out that the answer depends on how well the payoffs on the existing set of securities "span" the set of states at each date. Let $p(s^t)$ denote the time t price of a history of shocks denoted s^t.[6] To see how we can generate a set of strictly positive event prices by sequential trades in the existing securities at each date, consider the strategy of purchasing security at date t and selling it at date $t+1$. The payoff on this strategy for any security with price $q(s^t)$ at t is given by $q(s^{t+1}) + x(s^{t+1})$.

[5] This issue is analyzed more generally by LeRoy and Werner [306] and by Duffie [161]. The latter author also considers the issue of dynamic spanning in economies with infinite-dimensional state spaces.

[6] In the parlance of Chapter 7, these prices will correspond to the contingent claims prices with sequential trading. The time-0 contingent claims can be obtained as the product of these prices, starting from $p(s_0) = 1$.

If contingent claims prices exist, it must be the case that the value of this strategy is given by:

$$-p(s^t)q(s^t) + \sum_{s^{t+1}\in S^t} p(s^{t+1})\left[q(s^{t+1}) + x(s^{t+1})\right] = 0, \tag{2.44}$$

starting from any $p(s_0) = 1$. Otherwise, there would exist an arbitrage opportunity. For the simple binomial model, we have two securities – a bond and a stock. Using the expressions for the prices in each event s^t and s^{t+1}, the condition for the bond is:

$$p(s^t)r^{-(T-t)} = r^{-(T-(t+1))}p(s^t, u) + r^{-(T-(t+1))}p(s^t, d),$$

where $p(s^t, u)$ and $p(s^t, d)$ denote the events at $t + 1$ such that the history of "up"s and "down"s is summarized by the history s^t up to period t and either "up" (u) or "down" (d) occurs at $t + 1$. We can simplify this further as:

$$p(s^t) = rp(s^t, u) + rp(s^t, d). \tag{2.45}$$

For the stock, the relevant condition is:

$$p(s^t)u^{t-n}d^n = u^{t+1-n}d^n p(s^t, u) + u^{t-n}d^{n+1}p(s^t, d), \quad 0 \leq n \leq t,$$

or

$$p(s^t) = up(s^t, u) + dp(s^t, d). \tag{2.46}$$

Now stack the resulting conditions in equations (2.46) and (2.47) as:

$$\begin{bmatrix} p(s^t) \\ p(s^t) \end{bmatrix} = \begin{bmatrix} r & r \\ u & d \end{bmatrix} \begin{bmatrix} p(s^t, u) \\ p(s^t, d) \end{bmatrix}. \tag{2.47}$$

Notice immediately that we can solve for the vector of event prices $p(s^{t+1}) = (p(s^t, u), p(s^t, d))'$ starting from $p(s_0) = 1$ if and only if the rank of the payoff (or equivalently, return) matrix for the existing securities is equal to the number of states. Since $u > d$, this condition is satisfied for the binomial model. Using the relation in Equation (2.47), we can find the event prices for each s^t such that the number of "down"s preceding t is n by:

$$p(s_n^t) = \left[\frac{u - r}{r(u - d)}\right]^n \left[\frac{r - d}{r(u - d)}\right]^{t-n}, \quad 0 \leq n \leq t. \tag{2.48}$$

The event prices are strictly positive if $u > r > d$, which requires the risk-free rate is between the high and low returns on the stock.

We can also price an option using the state prices or equivalently, the risk-neutral probabilities along the event tree. Recall that the number of events with n "down"s between dates 0 and T is given by $\binom{T}{n}$. Hence, the price of an option at date 0 that matures at date T is given by:

$$q_o(s_0) = \sum_{n=0}^{T} \binom{T}{n} \max(u^{T-n}d^d - K, 0)p(s_n^t). \tag{2.49}$$

Example 2.8 Suppose there are four dates, 0, 1, 2, 3, and at each date t there are two states. There are two securities that can be traded in this economy, a pure discount bond maturing at date 3 and a stock whose price can move "up" or ""down" in each period. The price of the stock at date 0 is \$20, that is $q_e(s_0) = 20$. In the first period, from date 0 to 1, the stock price can go up by 10% and go down by 10%. Over time, the stock price volatility decreases so that "up" and "down" movements are expected to be 8% for the second period and 5% for the last period. The risk-free interest rate is 1% per period. The investor holds 100 units of the bond.

We will use the binomial model of securities markets to find the value of a European call option with a strike price of \$21 that will expire at date 3. First, we will calculate the evolution of the stock price given the assumptions above. In the first period, the stock price can increase by 10% or decrease by 10%, leading to the two nodes of \$22 or \$18. In the second period, it can now increase or decrease by 8%. Thus, if the stock price was \$22 and it increased in the second period, we obtain the node of \$23.76 and so on. To price the option, we need to find the final nodes for which the option has a positive payoff. Since the call option gives the holder the right to buy the stock at the exercise price, the call option will have a positive payoff when the stock price at $t = 3$ is greater than the exercise price. With an exercise price of \$21 for the option, Table 2.1 shows that there are only three final nodes in which the option will be exercised. These nodes correspond to the histories $(s_0, u, u, u)'$, $(s_0, u, u, d)'$, and $(s_0, u, d, u)'$. Denote the payoffs for these histories by:

$$x(s_0, u, u, u) = 24.948 - 21 = 3.948$$

$$x(s_0, u, u, d) = 22.572 - 21 = 1.572$$

$$x(s_0, u, d, u) = 21.252 - 21 = 0.252$$

Finding the state prices for the set of histories that leads to these nodes is enough to determine the current price of this option.

Here we will use a backwards solution to solve for the relevant state-prices using (2.47). Recall that the state price at each date "discounts" the future payoffs to the current price of an asset, that is,

$$q(s^t) = x(s^t, u)p(s^t, u) + x(s^t, d)p(s^t, d) \tag{2.50}$$

Table 2.1. *An economy with four dates and two states*

$t=0$	$t=1$	$t=2$	$t=3$	Option payoff
			24.948	3.948
		23.76		
			22.572	1.572
	22			
			21.252	0.252
		20.24		
			19.228	0
20				
			20.412	0
		19.44		
			18.468	0
	18			
			17.388	0
		16.56		
			15.732	0

for any asset, where s^t denotes the history at date t. At time 1, the possible histories of the shocks are $(s_0, u)'$ and $(s_0, d)'$. Denote the prices associated with these histories by $p(s_0, u)$ and $p(s_0, d)$. These state prices satisfy the following conditions:

$$101p(s_0, u) + 101p(s_0, d) = 100$$

$$22p(s_0, u) + 18p(s_0, d) = 20,$$

where the (gross) payoff on the bond that is worth \$100 at time 0 is \$101 at time 1, and likewise the (gross) payoffs on the stock that is worth \$20 at time 0 are \$22 and \$18, respectively. The solution is

$$p(s_0, u) = 0.5446, \quad p(s_0, d) = 0.4455. \tag{2.51}$$

In the second period, we are interested only in the histories $(s_0, u, u)'$ and $(s_0, u, d)'$. The state prices for these histories satisfy:

$$102.01p(s_0, u, u) + 102.01p(s_0, u, d) = 101$$

$$23.76p(s_0, u, u) + 20.24p(s_0, u, d) = 22$$

The solution is

$$p(s_0, u, u) = 0.5538, \quad p(s_0, u, d) = 0.4368. \tag{2.52}$$

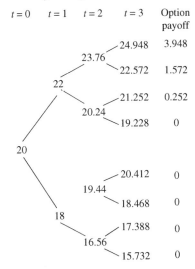

For the third period, we are interested in the histories $(s_0, u, u, u)'$, $(s_0, u, u, d)'$, $(s_0, u, d, u)'$, and $(s_0, u, d, d)'$. The state prices for these histories satisfy:

$$103.03p(s_0, u, u, u) + 103.03p(s_0, u, u, d) = 102.01$$

$$24.948p(s_0, u, u, u) + 22.572p(s_0, u, u, d) = 23.76$$

and

$$103.03p(s_0, u, d, u) + 10.03p(s_0, u, d, d) = 102.01$$

$$21.252p(s_0, u, d, u) + 19.228p(s_0, u, d, d) = 20.24$$

which yield:

$$p(s_0, u, u, u) = p(s_0, u, d, u) = 0.594, \tag{2.53}$$

$$p(s_0, u, u, d) = p(s_0, u, d, d) = 0.396. \tag{2.54}$$

So, the price of the call option at $t = 1$ and conditional on the event s_0, u, is given by:

$$\begin{aligned} q_c(s_0, u) &= p(s_0, u, u)q_c(s_0, u, u) + p(s_0, u, d)q_c(s_0, u, d) \\ &= p(s_0, u, u)[x(s_0, u, u, u)p(s_0, u, u, u) + x(s_0, u, u, d)p(s_0, u, u, d)] \\ &\quad + p(s_0, u, d)[x(s_0, u, d, u)p(s_0, u, d, u) + x(s_0, u, d, d)p(s_0, u, d, d)] \\ &= 0.5538\,[3.948(0.594) + 1.572(0.396)] + 0.4368\,[0.252(0.594)] \\ &= 1.7088. \end{aligned}$$

Discounting back the price at time 1, the price of the option at time 0 is

$$\begin{aligned} q_c(s_0) &= p(s_0, u)q_c(s_0, u) = 0.5446(1.7088) \\ &= 0.9306. \end{aligned} \tag{2.55}$$

We can also find the value of a American call option with a strike price of \$21 that will expire at date 3. [American options give the right to exercise the option early so that the holder of the option can buy or sell (depending on the type of the option) the underlying stock before the option expires, whereas European options can be exercised *only* at the maturity.] Note that the European and American call options have the same current value because early exercise is never profitable compared with the value of waiting. In order to see this, one should compare the value of the option and its payoff at all nodes of the tree. Notice that in states (s_0, u) and (s_0, u, u), exercising the option has a positive payoff since $q_e(s_0, u) = 22 > 21$ and $q_e(s_0, u, u) = 23.76 > 21$. However, the value of waiting until the option expires is greater than instantaneous exercise.

To see this, notice that for $t = 2$ in state s_0, u, u, the value of early exercise is $23.76 - 21 = 2.76$, which is smaller than the value of waiting, given by $[3.948(0.594) + 1.572(0.396)] = 2.9676$. Similarly, the value of the option at time $t = 1$ in state s_0, u is 1.7088, whereas exercising this option at this point will give a payoff of $22 - 21 = 1$, which is smaller than waiting. In this example, there is no node at which early exercise is preferred to waiting so that the value of the European option is equal to that of the American.

2.4. CONCLUSIONS

In this chapter, we showed that the existence of a strictly positive discount factor can be derived from relatively weak assumptions, namely, various assumptions regarding the absence of arbitrage in securities markets. We also showed that the existence of the discount factor does not depend on the assumption of complete markets. Under incomplete markets, however, while a strictly positive discount factor can be shown to exist, it is not unique. In Chapter 1, we characterized the pricing function for economies with a complete set of contingent claims by studying the equilibrium for those economies explicitly. In later chapters, we will illustrate the pricing function for economies with incomplete markets. In this chapter, we have abstracted from other frictions such as bid-ask spreads or short sales constraints. We discuss the impact of these factors in Part IV where we consider transactions costs.

This chapter also serves to illustrate the role of the absence of arbitrage in securities markets more generally. The approach that we have outlined here has found much use in the pricing of derivative instruments such as forward and future contracts and options. Absence of arbitrage arguments has also been used to develop an asset-pricing approach by putting further structure on the payoffs of primary assets, which are assets in net positive supply to the public, or equivalently which are part of the market portfolio. We discuss this approach, which has become known as the arbitrage pricing theory (APT), in Chapter 4 alongside another well-known asset-pricing model, the capital asset-pricing model (CAPM). The notions of the absence of arbitrage that we have developed in this chapter will prove useful when analyzing the implications of these models for pricing a variety of assets.

2.5. EXERCISES

1. Suppose there is one date and two states in the economy. The traded securities are two stocks. The current prices of the stocks are given by $q = (q_1, q_2)' = (\$80, \$88)'$ and their prices next period for each possible

state satisfy:

$$\begin{bmatrix} \$120 & \$80 \\ \$160 & \$60 \end{bmatrix}.$$

A *replicating portfolio* is a portfolio which allows us to obtain a given set of payoffs in the existing states of nature.

(a) What is a replicating portfolio that will yield \$100 in each state of nature?

(b) What is the value of this portfolio today? What is the risk-free rate in this economy?

(c) Find the state prices and the risk-neutral probabilities.

(d) A *put option* gives the owner the right to sell a stock at a given strike price. Find the value of a put option today written on the second stock with an exercise price of \$80.

2. Suppose there is one date and three states of nature. Suppose also that there exists a portfolio of stocks that has the payoffs 5, 8, and 15 in the three states. Such a portfolio is sometimes known as a *state index* security.

(a) Show how you can complete this market with the addition of two options. What are the exercise prices of the options?

(b) Assume that there are two individuals in the economy. Individual 1 receives the endowments (1, 0, 1) in the three states and individual 2 receives the endowments (1, 1, 0). Can consumers insure against endowment risk? If so, which asset allocation should each individual make to achieve this?

(c) Now suppose that there are six states of the economy. The overall economic conditions may be "good," "normal," or "bad." Depending on overall conditions, individuals receive two different values of their endowment, high (H) or low (L). Let s denote the aggregate state of the economy, and let j denote the individual state. Hence, individual i receives the endowment $\omega^i_{j,s}$ for $s = 1, 2, 3$ and $j = 1, 2$. Suppose that the portfolio of stocks pays off the amounts x_s in each aggregate state, regardless of the realization of the individual states. Can individuals insure against endowment risk in this economy?

3. A *collateral constraint* is a constraint to ensure that an investor's endowment is sufficient to cover the value of his borrowings (or short sales) in a given state of nature. Suppose there are S states of the economy and J traded securities. The agent's endowment in state s is denoted ω_s. Let $x_{j,s}$ denote the payoff on the jth security in state s. Purchases (or sales) of the first J' securities are subject to a collateral constraint as:

$$\theta_j x_{j,s} + f_j \omega_s \geq 0, \quad j \in J',$$

where f_j is a number strictly between 0 and 1.

(a) Show that the collateral constraints can equivalently be written as *short sales constraints* restricting the holdings of security j as:

$$\theta_j \geq -b_j, \quad j \in J'.$$

(b) Assume that there are three states of nature, and suppose that one of the securities that is subject to a short sales constraint is a stock. Assume that the payoff on the stock is its price in the different states with $x_{1,1} = \$80$, $x_{1,2} = \$100$, and $x_{1,3} = \$125$. Let $\omega_1 = \$500$, $\omega_2 = \$1,500$, and $\omega_3 = \$5,000$. What is the maximum amount of borrowing that the investor can engage in at date 0?

4. Short Sales Constraints and the Law of One Price

There are two countries, Home and Foreign, in the world economy. Representative agents in these countries both maximize their two-period lifetime utilities, where there are two states of nature in the second period. The expected lifetime utility of each representative agent is given by:

$$U_i = \ln(c_1^i) + \beta \sum_{s=1}^{2} \pi(s) \ln[c_2^i(s)] \quad \text{for } i = 1, 2.$$

Agents are able to trade Arrow-Debreu securities for consumption in each state. The budget constraint for the first period is given by:

$$p(1)z^i(1) + p(2)z^i(2) + p(3)z^i(3) = y_1^i - c_1^i, \quad i = 1, 2,$$

and for the second period:

$$c_2^i(s) = y_2^i(s) + z^i(s) + z^i(3), \quad s = 1, 2,$$

where $z^i(s)$ denotes the number of claims that country i holds for consumption in state s and $z^i(3)$ denotes the holdings of a risk-free asset that pays off one unit of consumption in each state. The output of each country in each period is $y^1 = (2, 4, 0)$ for Home and $y^2 = (2, 0, 4)$ for Foreign. Assume that states are equally likely such that $\pi(1) = \pi(2) = 1/2$ and $\beta = 3/4$.

(a) Suppose that there are no frictions in this economy (i.e. short sales constraints, transaction costs, etc.). Find the equilibrium consumption allocations and prices that solve each representative agent's maximization problem.

(b) Now, assume that agents are subject to short sales constraint such that $z^i(s) \geq -1$. Show that under the short sales constraint, the law of one price does not hold.

5. Put-call parity

A European call option gives the holder the right to buy one share of a stock for a certain price denoted the strike price or exercise price X at the maturity date T. A European put option gives the holder the right to sell one share of the stock for X at the maturity date T. Let c denote the price of the call option and p denote the price of the put option at date t and let r denote the real risk-free return on cash holdings.

Consider the following two portfolios:

- Portfolio A: one European call option plus an amount of cash equal to X/r^{T-t}.
- Portfolio B: one European put option plus one share.

Show that the price of the call and put options are related as:

$$c + X/r^{T-t} = p + S_t, \tag{2.56}$$

where S_t denotes the share price.

CHAPTER 3

Expected utility

In a stochastic environment, consumer preferences reflect their attitudes toward risk. These attitudes affect equilibrium asset prices and the nature of the equilibrium allocations. In this chapter, we describe expected utility preferences, which are additive across possible states of the world. We also define alternative measures of risk aversion and show their relationship to consumers' optimal portfolio choices.

Alternative utility functions imply different attitudes to risk by consumers. We examine the implications of risk aversion for a commonly used set of utility functions. We also discuss such concepts of increasing risk as stochastic dominance and a mean-preserving spread. These notions make precise the idea that a given situation under uncertainty is more risky relative to another, and allow us to examine the impact of increases in risk on consumer choices.

3.1. EXPECTED UTILITY PREFERENCES

The vast majority of consumer choice under uncertainty assumes expected utility maximization by consumers. In our previous analysis, we merely postulated the existence of expected utility preferences.

3.1.1. Some definitions

Expected utility preferences may be derived in an axiomatic way in a manner that is similar to the derivation of standard utility functions. According to the approach followed by von Neumann and Morgenstern [439], agents are assumed to have preferences over lotteries which are specified in terms of a set of payoffs and their probabilities. Under an alternative derivation of expected utility preferences due to Savage [386], the choices are modeled over state-contingent outcomes directly and the existence of the probabilities together with the utility function forming the expected utility representation are derived based on an axiomatic approach. Hence, this latter approach allows the subjective beliefs of agents to differ from some objectively defined probabilities.

We start with a definition. Suppose there are S states of nature, and denote by $\pi = (\pi_1, \ldots, \pi_S)'$ with $\pi_s \geq 0$ and $\sum_{s=1}^{S} \pi_s$ as the associated probability distribution on S.

Definition 3.1 *A function* $u : \Re_+^S \to \Re$ *provides an expected utility representation for preferences if for any state-contingent consumption vector* $c \in \Re_+^S$, *c is preferred to* c' *if and only if* $E[u(c)] = \sum_{s=1}^{S} \pi_s u(c_s) \geq E[u(c')] = \sum_{s=1}^{S} \pi_s u(c'_s)$.

This definition shows that expected utility preferences are *state independent*: that is, expected utility $E[u(c)]$ depends on c_s only through the probability distribution π_s, and not through any changes in the underlying utility index u as a function of the state s.

The expected utility model implies that for a given set of prizes, indifference curves are linear in the underlying probabilities. By construction of expected utility, $u(\cdot)$ is an increasing and continuous function. Suppose that there are three prizes, c_1, c_2, c_3. Then the indifference curve is given by:

$$\bar{u} = \sum_{i=1}^{3} \pi_i u(c_i) = \pi_1 u(c_1) + (1 - \pi_1 - \pi_3) u(c_2) + \pi_3 u(c_3),$$

where we have imposed the fact that $\sum_{i=1}^{3} \pi_i = 1$. This can be written as

$$\pi_3 = \frac{u(c_2) - u(c_1)}{u(c_3) - u(c_2)} \pi_1 + \frac{\bar{u} - u(c_2)}{u(c_3) - u(c_2)}. \tag{3.1}$$

Under the assumption that $u(\cdot)$ is an increasing function, the slope of the indifference curve is positive so that the direction of increasing preference in Figure 3.1 is northwest.

Next, consider the relation between indifference curves and iso-expected lines in terms of the underlying probabilities. Considering the same three prizes as before, these are given by

$$\bar{c} = \pi_1 c_1 + (1 - \pi_1 - \pi_3) c_2 + \pi_3 c_3,$$

or

$$\pi_3 = \frac{c_2 - c_1}{c_3 - c_2} \pi_1 + \frac{\bar{c} - c_2}{c_3 - c_2}. \tag{3.2}$$

Consider a change in the probabilities that leaves the expected value $\bar{c}$ the same but increases the probabilities of the first and third outcomes. This is known as a *mean-preserving spread*, and it is an example of an increase in risk in the sense of Rothschild and Stiglitz [374, 375]. Such a shift implies a northeast move along the iso-expected value line. If $u_{11} < 0$ so that the function $u(\cdot)$ is concave, then its indifference curve will be steeper than

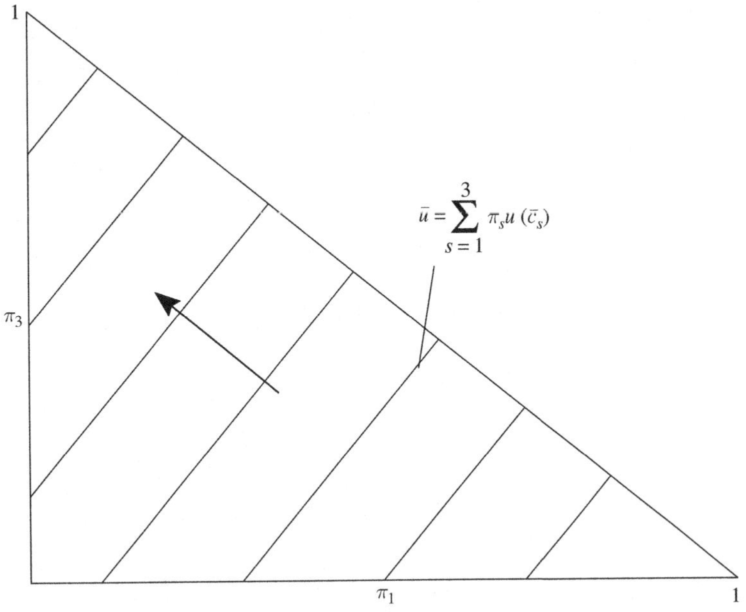

Figure 3.1. Expected utility indifference curves

the iso-expected line, and conversely if $u_{11} > 0$ so that $u(\cdot)$ is convex. That is, whenever $c_1 < c_2 < c_3$,

$$\frac{u(c_2) - u(c_1)}{u(c_3) - u(c_2)} > \frac{c_2 - c_1}{c_3 - c_2} \text{ if } u(\cdot) \text{ is concave,}$$

and conversely if $u(\cdot)$ is convex. Thus, such increases in risk will lead to lower (higher) utility if $u(\cdot)$ is concave (convex). We discuss the impact of increases in risk further in Section 3.3.

One of the most important axioms for deriving expected utility based on this approach is the *independence axiom*, which says that it is the utility of the subsequent reward that matters and not the mechanism for obtaining it. When this axiom is violated, the indifference curves become non-linear in the underlying probabilities. This axiom has been the source of several challenges to expected utility theory. One set of challenges derives from experimental evidence on individuals' choices over alternative lotteries. The famous challenge is known as the *Allais paradox* based on Allais [14]. Consider an individual who faces the prospect of three different monetary prizes as:

$$\text{First prize}: \$2,500,000$$

$$\text{Second prize}: \$500,000$$

$$\text{Third prize}: \$0.$$

Suppose the decision-maker is confronted with the following choices: choose \$500,000 with certainty or face the lottery which yields \$2,500,000 with probability 0.1, \$500,000 with probability 0.89 and 0 with probability 0.01. We can represent these choices as choices between the lotteries $L_1 = (0, 1, 0)'$ and $L_1' = (0.1, 0.89, 0.01)'$. The second choice involves choosing between another set of lotteries: choose between receiving \$2,500,000 with probability 0.1 and 0 with probability of 0.9 or receiving \$500,000 with probability 0.11 and 0 with 0.89. We can represent these lotteries as: $L_2 = (0.1, 0, 0.9)$ and $L_2' = (0, 0.11, 0.89)$.

In an experimental context, it is common for individuals to choose L_1 over L_1', that is, choosing the sure prize of \$500,000 over a lottery with a slightly greater expected reward, and L_2 over L_2', that is, choosing the possibility of a very large gain over the possibility of a gain that is five times less with a slightly higher probability. However, it turns out these choices are inconsistent with expected utility theory. To show this, suppose that there is a von Neumann–Morgenstern expected utility function $u(\cdot)$. Let u^{25}, u^{05}, and u^0 denote the utility associated with the three outcomes. Notice that L_1 being preferred to L_1' implies that the following must hold:

$$u^{05} > 0.1u^{25} + 0.89u^{05} + 0.01u^0.$$

Now add the quantity $0.89u^0 - 0.89u^{05}$ to both sides of this relation:

$$0.89u^0 + 0.11u^{05} > 0.1u^{25} + 0.9u^0,$$

implying that if the expected utility model is correct, L_2' should be preferred to L_2. However, the experimental evidence indicates that when confronted with two different lotteries in which the non-zero reward in one is fivefold higher than the other lottery but the probability of gain is negligibly lower, individuals opt for the lottery with the higher prize. One way of interpreting these results is that it is not just the lottery over an outcome that governs individual choices but rather considerations outside of the domain of expected utility analysis, such as the regret of having passed up the sure reward of a large sum in the first case whereas no such considerations exist in the second case. Machina [329] discusses the evidence against the expected utility model. Chew [102] and Dekel [144] derive a class of non-expected utility preferences that does not rely on the independence axiom. With non-expected utility preferences, the indifference curves in the underlying probability space become non-linear. (See Exercise 4.)

3.2. RISK AVERSION

Suppose we establish a gamble between two prospects, ϵ_1 and ϵ_2. Let the gamble be represented by the random variable $\tilde{\epsilon}$ such that the gamble yields ϵ_1 units of wealth with probability p and ϵ_2 units with probability $(1 - p)$.

The question is whether the consumer will prefer the actuarial value of the gamble (or its expected average value) with certainty or the gamble itself.

The actuarial value of the gamble is its expected value:

$$E(\tilde{\epsilon}) = p\epsilon_1 + (1-p)\epsilon_2. \tag{3.3}$$

An actuarially fair gamble satisfies

$$E(\tilde{\epsilon}) = p\epsilon_1 + (1-p)\epsilon_2 = 0, \tag{3.4}$$

which requires that $p/(1-p) = -\epsilon_2/\epsilon_1$.

Suppose that the consumer has a strictly increasing and continuous utility function U defined on wealth W.[1] Using the definition of the actuarially fair gamble, the expected utility of receiving W plus the expected value of an actuarially fair gamble is:

$$U[W + E(\tilde{\epsilon})] = U[W + p\epsilon_1 + (1-p)\epsilon_2].$$

We say that a consumer is strictly *risk averse* (*risk loving*) if she is unwilling (prefers) to accept an actuarially fair gamble. When the consumer is risk averse (risk loving), the utility of receiving the sure thing $W + E(\tilde{\epsilon})$ is greater (less) than the utility of receiving $W + \epsilon_1$ with probability p and $W + \epsilon_2$ with probability $1 - p$:

$$U[W + E(\tilde{\epsilon})] > (<) pU(W + \epsilon_1) + (1-p)U(W + \epsilon_2). \tag{3.5}$$

Under the assumption that the utility function has only one argument, strict risk aversion (risk loving) implies that the utility function is strictly concave (convex).

We can use Jensen's Inequality to show the converse, namely, that concavity (convexity) of the utility function implies risk aversion (risk loving).

Definition 3.2 *Jensen's Inequality: For a random variable x with mean $E(x)$ and a concave (convex) function $g(\cdot)$,*

$$E[g(x)] < g[E(x)] \quad (E[g(x)] > g[E(x)]).$$

Because U is concave (convex), it follows that

$$E[U(W + \tilde{\epsilon})] < (>) U[W + E(\tilde{\epsilon})] = U(W). \tag{3.6}$$

[1] The monotonicity of the utility function reflects *stochastic dominance preference*, which is the stochastic analogue of "more is better than less." A lottery is said to stochastically dominate another lottery if it is obtained from the first by shifting the probability from lower to higher outcomes. We discuss this notion further in the next section.

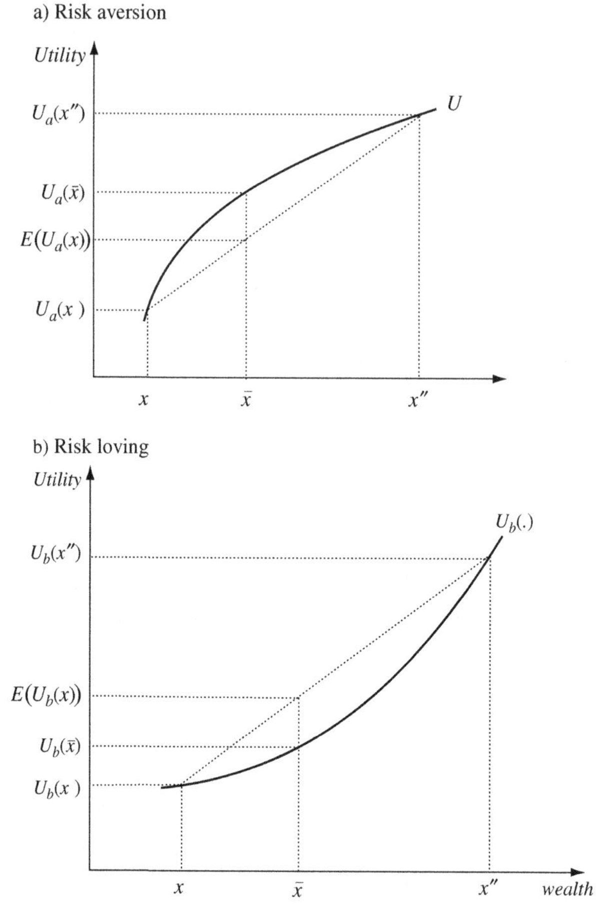

Figure 3.2. Attitudes toward risk

Hence, under the assumption that utility is a function of a single argument, strict concavity (convexity) implies that the agent is *risk averse (risk loving)*, using Jensen's Inequality. If

$$E[U(W+\tilde{\epsilon})] = U[W+E(\tilde{\epsilon})] = U(W), \tag{3.7}$$

then we say the consumer is *risk neutral.* Figure 3.2 shows that when $U[W]$ is strictly concave (convex), $U[E(W)]$ is strictly greater (less) than $E[U(W)]$.

3.3. ONE-PERIOD EXPECTED UTILITY ANALYSIS

A consumer has a choice of holding a risk-free asset with a constant return of r^f and a risky asset with a return of r, where r is a random variable with mean μ and variance σ^2. Assume that $\mu = r^f$.

Suppose that there are two possible outcomes r_1 and r_2 with probabilities π_1 and π_2. Then, for a *fair gamble*,

$$E(r - r^f) = \pi_1(r_1 - r^f) + \pi_2(r_2 - r^f) = 0.$$

For future reference, we can also calculate the variance of the return as

$$\begin{aligned} V(r) &= E[r - E(r)]^2 \\ &= \pi_1(r_1 - \mu)^2 + \pi_2(r_2 - \mu)^2 = \sigma^2. \end{aligned}$$

Consider the decision regarding whether to take part in the fair gamble or not, i.e. whether to hold the risky asset versus the risk-free asset, where $E(r) - r^f = 0$. Suppose the consumer's initial wealth is W_0.

- If the consumer holds the risk-free asset, then end-of-period wealth is $W_1 = W_0(1 + r^f)$, and
$$E(W_1) = W_0(1 + r^f) \quad \text{and} \quad V(W_1) = 0.$$
- If the consumer holds the risky asset, then $W_1 = W_0(1 + r)$, and
$$E(W_1) = W_0[1 + E(r)] \quad \text{and} \quad V(W_1) = W_0^2 V(r).$$

Suppose the investor's objective is to maximize the expected utility of wealth, $E[U(W)]$. The expected utilities from the alternative investment strategies are

$$E[U(W)] = \begin{cases} U[W_0(1 + r^f)] & \text{if invest in the risk-free asset} \\ E[U(W_0(1 + r))] & \text{if invest in the risky asset.} \end{cases}$$

We can approximate $U(x)$ around $x_0 = E(x)$ as

$$U(x) \approx U(x_0) + (x - x_0)U'(x_0) + \frac{(x - x_0)^2}{2} U''(x_0).$$

Consider $x = W_1 = W_0(1 + r)$, and approximate around $x_0 = E(x)$. Taking expectations of both sides yields

$$\begin{aligned} E[U(W_1)] &= U[W_0(1 + r^f)] + W_0 E(r - r^f) U'[W_0(1 + r^f)] \\ &\quad + \frac{W_0^2 E(r - r^f)^2}{2} U''[W_0(1 + r^f)] \\ &= U[W_0(1 + r^f)] + W_0^2 \frac{V(r)}{2} U''[W_0(1 + r^f)] \\ &< U[W_0(1 + r^f)], \end{aligned} \tag{3.8}$$

if $U'' < 0$. This result shows that the expected utility of the gamble is less than the utility of the risk-free asset if investors are risk-averse. If $U'' = 0$, we say that the investor is risk neutral, in which case the investor is indifferent between taking the gamble and the risk-free strategy.

3.3.1. *The risk premium*

Consider a slightly more general setup such that the consumer's end-of-period wealth can take on $s = 1, \ldots, S$ values. Let W_s denote the consumer's wealth if state s occurs and define

$$\tilde{\epsilon} \equiv W_s - E(W_s)$$

as the difference between the realized and expected value of wealth. Implicitly define the quantity $\rho > 0$ by

$$U[E(W_s) - \rho] = E[U(W_s)]. \tag{3.9}$$

Intuitively, ρ measures the amount by which certain wealth must be decreased to attain the same expected utility when wealth is risky, or the *risk premium.*

Expand both sides of the equation around $E(W_s)$. For the left side, we obtain

$$U[E(W_s) - \rho] \approx U[E(W_s)] - \rho U'[E(W_s)]. \tag{3.10}$$

For the right side, we approximate $U(W)$ around $E(W_s)$ by making use of the definition of $\tilde{\epsilon}$ and take expectations of the resulting expression as

$$\begin{aligned} E[U(W_s)] &\approx E\left\{U[E(W_s)] + \tilde{\epsilon} U'[E(W_s)] + \frac{1}{2}\tilde{\epsilon}^2 U''[E(W_s)]\right\} \\ &= U[E(W_s)] + \frac{1}{2}E(\tilde{\epsilon}^2)U''[E(W_s)] \end{aligned} \tag{3.11}$$

since $E(\tilde{\epsilon}) = 0$. Noting that $E(\tilde{\epsilon}^2) = \text{Var}(W_s)$, setting these approximations equal and solving for ρ, we have

$$\rho = \frac{\text{Var}(W_s)}{2}\left(-\frac{U''[E(W_s)]}{U'[E(W_s)]}\right). \tag{3.12}$$

Thus, the risk premium ρ will be larger a) the larger is $\text{Var}(W_s)$, and b) the larger is the curvature of the utility function. Note that for a risk-neutral investor, $U'' = 0$ and $\rho = 0$. If the risk premium is measured as a proportion of wealth, then we obtain the relationship

$$\rho^\star = \frac{\text{Var}(W_s)}{2}\left(-\frac{W_s U''[E(W_s)]}{U'[E(W_s)]}\right). \tag{3.13}$$

3.3.2. *Measures of risk aversion*

We can use the expression for the risk premium to define alternative measures of risk aversion. In Equation (3.12), the coefficient of *absolute risk aversion* $\mathcal{A}(W)$ is defined as

$$\mathcal{A}(W) = -\frac{U''(W)}{U'(W)}. \tag{3.14}$$

The quantity $\mathcal{A}$ measures risk aversion for a given level of wealth. The measure of absolute risk aversion will most likely fall as wealth increases. For example, a \$1000 gamble would be trivial for a billionaire, but a poor person would be very averse toward it. For U concave and increasing, $\mathcal{A}(W) \geq 0$. Absolute risk aversion is:

- decreasing if $\mathcal{A}'(W) < 0$,
- constant if $\mathcal{A}'(W) = 0$,
- increasing if $\mathcal{A}'(W) > 0$.

Differentiating $\mathcal{A}(W)$ with respect to W, we find that

$$\frac{d\mathcal{A}(W)}{dW} = \frac{(U''(W))^2 - U'''(W)U'(W)}{(U'(W))^2}. \tag{3.15}$$

Hence, the third derivative of the utility function determines whether absolute risk aversion is decreasing, constant, or increasing. If $U''' > 0$ and $(U''(W))^2 < U'''(W)U'(W)$ so that $\mathcal{A}'(W) < 0$, the implication is that as an agent's wealth increases, her aversion to risk decreases, which is intuitively plausible. This is a measure that was first defined by Arrow [32]. The properties of the coefficient of absolute risk aversion are described by Pratt [362].

We can multiply the coefficient of absolute risk aversion by wealth to obtain the coefficient of *relative risk aversion* $\mathcal{R}(W)$ as

$$\mathcal{R}(W) \equiv -\frac{U''(W)W}{U'(W)}. \tag{3.16}$$

The coefficient of relative risk aversion implies that an individual may have constant risk aversion to a proportionate loss in wealth even though absolute risk aversion decreases. We can derive this function using the same steps described above by considering risks $\tilde{\epsilon}$ that are measured as a proportion of assets. As in the case of absolute risk aversion, relative risk aversion is:

- decreasing if $\mathcal{R}'(W) < 0$,
- constant if $\mathcal{R}'(W) = 0$,
- increasing if $\mathcal{R}'(W) > 0$.

We can examine attitudes toward risk implied by various utility functions as follows:

1. Quadratic utility:

$$U(W) = aW - bW^2 \quad \text{for } W \leq a/2b. \tag{3.17}$$

$$\mathcal{A}(W) = -\frac{U''(W)}{U'(W)} = -\frac{-2b}{a - 2bW} = \frac{2b}{a - 2bW} > 0,$$

and

$$\mathcal{R}(W) = -\frac{WU''(W)}{U'(W)} = -\frac{-2bW}{a - 2bW} = \frac{2bW}{a - 2bW} > 0.$$

Thus, both the measure of absolute risk aversion and relative risk aversion are increasing in wealth, which does not make intuitive sense. For example, an individual with increasing $\mathcal{R}(W)$ would be more averse to a proportionate loss in wealth as wealth increases. Thus, a billionaire who loses half his wealth would lose more utility than someone who started out with $20,000 and lost $10,000.

2. Power utility:

$$U(W) = \frac{W^{1-\gamma} - 1}{1-\gamma}, \quad \gamma \geq 0. \tag{3.18}$$

Now we have that

$$\mathcal{A}(W) = -\frac{-\gamma W^{-\gamma-1}}{W^{-\gamma}} = \frac{\gamma}{W},$$

and

$$\mathcal{R}(W) = -\frac{-W\gamma W^{-\gamma-1}}{W^{-\gamma}} = \gamma.$$

Now we have that the measure of absolute risk aversion is decreasing in wealth, and the coefficient of relative risk aversion is constant. This is consistent with evidence obtained using data on individuals' portfolios, which shows that absolute risk aversion is decreasing and the relative risk aversion is around 2.

3. Logarithmic utility:

$$U(W) = \ln(W). \tag{3.19}$$

We obtain using L'Hospital's Rule as

$$\lim_{\gamma \to 1} \left[\frac{W^{1-\gamma} - 1}{1-\gamma} \right] = \lim_{\gamma \to 1} \left[\frac{-W^{1-\gamma} \ln(W)}{-1} \right] = \ln(W).$$

For the logarithmic utility function,

$$\mathcal{A}(W) = -\frac{-1/W^2}{1/W} = \frac{1}{W},$$

and

$$\mathcal{R}(W) = -\frac{-1/W}{1/W} = 1.$$

This demonstrates that the results for the log utility function follow as a special case for the power utility function.

4. Negative exponential:

$$U(W) = -\exp(-\theta W), \quad \theta > 0. \tag{3.20}$$

$$\mathcal{A}(W) = -\frac{-\theta^2 \exp(-\theta W)}{\theta \exp(-\theta W)} = \theta,$$

$$\mathcal{R}(W) = -\frac{-W\theta^2 \exp(-\theta W)}{\theta \exp(-\theta W)} = \theta W.$$

Whereas the power utility function displays constant relative risk aversion, the negative exponential has constant absolute risk aversion.

5. Hyperbolic absolute risk aversion (HARA):

$$U(W) = \frac{1-\sigma}{\sigma}\left[\frac{\alpha W}{1-\sigma} + \beta\right]^{\sigma}, \quad \alpha > 0, \beta > 0, 0 < \sigma < 1. \tag{3.21}$$

$$\mathcal{A}(W) = \frac{\alpha}{(\alpha W)/(1-\sigma) + \beta},$$

$$\mathcal{R}(W) = \frac{\alpha W}{(\alpha W)/(1-\sigma) + \beta}.$$

All of the utility functions are special cases of the HARA class. We obtain the quadratic utility function for $\sigma = 2$, the negative exponential for $\sigma = -\infty$ and $\beta = 1$, power utility with $\beta = 0$ and $\sigma = 1 - \gamma < 1$, and logarithmic utility with $\beta = \sigma = 0$. The HARA class of preferences admit conditions for the exact aggregation of asset-pricing relations. They also provide a tractable representation of risk preferences, and as a consequence, they have been used in many applications in the recent asset-pricing literature.

3.3.3. *Risk aversion in a portfolio choice problem*

We now demonstrate the effects of risk aversion on a consumer's optimal portfolio choices. For this purpose, we consider an economy with two dates and S states at each date. The consumer has preferences over current and future consumption c_0 and c_1. In period 1, she can allocate her current wealth denoted W_0 among current consumption, a risk-free security, and a risky security. In period 2, she consumes her end-of-period wealth. The risk-free security has the rate of return r^f and the risky security has the rate of return r_s if the state s is realized. Let β denote the quantity of initial wealth net of consumption allocated to the risk-free security and δ the quantity allocated to the risky security. The budget constraint in period 1 is

$$c_0 + \beta + \delta = W_0.$$

Then the consumer's end-of-period wealth in state s is

$$W_s = (W_0 - c_0)(1 + r^f) + \delta(r_s - r^f).$$

The consumer has expected utility preferences,

$$U(c_0) + E[V(W_s)], \tag{3.22}$$

so that utility is additively separable over consumption and future wealth. We assume that U and V are strictly increasing and strictly concave. We denote by $\pi_s > 0$ the probability that the consumer attaches to the occurrence of state s. Substituting for W_s in preferences, the first-order necessary and sufficient conditions for an optimum with respect to c_0 and δ include the conditions:

$$U'(c_0) = (1 + r^f)E[V'(W_s)], \tag{3.23}$$

$$E[V'(W_s)(r_s - r^f)] = 0. \tag{3.24}$$

We can use the solution to the consumer's portfolio choice problem to examine the demand for the risky asset and to relate the properties of an agent's absolute risk aversion to this demand. When utility is a function of one argument, Pratt [362] and Sandmo [382] have shown that decreasing absolute risk aversion is a sufficient condition for the risky asset to be a normal good. To show this result, we totally differentiate first-order condition in Equation (3.24) as:

$$(1 + r^f)E[V''(W_s)(r_s - r^f)]dW_0 + E[V''(W_s)(r_s - r^f)^2]d\delta = 0.$$

Solving for $d\delta/dW_0$ yields

$$\frac{d\delta}{dW_0} = -\frac{E[V''(W_s)(r_s - r^f)]}{E[V''(W_s)(r_s - r^f)^2]}(1 + r^f). \tag{3.25}$$

In this expression, the denominator is clearly negative since V is a concave function. It turns out that the sign of the numerator depends on whether absolute risk aversion is decreasing or not. To determine the sign of $d\delta/dW_0$, we prove the following lemma.

Lemma 3.1

$$\frac{\partial}{\partial W_s}\left(-\frac{V''(W_s)}{V'(W_s)}\right) \leq 0$$

implies $E[V''(W_s)(r_s - r^f)] \geq 0$ *if* $\delta \geq 0$ *and* $E[V''(W_s)(r_s - r^f)] \leq 0$ *if* $\delta \leq 0$.

PROOF

Recall that

$$W_s = (W_0 - c_0)(1 + r^f) + \delta(r_s - r^f).$$

Define

$$W_s^0 = (W_0 - c_0)(1 + r^f).$$

Since $W_s = W_s^0 + \delta(r_s - r^f)$ and $-V''(W_s)/V'(W_s)$ is decreasing in W_s, we have that

$$-\frac{V''(W_s)}{V'(W_s)} \leq -\frac{V''(W_s^0)}{V'(W_s^0)} \quad \text{if } r_s \geq r^f \text{ and } \delta \geq 0. \tag{3.26}$$

Trivially,

$$-V'(W_s)(r_s - r^f) \leq 0 \quad \text{if } r_s \geq r^f. \tag{3.27}$$

Multiply Equation (3.26) by $-V'(W_s)(r_s - r^f)$. The inequality is reversed:

$$V''(W_s)(r_s - r^f) \geq \left(\frac{V''(W_s^0)}{V'(W_s^0)}\right) V'(W_s)(r_s - r^f) \tag{3.28}$$

if $r_s \geq r^f$ and $\delta \geq 0$. Suppose $r_s \leq r^f$. Then the inequalities in both (3.26) and (3.27) are reversed, and the inequality (3.28) holds for all r_s. Since $V''(W_s^0)/V'(W_s^0)$ is not a random variable, we can take expectations of both sides of the above relation to obtain

$$E[V''(W_s)(r_s - r^f)] \geq \left(\frac{V''(W_s^0)}{V'(W_s^0)}\right) E[V'(W_s)(r_s - r^f)]. \tag{3.29}$$

But the right side is zero because of the first-order condition in Equation (3.24). Hence, the result is proved if $\delta \geq 0$. A similar proof with $\delta \leq 0$ (which allows for short sales) can be used to prove the second part of the lemma. ∎

Returning now to the condition in Equation (3.25) and using the result in Lemma 3.1, we find that the consumer will demand more of the risky asset when her wealth increases if absolute risk aversion is decreasing in wealth. Thus, as stated above, decreasing absolute risk aversion is a sufficient condition for the risky asset to be a normal good. From our examples of utility functions, we note that the class of power utility functions displays decreasing absolute risk aversion in wealth, and hence satisfies the conditions in the lemma. We also note that the sign of absolute risk aversion depends on the sign of the third derivative of utility, which determines whether marginal utility is concave or convex. The concavity or convexity of marginal utility has also been studied by Kimball [276], who defines a measure of "prudence" which shows how precautionary savings vary as wealth increases. We discuss precautionary savings in Chapter 5.

3.4. MEASURES OF INCREASING RISK

In this section, we formalize the concepts of increasing risk that we presented in Section 3.1. We begin with some definitions.

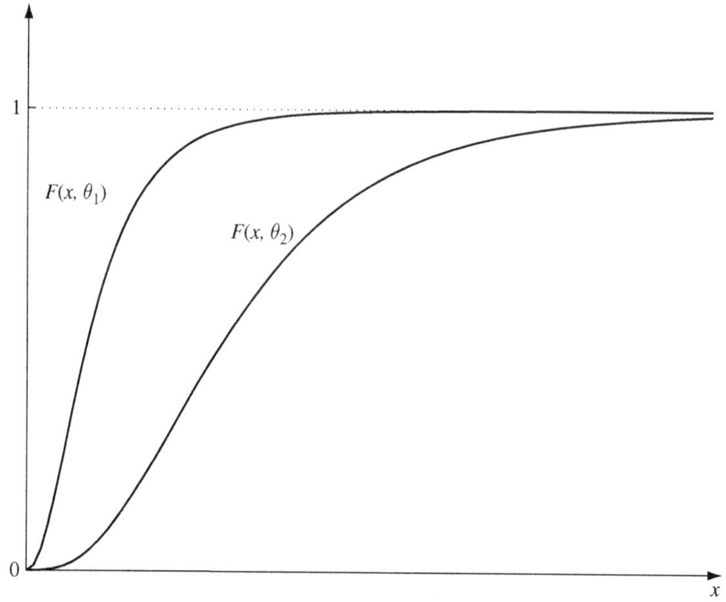

Figure 3.3. First-order stochastic dominance

The first concept is first-order stochastic dominance (FSD). Consider a family of probability distribution functions $F(x, \theta)$ for a random variable $x : \Omega \rightarrow X$ where $X \equiv [\underline{x}, \bar{x}]$ and θ is a parameter.

Definition 3.3 *For any non-decreasing function $u : \Re \rightarrow \Re$, $F(x, \theta_2)$ is said to have first-order stochastic dominance over $F(x, \theta_1)$ if*

$$\int_X u(x) dF(x, \theta_2) \geq \int_X u(x) dF(x, \theta_1).$$

Suppose $\theta_2 > \theta_1$ and $F(x, \theta_2)$ is derived from $F(x, \theta_1)$ such that

$$F(\underline{x}, \theta_1) = F(\underline{x}, \theta_2) = 0, \tag{3.30}$$

$$F(\bar{x}, \theta_1) = F(\bar{x}, \theta_2) = 1, \tag{3.31}$$

$$F(x, \theta_2) \leq F(x, \theta_1), \tag{3.32}$$

for all $x \in X$. Then it can be shown that $F(x, \theta_2)$ FSD dominates $F(x, \theta_1)$. See Figure 3.3.

A second concept of increasing risk is a mean-preserving spread, which describes an increase in the riskiness of a random variable, holding its mean constant. We consider the family of CDFs $F(x, \theta)$ indexed by the parameter θ defined earlier and suppose that $F(x, \theta_2)$ is derived from $F(x, \theta_1)$

by taking probability mass from the center of the probability density function and shifting it to the tails in such a way that the mean is unchanged. Intuitively, $F(x, \theta_2)$ represents a riskier situation than $F(x, \theta_1)$.

Definition 3.4 *For any two distributions $F(x, \theta_1)$ and $F(x, \theta_2)$ with the same mean, $F(x, \theta_1)$ second-order stochastic dominance (SSD) dominates $F(x, \theta_2)$ if for any non-decreasing, concave function $u : \Re \rightarrow \Re$,*

$$\int_X u(x)dF(x, \theta_1) \geq \int_X u(x)dF(x, \theta_2).$$

An example of an SSD shift is a *mean-preserving spread* (MPS). Suppose the distributions $F(x, \theta_1)$ and $F(x, \theta_2)$ satisfy the following conditions:

$$\int_X [F(x, \theta_2) - F(x, \theta_1)] = 0, \tag{3.33}$$

which ensures that the processes have the same mean, and there exists an $\hat{x}$ such that

$$F(x, \theta_2) - F(x, \theta_1) \leq (\geq) \, 0 \quad \text{when} \quad x \geq (\leq) \, \hat{x}, \tag{3.34}$$

which ensures that the two distributions cross only once. Then we say that the distribution $F(x, \theta_2)$ is an MPS over $F(x, \theta_1)$. To ensure that the mean of the two distributions remains the same, the areas A and B are equal in Figure 3.4. A mean-preserving increase in risk is defined and applied by Rothschild and Stiglitz [374, 375]. The effects of a mean-preserving spread on the behavior of risk-averse consumers are discussed by Diamond and Stiglitz [153].

Now consider the effect of an increase in the random variable θ that satisfies the conditions for first-order stochastic dominance. We consider the problem of a consumer who lives for two periods and starts the initial period with wealth W_0 and receives no exogenous wealth in the second period. All consumption in the second period is financed by savings, which pay a random return $\tilde{r}$ that takes values on $R \equiv [\underline{r}, \bar{r}]$ where $\underline{r} > 0$ and $\bar{r} < \infty$, and has a probability distribution function $F(r, \theta)$ parameterized by θ. The associated probability density function is denoted $f(r, \theta)$. The consumer solves the problem:

$$\max_{c_0} \left\{ U(c_0) + \int_R V[(W_0 - c_0)(1 + r)]f(r, \theta)dr \right\} \tag{3.37}$$

where the budget constraint $c_1 = S_0(1 + r)$ with $S_0 = W_0 - c_0$ has already been substituted into the objective function. Assume that U and V are increasing and strictly concave. The first-order condition is

$$0 = U'(c_0) - \int_R V'(c_1)(1 + r)f(r, \theta)dr \tag{3.38}$$

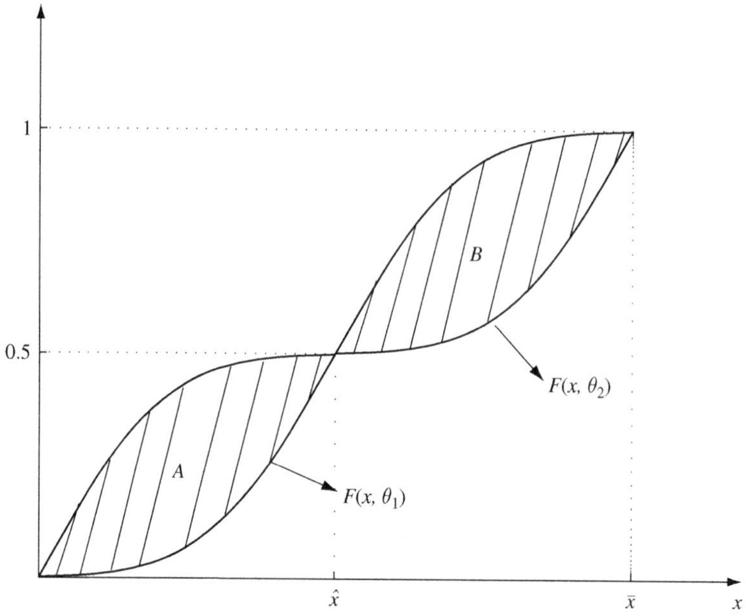

Figure 3.4. Mean-preserving spread

Notice that $U'(c_0)$ is strictly decreasing and that $V'(c_1)$ is strictly increasing in c_0 so that there is a solution to this equation, $c_0^\star \equiv c^\star(W_0, \theta)$.

To start, implicitly differentiate Equation (3.38) with respect to θ and solve for $\partial c^\star/\partial\theta$ to result in

$$\frac{\partial c^\star(W_0, \theta)}{\partial\theta} = \frac{\int_R V'(c_1)(1+r)f_\theta(r,\theta)dr}{U''(c_0) + E[V''(c_1)(1+r)^2]}. \tag{3.39}$$

We are assuming that the probability density function is differentiable in the parameter θ. The denominator of the right side is negative so that the sign of the left side is the same as the sign of the numerator on the right side. Using integration by parts on the numerator, we have

$$\int_R V'(c_1)(1+r)f_\theta(r,\theta)dr = V'(c_1)(1+r)F_\theta(r,\theta) \mid_{\underline{r}}^{\bar{r}}$$

$$- \int_R [V''(c_1)c_1 + V'(c_1)]F_\theta(r,\theta)dr$$

$$= - \int_R [V''(c_1)c_1 + V'(c_1)]F_\theta(r,\theta)dr,$$

where $F_\theta(r,\theta)$ is the derivative of the probability distribution function for $\tilde{r}$ with respect to the parameter θ. Notice that

$$F_\theta(\bar{r},\theta) = F_\theta(\underline{r},\theta) = 0$$

by Equations (3.30) and (3.31). Hence the sign depends on the sign of $V''(c_1)c_1 + V'(c_1)$, which can be expressed as $V'(c_1)[V''(c_1)c_1/V'(c_1) + 1]$. We can use the coefficient of relative risk aversion to express this as:

$$V''(c_1)c_1 + V'(c_1) = -V'(c_1)[\mathcal{R}(c) - 1].$$

Hence the effect of a parametric change that displays FSD on first-period consumption depends on the size of the coefficient of relative risk aversion. If relative risk aversion is less than 1, then current consumption increases, while it remains unchanged when relative risk aversion is equal to 1. Finally, current consumption decreases when relative risk aversion is greater than 1.

3.5. CONCLUSIONS

In this chapter, we have discussed expected utility analysis for simple static economies, and examined notions of risk aversion and increasing risk. In the next chapter, we will discuss notions of intertemporal substitution. We will initially consider preferences that are additively separable over time as well as over states. The focus on such preferences is not without merit because much of the recent macroeconomics literature has employed additively-separable preferences to describe consumers' choices over states and over time.

Nevertheless, it is worth considering deviations from these assumptions. Preferences may not be separable over states. In a multi-period context, agents may not be indifferent to the resolution of uncertainty over time. It may also be the case that agents do not have a single probability assessment over the alternative rewards but entertain a set of possible probabilities. In this case, the agent's objective function will involve minimizing expected utility over the set of possible probability measures. We provide a simple example of these preferences in Exercise 5 in this chapter in terms of the Gilboa–Schmeidler [202] preferences. These preferences exhibit *uncertainty aversion* in that the consumer's utility is increasing with greater information about the underlying probabilities. We discuss the implications of alternative preference specifications further in Chapter 9.

3.6. EXERCISES

1. Deriving a von Neumann–Morgenstern (VNM) utility function.

   Expected utility preferences of the VNM variety are based on consumers' rankings over alternative gambles or "lotteries." Let L denote a lottery that is characterized by a set of rewards $(x_1, \ldots, x_m)$ and the associated probabilities $(\pi_1, \ldots, \pi_m)'$. As in standard utility theory the axioms of completeness, reflexivity, transitivity, and continuity are assumed to hold for the pre-ordering over underlying rewards. To derive an *ordinal* utility function over "lotteries" or distributions, the pre-ordering over lotteries is also required to satisfy the axioms of completeness, reflexivity, and transitivity.

These are given by:

Axiom 3.1 *(Completeness) For every pair of lotteries, either* $L_1 \succeq L_2$ *or* $L_2 \succeq L_1$.

Axiom 3.2 *(Reflexivity) For every lottery,* $L \succeq L$.

Axiom 3.3 *(Transitivity) If* $L_1 \succeq L_2$ *and* $L_2 \succeq L_3$, *then* $L_1 \succeq L_3$.

Some additional axioms are necessary to obtain a *cardinal* utility function.

Axiom 3.4 *(Independence) Let* $L_1 = ((x_1, \ldots, x_m), \pi)$. *If* $x_\xi \sim u$, *then* $L_1 \sim L_2$. *If* u *is a lottery such that* $u = (x_1^\xi, \ldots, x_n^\xi, \pi^\xi)$, *then*

$$L_1 \sim L_2 \sim [(x_1, \ldots, x_{\xi-1}, x_1^\xi, \ldots, x_n^\xi, x_{\xi+1}, \ldots, x_m),$$

$$(\pi, \ldots, \pi_{\xi-1}, \pi_\xi \pi_1^\xi, \ldots, \pi_\xi \pi_n^\xi, \pi_{\xi+1}, \ldots, \pi_m)'].$$

Axiom 3.5 *(Continuity) If* $x_1 \succeq x_2 \succeq x_3$, *then there exists a probability* π *such that* $x_2 \sim ((x_1, x_3), \pi, (1 - \pi))$. *The probability is unique unless* $x_1 \sim x_3$.

Axiom 3.6 *(Dominance) Let* $L_1 = ((x_1, x_2), (\pi_1, 1 - \pi_1))$ *and* $L_2 = ((x_1, x_2), (\pi_2, 1 - \pi_2))$. *If* $x_1 \succ x_2$, *then* $L_1 \succ L_2$ *if and only if* $\pi_1 > \pi_2$.

Show that there exists a utility function u which satisfies Definition 3.1.

2. Consider an investor who maximizes the expected utility of end-of-period wealth by choosing how much to hold of a risky asset versus a risk-free asset. Let x denote the proportion of initial wealth W_0 held in the risky asset. Then, end-of-period wealth W_1 is given by

$$\begin{aligned} W_1 &= W_0 \left[x(1 + r) + (1 - x)(1 + r^f) \right] \\ &= W_0 \left[(1 + r^f) + x(r - r^f) \right], \end{aligned}$$

where r, r^f denotes the returns on the risky and risk-free assets.

The investor's problem is to solve:

$$\max_x E[U(W_1)] = E\left[U\left(W_0(1 + r^f + x(r - r^f)) \right) \right].$$

(a) Find the first-order condition with respect to x. Can you solve for the optimal x denoted $x^\star$?

(b) Consider a first-order Taylor approximation to $U'(W_1)(r - r_f)W_0$ around $x = 0$. Take the expectation of the resulting expression to solve for $x^\star$.

(c) Interpret the expression for $x^\star$. How does $x^\star$ vary with:

i. $E(r - r^f)$

ii. $Var(r)$

iii. the investor's coefficient of relative risk aversion?

3. A certainty equivalent approach to risk.

Suppose there are S states of nature. Let U denote a function that yields the utility of state-contingent consumption as:

$$U(\{c(s)\}) = U[c(1), c(2), \ldots, c(S)].$$

Consider the certain value of consumption or the *certainty equivalent* μ that yields the same utility as a given consumption stream:

$$U[\mu, \mu, \ldots, \mu] = U[c(1), c(2), \ldots, c(S)].$$

Suppose that U is increasing in all its arguments. Then we can solve for the certainty equivalent function as $\mu(\{c(s)\})$.

(a) Suppose we have expected utility preferences as:

$$U(\{c(s)\}) = \sum_{s=1}^{S} p(s)u(c(s)),$$

where $0 < p(s) < 1$, $\sum_s p(s) = 1$ and $u(\cdot)$ is strictly increasing and strictly concave.

Find an expression for the certainty equivalent of a given consumption stream $\{c(s)\}_{s=1}^{S}$. What is the appropriate measure of risk in this case?

(b) Suppose the utility function has the form:

$$u(c) = \frac{c^{1-\gamma} - 1}{1 - \gamma}, \quad \gamma = \frac{1}{2}.$$

Assume that $S = 2$ and $p(1) = \frac{1}{4}$ and $p(2) = \frac{3}{4}$. Find the certainty equivalent for the consumption stream $\{1, 4\}$.

4. A risk aggregator.

An alternative specification for preferences under uncertainty that allows us to relax the independence assumption can be expressed as:

$$\mu = \sum_{s=1}^{S} p(s)M[c(s), \mu],$$

where the function M has the following properties: (i) $M(m, m) = m$ (the certainty equivalent of a sure stream is itself); (ii) M is increasing in its first argument (stochastic dominance); (iii) M is concave in its first argument (risk aversion, see below); (iv) $M(kc, km) = kM(c, m)$ for $k > 0$ (linear homogeneity).

(a) Suppose

$$M(c, m) = \frac{c^{\alpha} m^{1-\alpha}}{\alpha} + m\left(1 - \frac{1}{m}\right), \quad \alpha \leq 1.$$

i. Derive the form of the certainty equivalent function μ. What class of models does this function belong to?

ii. Suppose that the agent is risk averse so that

$$\mu = u^{-1}\{E(u(c))\} > E(c)$$

holds. Show that this is equivalent to having M concave in its first argument.

(b) Consider two alternative specifications of non-expected utility preferences:

i. *Weighted utility*

$$M(c, m) = \frac{(c/m)^{\gamma} c^{\alpha} m^{1-\alpha}}{\alpha} + m\left(1 - \frac{(c/m)^{\gamma}}{\alpha}\right),$$

with (i) $0 < \gamma < 1$ and $\alpha + \gamma < 0$ or

(ii) $\gamma < 0$ and $0 < \alpha + \gamma < 1$.

ii. *Disappointment aversion*

$$M(c, m) = \begin{cases} \dfrac{c^{\alpha} m^{1-\alpha}}{\alpha} + m\left(1 - \dfrac{1}{m}\right) & c \geq m \\ \dfrac{c^{\alpha} m^{1-\alpha}}{\alpha} + m\left(1 - \dfrac{1}{m}\right) + \delta \dfrac{(c^{\alpha} m^{1-\alpha} - m)}{\alpha} & c \leq m, \end{cases}$$

with $\delta \geq 0$.

Derive the form of the certainty equivalent function μ for each specification. Interpret these functions. How do they differ from the standard expected utility formulation?

(c) Are the indifference curves linear in the probabilities? Try drawing the indifference for weighted utility and disappointment aversion when $S = 2$.

5. Max-min expected utility.

Gilboa and Schmeidler [202] provided an axiomatic derivation for preferences that allow for multiple probability assessments over state-contingent consumption. Suppose there are $s = 1, \ldots, S$ states of nature.

Let Π denote the set of prior probability distributions across consumption in the different states, c_s for $s = 1, \ldots, S$. The Gilboa–Schmeidler max-min preferences are defined as:

$$U = \min_{\pi \in \Pi} \sum_{s=1}^{S} \pi_s u(c_s) = \min_{\pi \in \Pi} E_\pi u(c). \tag{3.40}$$

In this setup, agents maximize preferences that have been minimized over alternative probability distributions or priors; hence the name "max-min."

Suppose there are two states of the world. States 1 and 2 are uncertain or ambiguous: the probability that state 2 occurs is given in the interval $\pi_1 = \frac{1}{2} - \gamma$ and $\pi_2 = \frac{1}{2} + \gamma$ for $-\frac{1}{4} \leq \gamma \leq \frac{1}{4}$. Suppose the utility of state-contingent consumption is given by $u(c) = c$.

(a) Suppose there are two securities, and assume that security i pays off one unit of the consumption in state i and nothing otherwise. Find the expected utility from owning each security.

(b) Compare the payoff from the securities (evaluated in utils) under the assumption that the probability of the two states is $\frac{1}{2}, \frac{1}{2}$.

CHAPTER 4

CAPM and APT

In Chapters 1 and 2, we introduced the general equilibrium approach to asset pricing, and presented a rationalization of the implied asset-pricing relations based on much weaker notions of the absence of arbitrage. Whereas these theoretical approaches provide intellectually appealing and elegant characterizations of asset pricing, the empirical finance literature has been dominated by two other approaches. These are the capital asset-pricing model (CAPM) of Sharpe [389], Lintner [311], and others, and the arbitrage pricing theory (APT) proposed by Ross [369]. The former approach exploits a risk-return relationship for the pricing of assets whereas the latter imposes a factor structure. These approaches also have implications for the theory of portfolio choice.

As is well known, the CAPM prices the riskiness of an individual asset in terms of its covariance with the market portfolio. By contrast, the APT prices assets in terms of an underlying set of risk factors. The CAPM typically exploits the implications of expected utility maximization with respect to end-of-period wealth whereas the APT has been derived based on absence of arbitrage arguments. We describe the alternative sets of assumptions under which these approaches can be derived, and compare their implications with the general equilibrium approach to asset pricing.

4.1. THE CAPITAL ASSET-PRICING MODEL

The CAPM has gained widespread use because it provides restrictions for investors' portfolios and asset prices and returns that appear to be validated by data on a variety of securities. The CAPM formulation can be derived in different ways. One approach is to start from the consumer's expected utility maximization problem by choice of risky and risk-free assets, given an initial wealth level. In what follows, we consider a derivation based on the stochastic discount factor approach.

4.1.1. The discount factor

Recall that the problem of asset pricing can be expressed in terms of the existence of a stochastic discount factor that prices any risky payoff. The implications of the CAPM can be illustrated very simply by assuming that the stochastic discount factor in the CAPM is given by:

$$m_{t+1} = c - dR^W_{t+1}, \tag{4.1}$$

where R^W_{t+1} denotes the return on the aggregate wealth portfolio and c, d are variables to be determined. To derive the CAPM representation, note that the price of the risk-free rate r^f is one:

$$1 = E\left[mr^f\right],$$

or

$$r^f = 1/E[m]. \tag{4.2}$$

To find the values of c and d, let $q^W = \theta^W \cdot q$ denote the market value of the portfolio, and $x^W = X^T\theta^W$ its payoff. Notice that both q^W and x^W are scalars. Hence, $R^W = x^W/q^W$. Using the pricing function derived in Chapters 1 and 2, we can write:

$$q^W = E\left[mx^W\right] \Rightarrow 1 = E\left[m\left(x^W/q^W\right)\right],$$

or

$$1 = E\left[mR^W\right] \tag{4.3}$$

A useful result that we will exploit throughout this book is the *covariance decomposition*:

$$\text{Cov}(X, Y) = E(XY) - E(X)E(Y),$$

where X, Y are any two random variables. Using this decomposition, we can write the right side of (4.3) as:

$$E\left[mR^W\right] = \text{Cov}(m, R^W) + E(m)E(R^W),$$

or

$$E(R^W) = \frac{1}{E(m)}\left(1 - \text{Cov}\left(m, R^W\right)\right). \tag{4.4}$$

Substituting the expression $m = c - dR^W$ into Equations (4.2) and (4.4), we obtain:

$$c = \frac{1}{r^f} + dE(R^W) \tag{4.5}$$

$$d = \frac{E(R^W) - r^f}{r^f\text{Var}(R^W)}. \tag{4.6}$$

Now consider pricing any asset l with this stochastic discount factor. Let R_l denote the return on the asset. Notice that it must satisfy the relation:

$$1 = E[mR_l].$$

Using a covariance decomposition on the right side of this expression and substituting for m, we obtain

$$\begin{aligned} E(R_l) &= r^f - r^f \mathrm{Cov}[c - dR^W, R_l] \\ &= r^f + dr^f \mathrm{Cov}[R^W, R_l], \end{aligned}$$

which implies that

$$E(R_l) - r^f = \frac{E(R^W) - r^f}{\mathrm{Var}(R^W)} \mathrm{Cov}[R^W, R_l].$$

According to this representation, the expected excess return on any security l is proportional to the covariance of the security return with the return on the wealth portfolio. This is known as the *beta* of the security:

$$\beta_l = \mathrm{Cov}(R^W, R_l). \tag{4.7}$$

Also define the term that multiplies the security's beta as the *price of risk*:

$$\text{price of risk} = \frac{E(R^W) - r^f}{\mathrm{Var}(R^W)}, \tag{4.8}$$

which shows the excess return on the wealth portfolio for each unit of risk. Hence, the CAPM prices the return on any security as the risk-free rate plus the product of the security's beta and the price of risk as:

$$E(R_l) = r^f + \beta_l \left(\frac{E(R^W) - r^f}{\mathrm{Var}(R^W)} \right). \tag{4.9}$$

We now show that this representation for the stochastic discount factor is consistent with expected utility maximization over end-of-period wealth.

4.1.2. *Expected utility maximization*

There are several alternative sets of assumptions on preferences and the distribution of returns that can yield a CAPM representation for asset returns. One set of sufficient conditions is to assume the joint normality of returns. Another sufficient condition involves the assumption that the utility function is quadratic. However, unlike the general equilibrium framework that we described in Chapter 1, the consumer's or investor's expected utility is defined over end-of-period wealth. In many utility maximizing formulations of the CAPM, the real interest rate is also taken as constant and labor income is ruled out.

Suppose that there are N securities where securities $1, \ldots, N-1$ are risky and security N is risk-free. Define the return on the N'th security by r^f. Also suppose that there are I different investors, each with initial wealth W_0^i, who maximize the expected value of utility from end-of-period wealth

W_s^i. Let $x_{n,s}$ be the payoff on security n in state s and $\theta^i = (\theta_1^i, \ldots, \theta_N^i)$ denote the portfolio of securities held by investor i. Then we can express the wealth for consumer i in state s as

$$W_s^i = \sum_{n=1}^{N} \theta_n^i x_{n,s}.$$

Let the price in the current period for security n be denoted by q_n.

Investor i solves

$$\max_{\{\theta_n^i\}_{n=1}^N} E\left[U\left(\sum_{n=1}^{N} \theta_n^i x_n\right)\right]$$

$$\text{subject to} \quad \sum_{n=1}^{N} q_n \theta_n^i \leq W_0^i.$$

Let λ denote the Lagrange multiplier on the budget constraint. The first-order conditions with respect to θ_n^i can be expressed as:

$$\lambda q_l = E\left[U'\left(\sum_{n=1}^{N} \theta_n^i x_n\right) x_l\right], \quad l = 1, \ldots, N. \tag{4.10}$$

To put further structure on this problem, assume that utility is quadratic or

$$U(W) = aW - bW^2, \quad W \leq a/2b.$$

Define the portfolio weights $w_n^i \equiv (\theta_n^i q_n)/W_0^i$ and let $R_{n,s} \equiv x_{n,s}/q_n$ equal the return on security n in state s. Recall that the N'th security is the risk-free asset with return r^f. Then we can express the first-order conditions as:

$$E\left[\left(a - 2bW_0^i \sum_{n=1}^{N} w_n^i R_n\right)(R_l - r^f)\right] = 0, \quad l = 1, \ldots, N-1. \tag{4.11}$$

Now write Equation (4.11) as

$$E\left[\left(\sum_{n=1}^{N} w_n^i R_n\right)(R_l - r^f)\right] = [E(R_l) - r^f]\frac{a}{2bW_0^i} n = 1, \ldots, N-1. \tag{4.12}$$

Let the return on the *wealth portfolio* in state s be defined as:

$$R_s^W \equiv \sum_{i=1}^{I} \sum_{n=1}^{N} w_n^i R_{n,s}. \tag{4.13}$$

To write the first-order condition in terms of the return on the aggregate wealth portfolio, sum over the investors $i=1,\ldots,I$. Then the first-order condition can be written as:

$$E\left[R^W(R_l - r^f)\right] = \left[E(R_l) - r^f\right] \sum_{i=1}^{I} \left(\frac{a}{2bW_0^i}\right) \quad l = 1,\ldots,N-1.$$

Using the covariance decomposition, the first-order conditions can be rewritten as:

$$\text{Cov}(R^W, R_l - r^f) = \left[E(R_l) - r^f\right] \left[\sum_{i=1}^{I} \left(\frac{a}{2bW_0^i}\right) - E(R^W)\right] \tag{4.14}$$

for $l=1,\ldots,N-1$. Define one of the securities as the wealth portfolio, in which case equation (4.14) becomes

$$\text{Var}(R^W) = \left[E(R^W) - r^f\right] \left[\sum_{i=1}^{I} \left(\frac{a}{2bW_0^i}\right) - E(R^W)\right], \tag{4.15}$$

where we have made use of the fact that $\text{Var}(R^W) = \text{Cov}(R^W, R^W - r^f)$. Taking the ratio of the conditions in equations (4.14) and (4.15) yields the CAPM representation as:

$$E(R_l - r^f) = \frac{E(R^W) - r^f}{\text{Var}(R^W)} \text{Cov}(R^W, R_l). \tag{4.16}$$

This representation is identical to the representation that we obtained when we priced the excess return $R_l - r^f$ using the stochastic discount factor $m = c - dR^W$ and the pricing function $1 = E(mR)$. Notice that the expected return depends on the risk-free rate and the covariance with the return on the wealth portfolio. Hence this model is known as the two-factor CAPM.

Figure 4.1 depicts the return on a security for different values of the *beta* of a security, given the risk-free rate r^f.[1] In Figure 4.1, asset A lies above the security market line (SML) and asset B below it. This means that A has a higher return and B has a lower return compared to assets with similar risk. In this case, we say that A is *underpriced* and B is *overpriced.*

[1] Notice we have graphed the relation in (4.16) by defining $\beta_i = \frac{\text{Cov}(R^W, R_l)}{\text{Var}(R^W)}$.

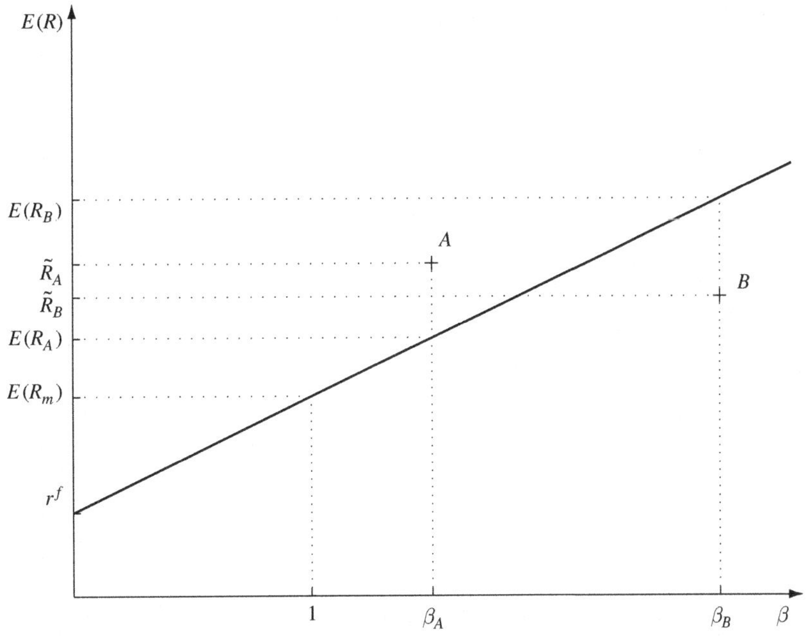

Figure 4.1. Security market line

Thus, the CAPM representation provides a way for pricing securities based on the covariance with the market portfolio. While the CAPM is widely used in the empirical finance literature to describe asset returns, it has been criticized on the grounds that the return on the wealth portfolio R^W is not observable. (See Roll [366].) In empirical applications, R^W is typically taken as the return on some stock market index such as the NYSE Composite Index.

4.1.3. Alternative derivations

The conditions under which the CAPM can be derived have been the topic of much controversy. The CAPM has received favor as an asset-pricing model because it express returns as linear functions of the return on the market portfolio, which is taken as a proxy for the wealth portfolio. Recall from Section 4.1 that the stochastic discount factor for the CAPM is given by:

$$m_{t+1} = c - dR^W_{t+1}.$$

One problem with this discount factor is that it is not guaranteed to be strictly positive. However, in Theorem 2.2 we showed that absence of arbitrage is equivalent to the existence of a strictly positive state-price vector or pricing function. Dybig and Ingersoll [165] discuss the relation of mean-variance pricing to a complete markets equilibrium and provide examples of arbitrage that can arise with the CAPM pricing function. To see how the CAPM leads to an arbitrage opportunity, consider the representation in equation (4.9). Recall that a return R_i is defined as $R_i = x_i/p_i$. Hence, we can write

$$E\left(x_i/p_i\right) - r^f = Cov\left(x_i/p_i, R^W\right)\lambda,$$

where $\lambda = [E(R^W) - r^f]/Var(R^W)$. Since p_i is known at the time of the security trade and is non-random, the price of an asset that has the payoff x_i can be expressed as:

$$\begin{aligned} p_i &= \frac{E(x_i) - \lambda Cov(x_i, R^W)}{r^f} \\ &= \frac{E(x_i) - \lambda\left[E(x_i R^W) - E(x_i)E(R^W)\right]}{r^f} \\ &= E\left[x_i\left(1 - \lambda(R^W - E(R^W))\right)\right]/r^f. \end{aligned} \tag{4.17}$$

To see how an arbitrage arises, consider the payoff that is positive in some states in which $R^W > E(R^W) + 1/\lambda$ and zero otherwise. Specifically, consider

$$z = \begin{cases} \left[\lambda\left(R^W - E(R^W)\right) - 1\right]^{-1} & \text{if } R^W > E(R^W) + 1/\lambda \\ 0 & \text{otherwise.} \end{cases} \tag{4.18}$$

Using the pricing relation in equation (4.17), the price of a security that has the payoff z is given by

$$\begin{aligned} p^z &= E\left(-1 | R^W > E(R^W) + 1/\lambda\right)/r^f \\ &= -Prob(R^W > E(R^W) + 1/\lambda)/r^f. \end{aligned}$$

Hence, provided that the probability on the last line is strictly positive (implying that the return on the wealth portfolio can achieve sufficiently high levels), the price of any asset with payoff z has a negative price. But this is equivalent to the existence of an arbitrage opportunity. One such opportunity is to purchase, at a negative price, the asset that has a payoff of z. This investment does not require any current cash outflow. Instead it generates a positive cash flow this period and possibly a positive cash outflow next period. Hence, it is an arbitrage. In the derivation leading up to equation (4.9), we assumed that investors have quadratic utility. In this case, it is possible to have unbounded payoffs (as described by equation (4.18)) and not have consumers capitalize on arbitrage opportunities as consumers with quadratic utility will be satiated. However, in all other derivations of mean-variance pricing that do not rely on quadratic utility, the presence of such unbounded returns will lead to arbitrage opportunities which are not consistent with equilibrium. Hence, to rule out such arbitrage, we need to generate a strictly positive discount factor that has the CAPM structure. One known case which accomplishes this is the log utility CAPM of Rubinstein [378]. This generates a strictly positive stochastic discount factor that depends only on the return on the aggregate wealth portfolio, R^W, where the wealth portfolio is defined as a claim to all future consumption.[2] We describe this approach more fully in Chapter 5.

In our discussion in Section 4.2, we provided a derivation of the CAPM based on the assumption of quadratic utility. However, an alternative derivation assumes that returns are jointly normal. (See Exercise 4 at the end of the chapter.) However, the normality assumption is typically inappropriate for derivative assets such as options, forward or future contracts. As a specific example, consider an option that is written on a stock whose payoff has a normal distribution given by $x \sim N(\mu, \sigma^2)$ with $\mu = 1$ and $\sigma^2 = 1$. Define a derivative asset as a call option with a strike price of \$1 on one share of the stock. The payoff on the option may be expressed as:

$$z = \max(x - 1, 0).$$

Thus, the payoff on the option follows a *truncated* normal distribution. Since $E(x) = 1$, the non-zero part of z is the right half of the normal distribution with mean 0 and variance 1. Notice that

$$Prob(z > 0) = 1 - \Phi(0),$$

and $f(z|z > 0)$, which denotes the density for a truncated normal distribution, is given by

$$f(z|z > 0) = \frac{f(z)}{1 - \Phi(0)} = \frac{(2\pi\sigma^2)^{-1} exp(-z^2/2\sigma^2)}{1 - \Phi(0)} = \frac{(1/\sigma)\phi\left(\frac{z}{\sigma}\right)}{1 - \Phi(0)},$$

where $\phi(\cdot)$ is the standard normal pdf. Hence, we can characterize the statistical properties of the option by making use of standard results on the truncated normal distribution as:

$$E(z|z > 0) = \sigma\lambda(0)$$

$$Var(z|z > 0) = \sigma^2[1 - \delta(0)]$$

[2] See Rubinstein [378].

where $\lambda(0) = \phi(0)/[1 - \Phi(0)]$ and $\delta(0) = \lambda(0)$.[3] In our application, $\lambda(0) = \sigma/\sqrt{2\pi}$, and $\delta(0) = \sigma^2/(2\pi)$. Using these results, we obtain

$$E(z) = \sigma/\sqrt{2\pi} \quad \text{and} \quad Var(z) = 1 - 1/(2\pi).$$

Thus, even if all assets in the economy are jointly normally distributed, derivative securities will not have normal distributions. This raises the issue of the pricing of derivative securities in a CAPM framework. Dybig and Ingersoll [165] show if all investors have quadratic utility preferences, the CAPM may still be used to price derivative assets even if their distributions are not normal. However, in the absence of the assumption that all investors have quadratic utility preferences, the introduction of derivative assets that are in net zero supply may even cause mispricing of the original assets. These results show that unless we are willing to make the assumption that investors' preferences are quadratic, alternative methods need to be found for pricing derivative assets.[4]

4.2. ARBITRAGE PRICING THEORY

The arbitrage pricing theory proposed by Ross [369] was motivated by the finding that security returns can be represented in terms of a set of risk factors common across different securities or portfolios plus a security- or portfolio-specific idiosyncratic risk term.

The APT assumes that the excess returns on assets that are in net zero supply or that are claims to the dividends of N technologies have the factor structure

$$R_{i,s} = \bar{R}_i + \sum_{k=1}^{K} \beta_{i,k}\delta_{k,s} + \epsilon_{i,s}, \quad i = 1, \ldots, N, \tag{4.19}$$

where $R_{i,s}$ denotes the return on the i'th security in state s, $\delta_{k,s}$ is systematic risk from factor k, $\epsilon_{i,s}$ is unsystematic or idiosyncratic risk specific to asset i, and $\bar{R}_i$ and $\beta_{i,k}$ are constants. We assume the following:

$$E(\delta_k) = 0, \quad E(\epsilon_i) = 0, \quad \text{Var}(\delta_k) = \sigma_k^2, \quad \text{Var}(\epsilon_i) = \sigma_i^2.$$

This states that the random variables denoting systematic and idiosyncratic risk have mean zero and finite variance. We also assume that random variables denoting the systematic and idiosyncratic risks are uncorrelated:

$$E(\epsilon_i\delta_k) = 0 \quad \text{for each } k \text{ and } i, \tag{4.20}$$

and that the idiosyncratic risks are mutually independent:

$$E(\epsilon_i\epsilon_j) = 0 \quad \text{for each } i, j = 1, \ldots, N. \tag{4.21}$$

[3] See, for example, Greene [214, p. 759].

[4] One approach that we outlined in Chapter 2 is based on the absence of arbitrage and the notion of risk-neutral pricing.

The notion behind the APT is that asset returns can be explained in terms of a small number of factors so that $K < N$.

Notice that $\bar{R}_{i,s}$ is the expected return on asset i. Let the N'th security be the risk-free security so that $R_{N,s} = r^f$ for all s. If we substitute the expression for returns into the first-order condition $E[U'(W)(R_i - r^f)] = 0$, we have

$$E\left[U'(W_s)\left(\bar{R}_i + \sum_{k=1}^{K} \beta_{i,k}\delta_k + \epsilon_i - r^f\right)\right] = 0, \tag{4.22}$$

where $W_s \equiv \sum_{j=1}^{N} \theta_j x_{j,s} = W_0 \sum_{j=1}^{N} w_j R_{j,s}$ denotes end-of-period wealth and $w_j = \theta_j q_j / W_0$ and $R_{j,s} = x_{j,s}/q_j$. This can be rewritten as:

$$\bar{R}_i - r^f = \sum_{k=1}^{K} \left\{ \frac{E[-U'(W_s)\delta_k]}{E[U'(W_s)]} \right\} \beta_{i,k} + \frac{E[-U'(W_s)\epsilon_i]}{E[U'(W_s)]}. \tag{4.23}$$

If all diversifiable risk is eliminated, then the ϵ_i term drops out. The excess return on any asset i relative to the risk-free rate is linear in the factor loadings, $\beta_{i,k}$, $k = 1, \ldots, K$.

The APT was originally promoted as a way of obtaining an asset-pricing model without relying on the economic structure imposed by the CAPM or the general equilibrium approach described in Chapter 1. The approach to deriving pricing relationships is to rely on the law of one price. Suppose that an *exact factor structure* characterizes payoffs. Consider the payoff on the ith asset:

$$x_i = E(x_i) \times 1 + \beta_i' f,$$

where f is a vector of factors. We may view this equivalently as a statistical decomposition that expresses payoffs on different assets in terms of a lower dimensional set of factors or as a statement that the payoff x_i can be expressed as a portfolio of the risk-free payoff and the factors. In the latter case, the *law of one price* states that the price of the payoff must be a linear combination of the price of the risk-free payoff and the factors:

$$q(x_i) = E(x_i)q(1) + \beta_i' q(f).$$

We can also derive a representation that is similar to the one in Equation (4.19) by considering returns R_i in place of payoffs:

$$1 = E(R_i)q(1) + \beta_i' q(f).$$

Notice that the risk-free rate is defined as $r^f = 1/q(1)$ so that we can write:

$$E(R_i) = r^f + \beta_i'[-r^f q(f)]. \tag{4.24}$$

Hence, we derive a representation for the return on the ith asset that is a linear function of the risk-free return and a term that is proportional to the prices of the factors. This is similar to the one in Equation (4.23) except that the factor representation holds exactly.

The literature on arbitrage pricing has investigated the conditions under which an *approximate* version of the APT, that is, one in which expected returns satisfy equation (4.23) even when the exact factor structure for returns does not hold exactly, can be derived.[5] First, our derivation of the APT makes clear that for given discount factor that prices the factors, the price of any security can be obtained as the price of the factors times the security-specific factor loadings as the number of securities gets arbitrarily large. More specifically, let the security payoffs be expressed as:

$$x_i = E(x_i) \times 1 + \beta_i' f + \epsilon_i, \quad i = 1, \ldots, N$$

where ϵ_i satisfy conditions (4.20) and (4.21). In a well-diversified portfolio, the idiosyncratic risk will be eliminated and the risk of the portfolio will depend on the risk emanating from the factors. Let x^p denote an equally weighted portfolio of the asset payoffs. Then

$$\begin{aligned} x^p &= \frac{1}{N} \sum_{i=1}^{N} x_i \\ &= \frac{1}{N} \sum_{i=1}^{N} E(x_i) + \frac{1}{N} \sum_{i=1}^{N} \beta_i' f + \frac{1}{N} \sum_{i=1}^{N} \epsilon_i \\ &= E(x^p) + \beta_p' f + \epsilon^p, \end{aligned}$$

where

$$Var(\epsilon^p) \to 0 \text{ as } N \to \infty$$

since the ϵ_i are mutually uncorrelated and have finite variance. Hence, under appropriate assumptions, we find that the payoff on an equally weighted portfolio can be priced using the factor representation. However, the content of the APT comes from assuming a specific form for the pricing function, $m = a + b'f$ where b is a $K \times 1$ vector. In the absence of a specific assumption regarding the pricing function m and for any finite-size economy with fixed N, a pricing function that prices the factors may not uniquely price the payoffs based solely on the law of one price. This is the notion behind Shanken's [387] original criticism of the so-called "empirical APT" model, and the basis for much further discussion on the issue. (See, for example, Shanken [388] or Dybig and Ross [166].)

[5] In the finance literature, a distinction is also made between a situation in which the factor structure is assumed to hold in the presence of idiosyncratic errors that are mutually uncorrelated (a *strict* factor structure) and one in which there is correlation between the idiosyncratic errors (an *approximate* factor structure). In our analysis, we ignore this distinction.

4.3. CONCLUSIONS

In this chapter, we have reviewed some alternative ways of deriving the CAPM and the APT. These models have served as the workhorses of empirical financial modeling despite various criticisms leveled at their underlying assumptions. The CAPM has been judged non-verifiable because the return on the aggregate wealth portfolio is difficult to measure. For the APT, the main criticism has to do with finding conditions under which exact factor pricing will hold for a finite economy. In his original contribution, Ross [369] advocated restricting the volatility of the discount factor in the APT pricing equation. There are other approaches that have been used to rationalize the APT for finite economies.[6] While the conditions under which the CAPM and APT can be derived as asset-pricing theories have generated much controversy, both models have provided useful frameworks for modeling risk. In the CAPM, the notion of risk is the covariance with the market or wealth portfolio. Likewise, the APT has led to alternative ways of thinking about the sources of macroeconomic or aggregate risk in the economy.

4.4. EXERCISES

1. Mean-Variance Frontier with Two Risky Assets
   Let r_i denote the return on risky asset i, and assume that returns are normally distributed as $r_i \sim N(\mu_i, \sigma_i^2)$ and $Cov(r_1, r_2) = \rho_{12}\sigma_1\sigma_2$. Let x denote the proportion of the first risky asset held by the investor and r_p denote the return on the portfolio as

$$r_p = xr_1 + (1 - x)r_2.$$

   Then

$$E(r_p) = xE(r_1) + (1 - x)E(r_2), \tag{4.25}$$

   and

$$Var(r_p) = x^2 Var(r_1) + (1 - x)^2 Var(r_2) + 2x(1 - x)\sigma_{12}. \tag{4.26}$$

   (a) Find the optimal value of x that minimizes $Var(r_p)$. Denote this value by x^*. What is the value of $Var(r_p)$ evaluated at x^*?
   (b) Define the correlation coefficient as

$$\rho_{12} = \frac{\sigma_{12}}{\sigma_1\sigma_2}.$$

[6] See, for example, Connor [115].

What are the optimal values of x and $Var(r_p)$ for
- perfectly positively correlated returns ($\rho_{12} = 1$)
- perfectly negatively correlated returns ($\rho_{12} = -1$)
- uncorrelated returns ($\rho_{12} = 0$)?

2. The Capital Market Line
The problem is to allocate wealth to n risky assets with returns $r_{i,t+1}$ and a risk-free asset with certain return r_t^f. We consider a two-period problem, and index the current period by t and the future period by $t+1$. Suppose an investor invests x_{it} in each risky asset i and the proportion x_t^f in the risk-free asset such that

$$\sum_{i=1}^{n} x_{it} + x_t^f = 1.$$

The consumer's wealth in period t is W_t, and wealth next period is

$$\begin{aligned} W_{t+1} &= W_t\left[\sum_{i=1}^{n} x_{it}(1 + r_{i,t+1}) + x_t^f(1 + r_t^f)\right] \\ &= W_t(1 + r_{t+1}^p), \end{aligned}$$

where r_{t+1}^p is the return on the portfolio. In matrix notation, let r_t denote the vector of the returns on the risky assets, and x_t denote the vector of portfolio weights on the risky assets where

$$r_t = \begin{bmatrix} r_{1t} \\ r_{2t} \\ \vdots \\ r_{nt} \end{bmatrix} \quad \text{and} \quad x_t = \begin{bmatrix} x_{1t} \\ x_{2t} \\ \vdots \\ x_{nt} \end{bmatrix}.$$

The conditional covariance matrix for the vector of risky returns given information at time t is then given by

$$Var_t(r_{t+1}) = E_t\left[(r_{t+1} - E_t(r_{t+1}))(r_{t+1} - E_t(r_{t+1}))'\right].$$

Define l to be the $n \times 1$ vector of ones, i.e., $l = (1, 1, \ldots, 1)'$.

(a) Find an expression for the investor's end-of-period wealth using these definitions.
(b) Suppose that the consumer maximizes the expected utility of next period's wealth $E_t[U(W_{t+1})]$. Show that maximizing expected utility is equivalent to maximizing a function of expected return and the variance of returns, where the two are traded off.
(c) Derive the first-order conditions with respect to x_t.
(d) Find an expression for the excess return on the optimal portfolio relative to the risk-free return.

(e) Assuming that all market investors have identical beliefs, in equilibrium the return on the portfolio r^p will be the *market* return r^m. Use this condition to characterize the risk and return on *efficient portfolios*, namely, those that have the lowest variance for a given return.

3. Deriving the CAPM
Consider the portfolio choice problem outlined in Exercise 2.
(a) Show that for a single asset the solution for this problem implies the risk-return relationship

$$E_t(r_{i,t+1}) - r_t^f = [E_t(r_{t+1}^m - r_t^f] \frac{Cov_t(r_{i,t+1}, r_{t+1}^m)}{V_t(r_{t+1}^m)}$$

$$= E_t(r_{t+1}^m - r_t^f)\beta_{it},$$

where β_{it} is called the *market beta* for asset i.
(b) What is the beta for the risk-free asset?
(c) What is the beta for the market portfolio?

4. The Joint Normality Assumption
Suppose that all traded assets are jointly normally distributed. A CAPM representation for expected returns can be obtained using Stein's lemma:

Lemma 4.1 *(Stein's lemma) If x, y are bivariate normal, $g(x)$ is differentiable, and $E|g'(x)| < \infty$, then*

$$Cov[g(x), y] = E[g'(x)]Cov(x, y).$$

Use equation (4.11) with an arbitrary utility function to derive an expected return-beta model that has the CAPM representation.

CHAPTER 5

Consumption and saving

Consumption and saving decisions affect asset and credit markets and are an important variable in determining investment. In this chapter, we will describe some key aspects of saving and consumption in a deterministic setting. We will then turn to uncertainty.

In the recent literature, there has been more emphasis placed on examining consumption and saving decisions and asset-pricing relations in a unified manner. As we have described in earlier chapters, the general equilibrium asset-pricing approach implies that random payoff streams are priced with respect to consumption risk. Thus, an asset is considered risky if it yields low returns in states when consumption is also low. The choice of consumption and saving in an environment with multiple assets is also a portfolio choice problem. Hence, it appears crucial to provide a simple framework to link these issues before proceeding to the more formal models considered in later parts of this book.

In this chapter, we provide an introduction to the study of optimal consumption and saving decisions in an intertemporal context. As part of this analysis, we define the notion of consumption smoothing and illustrate the role of saving in the consumer's intertemporal choice problem. We also generalize the simple portfolio choice problem that we used to derive the CAPM, and consider the joint determination of consumption and asset choices with labor income. Finally, we use the consumer's intertemporal choice problem under uncertainty to examine the role of uncertainty and precautionary saving.

5.1. A DETERMINISTIC ECONOMY

To start, let's consider a simple two-period world where a household supplies one unit of labor inelastically and receives wage income, which it can consume or save at a constant interest in period 1. In period 2, consumption satisfies $c' = (1 + r)S$. The household's problem is

$$\max_{c,S} \left\{ U(c) + W(c') \right\}$$

subject to

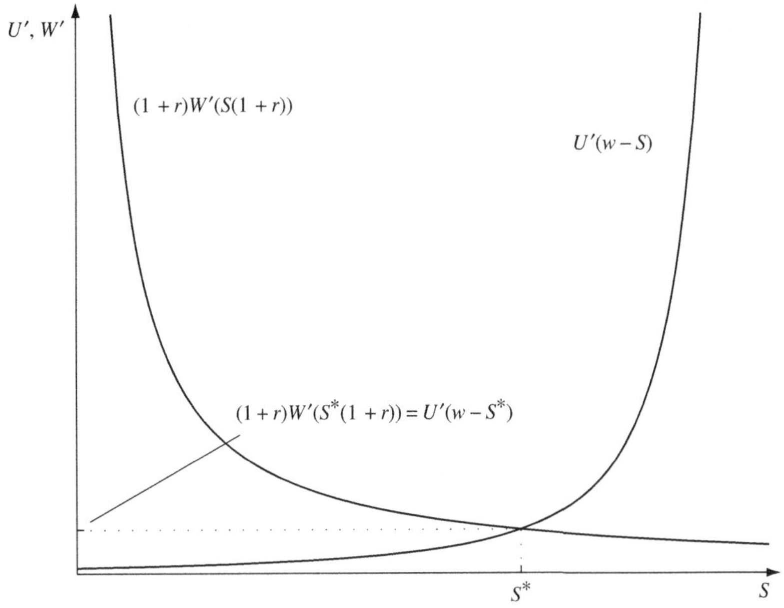

Figure 5.1. Consumer's first-order conditions

$$c + S \leq w \tag{5.1}$$

$$c' \leq (1 + r)S. \tag{5.2}$$

In this expression, U, W are the first- and second-period utility functions, both assumed to be continuous, twice continuously differentiable, and strictly concave. The variable w is the real wage, r is the interest rate, S is saving, and c and c' are consumption in periods 1 and 2, respectively. We also have the Inada conditions,

$$\lim_{c \to 0} U'(c) \to \infty \text{ and } \lim_{c \to 0} W'(c) \to \infty,$$

$$\lim_{c \to \infty} U'(c) \to 0 \text{ and } \lim_{c \to \infty} W'(c) \to 0.$$

With this assumption, we can rule out zero consumption at the consumer's optimum.

We can use this problem to examine the effect of an increase in the interest rate. Assuming that the budget constraints hold with equality, the consumer's problem can be expressed as

$$\max_{S} \left[U(w - S) + W(S(1 + r)) \right]. \tag{5.3}$$

The first-order condition is

$$-U'(w - S) + W'(S(1 + r))(1 + r) = 0.$$

Figure 5.1 provides a graphical depiction of the first-order condition.

Define the function $V(S,r) = -U'(w-S)+W'(S(1+r))(1+r)$. Taking the derivative of $V(S,r)$ with respect to S yields:

$$\frac{\partial V(S,r)}{\partial S} = U''(w-S) + W''(S(1+r))(1+r)^2 < 0.$$

By assumption the second derivatives of U and W exist so that $V(S,r)$ is strictly decreasing in S. Applying the inverse function theorem, there is a solution for saving, S, denoted

$$S^o = S(r,w) \tag{5.4}$$

solving the maximization problem. We refer to this as the *saving function.* Notice that the solution can be characterized as the value of S that sets the function $V(S,r)$ equal to zero.

5.1.1. *Properties of the saving function*

To determine how saving responds to a change in the interest rate, substitute the solution function into the first-order condition and then differentiate with respect to r to obtain

$$\frac{\partial S}{\partial r} = \frac{[W''(1+r)S + W']}{-(U'' + (1+r)^2 W'')}. \tag{5.5}$$

The denominator is positive because both U and W are concave. The sign of the numerator depends on the relative curvature of the second-period utility function. Recall that an increase in the real rate r has both a *substitution* and an *income* effect. When r increases, consumption in period 1 becomes more expensive relative to consumption in period 2, and the household tends to save more. However, there is also an income effect in that an increase in r will reduce the household's present value of income, or wealth. If the numerator is positive, then the substitution effect outweighs the income effect and saving increases with r. If it is negative, then the wealth effect outweighs the substitution effect and saving falls with r.

Suppose that the utility function is of the form

$$W(c) = U(c) = \frac{c^{1-\gamma} - 1}{1-\gamma}, \quad \gamma \geq 0.$$

How does optimal saving respond to changes in the interest rate for different values of γ? To answer this question, we use the result in Equation (5.5). Evaluating the partial derivative of U and W with respect to c, we have that

$W'(c)=c^{-\gamma}$ and $W''(c)=U''(c)=-\gamma c^{-\gamma-1}$. Substitute these values into the equation (5.5). This yields

$$\frac{\partial S}{\partial r}=\frac{c_2^{-\gamma}-\gamma c_2^{-\gamma-1}\overbrace{(1+r)S}^{c_2}}{-[-\gamma c_1^{-\gamma-1}-\gamma c_2^{-\gamma-1}(1+r)^2]}=\frac{(1-\gamma)c_2^{-\gamma}}{\underbrace{\gamma c_1^{-\gamma-1}}_{>0}+\underbrace{\gamma c_2^{-\gamma-1}(1+r)^2}_{>0}}.$$

We observe that the sign of $\partial S/\partial r$ depends on γ. If $\gamma<1$, the numerator of the above result is positive; correspondingly $\partial S/\partial r>0$. If $\gamma>1$, the numerator is negative, and $\partial S/\partial r<0$. Finally, if $\gamma=1$, numerator is zero and $\partial S/\partial r=0$.

To interpret these results, we note that the elasticity of intertemporal substitution in consumption is defined as

$$EITS=-\left(\frac{\partial\ln(c_1/c_2)}{\partial\ln(MU_1/MU_2)}\right)$$

where c_1 and c_2 denote consumption in periods 1 and 2, and MU_1 and MU_2 the marginal utility of consumption in the two periods. The intertemporal substitution elasticity shows consumers' attitudes toward smoothing consumption over time. To calculate the intertemporal elasticity:

$$\mathrm{MU}_i=\frac{\partial U(c_i)}{\partial c_i}=c_i^{-\gamma},\quad i=1,2.$$

Hence,

$$\frac{MU_1}{MU_2}=\left(\frac{c_1}{c_2}\right)^{-\gamma},$$

or

$$\ln\left(\frac{MU_1}{MU_2}\right)=-\gamma\ln\left(\frac{c_1}{c_2}\right).$$

Therefore,

$$-\left(\frac{\partial\ln(c_1/c_2)}{\partial\ln(MU_1/MU_2)}\right)=\frac{1}{\gamma}. \tag{5.6}$$

These results show that when $\gamma<1$, the intertemporal elasticity is greater than 1 and consumers are more willing to substitute consumption across periods. Hence, the substitution effect of an increase in the interest rate dominates the wealth effect. Thus, saving increases in response to an increase in the interest rate. By contrast, when $\gamma>1$, consumers prefer a smooth consumption profile. In this case, the wealth effect dominates the substitution effect, and saving falls when the interest rate rises. For the case with $\gamma=1$ which corresponds to logarithmic utility, we find that the substitution effect equals the wealth effect and saving does not change with changes in r. Hence, we find that optimal saving behavior can vary as a function of consumers' attitudes toward intertemporal substitution in the economy.

5.1.2. Optimal consumption over time

Suppose first that the household lives for T periods and has the preferences:

$$\sum_{t=0}^{T} \beta^t U(c_t), \quad 0 < \beta < 1. \tag{5.7}$$

The household receives the exogenous labor income $y \in (0, \bar{y}]$ where $\bar{y} < \infty$ in each period of its life. Also assume that it can borrow and lend at the interest rate $r \in (-1, \infty)$. Then it faces the sequence of budget constraints:

$$c_t + S_{t+1} \leq y_t + (1+r)S_t, \quad t \geq 0, \tag{5.8}$$

given initial saving S_0. Notice that in a finite horizon economy, savings in the last period of life must be zero, $S_{T+1} = 0$. As a consequence, consumption at date T must equal income at date T plus savings from $T-1$,

$$c_T = y_T + (1+r)S_{T-1}.$$

Let λ_t denote the Lagrange multiplier on the per-period budget constraint. The first-order conditions with respect to c_t and S_{t+1} for $t = 0, \ldots, T-1$ are

$$U'(c_t) = \lambda_t,$$

$$\lambda_t = \beta \lambda_{t+1}(1+r).$$

Combining these equations to eliminate the Lagrange multiplier yields the condition:

$$U'(c_t) = \beta(1+r)U'(c_{t+1}). \tag{5.9}$$

Suppose the utility function is given by $u(c) = (c^{1-\gamma} - 1)/(1-\gamma)$, $\gamma \geq 0$. Then this condition can be expressed as:

$$c_t^{-\gamma} = \beta(1+r)c_{t+1}^{-\gamma},$$

or

$$c_{t+1} = (\beta(1+r))^{\frac{1}{\gamma}} c_t,$$

$$\Rightarrow c_t = (\beta(1+r))^{\frac{t}{\gamma}} c_0, \quad t = 0, \ldots, T-1. \tag{5.10}$$

The per-period budget constraints can be simplified recursively as:

$$c_t + S_{t+1} = y_t + (1+r)S_t$$

$$c_t + \frac{c_{t+1} + S_{t+2} - y_{t+1}}{1+r} = y_t + (1+r)S_t$$

$$\vdots = \vdots$$

$$\sum_{j=0}^{T-t} \frac{c_{t+j}}{(1+r)^j} + \frac{S_{T+1}}{(1+r)^{T-t}} = \sum_{j=0}^{T-t} \frac{y_{t+j}}{(1+r)^j} + (1+r)S_t.$$

Setting $t=0$ in the above equation and noticing that $S_{T+1}=0$ yields the lifetime budget constraint as

$$\sum_{t=0}^{T} \frac{c_t}{(1+r)^t} = \sum_{t=0}^{T} \frac{y_t}{(1+r)^t} + (1+r)S_0. \tag{5.11}$$

Substituting for c_t using the left side of (5.10) yields

$$\sum_{t=0}^{T} \frac{c_t}{(1+r)^t} = \sum_{t=0}^{T} \frac{(\beta(1+r))^{\frac{t}{\gamma}} c_0}{(1+r)^t}.$$

Provided $\eta \equiv (\beta(1+r))^{\frac{1}{\gamma}}/(1+r) < 1$, we can simplify this last result as

$$\sum_{t=0}^{T} \eta^t c_0 = \frac{1}{1-\eta}(1-\eta^{T+1})c_0.$$

Therefore,

$$c_0 = \frac{1-\eta}{1-\eta^{T+1}} \left[\sum_{t=0}^{T} \frac{y_t}{(1+r)^t} + (1+r)S_0 \right],$$

which implies that

$$c_t = [(\beta(1+r))^{\frac{t}{\gamma}}] \frac{1-\eta}{1-\eta^{T+1}} \left[\sum_{t=0}^{T} \frac{y_t}{(1+r)^t} + (1+r)S_0 \right]. \tag{5.12}$$

Thus, we find that the optimal consumption policy involves consuming a fraction of lifetime income at each date t. This condition allows us to make predictions regarding the optimal consumption policy over time.

1. A consumer who lives longer will consume a smaller fraction of his lifetime income, i.e.

$$[(\beta(1+r))^{\frac{t}{\gamma}}] \frac{1-\eta}{1-\eta^{\tilde{T}+1}} < [(\beta(1+r))^{\frac{t}{\gamma}}] \frac{1-\eta}{1-\eta^{T+1}}$$

for $\tilde{T} > T$ since η^{T+1} is decreasing in T.

2. Recall that subjective discount factor can be written as $\beta = 1/(1+\rho)$, where ρ is the subjective discount rate. The optimal consumption policy states that if the subjective rate of time preference ρ is greater than the interest rate r, then the consumer will consume more today relative to tomorrow, $c_t > c_{t+1}$ whereas if $\rho < r$, then the consumer will prefer to delay consumption so that $c_t < c_{t+1}$. If $\rho = r$, then the optimal consumption path is constant, $c_t = \bar{c}$. (See Equation 5.10.) Thus, the consumption profile depends on how patient consumers are.
3. The optimal consumption profile also depends on the real interest rate. The higher is r, the higher will be consumption growth.
4. In the case with $\rho = r$, the consumer consumes a fixed fraction of his lifetime in each period denoted $(1-\eta)/(1-\eta^{T+1})$.

Now suppose that T goes to infinity. We can iterate the one-period budget constraint forward to obtain the lifetime budget constraint as:

$$\sum_{t=0}^{\infty} \frac{c_t}{(1+r)^t} = \sum_{t=0}^{\infty} \frac{y_t}{(1+r)^t}, \tag{5.13}$$

assuming $S_0 = 0$. To obtain this budget constraint, we also impose the condition that the discounted value of last-period savings goes to zero as the horizon gets longer:

$$\lim_{T\to\infty} \frac{S_{T+1}}{(1+r)^T} \to 0.$$

Suppose also that a household's income follows a known sequence $\{y_l, y_h, y_l, y_h, \ldots\}$, where $y_l < y_h$. The relative frequency of y_l and y_h is 0.5 (so that half of the time income is y_h and the other half, it is y_l). See Figure 5.2. Suppose that the household just consumes its endowment each period, so in low periods utility is $U(y_l)$ and in high periods it is $U(y_h)$. By Jensen's Inequality for concave functions, average utility is below the utility function evaluated at the average level of income, $\bar{y} = 0.5y_h + 0.5y_l$. That is,

$$0.5U(y_l) + 0.5U(y_h) < U(\bar{y}).$$

The household is much better off, in terms of higher utility, in smoothing consumption over time. How does it do this? By allowing saving to increase or decrease to maintain optimal consumption.

To further illustrate these results, suppose that real interest rate satisfies that $\beta(1+r) = 1$. Then

$$U'(c_t) = U'(c_{t+1}), \tag{5.14}$$

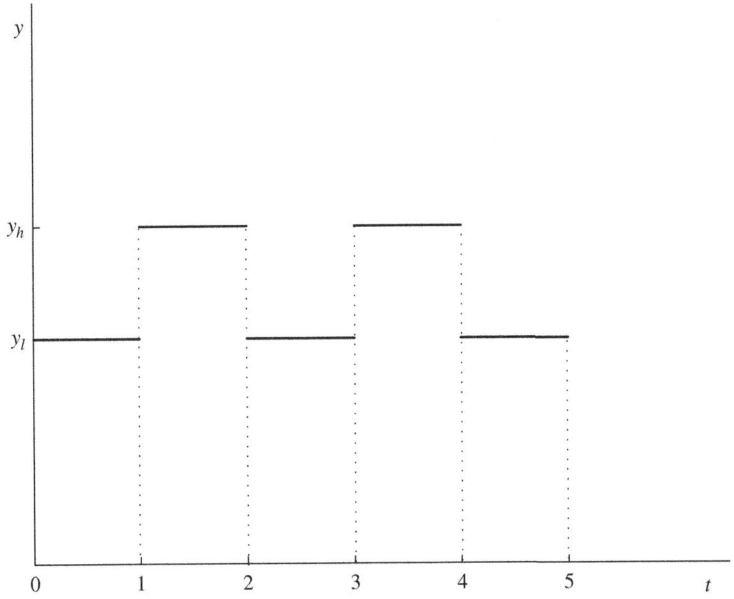

Figure 5.2. Alternating deterministic endowment

which implies that $c_t = c_{t+1} = \bar{c}$ for all t. The present value of lifetime income is:

$$PV_t(y) = \sum_{i=0}^{\infty} \left(\frac{1}{1+r}\right)^i y_{t+i},$$

where $y_t = y_l$ if t is odd and equal to y_h if t is even. This can be simplified as:

$$\begin{aligned} PV_0(y) &= \sum_{t=1}^{\infty} \left(\frac{1}{1+r}\right)^{2t} y_h + \sum_{t=1}^{\infty} \left(\frac{1}{1+r}\right)^{2t-1} y_l \\ &= y_h \left(\frac{1}{1 - 1/(1+r)^2}\right) + y_l \left(\frac{1}{1+r}\right)\left(\frac{1}{1 - 1/(1+r)^2}\right) \\ &= \frac{(1+r)^2}{r(2+r)} y_h + \frac{(1+r)}{r(2+r)} y_l. \end{aligned}$$

The present value of consumption expenditures is:

$$PV_0(c) = \bar{c} \sum_{t=0}^{\infty} \left(\frac{1}{1+r}\right)^t = \left(\frac{1+r}{r}\right) \bar{c}.$$

Setting this equal to the PV of income, we can solve for $\bar{c}$ as:

$$\bar{c} = \frac{r}{1+r} PV_0(y) = \frac{y_h(1+r)+y_l}{2+r}.$$

Notice that if $y_h = y_l = \bar{y}$, the consumer merely consumes $\bar{c} = \bar{y}$ in each period and saving is zero. By contrast, if there are variations in income, then saving adjusts to provide a constant consumption stream to the household. Assuming that the household's initial saving is zero, saving under a constant consumption policy evolves as

$$S_{t+1} = \begin{cases} y_l + (1+r)S_t - \bar{c} & \text{if } t \text{ is odd} \\ y_h + (1+r)S_t - \bar{c} & \text{if } t \text{ is even,} \end{cases}$$

given $S_1 = y_l - \bar{c}$. Hence, saving is the residual that fluctuates so that consumption can be constant. We discuss the properties of optimal consumption and saving further after we introduce uncertainty.

5.2. PORTFOLIO CHOICE UNDER UNCERTAINTY

We can extend this framework to allow for random variation in the next period's wealth. In what follows, we first consider a portfolio choice problem with a risky and risk-free asset. In a later section, we consider a more general saving-consumption problem under uncertainty.

Now suppose that the return on one of the assets that the agent holds is uncertain. In particular, suppose that there are two assets, A and B, and that A pays a certain return of r_a while B pays an uncertain return r_b. The consumer lives two periods, and obtains consumption $c = w - s_a - s_b$ in the first period and $c' = r_a s_a + r_b s_b$ in the second period. The consumer solves

$$\max_{s_a, s_b} U(w - s_a - s_b) + E[W(r_a s_a + r_b s_b)]. \tag{5.15}$$

The first-order conditions with respect to s_a, s_b are

$$U'(w - s_a - s_b) = E[W'(r_a s_a + r_b s_b) r_a] \tag{5.16}$$

$$U'(w - s_a - s_b) = E[W'(r_a s_a + r_b s_b) r_b]. \tag{5.17}$$

Divide both sides of each equation by U' to obtain

$$1 = \frac{E[W'(r_a s_a + r_b s_b) r_a]}{U'(w - s_a - s_b)} = \frac{E[W'(r_a s_a + r_b s_b) r_b]}{U'(w - s_a - s_b)}. \tag{5.18}$$

Hence each asset is held so that the expected weighted return is equalized across assets. The weight is the intertemporal marginal rate of substitution in consumption:

$$m_{t+1} = W'(c_{t+1})/U'(c_t),$$

This is the *stochastic discount factor* that we defined in Chapter 1. It is the rate at which future (random) income is discounted.

We will use the covariance decomposition property to rewrite our first-order conditions. Recall that for two random variables x, y, the covariance decomposition is $\mathrm{Cov}(x, y) = E(xy) - E(x)E(y)$ where $E(\cdot)$ is the unconditional expectations operator. Recall that the return to asset A is known with certainty so that we can move r_a from the expectations operator, so that

$$r_a = \left[\frac{E(W'(c'))}{U'(c)}\right]^{-1}. \tag{5.19}$$

According to the covariance property, the first-order condition for holdings of asset B can be expressed as:

$$\mathrm{Cov}\left(\frac{W'(c')}{U'(c)}, r_b\right) = 1 - E\left(\frac{W'(c')}{U'(c)}\right) E(r_b),$$

This can be rewritten as:

$$\frac{E[W'(c')]}{U'(c)} E(r_b) = 1 - \mathrm{Cov}\left(\frac{W'(c')}{U'(c)}, r_b\right). \tag{5.20}$$

Divide both sides by $E[W'(c')]/U'(c)$ and re-arrange

$$E(r_b) - r_a = -r_a \mathrm{Cov}\left(\frac{W'(c')}{U'(c)}, r_b\right). \tag{5.21}$$

The left side is the risk premium, $E(r_b) - r_a$ – the excess return over the certain return that the agent needs to be compensated to hold the risky asset. Hence, the portfolio choice problem under uncertainty yields a representation for the risk premium based on the covariance of the risky return with the intertemporal marginal rate of substitution. By contrast, the static CAPM yields a representation for the risk premium in terms of the covariance of the return with the wealth portfolio, R^W. It is this feature which separates much of the new literature of asset pricing from the earlier empirical literature. We will discuss these issues further in later chapters.

5.3. A MORE GENERAL PROBLEM

At the beginning of period t, the agent has an endowment y_t that can be allocated between consumption c_t or borrowing and lending, b_{t+1}. Assume that the endowment and the (net) return to borrowing or lending is stochastic. In particular, let $s \in S$ be a state variable. The endowment process is a function $y : S \to Y$ where $Y = (0, \bar{y}]$. The return process, which is determined endogenously in a general equilibrium model but which we will treat as exogenous, is function $r : S \to (-1, \infty)$. Assume that s follows a first-order Markov process. Assume for convenience that the state space is continuous.

The consumer's objective function at time t is:

$$E_0 \left\{ \sum_{t=0}^{\infty} \beta^t U(c_t) \right\}, \tag{5.22}$$

where $0 < \beta < 1$ is the subjective discount factor. Here the expectation operator is written as conditional on information at time t. Notice that as we go forward in time, the household will continuously update this information set, conditioning on all information available at the time the decision is made. The utility function $U : \Re_+ \to \Re$ is bounded, strictly increasing, strictly concave, and continuously differentiable with $\lim_{c\to 0} U'(c) = \infty$ and $\lim_{c\to\infty} U'(c) \to 0$. The budget constraints are:

$$c_t + b_{t+1} = y(s_t) + b_t(1 + r(s_t)), \tag{5.23}$$

for all $t \geq 0$.

The consumer's problem involves choosing sequences for consumption and bond holdings denoted $\{c_t\}_{t=0}^{\infty}$ and $\{b_{t+1}\}_{t=0}^{\infty}$ to maximize Equation (5.22) subject to a sequence of budget constraints and given initial bond holdings, b_0, and the initial state, s_0. In the next chapter, we show how to formulate this problem using a recursive approach and examine the conditions under which it has a solution. For now assume a solution exists. Let $\{\lambda_t\}_{t=0}^{\infty}$ denote the sequence of Lagrange multipliers corresponding to the one-period budget constraints. The first-order conditions characterizing the optimal consumption and bond-holding choices are as follows:

$$U'(c_t) = \lambda_t, \tag{5.24}$$

$$\lambda_t = E_t(\lambda_{t+1}(1 + r(s_{t+1}))) \tag{5.25}$$

for $t \geq 0$. Substituting for λ_t using the first condition yields:

$$U'[c_t] = \beta E_t\{U'[c_{t+1}](1 + r(s_{t+1}))\}. \tag{5.26}$$

We now examine the implications of Equation (5.26) for some special cases.

(i) *Constant real interest rate with* $\beta(1 + r) = 1$. In this case, the only randomness in the consumer's problem derives from income fluctuations whereas the interest rate is risk free, meaning that it is constant over time. Furthermore, the real interest rate is given by

$$(1 + r) = \frac{1}{\beta} = 1 + \rho \quad \text{or} \quad r = \rho,$$

where $\rho > 0$ is the subjective rate of time preference. Making these substitutions in the first-order condition yields

$$U'(c_t) = E_t[U'(c_{t+1})]. \tag{5.27}$$

Thus, we have that the marginal utility of consumption follows a *martingale*. This means that the best predictor of next period's marginal utility is this period's marginal utility.

(ii) *Independently and identically distributed income shocks.* If the random shocks s_t are independently and identically distributed each period, then the first-order condition (5.26) can be written as:

$$U'(c_t) = \beta E[U'(c_{t+1})(1 + r(s_{t+1}))]. \tag{5.28}$$

If the random state s_t is distributed as i.i.d. each period, then the expectation does not depend on which state is considered. In this case, current realizations of the state s_t are not useful for predicting future realizations.

(iii) *Constant interest rate with $\beta(1 + r) = 1$ and i.i.d. income shocks.* Now conditions (i) and (ii) hold together. In this case the expectation of marginal utility is a constant, and so is optimal consumption:

$$U'(c_t) = E[U'(c_{t+1})] \quad \Rightarrow \quad c = \bar{c}. \tag{5.29}$$

Let $\bar{U} = E[U'(c_{t+1})]$. Setting this equal to $U'(c_t)$ and solving for c_t yields $\bar{c} = (U')^{-1}(\bar{U})$. As in Section 5.1, the consumer borrows at the constant interest rate to smooth income shocks, so that optimal saving evolves as:

$$b_{t+1} = y(s_t) + (1 + r)b_t - \bar{c}, \tag{5.30}$$

given an initial b_0.

(iv) *Quadratic utility and $\beta(1 + r) = 1$.* Let the utility function have the form $U(c) = ac - bc^2/2$ so that marginal utility is linear in consumption, $U'(c) = a - bc$. The optimal consumption sequence satisfies Equation (5.27) with

$$c_t = E_t[c_{t+1}]. \tag{5.31}$$

This is referred to as the *random walk of consumption* due to Hall [223] and Flavin [187]. It has the strong implication that the best predictor of next period's consumption is this period's consumption. Thus, future consumption will vary only as a function of news or unanticipated shocks.

Let us use the sequence of budget constraints in (5.23) to derive an alternative representation by recursively substituting for next period's bond holdings into the current budget constraint:

$$c_t + b_{t+1} = y(s_t) + b_t(1 + r(s_t)),$$

which implies

$$c_t + \frac{c_{t+1}}{(1 + r(s_{t+1}))} + \frac{b_{t+2}}{(1 + r(s_{t+1}))} =$$
$$y(s_t) + \frac{y(s_{t+1})}{(1 + r(s_{t+1}))} + b_t(1 + r(s_t)).$$

Iterating forward up to period $t+h$ and defining the discount factor γ_{t+i} as

$$\gamma_t = 1, \quad \gamma_{t+i} \equiv \frac{1}{\prod_{j=1}^{i}(1 + r(s_{t+j}))} \quad \text{for } i > 0,$$

we have:

$$\sum_{i=0}^{h} \gamma_{t+i} c_{t+i} + \gamma_{t+h} b_{t+h+1} = \sum_{i=0}^{h} \gamma_{t+i} y(s_{t+i}) + b_t(1 + r(s_t)).$$

Taking the limit as $h \to \infty$ implies the consumer's intertemporal budget constraint:

$$\sum_{i=0}^{\infty} \gamma_{t+i} c_{t+i} = \sum_{i=0}^{\infty} \gamma_{t+i} y(s_{t+i}) + b_t(1 + r(s_t)), \tag{5.32}$$

where we have imposed the limiting condition:

$$\lim_{h \to \infty} \gamma_{t+h} b_{t+h+1} \to 0. \tag{5.33}$$

This says that the present value of the consumer's expenditures must equal the present value of the consumer's income plus any initial wealth $b_t(1 + r(s_t))$ for any given realization of the shocks $\{s_{t+i}\}_{i=0}^{\infty}$. Thus, consumers are required to have a balanced budget for each history of the shocks.

Now take expectations of both sides of the present value budget constraint conditional on information at time t. Also use the first-order condition which states that $E_t(c_{t+i}) = c_t$, assuming that the real interest rate is a constant:

$$\sum_{i=0}^{\infty} \frac{c_t}{(1 + r)^i} = E_t \left\{ \sum_{i=0}^{\infty} \frac{y(s_{t+i})}{(1 + r)^i} \right\} + b_t(1 + r). \tag{5.34}$$

Notice that we can simplify this expression as:

$$c_t = \frac{r}{1 + r} \left\{ E_t \left[\sum_{i=0}^{\infty} \frac{y(s_{t+i})}{(1 + r)^i} \right] + b_t(1 + r) \right\}. \tag{5.35}$$

The expression on the right side of this relation is called the consumer's *permanent income* and the relationship summarized by this equation is referred to as the *permanent income hypothesis* following Friedman [190], who argued that consumers would choose their consumption as a function of their permanent income or wealth. Hence, under the assumption that utility is quadratic and that the real interest rate is a constant and equal to the consumer's rate of subjective time preference, we find that optimal consumption is proportional to permanent income or wealth.

One implication of this representation is that permanent changes in income lead to permanent changes in consumption. We can show this using the solution for the model in case (iv). Suppose, in particular, that income at all dates increases by Δy. Then notice from the expression on the right side of Equation (5.35) that the change in permanent income is:

$$\frac{r}{1+r}\Delta y \sum_{i=0}^{\infty} \frac{1}{(1+r)^i} = \Delta y.$$

Hence, it must be the case that consumption also responds by the same amount at each date t.

We can use the framework of this section to examine the response of consumption to *permanent* versus *temporary* shocks. First, assume that households face income shocks that are transitory (temporary) and permanent. If households can easily borrow and save, then they will do so to smooth over transitory income shocks. The case with identically and independently distributed income shocks corresponds to a situation in which income shocks are purely transitory. If we assume that the real interest rate is constant and for simplicity satisfies $\beta(1+r)=1$, then Equations (5.29)–(5.30) imply that *all* income shocks will be smoothed away, and the optimal consumption sequence will be constant through time. If income shocks are permanent, then consumption will respond to permanent income shocks because consumption expenditures cannot exceed the income stream in discounted present value (so lifetime budget constraints must hold). Hence the empirical implications are clear: consumption does not respond to transitory income shocks while it does respond to permanent shocks.

The permanent income/life cycle hypothesis has been subject to much empirical testing. In the data, consumption typically responds strongly to permanent income shocks and this response tends to be much stronger than the response of consumption to transitory shocks. However, the response to transitory shocks is much larger than we would predict from the consumption smoothing model (sometimes called the *life-cycle model*). (See, for example, Flavin [187].) Such findings have been taken to be evidence against the consumption smoothing model. According to one view, the assumption that capital markets are perfect, specifically that consumers can easily borrow against future income, is not correct and consumers are subject to liquidity constraints. Others have argued that some of the findings may be explained by the presence of precautionary saving effects. (See, for example, Zeldes [452].) Pemberton [359] reviews the performance of multi-period stochastic dynamic programming models of household consumption and savings, and concludes that another problem with the application of such models for modeling actual behavior lies in their sheer complexity. He argues more attention should be paid to issues of consumers' ignorance or uncertainty and to learning. In later chapters, we address some of the criticisms leveled against the simple model by considering models with borrowing constraints and market incompleteness.

5.3.1. Precautionary saving

To extend our analysis of the previous section, we now examine the response of consumption and saving to income and interest rate uncertainty. We are interested in answering the following question: How does the solution for saving under uncertainty differ from the solution under certainty? In particular, does saving increase or decrease with uncertainty? It may be that the greater risk about the return to saving or about future income may lead the consumer to substitute away from consumption tomorrow by saving less and consuming more today. Or the increased uncertainty next period may lead to reduced consumption today and increased saving. Fearful of a very low return or income, the consumer may respond by increasing saving today to insure against a bad outcome tomorrow. When the latter occurs, we say that households have a *precautionary motive* to save.

This issue was considered by Leland [304] in a two-period model with income risk. Leland showed that the standard Arrow-Pratt measures of risk aversion did not suffice to determine the impact of greater uncertainty on the optimal saving decision. Instead he showed that the answer depends on the concavity or the convexity of the marginal utility function. Notice that the concavity or convexity of the utility function does not tell anything about whether *marginal utility* is concave or convex. Leland showed that whereas the Arrow-Pratt measures of risk aversion depend on the second derivative of the utility function, the notion of precautionary saving depends on its third derivative.

Returning to our simple two-period example in Section 5.1, we found that the solution was a saving function S^o that depends on the real interest rate and real wage. Now suppose that the return is stochastic, $r(s)$ and for simplicity, that it is i.i.d. Also define the gross rate of interest by $R(s) = 1 + r(s)$ and assume that w is constant. The first-order condition is:

$$U'(w - S) = E\left[W'(R(s)S)R(s)\right], \tag{5.36}$$

where $E(\cdot)$ denotes unconditional expectation. Let $\hat{S} = S(w, R(s))$ denote the solution to Equation (5.36). Likewise, the first-order condition under certainty can be written as:

$$U'(w - S) = W'(RS)R, \tag{5.37}$$

where $R = 1 + r$ and w are both non-stochastic. Write the solution under certainty as $S^o = S(w, R)$.

To illustrate the impact of uncertainty about the interest rate on the optimal saving decision, assume further that $R = E(R(s))$ and multiply both sides of Equations (5.36) and (5.37) by saving, S. Then the first-order conditions become:

$$U'(w - S)S = E\left[W'(R(s)S)R(s)S\right], \tag{5.38}$$

and

$$U'(w - S)S = W'(RS)RS. \tag{5.39}$$

We are interested in whether the marginal (utility) cost of additional saving in period 1 evaluated under the certainty solution S^o is less than the expected marginal benefit of this saving when there is interest rate uncertainty:

$$U'(w - S^o)S^o = W'(RS^o)RS^o < E\left[W'(R(s)S^o)R(s)S^o\right]. \tag{5.40}$$

If this is the case (and the second-order condition holds for the case with uncertainty), then utility can be increased by increasing saving above the case with certainty. In this case, we say that there exists a *precautionary* motive in the face of interest rate uncertainty. To determine the condition under which this is true, evaluate the right side of Equation (5.38) at the certainty solution S^o as $E\left[W'(R(s)S^o)R(s)S^o\right]$. Define $x = R(s)S^o$ and $x^o = RS^o$ and evaluate $E[W'(x)x]$ by expanding $W'(x)x$ around x^o as:

$$E\left[W'(x)x\right] = E\Bigg\{W'x^o + (x - x^o)\left[W''x^o + W'\right] + \frac{(x - x^o)^2}{2}\left[W'''x^o + 2W''\right]\Bigg\}.$$

Substituting back for $x = R(s)S^o$ and $x^o = RS^o$ and taking expectation of the right side, we obtain the result

$$E\left[W'(R(s)S^o)R(s)S^o\right] = W'(RS^o)RS^o + \frac{(S^o)^2 Var(R(s))}{2}\left[W'''(RS^o)(RS^o) + 2W''(RS^o)\right]. \tag{5.41}$$

Equation (5.41) implies that there exists a precautionary saving motive, or equivalently, Equation (5.40) holds, provided

$$\frac{(S^o)^2 Var(R(s))}{2}\left[W'''(RS^o)RS^o + 2W''(RS^o)\right] > 0.$$

Since the term $(S^o)^2 Var(R(s))$ is always positive, this condition simplifies as:

$$W'''(RS^o)RS^o > -2W''(RS^o).$$

Assuming the strict concavity of the utility function, we have that $W'' < 0$. Hence, a necessary (but not sufficient) condition for saving to be increasing in interest rate uncertainty is that the third derivative of the utility be positive, $W''' > 0$.

In a related analysis, Kimball [276] has defined measures of "prudence" that allow us to determine the impact of second-period uncertainty on the optimal first-period consumption decision. It is easier to illustrate Kimball's results using measures of income uncertainty. For simplicity, consider a two-period version of the problem with varying income. Assume that the consumer has labor income in the first and second periods of his life. Let the real interest be constant and equal to zero, $r = 0$. Define A as the sum of first-period assets plus first-period income and denote by $y(s)$ as the second-period income, where $y(s)$ is a random variable that varies as a function of the state s. Let consumption in period 1 be defined as c. We can define saving as $S = A - c$. Hence, consumption in period 2 is given by $A - c + y(s)$. We are interested in the impact of uncertainty on the consumer's optimal saving choice. The first-order condition under uncertainty is given by:

$$U'(c) = E\left[W'(A - c + y(s))\right]. \tag{5.42}$$

Proceeding in a manner similar to the derivation of the risk premium, Kimball defines the *compensating precautionary premium* to satisfy

$$W'(A - c + y) = E[W'(A - c + y(s) + \psi^*)]. \tag{5.43}$$

Thus, if there exists some quantity ψ^* that can compensate for the effect of income risk on second-period consumption, then the optimal solution for consumption (or saving) in period 1 would remain unaltered. Likewise, the *equivalent precautionary premium* satisfies

$$W'(A - c + y - \psi) = E[W'(A - c + y(s))]. \tag{5.44}$$

In this case, the existence of the quantity ψ that eliminates the effect of income risk on second-period consumption at a given cost to the consumer would leave first-period consumption (or saving) unchanged.

To find ψ^* or ψ, we proceed as before and solve for these quantities by taking approximations to the functions that appear on the left and right sides of (5.43) or (5.44). Also assume that the constant income in the certainty solution is equal to the mean of the stochastic income, $E(y(s)) = y$, and consider Equation (5.44). Approximating the left side around $\psi = 0$, we have

$$W'(A - c + y) - \psi W''(A - c + y).$$

Approximating the function on the right side around $y(s) = y$ and taking expectation, we have

$$W'(A - c + y) + \frac{\text{Var}(y(s))}{2} W'''(A - c - y).$$

Solving for ψ we obtain

$$\psi = \frac{\text{Var}(y(s))}{2} \left(-\frac{W'''}{W''} \right). \tag{5.45}$$

The second term denotes the *index of absolute prudence*, and it shows how the cost of reducing uncertainty to the consumer varies. It plays an analogous role as the coefficient of absolute risk aversion. Notice that $W''' < 0$ if W' is concave, and $W''' > 0$ if W' is convex. If W' is convex, then the consumer is willing to pay a positive premium to reduce uncertainty in the second period. If $W''' = 0$ (which occurs for quadratic utility), then we have that $\psi = 0$ and $E\left[W'(A - c + y(s))\right] = W'(A - c + y)$. We say that the *certainty equivalent property* holds when this is the case. (See Exercise 1.)

5.4. CONCLUSIONS

In this chapter we have established properties of optimal consumption and saving decisions, taking as given the interest rate and the income processes. Our results suggest that the desire to smooth consumption over time, whether in a deterministic or stochastic environment, has some strong implications. We have also shown how the consumption and saving model can be interpreted in terms of the consumer's portfolio choice problem. The consumption and saving model provides both an asset-pricing theory and a theory of risk. Furthermore, in a general equilibrium framework, rates of return on alternative assets are jointly determined with consumption and savings allocations. Hence, consumers' desire to smooth consumption affects the return on alternative assets. Production and capital accumulation aid in fulfilling consumption smoothing and provide an additional mechanism through which assets returns are affected. Such factors are further highlighted depending on the nature of market incompleteness in the economy. We defer discussion of some of these issues to Parts II and IV.

5.5. EXERCISES

1. Certainty Equivalent Solution
Consider the simple two-period model with income uncertainty and saving. Suppose that the two-period utility function is given by:

$$U(c_1) + \beta U(c_2),$$

where $0 < \beta < 1$ is the subjective discount rate. Assume further that U is quadratic:

$$U(c) = ac - bc^2/2, \quad c < a/2b.$$

Let the constant interest rate be equal to r, and define the consumer's budget constraints in periods 1 and 2 by:

$$c_1 + S \leq y_1$$

$$c_2 \leq y_2 + (1 + r)S,$$

where S denotes saving.
Show that the optimal choice of consumption and saving exhibits the *certainty equivalent property*, that is, the solution under uncertainty can be obtained from the solution under certainty by replacing random variables with their expectations.

2. Log Utility CAPM
Suppose that an infinitely lived consumer has preferences over random consumption streams defined as:

$$\sum_{i=0}^{\infty} \beta^i \ln(c_{t+i}).$$

(a) What is the intertemporal MRS or stochastic discount factor?
(b) Consider a claim to all future consumption. This may be defined as the *wealth portfolio*. The price of the wealth portfolio at date t satisfies:

$$p_t^W = E_t \left[\sum_{j=1}^{\infty} \frac{\beta^j U'(c_{t+j})}{U'(c_t)} c_{t+j} \right].$$

Find p_t^W.
(c) Define the return on the wealth portfolio as:

$$R_{t+1}^W = \frac{p_{t+1}^W + c_{t+1}}{p_t^W}.$$

Show that the intertemporal MRS for the log utility model is the inverse of the return on the wealth portfolio:

$$m_{t+1} = \frac{1}{R^W_{t+1}}.$$

3. An Intertemporal Model of the Current Account
Consider a small open economy that is populated by an infinitely lived representative consumer with preferences given by

$$E_0 \left\{ \sum_{t=0}^{\infty} \beta^t U(c_t) \right\}, \tag{5.46}$$

where E_0 is the expectations operator conditional on information at date zero, β is a subjective discount factor with $0 < \beta < 1$, $U(\cdot)$ is a strictly increasing, strictly concave utility function, and c_t denotes private consumption.

The country can borrow or lend at the constant real interest r with the rest of the world. Let b_t denote net foreign liabilities at t, y_t denote gross domestic product, i_t real investment, and g_t government expenditures. The following equation characterizes the accumulation of net foreign liabilities by the country:

$$\Delta b_{t+1} = c_t + i_t + g_t - y_t + rb_t, \quad t \geq 0. \tag{5.47}$$

The current account (CA) for the country is given by

$$CA_t = nf_t - c_t - rb_t,$$

where nf_t denotes national cash flow $nf_t = y_t - i_t - g_t$.

(a) Assuming a quadratic utility function and imposing the terminal condition that the discounted value of borrowing goes to zero as t goes to infinity, find the optimal value of consumption denoted c_t^* that maximizes Equation (5.46) subject to the budget constraint:

$$b_{t+1} + y_t = c_t + i_t + g_t + (1 + r)b_t, \quad t \geq 0.$$

(b) Using your answer to part (a), find the optimal consumption-smoothing current account CA_t^*.

(c) Discuss the impact of permanent versus transitory changes in (i) gross domestic product, (ii) investment, (iii) government expenditures on CA_t^*.

4. A household solves

$$\max_{\{c_t, l_t, S_t\}} \sum_{t=0}^{\infty} \beta^t U(c_t, l_t) \tag{5.48}$$

where c_t is consumption and l_t is leisure, subject to the time constraint

$$l_t + n_t = 1 \tag{5.49}$$

and the budget constraint

$$w_t n_t + (1 + r)S_t = c_t + S_{t+1} \tag{5.50}$$

where n_t is the labor supply, $\{w_t\}$ is a known sequence of wage rates, r is the real and constant interest rate, S_t is savings, and S_0 is given. The function U is continuous, increasing, and strictly concave in both arguments. Consumption and leisure are normal goods. Households maximize the discounted present value of utility by choosing consumption and leisure.

(a) Set up the maximization problem and derive the first-order conditions using the sequential approach with Lagrange multipliers. Demonstrate that optimal labor supply can be expressed as a function:

$$n_t = H(c_t, w_t).$$

Describe the properties of the function H.

(b) Assume that $\beta(1 + r) = 1$. Describe the behavior of consumption and savings over time, given the sequence of wages.

(c) Suppose that the utility function takes the form

$$\alpha_1 \ln(c_t) + \alpha_2 \ln(l_t).$$

Find the optimal consumption, savings, leisure, and labor supply expressed as a function of wages and past savings.

(d) Suppose that the wage rate follows a specific pattern: in even periods let $w_t = w^h$ and in odd periods $w_t = w^l$ where $w^h > w^l$. Describe how consumption, saving, and labor move over time.

PART II

Recursive models

CHAPTER 6

Dynamic programming

In this chapter, we provide a brief description of the dynamic programming approach. We consider the consumption/saving problem that we introduced in Chapter 5 and a deterministic growth problem. We illustrate the Principle of Optimality and introduce methods for solving a dynamic stochastic optimization problem using a recursive approach. In later chapters, we illustrate the dynamic programming approach in a variety of applications.

6.1. A DETERMINISTIC GROWTH PROBLEM

Suppose there is a representative infinite-lived household with time additive preferences over infinite consumption sequences $\{c_t\}_{t=0}^{\infty}$. The consumer maximizes

$$\sum_{t=0}^{\infty} \beta^t U(c_t)$$

where $0 < \beta < 1$ is the constant discount factor used to evaluate future utility. The utility function $U(\cdot)$ is increasing, strictly concave, and twice-continuously differentiable. The Inada conditions are assumed to hold.

Suppose that output is produced according to the production technology:

$$y_t = \theta f(k_t), \tag{6.1}$$

where $f(\cdot)$ is strictly increasing, strictly concave, and twice-continuously differentiable and θ is a known productivity parameter. Assume that households own the capital stock and that the resource constraint facing a household is

$$c_t + k_{t+1} = \theta f(k_t) + (1 - \delta)k_t, \tag{6.2}$$

where δ denotes the depreciation on capital with $0 < \delta < 1$.

The problem of the consumer can be expressed as:

$$(SS) \quad \max_{\{c_t\}_{t=0}^{\infty}, \{k_{t+1}\}_{t=0}^{\infty}} \sum_{t=0}^{\infty} \beta^t U(c_t)$$

subject to the sequences of constraints

$$c_t + k_{t+1} = \theta f(k_t) + (1 - \delta)k_t, \quad t \geq 0,$$

$$c_t \geq 0, \quad k_{t+1} \geq 0,$$

given the initial capital stock k_0.

Suppose we could solve the problem in (SS) for all possible values of k_0. Then we could define a function

$$V : \Re \rightarrow \Re$$

by taking $V(k_0)$ as the maximized value of the objective function in (SS) for all t, given k_0. The function V is known as the *value function*. If the function V were known for each state (k), we could evaluate the maximum utility that can be attained with the initial capital stock k_1 by $V(k_1)$. Define the set of feasible consumption and capital stock allocations at time 0 by:

$$\Gamma(k_0) \equiv \{(c_0, k_1) : c_0 + k_1 \leq \theta f(k_0)\}.$$

Given the function V, we can replace the dynamic optimization problem described by (SS) with the problem:

$$\max_{c_0, k_1 \in \Gamma(k_0)} \{U(c_0) + \beta V(k_1)\}. \tag{6.3}$$

If the function V were known, we could use Equation (6.3) to define the *policy functions* for the optimal choice of consumption and saving by:

$$g : \Re \rightarrow \Re_+$$

$$h : \Re \rightarrow \Re_+.$$

Thus, for each k_0, $c_0 = g(k_0)$ and $k' = h(k_0)$ show the values of consumption and capital that attain the maximum in Equation (6.3). The policy functions describe the optimal choice of consumption and capital as a function of the *state variable*, k_0.[1] Given the functions g and h, we can describe the evolution of the consumer's consumption and capital choices as $c_t = g(k_t)$ and $k_{t+1} = h(k_t)$ and for all $t \geq 0$, given k_0.

We assumed above that V shows the maximized value of the objective function for the problem in (SS) for the initial state (k_0). If the function V in Equation (6.3) also solves that problem for (k_1), then it must be the case that

$$(FE) \quad V(k_0) = \max_{c_0, k_1 \in \Gamma(k_0)} \{U(c_0) + \beta V(k_1)\}.$$

[1] In many applications, it is sufficient to restrict attention to stationary policies, specifically policies that do not have the time index as an argument and that is what we assume here.

This equation is known as the *Bellman equation* and it is a functional equation in the unknown function V. The study of dynamic optimization problems through the analysis of such functional equations is termed *dynamic programming.*

We motivate the study of the problem in (FE) by noting that the solution to this functional equation is the supremum function for the sequence space problem. The main issue that must be answered is the relation between the solutions for the sequence space problem denoted (SS) and the recursive formulation of the problem denoted (FE). Specifically, the value function V which solves the functional equation in (FE) yields the supremum for the sequence space problem described by (SS), for a given initial state (k_0), and conversely, sequences $\{c_t^\star\}_{t=0}^{\infty}$ and $\{k_{t+1}^\star\}_{t=0}^{\infty}$ attain the supremum (or maximum) for (SS) if and only if they satisfy the functional equation in (FE):

$$V(k_t^\star) = U(c_t^\star) + \beta V(k_{t+1}^\star), t = 0, 1, \ldots$$

where $c_t^\star = y_t + (1 - \delta)k_t^\star - k_{t+1}^\star$. These ideas are known as the *Principle of Optimality* due to R. Bellman, and they constitute the basis for the dynamic programming approach.

The conditions under which the Principle of Optimality holds are studied more formally by Stokey and Lucas [418], Chapters 4 and 9. In a deterministic setting, the supremum function for the problem in (SS) satisfies the functional equation in (FE) under some relatively mild assumptions. These require that the set of feasible allocations are non-empty and that all feasible allocations can be evaluated using the objective function in (6.34). Proving the converse statement requires that a certain boundedness property for the value function V holds. The issue is now to find the unknown function V. In what follows, we describe two simple methods for doing this. In the next section, we describe a more formal method for showing the existence of a function V satisfying Bellman's equation and for numerically solving for it.

6.1.1. Guess-and-verify

Under some configurations for preferences and the production function, we can use a guess-and-verify technique and solve for the unknown value using the method of undetermined coefficients. This approach is useful for solving models in which preferences are of the CRRA variety and the production technology is Cobb-Douglas or models with quadratic objective functions and linear constraints.

Suppose preferences and the production technology satisfy:

$$U(c) = \ln(c), \tag{6.4}$$

$$\theta f(k) = \theta k^{\alpha}, \quad \alpha < 1. \tag{6.5}$$

Also assume that capital depreciates 100% each period so that $\delta = 1$.

Notice that the capital stock and the technology parameter enter multiplicatively. Hence, instead of k, we take the state variable to be y and guess that the value function has the form:

$$V(y) = G + F\ln(y).$$

Bellman's equation is given by:

$$V(y) = \max_{c,k'} \left\{\ln(c) + \beta[G + F\ln(y')]\right\}$$

subject to $c + k' \leq \theta k^{\alpha}$. Let λ denote the multiplier for the resource constraint. The first-order conditions are given by:

$$\frac{1}{c} = \lambda,$$

$$\lambda = \beta\left[\frac{F\alpha\theta'(k')^{\alpha-1}}{y'}\right].$$

Combining these conditions yields the optimality condition:

$$\frac{1}{c} = \beta\left[\frac{F\alpha\theta'(k')^{\alpha-1}}{y'}\right].$$

Substitute for the resource constraint and for output into this equation:

$$\frac{1}{\theta k^{\alpha} - k'} = \beta\left[\frac{F\alpha\theta'(k')^{\alpha-1}}{\theta'(k')^{\alpha}}\right] = \beta\left[\frac{F\alpha}{k'}\right].$$

Solving this equation for k' and making use of the resource constraint, we can write the optimal policy functions as:

$$k' = \frac{\alpha\beta F k^{\alpha}\theta}{1 + \alpha\beta F}$$

$$c = \frac{\theta k^{\alpha}}{1 + \alpha\beta F}.$$

Now substitute these results back into the definition of the value function as:

$$G + F\ln(y) = \ln\left(\frac{y}{1 + \alpha\beta F}\right) + \beta[G + F\ln(y')].$$

Equating the coefficients on the constant term and on $\ln(y)$ allows us to solve for F and G as:

$$F = \frac{1}{1 - \alpha\beta} \tag{6.6}$$

$$G = \frac{\ln(1 - \alpha\beta)}{1 - \beta} + \frac{\alpha\beta \ln(\alpha\beta)}{(1 - \beta)(1 - \alpha\beta)} + \frac{\beta \ln(\theta)}{(1 - \beta)(1 - \alpha\beta)}. \tag{6.7}$$

Substituting the result for F back into the expressions for k' and c yields:

$$k' = h(y) = \alpha\beta y,$$

$$c = g(y) = (1 - \alpha\beta)y.$$

Since consumption must be strictly positive, we have the restriction that $\alpha\beta < 1$. Notice that the process of solving for the value function also yields the optimal policy functions.

The solution also illustrates a well-known result, namely, that an agent with logarithmic preferences will consume (and invest) a fixed fraction of her wealth. The higher is β (so that consumers are more patient), the lower is the current consumption and the higher investment. Likewise, as α increases (so that the production technology becomes more productive), investment and output increase.

6.1.2. Finite horizon economies

Another approach to deriving a solution to the infinite horizon problem is to consider the solution to a finite horizon version of the problem and to let the time period go to infinity. This approach is known as *backward induction*. There may also be independent interest in finding the solution to finite horizon economies. We consider economies with the parametric class of preferences and production technologies given in the previous section.

Consider a deterministic optimal growth problem where the objective of the social planner is to maximize:

$$\sum_{t=0}^{T} \beta^t U(c_t),$$

where $\beta < 1$. The resource constraint for the social planner is given by

$$c_t + k_{t+1} \leq \theta f(k_t) + (1 - \delta)k_t.$$

As before, we assume that there is 100% depreciation such that $\delta = 1$ and the technology shock θ is non-random. Also preferences and the production technology satisfy (6.4) and (6.5).

In the finite horizon setup, we solve the social planner's problem starting with the last period, and work backwards from period T.

At time $t = T$, the value function at time T has the form:

$$V(k_T) = \max_{k_{T+1}} \{\ln(c_T) + \beta V(k_{T+1})\}. \tag{6.8}$$

Since the world ends at time T, the value of capital at date $T+1$ is zero:

$$V(k_{T+1}) = 0. \tag{6.9}$$

Thus, the problem at time $t = T$ reduces to:

$$V(k_T) = \ln(c_T) = \ln[\theta k_T^\alpha - k_{T+1}].$$

The capital stock that solves this maximization problem is $k_{T+1} = 0$ and the value function at time T is

$$V(k_T) = \ln(\theta k_T^\alpha). \tag{6.10}$$

The optimal consumption behavior is to consume the whole output $c_T = \theta k_T^\alpha$.

At time $t = T - 1$ the social planner solves

$$V(k_{T-1}) = \max_{k_T} \{\ln(c_{T-1}) + \beta V(k_T)\}. \tag{6.11}$$

Substituting for $V(k_T)$ and feasibility constraints yields:

$$V(k_{T-1}) = \max_{k_T} \left\{\ln[\theta k_{T-1}^\alpha - k_T] + \beta \ln[\theta k_T^\alpha]\right\}.$$

The first-order condition with respect to k_T is:

$$\frac{1}{\theta k_{T-1}^\alpha - k_T} = \frac{\alpha\beta}{k_T}.$$

Solving for k_T yields:

$$k_T = \frac{\alpha\beta\theta}{1+\alpha\beta} k_{T-1}^\alpha. \tag{6.12}$$

Using the feasibility constraint, the optimal consumption is given by:

$$c_{T-1} = \frac{\theta}{1+\alpha\beta} k_{T-1}^\alpha. \tag{6.13}$$

Substituting for k_T yields an expression for the value function at time $T - 1$ as:

$$V(k_{T-1}) = \alpha(1+\alpha\beta)\ln(k_{T-1}) + (1+\alpha\beta)\ln\left(\frac{\theta}{1+\alpha\beta}\right) + \alpha\beta\ln(\alpha\beta) + \beta\ln\theta. \tag{6.14}$$

Continuing in this way, at $t = T - 2$ the Bellman equation is:

$$V(k_{T-2}) = \max_{k_{T-1}} \{\ln (c_{T-2}) + \beta V(k_{T-1})\}. \tag{6.15}$$

Substituting for $V(k_{T-1})$ and taking the derivative with respect to k_{T-1} yields:

$$k_{T-1} = \frac{\theta\alpha\beta(1+\alpha\beta)}{1+\alpha\beta(1+\alpha\beta)} k_{T-2}^{\alpha}. \tag{6.16}$$

The optimal consumption policy is:

$$c_{T-2} = \frac{\theta}{1+\alpha\beta(1+\alpha\beta)} k_{T-2}^{\alpha}. \tag{6.17}$$

Now we can generalize these results for all t as:

$$k_{t+1} = \frac{\theta\alpha\beta \sum_{i=0}^{T-t-1} (\alpha\beta)^i}{1+\alpha\beta \sum_{i=0}^{T-t-1} (\alpha\beta)^i} k_t^{\alpha}, \tag{6.18}$$

$$c_t = \frac{\theta}{1+\alpha\beta \sum_{i=0}^{T-t-1} (\alpha\beta)^i} k_t^{\alpha}. \tag{6.19}$$

Now consider the limit of the optimal policies as T goes to infinity:

$$\begin{aligned} \lim_{T\to\infty} k_{t+1}^F &= \lim_{T\to\infty} \frac{\theta\alpha\beta \sum_{i=0}^{T-t-1} (\alpha\beta)^i}{1+\alpha\beta \sum_{i=0}^{T-t-1} (\alpha\beta)^i} k_t^{\alpha} \\ &= \frac{\theta\alpha\beta \frac{1}{1-\alpha\beta} k_t^{\alpha}}{1+\alpha\beta\frac{1}{1-\alpha\beta}} = \alpha\beta\theta k_t^{\alpha} = k_{t+1}^I, \end{aligned} \tag{6.20}$$

and

$$\begin{aligned} c_t^F &= \lim_{T\to\infty} \frac{\theta}{1+\alpha\beta \sum_{i=0}^{T-t-1} (\alpha\beta)^i} k_t^{\alpha} \\ &= \frac{\theta k_t^{\alpha}}{1+\alpha\beta\frac{1}{1-\alpha\beta}} = (1-\alpha\beta)\theta k_t^{\alpha} = c_t^I. \end{aligned} \tag{6.21}$$

Hence, the decision rules as the horizon goes to infinity will be identical to those found for the infinite horizon case. However, in a finite horizon context, the form of these decision rules will not be time-invariant or stationary.

6.2. MATHEMATICAL PRELIMINARIES

In the next section, we will describe a simple consumption-saving example in which the agent's endowment or income and the return to saving is random. We will assume that the uncertainty in the economy evolves a Markov process and study the formulation of the agent's dynamic optimization problem as a dynamic programming problem. However, since the notion of Markov processes is used throughout this book, we will begin with a discussion of Markov processes. We will then provide a discussion of vector space methods and the contraction mapping approach.

6.2.1. Markov processes

A discrete parameter stochastic process $\{X(t), t = 0, 1, 2, \ldots\}$ is said to be a *Markov process* if, for any set of n points $t_1 < t_2 < \cdots t_n$, the conditional distribution of $X(t_n)$, for given values of $X(t_1), \ldots, X(t_{n-1})$ depends only on $X(t_{n-1})$, the most recent value; more precisely, for any real numbers $x_1, \ldots, x_n$,

$$\Pr(X(t_n) \leq x_n \mid X(t_1) = x_1, \ldots, X(t_{n-1}) = x_{n-1})$$
$$= \text{Prob}(X(t_n) \leq x_n \mid X(t_{n-1}) = x_{n-1}). \tag{6.22}$$

Discrete Markov chains are a special case of Markov processes. Consider a discrete parameter Markov process denoted by $\{s_t, t = 0, 1, 2, \ldots\}$. Then each s_t is assumed to take on integer values in the set $S = \{1, \ldots, k\}$ and we say that $\{s_t\}_{t=0}^{\infty}$ follows a *Markov chain* if

$$\Pr(s_{t+1} = j \mid s_t = i, \ldots, s_0 = k) = \Pr(s_{t+1} = j \mid s_t = i). \tag{6.23}$$

A Markov chain is said to be *time-invariant* if

$$\Pr(s_{t+1} = j \mid s_t = i) = \text{Prob}(s_{t+l+1} = j \mid s_{t+l} = i) \ \ \forall t, l \text{ and } i, j \in S.$$

For any i and j, let $p_{ij} \in [0, 1]$ denote the (constant) probability that $s_{t+1} = j$ will occur at $t + 1$ conditional on $s_t = i$ having occurred at date t:

$$\text{Prob}(s_{t+1} = j | s_t = i) = p_{ij}.$$

For each i, $p_{i1} + p_{i2} + \cdots p_{ik} = 1$. Also for the state of the system at time zero, we have that $\text{Prob}(s_0 = i) = \pi_{0i}$ for $i = 1, \ldots, k$, with $\sum_{i=1}^{k} \pi_{0i} = 1$. The *transition matrix* for the first-order discrete Markov chain can be written as:

$$\Pi = \begin{bmatrix} \pi_{11} & \pi_{12} & \ldots & \pi_{1k} \\ \pi_{21} & \pi_{22} & \ldots & \pi_{2k} \\ \vdots & \vdots & \ldots & \vdots \\ \pi_{k1} & \pi_{k2} & \ldots & \pi_{kk} \end{bmatrix}.$$

Thus, row i, column j gives the transition probability p_{ij}.

Example 6.1 Suppose that the random variable $s_t \in \{1, 2, 3\}$ follows a three-state first-order Markov process with transition matrix:

$$\Pi = \begin{bmatrix} 1/3 & 1/3 & 1/3 \\ 1/5 & 2/5 & 2/5 \\ 1/2 & 1/6 & 1/3 \end{bmatrix}.$$

Suppose $s_0 = 1$. Find the probability that the history of shocks $\tilde{s}^3 = (s_1 = 3, s_2 = 1, s_3 = 1)$, conditional on $s_0 = 1$.

Notice that

$$\begin{aligned}\Pr(\tilde{s}^3|s_0) &= \Pr(s_3 = 1|s_2 = 1)\Pr(s_2 = 1|s_1 = 3)\Pr(s_1 = 3|s_0 = 1)\\ &= \pi_{11}\pi_{31}\pi_{13} = (1/3)(1/2)(1/3) = 1/18.\end{aligned}$$

Markov chains may be *reducible* or *irreducible*. A reducible Markov chain is one in which should the process enter a given state, the probability of remaining in that state is unity. Formally, a Markov chain is said to *reducible* if the transition matrix can be written as:

$$\Pi = \left[\begin{array}{c|c} \Pi_0 & \Pi_1 \\ \hline 0 & \Pi_2 \end{array}\right],$$

where Π_0 and Π_2 are square matrices. Consider a two-state Markov chain with transition matrix:

$$\Pi = \begin{bmatrix} \pi_{11} & 1 - \pi_{11} \\ 1 - \pi_{22} & \pi_{22} \end{bmatrix}.$$

Suppose that $\pi_{22} = 1$. Then should state 2 occur, the probability of transiting back to state 1 is zero. State 2 is known as an *absorbing state*, and the Markov process is said to be reducible.

A Markov chain is said to be *irreducible* if it is not reducible. An irreducible Markov chain has transition probability matrix with elements that are strictly between 0 and 1. In the two-state case, we require that $0 < \pi_{11} < 1$ and $0 < \pi_{22} < 1$. Consider an irreducible Markov chain with transition matrix Π. Only an irreducible Markov chain has a unique stationary distribution. This is known as the *Perron-Frobenius Theorem.* To motivate the derivation of the stationary distribution further, notice that the rows of the transition matrix must sum to 1:

$$\Pi\mathbf{1} = \mathbf{1}, \tag{6.24}$$

where $\mathbf{1}$ denotes a $k \times 1$ vector of 1's. Hence, the relation $\Pi\mathbf{1} = \mathbf{1}$ implies that 1 is an eigenvalue of Π, and the vector of 1's the associated eigenvector.[2] Suppose that the transition matrix Π has one eigenvalue equal to 1 and all the other eigenvalues less than 1. Then the Markov chain is said to be *ergodic*. The $k \times 1$ vector of ergodic probabilities satisfies:

$$\Pi'\pi = \pi, \tag{6.26}$$

[2] Recall that the eigenvalues and eigenvectors of a $k \times k$ matrix satisfy:

$$Ax = \lambda x \Leftrightarrow (A - \lambda I_k)x = 0, \tag{6.25}$$

where I_k is the $k \times k$ identity matrix.

where π is an eigenvector which has been normalized so that $\mathbf{1}'\pi = 1$. Furthermore, if Π is the transition matrix for an ergodic Markov chain, then

$$\lim_{m\to\infty} (\Pi')^m = \pi\mathbf{1}'. \tag{6.27}$$

Example 6.2 The stationary probabilities associated with the matrix Π defined above are found from the relation:

$$\Pi'\pi = \begin{bmatrix} 1/3 & 1/5 & 1/2 \\ 1/3 & 2/5 & 1/6 \\ 1/3 & 2/5 & 1/3 \end{bmatrix} \begin{bmatrix} \pi_1 \\ \pi_2 \\ \pi_3 \end{bmatrix} = \begin{bmatrix} \pi_1 \\ \pi_2 \\ \pi_3 \end{bmatrix},$$

with $\mathbf{1}'\pi = 1$. This yields two equations in two unknowns as:

$$(1/3)\pi_1 + (1/5)\pi_2 + (1/2)(1 - \pi_1 - \pi_2) = \pi_1,$$

$$(1/3)\pi_1 + (2/5)\pi_2 + (1/6)(1 - \pi_1 - \pi_2) = \pi_2.$$

This yields the solution $\pi_1 = \pi_3 = 6/17$ and $\pi_2 = 5/17$.

6.2.2. Vector space methods

A *(real) vector space* X is a set of elements (vectors) together with two operations, addition and multiplication, such that for all $x, y \in X$, $x + y \in X$ and for any $\alpha \in \Re$ and $x \in X$, $\alpha x \in X$, where the operations obey the usual algebraic laws. A *metric space* is a set X, together with a *metric or distance function* $\rho : X \times X \to \Re$ such that for all $x, y, z \in X$:

(*i*) *Positivity* : $\rho(x, y) \geq 0$ with equality if and only if $x = y$;

(*ii*) *Symmetry* : $\rho(x, y) = \rho(y, x)$;

(*iii*) *Triangle Inequality* : $\rho(x, z) \leq \rho(x, y) + \rho(y, z)$.

Some examples of metric spaces are as follows:

Example 6.3 The set of all ordered n-tuples $(x_1, \ldots, x_n)'$ with distance function

$$\rho(x, y) = \left(\sum_{k=1}^{n} (x_k - y_k)^2 \right)^{\frac{1}{2}}.$$

is a metric space known as $\Re^n$ and denoted n-dimensional Euclidean space.

Example 6.4 The set of bounded infinite sequences of real numbers

$$(x_1, x_2, \ldots, x_k, \ldots)'$$

with distance function $\rho(x, y) = \sup_t |x_t - y_t|$.

Example 6.5 The set of all infinite sequences satisfying the convergence criterion

$$\sum_{k=1}^{\infty} x_k^2 < \infty,$$

with the distance function

$$\rho(x,y) = \left(\sum_{k=1}^{\infty} (x_k - y_k)^2\right)^{\frac{1}{2}}$$

is denoted by l_2. This space figures in applications involving stationary economic time series.

We can use the distance function ρ to define concepts of continuity and convergence for elements of the space X. We say that a sequence $\{x_n\}_{n=0}^{\infty}$ in X *converges* to $x \in X$ if for each $\epsilon > 0$, there exists N_ϵ such that

$$\rho(x_n, x) < \epsilon \quad \text{for } n \geq N_\epsilon,$$

and that $\{x_n\}_{n=0}^{\infty}$ is a *Cauchy sequence* if for each $\epsilon > 0$, there exists N_ϵ such that

$$\rho(x_n, x_m) < \epsilon \quad \text{for } n, m \geq N_\epsilon.$$

We say that a mapping $T : X \to X$ is *continuous at the point* $x_0 \in X$ if for every real number $\epsilon > 0$, there exists a real number $\delta > 0$ such that

$$\rho(Tx, Tx_0) < \epsilon \quad \text{whenever} \quad \rho(x, x_0) < \delta.$$

We say that a metric space (X, ρ) is *complete* if every Cauchy sequence in (X, ρ) converges to an element in that space.[3]

The following two examples show that not every metric space will be a complete metric space. The key is that a Cauchy sequence in a given metric space converges to an element of that space.

Example 6.6 A complete metric space

Let $\{x_n(t)\}$ be a Cauchy sequence in the function (and metric) space $C[a, b]$, the set of all continuous functions defined on the closed interval $[a, b]$, with distance $\rho[f(t), g(t)] = \max_{a \leq t \leq b} |f(t) - g(t)|$. Then, given any $\epsilon > 0$, there is an N_ϵ such that

$$|x_n(t) - x_{n'}(t)| < \epsilon \quad \text{for } n, n' > N_\epsilon \text{ and all } t \in [a, b].$$

[3] For a further discussion of metric spaces, see Naylor and Sell [351, Chapters 3 and 5].

It follows that the sequence $\{x_n(t)\}$ is uniformly convergent. Let $x(t)$ denote the limit function. By uniform convergence,

$$|x_n(t_1) - x(t_1)| < \epsilon \quad \text{for } n > N_\epsilon \text{ and } t_1 \in [a, b]$$

$$|x_n(t_0) - x(t_0)| < \epsilon \quad \text{for } n > N_\epsilon \text{ and } t_0 \in [a, b].$$

We want to show that the limit function $x(t) \in C[a, b]$. By the Triangle Inequality,

$$|x(t) - x(t_0)| \leq |x(t) - x_n(t)| + |x_n(t) - x_n(t_0)| + |x_n(t_0) - x(t_0)|.$$

It follows by uniform convergence that

$$|x(t) - x_n(t)| < \epsilon/3 \quad \text{for} \quad n > N_\epsilon \tag{6.28}$$

$$|x_n(t_0) - x(t_0)| < \epsilon/3 \quad \text{for} \quad n > N_\epsilon \tag{6.29}$$

and by continuity of $x_n(t)$, there exists a $\delta > 0$ such that

$$|x_n(t) - x_n(t_0)| < \epsilon/3 \quad \text{for} \quad |t - t_0| < \delta. \tag{6.30}$$

Then, combining (6.28), (6.29) and (6.30) yields

$$|x(t) - x(t_0)| < \epsilon \quad \text{for} \quad |t - t_0| < \delta$$

Therefore, $x(t)$ is continuous on the interval $[a, b]$, and $C[a, b]$ is a complete metric space.

Example 6.7 An incomplete metric space

Consider the space $C^2[-1, 1]$ of continuous functions on the interval $[-1, 1]$ with the metric:

$$\rho(f, g) = \left(\int_{-1}^{1} [f(t) - g(t)]^2 dt \right)^{\frac{1}{2}}.$$

Let $\{\varphi_n(t)\}$ be a sequence in $C^2[-1, 1]$, whose elements are defined by:

$$\varphi_n(t) = \begin{cases} -1 & \text{if} \quad -1 \leq t \leq -\frac{1}{n} \\ nt & \text{if} \quad -\frac{1}{n} \leq t \leq \frac{1}{n} \\ 1 & \text{if} \quad \frac{1}{n} \leq t \leq 1 \end{cases}$$

See Figure 6.1. Then, $\{\varphi_n(t)\}$ is a Cauchy sequence since,

$$\int_{-1}^{1} [\varphi_n(t) - \varphi_{n'}(t)]^2 \, dt = \int_{-1}^{\min\left(-\frac{1}{n}, -\frac{1}{n'}\right)} (-1 + 1)^2 dt$$

$$+ \int_{\min\left(-\frac{1}{n}, -\frac{1}{n'}\right)}^{\max\left(-\frac{1}{n}, -\frac{1}{n'}\right)} [1 - \min(n, n')t]^2 dt + \int_{\max\left(-\frac{1}{n}, -\frac{1}{n'}\right)}^{\min\left(\frac{1}{n}, \frac{1}{n'}\right)} (n - n')^2 t^2 dt$$

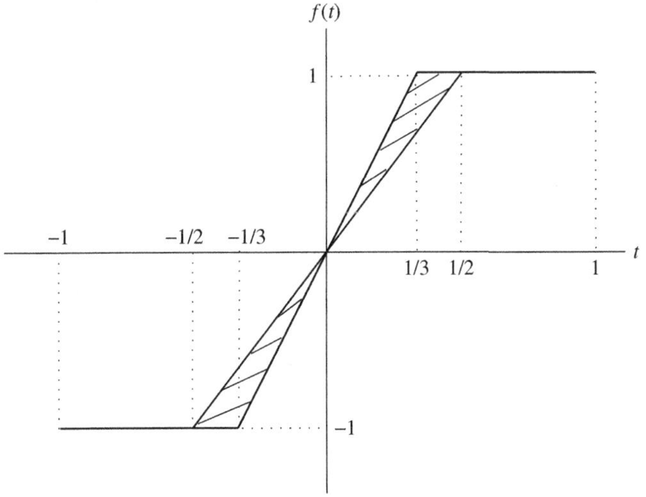

Figure 6.1. Plots of $\varphi_n(t)$ for $n = 2, 3$

$$
\begin{aligned}
&+ \int_{\min\left(\frac{1}{n},\frac{1}{n'}\right)}^{\max\left(\frac{1}{n},\frac{1}{n'}\right)} [1 - \min(n, n')t]^2 dt + \int_{\max\left(\frac{1}{n},\frac{1}{n'}\right)}^{1} (-1+1)^2 dt \\
&= 2\int_{\min\left(\frac{1}{n},\frac{1}{n'}\right)}^{\max\left(\frac{1}{n},\frac{1}{n'}\right)} [1 - \min(n, n')t]^2 dt + 2\int_{0}^{\min\left(\frac{1}{n},\frac{1}{n'}\right)} (n - n')^2 t^2 dt \\
&\leq \frac{2}{\min(n, n')}.
\end{aligned}
$$

We want to show that $\{\varphi_n(t)\}$ cannot converge to a function in $C^2[-1, 1]$. Let

$$
\psi(t) = \begin{cases} -1 & \text{if } t < 0 \\ 1 & \text{if } t \geq 0 \end{cases}
$$

be a discontinuous function. Then, for any function $f \in C^2[-1, 1]$, the Triangle Inequality suggests that

$$
\left(\int_{-1}^{1} [f(t) - \psi(t)]^2 dt\right)^{\frac{1}{2}} \leq \left(\int_{-1}^{1} [f(t) - \varphi_n(t)]^2 dt\right)^{\frac{1}{2}} + \left(\int_{-1}^{1} [\varphi_n(t) - \psi(t)]^2 dt\right)^{\frac{1}{2}} \quad (6.31)
$$

By the continuity of f, the integral on the left is different from zero. Notice that

$$\int_{-1}^{1} [\varphi_n(t) - \psi(t)]^2 dt = \int_{-\frac{1}{n}}^{0} (nt + 1)^2 dt + \int_{0}^{\frac{1}{n}} (nt - 1)^2 dt$$

$$= \left(\frac{n^2 t^3}{3} - nt^2 + t \right) \Big|_0^{\frac{1}{n}} + \left(\frac{n^2 t^3}{3} + nt^2 + t \right) \Big|_0^{\frac{1}{n}}$$

It is easy to see that in the limit, the value of this integral goes to zero as n goes to infinity such that

$$\lim_{n\to\infty} \int_{-1}^{1} [\varphi_n(t) - \psi(t)]^2 dt = 0.$$

Substituting this back into the Equation (6.31), we conclude that $\{\varphi_n(t)\}$ cannot converge in $C^2[-1, 1]$,

$$\lim_{n\to\infty} \int_{-1}^{1} [f(t) - \varphi_n(t)]^2 dt \neq 0.$$

Hence, $C^2[-1, 1]$ is not a complete metric space.

For vector spaces, metrics are usually defined such that the distance between any two points is equal to the distance of their difference from the zero point. Notice that for any $x, y \in X$, the point $x - y \in X$ also. Hence, the metric on the vector space X is defined such that $\rho(x, y) = \rho(x - y, 0)$. This yields the concept of a norm.

A *normed vector space* is a vector space X together with a *norm* $\| \cdot \| : X \to \Re$ such that for all $x, y \in X$ and $\alpha \in \Re$:

(i) $\|x\| \geq 0$ with equality if and only if $x = 0$;

(ii) $\|\alpha x\| = |\alpha| \|x\|$;

(iii) $\|x + y\| \leq \|x\| + \|y\|$.

Define $C(S)$ as the space of continuous and bounded functions $\{f : S \to \Re\}$ equipped with the sup norm $\|f\| \equiv \sup_{s\in S} |f(s)|$. An important property of the space of bounded, continuous, real-valued functions equipped with the sup norm is that it is a *complete normed, vector space* or a *Banach space*. This space figures importantly in applications of the Contraction Mapping Theorem, to which we turn next.

6.2.3. *Contraction mapping theorem*

We now study a particular type of operator known as a *contraction mapping*. Let (X, ρ) be a metric space and T be an operator that maps elements of X into itself, $T : X \to X$. We say that T is a contraction or a *contraction mapping* of modulus β if there is a real number β, $0 \leq \beta < 1$, such that

$$\rho(Tf, Tg) \leq \beta \rho(f, g) \quad \text{for all } f, g \in X. \tag{6.32}$$

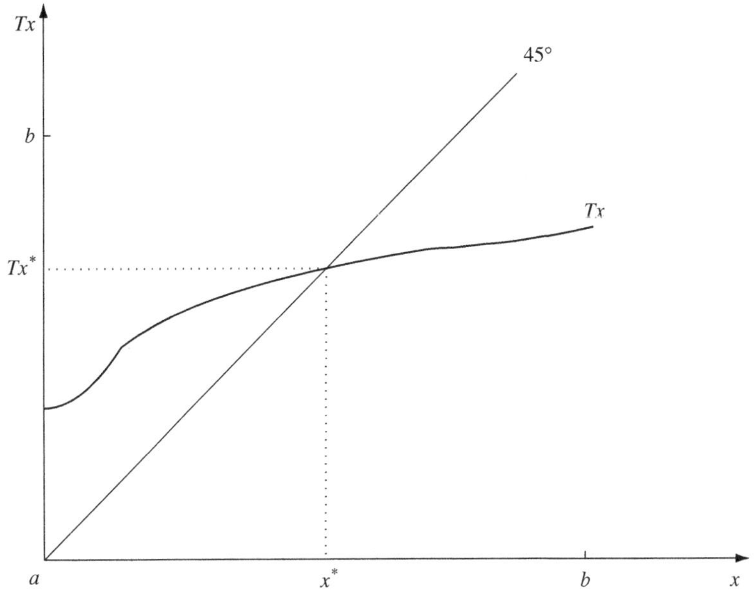

Figure 6.2. A fixed point on the real line

Example 6.8 Suppose that the set X is the closed interval $[a, b]$ and $\rho(x, y) = |x - y|$. Then we say that $T : X \to X$ is a contraction if for some $0 < \beta < 1$,

$$\frac{|Tx - Ty|}{|x - y|} \leq \beta < 1 \text{ for all } x, y \in X, \text{ with } x \neq y.$$

Thus, T is a contraction if it has slope uniformly less than one in absolute value.

The fixed points of T are those elements of X such that $Tx = x$. For this simple example above, they can be found as the intersections of Tx with the 45-degree line, which implies that the fixed point of a contraction T defined on the interval $[a, b]$ is unique. See Figure 6.2.

The following theorem shows that this result holds more generally.

Theorem 6.1 *(Contraction Mapping Theorem* [326, p. 272]*) Let (X, ρ) be a complete metric space and let $T : X \to X$ be a contraction with modulus β. Then (i) T has exactly one fixed point $v \in X$, (ii) for any $v_0 \in X$, $\rho(T^n v_0, v) \leq \beta^n \rho(v_0, v)$, $n = 1, 2, \ldots$*

PROOF

To prove part (i), we define the iterates of T, which are the sequence of mappings $\{T^n\}$, by $T^0 X = X$ and $T^n X = T(T^{n-1} X)$, $n = 1, 2, \ldots$ Choose

$v_0 \in X$ and define $\{v_n\}_{n=0}^{\infty}$ by $v_n = Tv_{n-1}$ so that $v_n = T^n v_0$. Since T is a contraction,

$$\rho(v_2, v_1) = \rho(Tv_1, Tv_0) \leq \beta\rho(v_1, v_0).$$

Continuing by induction, we have

$$\rho(v_{n+1}, v_n) \leq \beta^n \rho(v_1, v_0), \quad n = 1, 2, \ldots. \tag{6.33}$$

Hence for any $m > n$,

$$\begin{aligned}
\rho(v_m, v_n) &\leq \rho(v_m, v_{m-1}) + \cdots + \rho(v_{n+2}, v_{n+1}) + \rho(v_{n+1}, v_n) \\
&\leq [\beta^{m-1} + \cdots + \beta^{n+1} + \beta^n]\rho(v_1, v_0) \\
&= \beta^n[\beta^{m-n-1} + \cdots + \beta + 1]\rho(v_1, v_0) \\
&\leq \frac{\beta^n}{1-\beta}\rho(v_1, v_0),
\end{aligned}$$

where the first line uses the Triangle Inequality and the second follows from Equation (6.33). Notice that $\{v_n\}$ is a Cauchy sequence. Since X is a complete metric space, there exists a $v \in X$ such that $v_n \to v$ as $n \to \infty$.

To show that $Tv = v$, notice that for all n and all $v_0 \in X$,

$$\begin{aligned}
\rho(Tv, v) &\leq \rho(Tv, T^n v_0) + \rho(T^n v_0, v) \\
&\leq \beta\rho(v, T^{n-1}v_0) + \rho(T^n v_0, v).
\end{aligned}$$

But we showed that both terms in the second line converge to zero as $n \to \infty$; therefore, $\rho(Tv, v) = 0$ or $Tv = v$.

To show that the fixed point is unique, suppose to the contrary that $\hat{v} \neq v$ is another solution. Then

$$0 < a = \rho(\hat{v}, v) = \rho(T\hat{v}, Tv) \leq \beta\rho(\hat{v}, v) = \beta a,$$

which cannot hold since $\beta < 1$. This proves part (i).

To prove part (ii), notice that for any $n \geq 1$,

$$\rho(T^n v_0, v) = \rho[T(T^{n-1}v_0), Tv] \leq \beta\rho(T^{n-1}v_0, v),$$

so that (ii) follows by induction. ∎

There are some useful corollaries to the Contraction Mapping Theorem. One additional result we can prove is this: suppose $T : \mathcal{C}(S) \to \mathcal{C}(S)$ is a contraction with a fixed point v, where $\mathcal{C}(S)$ is the space of bounded, continuous functions with the sup norm defined earlier. Suppose $\mathcal{C}'(S)$ is the space of bounded, continuous, concave functions. Notice that $\mathcal{C}'(S)$ is a closed subset of $\mathcal{C}(S)$ and it is a complete normed linear space. If T is a contraction on $\mathcal{C}(S)$ and T maps the space of bounded, continuous, concave functions into itself, then the fixed point v is an element of the smaller space. We have the following corollary.

Corollary 6.1 *Let (X, ρ) be a complete metric space and $T : X \to X$ be a contraction mapping with fixed point $v \in X$. If X' is a closed subset of X and $T(X') \subseteq X'$ (where $T(X')$ is the image of X' under T), then $v \in X'$.*

PROOF
Choose $v_0 \in X'$. Notice that $\{T^n v_0\}$ is a sequence in X' converging to v. Since X' is closed, it follows that $v \in X'$. ∎

This result is useful for verifying some additional properties of the value function, such as concavity. We apply this result in applications described in Chapters 8 and 10. A second corollary of the Contraction Mapping Theorem is given as follows.

Corollary 6.2 *(N-Stage Contraction Mapping Theorem [326, p. 275]) Let (X, ρ) be a complete metric space, let $T : X \to X$ and suppose that for some integer N, $T^N : X \to X$ is a contraction mapping with modulus β. Then (i) T has exactly one fixed point in X, (ii) for any $v_0 \in X$, $\rho(T^{kN} v_0, v) \leq \beta^k \rho(v_0, v), k = 0, 1, 2, \ldots$.*

PROOF
We show that the unique fixed point of T^N is also the fixed point of T. Notice that

$$\rho(Tv, v) = \rho[T(T^N v), T^N v] = \rho[T^N(Tv), T^N v] \leq \beta\rho(Tv, v).$$

Since $0 < \beta < 1$, this implies that $\rho(Tv, v) = 0$ so v is a fixed point of T. To show uniqueness, note that any fixed point of T is also a fixed point of T^N. Part (ii) is established as in the previous theorem. ∎

To apply these results, we need to verify whether a mapping or an operator defines a contraction. We can do this by verifying the condition in Equation (6.32) directly. An alternative method that turns out to be useful in many applications is to verify Blackwell's Sufficient Conditions for a Contraction Mapping [67].

Theorem 6.2 *(Blackwell's Conditions for a Contraction Mapping) Let $\mathcal{B}(S)$ be the space of bounded functions $f : S \to \Re$ with the sup norm. Let $T : \mathcal{B}(S) \to \mathcal{B}(S)$ be an operator defined on $\mathcal{B}(S)$ satisfying*

(i) (Monotonicity) Let $f, g \in \mathcal{B}(S)$. For each $s \in S$, $f(s) \geq g(s)$ implies that $Tf(s) \geq Tg(s)$;

(ii) (Discounting) Let $0 < a < \infty$ be a constant. There is some $0 < \beta < 1$ such that, for $f \in \mathcal{B}(S)$, $T(f + a)(s) \leq Tf(s) + \beta a$.

If $T : \mathcal{B}(S) \to \mathcal{B}(S)$ and satisfies (i)–(ii), then T is a contraction with modulus β.

PROOF

If $f(s) \leq g(s)$ for all $s \in S$, then we say that $f \leq g$. For any $f, g \in \mathcal{B}(S)$, notice that by definition of the metric $\|\cdot\|$, $f \leq g + \|f - g\|$. Using properties (i) and (ii),

$$Tf \leq T\left(g + \|f - g\|\right) \leq Tg + \beta\|f - g\|.$$

Reversing the roles of f and g yields

$$Tg \leq T\left(f + \|f - g\|\right) \leq Tf + \beta\|f - g\|.$$

Combining these inequalities, $\|Tf - Tg\| \leq \beta\|f - g\|$, as was to be shown. ∎

6.3. A CONSUMPTION-SAVING PROBLEM UNDER UNCERTAINTY

Now consider the consumption-saving problem described in Chapter 5. At the beginning of period t, the agent has an endowment y_t that can be allocated between consumption c_t or borrowing and lending, b_{t+1}. We assume that the endowment and the (net) return to borrowing or lending is stochastic. In particular, let $s \in S = \{1, \ldots, n\}$ be a random shock. The endowment process is a function $y : S \rightarrow Y$ where $Y = (0, \bar{y}]$. The return process, which is determined endogenously in a general equilibrium model but which we will treat as exogenous, is a function $r : S \rightarrow (-1, \infty)$. We assume that s follows a discrete first-order Markov process or a Markov chain. According to this specification, to make a prediction of y and r next period, we need to make a prediction of s_{t+1}. The only information we need from the current period to make that prediction is s_t. This suggests that s_t is a good candidate for a state variable.

Consider the problem:

$$\max_{\{c_t, b_{t+1}\}_{t=0}^{\infty}} E_0 \left\{ \sum_{t=0}^{\infty} \beta^t U(c_t) \right\}, \tag{6.34}$$

subject to

$$c_t + b_{t+1} \leq y(s_t) + (1 + r(s_t))b_t, \quad t \geq 0 \tag{6.35}$$

given the initial conditions b_0 and s_0. We assume that $U(\cdot)$ is strictly increasing, strictly concave, twice differentiable, and bounded. In this expression, the expectation of the objective function, which is conditional on the realization of the state s_0 at date zero, is evaluated using the transition probabilities for s_t. Notice that savings can be positive (if the consumer is a lender) or negative (if the consumer is a borrower). For simplicity, we assume that $b_{t+1} \in \Re$. By contrast, $c_t \in \Re_+$.

Define the set of feasible consumption and saving allocations at time 0 by:

$$\Gamma(b_0, s_0) \equiv \{(c_0, b_1) : c_0 + b_1 \leq y_0 + (1 + r_0)b_0\}.$$

Following the approach that we outlined in Section 6.1, the Bellman equation for the consumer's problem is given by:

$$V(b_t, s_t) = \max_{c_t, b_{t+1} \in \Gamma(b_t, s_t)} \{U(c) + \beta \sum_{s_{t+1} \in S} \pi(s_{t+1} \mid s_t) V(b_{t+1}, s_{t+1})\}. \tag{6.36}$$

Given the recursive representation of the problem, drop the time subscripts on all variables because the problem has now been reduced to a two-period problem. We let variables without primes denote current state or choice variables and primed variables denote future values. We will analyze the problem in (6.36) using the contraction mapping approach.

Define a *fixed point* to this mapping as a function $V^\star$ such that

$$V^\star = TV^\star, \tag{6.37}$$

which means that if we apply T to the function $V^\star$, we obtain the same function $V^\star$. We would like to know under what conditions such a fixed point exists and whether it is unique. What are some methods for determining the existence and uniqueness of a fixed point to the operator or mapping defined by T? One way is to show that the mapping is a contraction.

Define $Z \equiv \Re \times S$ and notice that $V : Z \to \Re_+$. Denote $\mathcal{C}(Z)$ as the space of bounded, continuous, real-valued functions equipped with the sup norm. For $V \in \mathcal{C}(Z)$, define an operator or mapping T from the right side of the functional equation in Equation (6.36) as:

$$(TV)(b, s) \equiv \max_{c, b' \in \Gamma(b,s)} \{U(c) + \beta \sum_{s' \in S} \pi(s' \mid s) V(b', s')\} \tag{6.38}$$

For any function $V \in \mathcal{C}(Z)$, $(TV)(b, s)$ assigns a value to the maximum utility that can be attained for each value of (b, s). In the current context, recall that bond holdings are not restricted to be positive. However, the utility function U is bounded and the constraint set $\Gamma(b, s)$ is continuous in (b, s). Hence, $(TV)(b, s)$ is well defined for any (b, s), i.e. a maximum exists. Since $U(c)$ is bounded and $V(b', s')$ is bounded, the maximum function TV is bounded and by the Theorem of the Maximum[4], it is continuous. Thus, T maps bounded, continuous functions into the same space, $T : \mathcal{C}(Z) \to \mathcal{C}(Z)$.

[4] See the Mathematical Appendix.

Next, notice that T is monotone. Given any two functions $u \in \mathcal{C}(Z)$, $w \in \mathcal{C}(Z)$ such that $u(b,s) \geq w(b,s)$ for all $b, s \in Z$,

$$\sum_{s' \in S} \pi(s'|s)u(b',s') \geq \sum_{s' \in S} \pi(s'|s)w(b',s')$$

so that $(Tu)(b,s) \geq (Tw)(b,s)$. To verify discounting, for any constant a, notice that

$$\begin{aligned}
T(V+a)(b,s) &= \max_{c,b'} \left\{ U(c) + \beta \sum_{s' \in S} \pi(s'|s)[V(b',s') + a] \right\} \\
&= \max_{c,b'} \left\{ U(c) + \beta \sum_{s' \in S} \pi(s'|s)V(b',s') \right\} + \beta a \\
&= (TV)(b,s) + \beta a.
\end{aligned}$$

Hence, T satisfies Blackwell's conditions for a contraction. Since $\mathcal{C}(Z)$ is a complete, normed, linear space, the Contraction Mapping Theorem implies that T has a unique fixed point and $\lim_{n\to\infty} T^n V_0 = V^\star$ for any $V_0 \in \mathcal{C}(Z)$.

Recall that if the mapping T is a contraction, then the fixed point function V^* can be found by repeated iterations on T as:

$$\begin{aligned}
V^{n+1}(b,s) &= (TV^n)(b,s) \\
&= \max_{c,b' \in \Gamma(b,s)} \{U(c) + \beta \sum_{s' \in S} \pi(s' \mid s)V^n(b',s')\},
\end{aligned}$$

starting from $V^0 = 0$, or $\lim_{n\to\infty} T^n V_0$. This is known as *value iteration* and it provides the basis for numerically calculating the solution to the dynamic programming problem.

The process of iteratively finding the optimal policy functions denoted $c = g(b,s)$ and $b' = h(b,s)$ is known as *policy iteration.* Just as we set up operators to iteratively find the value function $V^\star$, we can also set up a recursive scheme to derive the optimal policy functions. For this purpose, define

$$\begin{aligned}
V^{n+1} &= TV^n, \\
g_n(b,s) &= argmax_{c \in \Gamma(b,s)}\{U(c) + \beta \sum_{s' \in S} \pi(s' \mid s)V^n(b',s')\}, \\
h_n(b,s) &= argmax_{b' \in \Gamma(b,s)}\{U(c) + \beta \sum_{s' \in S} \pi(s' \mid s)V^n(b',s')\}.
\end{aligned}$$

Thus, the policy functions at stage n are found as the feasible values of c and b' that attain the maximum for the value function at that stage, V^n, conditional on the state (b, s). We illustrate how these approaches can be used to numerically solve dynamic programming problems in later chapters.

Once the fixed-point function $V^\star$ has been found, the problem involves solving a simple calculus problem. To further characterize the policy functions g and h, suppose that the value function is differentiable. Since the utility function is strictly increasing, the budget constraint holds with equality. Substituting for c in the utility function using the budget constraint, the first-order condition evaluated at the optimal policy is:

$$U'[g(b,s)] = \beta E_s \left\{ \frac{\partial V^\star[h(b,s), s']}{\partial b'} \right\}. \tag{6.39}$$

Our final task is to find an expression for $\partial V^\star / \partial b'$. Using Equation (6.36) evaluated at the optimal policy, we have

$$\begin{aligned} \frac{\partial V^\star(b,s)}{\partial b} &= U'[g(b,s)](1 + r(s)) \\ &\quad - \left\{ U'[g(b,s)] - \beta E_s \left(\frac{\partial V^\star(b', s')}{\partial b'} \right) \right\} \frac{\partial h(b,s)}{\partial b} \\ &= U'[g(b,s)](1 + r(s)), \end{aligned}$$

where the term in braces equals zero using the first-order condition. This is the *envelope condition*. Given the definition of $g^\star(b,s)$, this can be used to express the first-order condition at the fixed point as:

$$U'[c(s)] = \beta E_s \{ U'[c(s')](1 + r(s')) \}. \tag{6.40}$$

This is identical to the first-order condition that we derived the Chapter 5, Section 5.3.

6.4. EXERCISES

1. Consider the framework in Section 6.1.2, where the technology shock θ_t is deterministic and the depreciation rate is 100%.
   (a) Find the optimal consumption and investment policies when

   $$U(c) = \frac{c^{1-\gamma} - 1}{1 - \gamma}, \quad \gamma \geq 0,$$

   $$\theta f(k) = \theta k.$$

   (b) Consider the finite horizon version of this problem. Using the same preferences and production technology as in part a), solve the social planner's problem in the finite horizon setup using the dynamic programming approach. Find the optimal capital stock and consumption policies.

(c) Show that when we take a limiting case as $T \to \infty$, the optimal policy function for the finite horizon case approaches to ones in the infinite horizon case.

2. A Discrete State, Discrete Control Problem[5]
Let X_i, $i=1,\ldots,r$ denote the set of states and u_i, $i=1,\ldots,m$ the set of controls. We assume that there is also a random disturbance in the model that takes on the finite values defined in terms of the set $\Theta=\{\theta_1,\ldots,\theta_k\}$ and that is identically and independently distributed over time. Let $\pi^l_{i,j}$ denote the transition probability for the state variable defined as:

$$\pi^l_{i,j} \equiv \text{Prob}(X_{t+1} = X_j | X_t = X_i, u_t = u_l).$$

The problem is to solve:

$$\max_{\{u_t\}_{t=0}} E_0 \left\{ \sum_{t=0}^{\infty} \beta^t v(X_t, u_t) \right\}, \quad 0 < \beta < 1,$$

subject to the law of motion, $X_{t+1}=f(X_t, u_t, \theta_t)$, $t=0,1,\ldots$ and given X_0. To make the problem well defined, we assume that $0 \leq v(X_t, u_t) \leq M < \infty$ for all X_t and u_t.

(a) Find an expression for $\pi^l_{i,j}$ using the law of motion for the state variable and the known probability distribution for the random shock, $G(\theta_t)$.

(b) Let $V_i \equiv V(X_i)$ and $v_{i,l} \equiv v(X_i, u_l)$. Show that the value function satisfies the equation:

$$V_i = \max_l [v_{i,l} + \beta \sum_{j=1}^{r} \pi^l_{i,j} V_j] \equiv (TV)_i. \tag{6.41}$$

(c) Suppose that when the state is X_i, the optimal control is:

$$U_i \in \text{argmax}_{u_l} [v_{i,l} + \beta \sum_{j=1}^{r} \pi^l_{i,j} V_j] \equiv (\mathcal{U} V)_i. \tag{6.42}$$

If U_i is the control in state X_i, then the return in that state is $S_i \equiv v(X_i, U_i)$. Let $V \equiv (V_1,\ldots,V_n)'$ and $S \equiv (S_1,\ldots,S_n)'$ and define the $n \times n$ matrix Π as the matrix of transition probabilities such that $\Pi_{i,j} = \pi^l_{i,j}$ if and only if $U_i = u_l$. Show that the solution for V is given by

$$V = (1 - \beta\Pi)^{-1} S.$$

(d) Describe how you would do *value function iteration* in this problem.

[5] This exercise is derived from Judd [269].

(e) *Policy function iteration* is implemented as follows:

$$
\begin{aligned}
&\text{(i)} \quad U^{n+1} = \mathcal{U}V^n,\\
&\text{(ii)} \quad S_i^{n+1} = v(X_i, U_i^{n+1}),\\
&\text{(iii)} \quad \Pi^{n+1} = \mathcal{P}U^{n+1},\\
&\text{(iv)} \quad V^{n+1} = (1 - \beta\Pi^{n+1})^{-1}S^{n+1},
\end{aligned}
$$

where the map $\mathcal{P}U$ is defined as $\Pi_{i,j} = \pi^l_{i,j}$ if and only if $U_i = u_l$ and the remaining maps are defined from the left sides of Equations (6.41) and (6.42). Describe the nature of this algorithm and compare it with value function iteration.

3. Error Bounds for Value Iteration
Let T denote a mapping defined on the space of bounded, continuous functions $\mathcal{C}(S)$ where S is some bounded set. Define the norm on $\mathcal{C}(S)$ as the sup norm, $\|\cdot\| \equiv \sup_{s\in S}|V(s)|$ for all $V \in \mathcal{C}(S)$.
(a) Show that if T is a contraction of modulus β, then

$$\|V^n - V_\infty\| \leq (1-\beta)^{-1}\|V^{n+1} - V^n\|, \tag{6.43}$$

where $V^n = T^n(V_0)$ for some $V_0 \in \mathcal{C}(S)$ and V^n converges uniformly to V_∞ as $n \to \infty$.
(b) Describe how you would use the result in Equation (6.43) to determine the error in approximating the true value function V_∞ by V^n. How would you compute the error bounds during the successive approximation or value iteration algorithm?

4. Approximating a Continuous Markov Process
Tauchen [428] proposes a simple method for approximating a continuous Markov process for some exogenous state variable by a discrete Markov model. Suppose the real-valued exogenous state variable s_t follows a first-order autoregressive process:

$$s_t = \rho s_{t-1} + \epsilon_t, \quad |\rho| < 1, \tag{6.44}$$

where ϵ_t is a white noise process with variance σ^2_ϵ and distribution function given by $\Pr[\epsilon_t \leq u] = F(u/\sigma)$. Here F is a cumulative distribution with unit variance.

Let $\tilde{s}_t$ denote the discrete-valued process that approximates $\{s_t\}$. Suppose the N discrete values that $\tilde{s}_t$ may take are defined to a multiple m of the unconditional standard deviation $\sigma_s = (\sigma^2_\epsilon/(1-\rho^2))^{1/2}$. Then let $\bar{s}^1 = -\bar{s}^N$ and let the remaining be equispaced over the interval

$[\bar{s}^1, \bar{s}^N]$. The transition probabilities $\pi_{j,k} = \Pr[\tilde{s}_t = \bar{s}^k | \tilde{s}^j_{t-1}]$ are calculated as follows. Let $w = \bar{s}^k - \bar{s}^{k-1}$. For each j, if k is between 2 and $N-1$, set

$$\begin{aligned}\pi_{j,k} &= \Pr[\bar{s}^k - w/2 \leq \rho\bar{s}^j + \epsilon_t \leq \bar{s}^k + w/2] \\ &= F\left[\sigma_\epsilon^{-1}(\bar{s}^k - \rho\bar{s}^j + w/2)\right] - F\left[\sigma_\epsilon^{-1}(\bar{s}^k - \rho\bar{s}^j - w/2)\right],\end{aligned}$$

otherwise,

$$\pi_{j,1} = F\left[\sigma_\epsilon^{-1}(\bar{s}^1 - \rho\bar{s}^j + w/2)\right],$$

and

$$\pi_{j,N} = 1 - F\left[\sigma_\epsilon^{-1}(\bar{s}^N - \rho\bar{s}^j - w/2)\right].$$

CHAPTER 7
Intertemporal risk sharing

In our earlier analysis of models with complete markets we have considered simple one- or two-period economies with a discrete number of states and commodities. We now consider complete contingent claims equilibrium in economies with an infinite number of dates. We describe how to price claims that have payoffs for all possible events and discuss the implications of perfect risk sharing for such economies.

We start with a complete contingent claims market in which all trading is done at time zero, before any events have occurred. The purpose is to illustrate an important property of contingent claims markets that are complete, namely that the resulting consumption path depends only on the current state and not on the history of the system. We examine an economy where there is aggregate uncertainty: the total endowment is stochastic and exogenous. In these types of economies, aggregate risk in output cannot be diversified away by the economy as a whole, but there are implications for optimal risk sharing that emerge from the contingent claims prices. Next we take the same economy, but now assume that trading is done sequentially over time, as we actually observe. We find remarkably that the consumption allocation chosen when all state-contingent trades are executed at time zero is identical to the consumption allocation under sequential trading.

We then turn to idiosyncratic risk – risk that is individual-specific. Under certain circumstances, agents can face idiosyncratic risk even though there is no aggregate risk. We derive the properties of optimal risk sharing in this setting. The next topic looks at models in which both aggregate and individual risk are present. The final section of the chapter is devoted to constructing assets such as equities and risk-free bonds that we observe in the market place using the contingent claims prices.

7.1. MULTI-PERIOD CONTINGENT CLAIMS

We first consider the role of aggregate uncertainty, and then examine models in which there is only idiosyncratic risk.

7.1.1. *Aggregate uncertainty*

Assume agents live an infinite number of periods and that there is only one commodity. Uncertainty is defined in terms of a random variable s_t that can take on S possible values in the set $\mathcal{S} = \{\bar{s}_1, \ldots, \bar{s}_S\}$. Thus, $s_t \in \mathcal{S}$ at each period. We assume that s_t follows a first-order Markov process so that the conditional distribution of s_{t+1} depends only on s_t, that is,

$$\text{Prob}(s_{t+1} \mid s_t, s_{t-1}, \ldots, s_0) = \text{Prob}(s_{t+1} \mid s_t) \tag{7.1}$$

for all t. Let the transition function for s_t be denoted by $\pi(s_{t+1}|s_t)$ and the initial distribution as $\bar{\pi}(s_0)$. The state of the economy is given by the history s^t of realizations of the random variable s_r for $r \leq t$, defined as

$$s^t \equiv (s_0, s_1, \ldots, s_t) = (s^{t-1}, s_t).$$

Let $\pi_t(s^t) \in [0, 1]$ denote the probability that $s^t \in \mathcal{S}^t$ occurs. Notice that

$$\sum_{s^t \in \mathcal{S}^t} \pi_t(s^t) = 1 \quad \forall t.$$

Then

$$\pi_t(s^t) = \pi(s_t \mid s_{t-1})\pi(s_{t-1} \mid s_{t-2}) \ldots \pi(s_2 \mid s_1)\pi(s_1 \mid s_0) \tag{7.2}$$

is the probability of a time path $s^t = (s_0, s_1, \ldots, s_t)$, conditional on the initial state s_0. If the initial state s_0 is also taken as random, then

$$\pi_t(s^t) = \pi(s_t \mid s_{t-1})\pi(s_{t-1} \mid s_{t-2}) \ldots \pi(s_2 \mid s_1)\pi(s_1 \mid s_0)\bar{\pi}(s_0). \tag{7.3}$$

Since the Markov process for the state s_t is stationary, the transition probabilities $\pi(s_{t+i}|s_{t+i-1})$ are time-invariant, and so is the probability of the history s^t, $\pi_t(s^t)$.

The endowment good is non-storable. Let $\omega^i(s_t)$ denote the endowment of agent i in state s_t, where the process is stationary and $\omega(s_t)$ is non-negative (so it might equal zero in some periods). Notice that we are allowing agents to have different endowments but we are assuming that all agents are affected by the same aggregate shock. The consumption of agent i at time t with history s^t is denoted $c_t^i(s^t)$. The t subscript is added to show that s^t is a t-dimensional vector. Let $p_t^0(s^t)$ denote the time-0 price of a unit of consumption at time t in history s^t and define $p^0 \equiv \{p_t^0(s^t)\}_{s^t \in \mathcal{S}^t, t=0}^{\infty}$ as the price system. Given p^0, agent $i \in I$ chooses $c^i \equiv \{c_t^i(s^t)\}_{t=0, s^t \in \mathcal{S}^t}^{\infty}$, to maximize

$$\sum_{t=0}^{\infty} \sum_{s^t \in \mathcal{S}^t} \beta^t \pi_t(s^t) U(c_t^i(s^t)) \tag{7.4}$$

subject to

$$\sum_{t=0}^{\infty} \sum_{s^t \in \mathcal{S}^t} p_t^0(s^t)[\omega^i(s_t) - c^i(s^t)] = 0. \tag{7.5}$$

What this means is that, for each time period t, there are S possible values that the state s_t can realize. Hence for each period t, there is a history of realizations up to that point in time, $\hat{s}^{t-1}$, for example. Given the history $\hat{s}^{t-1}$, an agent picks $c_t(s_1, \hat{s}^{t-1}), \ldots, c_t(s_S, \hat{s}^{t-1})$, where the optimal consumption choice at time t is allowed to depend on the history of past states. Hence at time 0, the agent is picking consumption for each time period over all of the possible histories of the state. All of these choices are state-contingent, and at time 0 all possible future time paths for the state variable, as well as the conditional probabilities, are known. Agents make these trades such that the budget constraint holds. Notice that the budget constraint for the consumer requires that the expected discounted present value of lifetime expenditures must equal the expected discounted present value of lifetime endowment. It does not require that the agent's budget be balanced for a particular history s^t.

A *time-0 contingent claims equilibrium* is a price system p^0 and an allocation $(c^1, \ldots, c^I)$ such that (i) given prices p^0, c^i solves agent i's problem; and (ii) markets clear:

$$\sum_{i=1}^{I} c_t^i(s^t) = \sum_{i=1}^{I} \omega^i(s_t), \quad s_t \in \mathcal{S}, t = 0, 1, \ldots$$

To solve the consumer's problem, let λ_i denote the Lagrange multiplier for the lifetime budget constraint for consumer i. Notice that the Lagrange multiplier is not indexed by time or state. The first-order condition is:

$$\frac{\beta^t \pi_t(s^t) U'(c_t^i(s^t))}{\lambda_i} = p_t^0(s^t) \;\; \forall t, \;\; \forall s^t \in \mathcal{S}^t, \;\; t \geq 0. \tag{7.6}$$

For two agents, $i, j \in I$ such that $i \neq j$, we have:

$$\frac{\beta^t \pi_t(s^t) U'(c_t^i(s^t))}{\lambda_i} = p_t^0(s^t) = \frac{\beta^t \pi_t(s^t) U'(c_t^j(s^t))}{\lambda_j}$$

This can be rewritten as:

$$\frac{p_t^0(s^t)}{\beta^t \pi_t(s^t)} = \frac{U'(c_t^i(s_t))}{\lambda^i} = \frac{U'(c_t^j(s_t))}{\lambda^j}. \tag{7.7}$$

This condition says that the weighted marginal utility of consumption is equated across consumers, where the weights are the Lagrange multipliers. Equivalently,

$$\frac{U'(c_t^i(s^t))}{U'(c_t^j(s^t))} = \frac{\lambda^i}{\lambda^j} \quad \forall i, j \tag{7.8}$$

Hence, for any history s^t, any time period t and any two distinct agents, the ratio of the marginal utilities of the agents is equal to a constant for all t, s^t. This condition illustrates a property of efficient risk sharing that the marginal rate of substitution across agents is equal to a constant across states. We refer to this feature of the complete contingent claims equilibrium as *complete risk sharing* or *full insurance*. Wilson [449] was one of the first to note that optimal sharing of risk by members of a risk-averse group is equivalent to the existence of a set of individual-specific weights such that individuals' marginal utility satisfies a version of Equation (7.7).[1]

The perfect risk-sharing hypothesis has been used in a variety of applications in the recent literature. These include the role of risk sharing in international business cycles (see Heathcote and Perri [247]), the interaction of risk sharing with specialization (see Kalemli-Ozcan, Sorensen, Yosha [270]), and the role of social security in aggregate risk sharing under incomplete markets (see Krueger and Kubler [291]). A variety of papers has also empirically examined the perfect risk-sharing hypothesis. Altug and Miller [18], [19] make use of this hypothesis to provide panel data estimates and tests of intertemporal models of consumption and labor supply with aggregate shocks. Cochrane [108], Mace [328], and Townsend [432] have used regressions of consumption growth on income growth to test the full risk-sharing hypothesis. Altonji, Hayashi, and Kotlikoff [15] test for full risk-sharing within families using a similar approach.

Idiosyncratic risk

Idiosyncratic risk refers to the situation in which any variation in individual endowments can be diversified away through trading among individuals in an economy. To examine the impact of idiosyncratic risk, suppose that there are only two types of agents, A and B. Let the endowment satisfy

$$\omega = \omega^a(s_t) + \omega^b(s_t), \tag{7.9}$$

where ω is constant for any date or state. Hence, there is no aggregate risk in this economy, which would occur if the aggregate endowment $\omega(s_t)$ were to vary as a function of the history s^t. Nevertheless, individuals experience variation in their endowment as a function of the state of the economy. Let $\pi(s_t)$, the probability of the state s_t, equal the quantity of output that goes

[1] See Wilson [449, pp. 123–24].

to agent A, so that $\omega^a(s_t) = \pi(s_t)$ and so $\omega^b(s_t) = 1 - \pi(s_t)$. For simplicity, we are assuming that the probability is i.i.d. However, there is no difficulty in assuming that it is Markov. Hence, the only uncertainty in this economy is how the total endowment is split between the two types of agents, and this is independent of the history of the economy at any date t.

The first-order condition is:

$$\frac{\beta^t \pi_t(s^t) U'(c_t^a(s_t))}{\lambda^a} = p_t^o(s^t) = \frac{\beta^t \pi_t(s^t) U'(c_t^b(s_t))}{\lambda^b}. \tag{7.10}$$

The goods market-clearing condition is:

$$\omega = c_t^a(s_t) + c_t^b(s_t). \tag{7.11}$$

Using this condition in the first-order condition and rewriting,

$$\frac{U'(c_t^a(s_t))}{U'(\omega - c_t^a(s_t))} = \frac{\lambda^a}{\lambda^b}. \tag{7.12}$$

Notice that the right side is constant over time and states. Also, since the total endowment is fixed, the solution to this equation, if λ^a/λ^b were known, has constant consumption $\bar{c}^a$. We can solve for the constant consumption using the inverse function theorem as:

$$c_t^a(s_t) = (U')^{-1}\left(\frac{\lambda^a}{\lambda^b} U'\left(\omega - c_t^a(s_t)\right)\right) = \bar{c}^a.$$

It follows from the feasibility condition that the consumption of type B is also constant, and equal to

$$c_t^b(s_t) = \bar{c}^b = \omega - \bar{c}^a.$$

Hence, if the only risk is idiosyncratic and if markets are complete, then agents can completely insure against endowment risk.

Aggregate risk

Of course the aggregate economy cannot diversify away *aggregate risk*. The best that can be done is to shift risk to those best able to bear it. Our model predicts that the marginal rate of substitution across agents at each point in time and in each state will be equal to a constant. Suppose that the aggregate endowment fluctuates randomly but that type A's fraction of output is constant. In particular, assume that

$$\omega^a(s_t) = \delta\omega(s_t), \quad 0 < \delta < 1.$$

Then using Equation (7.12), we can solve for the consumption of agent A for any given history of the shocks s^t as:

$$c_t^a(s_t) = (U')^{-1}\left(\frac{\lambda^a}{\lambda^b} U'\left(c_t^b(s_t)\right)\right),$$

and

$$c_t^b(s_t) = \omega(s_t) - c_t^a(s^t).$$

Hence, we observe that the aggregate economy is affected. Even with complete risk sharing, the allocations of individual agents vary with fluctuations in the aggregate economy. If, as we have assumed, output is non-storable, the economy cannot insure against aggregate fluctuations. The best it can do is to share the risk efficiently, which is achieved when the marginal rate of substitution across agents is equal to a constant for all states.

Finding a solution

Now return to the version with I consumers. Choose one of the consumers as a numeraire – say consumer 1 – and define the ratio of the Lagrange multipliers as:

$$\hat{\lambda}^i \equiv \frac{\lambda^i}{\lambda^1}, \quad i = 2, \ldots, I.$$

Notice that we can write the consumption allocation of consumer i as:

$$c_t^i(s^t) = (U')^{-1}\left(U'\left(c_t^1(s^t)\right)\hat{\lambda}^i\right) \quad i = 2, \ldots, I. \tag{7.13}$$

Now substitute this relation into the goods market-clearing condition to obtain:

$$\sum_{i=1}^{I}(U')^{-1}\left(U'\left(c_t^1(s^t)\right)\hat{\lambda}^i\right) = \sum_{i=1}^{I}\omega^i(s_t). \tag{7.14}$$

Notice that the right side of Equation (7.14) depends only on the current realization of s_t. Hence, so must the consumption allocation:

$$c_t^i(s^t) = c^i(s_t) \quad s^t \in \mathcal{S}^t. \tag{7.15}$$

This says that in a stationary environment, consumption allocations in a complete contingent claims equilibrium are not *history dependent*.

To further characterize the solution, notice that the left side of (7.14) is strictly increasing in c^1. Hence, there exists a solution for $c^1(s_t)$ and using (7.13), for $c^i(s_t), i=2,\ldots,I$ as a function of the ratio of the Lagrange multipliers $\hat{\lambda}^i$, $i=2,\ldots,I$ and the aggregate endowment, $\omega(s_t) = \sum_{i=1}^{I}\omega^i(s_t)$. Define $\hat{\lambda} = (\hat{\lambda}^2,\ldots,\hat{\lambda}^I)'$. The solution for the optimal consumption allocation can be written as $c^i(s_t) = c_i^\star(\hat{\lambda}, \omega(s_t))$, $i=1,\ldots,I$. Substituting for these functions in the individuals' budget constraints, using the definition of the contingent claims prices in (7.6), and multiplying the resulting expression through by λ^i allows us to solve for the ratio of the individual-specific Lagrange multipliers as:

$$\sum_{t=0}^{\infty}\sum_{s^t\in\mathcal{S}^t}\beta^t\pi(s^t)U'(c_i^\star(\hat{\lambda},\omega(s_t))[\omega^i(s_t)-c_i^\star(\hat{\lambda},\omega(s_t))]=0,\quad i=1,\ldots,I.$$

We will use these results in what follows when examining further the properties of competitive equilibrium with a complete set of contingent claims markets.

7.1.2. *Central planning problem*

It is useful to relate the competitive equilibrium allocation to the Pareto optimal allocation. We can determine the Pareto optimal allocation by setting Pareto weights $0<\phi_i$ for each $i\in I$. The central planning problem is to maximize

$$\sum_{i\in I}\phi_i\sum_{t=0}^{\infty}\sum_{s^t\in S^t}\beta^t\pi_t(s^t)U(c_t^i(s^t)) \tag{7.16}$$

subject to the resource constraint

$$\sum_i[\omega^i(s_t)-\sum_i c_t^i(s^t)]\leq 0. \tag{7.17}$$

Let $\Lambda_t(s^t)$ denote the Lagrange multiplier for the resource constraint. The first-order condition is:

$$\phi_i\beta^t\pi_t(s^t)U'\left(c_t^i(s^t)\right)=\Lambda_t(s^t) \tag{7.18}$$

Stationary solutions can be determined by assuming that

$$\hat{\Lambda}(s_t)\equiv\frac{\Lambda_t(s^t)}{\beta^t\pi_t(s^t)}$$

is stationary: we make this assumption. In this case,

$$U'(c_t^i(s^t))=\frac{\hat{\Lambda}(s_t)}{\phi_i}.$$

Notice that this equation can be used to define consumption as a function of $(\hat{\Lambda},s_t,\phi)$. Then the consumption for each agent can be substituted into the resource constraint, which is now an equation in the unknown variable $\hat{\Lambda}$. In this case, for agents $i,j\in I$ such that $i\neq j$,

$$\frac{U'(c^i(s_t))}{U'(c^j(s_t))}=\frac{\phi_j}{\phi_i}. \tag{7.19}$$

Recall in the competitive equilibrium, we showed that

$$\frac{U'(c^i(s_t))}{U'(c^j(s_t))} = \frac{\lambda_i}{\lambda_j}. \tag{7.20}$$

Hence, we have an application of the First Welfare Theorem, which states that a competitive equilibrium is Pareto optimal. Notice that, if the Pareto weights are determined such that

$$\frac{\phi_j}{\phi_i} = \frac{\lambda_i}{\lambda_j},$$

then the competitive equilibrium allocation coincides with the allocation under the central planning problem.

For an arbitrary set of Pareto weights, the Pareto optimal allocation can be determined as described above. According to the Second Welfare Theorem, under certain conditions the Pareto optimal allocation can be decentralized as a competitive equilibrium with a price system, assuming that transfers can be implemented. To understand this, suppose that the Pareto weights have the property that

$$\phi_i = \phi$$

so that all agents are treated identically by the central planner. Then, returning to our competitive allocation, for this allocation to be the solution to our contingent claims problem, it must be the case that the λ are equal across agents. This occurs if the expected discounted present value of lifetime endowment is equal across agents. Since we did not impose that, a set of endowment transfers is necessary for a Pareto optimal allocation with equal Pareto weights to be supported as a competitive equilibrium.

7.1.3. Sequential trading

The discussion above assumes that all of the contracts are negotiated at time 0. Once time progresses and the economy moves along a sample path s^t, there will be no need to renegotiate a contract and the state-contingent trades are carried out. This is not to say that we rule out any renegotiation, but rather to say that, given an opportunity to renegotiate, agents will choose the same state-contingent contracts.

Suppose now that consumers can trade one-period contingent claims at each date. One could ask whether the resulting equilibrium is identical to the one that is obtained with a time-0 trading scheme. To answer this question, we examine the case with sequential trading.

The aggregate endowment fluctuates randomly and the uncertainty follows a Markov process, as described in (7.1). We define $q(s_{t+1}, s_t)$ as the time t price in state s_t of a unit of consumption to be delivered in state

s_{t+1} at time $t+1$. Hence, $q(s_{t+1}, s_t)$ denotes the price of a one-period contingent claim. Likewise, let $z^i(s_{t+1}, s_t)$ denote the number of units of the consumption good that agent i receives ($z^i > 0$) or pays out ($z^i < 0$) if state s_{t+1} occurs. This has been written as a function of both s_{t+1} and s_t. However, to carry out the state-contingent trades, it will suffice to know the trade (amount and the sign – plus or minus) that must be transferred in each state. Hence, a vector $\{z^i(1), \ldots, z^i(S)\}$ summarizes the trades. Notice that this vector is independent of the state which occurred last period. So henceforth, we drop the additional state variable. Agent i has a budget constraint in period t:

$$c^i(s_t) + \sum_{s_{t+1} \in \mathcal{S}} q(s_{t+1}, s_t) z^i(s_{t+1}) \leq z^i(s_t) + \omega^i(s_t). \tag{7.21}$$

Let z^i_t denote the S-dimensional vector of contingent claims.

In the sequential version of the complete contingent claims equilibrium, we need to impose some debt limits to rule out Ponzi schemes. This rules out a situation in which the consumer can obtain unlimited consumption by infinitely rolling his/her existing debt. Observe that conditional on history $\hat{s}^t$, the agent's expected discounted present value of lifetime income is

$$A^i_t(\hat{s}^t) = \sum_{\tau=t}^{\infty} \sum_{s^\tau | \hat{s}^t} \beta^{\tau - t} p^t_\tau(s^\tau) \omega^i(s_\tau), \tag{7.22}$$

where $p^t_\tau(s^\tau)$ denotes the time-t contingent claims price for history s^τ.[2] Thus, $A_t(\hat{s}^t)$ shows the maximum amount an agent can repay at time t, conditional on the history $\hat{s}^t$. In this sense, we can view $A^i_t(\hat{s}^t)$ as a *natural debt limit* for consumer i conditional on history $\hat{s}^t$. Any borrowing by the agent at time t must be below the expected discounted present value of future endowment, which is $A^i_t(\hat{s}^{t+1})$. If the agent borrows $A^i_t(\hat{s}^{t+1})$ at time t, then consumption in period $t+1$ and all subsequent periods is equal to zero. Hence, in the sequential interpretation of the complete markets equilibrium, we also have the constraint:

$$-z^i(s_{t+1}) \leq A^i_{t+1}(s^{t+1}). \tag{7.23}$$

A *contingent claims equilibrium with sequential trading* is a sequence of one-step-ahead contingent claim prices, $q \equiv \{q(s_{t+1}, s_t)\}_{t=0}^{\infty}$ and consumption and portfolio allocations, $\{c^i(s_t)\}_{t=0}^{\infty}$ and $\{z^i(s_{t+1})\}_{t=0}^{\infty}$ for all

[2] The relationship between time-0 and time-t contingent claims prices is as follows:

$$p^t_\tau(s^\tau) = \frac{p^0_\tau(s^\tau)}{p^0_t(s^t)} = \frac{\beta^\tau U'(c_\tau(s^\tau))\pi(s^\tau)}{\beta^t U'(c_t(s^t))\pi(s^t)} = \beta^{\tau-t} \frac{U'(c_\tau(s^\tau))}{U'(c_t(s^t))} \pi(s^\tau \mid s^t).$$

Notice that $p^t_t(s^t) = 1$ for all $t \geq 0$.

$s_t, s_{t+1} \in \mathcal{S}$, $i \in I$ such that (i) given prices q, $\{c^i(s_t)\}_{t=0}^{\infty}$ and $\{z^i(s_{t+1})\}_{t=0}^{\infty}$ maximize

$$\sum_{t=0}^{\infty} \sum_{s^t \in \mathcal{S}^t} \beta^t \pi_t(s^t) U\left(c^i(s_t)\right) \tag{7.24}$$

subject to the sequence of budget constraints in (7.21) and the borrowing constraints in (7.23); and (ii) the goods and asset markets clear:

$$\sum_{i=1}^{I} c^i(s_t) = \sum_{i=1}^{I} \omega^i(s_t), \tag{7.25}$$

$$\sum_{i=1}^{I} z^i(s_{t+1}) = 0 \tag{7.26}$$

for all $s_t, s_{t+1} \in \mathcal{S}$, $t = 0, 1, \ldots,$.

To solve the consumer's problem, form the Lagrangian function:

$$\mathcal{L} = \sum_{t=0}^{\infty} \sum_{s^t \in \mathcal{S}^t} \beta^t \pi_t(s^t) \left\{ U(c^i(s_t)) \right.$$
$$\left. + \lambda_i(s_t) \left[z^i(s_t) + \omega^i(s_t) - c^i(s_t) - \sum_{s_{t+1} \in \mathcal{S}} q(s_{t+1}, s_t) z^i(s_{t+1}) \right] \right\},$$

where $\lambda_i(s_t)$ denotes the Lagrange multiplier for the period-by-period budget constraints.[3] The first-order conditions are:

$$U'(c^i(s_t)) = \lambda_i(s_t) \tag{7.27}$$

$$\pi_t(s^t)\lambda_i(s_t)q(s_{t+1}, s_t) = \beta \pi_{t+1}(s^{t+1})\lambda_i(s_{t+1}). \tag{7.28}$$

Notice that we are picking state-contingent trades, so that there is no expectations operator in the second equation. Eliminating the Lagrange multiplier and making use of the fact that $\pi_{t+1}(s^{t+1})/\pi_t(s^t) = \pi(s_{t+1} \mid s_t)$ yields

$$U'(c^i(s_t))q(s_{t+1}, s_t) = \beta \pi(s_{t+1} \mid s_t) U'(c^i(s_{t+1})). \tag{7.29}$$

Rewriting, observe that

$$q(s_{t+1}, s_t) = \frac{\beta \pi(s_{t+1} \mid s_t) U'(c^i(s_{t+1}))}{U'(c^i(s_t))} \tag{7.30}$$

for all agents.

[3] Given the Markov structure of uncertainty, it is more natural to formulate the sequential version of the complete markets equilibrium in a recursive fashion. We follow this approach in Section 7.2.

How is this price, which is the price of a unit of consumption to be delivered at time $t+1$ in state s_{t+1} determined in time t, conditional on the state s_t occurring, related to the time 0 price in (7.6)? To answer this, solve (7.6) for $U'(c^i(s^t))$ and substitute into (7.30) and then update by one time period and substitute for $U'(c^i(s^{t+1}))$ to obtain

$$q(s_{t+1}, s_t) = \left[\frac{\beta\pi(s_{t+1} \mid s_t)p^0_{t+1}(s^{t+1})\lambda_i}{\beta^{t+1}\pi_{t+1}(s^{t+1})}\right]\left[\frac{p^0_t(s^t)\lambda_i}{\beta^t\pi_t(s^t)}\right]^{-1}$$

$$= \frac{p^0_{t+1}(s^{t+1})}{p^0_t(s^t)}. \tag{7.31}$$

Hence, we find that the one-period contingent claims price for state s_{t+1} conditional on s_t occurring in period t is a ratio of the contingent claims prices that are negotiated at time zero for the histories s^{t+1} and s^t. Under this representation for prices, it follows that the first-order conditions for the time-0 version of the problem are equal to the first-order conditions for the problem with sequential trading. To show that the allocations for the sequential version of the problem are equivalent to those for the time-0 problem, we also need to show that the former allocations satisfy the time-0 version of the consumer's budget constraint evaluated at these prices. For this purpose, define

$$\Gamma^i_t(s^t) = \sum_{\tau=t}\sum_{s^\tau|s^t} p^t_\tau(s^\tau)[c^i(s_\tau) - \omega^i(s_\tau)] \tag{7.32}$$

as consumer i's wealth, or the value of all its current and future net claims, expressed in units of the date t, history s^t consumption good. The proof of the equivalence of the time-0 and sequential versions of the contingent claims equilibrium hinges on two conjectures. The first requires that the distribution of initial asset holdings satisfies $z^i(s_0) = 0$ for all $i \in I$, implying that consumers must finance their consumption allocations in the problem with sequential trading based on their lifetime income just as in the time-0 version of the problem. The second requires that the consumer's asset holdings in the equilibrium with sequential trading satisfy:

$$z^i(s_{t+1}) = \Gamma^i_{t+1}(s^{t+1}). \tag{7.33}$$

Consider the budget constraint at time-0 for the model with sequential trading and use the relation among the prices for the sequential versus time-0 version of the problem in Equation (7.31) to write this as:

$$\omega^i(s_0) - c^i(s_0) - z^i(s_0) = \sum_{s_1\in\mathcal{S}} q(s_1, s_0)z^i(s_1)$$

$$\Rightarrow \omega^i(s_0) - c^i(s_0) - z^i(s_0) = \sum_{s_1\in\mathcal{S}} \frac{p^0_1(s^1)}{p^0_0(s_0)} z^i(s_1).$$

Normalizing $p_0^0(s_0) = 1$ and substituting for $z^i(s_1)$ from Equation (7.33) yields:

$$z^i(s_0) + \sum_{j=0}^{\infty} \sum_{s^j \in S^j} p_j^0(s^j)[\omega^i(s_j) - c^i(s^j)] = 0. \tag{7.34}$$

Thus, the allocations of the problem with sequential trading solve the time-0 budget constraint under the distribution on initial wealth $z^i(s_0) = 0$. For periods $t > 0$, observe that

$$\begin{aligned}
\sum_{s_{t+1} \in S} q(s_{t+1}, s_t) z^i(s_{t+1}) &= \frac{p_{t+1}^t(s^{t+1})}{p_t^t(s^t)} \sum_{\tau=t+1} \sum_{s^\tau | s^{t+1}} p_\tau^{t+1}(s^\tau)[c^i(s_\tau) - \omega^i(s_\tau)] \\
&= p_{t+1}^t(s^{t+1}) \sum_{\tau=t+1} \sum_{s^\tau | s^{t+1}} p_\tau^{t+1}(s^\tau)[c^i(s_\tau) - \omega^i(s_\tau)] \\
&= \sum_{\tau=t+1} \sum_{s^\tau | s^{t+1}} p_\tau^t(s^\tau)[c^i(s_\tau) - \omega^i(s_\tau)] \\
&= \Gamma_t^i(s^t) - [c^i(s_t) - \omega^i(s_t)].^{4}
\end{aligned} \tag{7.35}$$

Recall that the budget constraints for the model with sequential trading can be written as:

$$c^i(s_t) + \sum_{s_{t+1} \in S} q(s_{t+1}, s_t) z^i(s_{t+1}) = \omega^i(s_t) + z^i(s_t).$$

Now substitute for the initial asset holdings as $z^i(s_t) = \Gamma_t^i(s^t)$ and use the result in (7.35), implying that the period-by-period budget constraint holds identically. Thus, the optimal asset allocation evaluated at the value of lifetime wealth based on the time-0 consumption allocation satisfies the period-by-period budget constraints. Hence, we conclude that the consumption allocation based on time-0 versus sequential trading is identical, $c_t^i(s^t) = c^i(s_t)$ for all dates and all histories.

To complete our argument, we also need to show that the consumer does not have an incentive to increase current consumption in the sequential equilibrium by reducing some component of the proposed asset allocation. This, in turn, depends on the existence of the debt limits imposed by the condition in (7.23). Suppose that the consumer wishes to attain a consumption stream $\{c^i(s^\tau)\}_{\tau=t+1}^{\infty}$ for all possible future events $s^\tau \in \mathcal{S}^\tau$. Then

[4] To obtain this result, we have used the fact that

$$p_{t+1}^t(s^{t+1}) p_\tau^{t+1}(s^\tau) = \frac{p_{t+1}^0(s^{t+1})}{p_t^0(s^t)} \frac{p_\tau^0(s^\tau)}{p_{t+1}^0(s^{t+1})} = p_\tau^t(s^\tau), \quad \tau > t.$$

it should subtract the value of this stream from the natural debt limit in (7.23) as:

$$-z^i(s_{t+1}) \leq A^i(s_{t+1}) - \sum_{\tau=t+1}^{\infty} \sum_{s^\tau | s^{t+1}} q_\tau^{t+1}(s^\tau) c^i(s^\tau)$$
$$= -\Gamma_{t+1}^i(s^{t+1}),$$

which implies that

$$z^i(s_{t+1}) \geq \Gamma_{t+1}^i(s^{t+1}).$$

But this says that the consumer should not increase current consumption by reducing next period's wealth below $\Gamma_{t+1}^i(s^{t+1})$ because that would prevent him from obtaining the optimal consumption plan satisfying the first-order conditions in (7.30).

These arguments show that the allocations which satisfy the first-order conditions and sequence of budget constraints for the time-0 problem also satisfy the first-order conditions and budget constraint for the sequential problem under the conjectured initial distribution of wealth and the state-by-state asset allocation. An important implication is that, after the contingent trades have been made at time 0, there is no interest in renegotiating any trades. This is despite the fact that the economy is moving along a particular sample path, whereas in the time-0 trading model, the lifetime budget constraint holds in present value over all sample paths.

7.1.4. *Implications for pricing assets*

In Section 1.2, we showed how a contingent claims equilibrium could be replicated by a security market equilibrium. The results of that section show that the prices of all assets will be a bundle of contingent claims prices. We can illustrate this result using the sequential interpretation of the contingent claims equilibrium.

Consider the price of a claim to one unit of the consumption good with certainty next period. Let b_t denote the amount of the asset you buy and let $Q(s_t)$ denote the price. Let us emphasize that we are not restricting $b_t > 0$. In particular, an agent can issue debt as a form of borrowing. The budget constraint is:

$$b_{t-1} + \omega_t \geq c_t + Q(s_t) b_t.$$

The first-order condition is:

$$U'(c_t) Q(s_t) = \beta \sum_{s_{t+1} \in S} \pi(s_{t+1} \mid s_t) U'(c_{t+1}).$$

Using the results of this section, we can express the price of the asset as:

$$\begin{aligned} Q(s_t) &= \sum_{s_{t+1}\in\mathcal{S}} q(s_{t+1}, s_t) \\ &= \sum_{s_{t+1}\in\mathcal{S}} \beta\pi(s_{t+1} \mid s_t)\frac{U'(c^i(s_{t+1}))}{U'(c^i(s_t))} \\ &= E\left[\beta\frac{U'(c^i(s_{t+1}))}{U'(c^i(s_t))} \mid s_t\right], \end{aligned} \tag{7.36}$$

where we have used the result in (7.30) to evaluate $q(s_{t+1}, s_t)$ in terms of the intertemporal MRS for any consumer i. To show that the allocation in this economy in which agents trade a one-period debt security b_t^i is not state contingent, observe that if the consumption sequence in the complete contingent claims equilibrium is $c_i^\star(s)$ for any agent i, then solving the budget constraint for contingent claims,

$$c_\star^i(s) = z^i(s) + w^i(s) - \sum_{s'} q(s' \mid s)z^i(s').$$

If

$$b_{t-1}^i - Q(s_t)b_t^i = z^i(s_t) + w^i(s_t) - \sum_{s_{t+1}} q(s_{t+1} \mid s_t)z^i(s_{t+1}),$$

then the allocations are identical. The point of this example is to show that, if markets are complete, then the securities prices are closely linked to the contingent claims prices. Hence, even though the menu of assets that we observe in markets looks very different from the contingent claims, the contingent claims prices are the basic building blocks for asset pricing in any complete market.

7.2. IDIOSYNCRATIC ENDOWMENT RISK

Idiosyncratic risk is risk that is faced by an individual agent, for example risk to an agent's health, and is risk that is not driven by a common shock to the economy. It is important to differentiate between risk sharing of idiosyncratic risk and risk-sharing arrangements for aggregate risk. We start with a pure endowment model in which all agents are *ex ante* identical. While agents face idiosyncratic endowment risk, aggregate endowment is deterministic. In this section, we study the role of *ex post* heterogeneity among individuals under alternative trading arrangements. Specifically, we consider the complete contingent claims equilibrium.

7.2.1. Notation

Each period, an agent draws a random endowment that is assumed to follow a first-order Markov chain. Let $\theta \in \Theta$, with $\Theta \equiv \{\underline{\theta}, \ldots, \bar{\theta}\}$, be a discrete random variable such that $\underline{\theta} \geq 0$ and $\bar{\theta}$ is finite. Let $g(\theta' \mid \theta)$ denote the probability of moving from state θ to θ' in one period. Define $\phi(\theta)$ as the *unconditional probability* of θ:

$$\phi(\theta') = \sum_{\theta \in \Theta} g(\theta' \mid \theta). \tag{7.37}$$

We have the following definition.

Definition 7.1 *The Markov process with transition probability function* $g : \Theta \times \Theta \to \Re_+$ *and unconditional probability function* $\phi : \Theta \to \Re_+$ *is said to be stationary if*

$$\phi(\theta') = \sum_{\theta \in \Theta} g(\theta' \mid \theta)\phi(\theta),$$

and invariant if

$$\phi(\theta) = \sum_{\theta' \in \Theta} g(\theta' \mid \theta)\phi(\theta').$$

Using these definitions, we can also define the following moments for the endowment process:

$$\text{unconditional mean} \quad \theta_m = \sum_{\theta \in \Theta} \phi(\theta)\theta,$$

$$\text{conditional mean} \quad \theta_m(\theta) = \sum_{\theta' \in \Theta} g(\theta' \mid \theta)\theta'.$$

Also define

$$g^j(\theta_j \mid \theta_0) = \prod_{h=1}^{j} \sum_{\theta_h \in \Theta} g(\theta_h \mid \theta_{h-1}) \tag{7.38}$$

as the *j-step ahead probability*, specifically the probability of $\theta = \theta_j$ in j periods when the current θ is θ_0. For example, the two-step probability function is given by:

$$g^2(\theta_j \mid \theta_i) = \sum_{\theta_h \in \Theta} g(\theta_j \mid \theta_h) g(\theta_h \mid \theta_i)$$

Finally, define

$$\theta_m^j(\theta) \equiv \sum_{\theta_j \in \Theta} g^j(\theta_j \mid \theta)\theta_j \tag{7.39}$$

as the *j-step ahead conditional mean.* As j increases, $\theta_m^j(\theta)$ tends to θ_m because the Markov process for θ is stationary and hence, exhibits mean reversion.

7.2.2. The economy

Assume there is a countable infinity of agents who receive a random endowment in each period. The reason that we make this assumption is that we wish to appeal to the Law of Large Numbers in our results. The idea is that if we have an infinite dimensional sample (here a countable infinity of agents), then the sample moments of the infinite sample are identical to the population moments of the distribution. This type of assumption is standard in the literature, although it is often assumed that there is a continuum of agents. There are certain technical issues with measurability that we wish to avoid so we assume there is a countable infinity of agents, but the assumptions basically serve the same purpose, namely to use the Law of Large Numbers.

The endowment process is a first-order Markov chain. Each agent receives an endowment drawn from Θ in every period so the history for agent i is denoted $\theta_i^t = \{\theta_{1,i}, \ldots, \theta_{t,i}\}$. An agent is characterized by his history $\theta^t \in \Theta^t$. The fraction of agents with history θ^t is identical to the probability of observing the history of the endowment shocks θ^t, and this is equal to $g_t(\theta^t) = g(\theta_t|\theta_{t-1})g(\theta_{t-1}|\theta_{t-2}) \cdots g(\theta_1|\theta_0)$, given θ_0. The unconditional probability of observing θ_t in the general population is $\phi(\theta_t)$ and, with a countable infinity of agents, the fraction of agents with θ is $\phi(\theta)$. To compute the aggregate endowment of the economy, observe that, with a countable infinity of agents, a fraction $\phi(\theta)$ of the agents have realized θ. The total endowment per capita of the economy each period is

$$\theta_m = \sum_{\theta \in \Theta} \phi(\theta)\theta = \sum_{\theta \in \Theta} \sum_{\theta_j \in \Theta} g(\theta \mid \theta_j)\phi(\theta_j)\theta, \tag{7.40}$$

so there is no aggregate uncertainty.

The *commodity space* for this economy consists of history-dependent sequences $\{c_t(\theta^t)\}_{t=0}^{\infty}$, where each element of the sequence denoted $c_t(\theta^t) \in \Re_+$ is indexed by the history of endowment shocks up to that date, $\theta^t \in \Theta^t$. Unlike the static model that we considered in Chapter 1, the commodity space is now infinite dimensional. The representative agent has lifetime preferences:

$$\sum_{t=0}^{\infty} \sum_{\theta^t \in \Theta^t} \beta^t g_t(\theta^t) U(c_{i,t}(\theta^t)). \tag{7.41}$$

Agents are identical at the beginning of time and become differentiated over time because of different endowment realizations.

The market-clearing conditions require that

$$\sum_{\theta_t \in \Theta} \sum_{\theta_{t-1} \in \Theta} g(\theta_t \mid \theta_{t-1})\phi(\theta_{t-1})[\theta_t - c_t(\theta^t)] = 0. \tag{7.42}$$

7.2.3. Complete contingent claims

As a baseline case, we start with the complete contingent claims solution and present both the time-0 and the dynamic programming versions of the problem.

Assume that agents can purchase contingent claims – in particular let $q_t(\theta^t)$ denote the time 0 price of a contingent claim paying one unit of the endowment good at time t conditional on history θ^t, so that $q_t : \Theta^t \rightarrow \Re_{++}$. The representative agent at time zero faces a lifetime budget constraint:

$$0 \leq \sum_{t=0}^{\infty} \sum_{\theta^t \in \Theta^t} q_t(\theta^t)[\theta_t - c_t(\theta^t)]. \tag{7.43}$$

Let λ denote the Lagrange multiplier for this constraint. Notice that λ is not indexed by an individual because all agents are identical at time 0, including in initial asset holdings, which are assumed to equal 0. The first-order conditions take the form:

$$\beta^t g_t(\theta^t)U'(c_i(\theta^t)) = \lambda q_t(\theta^t) \quad \text{for all } \theta^t \in \Theta^t, i = 1, 2, \ldots. \tag{7.44}$$

As written, the price depends on the entire history θ_i^t for each i. An agent with history $\tilde{\theta}^t$ faces a price $q_t(\tilde{\theta}^t)$ while an agent with history $\hat{\theta}^t$ faces price $q_t(\hat{\theta})$. Observe that the price depends on a growing sequence of histories, which varies across agents. This suggests that over time, the number of different prices is growing rapidly.

Given the stationary Markov property for the endowment process, however, we can examine a stationary solution to this problem without loss of generality. This will simplify considerably the space over which prices are defined. Under the Markov property, notice that given θ_{t-1}, the history of shocks θ^{t-2} is irrelevant for predicting θ_t. With this in mind, consider solutions in which consumption and prices depend only on the current $\theta_{i,t}$ and recent past $\theta_{i,t-1}$ endowments for agent i. Let $q_t(\theta_t, \theta_{t-1})$ denote the time 0 price of a unit of consumption conditional on θ_t at time t and θ_{t-1} at time $t-1$. If we sum the first-order condition over all possible histories up to time $t-2$ for agent i, then conditional on (θ_t, θ_{t-1}) the first-order condition becomes:

$$\sum_{\theta^{t-2} \in \Theta^{t-2}} \beta^t g_t(\theta^t)U'(c_i(\theta_t, \theta_{t-1})) = \lambda q_t(\theta_t, \theta_{t-1}). \tag{7.45}$$

This result says that for all possible histories that reach θ_{t-1} at $t-1$ and θ_t at t, the price will be $q(\theta_t, \theta_{t-1})$. If the contingent claims prices are set to satisfy

$$q_t(\theta_t, \theta_{t-1}) = \beta^t g(\theta_t \mid \theta_{t-1}),$$

then the first-order condition reduces to

$$U'(c(\theta_t, \theta_{t-1})) = \lambda,$$

which implies consumption is constant, $(U')^{-1}(\lambda) = c$. Using the resource constraint,

$$\sum_{\theta_j} \sum_{\theta_i} g(\theta_j \mid \theta_i)\phi(\theta_i)[\theta_j - c] = \theta_m - c = 0,$$

observe that a solution for the constant level of c is given by

$$c = \theta_m. \tag{7.46}$$

This is the *optimal consumption* whether the individual's endowment follows an i.i.d. process or a Markov process.

The lifetime budget constraint for the representative agent then becomes:

$$0 = \sum_{t=0}^{\infty} \sum_{\theta_t \in \Theta} \sum_{\theta_{t-1} \in \Theta} \beta^t g(\theta_t \mid \theta_{t-1})[\theta_t - \theta_m],$$

where we have substituted for $q_t(\theta_t, \theta_{t-1}) = \beta^t g(\theta_t \mid \theta_{t-1})$. Notice that borrowing or saving over time, given by $\theta_t - c = \theta_t - \theta_m$, is the deviation of the endowment from its unconditional mean.

We can also define a measure of net wealth for each consumer i as the expected value of future consumption claims net of all liabilities. Conditional on a particular history $\hat{\theta}_i^t$ for agent i up to time t, observe that the agent's expected future net claims under the consumption policy $c = \theta_m$ are:

$$\Lambda_t^i(\hat{\theta}_i^t) = \sum_{\tau=t+1}^{\infty} \sum_{\theta^\tau \mid \hat{\theta}_i^t} \beta^{\tau-t} g_\tau(\theta^\tau \mid \hat{\theta}_i^t)[\theta_m - \theta_\tau]. \tag{7.47}$$

In lieu of the market-clearing conditions, we have that

$$\sum_{\theta^t \in \Theta^t} g_t(\theta^t)\Lambda_t(\theta^t) = 0. \tag{7.48}$$

Observe that conditional on history $\hat{\theta}^t$, the agent's expected discounted present value of lifetime income is

$$A_t(\hat{\theta}_i^t) = \sum_{\tau=t}^{\infty} \sum_{\theta^\tau \mid \hat{\theta}_i^t} \beta^{\tau-t} g_\tau(\theta^\tau \mid \hat{\theta}_i^t)\theta_\tau. \tag{7.49}$$

For $\tau > t$ in the i.i.d. case, the expected discounted present value of lifetime income is identical across agents. Fluctuations in expected lifetime income are due entirely to temporary deviations from the unconditional mean θ_m in the current period.

7.2.4. Dynamic programming

To describe this problem, let $q(\theta', \theta)$ denote the time-t price of a one-period contingent claim that pays off contingent on all possible states $\theta' \in \Theta$ next period.

$$c + \sum_{\theta' \in \Theta} q(\theta', \theta) z(\theta', \theta) \leq \theta + z, \tag{7.50}$$

where $z(\theta', \theta)$ is the claim to a unit of consumption in the event that θ' occurs, conditional on θ. In the sequential version of the complete contingent claims equilibrium, we need to impose some debt limits to rule out Ponzi schemes. Any borrowing by the agent at time t with history $\hat{\theta}_i^t$ must be below the expected discounted present value of current and future endowment $A_t(\hat{\theta}_i^t)$, which is the maximum amount an agent can repay at time t, conditional on the history $\hat{\theta}_i^t$. If the agent borrows $A_t(\theta_i^t)$ at time t, then consumption in period $t + 1$ and all subsequent periods is equal to zero. In this sense, we can view $A_t(\hat{\theta}_i^t)$ as a *natural debt limit* for consumer i conditional on history $\hat{\theta}^t$. Hence, in the sequential interpretation of the complete markets equilibrium, we also have the constraint:

$$z(\theta_{t+1}) \geq -A_{t+1}(\theta^{t+1}). \tag{7.51}$$

The Bellman equation for the dynamic programming version of the problem is:

$$V(z, \theta) = \max_{c,z'} [U(c) + \beta \sum_{\theta' \in \Theta} g(\theta' \mid \theta) V(z', \theta')] \tag{7.52}$$

subject to (7.50), (7.51), and $c \geq 0$. Let $\lambda(\theta)$ denote the Lagrange multiplier on the budget constraint. The first-order and envelope conditions are given by:

$$U'(c) = \lambda(\theta), \tag{7.53}$$

$$\lambda(\theta) q(\theta', \theta) = \beta g(\theta' | \theta) V_z(z', \theta'), \tag{7.54}$$

$$V_z(z, \theta) = \lambda(\theta). \tag{7.55}$$

The simplified first-order condition is:

$$q(\theta', \theta) U'(c) = \beta g(\theta' | \theta) U'(c'). \tag{7.56}$$

As before, if $q(\theta', \theta) = \beta g(\theta' | \theta)$, then consumption is constant, that is, $U'(c) = U'(c')$ implies that $c = c' = \bar{c}$.

Suppose that $c = \theta_m$. Under this consumption policy, the agent's budget constraint can be expressed as

$$z(\theta_t) = \theta_m - \theta_t + \beta \sum_{\theta_{t+1} \in \Theta} g(\theta_{t+1} \mid \theta_t) z(\theta_{t+1}, \theta_t). \tag{7.57}$$

Solving this equation forward in $z(\theta)$, observe that

$$\begin{aligned} z(\theta_t) &= \theta_m - \theta_t + \beta \sum_{\theta_{t+1} \in \Theta} g(\theta_{t+1} \mid \theta_t) [(\theta_m - \theta_{t+1}) \\ &\quad + \beta \sum_{\theta_{t+2} \in \Theta} g(\theta_{t+2} \mid \theta_{t+1}) z(\theta_{t+2}, \theta_{t+1})] \\ &= \theta_m - \theta_t + \sum_{j=1}^{\infty} \beta^j \sum_{\theta_{t+j} \in \Theta} g^j(\theta_{t+j} \mid \theta_t)[\theta_m - \theta_{t+j}], \end{aligned} \tag{7.58}$$

where $g^j(\theta_{t+j}|\theta_t)$ is the j-step ahead probability, conditional on θ_t. There are two cases.

i.i.d. endowment

Assume that θ is i.i.d. with probability $g(\theta)$. In this case, forecasts of future endowment equal θ_m, regardless of the current θ_t. Consider the expression for $z(\theta_t)$ from Equation (7.58) under this assumption:

$$\begin{aligned} z(\theta_t) &= \theta_m - \theta_t + \sum_{j=1}^{\infty} \beta^j \sum_{\theta_{t+j} \in \Theta} g^j(\theta_{t+j} \mid \theta_t)[\theta_m - \theta_{t+j}] \\ &= \theta_m - \theta_t, \end{aligned}$$

where the last term on the first line is zero because the j-step ahead conditional mean of θ_{t+j} is just equal to the unconditional mean, θ_m. Hence, the distribution of wealth is just equal to the deviation of the endowment from the unconditional mean, $\{z(\theta_t^i)\}_{i \in I} = \{\theta_m - \theta_t^i\}_{i \in I}$. An agent's wealth over time is thus uncorrelated since $\theta_m - \theta_{t-1}^i$ and $\theta_m - \theta_t^i$ are uncorrelated. Notice that the agent's *permanent income*, that is, the level of income necessary to yield a constant consumption path, is θ_m. Consumption is equal to θ_m, and all fluctuations in wealth are transitory.

If the endowment process is i.i.d., then for any $\tau > t$, the expected value of $\theta_m - \theta_\tau$ is equal to 0. Hence, for this case, the distribution of wealth is determined by the distribution of the deviation from the unconditional mean $\theta_m - \theta_t^i$. The probability of achieving a given level of wealth, $\theta_m - \theta_t^i$, is identical across agents at a point in time and over time. This is not true if the endowment process is Markov.

Markov endowment

Now assume that θ_t is Markov. Observe that

$$z(\theta_t) = \theta_m - \theta_t + \sum_{j=1}^{\infty} \beta^j \sum_{\theta_{t+j} \in \Theta} g^j(\theta_{t+j} \mid \theta_t)[\theta_m - \theta_{t+j}]$$

$$= \theta_m - \theta_t + \sum_{j=1}^{\infty} \beta^j [\theta_m - \theta_m^j(\theta_t)]. \tag{7.59}$$

The discounted present value of future net claims, defined in (7.47) is

$$\Lambda_t^i(\hat{\theta}_i^t) = \sum_{\tau=t+1}^{\infty} \sum_{\theta_\tau \mid \hat{\theta}_i^t} \beta^{\tau-t} g_\tau(\theta_\tau \mid \hat{\theta}_i^t)[\theta_m - \theta_\tau].$$

Thus, the distribution of wealth depends on the entire path of the deviation of the conditional mean $\theta_m^j(\theta_t)$ from θ_m, that is, $\{z(\theta_t^i)\}_{i\in I}$ defined in Equation (7.59). This implies that the wealth distribution for the Markov economy is much richer over time. However, observe that the distribution is still a function of only the current endowment shock θ_t^i. The distribution of an agent's wealth next period will be determined only by the endowment realization θ_{t+1}^i. Furthermore, while the distribution of wealth varies across agents due to different realizations of θ_t^i at a point in time, the cross-sectional distribution is unchanged over time. This occurs because the cross-sectional distribution of wealth is indexed by different realizations of θ_t^i, which come from the same distribution in each period. In models with incomplete markets, we will see that the cross-section distribution of wealth may also change over time.

7.3. RISK SHARING WITH IDIOSYNCRATIC AND AGGREGATE RISK

We end this chapter with an example that we think illustrates one feature in the relationship between idiosyncratic and aggregate risk. In our discussion so far we have treated two extreme versions: all risk is aggregate or all risk is idiosyncratic with no aggregate uncertainty. In reality, the relationship is more complicated. The example below illustrates some of the issues.

As before, assume there is a countable infinity of agents. Instead of assuming that they are identical, we now assume that there are J types of agents. A fraction α_j of the population is a type j agent where $\alpha_j \geq 0$ and

$$\sum_{j=1}^{J} \alpha_j = 1.$$

Typically in the discussion below, $J = 2$.

Uncertainty is introduced through an endowment shock that is correlated across agents. Let $S = \{\underline{s}, \ldots, \bar{s}\}$ such that there are N possible values of s. Let $s \in S$ be a discrete random variable such that $\underline{s} \geq 0$ and $\bar{s}$ is finite. Let $\pi(s' \mid s)$ denote the probability of moving from state s to s' in one period. Define $\Pi(s)$ as the unconditional probability of s

$$\Pi(s') = \sum_{s} \pi(s' \mid s)\Pi(s). \tag{7.60}$$

The Markov process is assumed to be *stationary* and *invariant*. A type j agent has endowment $\theta_j(s)$ when the aggregate state is s. Total endowment in state s is

$$y(s) \equiv \sum_{j=1}^{J} \alpha_j \theta_j(s). \tag{7.61}$$

Hence, total endowment is possibly stochastic, depending on the properties of s.

Agents are assumed to have identical preferences, regardless of type. An agent of type j has preferences

$$\sum_{t=0}^{\infty} \sum_{s^t \in S^t} \beta^t \pi(s^t) U(c_{jt}(s^t)). \tag{7.62}$$

An agent of type j faces a lifetime budget constraint

$$\sum_{t=0}^{\infty} \sum_{s^t \in S^t} q_t(s^t)[\theta_j(s_t) - c_{jt}(s^t)] = 0. \tag{7.63}$$

Hence, agents differ only because of the impact of the aggregate state s on their endowment.

Finally, the market-clearing conditions require that

$$\sum_{j=1}^{J} \alpha_j c_{jt}(s^t) = \sum_{j=1}^{J} \theta_j(s_t) = y(s_t). \tag{7.64}$$

7.3.1. *First-best solution*

The representative type j agent maximizes (7.62) subject to the budget constraint (7.63). Let λ_j denote the Lagrange multiplier for the budget constraint. The first-order condition takes the form

$$\beta^t \pi(s^t) U'(c_{j,t}(s^t)) = \lambda_j q_t(s^t). \tag{7.65}$$

Solve this for the price $q_t(s^t)$ and observe for two types of agents $i \neq j$, that

$$\frac{q_t(s^t)}{\beta^t \pi(s^t)} = \frac{U'(c_{j,t}(s^t))}{\lambda_j} = \frac{U'(c_{i,t}(s^t))}{\lambda_i}. \tag{7.66}$$

This condition says that the weighted marginal utilities of consumption are equated across individuals but consumption allocations need not be, as the aggregate risk may affect individuals differently. To study the implications of aggregate risk further, re-write the above condition as

$$\frac{\lambda_j}{\lambda_i} = \frac{U'(c_{j,t}(s^t))}{U'(c_{i,t}(s^t))}. \tag{7.67}$$

Choose a numeraire consumer – say type 1 – and define

$$\hat{\lambda}_j = \frac{\lambda_j}{\lambda_1}.$$

If the endowment process is stationary, say follows a stationary first-order Markov process, then the consumption of each type of agent is also stationary. Define the consumption of a representative type 1 agent as $c_1(s)$ for all $s \in S$. Next, define the function $\hat{c} : S \times \Re_+ \rightarrow \Re_+$ as the solution $c_j = \hat{c}(c_1(s), \hat{\lambda}_j)$ to

$$\hat{\lambda}_j = \frac{U'(c_j)}{U'(c_1(s))}, \quad j = 2, \ldots, J. \tag{7.68}$$

The next step is to substitute for $c_j = \hat{c}(c_1(s), \hat{\lambda}_j)$ into the resource constraints

$$\sum_{j=1}^{J} \alpha_j \theta_j(s) = \sum_{j=2}^{J} \alpha_j \hat{c}(c_1, \hat{\lambda}_j) + \alpha_1 c_1(s) \tag{7.69}$$

for each $s \in S$. Notice that the right side is strictly increasing in c_1. Let $c_1^\star$ denote the solution. Since the solution for c_1 depends on the total endowment $y(s) = \sum_{j=1}^{J} \alpha_j \theta_j(s)$ and the ratio of multipliers $\hat{\lambda} \equiv (\hat{\lambda}_2, \ldots, \hat{\lambda}_J)'$, so do the solutions for c_j. Now use the type j's budget constraint and multiply both sides of the equation by λ_j to eliminate λ_j from the denominator.

$$0 = \sum_{t=0}^{\infty} \sum_{s^t \in S} \beta^t \pi(s^t) U'(\hat{c}(c_1(s_t), \hat{\lambda}_j))[\theta_j(s_t) - \hat{c}(c_1(s_t), \hat{\lambda}_j)] \tag{7.70}$$

Notice that the right side is strictly increasing in $\hat{\lambda}_j$. Let $\hat{\lambda}_j^\star$ denote the solution. Thus, the optimal consumption allocations are given by $c_j^\star = \hat{c}(\hat{\lambda}^\star, y(s))$ for $j = 1, \ldots, J$.

We now describe how to compute the complete contingent claims allocations and prices using this approach. For discussion's sake, assume that $J=2$ and $S=1,2$. Furthermore, for simplicity, assume that aggregate endowment shocks in each period are identically and independently distributed such that $Pr(s_t=1)=\pi$ and $Pr(s_t=2)=1-\pi$ for all t. If $s=1$, assume that $\theta_1(1)=0$ and $\theta_2(1)=1$ while if $s=2$, then $\theta_1(2)=1$ and $\theta_2(2)=0$. Hence the idiosyncratic endowment shocks are negatively correlated: if agent 1 has a high endowment realization then agent 2 has a low endowment realization and conversely. The resource constraint for $s=1,2$ becomes:

$$y(s_t) \equiv \alpha\theta_1(s_t)+(1-\alpha)\theta_2(s_t) = \alpha_1 c_1(s_t)+\alpha_2 c_2(s_t), \quad s_t = 1,2. \tag{7.71}$$

We consider some special cases.

- **Case 1:** $\pi(1)=\pi(2)=1/2$ **and** $\alpha=1/2$: Under this assumption, each period, half of the agents are productive and each type of agent expects to be productive with the same probability as any other agent. The resource constraints in Equation (7.71) become:

$$y(1) = 1 = c_1(1) + c_2(1)$$

$$y(2) = 1 = c_1(2) + c_2(2).$$

Notice that the aggregate endowment is constant over time and across states, so that there is no uncertainty at the aggregate level. Hence, the history of shocks is irrelevant for prices and decisions at time t. Thus, the first-order condition in Equation (7.66) can be written as:

$$\frac{q(s_t)}{\beta^t\pi(s_t)} = \frac{U'(c_1(s_t))}{\lambda_1} = \frac{U'(c_2(s_t))}{\lambda_2}. \tag{7.72}$$

Since agents are *ex ante* alike in all respects, including their preferences and their probabilities of receiving different endowments, it seems natural to seek a stationary solution to the problem with $\lambda_1=\lambda_2$. Notice that this implies that the time-0 price of consumption in state s_t is equal to the (discounted) probability of consumption in that state, $q(s_t)=\beta^t\pi(s_t)$. Also, using the first-order conditions evaluated under these assumptions, we have that

$$U'(c_1(s_t)) = U'(c_2(s_t)) \;\Rightarrow\; c_1(s_t) = c_2(s_t) = \bar{c}, \quad s_t = 1,2, \forall t.$$

In this case, both individuals consume a constant amount equal to $\bar{c}$ at all dates and in all states. Since there are an equal number of productive and unproductive individuals at each date, with identical preferences across agents, productive agents end up insuring unproductive agents so that all agents can consume a constant amount in each state. Output is constant and equal to $2\bar{c}=1$. This is the case of complete insurance in which the opportunities to pool risks enable all agents to consume a fixed amount regardless of the particular realization s_t which determines their earnings stream.

- **Case 2:** $\pi(1)=2/3$, $\pi(2)=1/3$ **and** $\alpha=1/2$: In this second case, one half of the agents are productive just as before. The resource constraint is the same and given by:

$$y(1) = 1 = c_1(1) + c_2(1)$$

$$y(2) = 1 = c_1(2) + c_2(2)$$

so that the aggregate endowment is certain, which is a result that follows from $\alpha=1/2$. Now suppose that preferences satisfy $U'(c_j(s))=c_j(s)^{-\gamma}$ for $j=1,2$. In a complete contingent claims equilibrium, we know that the ratio of weighted marginal utility of consumers is equated across states for all dates:

$$\frac{U'(c_1(s_t))}{U'(c_2(s_t))} = \frac{\lambda_1}{\lambda_2}, \quad \forall t, s_t = 1, 2.$$

Using the approach described earlier, we can simplify this expression as:

$$c_1(s_t) = c_2(s_t)\left(\frac{\lambda_1}{\lambda_2}\right)^{-1/\gamma} = c_2(S_t)k, \forall t \text{ and } s_t = 1, 2.$$

Substituting this back into the feasibility constraint yields:

$$c_1(s_t) = \bar{c}_1 = \frac{k}{1+k} \text{ and } c_2(s_t) = \bar{c}_2 = \frac{1}{1+k}, \quad \forall t, \quad s_t = 1, 2.$$

Again, agents prefer to smooth out their consumptions over time and across states. Since the consumption of each agent is constant across states, the ratio of the first-order conditions in Equation (7.72) shows that the price system should satisfy:

$$\frac{q(1)}{\beta^t \pi(1)} = \frac{q(2)}{\beta^t \pi(2)},$$

or

$$q(1) = 2q(2) \;\; \forall t. \tag{7.73}$$

Using the lifetime budget constraints evaluated at these prices yields:

$$\bar{c}_1 = 1 - \pi = \frac{1}{3} \text{ and } \bar{c}_2 = \pi = \frac{2}{3}.$$

In this case, consumption is not equated across agents at a point in time. Instead the agent with a lower probability of being productive at each date also receives a lower consumption. However, agents experience a constant consumption stream over time, and aggregate output is also constant over time. There is no market incompleteness here and risks are pooled.

- **Case 3:** $\pi(1)=\pi(2)=1/2$ **and** $\alpha=2/3$: Now, let us analyze the case when any individual agent expects to be productive with the same probability as any other agent but the proportion of agents that are productive varies so that aggregate output fluctuates across states because of the concentration of the productivity shock. In this case, the aggregate endowment in each state is given by:

$$y(1) = 1 - \alpha = \alpha c_1(1) + (1 - \alpha)c_2(1)$$

$$y(2) = \alpha = \alpha c_1(2) + (1 - \alpha)c_2(2),$$

where the economy experiences uncertainty both at an aggregate and at individual level. As in the previous case, consumption of agent 1 in state s_t satisfies

$$c_1(s_t) = c_2(s_t)\left(\frac{\lambda_1}{\lambda_2}\right)^{-1/\gamma}.$$

Substituting this result into the feasibility conditions yields:

$$1 - \alpha = \alpha c_2(1)\left(\frac{\lambda_1}{\lambda_2}\right)^{-1/\gamma} + (1 - \alpha)c_2(1)$$

$$\alpha = \alpha c_2(2)\left(\frac{\lambda_1}{\lambda_2}\right)^{-1/\gamma} + (1 - \alpha)c_2(2).$$

Solving for $c_i(s_t)$ yields:

$$c_i(1) = \left(\frac{1-\alpha}{\alpha}\right)c_i(2), \quad i = 1, 2. \tag{7.74}$$

Hence, consumption in the first state for each agent is proportional to consumption in the second state, with the factor of proportionality reflecting the fraction of agents who receive an endowment in each state. Substituting this result into the first-order conditions for consumer 1 (or equivalently, consumer 2) yields:

$$\frac{q(1)}{\beta^t\pi(1)} = \frac{\left(\left(\frac{1-\alpha}{\alpha}\right)c_1(2)\right)^{-\gamma}}{\lambda_1}$$

$$\frac{q(2)}{\beta^t\pi(2)} = \frac{(c_1(2))^{-\gamma}}{\lambda_1}$$

Dividing each side of these conditions, we can solve for the ratio of the state prices as:

$$\frac{q(1)}{q(2)} = \left(\frac{1-\alpha}{\alpha}\right)^{-\gamma} = \left(\frac{\alpha}{1-\alpha}\right)^{\gamma}. \tag{7.75}$$

For $\alpha = 2/3$, we find that $c_i(1) = \frac{1}{2}c_i(2)$ and $q(1) = 2^{\gamma} q(2)$. If we substitute these findings into lifetime budget constraints, we can solve for consumption allocations as:

$$\sum_{t=0}^{\infty} \beta^t \left[q(2)2^{\gamma}(-c_1(1)) + q(2)(1 - 2c_1(1)) \right] = 0$$

$$\sum_{t=0}^{\infty} \beta^t \left[q(2)2^{\gamma}(1 - c_2(1)) - q(2)2c_2(1) \right] = 0,$$

which implies that

$$c_1(1) = \frac{1}{2 + 2^{\gamma}}, \quad c_2(1) = \frac{2^{\gamma}}{2 + 2^{\gamma}}, \quad c_i(2) = 2c_i(1). \tag{7.76}$$

When agents have the same discounted present value of labor income, then they can borrow and lend to smooth consumption to an extent that the agent's consumption is no longer dependent on the particular time path of his wealth. When agents are no longer identical in expected present value, agents can no longer guarantee an identical consumption stream. When $\pi = 2/3$, agent 1 receives a lower consumption than agent 2 compared with the case where $\pi = 1/2$. This occurs because consumer 1's lifetime income is lower relative to consumer 2's. A similar result holds if $\pi = 1/2$ and $\alpha = 2/3$. In that case, although any individual agent expects to be productive with the same probability as any other agent, the proportion of agents that are productive varies so that agents' consumption fluctuates because of the concentration of the productivity shocks across the population. Hence, we find that an aggregate shock can cause variation in consumption allocations across agents. In our analysis up to this point, we have not considered variation in the aggregate shocks over time. Typically, this will also lead to variation in the individual allocations over time.

7.4. CONCLUSIONS

In this chapter, we have examined several versions of complete contingent claims markets and the implications for risk sharing. The material in this chapter is particularly useful in understanding what happens when markets are incomplete. In Chapter 16 on borrowing constraints, we discuss the implications of market frictions such as trading frictions and borrowing constraints. This chapter serves as a useful benchmark to understanding the implications for risk sharing when markets are incomplete.

7.5. EXERCISES

1. Multi-period Contingent Claims
Consider an economy under uncertainty such that there are T dates and S possible events at each date. Suppose there exists only one type of commodity. Assume that there are I individuals. Agents are identical in every way except their endowment.
Uncertainty is defined in terms of a random variable s_t that can take on S possible values at each date (this means $s_t \in (x_1, \ldots x_S) \equiv \mathcal{S}$ at each period). The state of the economy is given by the history s^t of realizations of the random variable s_r for $r \leq t$, defined as $s^t \equiv (s_1, \ldots, s_t) = (s^{t-1}, s_t)$. Let $\pi_t(s^t) \in [0, 1]$ denote the probability that $s^t \in \mathcal{S}^t$ occurs. Let $\pi(s_{t+1} = x_j \mid s_t = x_i)$ denote the probability of moving from state x_i to state x_j in one period. Then
$$\pi_t(s^t) = \pi(s_t \mid s_{t-1})\pi(s_{t-1} \mid s_{t-2}) \ldots \pi(s_2 \mid s_1)$$
is the probability of a time path $s^t = (s_1, \ldots, s_t)$.
The endowment good is non-storable. Let $w^i(s_t)$ denote the endowment of agent i in state s_t, where the process is stationary and $w(s)$ is non-negative (so it might equal 0 in some periods). Agent $i \in I$ maximizes
$$\sum_{t=1}^{T} \sum_{s^t \in \mathcal{S}^t} \beta^t \pi_t(s^t) U(c^i(s^t)). \tag{7.77}$$
   (a) Define the commodity space.
   (b) Let $p_t(s^t)$ denote the price of a contingent claim that pays one unit of the consumption good, conditional on the history s^t occurring. Assume that all trading takes place at time 0. Define a complete contingent claims equilibrium.
      i. Along a particular time path $\hat{s}^T$, does an agent have a balanced budget at time T? Specifically, does
$$\sum_{t=1}^{T} p_t(\hat{s}^t)[w^i(\hat{s}_t) - c^i(\hat{s}^t)] = 0?$$
      ii. If an agent can expire at the end of date T in debt, then what can we say about the asset position of some other agent $j \neq i$ in the economy?
      iii. What is the expected value of total endowment in this economy? Is it finite?
2. Now compare the allocations with the contingent claims solution (all trading at time 0) with the sequential trading.
   (a) Under what condition on prices and interest rates will the two allocations be equivalent?

(b) In this part of the problem, you are asked to examine the no-Ponzi game solution. First write the sequential budget constraints as a single lifetime constraint. (Hint: Let a^i_{t-1} denote the savings of agent i at the beginning of period t. The constraint will contain a term a^i_t, which is savings at the end of period t – solve for a^i_{t-1} and solve the equation forward.)

(c) Use your answer to the previous part of this question. Now suppose that $T \to \infty$. What is the no-Ponzi scheme condition in this model? What is the restriction on the interest rate process?

3. Formulate the social planning problem for this economy. The social planner maximizes a weighted sum of individual utilities subject to an aggregate feasibility constraint.
   Compare the first-order conditions for the social planning problem with the optimality conditions in the complete contingent claims equilibrium.
4. There are two consumers. Type A receives endowment y_t in period t while type B receives endowment x_t. The endowments are exogenous and stochastic. Assume that the mean of y is greater than the mean of x. Both types have the same utility function and maximize

$$\sum_{t=0}^{\infty} \beta^t U(c_t).$$

Assume that the initial wealth of each agent equals 0.

(a) Assume that each agent can borrow by issuing contingent claims and save by purchasing contingent claims from the other type of agent. Derive the contingent claims equilibrium.

(b) Suppose that x_t, y_t are negatively correlated. What type of trading would you expect?

(c) Suppose they are positively correlated. How does that affect the trading?

(d) Which agent has higher permanent income?

CHAPTER 8

Consumption and asset pricing

In this part we turn our attention to the analysis of dynamic economies using a recursive equilibrium approach. We begin our analysis with the consumption-based capital asset-pricing model of Lucas [319], Breeden [74], and others. We assume that there is a representative consumer and output evolves according to an exogenous Markov process. There is a rich array of assets traded in economies with well-developed capital markets. We show how this framework can be used for pricing such assets as equities which yield a random dividend stream, bonds of different maturities, and options on various underlying assets.

The remainder of this chapter is organized as follows. First, we demonstrate the existence of a recursive competitive equilibrium for a pure endowment economy based on Lucas [319]. We show the existence of a value function and the equilibrium asset-pricing function, and examine their properties. Second, we use this framework to derive the prices for a variety of assets, including pure-discount bonds of various maturities and derivative instruments such as options and forward contracts. Third, we describe asset pricing in a non-stationary environment when the aggregate endowment is growing. We also introduce a diagnostic tool known as volatility bounds for intertemporal MRSs or stochastic discount factors that allow a convenient way for examining the implications of alternative asset-pricing models.

8.1. THE CONSUMPTION-BASED CAPM

In this chapter we consider a pure endowment economy in which there is a representative consumer and output is exogenous. The issue is to derive equilibrium allocations and pricing functions under alternative assumptions about preferences and the stochastic properties of output.

Uncertainty is introduced by assuming that there are m exogenous shocks, $s_t \in S \subset \Re^m$ in each period. The endowment is a function of the shocks or exogenous state variables. The vector of shocks, s_t, follows a first-order Markov process with transition function F. The set S is assumed to be compact and $F : S \times S \rightarrow [0, 1]$ such that $F(s, s') \equiv \Pr(s_{t+1} \leq s' | s_t = s)$. We have the following assumption.

Assumption 8.1 *The transition function F has the Feller property so that for any bounded, continuous function $h : S \rightarrow \Re$, the function $Th(s) = \int_S h(s')F(s, ds')$ is continuous. The process defined by F has a stationary distribution Φ.*

The endowment is a time-invariant function of the shocks, $y_t \equiv y(s_t)$. Thus, the endowment also follows a stationary first-order Markov process and the evolution of y_t can be described in terms of the transition function F for s_t. The next assumption ensures that the endowment takes values in a compact set.

Assumption 8.2 *Define $\mathcal{Y} \equiv [\underline{y}, \bar{y}]$ with $\underline{y} > 0$ and $\bar{y} < \infty$. The function $y : S \rightarrow \mathcal{Y}$ is a continuous function that is bounded away from zero.*

The preferences of the representative consumer over sequences of consumption $\{c_t\}_{t=0}^{\infty}$ are given by:

$$E_0 \left\{ \sum_{t=0}^{\infty} \beta^t U(c_t) \right\}, \tag{8.1}$$

where $0 < \beta < 1$ denotes the subjective discount factor and E_0 is expectation conditional on information available at time zero. Notice that preferences are additively separable with respect to consumption at different dates. The following assumption characterizes the utility function.

Assumption 8.3 *The utility function $U : S \rightarrow \Re_+$ is continuous, continuously differentiable, strictly increasing, strictly concave with $U(0) = 0$ and $\lim_{c \rightarrow 0} U'(c) = \infty$.*

Next, consider the nature of securities trading. In this economy, consumers trade in shares to the exogenous output process and also buy and sell real risk-free bonds that are in zero net supply. Let q_t^e denote the price of a share after the dividends on the share have been paid. This price is referred to as the *ex-dividend price*. Let Q_t^1 denote the price at time t of a bond that pays off a sure unit of output at time $t + 1$. This is typically referred to as a *pure discount bond*; hence, $Q_t^1 \leq 1$. Let z_t denote a consumer's beginning-of-period share holdings and b_t the beginning-of-period bond holdings. Also assume that there is one perfectly divisible outstanding share.

The consumer faces the following sequence of budget constraints:

$$c_t + q_t^e z_{t+1} + Q_t^1 b_{t+1} \leq (y_t + q_t^e) z_t + b_t, \quad t = 0, 1, \ldots, \tag{8.2}$$

where y_t denotes dividends paid in period t and z_0 and b_0 are given. Prior to any securities trading in period t, the consumer observes the current value of output. She also knows all past values of output, y_r for $r < t$. The consumer takes the sequences for the prices of equities and bonds as given and chooses sequences for consumption and equity and bond holdings to maximize the objective function in (8.1) subject to the sequence of budget constraints (8.2) and the constraints that $c_t \geq 0$, $0 \leq z_{t+1} \leq \bar{z}$ where $\bar{z} > 1$ and $b_{t+1} \geq 0$ for all t.

The market-clearing conditions for $t = 0, 1, \ldots,$ are:

$$c_t = y_t, \tag{8.3}$$

$$z_{t+1} = 1, \tag{8.4}$$

$$b_{t+1} = 0. \tag{8.5}$$

8.1.1. Recursive competitive equilibrium

We follow the approach in Lucas [319] for showing the existence of a *recursive competitive equilibrium* in which prices can be expressed as time-invariant functions of variables that summarize the current state of the economy. In equilibrium, consumption equals the exogenous output at each date.

Note first that the consumer's expected discounted utility is well defined and finite under this allocation.

Lemma 8.1 *Under Assumptions 8.1 through 8.3, for any consumption sequence $\{c_t\}_{t=0}^{\infty}$ such that $c_t \leq y_t$, then*

$$E_0 \left\{ \sum_{t=0}^{\infty} \beta^t U(c_t) \right\} \leq \mathcal{U} < \infty.$$

PROOF

Notice that for any feasible c_t, $c_t \in [0, \bar{y}]$ where $y_t \leq \bar{y}$. Since U is continuous and takes a compact set into $\Re_+$, we can define an upper bound $\mathcal{U} \equiv \sum_{t=0}^{\infty} \beta^t U(\bar{y}) < \infty$. ∎

The Markov nature of uncertainty allows us to formulate the consumer's problem as a stationary dynamic programming problem. The consumer's state is summarized by its beginning-of-period equity holdings, z_t, its beginning-of-period bond holdings b_t, and the current shock s_t. Note that the consumer's choices take values in a compact set. Because there is one equity share outstanding, z_{t+1} will equal exactly one in equilibrium and so define an interval $Z = [0, \bar{z}]$ where $\bar{z} > 1$ such that $z_{t+1} \in Z$. In equilibrium, $b_{t+1} = 0$ and so defines an interval $B = [-b, b]$ where $b > 0$ such that $b_{t+1} \in B$.

We will seek an equilibrium in which the price of equities and the price of the risk-free asset are continuous, strictly positive functions of the exogenous shocks,

$$q^e : S \to \Re_{++} \tag{8.6}$$

$$Q^1 : S \to \Re_{++}. \tag{8.7}$$

To emphasize the recursive nature of the problem, let variables without primes denote current state or decision variables and variables with primes denote future values. Define $v(z, b, s)$ as the expected discounted utility of the consumer, given initial equity holdings z, bond holdings b, and the current shock s. By Lemma 8.1, this is well defined and finite. Given the price functions $q^e(\cdot)$ and $Q^1(\cdot)$, the value function for the consumer's problem satisfies the Bellman equation:

$$v(z, b, s) = \max_{c, z', b'} \left\{ U(c) + \beta \int_S v(z', b', s') F(s, ds') \right\} \tag{8.8}$$

subject to

$$c + q^e(s) z' + Q^1(s) b' \leq [y(s) + q^e(s)] z + b, \tag{8.9}$$

$$c \geq 0, \quad z' \in Z, \quad b' \in B. \tag{8.10}$$

Definition 8.1 *A recursive competitive equilibrium is a set of price functions $q^e : S \to \Re_{++}$ and $Q^1 : S \to \Re_{++}$ and a value function $v : Z \times B \times S \to \Re_+$ such that (i) given $q^e(s)$ and $Q^1(s)$, $v(z, b, s)$ solves the consumer's problem; (ii) markets clear.*

Notice that the price functions that the consumer takes as given are identical to the equilibrium price functions. This is the property of *rational expectations* which imposes a consistency between subjective beliefs about prices and the objective distributions for prices that arise in equilibrium.

Consider first the consumer's problem for given price behavior. Define the set $\mathcal{S} \equiv Z \times B \times S$. Let $C(\mathcal{S})$ denote the space of bounded, continuous functions $\{v : \mathcal{S} \to \Re_+\}$ equipped with the sup norm:

$$\|u\| \equiv \sup_{z, b, s \in \mathcal{S}} |u(z, b, s)| \quad \text{for any } u \in C(\mathcal{S}).$$

Proposition 8.1 *Under Assumptions 8.1 through 8.3, there exists a unique solution $v^* \in C(\mathcal{S})$ to the functional equation defined by Equation (8.8). The function v^* is concave, increasing in (z, b).*

PROOF

For $v \in \mathcal{C}(\mathcal{S})$, define the operator T by:

$$(Tv)(z, b, s) = \max_{c,z',b'} \left\{ U(c) + \beta \int_S v(z', b', s')F(s, ds') \right\}$$

subject to the constraints (8.9) and (8.10). Since $0 \leq c \leq y$, $z' \in \mathcal{Z}$ and $b' \in B$, the constraint set is compact. By Assumption 8.3, the utility function U is continuous in c and the function v is jointly continuous in (z, b, s) since $v \in \mathcal{C}(\mathcal{S})$. Hence, Tv involves maximizing a continuous function over a compact set so that it is well defined; that is, a maximum exists. Since $U(c)$ is bounded for $0 \leq c \leq y$ and $v(z', b', s')$ is bounded, the maximum function Tv is bounded and by the Theorem of the Maximum, it is continuous. Thus, T maps bounded, continuous functions into the same space, $T : \mathcal{C}(\mathcal{S}) \rightarrow \mathcal{C}(\mathcal{S})$.

Next, notice that T is monotone. Given any two functions $u \in \mathcal{C}(\mathcal{S})$, $w \in \mathcal{C}(\mathcal{S})$ such that $u(z, b, s) \geq w(z, b, s)$ for all $z, b, s \in \mathcal{S}$,

$$\int_S u(z', b', s')F(s, ds') \geq \int_S w(z', b', s')F(s, ds')$$

so that $(Tu)(z, b, s) \geq (Tw)(z, b, s)$. To verify discounting, for any constant a, notice that

$$\begin{aligned} T(v + a)(z, b, s) &= \max_{c,z',b'} \left\{ U(c) + \beta \int_S [v(z', b', s') + a]F(s, ds') \right\} \\ &= \max_{c,z',b'} \left\{ U(c) + \beta \int_S v(z', b', s')F(s, ds') \right\} + \beta a \\ &= (Tv)(z, b, s) + \beta a. \end{aligned}$$

Hence, T satisfies Blackwell's conditions for a contraction. Since $\mathcal{C}(\mathcal{S})$ is a complete, normed, linear space, the Contraction Mapping Theorem implies that T has a unique fixed point and $\lim_{n\to\infty} T^n v_0 = v^\star$ for any $v_0 \in \mathcal{C}(\mathcal{S})$.

To show that $v^\star$ is increasing, let $\mathcal{C}'(\mathcal{S})$ be the space of continuous, bounded, increasing, and concave real-valued functions defined on $\mathcal{S}$ equipped with the sup norm. Notice that $\mathcal{C}'(\mathcal{S})$ is a closed subset of $\mathcal{C}(\mathcal{S})$ and it is a complete, normed, linear space. Choose some $w \in \mathcal{C}'(\mathcal{S})$. Notice that for any $w(z_1, b, s) < w(z_2, b, s)$ for $z_1 < z_2$ implies $Tw(z_1, b, s) < Tw(z_2, b, s)$ and similarly for b.

To show that T preserves concavity, let (z_0, b_0) and (z_1, b_1) be given, let $0 \leq \theta \leq 1$, and define $z_\theta = \theta z_0 + (1 - \theta)z_1$ and $b_\theta = \theta b_0 + (1 - \theta)b_1$. Let (c_i, z_i', b_i') attain $(Tw)(z_i, b_i, s)$, $i = 0, 1$. Now, $(c_\theta, z_\theta', b_\theta')$ satisfies the budget constraint because (c_0, z_0', b_0') and (c_1, z_1', b_1') are both feasible. Therefore,

$$(Tw)(z_\theta, b_\theta, s) \geq U(c_\theta) + \beta \int_S w(z'_\theta, b'_\theta, s')F(s, ds')$$

$$\geq \theta U(c_0) + (1-\theta)U(c_1) + \theta\beta \int_S w(z'_0, b'_0, s')F(s, ds')$$

$$+ (1-\theta)\beta \int_S w(z'_1, b'_1, s')F(s, ds')$$

$$\geq \theta(Tw)(z_0, b_0, s) + (1-\theta)(Tw)(z_1, b_1, s).$$

The second line follows by the concavity of U and w while the third line follows since (c_i, z'_i, b'_i) attains $(Tw)(z_i, b_i, s)$ for $i = 0, 1$. Hence, $(Tw)(z, b, s)$ is concave in (z, b).

Because $\mathcal{C}'(\mathcal{S})$ is a closed subset of $\mathcal{C}(\mathcal{S})$ and we have shown that T is a contraction on $\mathcal{C}(\mathcal{S})$ (so that, for any initial guess $v^0 \in \mathcal{C}(\mathcal{S})$, repeated applications of T result in v^*), we can conclude that v^* is an element of $\mathcal{C}'(\mathcal{S})$. ∎

These results establish the existence of a solution to the consumer's problem, given the price functions q^e and Q^1. They also show that the value function is concave, increasing in shares and bond holdings. Intuitively, increases in number of shares and bonds increase the consumer's wealth and hence the maximum utility that can be achieved.

8.1.2. Asset-pricing functions

To derive further results about the nature of the price functions, consider the optimality conditions for this problem, given the fixed point v^*. Define v_z^* and v_b^* as the partial derivative of v^* with respect to z and b, respectively.[1] Let $\lambda(s)$ denote the Lagrange multiplier for the representative consumer's budget constraint. The first-order conditions with respect to c, z', and b' and envelope conditions with respect to z and b are given by:

$$U'(c) = \lambda(s) \tag{8.11}$$

$$q^e(s)\lambda(s) = \beta E_s[v_z(z', b', s')] \tag{8.12}$$

$$Q^1(s)\lambda(s) = \beta E_s[v_b(z', b', s')] \tag{8.13}$$

$$v_z(z, b, s) = U'(c)[y(s) + q^e(s)] \tag{8.14}$$

$$v_b(z, b, s) = U'(c). \tag{8.15}$$

[1] For a proof of the differentiability of the value function, see Lucas [317, pp. 1433–1434]. Benveniste and Scheinkman [56] have shown that under fairly general conditions the value function is *once* differentiable. For a further discussion of this issue, see Stokey and Lucas [418, pp. 84–85 and 266].

Define the policy functions $c^\star(z,b,s)$, $z^\star(z,b,s)$, and $b^\star(z,b,s)$ that are associated with the value function $v^\star(z,b,s)$. In equilibrium, $z'=1$, $b'=0$, and consumption equals output so that we need to determine the price functions such that the associated policy functions satisfy $c^\star(1,0,s)=y(s)$, $z^\star(1,0,s)=1$, and $b^\star(1,0,s)=0$. To determine these price functions, we study the first-order conditions together with the envelope conditions when markets clear as:

$$U'(y(s))q^e(s) = \beta \int_S U'(y(s'))[y(s') + q^e(s')]F(s,ds'), \tag{8.16}$$

$$U'(y(s))Q^1(s) = \beta \int_S U'(y(s'))F(s,ds'). \tag{8.17}$$

These equations are known as the intertemporal Euler equations and they are satisfied for the optimal choice of consumption and equity and bond holdings. Many recent tests of the consumption-based asset-pricing model have been based on such optimality conditions.

Notice that Equation (8.16) defines a functional equation for the unknown equity price $q^e(s)$. To complete the proof of the existence of a recursive competitive equilibrium, we need to show that given the consumer's value function v, there exists a unique solution for the equity price $q^e(s)$. Let $C_q(S)$ denote the space of bounded, continuous functions $\{\phi : S \to \Re_+\}$ equipped with the sup norm. Define the function $\gamma : S \to \Re_+$ by:

$$\gamma(s) \equiv \beta \int_S U'(y(s'))y(s')F(s,ds').$$

Instead of seeking a solution for the function $q^e(s)$, define the function $\phi(s) \equiv U'(y(s))q^e(s)$. Notice that $y(s)$ is exogenous and U is strictly increasing so that finding ϕ is equivalent to finding q^e. Notice that for any $\phi \in C_q(S)$, we can define an operator T_q from the right side of Equation (8.16) as:

$$(T_q\phi)(s) = \gamma(s) + \beta \int_S \phi(s')F(s,ds'). \tag{8.18}$$

We have the following proposition.

Proposition 8.2 *There is a unique, continuous and bounded solution $\phi^\star$ to $T_q\phi=\phi$. For any $\phi_0 \in C_q(S)$, $\lim_{n\to\infty} T_q^n\phi_0 = \phi^\star$.*

PROOF

The first expression on the right side of Equation (8.18) is non-negative since U is an increasing function and $y(s) > 0$ for all $s \in S$. Since $y(s)$ takes values in the compact set $\mathcal{Y}$ and U is continuous, we know that U is bounded. We first show that if U is bounded on $\mathcal{Y}$, then $\gamma(s)$ is bounded. By the concavity of U, we have

$$U(y) - U(0) \geq U'(y)(y - 0) = U'(y)y.$$

Thus, there exists a $\bar{U}$ such that $U'(y)y \leq \bar{U}$ for all $y \in \mathcal{Y}$, which implies that $\gamma(s) = \beta \int_S U'(y(s'))y(s')F(s, ds') \leq \beta\bar{U}$. Since ϕ is bounded, T_q maps bounded functions into bounded functions. Assumption 8.1 implies that both terms on the right side of Equation (8.18) are continuous. Thus, the operator T_q maps elements of the space of bounded, continuous functions into itself, $T_q : \mathcal{C}_q(S) \to \mathcal{C}_q(S)$.

Notice that T_q is monotone since given any $\psi \geq \phi$, $T_q\psi \geq T_q\phi$. For any constant a, notice that

$$\begin{aligned} T_q(\phi + a)(s) &= \gamma(s) + \beta \int_S [\phi(s') + a]F(s, ds') \\ &= (T_q\phi)(s) + \beta a \end{aligned}$$

so that T_q discounts. Thus, T_q satisfies Blackwell's conditions to be a contraction. Since $\mathcal{C}_q(S)$ is a complete normed, linear space, the Contraction Mapping Theorem implies that Equation (8.18) has a unique fixed point. ∎

Define the fixed point function by $\phi^\star$. The equilibrium equity price is determined as:

$$q^e(s) = \frac{\phi^\star(s)}{U'(y(s))}. \tag{8.19}$$

The pricing function in this model depends on consumers' attitudes toward risk, their rate of time preference, and the stochastic properties of output or consumption.

There are different methods for finding the unknown asset-pricing functions. In some cases, we can generate exact solutions for various asset prices under CRRA preferences and a joint log-normality assumption. We provide examples of this approach in Exercises 2 and 3. The method of *successive approximation* allows us to numerically compute the asset-pricing functions by making use of the contraction property underlying the asset-pricing equations. This approach can also be used in cash-in-advance type models to derive the form of the inverse velocity function, an issue that we describe in Chapter 13. We illustrate this method in the context of i.i.d. shocks for the random endowment.

Example 8.1 Independently and Identically Distributed Shocks

Let $\{y_t\}_{t=0}^{\infty}$ be a sequence of independent and identically distributed random variables with cumulative distribution function $\Phi(y)$ defined on the set Y. Recall that the equity price satisfies Equation (8.16). Under the assumption of i.i.d. shocks, this simplifies as

$$U'(y)q^e = \beta \int_Y \left[U'(y')(y' + (q^e)')d\Phi(y') \right].$$

To solve this equation for the unknown function q^e, define the new function $\bar{\phi}$ as

$$\bar{\phi} \equiv \beta E[y' U'(y')] \tag{8.20}$$

where $\bar{\phi}$ is a constant. Also define the mapping:

$$\phi_n(y) = (T_q \phi_{n-1})(y) = \bar{\phi} + \beta \int \phi_{n-1}(y') d\Phi(y'), \tag{8.21}$$

where $\phi(y) = U'(y)q^e$. In Proposition 8.2, we showed the mapping T_q is a contraction. Consequently, by the Contraction Mapping Theorem, repeated iterations on T_q will converge to the true solution for ϕ. Hence, beginning with $\phi_0(y) = 0$, consider

$$\phi_1(y) = (T_q \phi_0)(y) = \bar{\phi} + \beta \int 0 \cdot d\Phi(y') = \bar{\phi},$$

$$\phi_2(y) = (T_q \phi_1)(y) = \bar{\phi} + \beta \int \bar{\phi} d\Phi(y') = \bar{\phi}(1 + \beta)$$

$$\vdots = \vdots$$

$$\phi_n(y) = (T_q \phi_{n-1})(y) = \bar{\phi} + \beta \int \bar{\phi}(1 + \beta + \ldots \beta^{n-2}) d\Phi(y')$$

$$= \bar{\phi} \sum_{i=0}^{n-1} \beta^i.$$

Notice that we can also write $\phi_n(y) = (T_q^{n-1} \phi_0)(y)$. Thus, letting $n \to \infty$, we have

$$\phi^*(y) = \lim_{n \to \infty} (T_q^{n-1} \phi_0)(y)$$

$$= \lim_{n \to \infty} \bar{\phi} \sum_{i=0}^{n-1} \beta^i = \bar{\phi}/(1 - \beta).$$

Using the definition of ϕ^*, the solution for the equity price can be obtained as $U'(y)q^e = \bar{\phi}/(1 - \beta)$ or

$$U'(y)q^e = \frac{\beta}{1 - \beta} E[y' U'(y')]. \tag{8.22}$$

We can use this solution to determine how the equity price varies with current output. For this purpose, totally differentiate both sides of Equation (8.22) as

$$U''(y)q^e dy + U'(y)dq^e = \frac{\beta}{1-\beta} dE[y' U'(y')] = 0$$

since $E[y' U'(y')]$ is independent of y. Thus,

$$\frac{dq^e y}{dy q^e} = -\frac{U''(y)y}{U'(y)}. \tag{8.23}$$

This expression shows that the elasticity of the equity price with respect to output depends on the consumer's relative risk aversion. If the utility function is of the constant relative risk aversion variety, then this elasticity is also constant. Otherwise, the response of the equity price to current changes in output will reflect changes in the consumer's degree of risk aversion.

8.1.3. Risk premia

Define the (gross) real return on the equity by

$$r_{t+1} \equiv (q^e_{t+1} + y_{t+1})/q^e_t.$$

Define the intertemporal marginal rate of substitution (MRS) in consumption between periods t and $t+1$ evaluated at the equilibrium quantities as

$$m_{t+1} = \beta \frac{U'(y_{t+1})}{U'(y_t)}. \tag{8.24}$$

Reverting to time subscripts in Equation (8.16), the real return on the equity satisfies

$$1 = E_t\left[m_{t+1} r_{t+1}\right], \tag{8.25}$$

where $E_t(\cdot)$ denotes expectation conditional on s_t. Similarly, the bond price is given by:

$$Q^1_t = E_t\left[m_{t+1}\right]. \tag{8.26}$$

These conditions show that the intertemporal marginal rate of substitution (MRS) in consumption for the representative consumer is used to price payoffs on all securities traded in this economy. Using our earlier definition, we denote this MRS as the stochastic discount factor.

Recall that the bond is a security that guarantees a sure unit of output in each period. Hence, we can define the (gross) risk-free return as

$$r^1_t = \frac{1}{Q^1_t} = \frac{1}{E_t(m_{t+1})}. \tag{8.27}$$

Thus, the risk-free return is equal to the inverse of expected value of the stochastic discount factor or the intertemporal marginal rate of substitution in consumption (MRS). If the MRS is high (so that consumption is low in period $t+1$ relative to period t), then consumers will still choose to save in equilibrium by holding the risk-free asset even if the real interest rate is low. By contrast, if the MRS is low (so that consumption is high in period $t+1$ relative to period t), then the real interest rate must be high to induce consumers to undertake any saving in period t.

Using a covariance decomposition, we can rewrite Equation (8.25) as:

$$E_t(r_{t+1}) = r_t^{\mathrm{I}}\left[1 - \mathrm{Cov}_t\left(m_{t+1}, r_{t+1}\right)\right]. \qquad (8.28)$$

We can use the expressions in Equation (8.28) to evaluate the *conditional equity premium* defined as:

$$E_t(r_{t+1}) - r_t^{\mathrm{I}} = -r_t^{\mathrm{I}}\mathrm{Cov}_t\left(m_{t+1}, r_{t+1}\right). \qquad (8.29)$$

This equation relates the excess expected return on a risky asset relative to the risk-free return to the covariance between the stochastic discount factor and the gross return on the risky asset. The right side of this expression is the *risk premium*.

How is the risk premium determined in the model with the stochastic discount factor? Notice that for the risk premium to be positive, we need $Cov_t(m_{t+1}, r_{t+1}) < 0$. Thus, the risk premium for an asset is positive if the random return on the asset r_{t+1} covaries negatively with the stochastic discount factor m_{t+1}, which is defined as the intertemporal marginal rate of substitution (MRS) in consumption. Hence, the notion of risk implied by Equation (8.29) states that it is the covariance of returns with future consumption that is important. This is the concept of riskiness suggested by Breeden [74]. Since the relevant pricing function that we have derived depends on the MRS in consumption, this asset-pricing model is referred to as the *consumption-based capital asset pricing (C-CAPM) model.*

In this model, we say that an asset is *risky* if for states of nature in which returns are low, the intertemporal marginal rate of substitution in consumption m_{t+1} is high. Since m_{t+1} will be high if future consumption is low, a risky asset is one which yields low returns in states for which consumers also have low consumption. To ensure that consumers are willing to hold such a risky asset, it must have an expected return that is higher than that of the risk-free asset, which has the same return in *all* states of nature. According to the C-CAPM, an *ideal* risky asset is one which pays a high return when consumption (or income) is low and future marginal utility is high. This asset would then provide insurance against bad income shocks. Such an asset would have a return whose covariance with the intertemporal MRS is low or even positive. Thus, the consumer would even be willing to incur a cost to hold such an asset in order to take advantage of its insurance properties. Notice also that the volatility of the asset ($\mathrm{Var}(r_{t+1})$) is not the quantity that gets "priced" in the asset-pricing formula. Rather it is its *covariance* with the intertemporal MRS. An asset that has a large idiosyncratic component that is uncorrelated with the intertemporal MRS would have only its "systematic" component priced in equilibrium.

A joint log-normality assumption

In certain situations, we can obtain a more convenient representation of asset-pricing relations under a joint log-normality assumption. We illustrate the basic approach, and employ versions of it in different applications to follow.

A random variable X is said to be log-normally distributed if $\ln(X)$ follows a normal distribution with mean μ and variance σ^2. If $\ln(X)$ is distributed as $N(\mu, \sigma^2)$ then the expected value and variance of X are given by

$$E(X) = \exp(\mu + \sigma^2/2),$$

$$Var(X) = \exp(2\mu + 2\sigma^2) - \exp(2\mu + \sigma^2).$$

The basic asset-pricing equation is given by

$$E_t[M_{t+1}R_{t+1}] = 1, \tag{8.30}$$

where M_{t+1} is the intertemporal MRS. Under the joint log-normality assumption, $M_{t+1} \equiv \ln(M_{t+1})$ and $r_{t+1} = \ln R_{t+1}$ are jointly normally distributed. [Note that $\ln(1+r_{t+1}) \approx r_{t+1}$ for small r_{t+1}.] Let $X_{t+1} = M_{t+1}R_{t+1}$. Then $\ln(X_{t+1}) = m_{t+1} + r_{t+1}$. Thus

$$E_t[\ln(X_{t+1})] = E_t(m_{t+1}) + E_t(r_{t+1})$$

and

$$Var_t[\ln(X_{t+1})] = Var_t(m_{t+1}) + Var_t(r_{t+1}) + 2Cov_t(m_{t+1}, r_{t+1}).$$

Therefore, the asset-pricing equation can be written as

$$E_t(X_{t+1}) = \exp\left[E_t(m_{t+1}) + E_t(r_{t+1}) + \frac{1}{2}Var_t(m_{t+1}) + \frac{1}{2}Var_t(r_{t+1}) + Cov_t(m_{t+1}, r_{t+1})\right] = 1.$$

Take the natural logarithm of both sides to obtain:

$$E_t(m_{t+1}) + E_t(r_{t+1}) + \frac{1}{2}Var_t(m_{t+1}) + \frac{1}{2}Var_t(r_{t+1}) + Cov_t(m_{t+1}, r_{t+1}) = 0. \tag{8.31}$$

This is the equation that we obtain under the joint log-normality assumption for intertemporal MRS and asset returns. The conditional variance of the intertemporal MRS and returns appears because of the Jensen effect. [The Jensen effect is due to the fact that $E[f(x)] \neq f[E(x)]$ unless $f(x)$ is linear.]

This equation is valid for all assets. Thus, let $r_{t+1} = r_t^f$. Then Equation (8.31) becomes:

$$E_t(m_{t+1}) + r_t^f + \frac{1}{2} Var_t(m_{t+1}) = 0.$$

Solving for r_t^f yields $r_t^f = -E_t(m_{t+1}) - \frac{1}{2} Var_t(m_{t+1})$. Substitute this back into Equation (8.31) to obtain:

$$E_t(r_{t+1}) - r_t^f + \frac{1}{2} Var_t(r_{t+1}) = -Cov_t(m_{t+1}, r_{t+1}). \tag{8.32}$$

This expression says that the expected excess return plus the variance of returns (due to the Jensen effect) equals the risk premium.

The intertemporal MRS or the stochastic discount factor (SDF) is given by

$$M_{t+1} = \frac{\beta U'(c_{t+1})}{U'(c_t)}. \tag{8.33}$$

We cannot evaluate the SDF unless we make specific assumptions about the utility functions. However, we can use a first-order Taylor approximation of $U'(c_{t+1})$ about c_t to obtain a linear expression for M_{t+1}. It is worth noting that this is a useful method for obtaining *log-linear pricing equations*. We will illustrate this approach in the next chapter when we consider preferences that are non-separable over time or states.

Using the first-order Taylor series approximation, we obtain:

$$U'(c_{t+1}) \approx U'(c_t) + U''(c_t)(c_{t+1} - c_t). \tag{8.34}$$

This yields:

$$\begin{aligned} M_{t+1} &\approx \beta \frac{[U'(c_t) + U''(c_t)(c_{t+1} - c_t)]}{U'(c_t)} \\ &= \beta \left[1 + \frac{U''(c_t) c_t}{U'(c_t)} \frac{\Delta c_{t+1}}{c_t} \right] \\ &\approx \beta [1 - CRRA_t \Delta \ln (c_{t+1})]. \end{aligned} \tag{8.35}$$

Using the fact that $\beta = 1/(1+\rho)$ and taking the logarithm of both sides of the above expression yields

$$\begin{aligned} \ln (M_{t+1}) &= -\ln (1+\rho) + \ln (1 - CRRA_t \Delta \ln (c_{t+1})) \\ &\approx -\left[\rho + CRRA_t \Delta \ln (c_{t+1}) \right]. \end{aligned} \tag{8.36}$$

Thus, the intertemporal CAPM implies that the stochastic discount factor depends on consumption growth rate $\Delta \ln(c_{t+1})$. Using the expression for the risk premium in Equation (8.32) implied by the log-normal model, the excess return on the risky asset relative to the risk-free asset is given by

$$E_t(r_{t+1} - r_t^f) + \frac{1}{2} Var_t(r_{t+1}) = CRRA_t Cov_t \left[\Delta \ln(c_{t+1}), r_{t+1} \right]. \quad (8.37)$$

This relation implies that the greater the correlation between consumption growth and the risky return, the higher the risk premium, e.g. low returns are associated with lower future consumption growth.

An alternative way of giving content to the asset pricing relation summarized by (8.31) is to assume that the logarithm of the intertemporal MRS is a linear function of some known state variables plus a random error term. The Vasicek [437] model is an example of this approach which assumes a normally distributed, homoscedastic error term to the intertemporal MRS. The Cox, Ingersoll, and Ross [128] model modifies the Vasicek model by assuming that the variance of the error term is conditionally heteroscedastic. These models are widely used for empirically characterizing the term structure of interest rates, a topic that we discuss below.

8.1.4. Volatility bounds for intertemporal MRSs

Suppose that we would like to further characterize the behavior of the risk premium. Notice that the risk premium depends on the conditional covariance of the intertemporal MRS and assets returns. The intertemporal MRS is, in general, an unknown function unless we are willing to make further assumptions about the form of preferences. Likewise, the conditional covariance depends on the joint distribution for the intertemporal MRS and assets returns.

In the earlier literature, asset pricing was typically phrased in terms of restrictions for investors' portfolios. However, the modern theory of asset pricing is based on the behavior of the intertemporal marginal rate of substitution (MRS) for consumption. Recently Hansen and Jagannathan [232] have shown how the restrictions of alternative asset-pricing models may be examined by constructing a *mean-variance frontier* for intertemporal MRSs. This mean-variance frontier is related to the mean-variance frontier for asset returns derived by Chamberlain and Rothschild [100]. The following derivation assumes that there are no short sales constraints, transactions costs, and other frictions. Volatility bounds with such frictions are studied by Luttmer [327] and He and Modest [246].

In our previous analysis, we showed that the expected return on a risky asset in excess of the risk-free return is given by

$$E_t(r_{t+1} - r_t^f) = -r_t^f Cov_t(m_{t+1}, r_{t+1}).$$

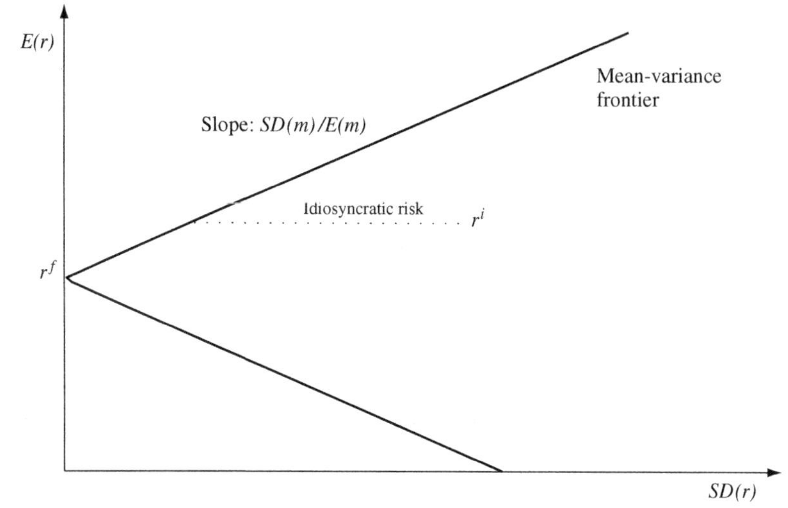

Figure 8.1. Mean-variance frontier for MRSs

However, using the definition of the correlation coefficient between m_{t+1} and r_{t+1}, $\rho_t(m_{t+1}, r_{t+1})$, we can express

$$Cov_t(m_{t+1}, r_{t+1})^2 = \rho_t^2(m_{t+1}, r_{t+1}) Var_t(m_{t+1}) Var_t(r_{t+1}).$$

Hence,

$$E_t(r_{t+1}) = r_t^f - \rho_t(m_{t+1}, r_{t+1}) \frac{SD_t(m_{t+1})}{E(m_{t+1})} SD_t(r_{t+1}), \tag{8.38}$$

where $SD_t(X_t)$ denotes the conditional standard deviation of X_t. Since $-1 \leq \rho_t(m_{t+1}, r_{t+1}) \leq 1$,

$$-\frac{SD_t(m_{t+1})}{E_t(m_{t+1})} \leq \frac{E_t(r_{t+1} - r_t^f)}{SD_t(r_{t+1})} \leq \frac{SD_t(m_{t+1})}{E_t(m_{t+1})}, \tag{8.39}$$

Figure 8.1 graphs the relation in Equation (8.38) in $E(r), SD(r)$ space.

This figure shows that the means and standard deviations of all asset returns must lie in the wedge-shaped area. The boundary of this area is known as the *mean-variance frontier*. The slope of the frontier is given by the ratio $SD_t(m_{t+1})/E(m_{t+1})$. All asset returns on the frontier satisfy the relation $|\rho_t(m_{t+1}, r_{t+1})| = 1$. Hence, they are perfectly correlated with the intertemporal MRS. Assets that lie on the upper portion of the frontier are risky assets in that their covariance with the intertemporal MRS is negative. Thus, their expected return exceeds the risk-free rate. Assets that lie on the lower portion of the frontier have returns that are positively correlated with the intertemporal MRS. Thus, they provide insurance against low consumption states and have expected returns that are less than the risk-free rate.[2] We can also consider assets that lie in the interior of the wedge-shaped region. Notice that an asset that has the same mean for a greater standard deviation contains idiosyncratic risk. We argued earlier that it is only the part of risk that is correlated with the intertemporal MRS, namely, the systematic part of risk, that gets priced in equilibrium. Hence, the idiosyncratic risk is just the horizontal distance between the frontier return and the actual return. The frontier returns have the property that they *span* the space of all mean-variance efficient returns. Also, all frontier returns are perfectly correlated with each other since they are perfectly correlated with the discount factor. Hence, any frontier return can be generated at the linear combination of the frontier return and the risk-free asset (which also lies on the mean-variance frontier). Suppose r^m lies on the mean-variance frontier. Then all frontier returns must satisfy:

$$r^{\phi,m} = r^f + a(r^m - r^f)$$

for some a. Since the discount factor m is perfectly correlated with each point on the mean-variance frontier, the discount factor itself may be generated from any frontier return and the risk-free rate. Since the stochastic discount factor is used to price any asset, mean-variance efficient returns contain all information that is relevant for pricing any asset.

Using the relation in Equation (8.39), it is also true that

$$SD_t(m_{t+1}) \geq \left[\frac{E_t(r_{t+1} - r_t^f)}{SD_t(r_{t+1})} \right] \frac{1}{r_t^f} \tag{8.40}$$

where the quantity

$$\frac{E_t(r_{t+1} - r_t^f)}{SD_t(r_{t+1})}$$

is known as the *Sharpe ratio* for asset returns. To understand this quantity, consider an investment strategy where you borrow money at the risk-free rate and invest in the risky security. The mean return on your investment increases but so does the standard deviation. Hence, the Sharpe ratio remains constant. Returning to Equation (8.40), we find that the standard deviation of the intertemporal MRS must be at least as great as a quantity that is proportional to the Sharpe ratio for risky assets. Recall that the stochastic discount factor m_{t+1} is not observable unless we make additional assumptions on consumers' utility functions. The bounds that we obtained in (8.39) and (8.40) can be used to characterize the stochastic behavior of m_{t+1} without specifying an explicit utility function.

[2] For a similar discussion with N risky assets and a risk-free asset, see Exercise 2 in Chapter 4.

8.1.5. The "equity premium puzzle"

The behavior of the observed equity premium has been studied by Mehra and Prescott [341], among others. These authors assume CRRA preferences and growing endowment to determine if a representative consumer model can generate an average equity premium that matches the average equity premium observed in the data. The mean-variance frontier for intertemporal MRSs allows a clear statement of the "equity premium puzzle."

Recall that the relation in Equation (8.40) places a lower bound on the standard deviation of the stochastic discount factor. Consider the model with time-separable preferences and power utility function. Suppose also that consumption growth is distributed as i.i.d. log-normal with $E[\ln(c_{t+1}/c_t)] = g$ and $Var[\ln(c_{t+1}/c_t)] = \sigma^2$. The intertemporal MRS is given by:

$$m_{t+1} = \beta \left(\frac{c_{t+1}}{c_t} \right)^{-\gamma}.$$

Using the formula for m_{t+1}, we can express the Hansen-Jagannathan bounds for the intertemporal MRS as:

$$\begin{aligned} \frac{E_t(r_{t+1} - r_t^f)}{SD_t(r_{t+1})} &\leq \frac{SD_t(m_{t+1})}{E_t(m_{t+1})} \\ &= \frac{[\exp(-2\gamma g + 2\gamma^2\sigma^2) - \exp(-2\gamma g + \gamma^2\sigma^2)]^{1/2}}{\exp(-\gamma g + \gamma^2\sigma^2/2)} \\ &= [\exp(\gamma^2\sigma^2 - 1)]^{1/2} \approx \gamma\sigma. \end{aligned} \tag{8.41}$$

Mehra and Prescott estimated the annual rate of return on the Standard and Poor's composite stock index for the 1889–1978 period to have mean 9.8% and standard deviation 16.54%. Likewise, they estimated the mean annual return on a relatively risk-free security to be around 1%, and the mean of the annual growth rate of per capita consumption for nondurables and services for the years 1889–1978 to be 1.83% with a standard deviation of 3.57% for the US economy. Substituting these values in the above relation, we obtain a Sharpe ratio (the left side of the above relation) of 0.3636. Substituting for the remaining values and solving for the value of the risk aversion parameter γ that satisfies the inequality in Equation (8.41) yields:

$$0.3636 \leq 0.0357\gamma \quad \Leftrightarrow \quad 10.186 \leq \gamma.$$

Thus, we find that the coefficient of relative risk aversion must be at least 10 for the volatility bound implied by the time-separable model to hold. This is the equity premium "puzzle," that is, the return on equity relative to the return on the risk-free rate can be reconciled in a representative consumer model with a time-separable utility specification only for high values of the risk aversion parameter γ.

For the CRRA utility function, the coefficient of intertemporal substitution is the inverse of the coefficient of relative risk aversion.[3] Thus, a high value of γ (which is needed to reconcile the equity premium puzzle) implies that the risk-free rate will be very high unless the value of β is set to be greater than unity. Using the expression for the risk-free rate, we have that

$$r_t^f = \frac{1}{\beta \exp(-\gamma g + \gamma^2 \sigma^2 / 2)}.$$

For example, with a $\gamma = 10$, we need a $\beta = 1.115$ to get a real interest rate of 1% (or $r_t^f = 1.01$). To understand this result, notice that a high value of γ implies that individuals are not willing to intertemporally substitute consumption. Thus, it is difficult to reconcile positive consumption growth with a low value of the real interest rate – unless consumers are also very patient. This is known as the "risk-free rate puzzle." In both cases, the problem arises from the fact that the variablity of non-durable consumption expenditures plus services is too low relative to stock return variability. Hence, a high relative risk-aversion parameter is necessary to make the smoothness of consumption expenditures consistent with the historical equity premium. Cochrane [109] and Campbell and Cochrane [93] show that for a shorter post-war sample of 50 years for the US, real stock returns have been around 9% with a standard deviation of 16% while the return on Treasury bills has been around 1%. This leads to a Sharpe ratio of 0.50. Likewise, the mean and standard deviation of aggregate consumption expenditures on non-durables and services have both been around 1%. Under these assumptions, the value of the risk aversion parameter that satisfies the volatility bound is around 50. For this value of γ, the value of the discount factor that satisfies the expression for the real risk-free rate is also much greater than unity.

The "equity premium puzzle" has led to a wide variety of studies seeking to explain it. One possible resolution is to drop the assumption of time-additive preferences in favor of preferences displaying habit persistence, consumption durability, or to assume a version of non-expected utility. We describe such preferences in the next chapter. An alternative direction is to introduce another source of uncertainty such as inflation risk. We study the role of inflation risk in Chapter 13. Another possible resolution is to assume that agents are heterogeneous and subject to borrowing constraints, limiting their ability to smooth consumption. There are several

[3] See Chapter 5.

other explanations that have been offered to explain this puzzle. We discuss potential resolutions of the "equity premium puzzle" in subsequent chapters.

8.2. PRICING ALTERNATIVE ASSETS

In actual capital markets, we observe many other types of assets being traded, including derivative instruments such as options, futures contracts, and forward contracts. We begin by describing the pricing of risk-free debt instruments and by defining some of the returns and premiums that are associated.

8.2.1. *Discount bonds and the yield curve*

The simplest type of debt instrument is a zero-coupon discount bond, which we defined above. This type of bond pays a fixed amount, which we assume is one unit of the consumption good, at some maturity date, and there are no coupons paid before the maturity date. Because there are no payments made to the bondholder before the maturity date, the bond sells for a real price that is below the real amount paid at the maturity date, or the bond sells at a discount. We can also price a coupon bond, which pays a coupon of c at regular intervals and the principal at maturity. Likewise, we could introduce a perpetuity or consol bond, which is a coupon bond with an infinite maturity date. There are many other types of debt instruments traded in actual capital markets.[4]

We now determine the prices for a variety of maturity lengths of zero-coupon discount bonds that are risk free. The household's initial wealth consists of the endowment and its portfolio of discount bonds $b_{j,t}$, where $b_{j,t}$ denotes the number of bonds held at the beginning of period t that mature in j periods and pay one unit of the endowment at time $t+j$ and Q_t^j is the price of a bond at time t which will mature in j periods. The agent's real wealth constraint at the beginning of period t is:

$$c_t + \sum_{j=1}^{N} b_{j,t+1} Q_t^j \leq y_t + \sum_{j=0}^{N-1} b_{j+1,t} Q_t^j,$$

where N is the longest maturity issue and $Q_t^0 = 1$. We assume that the discount bonds are in zero net supply so that, in equilibrium, $b_{j,t+1} = 0$

[4] These are typically differentiated in terms of default risk, convertibility provisions (providing the option to convert to another financial instrument), call provisions (allowing debt to be paid off before the maturity date), and other features.

for all j and t. We also have that $c_t = y_t$ so that the equilibrium first-order conditions with respect to bond holdings $b_{j,t+1}$ are:

$$U'(y_t)Q_t^j = \beta E_t\left[U'(y_{t+1})Q_{t+1}^{j-1}\right], \quad j = 1, \ldots, N. \tag{8.42}$$

Re-write this condition as

$$Q_t^j = \beta E_t\left[\frac{U'(y_{t+1})}{U'(y_t)}Q_{t+1}^{j-1}\right].$$

Define

$$m_{t,\tau} = \beta^\tau\left[\frac{U'(y_{t+\tau})}{U'(y_t)}\right]$$

as the intertemporal MRS between periods t and τ. Substituting recursively in this condition, we can express the equilibrium price of an indexed discount bond maturing in τ periods by:

$$Q_t^\tau = E_t[m_{t,\tau}], \quad \tau = 1, \ldots, N \tag{8.43}$$

where we have used the fact that $Q_t^0 = 1$. Define the real return on this bond as $r_t^\tau \equiv 1/Q_t^\tau$.

The returns to the bonds at various maturity dates are not directly comparable because the number of periods over which the bond is held is not the same. One way to make the returns comparable is to compute the yield to maturity, i_t^τ, and a particularly convenient way to do this is to define the continuously compounded yield:

$$i_t^\tau = -\frac{1}{\tau}\log Q_t^\tau. \tag{8.44}$$

Given the price Q_t^τ, the yield to maturity i_t^τ at time t on a discount bond maturing τ periods later is the steady rate at which the price should increase if the bond is to be worth one unit of output at $t+\tau$. Thus, i_t^τ satisfies the relation $Q_t^\tau \exp(-\tau i_t^\tau) = 1.00$, which yields Equation (8.44). An alternative method is to define the yield as

$$i_t^\tau = (Q_t^\tau)^{-\frac{1}{\tau}}. \tag{8.45}$$

By defining the yield for bonds of various maturities, we can construct a *yield curve* or *term structure* by varying τ. The *slope* of the yield curve (or the yield spread) is $i_t^\tau - i_t^{\tau-1}$.

We can also derive the prices of *forward contracts* on pure-discount bonds of various maturities. A forward contract on a τ-period pure-discount bond to be delivered at date $t+n$ where $n \leq \tau$ is an agreement to buy or sell the bond at that date, which is called the *maturity date.* We denote the price at date t of such a forward contract by $F_{t,n}^\tau$, which is called the *delivery price.* At the time the contract matures, an agent holding the contract must buy or sell the bond at the delivery price. Entering into a forward contract at date t which is to be delivered at some time in the future has no effect on the agent's time t budget constraint. If the agent must deliver the bond (so he has a short position), then he must purchase the bond at the current spot price. He profits if the spot price is less than the delivery price. Similarly, the agent in the long position is obligated to purchase the bond at the delivery price. He profits if the spot price is greater than the delivery price. The net profit of the short and long positions is zero.

The spot price on the bond at time $t+n$ is $Q_{t+n}^{\tau-n}$. The payoff on a *long position* in a forward contract on one unit of the discount bond at time $t+n$ is

$$Q_{t+n}^{\tau-n} - F_{t,n}^{\tau}.$$

In equilibrium, the expected discounted present value of that payoff is equal to zero, or

$$0 = E_t\left[m_{t,n}(Q_{t+n}^{\tau-n} - F_{t,n}^{\tau})\right]. \tag{8.46}$$

Notice that the equilibrium delivery price satisfies

$$F_{t,n}^{\tau} = E_t(m_{t,n})^{-1}E_t(m_{t,n}Q_{t+n}^{\tau-n}) = Q_t^{\tau}/Q_t^{n}, \tag{8.47}$$

where we have made use of Equations (8.42) and (8.43) to obtain the second equality. Notice also that $F_{t,n}^{\tau}$ and $m_{t,n}$ are independent because the forward price $F_{t,n}^{\tau}$ is determined at time t.

The forward price provides information about the expected spot price. To see this, use Equation (8.47) and the conditional covariance decomposition to express the forward rate as:

$$\begin{aligned}
F_{t,\tau-1}^{\tau} &= E_t(m_{t,\tau-1})^{-1}E_t(m_{t,\tau-1}Q_{t+\tau-1}^{1}) \\
&= E_t(m_{t,\tau-1})^{-1}\left[Cov_t(m_{t,\tau-1}Q_{t+\tau-1}^{1}) + E_t(m_{t,\tau-1})E_t(Q_{t+\tau-1}^{1})\right] \\
&= r_t^{\tau-1}\mathrm{Cov}_t\left(m_{t,\tau-1}, Q_{t+\tau-1}^{1}\right) + E_t(Q_{t+\tau-1}^{1}).
\end{aligned} \tag{8.48}$$

Clearly, if the conditional covariance between the marginal utility at time $t+\tau-1$ and the spot price at time $t+\tau-1$ is positive (negative), then the forward price is greater than (less than) the expected spot price. The *forward premium* is defined as the difference between the expected spot price and the forward price, or

$$E_t(Q_{t+\tau-1}^{1}) - F_{t,\tau-1}^{\tau}$$

so that the forward premium is the negative of the conditional covariance times $r_t^{\tau-1}$ in Equation (8.48).[5]

[5] This is the premium in the forward price. The premium on the implied return is $1/F_{t,\tau-1}^{\tau} - E_t(r_{t+\tau-1}^{1})$, where r^1 is the spot return. Notice that if the conditional covariance in Equation (8.48)

We now turn to the one-period expected *holding return*. This is the expected return to holding a bond for one period and then selling it in the secondary market. The (gross) return to holding a bond maturing in τ periods for one period and selling is:

$$h^{\tau}_{t+1} \equiv Q^{\tau-1}_{t+1}/Q^{\tau}_{t}. \tag{8.49}$$

From the first-order condition and using the conditional covariance decomposition, the expected one-period holding return satisfies

$$E_t(h^{\tau}_{t+1}) - r^1_t = -r^1_t \text{Cov}_t(m_{t,1}, h^{\tau}_{t+1})$$

where r^1_t is the certain return on a one-period bond. If the conditional covariance is non-zero, then there exists a *term risk premium*. Since the real payoff to the one-period bond is certain, this bond provides a convenient benchmark for measuring riskiness. A bond is risky relative to the benchmark bond if its risk premium is positive. Since the risk premium is proportional to the conditional covariance between the MRS and the bond's return, this measure of riskiness refers to the usefulness of the payoff in smoothing consumption over time. If a payoff is high when next period's consumption is high (so that $m_{t,1}$ is low), then the covariance is negative and the risk premium is positive because the bond is a poor instrument for smoothing consumption over time.

The (gross) return to holding a bond maturing in τ periods for n periods and selling is:

$$h^{\tau}_{t+n} \equiv Q^{\tau-n}_{t+n}/Q^{\tau}_{t} \quad \text{for } 0 < n < \tau. \tag{8.50}$$

This satisfies the relation:

$$1 = E_t\left(m_{t,n} h^{\tau}_{t+n}\right), \quad 0 < n < \tau.$$

Using the conditional covariance decomposition, we have

$$E_t(h^{\tau}_{t+n}) - r^n_t = -r^n_t \text{Cov}_t\left(m_{t,n}, h^{\tau}_{t+n}\right), \tag{8.51}$$

where once again, if the conditional covariance on the right side is zero, then expected holding returns on all assets are equalized. Otherwise, there exists a term risk premium and this premium depends on the holding period n as well as the time to maturity τ. We discuss the implications of real and nominal equilibrium asset-pricing models in reconciling the observations on the term structure of interest rates in Chapter 13.

is zero, then the forward premium on the return is negative because of Jensen's inequality. Hence, in the case where the covariance is negative, there may be some indeterminacy about the sign of the premium.

Expectations theory of the term structure
A long-standing hypothesis about the way interest rates of different maturities are determined is given by the *expectations theory* of the term structure of interest rates. This theory says that the slope of the term structure or yield curve depends on changing expectations for future interest rates. Loosely speaking, downward-sloping term structures are taken to indicate expectations of a decline in interest rates and upward-sloping ones of a rise. Shiller [399] describes empirical evidence that has been obtained on the term premium. Many of these tests assume that term risk premia are constant.

To provide a simple derivation of the expectations hypothesis, consider an investment strategy of rolling over a sequence of one-period bonds over n periods. Proceeding analogously as above, the return on this strategy is

$$h_{t+n} \equiv \frac{1}{Q_t^1}\frac{1}{Q_{t+1}^1}\cdots\frac{1}{Q_{t+n-1}^1}. \tag{8.52}$$

This return satisfies the condition:

$$1 = E_t\left(m_{t,n}h_{t+n}\right). \tag{8.53}$$

Using a covariance decomposition,

$$r_t^n = E_t\left[h_{t+n}\right] + r_t^n Cov_t(m_{t,n}h_{t+n}), \tag{8.54}$$

where $r_t^n = 1/E_t(m_{t,n})$. Suppose that the term risk premium is zero, that is, $r_t^n Cov_t(m_{t,n}h_{t+n}) = 0$. Then the return on a n-period bond can be written as:

$$\begin{aligned} r_t^n &= E_t\left[h_{t+n}\right] \\ &= E_t\left[\frac{1}{Q_t^1}\frac{1}{Q_{t+1}^1}\cdots\frac{1}{Q_{t+n-1}^1}\right] \\ &= r_t^1 E_t(r_{t+1}^1\cdots r_{t+n-1}^1), \end{aligned} \tag{8.55}$$

where we have made use of the fact that $(Q_{t+i}^1)^{-1} = r_{t+i}^1$. To further simplify this expression, note that $\ln(r_t^h) = \ln(1+\tilde{r}_t^h) \approx \tilde{r}_t^h$ where $\tilde{r}_t^h$ is the *net* real interest rate.

We derive a linear pricing relationship by making an assumption that can be used in a variety of contexts. This is the *joint log-normality assumption*. Specifically, we assume that conditional on information at date t, the one-period interest rates $r_{t+1}^i, i = 1, \ldots, n$ are jointly log-normally distributed. Define the constant conditional variances and covariances of the net one-period interest rates as:

$$\sigma_i^2 \equiv Var_t(\tilde{r}^1_{t+i})$$

$$\sigma_{ij} \equiv Cov_t(\tilde{r}^1_{t+i}, \tilde{r}^1_{t+j}), \quad i \neq j.$$

Now evaluate the expectation in (8.55) as:

$$E_t\left[\prod_{i=1}^{n-1} r^1_{t+i}\right] = \exp\left[\sum_{i=1}^{n-1}(E_t\tilde{r}^1_{t+i} + \sigma_i^2/2) + \sum_{i,j=1,i\neq j}^{n-1} \sigma_{ij}\right].$$

Taking logarithms of both sides of (8.55) then yields

$$\tilde{r}^n_t - \tilde{r}^1_t = \sum_{i=1}^{n-1} E_t(\tilde{r}^1_{t+i}) + \bar{r}, \tag{8.56}$$

where $\bar{r} = \sum_{i=1}^{n-1}\sigma_i^2/2 + \sum_{i,j=1,i\neq j}^{n-1}\sigma_{ij}$. This relation says that the spread between the current long- and short-term rates should predict future changes in the short-term rate. Let us illustrate this relation with a simple example. Let $\tilde{r}^2_t$ denote the current yield on a two-year bond and similarly, $\tilde{r}^1_t$ the current yield on a one-year bond. The expectations theory predicts that the spread between the one-year and the two-year bonds should be equal to the expectation of the yield on the one-year bond next period, $E_0(\tilde{r}^1_{t+1})$ plus some constant. If the expectations theory holds, then the current yield on the two-year bond should be determined by the average of returns on the current and future short-term bonds.

Campbell and Shiller [97], Fama and Bliss [179], and others have used different econometric methods in order to test the empirical validity of the expectations theory. In most of these studies, the expectations theory of the term structure is statistically rejected, but some of them find evidence on the predictive power of the spread between long- and short-term rates for future interest rate movements. Fama and Bliss [179] showed that when the short-term yield is one year, as the maturity of the long-term yield increases, the forecasting power of the term structure improves. Shiller, Campbell, and Schoenholtz [400] used bonds with maturity less than a year and found that the spread between 3- and 6-month Treasury bill rates helps to forecast the change in the 3-month bill rate. Finally, Campbell and Shiller [97] find that for different pairs of long- and short-term yields, varying from one month to ten years, a relatively high spread is followed by rising short-term interest rates over the life of the long-term bond, in accordance with the expectations theory. On the other hand, they show that the yield on the long-term bond tends to fall over the life of the short-term bond, which is in contradiction to the predictions of the expectations theory.

8.2.2. *Pricing derivative instruments*

A derivative security has a value that depends on other underlying securities such as forward contracts, stocks, and bonds. We examine just a few of the derivative securities that are now traded in the market.[6]

We begin by describing options pricing. There are two types of options:

- The *call option* gives the holder the right to buy the asset by a certain date for a certain price.
- The *put option* gives the holder the right to sell the underlying asset by a certain date for a certain price.

The price of the option is known as the exercise price or *strike price* and the date at which the option is exercised is known as the *expiration date.* There are two categories of options: the *American option* and the *European option.* The American option can be exercised any time up to the expiration date. The European option can be exercised only on the expiration date. Most of the options that are traded are American. Unlike futures or forward contracts where the holder is obligated to buy or sell, the holder of the option does not have to exercise the option; he may simply hold it until it expires. Entering into a futures or forward contract does not affect the current budget constraint of the agent while buying or selling an option does affect the current budget constraint.

A *stock option* entitles the holder to buy (or sell) an equity at a certain date for a certain price. To determine the price of a one-period stock option, we have to determine the price at time t that someone would pay to buy an equity at a price $\bar{q}$ at time $t+1$. In equilibrium, the stock price satisfies:

$$q^e(s_t) = \beta \int_S \frac{U'(y(s_{t+1}))}{U'(y(s_t))}[q^e(s_{t+1}) + y(s_{t+1})]F(s_t, ds_{t+1}).$$

What is the price that someone would pay for the option of buying the equity next period for the price $\bar{q}$ – the price of a one-period call option? If the price next period is greater than the strike price $q^e(s_{t+1}) > \bar{q}$, then the agent will exercise the option, while if $q^e(s_{t+1}) < \bar{q}$, the agent will not. The equilibrium price of a call option is:

$$\begin{aligned} P^c_{s,t} &= \beta \int_{\bar{q} \leq q^e(s_{t+1})} \frac{U'(y(s_{t+1}))}{U'(y(s_t))}[q^e(s_{t+1}) - \bar{q}]F(s_t, ds_{t+1}) \\ &\quad + \beta \int_{\bar{q} \geq q^e(s_{t+1})} \frac{U'(y(s_{t+1}))}{U'(y(s_t))} \cdot 0 \cdot F(s_t, ds_{t+1}) \\ &= E_t \left[m_{t,1} \cdot \max(0, q^e_{t+1} - \bar{q}) \right]. \end{aligned} \tag{8.57}$$

[6] Useful books on derivative securities include Rubinstein and Cox [380], Hull [259], and Stoll and Whaley [421]. Some of our discussion is based on Turnbull and Milne [434]. A useful book on futures markets is by Duffie [160].

The price of the put option is then equal to

$$P^p_{s,t} = E_t\left[m_{t,1} \cdot \max\left(0, \bar{q} - q^e_{t+1}\right)\right]. \tag{8.58}$$

In Chapter 2, we described the binomial model of option pricing that allows us to find the option price using a certainty equivalent approach to asset pricing. In that approach, we were able to circumvent the problem of evaluating the non-linear second moment that appears in Equations (8.57) and (8.58).

We can also price *interest rate options* using the same approach. Consider now the price of a European option on a pure discount bond that matures in τ periods. Suppose that the expiration date is $t+n$ where $n \leq \tau$ and the strike price is $\bar{Q}$. A European option can be exercised only at time $t+n$. The price of a call option at time t when the expiration date is time $t+n$ is:

$$P^c_{d,t}(n,\tau) = E_t\left[m_{t,n} \cdot \max\left(0, Q^{\tau-n}_{t+n} - \bar{Q}\right)\right], \tag{8.59}$$

where $Q^{\tau-n}_{t+n}$ is the price at time $t+n$ of a discount bond that matures in $\tau - n$ periods.

Now consider an American call option on a pure discount bond that matures in τ periods. This is much more complicated for the obvious reason that the holder can exercise the option at any time up to and including the expiration date. At time $t+n-1$ when there is one period until the option expires, the price of the American option and the European option are the same, or

$$S^c_{1,t+n-1} = E_{t+n-1}\left[m_{t+n-1,1} \cdot \max\left(0, Q^{\tau-n}_{t+n} - \bar{Q}\right)\right].$$

Now consider the choices of the holder of an American call option at time $t+1$. These are as follows: (i) The agent can continue to hold the option, which has the value $S^c_{n-1,t+1}$. (ii) He can exercise the option to buy a bond that matures at time $t+\tau$ at the exercise price of $\bar{Q}$ instead of paying the current price $Q^{\tau-1}_{t+1}$. The value of an n-period call option on a discount bond maturing in τ periods is:

$$S^c_{n,t} = E_t\left[m_{t,1} \cdot \max\left(S^c_{n-1,t+1}, Q^{\tau-1}_{t+1} - \bar{Q}\right)\right]. \tag{8.60}$$

Comparing the expressions for European versus American options, we note that for the latter the options price $S^c_{n,t}$ satisfies an nth order non-linear difference equation.

It is also possible to price options on derivative instruments such as a forward or futures contract. Consider the price of an m-period European call option on an n-period forward contract where the underlying asset on which the contract is written is a τ-period discount bond. We have shown that the price of the n-period forward contract written on a discount bond maturing in τ periods at time $t+m$ is $F^{\tau}_{t+m,n} = Q^{\tau}_{t+m}/Q^{n}_{t+m}$. The European call option on the forward contract gives the holder the right to buy the n-period contract in m periods ($m \leq n$) at the strike price $\bar{F}$. Because the only time at which the option can be exercised is period $t+m$, the price of the call option is:

$$S^c_{f,t}(m,n) = E_t\left[m_{t,m} \cdot \max(0, F^{\tau}_{t+m,n} - \bar{F})\right]. \tag{8.61}$$

Because the European option cannot be exercised before the date $t+m$, it is straightforward to price.

8.2.3. The Black-Scholes options pricing formula

One of the best known results in the finance literature has to do with the Black-Scholes options pricing formula. The original derivation relied on absence of arbitrage arguments with continuous time diffusion processes for the stock price and a constant interest rate. In this section, we show how the discrete time consumption-based asset-pricing model can be used to derive an exact solution for the options price under some additional assumptions.

Recall that the price of a *call option* satisfies the relation:

$$P^c_{s,t} = E_t\left[m_{t,1} \cdot \max(0, q^e_{t+1} - \bar{q})\right], \tag{8.62}$$

where q^e_t is the price of the underlying stock, $\bar{q}$ is the exercise or strike price and $m_{t,1} = \beta U'(y_{t+1})/U'(y_t)$. To derive the Black-Scholes formula, we make some additional assumptions.

Assumption 8.4 *Preferences are of the CRRA variety:*

$$U(c) = \frac{c^{1-\gamma} - 1}{1-\gamma}, \gamma \geq 0. \tag{8.63}$$

Assumption 8.5 *(c_t, q^e_t) are jointly log-normally distributed.*

Under the first assumption, the intertemporal MRS can be evaluated as:

$$m_{t,1} = \beta\left(\frac{c_{t+1}}{c_t}\right)^{-\gamma}. \tag{8.64}$$

Hence, the options price can be evaluated as

$$P^c_{s,t} = \beta E_t\left[\left(\frac{c_{t+1}}{c_t}\right)^{-\gamma} \max(0, q^e_{t+1} - \bar{q})\right]. \tag{8.65}$$

Under the second assumption, $\ln(q^e_{t+1})$ and $\ln(c_{t+1})$ are normally distributed with means $\bar{\mu}_q, \bar{\mu}_c$ and covariance matrix

$$\bar{\Sigma} = \begin{bmatrix} \sigma^2_q & \rho\sigma_q\bar{\sigma}_c \\ \rho\sigma_q\bar{\sigma}_c & \bar{\sigma}^2_c. \end{bmatrix},$$

where ρ is the correlation coefficient between $\ln(q^e_{t+1})$ and $\ln(c_{t+1})$. Hence, conditional on information at t, q^e_{t+1}/q^e_t and $\beta(c_{t+1}/c_t)^{-\gamma}$ are jointly log-normally distributed with means

$$\begin{bmatrix} \mu_q \\ \mu_c \end{bmatrix} = \begin{bmatrix} \bar{\mu}_q - \ln(q^e_t) \\ \ln(\beta) - \gamma\bar{\mu}_c + \gamma\ln(c_t) \end{bmatrix}$$

and covariance matrix

$$\Sigma = \begin{bmatrix} \sigma^2_q & \rho\sigma_q\sigma_c \\ \rho\sigma_q\sigma_c & \sigma^2_c. \end{bmatrix} = \begin{bmatrix} \sigma^2_q & -\gamma\rho\sigma_q\bar{\sigma}_c \\ -\gamma\rho\sigma_q\bar{\sigma}_c & \gamma^2\bar{\sigma}^2_c. \end{bmatrix}.$$

Now we can write Equation (8.65) as

$$P^c_{s,t} = q^e \int_{-\infty}^{\infty}\int_{\ln(\bar{q}/q^e)}^{\infty} \left(\exp(z) - \bar{q}/q^e\right)\exp(y) f(z,y)\,dz\,dy, \quad (8.66)$$

where $f(z,y)$ is the joint density function for $z \equiv \ln((q^e)'/q^e)$ and $y \equiv \ln(\beta(c'/c)^{-\gamma})$. This last relation may be expressed as the difference between two indefinite integrals as:

$$P^c_{s,t} = q^e \int_{-\infty}^{\infty}\int_{\ln(\bar{q}/q^e)}^{\infty} \exp(z+y) f(z,y)\,dz\,dy$$
$$- \bar{q}\int_{-\infty}^{\infty}\int_{\ln(\bar{q}/q^e)}^{\infty} \exp(y) f(z,y)\,dz\,dy. \quad (8.67)$$

Rubinstein [378] shows the two integrals may be evaluated as:

$$\int_{-\infty}^{\infty}\int_{\ln(\bar{q}/q^e)}^{\infty} \exp(y) f(z,y)\,dz\,dy$$
$$= \exp\left[\mu_c + \frac{\sigma^2_c}{2}\right]\Phi\left(\frac{-\ln(\bar{q}/q^e) + \mu_q}{\sigma_q} + \rho\sigma_c\right),$$

and

$$\int_{-\infty}^{\infty}\int_{\ln(\bar{q}/q^e)}^{\infty} \exp(z+y) f(z,y)\,dz\,dy$$
$$= \exp\left[\mu_q + \mu_c + \left(\frac{\sigma^2_q + 2\rho\sigma_q\sigma_c + \sigma^2_c}{2}\right)\right]\Phi\left(\frac{-\ln(\bar{q}/q^e) + \mu_q}{\sigma_q} + \rho\sigma_c + \sigma_q\right),$$

where $\Phi(\cdot)$ is the distribution function of a standard normal variable and $\phi(\cdot)$ is the standard normal density.

$$\Phi(z) \equiv \frac{1}{\sqrt{(2\pi)}} \int_{-\infty}^{z} e^{-v^2} dv,$$

$$\phi(z) \equiv \frac{1}{\sqrt{(2\pi)}} e^{-z^2}.$$

Under the distributional assumptions for consumption, we have that

$$E\left[\beta \left(\frac{c'}{c}\right)^{-\gamma}\right] = \exp\left(\mu_c + \sigma_c^2/2\right), \tag{8.68}$$

and

$$E\left[\beta \left(\frac{c'}{c}\right)^{-\gamma} \frac{(q^e)'}{q^e}\right] = \exp[\mu_q + \mu_c + (\sigma_q^2 + 2\rho\sigma_q\sigma_c + \sigma_c^2)/2]. \tag{8.69}$$

But the left side of Equation (8.68) is equal to the inverse of the risk-free rate according to C-CAPM. Likewise, the left-side of (8.69) is just equal to 1 by the optimality condition characterizing the return for a risky security:

$$\exp[\mu_c + \sigma_c^2/2] = \left(r^f\right)^{-1}, \tag{8.70}$$

and

$$\exp[\mu_q + \mu_c + (\sigma_q^2 + 2\rho\sigma_q\sigma_c + \sigma_c^2)/2] = 1. \tag{8.71}$$

Using these results, we can express the price of the call option as

$$P_{s,t}^c = q^e \Phi(A + \sigma_q) - \left(r^f\right)^{-1} \bar{q}\Phi(A), \tag{8.72}$$

where

$$A \equiv \frac{\ln(q^e/\bar{q}) + (\mu_q + \rho\sigma_q\sigma_c)}{\sigma_q}.$$

Likewise, taking the logarithm of both sides of Equations (8.70) and (8.71) and equating, we obtain:

$$\mu_q + \rho\sigma_q\sigma_c = \ln(r^f) - \frac{1}{2}\sigma_q^2.$$

Using this result, we obtain

$$A = \frac{\ln(q^e/\bar{q}) + \ln(r^f)}{\sigma_q} - \frac{1}{2}\sigma_q.$$

If we substitute this result back into (8.72), we obtain the *Black-Scholes options pricing formula*, which has found wide use in options pricing.

8.3. A GROWING ECONOMY

In many applications, we need to allow for growth in the underlying variables. In this section, we consider a version of the basic asset-pricing model with unbounded utility and growing endowment. Since expected discounted utility becomes unbounded in this case, the approach for proving the existence and uniqueness of the representative consumer's value function and the equilibrium asset price functions must be modified.

There is a vector of exogenous shocks to the economy that satisfies Assumption 8.1. The law of motion for the endowment is

$$y_t = \lambda(s_t)y_{t-1}. \tag{8.73}$$

Notice that in general, the growth rate of the endowment depends on the shock.

Assumption 8.6 *Define $\mathcal{L} \equiv [\underline{\lambda}, \bar{\lambda}]$ where $\underline{\lambda} > 0$ and $\bar{\lambda} < \infty$. The set S is compact and the function $\lambda : S \rightarrow \mathcal{L}$ is a continuous function that is bounded away from zero.*

The following assumption characterizes the utility function.

Assumption 8.7 *The utility function is given by*

$$U(c) = (c^{1-\gamma} - 1)/(1 - \gamma) \quad \textit{for } \gamma \geq 0.$$

If $\gamma = 1$, $U(c) = \ln(c)$. When $\gamma \leq 1$, the utility function is unbounded above on $\Re_{++}$ and unbounded below when $\gamma \geq 1$. Notice that there is an unbounded return function and unbounded endowment process. We have an additional restriction on endowment growth.

Assumption 8.8 *For all $s \in S$, $\beta \int_S \lambda(s')^{1-\gamma} F(s, ds') < 1$, $\gamma \neq 1$.*

The restriction is on the conditional expectation of $\lambda(s')$ so that it holds for each $s \in S$. In later chapters, we describe how this assumption can be weakened so that discounted utility is less than one on average and not for every realization of the shock. Because endowment is growing and prices are measured in units of the endowment good, prices are also growing. In general, the equity price q^e is a function of the endowment level $y \in \Re_{++}$ and the current shock $s \in S$. We will restrict our attention to price functions such that the *price-dividend ratio* and risk-free bond price defined respectively as

$$q^e(y, s)/y \quad \text{and} \quad Q^1(s)$$

are functions of s only. Further, we assume that they are elements of the space of continuous and bounded real-valued functions defined on S,

$$q^e(y,s)/y \in \mathcal{C}_q(S) \quad \text{and} \quad Q^1(s) \in \mathcal{C}_q(S),$$

and that q^e is continuous with respect to y.

The representative consumer's problem is identical to that described in Section 8.1 aside from the fact that the equity price depends on both the level of the endowment y and the current shock s, $q^e(y,s)$. Feasible consumption levels are those that satisfy $0 \leq c \leq y$. The discounted expected utility from consuming the endowment process by setting $c_t = y_t$ for all t is given by:

$$W(y_0) \equiv \frac{1}{1-\gamma} E_0 \left[\sum_{t=0}^{\infty} \beta^t y_t^{1-\gamma} \right]$$

$$= \frac{1}{1-\gamma} y_0^{1-\gamma} E_0 \left[1 + \sum_{t=1}^{\infty} \beta^t \left(\prod_{i=1}^{t} \lambda_i \right)^{1-\gamma} \right], \tag{8.74}$$

where the constant term $-1/[(1-\gamma)(1-\beta)]$ has been omitted. Using an iterated expectation argument, notice that:

$$E_0 \left\{ \beta^t \left(\prod_{i=1}^{t} \lambda_i \right)^{1-\gamma} \right\} = E_0 \left\{ \beta \lambda_1^{1-\gamma} \cdots E_{t-1} \left\{ \beta \lambda_t^{1-\gamma} \right\} \right\} \leq \alpha^t,$$

where

$$\alpha = \sup_{s \in S} \left\{ \beta \int_S \lambda(s')^{1-\gamma} F(s, ds') \right\}.$$

Since $\alpha < 1$ by Assumption 8.8, this result shows that the term in square brackets in Equation (8.74) is finite. Consequently, $W(y_0)/y_0^{1-\gamma}$ is finite even though total expected discounted utility is not.

For this application, the value function depends on the level of the endowment. More precisely, given the price functions $q^e(y,s)$ and $Q^1(s)$, the consumer's value function satisfies:

$$V(z,b,s,y) = \max_{c,z',b'} \left\{ U(c) + \beta \int_S V(z',b',s',y') F(s,ds') \right\}$$

subject to

$$c + q^e(y,s)z' + Q^1(s)b' \leq [y + q^e(y,s)]z + b, \tag{8.75}$$

$$0 \leq c \leq y, \quad z' \in Z, \quad b' \in B. \tag{8.76}$$

Since the endowment is growing, we cannot choose the value function V to be an element of the space of bounded, continuous functions on $Z \times B \times S$. Instead the result in Equation (8.74) suggests that we should restrict our attention to value functions V that grow no faster than $y^{1-\gamma}$.

To describe the space of such functions, let $\mathcal{Z} = Z \times B \times S \times \Re_{++}$ and define $\mathcal{B}$ as the space of functions $g : \mathcal{Z} \to \Re$ that are jointly continuous in the arguments (z, b, s, y). Notice that Z, B, S are compact and $y \in \Re_{++}$. Define the norm for elements of $\mathcal{B}$ by:

$$\|g\|_{\varphi} = \sup_{z,b,s,y \in \mathcal{Z}} \left| \frac{g(z, b, s, y)}{\varphi(y)} \right| < \infty,$$

where $\varphi \in \mathcal{B}$; in our case, we choose $\varphi(y) = y^{1-\gamma}$. This function is still an element of $\mathcal{B}$ even though it is not an explicit function of (z, b, s). We say that a function $g \in \mathcal{B}$ is φ-bounded if the φ-norm $\|g\|_{\varphi}$ is finite. We can show that the space $\mathcal{B}$ is a complete, normed, linear space.

To show the existence of a fixed point to the functional equation above, we use a modification of the Contraction Mapping and Blackwell's conditions, known as the Weighted Contraction Mapping Theorem (see Boyd [71]). Suppose T is an operator that maps the space $\mathcal{B}$ into itself, where $\mathcal{B}$ is a complete, normed, linear space. According to this theorem, if (i) T is monotone ($f \geq g$ implies that $Tf \geq Tg$ for $f, g \in \mathcal{B}$); (ii) T discounts ($T(g + a\varphi) \leq Tg + \delta a \varphi$ for some constant $0 < \delta < 1$ and $a > 0$); and (iii) $T(0) \in \mathcal{B}$, then T has a unique fixed point in $\mathcal{B}$.

To apply this result for our problem, for $V \in \mathcal{B}$ define the operator T by:

$$(TV)(z, b, s, y) = \max_{c,z',b'} \left\{ U(c) + \beta \int_S V(z', b', s', y') F(s, ds') \right\} \tag{8.77}$$

subject to Equations (8.75) and (8.76). We have the following proposition.

Proposition 8.3 *Under Assumptions 8.1, 8.6, 8.7, and 8.8, there exists a unique solution $V^{\star} \in \mathcal{B}$ to Equation (8.77).*

PROOF

First, we need to show that the operator T maps the space of bounded, continuous functions with the φ-norm into itself. This requires that for any $V \in \mathcal{B}$, TV is bounded (so that $\|(TV)\|_{\varphi} < \infty$) and that it is jointly continuous in its arguments.

From the budget constraint, notice that

$$\frac{c}{y} \leq \frac{b}{y} + z \left(\frac{q^e(s, y)}{y} + 1 \right) - z' \frac{q^e(s, y)}{y} - \frac{Q(s) b'}{y}.$$

We have restricted $b' \in B, z' \in Z$ and feasible c such that $0 \leq c \leq y$. For any c such that $0 \leq c \leq y$, current utility (which is continuous in c) is also φ-bounded and continuous. If $V \in \mathcal{B}$, then $\beta E_s[V(z', b', s', y')]$ is φ-bounded because

$$\begin{aligned}
&\frac{\varphi(y)}{\varphi(y)}\beta \int_S \varphi(y') \frac{V(z', b', s', y')}{\varphi(y')} F(s, ds') \\
&= \varphi(y)\beta \int_S \lambda(s')^{1-\gamma} \frac{V(z', b', s', y')}{\varphi(y')} F(s, ds') \\
&\leq \varphi(y)\bar{B}\beta \int_S \lambda(s')^{1-\gamma} F(s, ds') \leq \varphi(y)\bar{B}
\end{aligned}$$

since V is φ-bounded and $\beta \int_S \lambda(s')^{1-\gamma} F(s, ds') < 1$. Furthermore, the function $\beta E_s[V(z', b', s', y')]$ is continuous since V is continuous and the transition function has the Feller property. Hence, TV involves maximizing a continuous function over a compact set so that it is well defined; that is, a maximum exists and it is bounded, and by the Theorem of the Maximum, it is continuous. Thus, $T : \mathcal{B} \to \mathcal{B}$.

Next, notice that T is monotone. Given any two functions $u \geq w$, it is straightforward to verify that $Tu \geq Tw$. Furthermore, for any constant $a > 0$,

$$\begin{aligned}
T(V + a\varphi)(z, b, s, y) \leq \max_{c, z', b'} \Bigg\{ y^{1-\gamma} \Bigg[&\frac{c^{1-\gamma} - 1}{y^{1-\gamma}(1-\gamma)} \\
&+ \beta \int_S \lambda(s')^{1-\gamma} \frac{V(z', b', s') + a\varphi(y')}{\varphi(y')} F(s, ds') \Bigg] \Bigg\} \\
\leq (TV)(z, b, s, y) + \delta a \varphi(y),
\end{aligned}$$

where $\delta = \beta \int_S \lambda(s')^{1-\gamma} F(s, ds') < 1$ by Assumption 8.8 so that T discounts. Finally, notice that $T(0) \in \mathcal{B}$ since U is φ-bounded and continuous for $0 \leq c \leq y$. Hence, T satisfies the conditions for a weighted contraction mapping and has a unique fixed point $V^* \in \mathcal{B}$. ∎

In equilibrium, $c = y$, $z' = 1$, and $b' = 0$. The equilibrium first-order conditions are given by:

$$q^e(s, y)U'(y) = \beta \int_S U'(y')[q^e(s', y') + y(s')]F(s, ds'), \tag{8.78}$$

$$Q^1(s)U'(y) = \beta \int_S U'(y')F(s, ds'). \tag{8.79}$$

We can use the fact that $U'(y) = y^{-\gamma}$ to derive a functional equation for the equilibrium price-dividend ratio, defined as $\psi(s) \equiv q^e(s, y)/y$. Equation (8.78) can be rewritten as:

$$\psi(s) = \beta \int_S \lambda(s')^{1-\gamma} \left[1 + \psi(s')\right] F(s, ds'). \tag{8.80}$$

Notice that $\psi : S \to \Re_+$. When endowment is growing, the equity is a claim to a growing dividend and it is not a stationary variable. However, the price-dividend ratio $\psi(s)$ is a function only of endowment growth $\lambda(s)$ and it is stationary. Under Assumptions 8.1, 8.6, 8.7, and 8.8, it is straightforward to demonstrate that for any $\psi \in C_q(S)$ an operator $T_q\psi$ defined from the right side of Equation (8.80) maps the space of bounded, continuous, real-valued functions into itself and satisfies Blackwell's conditions for a contraction. By the Contraction Mapping Theorem, we can show that there exists a unique fixed point to Equation (8.80) denoted ψ^*. It also follows from the equilibrium first-order conditions that the risk-free bond price is:

$$Q^1(s) = \beta E_s[\lambda(s')^{-\gamma}]. \tag{8.81}$$

8.3.1. Cointegration in asset-pricing relations

An implication of the model with a growing endowment is that the stock price and dividends form a *cointegrated* process, that is, both the stock price and the dividend process are stationary in first differences but there exists at least one linear combination of them, which is stationary. In the literature, cointegration in asset-pricing relations has been studied in the context of *present value models*. Such models have been used to formalize the expectations theory for interest rates, the present value model of stock prices, and permanent income theory of consumption. The present value model is used, amongst others, by Shiller [398, 392], LeRoy and Porter [305], and West [448] to study the relation between stock prices and dividends and by Singleton [404] and Shiller, Campbell, and Schoenholtz [400] to model the behavior of long- and short-term bonds.

The general form of the model is given by:

$$\zeta_t = \theta(1-\beta)\sum_{i=0}^{\infty} \beta^i E_t(y_{t+i}) + c \tag{8.82}$$

where θ is the coefficient of proportionality, β is the discount factor and c is a constant. In this model, ζ_t can denote the long-term bond yield, current stock price or current consumption, depending on the model of interest. Similarly, y_t is the one-period (or short-term) bond yield, payments of dividend or current income.[7] To illustrate the cointegration approach, suppose that $\{y_t\}_{t=0}^{\infty}$ follows a non-stationary process. In this case, $\{\zeta_t\}$ also becomes non-stationary. Thus, while the model is simple, the non-stationarity of y_t

[7] In the context of our framework, the present value model of stock prices can be obtained under the assumption of risk neutrality. In this case, future dividends y_t are discounted with constant discount factor $\beta = 1/(1+r)$, yielding a representation similar to (8.82). See Exercise 1.

and ζ_t requires some transformations. Campbell and Shiller [95] test the present value model by defining the variable $S_t = \zeta_t - \theta y_t$, which denotes the *spread* between the long- and short-term interest rates in the case of term structure, and the difference between the stock price and a multiple of dividends when the stock price is of interest.[8] Hence, a test of the present value model can be obtained by using the theory of cointegrated vectors. Campbell and Shiller [95] find evidence for cointegration between stock prices and dividends but it is weaker than the evidence found for the cointegration between long- and short-time interest rates. They also find evidence against the present-value model for both bonds and stocks. However, while the deviations from the present-value model for bonds appear transitory, they find that the spread between stocks and dividends moves too much and that the deviations from the present value model are quite persistent.

Campbell and Shiller [96] provide an alternative representation for the logarithm of the price-dividend ratio in terms of the logarithm of future dividends and future returns. For simplicity, define variables in capital letters to be measured as levels and small letters to be measured in logs. To derive this model, notice that we can write log returns

$$\ln(R_{t+1}) = \ln(1 + r_{t+1}) \approx r_{t+1} = \ln(Q^e_{t+1} + D_{t+1}) - \ln(Q^e_t).$$

Then

$$\begin{aligned} r_{t+1} &= \ln(Q^e_{t+1}) - \ln(Q^e_{t+1}) + \ln(Q^e_{t+1} + D_{t+1}) - \ln(Q^e_t) \\ &= q^e_{t+1} - q^e_t + \ln\left[\frac{Q^e_{t+1} + D_{t+1}}{Q^e_{t+1}}\right] \\ &= q^e_{t+1} - q^e_t + \ln\left[1 + \exp\left(\ln\left(\frac{D_{t+1}}{Q^e_{t+1}}\right)\right)\right]. \end{aligned} \tag{8.83}$$

Next, approximate the last term in (8.83) using a first-order Taylor series approximation around the average log dividend-price ratio, $\overline{d - q^e} = \ln(\overline{D/Q^e})$ as

[8] To obtain the present value model of stock prices, we take $\theta = \beta/(1-\beta)$. Notice that

$$\begin{aligned} S_t = \zeta_t - \frac{\beta}{1-\beta}y_t &= \beta\sum_{i=0}^{\infty}\beta^i E_t(y_{t+i}) + c - \frac{\beta}{1-\beta}y_t \\ &= \beta\sum_{i=0}^{\infty}\beta^i E_t(y_{t+i} - y_t) + c, \end{aligned}$$

which is stationary.

$$\ln\left(1 + \exp\left(d_{t+1} - q^e_{t+1}\right)\right)$$
$$\approx \kappa + (1-\rho)d_{t+1} - (1-\rho)q^e_{t+1},$$

where

$$\rho \equiv \frac{1}{1 + \exp\left(\overline{d - q^e}\right)}$$

$$\kappa = -\ln(\rho) - (1-\rho)\ln\left(\frac{1}{\rho} - 1\right).$$

Thus, we can write r_{t+1} as

$$r_{t+1} = \kappa + \rho q^e_{t+1} + (1-\rho)d_{t+1} - q^e_t. \tag{8.84}$$

When the dividend-price ratio is constant, then $\rho = 1/(1 + D/Q^e)$, which equals the reciprocal of one plus the dividend-price ratio. For the US over the period 1926–1994, the average dividend-price ratio has been around 4%, implying that $\rho = 0.96$ for annual data or around 0.997 for monthly data. Thus, the approximation in (8.84) assigns a weight that is close to one to the log price, and a weight close to zero to log dividends because dividends are much smaller than the stock price. The approximation in (8.84) will be accurate provided the variation in the log dividend-price ratio is not too great. In general, a comparison of actual returns and the returns implied by (8.84) are very close, implying that the approximation is, in general, very accurate.

Now solve the relation in (8.84) forward by imposing the terminal condition

$$\lim_{j\to\infty}\rho^j q^e_{t+j} = 0.$$

This yields

$$q^e_t = \frac{\kappa}{1-\rho} + \sum_{j=0}^{\infty}\rho^j\left[(1-\rho)d_{t+1+j} - r_{t+1+j}\right]. \tag{8.85}$$

This is a dynamic accounting condition which has been obtained by solving forward an identity and imposing a terminal condition. It holds *ex post* but it also holds *ex ante* as

$$q^e_t = \frac{\kappa}{1-\rho} + E_t\left[\sum_{j=0}^{\infty}\rho^j[(1-\rho)d_{t+1+j} - r_{t+1+j}]\right]. \tag{8.86}$$

This condition says that if the stock price is high, then investors must be expecting some combination of future high dividends and low future returns. Notice that we obtain the present value model with constant discount factors by setting $r_{t+1+j} = r$, where r is a constant. In the model summarized by (8.86), stock prices are high when dividends are expected to grow or when they are discounted at a low rate.

We can also express (8.86) in terms of the log dividend-price ratio as

$$d_t - q_t^e = -\frac{\kappa}{1-\rho} + E_t\left[\sum_{j=0}^{\infty} \rho^j[-\Delta d_{t+1+j} + r_{t+1+j}]\right]. \quad (8.87)$$

This relation says that the dividend-price ratio is high when dividends are expected to grow only slowly or when future stock returns are expected to be high. This relation is also convenient because the dividend-price ratio is a stationary random variable if dividends follow a log-linear unit-root process and returns are stationary. In this case, log stock prices and dividends are cointegrated, and the stationary linear combination of these variables involves no unknown parameters. Another reason for considering the model with time-varying stock returns is that the dividend-price ratio appears to be a good predictor of long-term real stock returns. (See, for example, Campbell and Shiller [96].) The relation in (8.87) can be used to rationalize the second set of findings under the assumption that expectations of future dividend growth are not too variable. Since the expectations on the right-hand side of (8.87) are over the infinite horizon, the log dividend-price ratio will, in general, be a better proxy over longer horizons. Finally, the relation in (8.87) can also be used to examine the implications of alternative theoretical models for the stochastic discount factor by linking r_{t+1+j} to observables implied by the theory. Campbell [90] provides a discussion of this approach in the context of accounting for alternative asset pricing anomalies, including the "equity premium puzzle."

8.4. CONCLUSIONS

In this chapter, we have set out the basic asset pricing for an endowment economy, and outlined the pricing of a variety of assets based on this model. We have also described solution procedures that can be used to examine numerically or quantitatively the implications of the model. The modern approach to asset pricing and dynamic macroeconomic analysis has made much use of this framework. In later chapters, we extend the basic framework to allow for non-separable preferences, production, investment, money, to name a few.

8.5. EXERCISES

1. Risk-Neutral Pricing

   Suppose output evolves as a stationary Markov process with transition function $F(s, s')$ and consumers are risk neutral, $U(c) = ac$. Show that the equilibrium price function satisfies:

$$q^e(y) = \sum_{s=1}^{\infty} \beta^s E(y_{t+s} | y_t = y). \tag{8.88}$$

   Suppose y_t evolves as $y_{t+1} = \mu_y + \rho y_t + \varepsilon_{t+1}$ where $|\rho| < 1$ and $E(\varepsilon_t) = 0$, $E(\varepsilon_t^2) = \sigma^2$, and $E(\varepsilon_t \varepsilon_{t-s}) = 0$ for $s > 0$. Show that the equity price is given by

$$q_t = \beta \rho y_t / (1 - \beta \rho).$$

   Interpret these results.
2. Consider the version of the model with CRRA preferences and growing endowment.
   (a) Show that Equation (8.80) can be solved forward to yield an expression for the price-dividend ratio as:

$$\frac{q_t^e}{y_t} = E_t \left[\sum_{i=1}^{\infty} \beta^i \left(\prod_{j=1}^{i} \lambda_{t+j}^{1-\gamma} \right) \right].$$

   (b) Suppose that dividend growth satisfies:

$$\lambda_t = \exp(\mu + \varepsilon_t), \quad \varepsilon_t \sim N(0, \sigma^2) \ \{\epsilon_t\} \ i.i.d.$$

   Show that the price-dividend ratio is given by:

$$\frac{q_t^e}{y_t} = \frac{\Omega}{1 - \Omega},$$

   where

$$\Omega = \beta \exp[(1 - \gamma)\mu + (1 - \gamma)^2 (\sigma^2/2)].$$

   (c) Show that the condition for the existence of a recursive competitive equilibrium with growing endowment is equivalent to the condition that $\Omega < 1$.
3. The Effects of a Mean-Preserving Spread

   We now study the effects of a mean-preserving spread in the distribution of dividend growth on the equilibrium price-dividend ratio. Consider the version of the model with CRRA preferences and a growing endowment. Suppose that dividend growth satisfies:

$$\lambda_t = \exp(\mu + \varepsilon_t), \quad \varepsilon_t \sim i.i.d. N(0, \sigma^2).$$

(a) Show that if the variance of dividend growth $Var(\lambda_t)$ changes, the mean of dividend growth $E(\lambda_t)$ also changes.

(b) Let μ be a function of a parameter ξ and similarly let σ^2 be a function also of ξ. Define a mean-preserving spread as a change in ξ such that

$$-\partial\mu(\xi)/\partial\xi = \partial(\sigma^2(\xi)/2)/\partial\xi.$$

Show that a mean-preserving spread satisfying the preceding condition decreases the price-dividend ratio if $\gamma > 1$ and increases it if $\gamma < 1$.

4. Pricing Coupon Bonds

Suppose that a coupon bond matures in τ periods at which time it pays one unit of the consumption good. It also pays a coupon equal to c in periods $t+1, \ldots, t+\tau-1$. Show that the price of such a bond satisfies:

$$Q^{\tau}_{c,t} = c\sum_{i=1}^{\tau-1} Q^{i}_{t} + Q^{\tau}_{t},$$

where Q^i_t is the price of a *pure discount bond* with maturity i for $i = 1, \ldots, \tau$.

5. Pricing a Forward Contract on Equity

The owner of an n-period forward contract purchases one share of the equity at the forward price where the forward price has been set such that the initial value of the contract is equal to zero. Let $\bar{S}$ denote the delivery price. The ex-dividend price of the equity at time $t+n$ is $q^e(s_{t+n})$. Derive an expression for the delivery price on the forward contract.

6. Discount Bonds and the Yield Curve

Assume that the utility function is given by:

$$U(c) = \frac{c^{1-\gamma} - 1}{1-\gamma}, \gamma \geq 0.$$

Suppose the endowment follows two different time series models. The first time series model is termed the *trend-stationary model* and it assumes that the logarithm of endowment follows a first-order autoregressive stationary process around a deterministic trend:

$$y_t = \exp(\delta_0 + \delta_1 t + \varepsilon_t), \quad \varepsilon_t = \delta_2\varepsilon_{t-1} + e_t \text{ with } |\delta_2| < 1.$$

The disturbance $\{e_t\}$ is assumed to be an i.i.d. normally distributed process with mean zero and variance σ_e^2.

The second model is termed the *difference-stationary model* and it assumes that the difference of the logarithm of the endowment is a stationary autoregressive process. The endowment evolves according to Equation (8.73) while endowment growth has the law of motion:

$$\log \lambda_t = \rho_0 + \rho_1 \log \lambda_{t-1} + u_t \text{ with } |\rho_1| < 1.$$

The innovation $\{u_t\}$ is assumed to be an i.i.d. normally distributed process with mean zero and variance σ_u^2.[9]

Find expressions for τ-period pure discount bond for each time-series model. Backus, Gregory, and Zin [41] show that the yield curve has a negative slope when the endowment process has a unit root. Demonstrate this result using your answer above. Suppose you use the trend-stationary model for the dividend growth. Does the yield curve have a positive or a negative slope?

7. Using the Black-Scholes option-pricing method, show that the price of a *put option* is given by:

$$P_t^p = \bar{q}(r^f)^{-1}\Phi(-A) - q^e\Phi(-A - \sigma_q), \tag{8.89}$$

where $\bar{q}$ is the exercise price, r^f is the (gross) risk-free rate, q^e is the current price of the stock, and σ_q is the standard deviation of the stock.

[9] Campbell and Mankiw [94], Eichenbaum and Christiano [168], and Stock [412], among others, discuss the adequacy of these time-series models for describing aggregate GNP or output. For an application of these models in an asset-pricing context, see Campbell [88].

CHAPTER 9

Non-separable preferences

In our framework the stochastic discount factor plays a key role in determining asset-pricing relations. Our analysis up to this point has examined models with preferences that are separable over time and over states. A number of recent studies have proposed alternative preference specifications that allow for non-separabilities. Non-expected utility preferences imply that preferences are non-additive over alternative states of the world. Models with habit persistence and consumption durability allow for non-separabilities over time.

Constantinides [118] and Ferson and Constantinides [183] among others consider models with habit persistence for explaining asset-pricing puzzles. Habit persistence captures the notion that consumers' well-being appears to depend on recent changes in consumption rather than its level. Abel [3] allows for the phenomenon of "keeping up with the Joneses" by modeling habit as being external to the household. Campbell and Cochrane [93] argue that many recent asset puzzles can be explained by allowing for models with an external habit. In a related literature, models with consumption durability have been used by Eichenbaum, Hansen, and Singleton [171], Dunn and Singleton [164], and Eichenbaum and Hansen [169] to model the behavior of consumption and leisure choices, to examine the implications of the term structure of interest rates, and to derive implications for durable goods prices. In this chapter we examine the role of preferences that are non-separable across time and states for explaining a variety of phenomena in the recent macroeconomics literature. These phenomena include asset-pricing puzzles.

9.1. NON-TIME-ADDITIVE PREFERENCES

When current utility depends on past consumption, we say that preferences are *non-additive over time*. Habit persistence and consumption durability are alternative ways of modeling the effect of past consumption choices on current utility. Consumption durability states that new consumption goods acquisitions at time t produce a flow of consumption services at time $t+\tau$. Habit persistence implies that the consumer's utility at time t depends on an internal or external level of "habit."

9.1.1. Habit persistence and consumption durability

Assume that the consumer has preferences over consumption services as:

$$E_0\left\{\sum_{t=0}^{\infty}\beta^t U\left(c_t^\star - x_t^\star\right)\right\}, \tag{9.1}$$

where $c_t^\star$ denotes consumption from services of durable goods and $x_t^\star$ denotes the internal habit level of consumption services. To illustrate the impact of consumption durability and habit persistence, we start with some simple cases.

- *Consumption durability but no habit persistence.* In this case, $x_t^* = 0$. Also suppose that services from consumption at time t depend positively on current and one lagged value of acquisitions of consumption goods:

$$c_t^\star = (1-b)c_t + bc_{t-1}, \quad b > 0. \tag{9.2}$$

  We can calculate the intertemporal MRS under this specification as:

$$\text{MRS}_{t,t+1} = \beta\frac{(1-b)U'(c_{t+1}^\star) + \beta bU'(c_{t+2}^\star)}{(1-b)U'(c_t^\star) + \beta bU'(c_{t+1}^\star)}.$$

  Hence, we find that the marginal utility of consumption at any date is a weighted average of current and future (discounted) marginal utility. Furthermore, the intertemporal MRS depends on a finite number of leads and lags of consumption choices.
- *Habit persistence but no consumption durability.* Now $c_t^* = c_t$. Suppose also that the habit can simply be represented by past consumption:

$$x_t^\star = hc_{t-1}, \quad h > 0. \tag{9.3}$$

  The habit parameter h shows the fraction of lagged consumption services that establishes a subsistence level of consumption.

  The intertemporal MRS can be written as:

$$\text{MRS}_{t,t+1} = \beta\frac{U'(c_{t+1} - x_{t+1}^\star) - \beta hU'(c_{t+2} - x_{t+2}^\star)}{U'(c_t - x_t^\star) - \beta hU'(c_{t+1} - x_{t+1}^\star)}.$$

  When consumption is lower relative to habit, the curvature of the utility function is higher compared with the case without a habit. Furthermore, the intertemporal MRS may fall if next period's consumption relative to habit is lower compared to this period's consumption relative to habit, that is, if $c_{t+i} - x_{t+i}^\star < c_{t+i-1} - x_{t+i-1}^\star$ for $i \geq 1$. This yields the possibility for greater variation in the intertemporal MRS compared to the case with time-separable preferences.

9.1.2. A more general specification

Ferson and Constantinides [183] analyze the impact of consumption and habit persistence on asset prices by considering a more general specification for $c_t^\star$ and $x_t^\star$:

$$c_t^\star = \sum_{s=0}^{\infty} b_s c_{t-s} \tag{9.4}$$

$$x_t^\star = h \sum_{s=1}^{\infty} a_s c_{t-s}^\star. \tag{9.5}$$

In these expressions, $\sum_{s=1}^{\infty} a_s = 1$, $\sum_{s=0}^{\infty} b_s = 1$ and $a_s \geq 0$, $b_s \geq 0$ for all $s \geq 0$. The consumer's preferences can be written as a function of c_t only by noting that

$$\begin{aligned} c_t^\star - x_t^\star &= \sum_{s=0}^{\infty} b_s c_{t-s} - h \sum_{\tau=1}^{\infty} \sum_{s=0}^{\infty} a_\tau b_s c_{t-s-\tau} \\ &= b_0 \sum_{s=0}^{\infty} \delta_s c_{t-s}, \end{aligned} \tag{9.6}$$

where

$$\delta_0 = 1 \tag{9.7}$$

$$\delta_s = \left(b_s - h \sum_{i=1}^{s} a_i b_{s-i} \right) \Big/ b_0. \tag{9.8}$$

Suppose $b_s = (1-b)b^s$ for $0 \leq b < 1$ and $a_s = (1-a)a^{s-1}$ for $0 \leq a < 1$. Then we can write:

$$\delta_s = \left(1 - \frac{(1-a)h}{b-a} \right) b^s + \frac{(1-a)h}{b-a} a^s, \quad s \geq 1. \tag{9.9}$$

If there is habit persistence but no consumption durability ($b = 0$), then

$$\delta_s = -(1-a)ha^{s-1} \tag{9.10}$$

and the coefficients δ_s are negative for $s \geq 1$. In the absence of habit persistence but with consumption durability ($h = 0$),

$$\delta_s = b^s \tag{9.11}$$

and δ_s are positive for $s \geq 1$.

When both habit persistence and consumption durability are present, the coefficients δ_s are positive or negative depending on the relative magnitudes of the durability parameter b and the habit parameters h and a.

- If $b \geq a + h(1 - a)$, the coefficient δ_s is positive for all s. To show this result, re-write the coefficient δ_s as

$$\delta_s = \left(\frac{b - a - h(1 - a)}{b - a}\right) b^s + \frac{(1 - a)h}{b - a} a^s, \quad s \geq 1.$$

It follows immediately that $\delta_s > 0$ whenever $b \geq a + h(1 - a)$.

- If $b \leq h(1 - a)$ then δ_s is negative for all s. To demonstrate this result, notice that δ_s can be equivalently written as:

$$\delta_s = b^s - h(1 - a)\left[\frac{b^s - a^s}{b - a}\right], \quad s \geq 1.$$

Notice that the term $b^s - a^s$ can be factored as:

$$b^s - a^s = (b - a)(b^{s-1} + ab^{s-2} + a^2 b^{s-3} + \cdots a^{s-3} b^2 + a^{s-2} b + a^{s-1}).$$

Therefore:

$$\begin{aligned}\delta_s &= b^s - (1 - a)h[b^{s-1} + ab^{s-2} + \cdots + a^{s-2} b + a^{s-1}] \\ &= b^{s-1}[b - h(1 - a)] - h(1 - a)[ab^{s-2} + \cdots + a^{s-2} b + a^{s-1}].\end{aligned}$$

Since the second term in square brackets is always positive, we have that $\delta_s < 0$ provided $b < (1 - a)h$.

- Finally, if $h(1 - a) < b < a + h(1 - a)$, then δ_s is positive for recent lags and negative for distant ones. To understand this result, notice that $\delta_1 = b - h(1 - a) > 0$ but the remaining coefficients are positive or negative depending on whether habit persistence or consumption durability is dominant. If, however, $\delta_\tau < 0$ for some τ, then $\delta_s < 0$ for $s > \tau$. That is, there is some threshold value τ such that whenever δ_τ is negative, then all the subsequent coefficients are also negative. To see this, consider the definition of δ_s and notice that $\delta_s < 0$ is equivalent to the statement that

$$b^s \leq h(1 - a)\left(\frac{b^s - a^s}{b - a}\right).$$

Using the definition for δ_s, we can write:

$$\begin{aligned}\delta_{s+1} &= b^{s+1} - h(1 - a)\left(\frac{b^{s+1} - a^{s+1}}{b - a}\right) \\ &\leq b\left[h(1 - a)\left(\frac{b^s - a^s}{b - a}\right)\right] - h(1 - a)\left(\frac{b^{s+1} - a^{s+1}}{b - a}\right) \\ &= -a^s h(1 - a)\left(\frac{b - a}{b - a}\right) = -a^s h(1 - a) < 0.\end{aligned}$$

In all of these cases, a change in consumption at date t has an effect on utility infinitely far out into the future. Whether this effect is positive or negative depends on which of the cases that we have described holds. Furthermore, the intertemporal MRS depends on an infinite number of leads and lags of consumption. We will examine the impact of these issues on asset-pricing relations in the next sections.

9.1.3. A recursive framework

We now analyze models with preferences that are non-additive over time using a recursive approach. We begin with a generalization of the first case above where purchases of past consumption goods lead to current consumption services. In this case, the effect of past consumption choices on current utility is always positive. We then describe how our approach can be extended to deal with the case when the effect of past consumption on current utility is negative and when it is positive or negative depending on the lag.

There are multiple consumption goods, and consumption services are produced using a vector of household capital stocks. Let k_{t-1} denote the m-dimensional vector of household capital stocks brought into period t. Given purchases of m new consumption goods at time t, k_t evolves as:

$$k_t = \Delta k_{t-1} + \Theta c_t, \tag{9.12}$$

where Δ is an $m \times m$ matrix whose eigenvalues are strictly less than one. Consumption services $c_t^\star$ are produced as:

$$c_t^\star = \Gamma k_t, \tag{9.13}$$

for an $m \times m$ matrix Γ. This is a dynamic version of the household service technology proposed by Gorman [210] and Lancaster [303], which views consumption goods as claims to future consumption services. In this more general setup, a vector of consumption goods at time t provides consumption services $\Gamma \Delta^\tau \Theta c_t$ at time $t + \tau$. To simplify the matter further, we assume that Δ, Θ, and Γ are diagonal matrices with diagonal elements δ_j, θ_j and γ_j for $j = 1, \ldots, m$ and that $0 < \delta_j < 1$ and $\theta_j > 0$ and $\gamma_j > 0$.

The output of consumption goods evolves as an exogenous stochastic process defined by:

$$y_t \equiv (y_{1,t}, \ldots, y_{m,t})'.$$

As before, we assume that each $y_{j,t}$ is a function of an m-dimensional vector of exogenous shocks $s_t \in S \subseteq \Re^m$, namely,

$$y_{j,t} \equiv y_j(s_t) \quad j = 1, \ldots, m.$$

The exogenous shocks s_t have a transition function F that satisfies Assumption 8.1. The endowment of each consumption good takes values in a compact set. Let

$$\mathcal{Y} \equiv [\underline{y}, \bar{y}]$$

where $\underline{y} > 0$ and $\bar{y} < \infty$. We assume that $y_j : S \to \mathcal{Y}$ are continuous functions that are bounded away from zero for $j = 1, \ldots, m$.

The representative consumer has preferences over sequences of consumption services $\{c_t^\star\}_{t=0}^\infty$ given by:

$$E_0 \left\{ \sum_{t=0}^{\infty} \beta^t U(c_t^\star) \right\}, \tag{9.14}$$

where $0 < \beta < 1$ and E_0 denotes expectation conditional on information available at time zero. The utility function $U : S \to \Re_+$ is continuous, continuously differentiable, strictly increasing, and strictly concave in $c^\star$. For all $c^\star \geq 0$, assume that $U(c^\star) \geq 0$. Define $\mathrm{MU}_j(c^\star) \equiv \partial U(c^\star)/\partial c_j^\star$ and assume that $\lim_{c_j^\star \to 0} \mathrm{MU}_j(c^\star)/\mathrm{MU}_i(c^\star) = \infty$ for all i and j. This ensures that all goods are consumed in equilibrium. Finally, the restrictions that $\theta_j > 0$ and $\gamma_j > 0$ imply that past consumption choices have a positive effect on current utility. An alternative expression for the vector of household capital stocks can be derived as:

$$k_t = \Theta c_t + \sum_{s=1}^{\infty} \Delta^s \Theta c_{t-s}. \tag{9.15}$$

This is well defined since the diagonal elements of Δ are less than one. The feasible consumption goods purchases satisfy

$$0 \leq c_{j,t} \leq y_{j,t}, \quad j = 1, \ldots, m.$$

Since each $y_{j,t}$ is bounded above by $\bar{y}$, the vector of capital stocks takes values in the compact set:

$$\mathcal{K} \equiv [0, (1-\delta_1)^{-1}\theta_1 \bar{y}] \times \cdots \times [0, (1-\delta_m)^{-1}\theta_m \bar{y}].$$

Consumers can trade in the market for used capital goods as well as make new purchases of consumption goods. The first consumption good is the numeraire so that its price is normalized as one. The consumer can also purchase equities that pay off in terms of each consumption good and a risk-free bond that pays off in terms of the numeraire good. For each j, denote by

$p_{j,t}^c$: the price of new capital goods

$p_{j,t}^k$: the price of used capital goods

$k_{j,t}^d$: the consumer's purchases of used capital goods

$q_{j,t}^e$: the equity price that pays off in units of good j

Q_t^1 : the price of the risk-free bond that pays off in units of the numeraire good

κ_{t-1} : the vector of aggregate or per capita capital holdings.

The consumer's state is summarized by its beginning-of-period capital stocks k_{t-1}, its equity holdings z_t, its beginning-of-period bond holdings b_t, the value of per capita capital stock κ_{t-1}, and the current shock s_t. The state of the economy is summarized by the current shock s_t and the per capita capital holdings, κ_{t-1}.

We seek an equilibrium in which all prices and the law of motion for the per capita capital stock can be expressed as time-invariant functions of the current state, s and κ. Define the strictly positive, continuous price functions $p^c : S \times \mathcal{K} \to \Re^m_{++}$, $p^k : S \times \mathcal{K} \to \Re^m_{++}$, $q^e : S \times \mathcal{K} \to \Re^m_{++}$, and $Q^1 : S \times \mathcal{K} \to \Re_{++}$. Assume that the per capita capital stock evolves according to

$$\kappa' = \bar{\kappa}(s, \kappa),$$

where $\bar{\kappa} : S \times \mathcal{K} \to \mathcal{K}$ are strictly positive, continuous functions and define the set of functions $\mathcal{P} \equiv (p^c, p^k, q^e, Q^1)$. Given $\mathcal{P}$ and the law of motion for capital $\bar{\kappa}$, the value function for the consumer's problem satisfies:

$$V(k, z, b, \kappa, s) = max_{c,k^d,z',b'} \left\{ U(c^\star) + \beta \int_S V(k', z', b', \kappa', s') F(s, ds') \right\}$$

subject to

$$p^c(s,\kappa) \cdot c + p^k(s,\kappa) \cdot k^d + q^e(s,\kappa) \cdot z' + Q^1(s,\kappa) b'$$

$$\leq p^k(s,\kappa) \cdot \Delta k + [y(s) + q^e(s,\kappa)] \cdot z + b, \tag{9.16}$$

$$k' = k^d + \Theta c, \tag{9.17}$$

$$c^\star = \Gamma k', \tag{9.18}$$

$$c \geq 0, \quad z' \in Z, \quad b' \in B, \quad k^d \in \mathcal{K}. \tag{9.19}$$

We can use the approach in Proposition 8.1 to show that there exists a bounded, continuous function $V : \mathcal{K} \times Z \times B \times \mathcal{K} \times S \to \Re_+$ that solves the consumer's problem.

The market-clearing conditions require that the goods market clears, $c_j = y_j$ for $j = 1, \ldots, m$, the used capital goods market clears, $k^d_j = \delta_j k_j$ for $j = 1, \ldots, m$, all shares are held $z' = \underline{1}$, and all bonds are held, $b' = 0$. A *recursive competitive equilibrium* for this economy is a set of price functions $\mathcal{P} \equiv (p^c, p^k, q^e, Q^1)$, a value function V, and a law of motion for the per capita capital stock $\bar{\kappa}$ such that (i) given $\mathcal{P}$ and $\bar{\kappa}$, V solves the consumer's problem; (ii) markets clear; (iii) the law of motion for the individual capital stock is equal to the law of motion for the per capita capital stock, $k'_j = \bar{\kappa}_j(\kappa, s)$ for $j = 1, \ldots, m$.

Let $\lambda(s,\kappa)$ be the multiplier on the budget constraint. Now substitute the envelope conditions into the first-order conditions for c, k^d, z' and b' to obtain:

$$\lambda(s,\kappa)p_j^c(s,\kappa) = \gamma_j\theta_j \mathrm{MU}_j(c^\star) + \beta E_s[\theta_j\delta_j\lambda(s',\kappa')p_j^k(s',\kappa')], \tag{9.20}$$

$$\lambda(s,\kappa)p_j^k(s,\kappa) = \gamma_j \mathrm{MU}_j(c^\star) + \beta E_s[\delta_j\lambda(s',\kappa')p_j^k(s',\kappa')], \tag{9.21}$$

$$\lambda(s,\kappa)q_j^e(s,\kappa) = \beta E_s\{\lambda(s',\kappa')[y_j(s') + q_j^e(s',\kappa')]\}, \tag{9.22}$$

$$\lambda(s,\kappa)Q^1(s,\kappa) = \beta E_s[\lambda(s',\kappa')]. \tag{9.23}$$

9.1.4. Pricing durable consumption goods

We can use this framework to derive the prices of durable consumption goods and consumption services. The conditions in Equations (9.20) and (9.21) imply that the price of used capital goods is proportional to the price of durable consumption goods:

$$p_j^k(s,\kappa) = \frac{1}{\theta_j}p_j^c(s,\kappa), \quad j = 1,\ldots,m.$$

We can use Equation (9.20) to show that the durable consumption goods prices satisfy:

$$\lambda(s,\kappa)p_j^c(s,\kappa) = \mathrm{MU}_j(c^\star)\gamma_j\theta_j + \beta\delta_j E_s[\lambda(s',\kappa')p_j^c(s',\kappa')]$$

for $j=1,\ldots,m$. These are functional equations in $\lambda(s,\kappa)p_j^c(s,\kappa)$. The vector of capital stocks k' carried into the next period is given once $c_j = y_j(s)$ and $k_j^d = \delta_j k$ are determined. Therefore, solving for an equilibrium involves solving for the asset-price functions. Since $\mathrm{MU}_j(c^\star)$ is bounded for any $0 < c^\star \leq \Gamma k'$ where $k' \in \mathcal{K}$ and $\beta\delta_j E_s[\lambda(s',\kappa')p_j^c(s',\kappa')]$ is bounded and continuous for any bounded, continuous $\lambda(s,\kappa)p_j^c(s,\kappa)$ for $j=1,\ldots,m$, we can find a fixed point for this equation using the Contraction Mapping Theorem. Assuming the fixed point has been found, we revert to time subscripts and solve this forward as:

$$\lambda_t p_{j,t}^c = \gamma_j\theta_j E_t\left[\sum_{s=0}^{\infty}(\beta\delta_j)^s \mathrm{MU}_j(c_{t+s}^\star)\right].$$

The price of the first consumption is normalized as one so that

$$\lambda_t = \gamma_1\theta_1 E_t\left[\sum_{s=0}^{\infty}(\beta\delta_1)^s \mathrm{MU}_1(c_{t+s}^\star)\right].$$

Substituting for λ_t from the previous expression yields the price of the jth consumption good as:

$$p^c_{j,t} = \frac{\gamma_j \theta_j E_t \left[\sum_{s=0}^{\infty} (\beta\delta_j)^s \mathrm{MU}_j(c^\star_{t+s})\right]}{\gamma_1 \theta_1 E_t \left[\sum_{s=0}^{\infty} (\beta\delta_1)^s \mathrm{MU}_1(c^\star_{t+s})\right]} \tag{9.24}$$

for $j = 1, \ldots, m$. Notice that the price of the jth durable consumption good is defined in terms of the future discounted value of the services from that good, expressed in units of the numeraire good.

We can also use this framework to derive the implicit price of consumption services. We can write the price of the jth durable good as:

$$p^c_{j,t} = \gamma_j \theta_j p^{c\star}_{j,t} + \beta\delta_j E_t \left(\frac{\lambda_{t+1}}{\lambda_t} p^c_{j,t+1} \right).$$

This expression says that the price of the jth durable good is equal to value of the services from that good obtained in period t plus the expected resale value of the durable good at date $t+1$, taking into account that $1-\delta_j$ units of the durable good are lost between t and $t+1$ due to depreciation. Hence, the price of a unit of services from the jth durable good is given by:

$$p^{c\star}_{j,t} = \frac{1}{\gamma_j \theta_j} \left[p^c_{j,t} - \beta\delta_j E_t \left(\frac{\lambda_{t+1}}{\lambda_t} p^c_{j,t+1} \right) \right], \tag{9.25}$$

Another way of understanding this result is to note that a claim to the jth durable consumption good for one period contributes $\gamma_j\theta_j$ units of services at date t so the value of a unit of services denoted $p^{c\star}_{j,t}$ is given by the expression in (9.25).

9.1.5. Asset-pricing relations

This framework can also be used to yield an asset-pricing formula. Consider first the rate of return on real risk-free bonds. From Equation (9.23), we have that

$$Q^1(s,\kappa) = \beta E_s \left[\frac{\lambda(s',\kappa')}{\lambda(s,\kappa)} \right]. \tag{9.26}$$

Likewise, the equity prices satisfy the relation:

$$q^e_j(s,\kappa) = \beta E_s \left\{ \frac{\lambda(s',\kappa')}{\lambda(s,\kappa)} [y_j(s') + q^e_j(s',\kappa')] \right\}, \quad j = 1, \ldots, m. \tag{9.27}$$

The relevant stochastic discount factor used to price payoffs on any security in this framework is the marginal rate of substitution for the numeraire consumption good, λ_{t+1}/λ_t. Using the expressions derived earlier, the stochastic discount factor is defined as:

$$m_{t+1} \equiv \frac{\beta E_{t+1}\left[\sum_{s=0}^{\infty} (\beta\delta_1)^s \mathrm{MU}_1(c^\star_{t+s+1})\right]}{E_t\left[\sum_{s=0}^{\infty} (\beta\delta_1)^s \mathrm{MU}_1(c^\star_{t+s})\right]}. \tag{9.28}$$

The relevant pricing function that is used to value risky payoffs depends on the discounted utility of all future services from consumption goods.

We can consider some variations of this framework. Suppose that $m = 1$ and the household capital stock k_t evolves as:

$$k_t = bk_{t-1} + c_t, \quad 0 < b < 1. \tag{9.29}$$

Using the representation in Equation (9.6), consumption services are proportional to the household capital stock as:

$$c^\star_t = (1-b)k_t = (1-b)\sum_{s=0}^{\infty} b^s c_{t-s}. \tag{9.30}$$

This is just the first case that we described in Section 9.1. Hence, the stochastic discount factor when there is only consumption durability has the form:

$$m_{t+1} \equiv \frac{\beta E_{t+1}\left[\sum_{s=0}^{\infty} (\beta b)^s \mathrm{MU}(c^\star_{t+s+1})\right]}{E_t\left[\sum_{s=0}^{\infty} (\beta b)^s \mathrm{MU}(c^\star_{t+s})\right]}. \tag{9.31}$$

Since the coefficient b is strictly positive, an increase in consumption c_t at date t has a strictly positive but decaying effect on future consumption services. Hence, the marginal utility of consumption expenditures is equal to the discounted value of marginal utility from future consumption services, the discounting being done with the strictly positive coefficients $(\beta b)^s$ for $s \geq 1$.

Now suppose that there is only habit persistence. Then we can reformulate the model with habit persistence by defining:

$$k_t = ak_{t-1} + c_t, \quad 0 < a < 1, \tag{9.32}$$

and

$$x^\star_t = h(1-a)k_{t-1}. \tag{9.33}$$

Then

$$\begin{aligned} c_t - x^\star_t &= c_t - h(1-a)k_{t-1} \\ &= c_t - h(1-a)[ak_{t-2} + c_{t-1}] \qquad (9.34) \\ &= c_t - h(1-a)\sum_{s=1}^{\infty} a^{s-1} c_{t-s}. \qquad (9.35) \end{aligned}$$

Hence, past values of consumption lead to consumption *disservices* through the effect of the habit variable. In this case, the stochastic discount factor has the form:

$$m_{t+1} \equiv \frac{\beta E_{t+1}\left[\mathrm{MU}_{t+1} - (h/a)(1-a)\sum_{s=1}^{\infty}(\beta a)^s \mathrm{MU}_{t+s+1}\right]}{E_t\left[\mathrm{MU}_t - (h/a)(1-a)\sum_{s=1}^{\infty}(\beta a)^s \mathrm{MU}_{t+s}\right]}. \tag{9.36}$$

Thus, an increase in consumption expenditures at date t reduces future consumption relative to habit by increasing the future habit level of consumption, $x^\star_{t+s}$ for $s \geq 1$. As a consequence, we see that an increase in current consumption has a negative effect on the future marginal utility of consumption net of the habit.

The third case analyzed in Section 9.1 involves both habit persistence and consumption durability. Recall that consumption services net of the habit evolve as:

$$\begin{aligned} c^\star_t - x^\star_t &= \sum_{s=0}^{\infty} b_s c_{t-s} - h\sum_{\tau=1}^{\infty}\sum_{s=0}^{\infty} a_\tau b_s c_{t-s-\tau} \\ &= b_0 \sum_{s=0}^{\infty} \delta_s c_{t-s}. \end{aligned}$$

In this case, an increase in current consumption will have a positive or negative effect on future consumption services depending on the sign of the coefficients on MU_{t+s}. Now the stochastic discount factor has the form:

$$m_{t+1} \equiv \frac{\beta E_{t+1}\left[\sum_{s=0}^{\infty} \beta^s \delta_s \mathrm{MU}(c^\star_{t+s+1})\right]}{E_t\left[\sum_{s=0}^{\infty} \beta^s \delta_s \mathrm{MU}(c^\star_{t+s})\right]}. \tag{9.37}$$

We cannot analyze this model using the simple recursive framework described above because it does not possess a finite number of state variables. However, if there is a finite number of lags for both consumption durability and the habit, then dynamic programming methods are still valid.

Models with intertemporal inseparabilities provide an important extension to the standard time-separable model because they break the link between intertemporal substitution and risk aversion.[1] By contrast, the time-separable model with CRRA preferences implies that the parameter that governs (relative) risk aversion is the inverse of the elasticity of intertemporal substitution. For this reason, non-separable preferences have been proposed in the recent asset-pricing literature for the purpose of rationalizing the "equity premium puzzle." We discuss the implications

[1] See Exercise 3.

of models with preferences that are non-separable over time and states at later points in the chapter.

9.1.6. Log-linear asset-pricing formulas

In the previous chapter, we described the role of the joint log-normality assumption in deriving log-linear pricing relations. In this section, we illustrate this approach when there exist time non-separabilities in preferences. We first illustrate a situation in which there exists an exact solution under a specific functional form for the single-period utility function. We also derive a solution based on a Taylor-series approximation to the utility function.

Consider the pricing of a strip asset. A *strip* is an asset that has a single-period payoff. Such assets are useful because they can be used as the basis for more complex assets such as equities. In a pure endowment economy, the dividend process $\{D_t\}$ on a stock is just equal to the exogenous endowment $\{Y_t\}$. We seek to find the price of a strip that pays off the dividend D_{t+k} at date $t+k$. Following our earlier notation, we will assume that the services from current consumption are denoted $C_t^\star$, and that the single-period utility function is of the CRRA variety:

$$U(C^\star) = \frac{(C^\star)^{1-\gamma} - 1}{1-\gamma}, \quad \gamma \geq 0.$$

We also assume that the marginal utility of consumption, $MU(C_{t+k})$, and dividends, D_{t+k}, are conditionally jointly lognormally distributed.

We can set up the household's problem as:

$$\max_{C_t} \; E_t \left\{ \sum_{t=0}^{\infty} \beta^t U(C_t) \right\}$$

subject to the budget constraint:

$$P_t S_t + C_t \leq D_t S_{t-k},$$

where S_t denotes the amount of strip purchased and P_t is the price of strip at time t that will pay k periods later. The first-order condition is given by:

$$\beta^k E_t[D_{t+k} MU(C_{t+k})] - P_t MU(C_t) = 0,$$

and the price of a strip that pays off the dividend at date $t+k$ is:

$$P_t = \frac{\beta^k E_t[D_{t+k} MU(C_{t+k})]}{MU(C_t)}. \tag{9.38}$$

Example 9.1 Time-separable Utility

Suppose that $C_t^\star = C_t$. For convenience, define $MU(C_{t+k}) \equiv C_{t+k}^{-\gamma}$, $\ln(MU(C_{t+k})) = -\gamma \ln(C_{t+k}) = -\gamma \ln(c_{t+k})$, and $d_{t+k} \equiv \ln(D_{t+k})$ for $k \geq 0$. Under the assumption of log-normality, we can evaluate the price of a strip as:

$$\begin{aligned} P_t &= \beta^k \exp(E_t[\ln(MU_{t+k}) - \ln(MU_t) + \ln(D_{t+k})] \\ &\quad + Var_t[\ln(MU_{t+k}) - \ln(MU_t) + ln(D_{t+k})]/2) \\ &= \beta^k \exp(E_t[-\gamma(c_{t+k} - c_t) + d_{t+k}] \\ &\quad + Var_t[-\gamma(c_{t+k} - c_t) + d_{t+k}]/2) \end{aligned}$$

Taking logarithms of both sides and denoting $p_t = \ln(P_t)$ yields:

$$\begin{aligned} p_t &= k\ln(\beta) - \gamma E_t[(c_{t+k} - c_t)] + E_t(d_{t+k}) + \gamma^2 Var_t[(c_{t+k} - c_t)]/2 \\ &\quad + Var_t(d_{t+k})/2 - \gamma Cov_t[(c_{t+k} - c_t), d_{t+k}]. \end{aligned} \tag{9.39}$$

Thus, under time-separable preferences, we can obtain a closed-form solution for the strip.

Example 9.2 Habit Persistence

Now suppose that $C_t^\star = C_t - hC_{t-1}$. In this case, the marginal utility of consumption becomes:

$$MU(c_{t+k}) = U'(C_{t+k}^\star) - h\beta U'(C_{t+k+1}^\star) \quad k \geq 0.$$

Then, the price of strip is given by:

$$P_t = \beta^k \frac{E_t[D_{t+k}(U'(C_{t+k}^\star) - h\beta U'(C_{t+k+1}^\star))]}{E_t[U(C_t^\star) - h\beta U'(C_{t+1}^\star)]}. \tag{9.40}$$

To evaluate the price of the strip in terms of consumption growth, we evaluate the marginal utility of consumption using the power utility function as:

$$\begin{aligned} MU(C_t) &= U'(C_t^\star) - h\beta U'(C_{t+1}^\star) \\ &= (C_t - hC_{t-1})^{-\gamma} - h\beta(C_{t+1} - hC_t)^{-\gamma}. \end{aligned}$$

However, this is non-linear in consumption. Hence, we cannot use log-linear pricing formulas as in the case with time-separable utility. Notice that we can write $\ln(MU(C_t))$ as:

$$\begin{aligned} \ln(MU(C_t)) &= \ln[(C_t - hC_{t-1})^{-\gamma} - h\beta(C_{t+1} - hC_t)^{-\gamma}] \\ &= \ln\Big[(\exp(\ln(C_t)) - h\exp(\ln(C_{t-1})))^{-\gamma} \\ &\quad - h\beta(\exp(\ln(C_{t+1})) - h\exp(\ln(C_t)))^{-\gamma}\Big]. \end{aligned}$$

Define $c_{t+i} = \ln(C_{t+i})$ for $i = -1, 0, 1$. Hence, we can linearize this expression around $c_{t+i} = \bar{c}$ for $i = -1, 0, 1$ using a first-order Taylor approximation as:

$$\ln(MU(C_t)) = \frac{\gamma h(\exp(\bar{c}) - h\exp(\bar{c}))^{-\gamma-1}\exp(\bar{c})}{(1-\beta h)(\exp(\bar{c}) - h\exp(\bar{c}))^{-\gamma}}(c_{t-1} - \bar{c})$$

$$+ \left[\frac{(-\gamma - \beta\gamma h^2)(\exp(\bar{c}) - h\exp(\bar{c}))^{-\gamma-1}\exp(\bar{c})}{(1-\beta h)(\exp(\bar{c}) - h\exp(\bar{c}))^{-\gamma}}\right](c_t - \bar{c})$$

$$+ \frac{\gamma\beta h(\exp(\bar{c}) - h\exp(\bar{c}))^{-\gamma-1}\exp(\bar{c})}{(1-\beta h)(\exp(\bar{c}) - h\exp(\bar{c}))^{-\gamma}}(c_{t+1} - \bar{c}).$$

Hence,

$$\ln(MU(C_t)) = \frac{\gamma h c_{t-1} - \gamma(1+\beta h^2)c_t + \beta\gamma h c_{t+1}}{(1-h)(1-\beta h)},$$

Now we can proceed to apply the log-normal distribution to evaluate the price of the strip.

Jermann [264] uses such log-linear pricing functions in a model with production. As in many recent applications, he linearizes the decision rules of the original growth model, and evaluates the log-linear pricing formulas that we developed above under these solutions. In Chapters 10 and 12, we discuss alternative numerical solution methods for determining optimal allocations and asset-pricing relations.

9.2. NON-EXPECTED UTILITY

In the recent macroeconomics and finance literature, a set of recursive preferences has been proposed that relaxes the assumptions of the standard time- and state-separable specification. In this section, we provide a brief description of these preferences in deterministic and stochastic settings.[2] This class of preferences includes non-expected utility preferences, which have found widespread use in different applications.

9.2.1. Recursive preferences under certainty

Consider first a deterministic setting. Let $\bar{c} \equiv \{c_t\}_{t=0}^{\infty}$ denote an arbitrary consumption sequence. In the absence of any restrictions on preferences, the utility from the consumption sequence $\bar{c}$ is defined as:

$$U(\bar{c}) = U(\{c_t\}) = U(c_0, c_1, c_2, \ldots). \tag{9.41}$$

[2] For further discussion, see Backus, Routledge, and Zin [42].

In general, the marginal rate of substitution between consumption at any two dates t, $t+1$ can depend on consumption at all past, present, and future dates. That is,

$$\text{MRS}_{t,t+1} = \frac{\partial U(\{c_t\})/\partial c_{t+1}}{\partial U(\{c_t\})/\partial c_t}$$

$$= f(\ldots, c_{t-1}, c_t, c_{t+1}, \ldots), \tag{9.42}$$

where $f(\cdot)$ is an arbitrary function. Typically a number of restrictions are placed on (9.41) to give content to economic relations. These restrictions also have implications for the form of the intertemporal MRS.

In the traditional time-separable case, we have that

$$U(\{c_t\}) = \sum_{t=0}^{\infty} \beta^t U(c_t)$$

and

$$\text{MRS}_{t,t+1} = \frac{\beta U'(c_{t+1})}{U'(c_t)}.$$

For a constant consumption path with $c_t = c$ for all t, note that

$$\text{MRS}_{t,t+1}(c) = \beta$$

also defines the subjective discount factor.

Koopmans [284] derives a class of stationary recursive preferences for a multi-dimensional consumption vector by imposing conditions on U. Let the consumption sequence starting at date t be defined by ${}_t\mathbf{c} = (c_t, c_{t+1}, \ldots)$. Preferences are assumed to be dynamically consistent in that preferences at all dates come from U:

$$U({}_0\mathbf{c}) = U(c_0, {}_1\mathbf{c}). \tag{9.43}$$

Koopmans [284] makes three additional assumptions. The first assumption involves history-independence, which means that choices over ${}_t\mathbf{c}$ do not depend on consumption at dates prior to t. (Notice that this class of preferences does not accommodate the types of temporal dependencies that we discussed in Section 9.1.) Hence, the utility function can be expressed in the form

$$U({}_0\mathbf{c}) = V[c_0, U_1({}_1\mathbf{c})] \tag{9.44}$$

for some time aggregator V. In the time-separable case, we have that $V(u, U) = u + \beta U$. The second assumption requires that preferences over c_t do not depend on ${}_{t+1}\mathbf{c}$. This implies

$$U({}_0\mathbf{c}) = V[u(c_0), U_1({}_1\mathbf{c})]. \tag{9.45}$$

Third, preferences are required to be stationary:

$$U({}_t\mathbf{c}) = V[u(c_t), U({}_{t+1}\mathbf{c})] \tag{9.46}$$

for all t. In this class of preferences, time preference is defined as a property of the aggregator function V. To see this, note that

$$\begin{aligned} \mathrm{MRS}_{t,t+1} &= \frac{\beta \partial U({}_t\mathbf{c})/\partial c_{t+1}}{\partial U({}_t\mathbf{c})/\partial c_t} \\ &= \frac{\beta V_2(u_t, U_{t+1}) V_1(u_{t+1}, U_{t+2})}{V_1(u_t, U_{t+1})}, \end{aligned} \tag{9.47}$$

where we have made use of the relation $U_t = V(u_t, U_{t+1}) = V[u_t, V(u_{t+1}, U_{t+2})]$. For a constant consumption path with period utility u, $U = V[u, U]$, which implies that $U = g(u) = V[u, g(u)]$. Hence,

$$\beta(c) = V_2[u, g(u)]. \tag{9.48}$$

Thus, in contrast to the time-separable case, discounting depends on the level of the period utility function, u. Typically, preferences are assumed to be increasing in consumption. This implies that u is increasing in c and that V is increasing in both its arguments, u and U. For consumption paths with constant consumption, U must be increasing in u. Therefore,

$$\begin{aligned} g'(u) &= V_1(u, g(u)) + V_2(u, g(u))g'(u) \\ &= \frac{V_1(u, g(u))}{1 - V_2(u, g(u))} > 0. \end{aligned}$$

Since $V_1 > 0$, $0 < V_2(u, g(u)) < 1$. Thus, the discount factor is between zero and one, and depends, in general, on u.

9.2.2. The role of temporal lotteries

Kreps and Porteus [288, 289] have shown that the Koopmans recursive preferences can be generalized to admit risk and uncertainty, and that this generalization leads to non-expected utility preferences. They motivate this class of preferences by noting that preferences for random income streams induced from preferences for random consumption streams have two properties. The first is that the resolution of uncertainty may be important in an intertemporal setting, and the second that induced preferences for random income streams may not satisfy the von Neumann-Morgenstern axioms.

To illustrate these results, we consider some simple examples from Kreps and Porteus [289]. The consumer has preferences over consumption at dates 0 and 1 given by:

$$U(c_0, c_1) = \ln(c_0) + \ln(c_1),$$

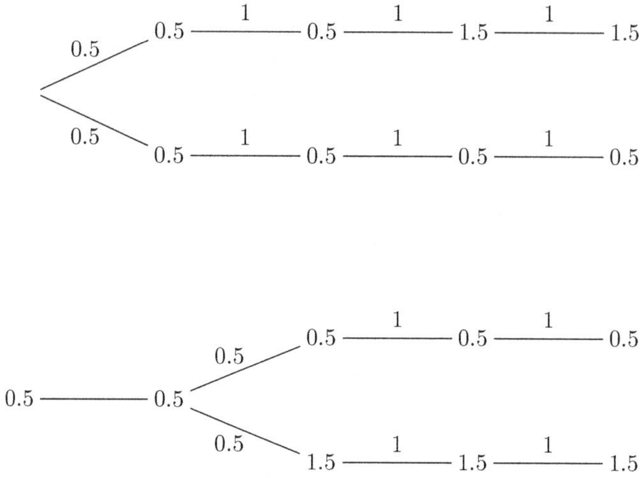

Figure 9.1. Early versus late resolution of uncertainty

and can borrow or lend at the zero interest rate. Suppose that the consumer's endowment is random and described by the random vector (y_0, y_1), which equals $(0.5, 0.5)$ or $(0.5, 1.5)$ with equal probabilities. Figure 9.1 depicts the lotteries available to the consumer.

Suppose first that uncertainty resolves *before* the time 0 consumption decision must be made. That is, the consumer knows for sure which random consumption vector he will be facing when making his period 0 consumption decision. In this case, we can solve the consumer's decision problem conditional on the state as:

$$\max_{c_0, c_1}\{\ln(c_0) + \ln(c_1)\}$$

subject to

$$c_0 + S \leq y_0$$

$$c_1 \leq y_1 + S,$$

where S denotes the saving decision. Substituting for c_0 and c_1 in the utility function and taking the derivative with respect to S yields the condition:

$$\frac{1}{c_0} = \frac{1}{c_1} \quad \Rightarrow \quad c_0 = c_1.$$

For the first income vector, this yields the solution $c_0 = c_1 = 0.5$ and for the second random vector, $c_0 = c_1 = 1$. Hence, expected utility is $0.5[\ln(0.5) + \ln(0.5)] + 0.5[\ln(1) + \ln(1)] = -0.693$.

Now suppose that uncertainty resolves *after* the time 0 consumption decision must be made. Now the consumer knows for certain that the time zero endowment is equal to $y_0 = 0.5$ but he must choose c_1 conditional on y_1 equal to 0.5 and 1.5 with probability 0.5 each. We can write the consumer's problem as:

$$\max_{c_0, c_{11}, c_{12}} \{\ln(c_0) + 0.5 \ln(c_{11}) + 0.5 \ln(c_{12})\}$$

subject to:

$$c_0 + S \leq y_0$$
$$c_{11} \leq y_{11} + S$$
$$c_{12} \leq y_{12} + S,$$

where c_{1i} and y_{1i}, $i = 1, 2$ denotes consumption and income conditional on state i occurring in period 1. Evaluating the utility function in terms of S using the budget constraints and differentiating yields the conditions:

$$-\frac{1}{0.5 - S} + \frac{0.5}{0.5 + S} + \frac{0.5}{1.5 + S} = 0.$$

This yields a quadratic equation in S which has the solution $S = -0.1096$. Note that the solution, $c_0 = 0.6096$, differs from the case when uncertainty resolves before the time 0 consumption decision. We can also show that $c_{11} = 0.3904$ and $c_{12} = 1.3904$. Evaluating expected utility under this assumption, we find that it equals $\ln(0.6096) + 0.5 \ln(0.3904) + 0.5 \ln(1.3904) = -0.8004$. Thus, the consumer prefers early resolution of uncertainty to late because it allows the consumer to adapt his choice of c_0 to the realization of his income at date 1.

The second property that Kreps and Porteus stress has to do with the violation of the von Neumann-Morgenstern independence axiom. To see this, consider again the situation where uncertainty resolves after c_0 is chosen. Assume that the time zero endowment is fixed at $y_0 = 0.5$ and suppose that the consumer faces the lotteries $(y_0, y_1) = (0.5, 0.1)$ or $(0.5, 6.202)$, each with probability 0.5. Following the same steps above, the consumer's choices at each date and state are given by $c_0 = 0.3957$, $c_{11} = 0.2043$, and $c_{12} = 6.3063$. In contrast to the former case, the consumer is now a saver instead of a borrower. The expected utility from this consumption allocation is -0.8004. Hence, the consumer is indifferent between the income lottery that yields $(0.5, 0.5)$ and $(0.5, 1.5)$ with probability 0.5 and the one that yields $(0.5, 0.1)$ and $(0.5, 6.202)$ again with probability 0.5. If the induced preferences of random income streams had the expected utility representation, then the consumer would also be indifferent between these lotteries and the lottery with prizes $(0.5, 0.5), (0.5, 1.5), (0.5, 0.1)$ and

(0. 5, 6. 202) each with probability one-quarter. Let $p_i = \frac{1}{4}$. The solution for the consumer's problem under this lottery is given by:

$$\max_{c_0, c_{1i}, i=1,\ldots,4} \{\ln(c_0) + \sum_i p_i \ln(c_{1i})\}$$

subject to

$$c_0 + S \leq y_0$$

$$c_{1i} \leq y_{1i} + S, \quad i = 1, \ldots, 4.$$

The solution for S is 0.05596 and the expected utility of the compound lottery is -0.85415. Hence, the consumer strictly prefers the former two lotteries to the latter (compound) lottery, thereby violating one of the main axioms of VNM expected utility.

9.2.3. Properties of non-expected utility preferences

In the standard expected utility model, preferences over random consumption streams are formulated in terms of an atemporal von Neumann-Morgenstern utility function. As our discussion in the previous section has shown, the assumption underlying the expected utility model is that individuals are indifferent to the timing of resolution of uncertainty for temporal lotteries. Furthermore, the axiomatic derivation of expected utility preferences assumes that the consumer cares only about the compound probability of each prize. When these assumptions are relaxed, preferences can be represented recursively as:

$$U_t = V(u_t, E_t[U_{t+1}]), \tag{9.49}$$

where U_t denotes lifetime utility at time t, V is an aggregator function (through which utility from current consumption and future utility are aggregated), and $E_t(\cdot)$ denotes expectation conditional on information available at time t. We say that consumers exhibit a preference for early (late) resolution of uncertainty over temporal lotteries depending on whether $V(c, \cdot)$ is convex (concave) in its second argument. When V is linear, we obtain the standard time and state-additive formulation of preferences.

Epstein and Zin [175] and Weil [445] have proposed a parametric class of preferences that satisfies the recursive structure of Equation (9.49). This class of preferences allows us to parameterize risk aversion and aversion to intertemporal substitution as two distinct aspects of a consumer's tastes.

Weil's specification

We first present the parameterization in Weil [445], which nests a variety of special cases.

$$U_t = W\left[c_t, E_t U_{t+1}\right]$$

$$= \frac{\left\{(1-\beta)c_t^{1-\frac{1}{\sigma}} + \beta[1+(1-\beta)(1-\gamma)E_t U_{t+1}]^{\frac{1-1/\sigma}{1-\gamma}}\right\}^{\frac{1-\gamma}{1-1/\sigma}} - 1}{(1-\beta)(1-\gamma)}$$

$$= \frac{\left\{(1-\beta)c_t^{1-\frac{1}{\sigma}} + \beta[1+(1-\beta)(1-\gamma)E_t U_{t+1}]^{\frac{1}{\theta}}\right\}^{\theta} - 1}{(1-\beta)(1-\gamma)}, \quad (9.50)$$

where $\gamma \geq 0$, $\sigma \geq 0$, and $0 \leq \beta \leq 1$ and $\theta = (1-\gamma)/(1-1/\sigma)$.

This class of preferences allows us to separate attitudes towards risk over temporal lotteries versus intertemporal substitution in consumption.

- The parameter σ represents the elasticity of intertemporal substitution for deterministic consumption paths. To show this, we note that the elasticity of intertemporal substitution (EITS) is given by:

$$\sigma = \text{EITS} = -\frac{d\ln(c_t/c_{t+1})}{d\ln(MU_t/MU_{t+1})}\Big|_{U=U_0} \quad (9.51)$$

To interpret this quantity, notice that in a deterministic economy in which the time prices of consumption are given p_t for $t \geq 0$, the ratio of the marginal utilities will equal the ratio of the time prices, $MU_t/MU_{t+1} = p_t/p_{t+1}$. This result shows that the elasticity of intertemporal substitution in consumption along a deterministic consumption path measures how changes in relative prices affect the relative magnitudes of current versus future consumption.

In our application,

$$MU_t = \frac{\partial U_t}{\partial c_t}$$

$$MU_{t+1} = \frac{\partial U_t}{\partial c_{t+1}} = \frac{\partial U_t}{\partial U_{t+1}}\frac{\partial U_{t+1}}{\partial c_{t+1}}.$$

Thus,

$$\frac{MU_t}{MU_{t+1}} = \frac{\partial U_t/\partial c_t}{(\partial U_t/\partial U_{t+1})(\partial U_{t+1}/\partial c_{t+1})}.$$

Next, we note that

$$[1+(1-\beta)(1-\gamma)U_t]^{\frac{1-1/\sigma}{1-\gamma}}$$
$$= (1-\beta)c_t^{1-1/\sigma} + \beta[1+(1-\beta)(1-\gamma)U_{t+1}]^{\frac{1-1/\sigma}{1-\gamma}}. \quad (9.52)$$

Thus,

$$(1-\beta)(1-\gamma)\left(\frac{1-1/\sigma}{1-\gamma}\right)[1+(1-\beta)(1-\gamma)U_t]^{\frac{1-1/\sigma}{1-\gamma}-1}\frac{\partial U_t}{\partial c_t}$$
$$=(1-\beta)\left(1-\frac{1}{\sigma}\right)c_t^{-\frac{1}{\sigma}},$$

which implies that

$$\frac{\partial U_t}{\partial c_t}=c_t^{-\frac{1}{\sigma}}[1+(1-\beta)(1-\gamma)U_t]^{1-\frac{1-1/\sigma}{1-\gamma}}. \tag{9.53}$$

Next, we have that

$$(1-\beta)(1-\gamma)\frac{1-1/\sigma}{1-\gamma}[1+(1-\beta)(1-\gamma)U_t]^{\frac{1-1/\sigma}{1-\gamma}-1}\frac{\partial U_t}{\partial U_{t+1}}$$
$$=\beta(1-\beta)(1-\gamma)\frac{1-1/\sigma}{1-\gamma}[1+(1-\beta)(1-\gamma)U_{t+1}]^{\frac{1-1/\sigma}{1-\gamma}-1},$$

which implies that

$$\frac{\partial U_t}{\partial U_{t+1}}=\beta\,[1+(1-\beta)(1-\gamma)U_{t+1}]^{\frac{1-1/\sigma}{1-\gamma}-1}$$
$$\times[1+(1-\beta)(1-\gamma)U_t]^{1-\frac{1-1/\sigma}{1-\gamma}}. \tag{9.54}$$

Therefore,

$$\frac{MU_t}{MU_{t+1}}=\frac{1}{\beta}\left(\frac{c_t}{c_{t+1}}\right)^{-\frac{1}{\sigma}}, \tag{9.55}$$

or

$$\ln\left[\frac{MU_t}{MU_{t+1}}\right]=-\ln(\beta)-\frac{1}{\sigma}\ln\left(\frac{c_t}{c_{t+1}}\right).$$

Hence,

$$-\frac{d\ln(c_t/c_{t+1})}{d\ln(MU_t/MU_{t+1})}=\sigma. \tag{9.56}$$

- The parameter γ is the constant coefficient of relative risk aversion over timeless gambles. It also represents the elasticity of the indirect marginal utility of wealth. (See Exercise 4.) Another way of interpreting the parameter γ is that the proportional premium that a consumer would be willing to pay to undertake a fair gamble on a permanent change in consumption is proportional to γ, with the proportionality factor reflecting the variance of the lottery.
- As $\gamma \to 1$ and $\sigma \to 1$, we obtain the logarithmic risk preferences and logarithmic intertemporal substitution preferences, respectively:

$$\ln(U_t)=\ln(c_t)+\beta E_t\ln(U_{t+1}).$$

Some further properties of these preferences are as follows. The parameter β is the subjective discount factor. To see this, use Equation (9.55) evaluated for a constant consumption path $c_t = c$ for all t as

$$MRS_{t,t+1}(c) = \frac{MU_{t+1}(c)}{MU_t(c)} = \beta. \tag{9.57}$$

When $\theta = 1$, we get $\gamma = 1/\sigma$. In this case, the coefficient of relative risk aversion for timeless gambles is equal to the inverse of the EITS. This implies standard additively separable preferences as:

$$U_t = E_t \left\{ \sum_{s=0}^{\infty} \beta^s \frac{c_{t+s}^{1-\frac{1}{\sigma}} - 1}{1 - 1/\sigma} \right\}.$$

When $\gamma = 0$, we get a constant elasticity of substitution (CES) representation for U_t as:

$$[(1-\beta)U_t + 1]^{1-\frac{1}{\sigma}} = (1-\beta)c_t^{1-\frac{1}{\sigma}} + \beta\left[1 + (1-\beta)E_t U_{t+1}\right]^{1-\frac{1}{\sigma}}.$$

This reflects the fact that σ is the elasticity of intertemporal substitution for deterministic consumption paths, a result that we have demonstrated more generally above.

When $\beta = 0$, we get the myopic preferences:

$$U_t = \frac{c_t^{1-\gamma} - 1}{1-\gamma}.$$

Hence, γ is associated with the curvature of the utility function and reflects consumers' attitudes toward risk over timeless gambles. When $\gamma = 0$, we get risk neutrality.

9.2.4. *Optimal consumption and portfolio choices*

Epstein and Zin [175] have considered a parametric class of non-expected utility preferences that satisfies the recursive structure of Equation (9.49). As in Weil's formulation, this class of preferences allows us to parameterize risk aversion and aversion to intertemporal substitution as two distinct aspects of a consumer's tastes. Unlike the time-separable model with expected utility preferences, these preferences allow for preferences over early versus late resolution of uncertainty. To define these preferences, let the aggregator function, W, be defined to be of the CES form:

$$W(c,z) = \left[(1-\beta)c^{\delta} + \beta z^{\delta}\right]^{1/\delta}, \quad 0 \neq \delta < 1, \tag{9.58}$$

$$W(c,z) = (1-\beta)\log(c) + \beta\log(z), \quad \delta = 0, \tag{9.59}$$

where $c, z \geq 0$ and $\beta = 1/(1+\rho)$, $\rho > 0$. When future consumption paths are deterministic, this aggregator function results in an intertemporal constant elasticity of substitution utility function with elasticity of substitution $1/(1-\delta)$ and rate of time preference ρ.

Recall that in Chapter 3 we introduced the notion of a certainty equivalent function which shows the certain value of a random consumption stream. The certainty equivalent function $\mu[U_{t+1}]$, which shows the certain value of the random utility stream U_{t+1} conditional on information available at time t, is specified to be a constant relative risk aversion expected utility function. For some random variable x, μ is given by:

$$\mu[x] = \left[Ex^{\alpha}\right]^{1/\alpha}, \quad 0 \neq \alpha < 1, \tag{9.60}$$

$$\log(\mu) = E\left[\log(x)\right], \quad \alpha = 0, \tag{9.61}$$

where $E(\,\cdot\,)$ is the expectation operator. In the current application, the random variable is the utility from consuming the uncertain consumption stream $\{\tilde{c}_{t+1}, \tilde{c}_{t+2}, \ldots\}$. Thus, we can derive a recursive specification for intertemporal utility as:

$$U_t = \left[(1-\beta)c_t^{\delta} + \beta(E_t U_{t+1}^{\alpha})^{\delta/\alpha}\right]^{1/\delta}, \quad \alpha \neq 0, \quad \delta \neq 0, \tag{9.62}$$

where $E_t(\,\cdot\,)$ is expectation conditional on information available at time t. If $\alpha < \delta$ then a consumer who satisfies the Kreps-Porteus axioms prefers early resolution of uncertainty to late and the opposite if $\alpha > \delta$. Notice that when $\alpha = \delta$, Equation (9.62) specializes to the expected utility specification $U_t^{\alpha} = (1-\beta)E_t\left\{\sum_{j=0}^{\infty}\beta^j c_{t+j}^{\alpha}\right\}$.[3]

Consider the problem of some representative consumer who makes optimal consumption and portfolio choices and whose preferences can be represented by Equation (9.62). The consumer is endowed with an initial stock of the consumption good, A_0, which can either be consumed or invested in assets traded on competitive markets. Suppose there are N assets available for trade. Let r_t denote an N-vector of returns with typical element $r_{j,t}$ which shows the gross, real return on an asset held throughout period t. Let ω_{jt} be the fraction of wealth invested in the jth asset. Each

[3] Notice that this specification can be obtained by considering a transformation of the non-expected utility preferences proposed by Weil as:

$$u_t = [1 + (1-\beta)(1-\gamma)U_t]^{\frac{1}{1-\gamma}}(1-\beta)^{1/\sigma - 1},$$

which implies that

$$u_t = \left\{(1-\beta)c_t^{1-\frac{1}{\sigma}} + \beta\left(E_t u_{t+1}^{1-\gamma}\right)^{\frac{1-1/\sigma}{1-\gamma}}\right\}^{\frac{1}{1-1/\sigma}}.$$

Letting $\delta = 1 - 1/\sigma$ and $\alpha = 1 - \gamma$ yields Equation (9.62) in the text.

$r_{j,t}$ has support $[\underline{r}, \bar{r}]$, $\underline{r} > 0$. We assume that (r_t, s_t) follows a first-order stationary Markov process with transition function F where s_t are variables that help to predict the future. The random vector (r_t, s_t) is observed at the beginning of period t before decisions are made.

When (r_t, s_t) follows a first-order Markov process, the state of the economy is summarized by $h_t \equiv (r_t, s_t)$. The state variables for the individual are her initial wealth and the current state of the economy. The consumer's problem can be formulated as a dynamic programming problem as follows:

$$V(A_t, h_t) \equiv \max_{c_t, \omega_t} \left\{ (1-\beta)c_t^{\delta} + \beta \left[E_t V(A_{t+1}, h_{t+1})^{\alpha} \right]^{\frac{\delta}{\alpha}} \right\}^{\frac{1}{\delta}}$$

subject to

$$A_{t+1} = (A_t - c_t)\omega_t' r_t$$

$$\sum_{j=1}^{N} \omega_{j,t} = 1.$$

The solution for this problem is a plan that expresses consumption and portfolio choices as a function of the state variables (A_t, h_t). Suppose there exists a solution that expresses (c_t, A_{t+1}) as homogeneous functions of the state variables; that is, for all (A_t, h_t), $g_t(1, h_t) = (c_t, A_{t+1})$ implies that $g_t(A_t, h_t) = (c_t A_t, A_{t+1})$. In this case, the consumer's value function is given by:

$$V(A_t, h_t) = \phi(h_t) A_t \equiv \phi_t A_t,$$

where

$$\phi_t A_t = \max_{c_t, \omega_t} \left\{ (1-\beta)c_t^{\delta} + \beta \left[E_t(\phi_{t+1} A_{t+1})^{\alpha} \right]^{\frac{\delta}{\alpha}} \right\}^{\frac{1}{\delta}} \tag{9.63}$$

subject to $A_{t+1} = (A_t - c_t)\omega_t' r_t$ and $\sum_{j=1}^{N} \omega_{j,t} = 1$. Substituting for A_{t+1} in Equation (9.63) and taking the derivative with respect to c_t yields:

$$\delta(1-\beta)c_t^{\delta-1} - \beta\delta(A_t - c_t)^{\delta-1}\mu^{\delta} = 0, \tag{9.64}$$

where

$$\mu = \left[E_t(\phi_{t+1} R_t^M)^{\alpha} \right]^{\frac{1}{\alpha}},$$

and R_t^M is the gross return on the optimal portfolio, $R_t^M = \omega_t' r_t$. Recall that consumption is proportional to wealth $c_t = \psi_t A_t$. Using this result in Equation (9.64), we can write the first-order condition as:

$$(1-\beta)(\psi_t A_t)^{\delta-1} = \beta(A_t - \psi_t A_t)^{\delta-1}\mu^{\delta}. \tag{9.65}$$

Now solve for μ^{δ} and substitute for it in Eq. (9.63) to obtain:

$$(\phi_t A_t)^{\delta} = (1-\beta)c_t^{\delta} + \beta(A_t - c_t)^{\delta}\left(\frac{1-\beta}{\beta}\right)\left(\frac{\psi_t}{1-\psi_t}\right)^{\delta-1}$$

$$(\phi_t A_t)^{\delta} = (1-\beta)\left[(\psi_t A_t)^{\delta} + (A_t - \psi_t A_t)^{\delta}\left(\frac{\psi_t}{1-\psi_t}\right)^{\delta-1}\right]$$

$$\phi_t^{\delta} = (1-\beta)[\psi_t^{\delta} + (1-\psi_t)\psi_t^{\delta-1}].$$

Thus,

$$\mu^{\delta} = \frac{1-\beta}{\beta}\left(\frac{\psi_t}{1-\psi_t}\right)^{\delta-1}$$

$$\phi_t = (1-\beta)^{\frac{1}{\delta}}\psi_t^{\delta-1} = (1-\beta)^{\frac{1}{\delta}}\left(\frac{c_t}{A_t}\right)^{\frac{\delta-1}{\delta}}.$$

We can re-write the Euler equation defined by Equation (9.65) by using the solution for μ^{δ} as:

$$(1-\beta)(\psi_t A_t)^{\delta-1} = \beta(A_t - \psi_t A_t)^{\delta-1}\left[E_t(\phi_{t+1}R_t^M)^{\alpha}\right]^{\frac{\delta}{\alpha}}$$

$$(1-\beta)\psi_t^{\delta-1} = \beta(1-\psi_t)^{\delta-1}\left\{E_t\left[(1-\beta)^{\frac{\alpha}{\delta}}\left(\frac{c_{t+1}}{A_{t+1}}\right)^{\frac{\alpha(\delta-1)}{\delta}}(R_t^M)^{\alpha}\right]\right\}^{\frac{\delta}{\alpha}}.$$

Substituting for $\psi_t = c_t/A_t$ and simplifying yields

$$\left(\frac{c_t}{A_t}\right)^{\delta-1} = \beta\left(\frac{A_t - c_t}{A_t}\right)^{\delta-1}\left\{E_t\left[\left(\frac{c_{t+1}}{A_{t+1}}\right)^{\frac{\alpha(\delta-1)}{\delta}}(R_t^M)^{\alpha}\right]\right\}^{\frac{\delta}{\alpha}}$$

$$\Rightarrow\quad c_t^{\delta-1} = \beta\left\{E_t\left[c_{t+1}^{\frac{\alpha(\delta-1)}{\delta}}(R_t^M)^{\frac{\alpha}{\delta}}\right]\right\}^{\frac{\delta}{\alpha}},$$

where we have substituted for $A_{t+1} = (A_t - c_t)R_t^M$ in the first line. Simplifying the last expression yields the consumption optimality equation as:

$$1 = \beta^{\frac{\alpha}{\delta}}E_t\left[\left(\frac{c_{t+1}}{c_t}\right)^{\frac{\alpha(\delta-1)}{\delta}}(R_t^M)^{\frac{\alpha}{\delta}}\right] \quad \alpha \neq 0,\ \delta \neq 0. \tag{9.66}$$

The optimal portfolio weights ω_t can be obtained by solving the problem:

$$\max_{\omega_t} \left[E_t(\phi_{t+1}\omega_t' r_t)^\alpha\right]^{\frac{1}{\alpha}} \quad \text{subject to} \quad \sum_{j=1}^{N} \omega_{j,t} = 1.$$

Let λ equal the Lagrange multiplier on the portfolio weight constraint. The first-order conditions with respect to $\omega_{j,t}$ are:

$$\frac{1}{\alpha}\left[E_t(\phi_{t+1}\omega_t' r_t)^\alpha\right]^{\frac{1}{\alpha}-1} E_t\left[(\phi_{t+1}\omega_t' r_t)^{\alpha-1}\phi_{t+1} r_{jt}\right] + \lambda = 0,$$

for $j = 1, \ldots, N$. Using one of these conditions to eliminate λ yields:

$$E_t\left[(\phi_{t+1}\omega_t' r_t)^{\alpha-1}\phi_{t+1}(r_{jt} - r_{1t})\right] = 0, \quad j = 2, \ldots, N.$$

Substituting for ϕ_{t+1}, we obtain:

$$E_t\left[\left(\frac{c_{t+1}}{A_{t+1}}\right)^{\frac{\alpha(\delta-1)}{\delta}} (R_t^M)^{\alpha-1}(r_{jt} - r_{it})\right] = 0$$

$$E_t\left[\left(\frac{c_{t+1}}{(A_t - c_t)R_t^M}\right)^{\frac{\alpha(\delta-1)}{\delta}} (R_t^M)^{\alpha-1}(r_{jt} - r_{it})\right] = 0$$

$$E_t\left[\left(\frac{c_{t+1}}{c_t}\right)^{\frac{\alpha(\delta-1)}{\delta}} (R_t^M)^{\frac{\alpha}{\delta}-1}(r_{jt} - r_{1t})\right] = 0, \quad j = 2, \ldots, N.$$

Multiplying the last expression by $\omega_{j,t}$, summing over j, and substituting from Equation (9.66) yields:

$$E\left[\beta^{\frac{\alpha}{\delta}}\left(\frac{c_{t+1}}{c_t}\right)^{\frac{(\delta-1)\alpha}{\delta}} (R_t^M)^{\frac{\alpha}{\delta}-1} r_{jt}\right] = 1, \quad j = 1, \ldots, N. \tag{9.67}$$

Notice that the intertemporal MRS or the stochastic discount factor that is used to price uncertain payoffs in this model is defined as:

$$m_{t+1} \equiv \left[\beta\left(\frac{c_{t+1}}{c_t}\right)^{\delta-1}\right]^{\frac{\alpha}{\delta}} \left(\frac{1}{R_t^M}\right)^{1-\frac{\alpha}{\delta}}, \tag{9.68}$$

which is a geometric average of the intertemporal MRS from the standard expected utility model and the intertemporal MRS from the logarithmic expected utility model.

If $\alpha = \delta$, then these first-order conditions become:

$$E_t\left[\beta\left(\frac{c_{t+1}}{c_t}\right)^{\delta-1} r_{jt}\right] = 1, \quad j = 1, \ldots, N,$$

which correspond to the first-order conditions for the expected utility model with constant relative aversion preferences. Hence, consumption growth is sufficient for discounting future payoffs as in the intertemporal asset-pricing model with time-additive preferences. Hence, the non-expected utility model yields similar implications as the expected utility model except that the elasticity of intertemporal substitution is no longer forced to be the inverse of the coefficient of relative risk aversion.

Another specialization that is of interest is logarithmic risk preferences, which occurs when $\alpha = 0$ but $\delta \neq 0$. Then the counterpart to Equation (9.67) is:

$$E_t\left[(R_t^M)^{-1} r_{jt}\right] = 1, \quad j = 1, \ldots, N.$$

In this case, the market return is sufficient for discounting uncertain payoffs as in the simple static CAPM. Notice that this specification imposes the same restrictions as those implied by the expected utility problem with logarithmic preferences.[4] One problem with this specification is that when $\alpha = 0$ (which corresponds to logarithmic risk preferences), the parameter δ (which governs intertemporal substitutability) cannot be identified from these equations. However, it can be identified from Equation (9.66). Write this equation as:

$$E_t\left[\frac{\{\beta(c_{t+1}/c_t)^{\delta-1} R_t^M\}^{\gamma} - 1}{\gamma}\right] = 0.$$

As α goes to zero, γ goes to zero and the above expression converges to:

$$\log(\beta) + (\delta - 1)E_t[\log(c_{t+1}/c_t)] + E_t[\log(R_t^M)] = 0,$$

which can be used to differentiate between the logarithmic expected utility model ($\alpha = \delta = 0$) and the non-expected utility model with logarithmic risk preferences ($\alpha = 0$, $\delta \neq 0$).

9.3. TESTS OF ASSET-PRICING RELATIONS

One of the most important applications of preferences that are non-additive over time or states has been in asset pricing. Initial tests of asset-pricing relations were based on the standard time-separable, expected utility model. The inability of this model to rationalize the joint behavior of consumption and asset returns led to the consideration of other specifications.

The influential study by Hansen and Singleton [237] provided estimates and tests for a single good, representative consumer model with time-additive preferences. These authors assume CRRA preferences with

[4] See Exercise 2 in Chapter 5.

$U(c) = (c^{1-\gamma} - 1)/(1 - \gamma)$, $\gamma \geq 0$, and considered one-period returns. Two measures of consumption are used: non-durables plus services and non-durables. The return series consists of the equally weighted average returns on all stocks listed on the New York Stock Exchange (NYSE), the value-weighted average return on stocks on the NYSE, and the equally weighted returns on the stocks of three two-digit SEC industries.[5] The sample period is from February, 1959 to December, 1978. The model is estimated by Generalized Method of Moments (GMM) using value-weighted and equally weighted stock returns separately and also by using the combinations of returns consisting of value-weighted and equally weighted stock returns, value-weighted returns and nominal risk-free bond returns, and the returns on three industry-average stock returns. The authors report greater evidence against the model when equally weighted returns were used. However, when the model is estimated with multiple returns, the orthogonality conditions are rejected at the 5% level for all sets of returns except for two sets of industry averages.

Tests of the representative consumer asset-pricing model have also been conducted by allowing for consumption and leisure choices (see Mankiw, Rotemberg, and Summers [332]), structural breaks (see Ghysels and Hall [199, 200]), alternative sample periods (Brown and Gibbons [82]), and the use of seasonally adjusted data (see Ferson and Harvey [184]). The results of these tests indicate that the single good, consumption-based asset-pricing model with time-additive preferences could not rationalize the joint time-series behavior of stock and bond returns. In particular, the strong rejections of the model involving stock returns and bond returns have been typically taken to imply that the common stochastic discount factor defined as the representative consumer's MRS cannot capture the relative risk structure of stocks versus bonds. In a related literature, Backus, Gregory, and Zin [41] and others demonstrate that the standard time-separable model cannot account for the risk premia in forward prices and holding returns on real and nominal risk-free bonds.

Partly in response to these results, models with preferences that are non-separable over time and states were put forward to account for various asset-pricing anomalies. Eichenbaum, Hansen, and Singleton [171], Eichenbaum and Hansen [169], and Dunn and Singleton [164] considered models with consumption durability, and estimated a positive impact of lagged consumption in Euler equations with monthly consumption data. Notice that under consumption durability, consumption expenditures are likely to exhibit negative autocorrelation. The reason is that a consumer who has purchased a durable consumption good in one period is

[5] In their revised estimates (published as "Errata" in 1984), they also use observations on a one-month, nominal risk-free bond return, converted to real returns by dividing by the implicit deflator associated with the measure of consumption.

unlikely to purchase another in following periods. By contrast, Ferson and Constantinides [183] find evidence for habit persistence using a broader instrument set and by measuring consumption at monthly, quarterly, and annual frequencies. These authors note that factors such as measurement error could induce negative autocorrelation in monthly consumption data and thereby lead to erroneous conclusions of consumption durability. They also find that the model with habit persistence is less likely to lead to rejections of the intertemporal Euler equations describing the joint behavior of consumption and asset returns. Various authors also estimated models with non-expected utility preferences. Epstein and Zin [177] use the framework described in Section 9.2.4 to provide tests of the intertemporal capital asset-pricing model. Although they obtained some favorable results with non-expected utility preferences, they find that these results are sensitive to the measure of consumption and the instrument set. Gregory and Voss [213] examine habit persistence and non-expected utility models to explain the term structure of interest rates. Braun, Constantinides, and Ferson [73] allow for both habit persistence and consumption durability for explaining asset returns and consumption data on an international basis.

These findings are related to the "equity premium puzzle" that we described earlier as well as the average real "risk-free rate puzzle" and the behavior of the term premia that have been studied using the approach proposed by Mehra and Prescott [341]. For example, the average real "risk-free rate puzzle" due to Weil [444] states that the average real risk-free return implied by a representative consumer model is too high relative to that in the data, a finding that also accounts for the "equity premium puzzle." The common cause of these findings is due to the fact that in the standard time-separable model, risk aversion and intertemporal substitution of consumption cannot be separately parameterized. As a consequence, the time-separable model that is calibrated using the observed moments for consumption growth and asset returns generates a consumption path that is too smooth to rationalize the variation in stock returns unless risk aversion is very high.

In the previous sections, we provided alternative specifications that relax the assumption that preferences are additive over time or states. These specifications go some way towards reconciling the puzzle. For example, Constantinides [118] shows that a habit that is 80% of normal consumption is sufficient to explain the equity premium puzzle. The intuition is straightforward: when there is a small drop in consumption, consumption *net* of the habit falls a lot, thus leading to a large drop in the intertemporal MRS. This type of variation makes it possible to explain the variation in the rates of return on equity relative to the risk-free asset without relying on high risk aversion. In other words, even though the observed consumption series is quite smooth, what matters for individuals' utility is not consumption *per se* but consumption *relative* to habit. Under the assumption of habit persistence in consumption, Constantinides [118] is able to generate a simulated equity premium that is in line with its observed magnitude for values of the risk aversion parameter around 2 or even lower. Another way of understanding this result is to note that preferences that are not additively separable over time or states break the relationship between risk aversion and intertemporal substitution in consumption.[6] As a consequence, the model with habit persistence can generate substantial variation in consumption growth even for low degrees of relative risk aversion.[7]

9.4. A MODEL WITH AN EXTERNAL HABIT

Campbell and Cochrane [93] argue that many existing asset-pricing phenomena can be explained using a model with an external habit. They also make use of the bounds on intertemporal MRSs.

In their model, the agent's utility function has the form:

$$U(C_t, X_t) = \frac{(C_t - X_t)^{1-\gamma} - 1}{1-\gamma}, \quad \gamma > 0. \tag{9.69}$$

where X_t denotes the level of the external habit. Define the *surplus consumption ratio* by:

$$S_t = \frac{C_t - X_t}{C_t}.$$

Thus, S_t increases with consumption C_t. The situation with $S_t = 0$ corresponds to a situation when actual consumption is equal to habit. As consumption rises above habit, the surplus consumption ratio approaches one. It is also possible to show that the curvature of the utility function is related to the surplus consumption ratio. To show this, consider:

[6] Consider a simple habit persistence model where current utility depends positively on current consumption and negatively on one lagged value of consumption with a coefficient $0 < h < 1$. As Exercise 4 shows, the product of the elasticity of intertemporal substitution ϵ and the coefficient of relative risk aversion *CRRA* is given by:

$$\epsilon \times CRRA = 1 - hR^{-1}$$

in the deterministic steady state. Under the restriction that $R > h$, it is easy to see that with habit persistence, this product may be substantially below one.

[7] However, this "resolution" may also have problems because the habit persistence model has unreasonable implications for consumption smoothing and optimal fiscal policy. See, for example, Lettau and Uhlig [308] or Ljungqvist and Uhlig [313].

$$-\frac{CU''(C,X)}{U'(C,X)} = \frac{\gamma C(C-X)^{-\gamma-1}}{(C-X)^{-\gamma}}$$
$$= \frac{\gamma C}{C-X}$$
$$= \frac{\gamma}{S}.$$

Hence, the lower is consumption relative to habit, the higher is the curvature of the utility function. Intuitively, a low surplus consumption ratio indicates a "recession" and a high surplus consumption ratio indicates a "boom."

The intertemporal MRS or stochastic discount factor for this model is given by:

$$m_{t+1} = \frac{\beta U_1(C_{t+1}, X_{t+1})}{U_1(C_t, X_t)} = \beta \left(\frac{S_{t+1}}{S_t} \frac{C_{t+1}}{C_t} \right)^{-\gamma}. \tag{9.70}$$

The intertemporal MRS varies not only with consumption growth but also with changes in the surplus consumption ratio, S_{t+1}/S_t. This feature of the model allows it to capture the impact of upturns and downturns in economic activity, as we discuss below.

The model is specified so that the habit is determined as a function of the history of aggregate consumption, C_t^a:

$$S_t^a = \frac{C_t^a - X_t}{C_t^a}.$$

However, for a representative consumer economy, individual consumption allocations equal the aggregate. Hence, we assume $S_t^a = S_t$ and $C_t = C_t^a$ in what follows. Let small-case letters denote the logarithm of the variable, $c = \ln(C)$, $x = \ln(X)$ and similarly for the other variables. To derive the empirical implications of this model, aggregate consumption growth is assumed to be an i.i.d. log-normal process, and the logarithm of the surplus consumption ratio is modelled as a first-order autoregressive conditionally heteroscedastic process:

$$\Delta c_{t+1} = g + v_{t+1}, \quad v_{t+1} \sim i.i.d, \quad N(0, \sigma^2)$$
$$s_{t+1} = (1-\phi)\bar{s} + \phi s_t + \lambda(s_t)(c_{t+1} - c_t - g),$$

where $\bar{s}$, ϕ, and g are parameters. These expressions show that the conditional variance of s_{t+1}^a varies with its own past:

$$Var_t(s_{t+1}) = \lambda(s_t)^2 Var(c_{t+1} - c_t - g) = \lambda(s_t)^2 \sigma^2.$$

Using these processes, the stochastic discount factor is expressed as:

$$\begin{aligned} m_{t+1} &= \beta\left(\frac{S_{t+1}}{S_t}\frac{C_{t+1}}{C_t}\right)^{-\gamma} \\ &= \beta G^{-\gamma}\exp\left(-\gamma(s_{t+1}-s_t+v_{t+1})\right) \\ &= \beta G^{-\gamma}\exp\left(-\gamma(\phi-1)(s_t-\bar{s})+[1+\lambda(s_t)]v_{t+1}\right), \end{aligned}$$

where $G = \exp(g)$.

Recall from the previous section that the slope of the mean-standard deviation frontier is given by:

$$\frac{E_t(R^e_{t+1})}{\sigma_t(R^e_{t+1})} \leq \frac{\sigma_t(m_{t+1})}{E_t(m_{t+1})},$$

where R^e denotes the excess return on any asset. Using the log-normality for m_{t+1}, we can express:

$$\max\frac{E_t(R^e_{t+1})}{\sigma_t(R^e_{t+1})} = [\exp(\gamma^2\sigma^2(1+\lambda(s_t))^2-1]^{1/2} \approx \gamma\sigma[1+\lambda(s_t)].$$

This relation is used to specify the model. In the data, the Sharpe ratios vary with time in that the conditional variance of returns changes but not on a one-for-one with the conditional means. This requires that $\lambda(s)$ must vary with s. Furthermore, there is evidence that risk premia increase in bad times. This requires that $\lambda(s)$ and hence, the volatility of s must increase as s falls. Notice that the conditional volatility in s_t is crucial in differentiating this model from the standard time-separable CRRA model. In particular, if $1+\lambda(s_t)$ is a constant, then the implications of the model with an external habit are very similar to the time-separable model except that $\gamma(1+\lambda)$ is substituted for γ.

The expression for the risk-free rate is also used to calibrate the model. Campbell and Cochrane [93] observe that the real risk-free rate is essentially constant over long horizons. Using the expression for the stochastic discount factor, the real interest rate is calculated as:

$$\begin{aligned} r^f_t &= \frac{1}{E_t(m_{t+1})} \\ &= -\ln(\beta)+\gamma g-\gamma(1-\phi)(s_t-\bar{s})-\frac{\gamma^s\sigma^2}{2}[1+\lambda(s_t)]^2. \end{aligned}$$

This equation shows the different factors that determine the real interest rate. The term $s_t-\bar{s}$ represents intertemporal substitution: when the surplus consumption ratio is significantly below its mean, the marginal utility of consumption is high, implying that consumers would like to borrow to consume more. However, as they do so, the real interest rate also rises. The second term reflects the effect of precautionary saving: as uncertainty (captured by the variable $\lambda(s_t)$) increases, consumers prefer to save, implying that the real interest rate falls. To generate a real interest rate with little or no variation over time, it must be the case that the intertemporal substitution effect in the real interest rate be offset by the precautionary saving effect.

Campbell and Cochrane [93] model the sensitivity function $\lambda(s_t)$ to ensure that i) the risk-free rate is a constant, ii) that habit is predetemined at the steady state, $(dx_t/dc_t)|_{s_t=\bar{s}}$, and iii) the habit moves positively everywhere with consumption, $d/ds\,(dx_t/dc_t)\,|_{s_t=\bar{s}}$. These authors consider two data sets. The first is comprised of the postwar (1947–95) value-weighted New York Stock Exchange stock index returns, three-month Treasury bill rate, and per capita non-durables and services consumption while the second is a long annual data set of Standard and Poor's 500 stock and commercial paper returns (1871–1993) and per capita consumption (1889–1992). They use the framework described above to price a consumption claim and a dividend claim, where the latter is assumed to evolve as an i.i.d. process. Their results indicate that both the price-dividend ratio for the dividend claim and the consumption claim rise with the surplus consumption ratio, S_t. When S_t is low (as in a "recession"), consumption is low relative to habit, implying that the curvature of the utility function is high. This tends to lower the intertemporal MRS, or pricing function, and to depress prices relative to dividends. Similarly, a decline in the surplus consumption ratio causes the expected return of the dividend and consumption claim to rise dramatically above the risk-free rate, and the conditional volatility of returns to rise.

Campbell and Cochrane [93] also discuss the resolution of the equity premium and the risk-free "puzzles" in the context of their model. As in the model with an internal habit or with non-expected utility preferences, the presence of the external habit breaks the relationship between risk aversion and intertemporal substitution in consumption. As we have discussed above, the curvature of the utility function in the model with an external habit is γ/S. Hence, a low value of γ is consistent with greater volatility in the intertemporal MRS. Likewise, in the time-separable model, a resolution of the risk-free rate "puzzle" requires a value of the discount factor β that exceeds one. By contrast, the model in Campbell and Cochrane [93] is able to generate a low risk-free rate with a low value of β. Unlike the specifications that we have described above, the model with an external habit implies that changes in current consumption do not have the effect of raising the future habit. Furthermore, the habit in their model adapts nonlinearly to consumption and hence, consumption never falls below habit whereas this is not the case with the simpler linear specifications considered in earlier sections.

9.5. CONCLUSIONS

Models with preferences that are non-separable over time and states have received increased attention in macroeconomics and finance in recent years. Such preferences allow for a richer specification of time and risk preferences than the standard case. As a consequence, they have featured in a variety of applications, including growth, consumption and saving, asset pricing, to name a few. In this chapter, we have provided a discussion of some commonly used preference specifications that allow for inseparabilities over time and states. Our discussion has highlighted some issues that are often important from the viewpoint of applied work, such as methods for measuring consumers' attitudes towards uncertain gambles over wealth versus their propensity to substitute consumption across different dates.

In this chapter, we have also described recursive frameworks for pricing durable consumption goods and characterized the representative consumer's portfolio choice problem under non-expected utility preferences. These results extend the basic asset-pricing model that we introduced in Chapter 8. However, in common with our discussion in Chapter 8, the frameworks analyzed in this chapter still pertain to a simple endowment economy. In the subsequent chapters, we introduce production and capital accumulation decisions. We also consider economies with incomplete markets, borrowing constraints, and other frictions. The consideration of such environments raises a variety of new issues such as the role of habit formation in an environment with production or the construction of volatility bounds with borrowing or short sales constraints. The groundwork that we have laid in this chapter provides the basis for considering such issues subsequently.

9.6. EXERCISES

1. Portfolio Separation

   Suppose that the consumer lives for two periods and has preferences of the form:

$$U(c) = -A\exp(-c/A), \quad A > 0.$$

   The consumer faces a complete set of contingent claims markets and maximizes the utility from current consumption c_0 and next period's state-contingent wealth W_s as:

$$\max_{c_0, \{W_s\}_{s=1}^{S}} U(c_0) + \beta \sum_{s=1}^{S} \pi_s U(W_s)$$

subject to

$$c_0 + \sum_{s=1}^{S} p_s W_s \leq W_0,$$

where p_s are the state-contingent prices, $0 < \pi_s < 1$ are the probabilities of each state, and W_0 is initial wealth that is given at date 0.

(a) Derive the following expression for next period's wealth:

$$W_s = (1+r^f)\left\{\frac{(\phi-1)\{W_0 - A\sum_{s=1}^{S} p_s \log(\pi_s\beta/p_s)\}}{\phi}\right\}$$

$$+\frac{\sum_{s=1}^{S}\log(\pi_s\beta/p_s)}{\sum_{s=1}^{S} p_s\log(\pi_s\beta/p_s)}\left\{A\sum_{s=1}^{S} p_s\log(\pi_s\beta/p_s)\right\}$$

where $\phi = 1 + \sum_{s=1}^{S} p_s$ and $1 + r^f \equiv (\sum_{s=1}^{S} p_s)^{-1}$.

(b) Show that the terms in braces sum to $W_0 - c_0$. Using this result, argue that the consumer holds her portfolio in two assets, one of which is risk free.

2. Consider a deterministic economy in which the representative consumer's preferences are given by:

$$\sum_{t=0}^{\infty} \beta^t \frac{(c_t - hc_{t-1})^{1-\gamma}}{1-\gamma}, \quad \gamma \geq 0, 0 < h < 1, 0 < \beta < 1.$$

The consumer has no labor income at any date. Let the consumer's initial wealth equal W_0 and the rate of return on wealth be R. Then:

$$W_t = (W_{t-1} - c_{t-1})R.$$

Further assume that initial wealth satisfies $W_0 - [hRc_{-1}/(R-h)] \geq 0$ and

$$1 < (\beta R)^{1/\gamma} < R, \quad h < R.$$

(a) Write down the value function for the consumer's problem. What are the state variables for the consumer's problem?

(b) What is the optimal consumption plan as a function of the state variables? Find an expression for the value function evaluated at the optimal consumption policy.

(c) Use the optimal consumption policy to solve for steady-state consumption.

(d) What is the coefficient of relative risk aversion (RRA) along an optimal path? In the steady state?

Hint: Use the expression for the value function evaluated at the optimal consumption policy.

(e) Find the elasticity of consumption with respect to the interest rate, i.e.:

$$\epsilon = \frac{\partial c_t}{\partial \ln(R)} \frac{1}{c_t}$$

along the optimal consumption path and in the steady state.

(f) How does the presence of habit persistence affect the value of RRA and ϵ?

3. Suppose that preferences are described according to the Weil specification in Equation (9.50). Suppose that the consumer's wealth evolves as:

$$A_{t+1} = R_t(A_t - c_t),$$

where $\{R_t\}_{t=0}^{\infty}$ is the stochastic interest rate which is distributed i.i.d.

(a) Show that the consumer's value function and optimal consumption policy can be written as:

$$V(A_t) = \frac{(\psi A_t)^{1-\gamma} - 1}{(1-\beta)(1-\gamma)},$$

$$c_t = \mu A_t,$$

where

$$\mu = 1 - \beta^{\sigma} \left[(E(R_t^{1-\gamma})^{1/(1-\gamma)} \right]^{\sigma(1-1/\sigma)},$$

$$\psi = [(1-\beta)\mu^{-1/\sigma}]^{1/(1-1/\sigma)}.$$

(b) What is the coefficient of relative risk aversion for wealth in this framework?

4. Let c_t denote purchases of non-durable consumption goods and d_t purchases of durable consumption goods, as defined in the National Income and Product Accounts, respectively. The service flow from non-durable consumption goods is given by:

$$c_t^{\star} = \alpha_0 c_t + \ldots + \alpha_m c_{t-m}, \quad m < \infty, \tag{9.71}$$

where $\alpha_j \geq 0$ and $\alpha_0 = 1$. Services from durable consumption goods are proportional to the sum of the stock of durable consumption goods at the beginning of period t (k_{t-1}) and durable goods purchases during period t (d_t):

$$d_t^{\star} = \theta(k_{t-1} + d_t), \quad 0 < \theta < 1. \tag{9.72}$$

The representative consumer owns the capital stock so that capital carried over into the next period k_t is equal to $k_{t-1} + d_t$ less the amount used to produce services:

$$k_t = (1-\theta)(k_{t-1} + d_t). \tag{9.73}$$

Preferences over sequences of consumption services $c_t^\star$ and $d_t^\star$ are given by:

$$E_0 \sum_{t=0}^{\infty} \beta^t U(c_t^\star, d_t^\star)$$

$$E_0 \left\{ \sum_{t=0}^{\infty} \beta^t \frac{\left(c_t^{\star\delta} d_t^{\star(1-\delta)}\right)^{1-\gamma} - 1}{1-\gamma} \right\}, \quad 0 < \delta < 1, \gamma \geq 0. \tag{9.74}$$

Let $p_{d,t}$ denote the price of durable consumption goods expressed in units of the numeraire good and $b_{j,t+1}$ the quantity of real risk-free bonds that are purchased at date t which mature in j periods. The longest maturity date is N and $Q_t^0 = 1$. The budget constraint for the representative consumer is given by:

$$c_t + p_{d,t} d_t + \sum_{j=1}^{N} b_{j,t+1} Q_t^j \leq y_t + \sum_{j=1}^{N} b_{j,t} Q_t^j, \tag{9.75}$$

where y_t is the endowment of the numeraire consumption good.

The representative consumer chooses sequences for c_t, d_t, and $b_{j,t+1}$, $j = 1, \ldots, N$ and $t \geq 0$ to maximize the objective function in Equation (9.74) subject to the constraints in Equations (9.71), (9.72), (9.73), and (9.75), given an initial capital stock k_{-1}.

(a) Formulate this problem as a dynamic programming problem.

(b) Let $\{\xi_t\}$ denote the sequence of Lagrange multipliers on the sequence of budget constraints in Equation (9.75). Derive the first-order conditions.

(c) Consider investment strategies that involve holding one-month Treasury bills for one month, holding three-month and six-month Treasury bills for three months, and rolling over a sequence of three one-month bills for three months. Let $h_{t,n}^k$ denote the gross holding return from following the kth investment strategy from date t to $t + n$, denominated in terms of the numeraire consumption good. Find expressions for $h_{t,n}^k$.

(d) Find expressions characterizing the behavior of the returns $h_{t,n}^k$ and the durable goods price $p_{d,t}$ in terms of observable measures of c_t and d_t, assuming the preferences in Equation (9.74).

CHAPTER 10

Economies with production

In the economies that we have studied up to this point, output has been taken as exogenous and no explicit consideration has been given to optimal investment decisions. Yet asset-pricing models such as the APT seek to model asset returns as a function of economy-wide sources of uncertainty, one of which may be technological uncertainty. There is also a large literature that seeks to link firms' investment decisions with their optimal financial structure. To address these issues, we now study investment and production decisions in an uncertain environment.

The one-sector optimal growth model has become the mainstay of dynamic macroeconomic modeling. Cass [99] and Koopmans [285] studied the long-run behavior of the deterministic one-sector optimal growth model, and showed the existence of a steady-state solution. This model was extended to the uncertainty case by Brock and Mirman [78], [79] and Mirman and Zilcha [344], who derived the optimal policy functions and the invariant distribution for capital stocks characterizing the stochastic steady state.

In Section 10.1, we provide a competitive equilibrium interpretation of the one-sector optimal growth model under uncertainty by considering first a setup where households own the capital stocks and make all investment decisions and second where they rent capital to firms on a period-by-period basis. This is similar to the approach in Brock [76], [77], who integrated the asset-pricing model with production, and Mehra and Prescott [340], who describe how to analyze dynamic competitive equilibrium models under uncertainty using a recursive approach. In this framework, the optimal allocations can be derived by exploiting the equivalence between the competitive equilibrium and the social planner's problem. However, when there are taxes, public goods, externalities, or other forms of distortions, this equivalence breaks down. In Section 10.2, we consider some extensions of the basic framework. First, we briefly describe some methods for solving for the competitive equilibrium in the presence of such distortions. We also analyze the model with correlated productivity shocks and examine the impact of changes in the current productivity shock on optimal savings behavior.

In Section 10.4, we show how the standard framework can be embedded in a more traditional and realistic setting in which firms own the capital stock and finance new investment by issuing equity and bonds. This framework allows us to analyze the optimal financial structure of a firm. If markets are complete and there are no other distortions, then we show that the Modigliani-Miller theorem holds and the corporate financial structure is irrelevant. In the presence of distortionary taxes, this result is no longer true. We use a version of the asset-pricing model with distortionary taxes to derive the latter result, and to show the nature of the firm's cost of capital variable. Our discussion follows Brock and Turnovsky [80]. Using this framework, we also derive the firm's optimal financial policy and show how it yields a version of Miller's [343] equilibrium with debt and taxes.

10.1. RECURSIVE COMPETITIVE EQUILIBRIUM WITH PRODUCTION

Suppose there exists a representative infinite-lived household with time additive preferences which supplies labor inelastically at one unit. The household maximizes

$$E_0 \left\{ \sum_{t=0}^{\infty} \beta^t U(c_t) \right\}, \quad 0 < \beta < 1, \tag{10.1}$$

where c_t denotes consumption of the single good and $E_0(\cdot)$ denotes expectation conditional on information at time zero. The following assumption characterizes the utility function.

Assumption 10.1 *The utility function $U : \Re_+ \to \Re_+$ is strictly concave, strictly increasing, and continuously differentiable with $U(0) = 0$, $U'(0) = \infty$ and $U'(\infty) = 0$.*

There is a single good that can be consumed or invested to produce new capital next period. Output of the single good is produced using the production technology:

$$y_t = f(k_t, \theta_t), \tag{10.2}$$

where θ_t is a random productivity shock and k_t is the capital stock.

Uncertainty is introduced by assuming that there are random shocks to productivity in each period. The following assumption characterizes the technology shock.

Assumption 10.2 *The technology shock takes values in the set $\Theta \equiv [\underline{\theta}, \bar{\theta}]$ with $\underline{\theta} > 0$ and $\bar{\theta} < \infty$ and follows a first-order Markov process with transition function F. The function $F : \Theta \times \Theta \to [0, 1]$ is defined such* *that* $F(\theta,\theta') \equiv \Pr(\theta_{t+1} \leq \theta' | \theta_t = \theta)$. *The transition function* F *satisfies Assumption 10.1.*

10.1.1. Households own the capital stock

Suppose first that the household owns the capital stock and makes all investment decisions. Let i_t denote gross investment and define $0 < \delta \leq 1$ as the depreciation rate of capital. The law of motion for the capital stock is:

$$k_{t+1} = (1-\delta)k_t + i_t. \tag{10.3}$$

The per capita resource or feasibility constraint states that total output is allocated between consumption and investment as:

$$c_t + i_t \leq f(k_t, \theta_t). \tag{10.4}$$

We can substitute for investment i_t using the law of motion to express the constraint facing a household as:

$$c_t + k_{t+1} - k_t \leq f(k_t, \theta_t) - \delta k_t. \tag{10.5}$$

In this expression,

- k_t denotes the per capita capital stock at the beginning of period t,
- $k_{t+1} - k_t = i_t - \delta k_t$ denotes *net* investment in the capital stock;
- $f(k_t, \theta_t) - \delta k_t$ is output net of depreciation.

We make the following assumption.

Assumption 10.3 *(i) The function* $f(\cdot, \theta)$ *is continuously differentiable, strictly increasing, and strictly concave on* $\Re_+$ *with* $f(0,\theta) = 0$, $f'(0,\theta) = \infty$, *and* $f'(\infty, \theta) = 0$. *(ii)* $f(k,\theta) - f'(k,\theta)k > 0$ *for all* $k > 0$.

The second part of this assumption ensures that profits are always positive. Notice that this assumption is consistent with a production function that displays constant returns to scale (CRTS) in capital and labor, where y and k are interpreted as the output per labor and capital per labor:

$$\begin{aligned} Y_t &= F(K_t, n_t, \theta_t) \\ &= n_t F(K_t/n_t, 1, \theta_t) \\ &= n_t f(k_t, \theta_t). \end{aligned}$$

Hence, $y_t = f(k_t, \theta_t)$ where $y_t = Y_t/n_t$ and $k_t = K_t/n_t$.

The household chooses (c_t, k_{t+1}) for $t = 0, 1, \ldots$ to solve

$$\max_{\{c_t, k_{t+1}\}} \left\{ E_0 \sum_{t=0}^{\infty} \beta^t U(c_t) \right\}, \tag{10.6}$$

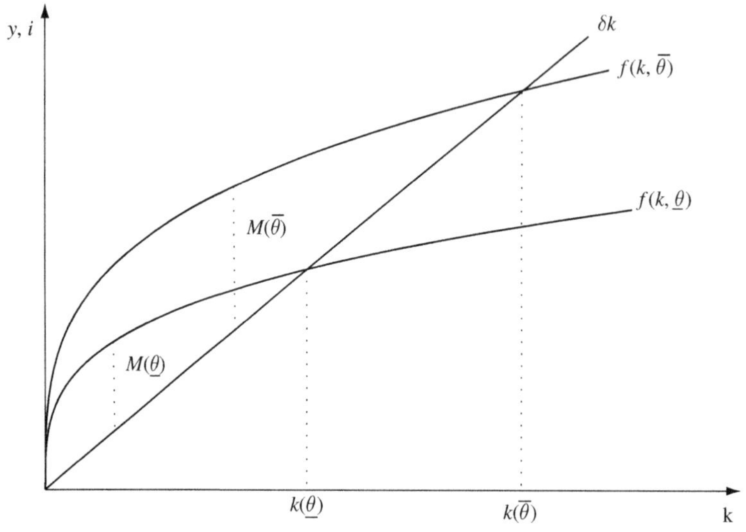

Figure 10.1. Configurations of capital stocks

subject to

$$c_t + k_{t+1} \leq f(k_t, \theta_t) + (1 - \delta)k_t, \tag{10.7}$$

$$c_t, k_{t+1} \geq 0, \tag{10.8}$$

given the fixed initial stock k_0 and the current realization of the technology shock θ_0. Notice that investment is reversible in this model because k_{t+1} may be less than $(1 - \delta)k_t$, implying that the household can consume the old capital stock. We drop this assumption in Chapter 11 when we consider a model with irreversible investment.

We now describe how to formulate this problem as a stationary dynamic programming problem. This approach yields solutions that are time-invariant functions of a finite set of state variables. We begin by showing that the set of feasible allocations $\Gamma(k_t, \theta_t)$, defined as pairs (c_t, k_{t+1}) satisfying Equation (10.7) is a compact set. Define $M(\theta)$ as

$$M(\theta) \equiv \max_k \left[f(k, \theta) - \delta k\right]$$

and let $\hat{k}(\theta)$ be the unique solution to

$$f(k, \theta) = \delta k.$$

Notice that f is increasing and strictly concave so that such a maximum exists. Define $\hat{k} \equiv \max_\theta \hat{k}(\theta)$ and $M \equiv \max_\theta M(\theta)$. These quantities are well defined because f is continuous and θ takes on values in the compact set $[\underline{\theta}, \bar{\theta}]$. Figure 10.1 illustrates the different quantities.

We have the following lemma.

Lemma 10.1 *If $\{k_t, c_t\}$ is any feasible plan for the problem in (10.6), then $0 \leq k_t \leq B$ and $0 \leq c_t \leq B + M$, where $B = \max(\hat{k} + M, \bar{k}_0)$.*

PROOF

First, $k_t \geq 0$ and $k_{t+1} \geq 0$ by assumption. Suppose $k_t > \hat{k}$, then $k_{t+1} < k_t$. This follows from the fact that $\hat{k}$ is the maximum sustainable capital stock. Using the budget constraint, it is also the case that:

$$k_{t+1} \leq f(k_t, \theta_t) - \delta k_t + k_t \leq k_t + M.$$

Define $B = \max(\hat{k} + M, \bar{k}_0)$ and $\bar{k}_0 = k_0$. Clearly, $k_0 = \bar{k}_0 \leq B$. Suppose $k_t \leq B$. If $k_t \leq \hat{k}$, then $k_{t+1} \leq k_t + M \leq \hat{k} + M \leq B$. If instead $k_t > \hat{k}$, then $k_{t+1} < k_t \leq B$ by assumption. Hence, $k_t \leq B$ for all t. Then it is straightforward to show that:

$$0 \leq c_t \leq f(k_t, \theta_t) - \delta k_t + k_t \leq M + B \;\; \forall t.$$

∎

We can also prove the following.

Lemma 10.2 *Under Assumptions 10.1–10.3, for any sequence $\{c_t, k_{t+1}\}$ such that (c_t, k_{t+1}) satisfy Equation (10.7) and the initial condition k_0, then*

$$E_0 \left\{ \sum_{t=0}^{\infty} \beta^t U(c_t) \right\} \leq \mathcal{U} < \infty. \tag{10.9}$$

PROOF

Define $\bar{C} = M + B$ and note that, for any feasible c_t, $c_t \in [0, \bar{C}]$. Because U is continuous and takes a compact set into $\Re_+$, we can define an upper bound $\mathcal{U} \equiv \sum_{t=0}^{\infty} \beta^t U(\bar{C}) < \infty$. ∎

In the following discussion, we drop the time subscripts on time t variables and let variables with primes, z', for example, denote variables at time $t + 1$. This notation emphasizes the recursive structure of the problem. The state variables for the problem consist of the current realization of the shocks θ and the beginning-of-period capital stock k. Since there is an upper (and lower) bound on the expected discounted present value of utility, the household's problem is well defined. Let $\mathcal{K} = [0, B]$. The valuation function $V : \mathcal{K} \times \Theta \rightarrow \Re_+$ for a dynamic programming problem satisfies the functional equation:

$$V(k, \theta) = \max_{(c,k') \in \Gamma(k,\theta)} \left\{ U(c) + \beta \int_{\Theta} V(k', \theta') dF(\theta, \theta') \right\}. \tag{10.10}$$

The maximization problem is to choose consumption and next period's capital stock subject to the aggregate resource constraint. Define $\mathcal{Y} \equiv \mathcal{K} \times \Theta$. Let $\mathcal{C}(\mathcal{Y})$ denote the space of continuous, bounded functions $\{V : \mathcal{Y} \to \Re\}$ equipped with the sup norm. Define the operator T by:

$$(TV)(k,\theta) = \max_{(c,k')\in\Gamma(k,\theta)} \left\{ U(c) + \beta \int_{\Theta} V(k',\theta')dF(\theta,\theta') \right\}. \tag{10.11}$$

We have the following theorem.

Theorem 10.1 *Let $T : \mathcal{C}(\mathcal{Y}) \to \mathcal{C}(\mathcal{Y})$ be defined by Equation (10.11). Under Assumptions 10.1–10.3, the operator is a contraction with unique fixed point $V^\star$, which is bounded, increasing, and concave. Further, there exist unique, bounded, and increasing optimal policy functions,*

$$c = g(k,\theta), \tag{10.12}$$

$$k' = h(k,\theta), \tag{10.13}$$

that satisfy

$$V^\star(k,\theta) = U(g(k,\theta)) + \beta \int_{\Theta} V^\star(h(k,\theta),\theta')dF(\theta,\theta'). \tag{10.14}$$

such that $g(k,\theta) + h(k,\theta) = y = f(k,\theta) + (1-\delta)k$.

PROOF
Notice that U is continuous and $\int_{\Theta} V(k',\theta')dF(\theta,\theta)$ is continuous for continuous V. Thus, applying T involves maximizing a continuous function over a compact set so that TV is well defined for any $V \in \mathcal{C}(\mathcal{Y})$. Since $U(c)$ is bounded because c is bounded and U is continuous, TV is bounded and hence continuous. Thus, for any $V \in \mathcal{C}(\mathcal{Y})$, the operator T takes continuous, bounded functions into continuous, bounded functions. The operator T is monotone; for any $V_1, V_2 \in \mathcal{C}(\mathcal{Y})$ such that if $V_1 > V_2$, then $TV_1 \geq TV_2$. Because $0 < \beta < 1$, the operator T also discounts, that is, $T(V+a) \leq TV + \beta a$ for $a \geq 0$. Hence, T satisfies Blackwell's conditions for a contraction. Thus, there exists a unique solution, $V^\star(k,\theta) = (TV^\star)(k,\theta)$.

To prove that $V^\star$ is increasing and concave, choose some $\bar{V} \in \mathcal{C}(\mathcal{Y})$ that is increasing and concave. Denote the space of continuous, bounded, increasing, and concave functions defined on $\mathcal{Y}$ by $\mathcal{C}'(\mathcal{Y})$. Applying the operator T to $\bar{V}$ notice that T preserves these properties so that $T : \mathcal{C}'(\mathcal{Y}) \to \mathcal{C}'(\mathcal{Y})$. Because the space of continuous, bounded, increasing, and concave functions $\mathcal{C}'(\mathcal{Y})$ is a subspace of the space of continuous and bounded functions $\mathcal{C}(\mathcal{Y})$ and we have shown that T is a contraction,

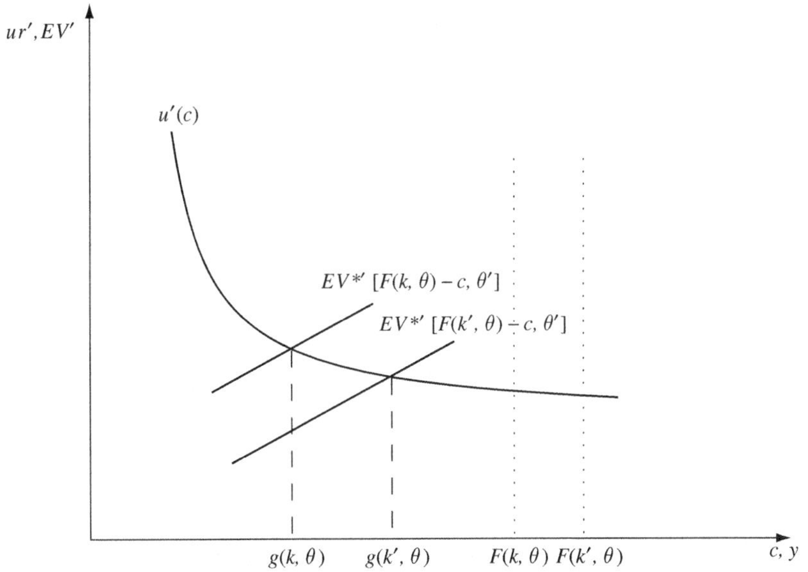

Figure 10.2. Optimal consumption and capital stocks

we can conclude that $V^\star$ is increasing and concave. This follows as an application of Corollary 6.1 in Chapter 6.

Because $V^\star$ is concave and U is strictly concave by assumption, we can conclude that the optimal policy (defined by the functions g and h) is unique and, by the Theorem of the Maximum, it is continuous and bounded. Finally, by the envelope theorem, we have that $V_k^\star(k,\theta) = U'(g(k,\theta)) > 0$. ∎

Since the valuation function $V^\star$ is strictly concave, the necessary and sufficient conditions for an optimum are given by:

$$U'(c) = \beta \int_\Theta U'(c') \left[f'(k',\theta') + (1-\delta) \right] dF(\theta,\theta'),$$

$$c + k' = y = f(k,\theta) + (1-\delta)k.$$

Define $F(k,\theta) = f(k,\theta) + (1-\delta)k$ and subsume β in the definition of $V(\cdot)$. Figure 10.2 illustrates the first-order condition for the household's (interior) optimum.

Reverting to time subscripts, we can re-write these conditions as

$$U'(c_t) = \beta E_t \left\{ U'(c_{t+1}) \left[f'(k_{t+1},\theta_{t+1}) + (1-\delta) \right] \right\}, \qquad (10.15)$$

where $c_t = f(k_t,\theta_t) + (1-\delta)k_t - k_{t+1}$.

Notice that the optimal policy function for the capital stock provides a way for describing the evolution over time of next period's capital, given this period's capital stock and the current shock. However, it does not allow us to make unconditional probability statements about the future capital stock. For this purpose, we need to derive the stationary distribution of the capital stock and to characterize this distribution. The characterization of this distribution is particularly important for non-linear models in which a deterministic steady state cannot be calculated explicitly. A formal derivation of the stationary distribution of the capital stock is in the appendix to this chapter.

10.1.2. *Households lease capital to firms*

We begin by solving the problem for the representative firm. In this formulation, we use the form of the CRTS production function F that depends on capital and labor. We assume that there is a firm that hires labor at real wage w_t and rents capital from households, paying a rental rate of r_t. The firm returns the undepreciated part of the capital denoted by $(1-\delta)K_t$ to the household at the end of period t.

The representative firm has profits each period determined by:

$$\max_{\{K_t,n_t\}} F(K_t, n_t, \theta_t) - w_t n_t - r_t K_t$$

The first-order conditions are:

$$F_1(K_t, n_t, \theta_t) = r_t, \tag{10.16}$$

$$F_2(K_t, n_t, \theta_t) = w_t, \tag{10.17}$$

which says that all factors are utilized up to the point where their marginal products equal the relevant factor prices.

The household supplies labor and rents capital to firms. Hence, it has the budget constraint:

$$c_t + K_{t+1} \leq w_t n_t + r_t K_t + (1-\delta)K_t. \tag{10.18}$$

This equation says that the household's consumption c_t and investment in new capital $K_{t+1} - (1-\delta)K_t$ must equal the sum of its wage income $w_t n_t$ and rental income $r_t K_t$. The Bellman equation is:

$$V(K_t, \theta_t) = \max_{\{c_t, K_{t+1}\}} [U(c_t) + \beta E_t V(K_{t+1}, \theta_{t+1})] \tag{10.19}$$

subject to the budget constraint in Equation (10.18). Let λ_t denote the Lagrange multiplier for the budget constraint. The first-order conditions with respect to c_t and K_{t+1} are:

$$U'(c_t) = \lambda_t, \tag{10.20}$$

$$\lambda_t = \beta E_t \left[V_k(K_{t+1}, \theta_{t+1}) \right]. \tag{10.21}$$

The envelope condition is:

$$V_k(K_t, \theta_t) = \lambda_t[r_t + (1 - \delta)] \tag{10.22}$$

We can derive the first-order condition that optimal consumption choices must satisfy by solving (10.20) for λ_t, substituting into (10.21) and (10.22). Increasing the time subscript by one unit in (10.22) and then substituting into (10.21) yields:

$$U'(c_t) = \beta E_t \left\{ U'(c_{t+1})[r_{t+1} + (1 - \delta)] \right\}. \tag{10.23}$$

There are three market-clearing conditions:
the *goods* market

$$c_t + K_{t+1} - (1 - \delta)K_t = F(K_t, n_t, \theta_t)$$

where output produced in period t is allocated to consumption plus investment;
the *labor* market

$$w_t = F_2(K_t, 1, \theta_t)$$

where the fixed labor supply $n_t = 1$ has been incorporated;
the *capital* market

$$r_t = F_1(K_t, 1, \theta_t)$$

where households rent out all of their capital. Note that the firm returns the undepreciated capital to the households.

To construct the equilibrium, we combine the household's and firm's first-order conditions and the market-clearing conditions. We substitute the market-clearing conditions for the labor market and capital rental market into the household's budget constraint and use the property of a CRTS production function to show that total factor payments equal output,

$$w_t n_t + r_t k_t = F(k_t, n_t, \theta_t).$$

Writing the real rental rate and the real wage in terms of the capital per labor production function, we also find that:

$$r_t = f'(k_t, \theta_t)$$

$$w_t = f(k_t, \theta_t) - f'(k_t, \theta_t)k_t.$$

Hence, the budget constraint is identical to the one in Equation (10.5). Equation (10.23) is now

$$U'(c_t) = \beta E_t \left\{ U'(c_{t+1})[f'(k_{t+1}, \theta_{t+1}) + (1 - \delta)] \right\}, \tag{10.24}$$

which is equivalent to the case when households own the capital stock.

10.2. EXTENSIONS

In the economies that we examined in the previous sections, the competitive equilibrium allocations could be characterized by exploiting the equivalence between competitive equilibrium and Pareto optimum. When there are distortions such as non-lump sum taxes, money, imperfectly competitive markets, borrowing constraints, or transaction costs, it is necessary to devise other methods for characterizing the equilibrium. This is the first topic that we address in this section. Second, we use the growth model to examine the role of expectations in determining optimal consumption and capital stock allocations.

10.2.1. Economies with distortions

In this section, we discuss the approach of constructing an *equivalent social planner's problem* whose allocations mimic those of the non-optimal competitive equilibrium. This discussion allows us to examine the impact of taxation on capital accumulation decisions. It also allows us to analyze the impact of distortionary taxation on equity prices. (See Exercise 2.) Danthine and Donaldson [134] provide a comprehensive discussion of the alternative approaches to finding equilibria in non-optimal economies. Under some circumstances, it may be possible to use a contraction-based approach for solving the intertemporal Euler equation. We illustrated this approach for the solution of the Lucas asset-pricing model in Chapter 8, and we will describe variants of it when we introduce monetary models. We will also describe a method for directly computing the equilibrium for an economy with borrowing constraints.

Consider an economy with a distortionary tax on capital income. The assumptions are identical to those in Section 10.1. The production function has the multiplicative form $f(k_t)\theta_t$, where k_t is the capital stock. Second, the stochastic technology shock θ_t follows a first-order Markov process that is characterized by Assumption 10.2. Finally, capital depreciates 100% each period.

Firms take the rental rate on capital r_t as given and choose how much capital to rent from households. Their problem is defined as:

$$\max_{k_t} \pi_t = f(k_t)\theta_t - r_t k_t.$$

The first-order condition for the firm's problem is given by:

$$f'(k_t)\theta_t = r_t. \tag{10.25}$$

Since firms solve a static problem, they choose how much capital to rent by maximizing one-period profits each period.

Households own the stocks of capital which they rent to firms. They are taxed on their capital income at the rate τ and receive a lump-sum transfer from the government. Their problem can be expressed as follows:

$$\max_{\{c_t, k_{t+1}\}_{t=0}^{\infty}} E_0 \left\{ \sum_{t=0}^{\infty} \beta^t U(c_t) \right\}$$

subject to $c_0 + k_1 = y_0$ where y_0 is given, and

$$c_t + k_{t+1} = (1 - \tau) r_t k_t + g_t,$$

where $(1 - \tau) r_t k_t$ denotes rental income net of taxes. Here k_t denotes the household's holdings of capital at the beginning of period t.

Let K_t denote the per capita aggregate capital stock. The government taxes capital and then redistributes its revenue in a lump-sum fashion:

$$g_t = \tau r_t K_t. \tag{10.26}$$

The per capita or aggregate capital stock is taken as given by households.

Let λ_t denote the Lagrange multiplier on the household's budget constraint. The first-order conditions with respect to c_t and k_{t+1} are given by:

$$U'(c_t) = \lambda_t, \tag{10.27}$$

$$\lambda_t = \beta(1 - \tau) E_t [r_{t+1} \lambda_{t+1}], \tag{10.28}$$

In equilibrium the individual holdings of capital equal the per capita holdings so that $k_t = K_t$. Furthermore, consumption plus investment equal total output, $c_t + K_{t+1} = f(K_t)\theta_t$. Recall that we are using the per capita form of the production function so that $n_t = 1$.

Using the market-clearing conditions in the household's and firm's problem, the optimal policy functions satisfy the condition:

$$U'(c_t) = \beta(1 - \tau) E_t \left[U'(c_{t+1}) f'(K_{t+1}) \theta_{t+1} \right], \tag{10.29}$$

where $c_t + K_{t+1} = f(K_t)\theta_t$

Now consider the following social planning problem:

$$\max_{\{c_t, K_{t+1}\}_{t=0}^{\infty}} E_0 \left\{ \sum_{t=0}^{\infty} \beta^t (1 - \tau)^t U(c_t) \right\}$$

subject to

$$c_t + K_{t+1} = f(K_t)\theta_t, \quad K_0 \text{ given.}$$

It is straightforward to see that the first-order conditions for the equivalent social planner's problem satisfy Equation (10.29). Since the allocations in the social planner's problem must be feasible, they also satisfy the market-clearing conditions. Hence, this approach shows that the equivalent social planner's problem provides a convenient way for obtaining the competitive equilibrium allocations for non-optimal economies. In this application, the distortionary tax has the effect of reducing the discount factor. As a result, investment is lower and the mean values of consumption, capital stock, and output are lower compared with an otherwise identical but untaxed economy. This is despite the fact that the government returns the tax proceeds in a lump-sum manner to the household.

Example 10.1 Assume that the model with a capital income tax has an i.i.d. technology shock $\{\theta_t\}_{t=0}^{\infty}$. Suppose the utility function is of the logarithmic variety, $U(c) = \ln(c)$, and that the production function satisfies $f(k,\theta) = k^\alpha \theta$ with $\alpha < 1$. Suppose that firms take the rental rate on capital r_t as given and choose how much capital to rent from households. Households own the stocks of capital which they rent to firms. They also trade in claims to the output produced by firms. They are taxed on their capital income at the rate τ and receive a lump-sum transfer from the government.

The firm's problem is defined as:

$$\max_{k_t} \pi_t = k_t^\alpha \theta_t - r_t k_t.$$

The first-order condition is:

$$\alpha k_t^{\alpha-1} \theta_t = r_t. \tag{10.30}$$

The household's problem can be expressed as follows:

$$\max_{\{c_t, k_{t+1}\}_{t=0}^{\infty}} E\left\{\sum_{t=0}^{\infty} \beta^t \ln(c_t)\right\}$$

subject to

$$c_t + k_{t+1} + q_t z_{t+1} = (1-\tau) r_t k_t + (q_t + d_t) z_t + g_t, \quad t \geq 0,$$

where q_t is the ex-dividend price of the equity, d_t is the dividend, g_t is the lump-sum transfer from the government, and y_0 is given. Here k_t denotes the household's holdings of capital at the beginning of period t and z_t and z_{t+1} are its share holdings at the beginning of t and $t+1$, respectively. We assume that the total number of shares in each period is one.

Let K_t denote the per capita aggregate capital stock. The government taxes capital and then redistributes its revenue in a lump-sum fashion:

$$g_t = \tau r_t K_t = \tau \alpha K_t^\alpha \theta_t. \tag{10.31}$$

In equilibrium the individual holdings of capital equal the per capita holdings so that $k_t = K_t$. Furthermore, $z_{t+1} = z_t = 1$ and consumption plus investment equal total output, $c_t + K_{t+1} = f(K_t)\theta_t$.

The optimal policy functions satisfy the first-order condition:

$$\frac{1}{c_t} = \beta(1-\tau)E\left[\frac{1}{c_{t+1}}\alpha K_{t+1}^{\alpha-1}\theta_{t+1}\right]. \tag{10.32}$$

Notice that this example falls within the class of problems described in Chapter 6. Hence, we guess that the policy functions for consumption and investment have the form, $c_t = \phi y_t$ and $K_{t+1} = (1-\phi)y_t$, where $y_t = f(K_t)\theta_t$ and ϕ is a constant to be determined. By our hypothesis,

$$c_{t+1} = \phi K_{t+1}^{\alpha}\theta_{t+1} = \phi[(1-\phi)y_t]^{\alpha}\theta_{t+1}.$$

Substituting these expressions in Equation (10.32) yields:

$$\frac{1}{\phi y_t} = (1-\tau)\beta E\left\{\alpha[(1-\phi)y_t]^{\alpha-1}\theta_{t+1}\frac{1}{\phi[(1-\phi)y_t]^{\alpha}\theta_{t+1}}\right\}.$$

This can be solved for $\phi = 1-\alpha\beta(1-\tau)$, yielding the solutions for c_t and K_{t+1} as:

$$c_t = [1-\alpha\beta(1-\tau)]y_t, \tag{10.33}$$

$$K_{t+1} = \alpha\beta(1-\tau)y_t. \tag{10.34}$$

To derive an expression for the equity price, we substitute for profits equal to $\pi_{t+i} = (1-\alpha)K_{t+i}^{\alpha}\theta_{t+i}$ and $c_{t+i} = \phi y_{t+i}$ into the equilibrium condition for shares. This yields:

$$\frac{q_t}{y_t} = \beta E\left[(1-\alpha) + \frac{q_{t+1}}{y_{t+1}}\right]. \tag{10.35}$$

We guess that the solution has the form, $q_t = \psi y_t$. Equating coefficients on both sides of Equation (10.35) yields $\psi = \beta(1-\alpha) + \beta\psi$, or $\psi = (1-\beta)^{-1}\beta(1-\alpha)$. Thus, the equity price is given by:

$$q_t = \frac{\beta}{1-\beta}(1-\alpha)\theta_t K_t^{\alpha}. \tag{10.36}$$

Notice that consumption, investment, output, and the equity price exhibit persistence because they depend on current capital. The capital tax rate also affects the entire time path of the endogenous variables although its effect on the equity price is indirectly through output and capital.

In the above framework, the tax rate is deterministic. Other studies that analyze the effects of distortionary taxation on capital accumulation include Judd ([267, 268]). Dotsey [158] studies the effect of production taxes in a stochastic growth model. In his model, the stochastic tax is assessed on the firm's profits and the tax rate is the only source of randomness. Coleman [113] studies the effect of a state-dependent income tax on the capital accumulation process. Bizer and Judd [66] also discuss the effects of distortionary taxation in a general equilibrium model. They show that the volatility of the investment tax credit around a constant mean induces substantial variability in investment, thus giving rise to a large welfare cost.

10.2.2. *The role of expectations*

The role of expectations in determining macroeconomic outcomes and equity prices is a topic of much recent interest. Even in the simple growth model that we considered in Section 10.1.1. with correlated shocks, there may exist interesting dynamics arising from the fact that the current realization of the shock conveys information as to future realizations. Donaldson and Mehra [155] have used such a framework to derive further implications of the model with correlated technology shocks. The role of expectations in mitigating or exacerbating the impact of changes in a stochastic investment credit on investment is studied by Altug, Demers, and Demers [21].

To simplify the model, we also assume that the technology shock has the multiplicative form as:

$$y_t = f(k_t)\theta_t.$$

We characterize the distribution with the following two assumptions.

Assumption 10.4 *Let $F : \Theta \times \Theta \rightarrow [0, 1]$ denote the transition for the technology shock where $\Theta = [\underline{\theta}, \bar{\theta}]$ where $0 < \underline{\theta} < \bar{\theta} < \infty$. For fixed θ_t, $F(\theta_{t+1}; \theta_t)$ denotes the probability distribution for next period's shock. Thus, for all θ_t,*

$$F(\theta_{t+1}; \theta_t) = 0, \quad \theta_{t+1} \leq \underline{\theta}$$

$$F(\theta_{t+1}; \theta_t) = 1, \quad \theta_{t+1} \geq \bar{\theta}.$$

The density function $dF(\cdot; \cdot)$ is continuous on $\Theta \times \Theta$, strictly positive, and there exists an $L > 0$ such that for all $\theta_1, \theta_2 \in \Theta$,

$$\int_{\Theta} |dF(\theta; \theta_2) - dF(\theta; \theta_1)| < L|\theta_2 - \theta_1|.$$

Assumption 10.5 *$F(\theta_{t+1}; \theta_t')$ stochastically dominates $F(\theta_{t+1}; \theta_t)$ in the first degree (in the sense of Rothschild and Stiglitz) whenever $\theta_t' > \theta_t$.*

This assumption captures the notion that it is more likely that tomorrow will be similar to today rather than different.

Consider the problem of solving

$$\max_{\{c_t, k_{t+1}\}_{t=0}^{\infty}} E_0 \left\{ \sum_{t=0}^{\infty} \beta^t U(c_t) \right\} \tag{10.37}$$

subject to

$$c_t + k_{t+1} \leq y_t = f(k_t)\theta_t, \tag{10.38}$$

given y_0. The state variables of the model are given by the beginning-of-period capital stock k and the current realization of the technology shock, θ. However, knowing k and θ also implies knowledge of current output y. Hence, we can equivalently choose the state variables as y_t and θ_t. Dropping time subscripts and denoting current values with unprimed variables and future values with primed variables, the associated dynamic programming problem can be written as:

$$V(y, \theta) = \max_{c,k'} \left\{ U(c) + \beta E_\theta [V(y', \theta')] \right\}$$

subject to (10.38) where $E_\theta(\cdot)$ denotes conditional expectation.

Let ξ denote the Lagrange multiplier on the aggregate resource constraint. The first-order and envelope conditions are:

$$U'(c) = \xi, \tag{10.39}$$

$$\xi = \beta E_\theta \left[\frac{\partial V(y', \theta')}{\partial k} \right], \tag{10.40}$$

$$\frac{\partial V(y, \theta)}{\partial k} = U'(c) f'(k)\theta. \tag{10.41}$$

The optimal policy is given by the functions $c = g(y, \theta)$ and $k' = h(y, \theta)$.

The issue to be investigated is the impact of changes in θ_t on the optimal consumption and capital accumulation (or saving) decisions. Such an effect is predicted because the current realization of θ_t conveys information about its future values. Consider the first-order condition in which the policy functions have been substituted as:

$$U'(g(y, \theta)) = \beta f'(k') \int V_1(f(k')\theta', \theta')\theta' dF(\theta'; \theta).$$

We consider a specialization of the model by assuming the preferences are of the constant relative risk aversion variety:

$$U(c) = (c^{1-\gamma} - 1)/(1 - \gamma), \quad \gamma > 0, \tag{10.42}$$

and the technology displays diminishing returns to scale:

$$f(k, \theta) = k^\alpha \theta, \quad 0 < \alpha < 1. \tag{10.43}$$

The first-order condition becomes:

$$g(y, \theta)^{-\gamma} = \beta \alpha (k')^{\alpha - 1} \int V_1((k')^\alpha \theta', \theta')\theta' dF(\theta'; \theta). \tag{10.44}$$

We are interested in determining the effect of changes in the current realization of the technology shock θ on optimal consumption and savings behavior. For this purpose, differentiate the first-order condition with respect to θ using the fact that $k' = y - g(y,\theta)$:

$$\left(-\frac{\partial g(y,\theta)}{\partial\theta}\right)\Big[-\gamma g(y,\theta)^{-\gamma-1} + \beta\alpha(\alpha-1)(k')^{\alpha-2}\int V_1((k')^{\alpha}\theta',\theta')\theta' dF(\theta';\theta)$$
$$+\beta\alpha^2(k')^{2(\alpha-1)}\int V_{11}((k')^{\alpha}\theta',\theta')(\theta')^2 dF(\theta';\theta)\Big]$$
$$+\lim_{\epsilon\to 0}\frac{\beta}{\epsilon}\alpha(k')^{\alpha-1}\int V_1((k')^{\alpha}\theta',\theta')\theta'\left[dF(\theta';\theta+\epsilon) - dF(\theta';\theta)\right] = 0.$$

To see the impact of changes in the current technology shock on optimal consumption and saving, write this condition as:

$$\Big[-\gamma c^{-\gamma-1} + \beta\alpha(\alpha-1)(k')^{\alpha-2}\int V_1((k')^{\alpha}\theta',\theta')\theta' dF(\theta';\theta)$$
$$+\beta\alpha^2(k')^{2(\alpha-1)}\int V_{11}((k')^{\alpha}\theta',\theta')(\theta')^2 dF(\theta';\theta)\Big]\frac{\partial g(y,\theta)}{\partial\theta}$$
$$= \lim_{\epsilon\to 0}\frac{\beta}{\epsilon}\alpha(k')^{\alpha-1}\int V_1((k')^{\alpha}\theta',\theta')\left[dF(\theta';\theta+\epsilon) - dF(\theta';\theta)\right]. \tag{10.45}$$

Recall that the value function V is increasing and concave in y so that the sign of $\partial c/\partial\theta$ depends on the sign of the term on the right side of equation (10.45). If this term is negative, then $\partial c/\partial\theta > 0$ and if this term is positive, then $\partial c/\partial\theta < 0$. Assuming the limit exists and ignoring the term $\beta\alpha(k')^{\alpha-1}$, we can integrate this expression by parts to obtain:

$$\int V_1((k')^{\alpha}\theta',\theta')\theta' dF_{\theta}(\theta';\theta)$$
$$= V_1((k')^{\alpha}\theta',\theta')\theta' F(\theta';\theta)\Big|_{\underline{\theta}}^{\bar{\theta}} - \int V_{1\theta}((k')^{\alpha}\theta',\theta')\theta' F(\theta';\theta). \tag{10.46}$$

Notice that $\partial c/\partial\theta < 0$ if $V_{1\theta} < 0$. To determine the sign of this cross-partial derivative, it is necessary to examine the behavior of the limit of the sequence of approximating functions $\{V_1^n\}$ to V_1.[1] We can illustrate the nature of the results by defining $V^n(y, \theta)$ to satisfy:

$$V^n(y,\theta) = \max_{c,k'} \left\{ \frac{c^{1-\gamma} - 1}{1-\gamma} + \beta \int V^{n-1}((k')^{\alpha}\theta', \theta') dF(\theta'; \theta) \right\}$$

subject to

$$c + k' \le y.$$

To give a flavor of the results that can be obtained, we consider the case with $n = 1$. In this case, we have that $V_1^1(y, \theta) = (k^{\alpha}\theta)^{-\gamma}$ so that

$$\frac{\partial V_1^1(k^{\alpha}\theta, \theta)\theta}{\partial \theta} = -\gamma(k^{\alpha}\theta)^{-\gamma-1}k^{\alpha}\theta + (k^{\alpha}\theta)^{-\gamma}$$

$$= (k^{\alpha}\theta)^{-\gamma}[-\gamma + 1] < 0$$

if and only if $\gamma > 1$. While the impact of θ on c_t is more complicated for V_1^n, we can nevertheless show that consumption will be increasing in the current realization of the technology shock provided the consumer displays "sufficient" risk aversion. The interpretation of these results is noteworthy. In economies where consumers are sufficiently risk averse, optimal saving behavior will tend to stabilize output and consumption. In a situation when a low current value of the technology shock signals a low future value, a highly risk-averse agent saves more the lower is the shock. This mitigates the effects of any future output declines. By contrast, less risk-averse consumers save less in response to a low realization of the technology shock. Since a low value of the shock today signals a low value of the shock tomorrow, this type of saving behavior tends to exacerbate the effects of future output declines by reducing investment today. In the case of logarithmic preferences, the optimal consumption/saving policies depend only on the current realization of the capital stock (or current output), implying no role for the current shock.

10.3. SOLVING MODELS WITH PRODUCTION

Up to this point, we have characterized the solutions for models with production. However, many recent applications also derive numerical solutions for dynamic equilibrium models, and examine how their predictions match up with the data. One approach to solving such models is to implement a log-linearization around a deterministic steady state to the first-order conditions of the model. However, this approach is not feasible

[1] See Danthine and Donaldson [155] or Altug, Demers, and Demers [21] for a similar proof in the context of an irreversible investment model with a stochastic investment tax credit.

if there exist non-negativity constraints for some of the choice variables. Another approach is to replace the original non-linear objective function with one which is quadratic around a deterministic steady state. We illustrate this approach in Chapter 12.

A more general approach is to employ numerical dynamic programming methods. This method has also been used for solving dynamic discrete choice models. Numerical dynamic programming is motivated by the fact that the valuation function characterizing agents' or the social planner's optimum typically satisfies a contraction mapping. The underlying theory is well understood.[2] One problem with this approach, however, is the so-called "curse of dimensionality." Typically, numerical dynamic programming involves discretizing the state space. As the number of state variables gets larger, it becomes impracticable, if not impossible, to implement this technique. Judd [269] and others have proposed alternative numerical solutions to circumvent this problem, such as those based on polynomial approximations.

In this section, we provide an illustration of numerical dynamic programming for a simple application based on value function iteration with a discretized state space. We consider a simple parametric example from Danthine, Donaldson and Mehra [135] that has been widely studied in this literature. This application allows us to numerically determine the impact of changes in shock persistence on optimal consumption and investment allocations, an issue that we discussed in more theoretical terms in Section 10.2.2.

10.3.1. A parametric model

Preferences are assumed to be of the constant relative risk variety,

$$U(c_t) = \frac{c_t^{1-\gamma} - 1}{1-\gamma}, \quad \gamma \geq 0$$

and the production function displays constant returns to scale with

$$z_t f(k_t) = A z_t k_t^{\alpha}, \quad 0 < \alpha < 1,$$

where z_t represents a technology shock. Among others, the following parameter values are considered:

- $\gamma \in \{0.5, 1, 3\}$ where $\gamma = 1$ is the case $U(c) = \ln(c)$;
- $A = 2/3$;
- $\alpha = 0.25$;
- $\beta = 0.9$.

[2] See Bertsekas [62] and Bertsekas and Shreve [63].

In this example, the productivity shock z_t is correlated and follows a first-order Markov process. Suppose that the technology takes on n discrete values. Define the $n \times n$ transition probability matrix for z_t by Φ:

$$\Phi = \begin{bmatrix} \phi_{11} & \cdots & \phi_{1n} \\ \vdots & & \vdots \\ \phi_{n1} & \cdots & \phi_{nn} \end{bmatrix},$$

where a typical element of Φ is given by:

$$\phi_{i,j} = \text{Prob}(z_{t+1} = z_j | z_t = z_i), \quad i,j = 1, \ldots, n.$$

We describe below how the distribution for z_t is parameterized.

In this problem, the state variables are the per capita capital stock k_t and the current value of the technology shock, z_t. Both variables take values on continuous intervals. To implement value function iteration, we need to discretize or partition the state space into a finite set of points. This implies that the control variables also take on a finite number of values. In their application, Danthine, Donaldson and Mehra [135] assume that the technology shock takes values in the set $z_t \in Z \equiv \{0.5, 1.0, 1.5\}$. They incorporate the persistence of the technology shock by assuming that Φ is symmetric ($\phi_{i,j} = \phi_{j,i}$) and that $\phi_{i,i} = a$ and $\phi_{i,j} = (1 - a)/2$ for $i \neq j$. The identical diagonal elements of the matrix Φ take values from the set $\phi_{i,i} \in \{0.333, 0.5, 0.7, 0.9\}$. As $\phi_{i,i}$ increases, the correlation of the shocks over time increases. Notice that this procedure substitutes a discrete Markov chain for the continuous Markov process for z_t.[3]

The remaining issue is how to discretize the endogenous state variable k_t. Because this is a recursive model, choosing a set of possible values for k_t also specifies the set of values from which the decision variable k_{t+1} at time t can be chosen; we will call this set K. To determine this set, we first determine the maximum sustainable capital stock. Using the resource constraint, optimal consumption and capital stocks must satisfy $c_t + k_{t+1} \leq \sup_{z \in Z} Azk_t^\alpha$, which implies that the steady-state capital stock satisfies the equation: $k_m = Az_t k_m^\alpha$. Recall that $A = 2/3$ and the maximum value of $z = 1.5$. Hence, $k_m = (2/3)k_m^\alpha(1.5)$. We know that $\alpha \leq 1$; hence the solution is $k_m = 1$. Hence we can conclude that capital takes values on $[0, 1]$. The next step is to define a partition of this range, such as $k_{i+1} - k_i = 0.01$. This creates an evenly spaced grid of 100 possible values for the capital stock and defines our feasible set K.

[3] See Exercise 4 in Chapter 6.

The problem now becomes one of solving the functional equation:

$$V^n(k_i, z_r) = \max_{k_j \in K} \left[U(Ak_i^\alpha z_r - k_j) + \beta \sum_{s=1}^{3} \phi_{r,s} V^{n-1}(k_j, z_s) \right] \tag{10.47}$$

subject to $k_j \leq Ak_i^\alpha z_r$, where $k_i \in K$ and $z_r, z_s \in Z$. A computer program can be written along the following lines.

1. Formulate an initial guess of the function V^0. For example, set $V^0 = 0$.
2. For each pair (k_i, z_r), compute the value function for each point k in the feasible set K that satisfies the constraint $k_j \leq Ak_i^\alpha z_r$; this will limit the set over which the value function must be computed. Given the initial guess V^0, choose the point $k_j^0 \in K$ that maximizes the right side of Equation (10.47); call this new value function $V^1(k_i, z_r)$.
3. Evaluate the value function for all pairs $(k_i, z_r) \in (K \times Z)$. There are 3×100 points in the range of $V^1(k_i, z_r)$ and the associated policy function is $k_j^1 = h^1(k_i, z_r)$.
4. Repeat steps 2. and 3. until $|V^{n+1}(k_i, z_r) - V^n(k_i, z_r)| \leq \epsilon_c$ for all $k_i \in K$ and all $z_r \in Z$ where ϵ_c is a convergence criterion.

There are different ways of choosing the convergence criterion. One possible convergence criterion is to choose $\epsilon_c = b\|K\|$ where b is a small positive constant and $\|K\|$ is the norm of the capital partition (equal to 0.01 in our example). The convergence criterion should be small but there is a tradeoff in terms of computation time. Notice that the set $(K \times Z)$ is compact so that the value function iteration described above is well defined. One problem with this procedure is that we run into the "curse of dimensionality." The accuracy of the solution can be increased by partitioning the state space in terms of a finer grid but at the cost of increased computing time.

In Table 10.1, we report decision rules for the optimal choice of capital accumulation or saving k_{t+1} for values of $\gamma = 0.5, 1, 3$ and $\phi_{ii} = 0.33, 0.7$. The decision rule shows the value of k_{t+1} for all possible (k_t, z_t) pairs. Notice that the current value of the technology shock z determines the current productivity of capital through the production function, and if it is serially correlated, through its impact on the expectation of future productivity. Considering initially the i.i.d. case (with $\phi_{ii} = 0.33$), we note that higher values of the shock and/or the capital stock lead to higher saving. When the shock is serially correlated, Table 10.1 shows that the optimal saving behavior depends on whether $\gamma < 1$ or $\gamma > 1$. For the case with $\gamma < 1$, an increase in persistence leads to lower saving for low values of z_t and to increased saving for high values of z_t. By contrast, we see the opposite behavior for the case with $\gamma > 1$. When $\gamma = 1$ which

Table 10.1. *Optimal savings levels as a function of* (k, z)

	$\gamma = 0.5$					
	$\phi = 0.33$			$\phi = 0.7$		
k	z_1	z_2	z_3	z_1	z_2	z_3
k_{10}	0.0600	0.0900	0.1100	0.0500	0.0900	0.1200
k_{20}	0.0600	0.1000	0.1200	0.0500	0.1000	0.1400
k_{30}	0.0700	0.1000	0.1300	0.0600	0.1000	0.1500
k_{40}	0.0700	0.1100	0.1400	0.0600	0.1100	0.1500
k_{50}	0.0700	0.1100	0.1400	0.0600	0.1100	0.1600
k_{60}	0.0700	0.1100	0.1500	0.0600	0.1100	0.1600
k_{70}	0.0800	0.1200	0.1500	0.0600	0.1200	0.1700
k_{80}	0.0800	0.1200	0.1500	0.0700	0.1200	0.1700
k_{90}	0.0800	0.1200	0.1500	0.0700	0.1200	0.1800
k_{100}	0.0800	0.1200	0.1600	0.0700	0.1200	0.1800
	$\gamma = 1$					
	$\phi = 0.33$			$\phi = 0.7$		
k	z_1	z_2	z_3	z_1	z_2	z_3
k_{10}	0.0400	0.0900	0.1300	0.0400	0.0900	0.1300
k_{20}	0.0500	0.1100	0.1600	0.0500	0.1100	0.1600
k_{30}	0.0600	0.1200	0.1700	0.0600	0.1200	0.1700
k_{40}	0.0600	0.1300	0.1900	0.0600	0.1300	0.1900
k_{50}	0.0700	0.1300	0.2000	0.0700	0.1300	0.2000
k_{60}	0.0700	0.1400	0.2100	0.0700	0.1400	0.2100
k_{70}	0.0700	0.1500	0.2200	0.0700	0.1500	0.2200
k_{80}	0.0700	0.1500	0.2200	0.0700	0.1500	0.2200
k_{90}	0.0800	0.1500	0.2300	0.0800	0.1500	0.2300
k_{100}	0.0800	0.1600	0.2400	0.0800	0.1600	0.2400
	$\gamma = 3$					
	$\phi = 0.33$			$\phi = 0.7$		
k	z_1	z_2	z_3	z_1	z_2	z_3
k_{10}	0.0300	0.1200	0.2200	0.0400	0.1100	0.2000
k_{20}	0.0500	0.1500	0.2900	0.0600	0.1500	0.2600
k_{30}	0.0600	0.1800	0.3300	0.0700	0.1700	0.3000
k_{40}	0.0700	0.2000	0.3700	0.0800	0.1900	0.3400
k_{50}	0.0700	0.2200	0.4000	0.0900	0.2100	0.3700
k_{60}	0.0800	0.2300	0.4300	0.0900	0.2300	0.3900
k_{70}	0.0800	0.2500	0.4500	0.1000	0.2400	0.4200
k_{80}	0.0900	0.2600	0.4700	0.1100	0.2500	0.4300
k_{90}	0.0900	0.2800	0.4900	0.1100	0.2600	0.4500
k_{100}	0.0900	0.2900	0.5100	0.1200	0.2800	0.4700

corresponds to the logarithmic utility case, changes in persistence have *no* effect on optimal saving behavior. To understand these results, notice that the expected return on saving is $f(k)E(z)$ and the variance of the return to saving is $[f'(k)]^2 Var(z)$. Evaluating these quantities, we have that $E(z' \mid z = z_1) = 0.7(0.5) + 0.15(1) + 0.15(1.5) = 0.7250 < E(z') = 1$ where $E(z')$ denotes the expectation of the technology shock in the i.i.d. case, and $E(z') < E(z' \mid z = z_3) = 0.15(0.5) + 0.15(1) + 0.7(1.5) = 1.2750$. We also have that $Var(z' \mid z = z_1) = Var(z' \mid z = z_3) = 0.1369$ and $Var(z') = 0.1667$. Combining these results with the form of the optimal decision rule for savings shows that an increase in the persistence of the shock on saving decreases the expected return to saving when z is low and increases its variance, and conversely when z is high. The effect of an increase in persistence is the sum of these two effects, as demonstrated by the numerical results.

10.3.2. The stationary distribution

We can also calculate the unconditional moments for consumption, saving, and output by generating the stationary distribution for the capital stock-technology shock pairs (k, z). The interest in generating such unconditional moments is that they have been used to match the model with the data in the RBC literature. To derive the unconditional moments, we first generate the conditional distribution for (k', z') given (k, z) by making use of the decision rule for the optimal capital stock $k' = g(k, z)$ and the transition probability matrix for the technology shock. Define $\mathcal{K}_j$ as the 100×100 matrix which has a one in the (l, i) position if $g(k_i, z_j) = l$ for $i, l = 1, \ldots, 100$ and $j = 1, \ldots, 3$. In other words, $\mathcal{K}_j$ shows the capital stock states that can be reached next period conditional on being in the state $k = k_i, z = z_j$ today. Now define $\mathcal{P}$ as

$$\mathcal{P} = \begin{bmatrix} \phi_{11}\mathcal{K}_1 & \phi_{12}\mathcal{K}_1 & \phi_{13}\mathcal{K}_1 \\ \phi_{21}\mathcal{K}_2 & \phi_{22}\mathcal{K}_2 & \phi_{23}\mathcal{K}_2 \\ \phi_{31}\mathcal{K}_3 & \phi_{32}\mathcal{K}_3 & \phi_{33}\mathcal{K}_3 \end{bmatrix}.$$

Notice that $\mathcal{P}$ is a 300×300 matrix with typical element given by $Prob(k' = k_l, z' = z_m \mid k = k_i, z = z_j)$ for $i, l = 1, \ldots, 100$ and $j, m = 1, \ldots, 3$. The *stationary distribution* for (k, z) satisfies the relation

$$\mathcal{P}'\Pi = \Pi,$$

where $\pi_{l,m} = \text{Prob}(k' = k_l, z' = z_m)$ for $l = 1, \ldots, 100$ and $m = 1, \ldots, 3$. In practice, the probability of many of the (k_l, z_m) pairs will be zero as the *ergodic set* for the joint distribution of the long-run capital stock and technology shock will be a strict subset of $K \times Z$. The stationary distribution for the (k, z) pairs is obtained by iterating on the relation

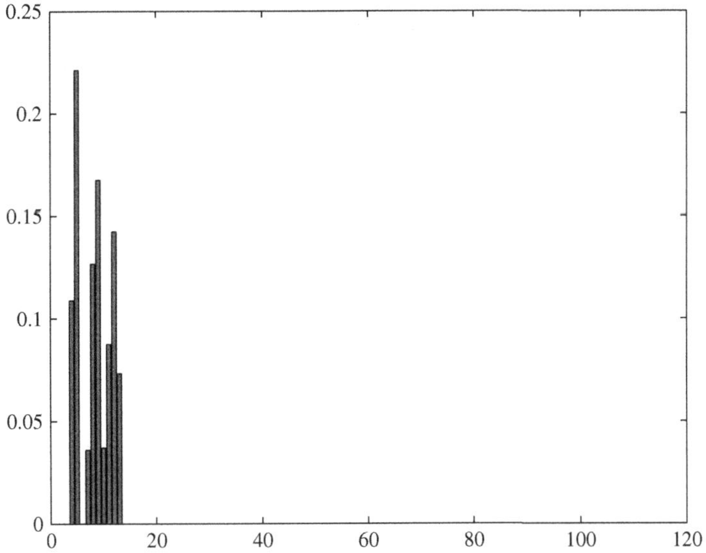

Figure 10.3. Stationary distribution for the capital stock

$\mathcal{P}'\Pi_n = \Pi_{n+1}$ beginning with Π_0. The invariant distribution for the capital stock is then obtained by summing π_{ij} over the possible realizations of z as $\pi_l^k = \sum_{m=1}^{3} \pi_{l,m}$. Figure 10.3 displays this distribution for the case of $\gamma = 0.25$ and $\phi = 0.33$.

The stationary distribution for the capital stock allows us to examine the unconditional moments of consumption, capital, and output. These are reported in Table 10.2. For the logarithmic utility case, an increase in variance leads to greater variability of all three series. Recall that there is no effect of changes in persistence on the optimal decision rule. Hence, changes in persistence affect the underlying moments only through changes in the stationary distribution for the economy. In contrast to the i.i.d. case, when there is a realization of a high productivity state, this will tend to last longer the more persistent is the shock. Consequently, the economy will continue to accumulate capital until the capital stock reaches the upper bound of the ergodic state. Similarly, when the economy experiences a low realization of the shock, the longer is the series of low shocks, the lower will be the values of capital, consumption, and output. When $\gamma < 1$, recall that saving is increased for high realizations of z and decreased for low realizations. This has the effect of reinforcing the direct effect of increased correlation, leading to higher variability in all three series as persistence is increased. By contrast, the impact of increased persistence on output, consumption, or capital volatility is not monotonic for the case with $\gamma > 1$.

Table 10.2. *Unconditional moments of consumption, capital stock and output*

		$\gamma = 0.5$		
ϕ		Consumption	Capital	Output
0.33	mean	0.2737	0.0814	0.3552
	var	0.0157	0.0005	0.0217
	coeff. var.	0.4575	0.2746	0.4147
0.7	mean	0.2773	0.0845	0.3618
	var	0.0180	0.0012	0.0283
	coeff. var.	0.4840	0.4045	0.4648
		$\gamma = 1$		
ϕ		Consumption	Capital	Output
0.33	mean	0.2702	0.0848	0.3551
	var.	0.0133	0.0013	0.0228
	coeff. var.	0.4265	0.4219	0.4249
0.7	mean	0.2759	0.0858	0.3617
	var.	0.0173	0.0018	0.0304
	coeff. var.	0.4771	0.4985	0.4818
		$\gamma = 3$		
ϕ		Consumption	Capital	Output
0.33	mean	0.2518	0.1281	0.3799
	var	0.0075	0.0080	0.0306
	coeff. var.	0.3434	0.6998	0.4608
0.7	mean	0.2644	0.1342	0.3987
	var	0.0132	0.0087	0.0429
	coeff. var.	0.4344	0.6966	0.5195

10.4. FINANCIAL STRUCTURE OF A FIRM

In Section 10.1, we assumed that households own the stocks of capital and make investment decisions and firms rent or buy capital from households on a period-by-period basis. In this section, we assume that firms own the physical stocks of capital and formulate the present-value maximization problem that they solve. Firms finance new investment by retained earnings, equity issue, and debt issue which we assume takes the form of one-period bonds. There is a single production process that uses labor and capital and that depends on the random technology shock. We use this framework to discuss the financial structure of a firm, to derive a Modigliani-Miller theorem about the irrelevance of debt versus equity financing, and to study market returns and risk. Our discussion is based on Brock and Turnovsky [80], who work with a continuous time version of the one-sector growth model.

The household supplies labor inelastically and chooses sequences for consumption, and bond and share holdings to solve:

$$\max_{\{c_t, z_{t+1}, b^d_{t+1}\}} E_0 \left\{ \sum_{t=0}^{\infty} \beta^t U(c_t) \right\} \qquad (10.48)$$

subject to

$$c_t + q_t z_{t+1} + b^d_{t+1} \leq w_t n^s_t + (1 + r_t) b^d_t + z_t(q_t + d_t), \qquad (10.49)$$

and the restriction that $0 \leq n^s_t \leq 1$. The household treats the stochastic processes for prices w_t, r_t, q_t, and dividends d_t as given. In this expression, the price of the bond being sold is assumed to be one for all periods. The left side of the household budget constraint in (10.49) gives total expenditures on consumption and payments on purchases of bond and stock. The right side denotes the total wealth accumulated during the period, which consists of labor income, the face value plus return of the bond purchased at the beginning of the period, and dividends plus resale value of the stock purchased at the beginning of the period.

Let λ_t denote the multiplier for the constraint in Equation (10.49). The first-order conditions with respect to c_t, z_{t+1} and b^d_{t+1} are:

$$\lambda_t = U'(c_t), \qquad (10.50)$$

$$q_t \lambda_t = \beta E_t[\lambda_{t+1}(q_{t+1} + d_{t+1})], \qquad (10.51)$$

$$\lambda_t = \beta E_t[\lambda_{t+1}(1 + r_{t+1})]. \qquad (10.52)$$

Define $m_{t+i} \equiv \beta^i U'(c_{t+i})/U'(c_t)$ as the intertemporal marginal rate of substitution in consumption. We assume that $0 \leq n^s_t \leq 1$ and because labor causes no disutility, $n^s_t = 1$ at the consumer's optimum.

On the production side, the firm owns the capital stock and chooses how much labor to hire, how much to produce, and how much to invest. The production function is given by $F(K_t, n_t, \theta_t)$ and it displays constant returns to scale. The technology shock is i.i.d. and has a distribution that satisfies the conditions of Assumption 10.6.

Assumption 10.6 *The technology shock* $\theta : \Omega \rightarrow \Theta$ *where* $\Theta = [\underline{\theta}, \bar{\theta}]$ *is i.i.d. with stationary distribution function G. The function G has the properties that* $G(\theta) = 0$ *for* $\theta \leq \underline{\theta}$ *and* $G(\theta) = 1$ *for* $\theta \geq \bar{\theta}$. *Also* $dG > 0$ *and* dG *is continuous.*

The firm sells output to consumers and to other firms for investment. In the absence of adjustment costs, irreversibilities in investment, and other frictions, the relative price of old and new capital equals one. Thus, the gross profit of the firm equals total sales (which we assume equals its output so that no inventories are held) minus its wage bill, or

$$\pi_t = F(K_t, n_t, \theta_t) - w_t n_t^d. \tag{10.53}$$

The receipts π_t are disbursed in various ways: either paid out as dividends, $z_t d_t$, as payments on bonds $(1 + r_t)b_t$, or held as retained earnings, RE_t. The following accounting identity holds:

$$\pi_t = RE_t + d_t z_t + (1 + r_t)b_t. \tag{10.54}$$

Because a firm is the owner of the capital stock, it must decide not only how much to invest but also how to finance this investment. A firm can finance investment by:

- issuing new bonds b_{t+1};
- issuing new equity shares $q_t(z_{t+1} - z_t)$; or
- its retained earnings, RE_t.

Hence, the firm's investment, $K_{t+1} - (1 - \delta)K_t$, satisfies:

$$K_{t+1} - (1 - \delta)K_t = b_{t+1} + (z_{t+1} - z_t)q_t + RE_t \tag{10.55}$$

Define *net cash flow (NCF)* from the firm to households as:

$$N_t = \pi_t - K_{t+1} + (1 - \delta)K_t, \tag{10.56}$$

which is the gross profit net of investment. By substituting the equations for π_t and investment in (10.54) and (10.55) into the definition of *NCF* above, we obtain:

$$N_t = d_t z_t + (1 + r_t)b_t + q_t(z_t - z_{t+1}) - b_{t+1}. \tag{10.57}$$

Thus, the net cash flow to households equals the sum of dividend and interest payments on outstanding shares and debt minus new share and debt issues. We will relate the firm's net cash flow to the value of the firm momentarily.

The *ex-dividend value of the firm*, or the value of the firm at the end of the period after all dividend and debt payments have been made, is defined as the value of its equity shares, $q_t z_{t+1}$, plus the value of its outstanding debt, b_{t+1}.

$$W_t^e \equiv q_t z_{t+1} + b_{t+1}. \tag{10.58}$$

We can also define the ex-dividend value as the total claims of shareholders and debtholders on the firm. The *value of the firm* at the beginning of period t is the sum of net cash flow in period t and the ex-dividend value:

$$\begin{aligned} W_t &\equiv N_t + W_t^e \\ &= N_t + q_t z_{t+1} + b_{t+1}. \end{aligned} \tag{10.59}$$

We now show that the value of the firm can be expressed as the expected discounted value of its future cash flows. Now

$$\begin{aligned} W_t^e &\equiv q_t z_{t+1} + b_{t+1} \\ &= E_t\{m_{t+1}[(q_{t+1} + d_{t+1})z_{t+1} + (1 + r_{t+1})b_{t+1}]\}, \end{aligned} \tag{10.60}$$

where we have substituted for $q_t z_{t+1}$ and b_{t+1} after multiplying Equations (10.51) and (10.52) by z_{t+1} and b_{t+1}, respectively. Now add and subtract $q_{t+1}z_{t+2}$ and b_{t+2} to the right side of Equation (10.60). Using the definition of W_{t+1}^e and NCF in Equation (10.57), we have:

$$\begin{aligned} W_t^e &= E_t\left\{m_{t+1}\left[W_{t+1}^e + d_{t+1}z_{t+1} + (1 + r_{t+1})b_{t+1}\right.\right. \\ &\qquad \left.\left. + q_{t+1}(z_{t+1} - z_{t+2}) - b_{t+2}\right]\right\} \\ &= E_t\left[m_{t+1}(W_{t+1}^e + N_{t+1})\right]. \end{aligned} \tag{10.61}$$

We can use this expression and solve Equation (10.61) forward to express the (ex-dividend) value of the firm as:

$$W_t^e = E_t\left[\sum_{i=1}^{\infty} m_{t+i}N_{t+i}\right] \tag{10.62}$$

assuming that the discounted value $\lim_{i\to\infty} E_t[m_{t+i}W_{t+i}^e] \to 0$. This shows that the ex-dividend value of the firm is the expected discounted value of future cash flows.

The present-value maximization problem of the firm involves choosing next period's capital stock and the labor input to maximize the firm's value today. At the beginning of period t, the firm solves:

$$W_t = \max_{\{K_{j+1}, n_j^d\}_{j=t}^{\infty}} \left\{N_t + E_t\left[\sum_{i=1}^{\infty} m_{t+i}N_{t+i}\right]\right\}, \tag{10.63}$$

subject to the law of motion for capital $K_{t+1} = (1 - \delta)K_t + i_t$, given the expression for net cash flows $N_t = F(K_t, n_t, \theta_t) - w_t n_t^d - i_t$ and the initial capital stock K_t.

The discount rate is treated parametrically by the firm although it depends on the representative household's behavior in equilibrium. Hence, we can model a firm as maximizing its value, defined as its expected discounted cash flow. This result holds more generally; if there exist complete contingent claims markets, the discount factor for the firm's problem is also given parametrically but it can be evaluated in terms of the intertemporal MRS in consumption for *any* consumer in the economy, which equals the ratio of the contingent claims prices.[4] We now demonstrate that the version of the problem in which firms own the capital stock is equivalent to the previous two versions studied in Sections 10.1.1 and 10.1.2. The firm solves the problem defined in Equation (10.63) subject to the constraints. The first-order conditions for the firm's problem are:

$$w_t = F_2(K_t, n_t, \theta_t), \tag{10.64}$$

$$1 = E_t \{m_{t+1} [F_1(K_{t+1}, n_{t+1}, \theta_{t+1}) + (1 - \delta)]\}. \tag{10.65}$$

Observe that the household's budget constraint can be rewritten as:

$$\begin{aligned} c_t &= w_t n_t^s + N_t \\ &= w_t n_t^s + F(K_t, n_t, \theta_t) - w_t n_t^d - [K_{t+1} - (1 - \delta)K_t] \\ &= F(K_t, n_t, \theta_t) - [K_{t+1} - (1 - \delta)K_t] \end{aligned}$$

Making use of the CRTS property of the production function and the fact that quantity of labor in equilibrium is one, $n_t^d = n_t^s = 1$, the first-order condition for the firm with respect to its choice of capital can be expressed:

$$U'(c_t) = \beta E_t \left\{ U'(c_{t+1})[f'(k_{t+1}, \theta_{t+1}) + (1 - \delta)] \right\}. \tag{10.66}$$

Hence, we have shown that different versions of the problem with production and capital accumulation in which households own the capital stocks, where they lease this capital to firms, or where firms own the capital stocks, yield equivalent solutions.

10.4.1. The irrelevance of debt versus equity financing

The Modigliani-Miller theorem says that if markets are complete, then firms are indifferent between debt and equity financing, so the debt-equity ratio is indeterminate. We can derive the Modigliani-Miller theorem regarding the irrelevance of the firm's financing decisions using this framework. (See Modigliani and Miller [345].) Notice that the firm's cash flow depends only on the firm's production decisions, such as how much labor to hire, how much to produce, and how much to invest. Under the assumption of constant returns to scale, gross profits are equal to $\pi_t = f'(k_t, \theta_t)k_t$, or the value of capital, which is the marginal product of capital times the capital stock per capita. Hence, the net cash flow is:

$$N_t = f'(k_t, \theta_t)k_t - [k_{t+1} - (1 - \delta)k_t].$$

[4] This is just a restatement of the implications of complete contingent claims equilibrium that we derived in Chapter 1. In the absence of a representative consumer or the complete markets assumption, we run into the problem of shareholder unanimity explored by Hart [241], Radner [364], and others in terms of determining the criterion function for the firm.

Hence, the firm's cash flow does not depend on the financing decisions made by the firm. In particular, it does not depend on the amount of equity issued, the debt-equity ratio, nor on the amount of retained earnings.

To show this result in a different way, add and subtract $q_{t+1}z_{t+2}$ and b_{t+2} from the right side of Equation (10.60) and use the definition of N_{t+1} to obtain:

$$\begin{aligned} W_t^e &= \left[q_t z_{t+1} + b_{t+1}\right] \\ &= E_t\left\{m_{t+1}[q_{t+1}z_{t+2} + b_{t+2} + N_{t+1}]\right\}. \end{aligned}$$

This expression shows that a person who owns all the equity and debt of the firm, simply someone who owns the firm, has a claim on next period's cash flow and the value of debt and equity. Re-writing this shows that the debt-equity ratio is irrelevant:

$$\begin{aligned} W_t^e &= E_t\left\{m_{t+1}[q_{t+1}z_{t+2} + b_{t+2} + N_{t+1}]\right\} \\ &= \left[q_t + \frac{b_{t+1}}{z_{t+1}}\right] z_{t+1}. \end{aligned} \tag{10.67}$$

Recall that q_t depends on the agent's intertemporal marginal rate of substitution. Thus, as long as the ex-dividend value of the firm W_t^e remains fixed, the division of this quantity between debt and equity is irrelevant. Consequently, if there are no other distortions such as taxation, bankruptcy, et cetera, the financing decisions do not affect the value of the firm.

10.4.2. The equity price and the equity premium

We now derive expressions for the equity price, equilibrium dividends, and the equity premium. Since there are no taxes or other distortions, the equilibrium allocation is optimal and can be found by solving the social planning problem. Let the solution take the form of time-invariant policy functions $c_t = g(k_t, \theta_t)$ and $k_{t+1} = h(k_t, \theta_t)$. We will construct supporting prices for the implied optimal allocations. In equilibrium, all shares are held, $z_{t+1} = 1$, all bonds are purchased, $b^d_{t+1} = b_{t+1}$, and consumption plus investment exhaust output, $c_t + k_{t+1} = f(k_t, \theta_t) + (1 - \delta)k_t$. Notice that the net cash flow, N_t, is equal to the cash that flows from the business sector to the household sector.

If we solve Equation (10.55) for retained earnings and substitute into Equation (10.54) and then solve for d_t, we have:

$$d_t = f'(k_t, \theta_t)k_t - [k_{t+1} - (1 - \delta)k_t] + b_{t+1} - (1 + r_t)b_t. \tag{10.68}$$

Increasing the time subscript by one in the preceding equation and then substituting for d_{t+1} into Equation (10.51), the equity price satisfies:

$$q_t = E_t \left\{ m_{t+1} \left[q_{t+1} + f'(k_{t+1}, \theta_{t+1}) k_{t+1} \right.\right.$$
$$\left.\left. - k_{t+2} + (1 - \delta) k_{t+1} + b_{t+2} - (1 + r_{t+1}) b_{t+1} \right] \right\}. \qquad (10.69)$$

Now multiply the first-order condition for the firm's choice of investment described by Equation (10.65) by k_{t+1} and use the resulting expression to substitute for the term $m_{t+1} f'(k_{t+1}, \theta_{t+1}) k_{t+1}$ in Equation (10.69). This yields:

$$q_t = E_t \left[m_{t+1}(q_{t+1} + b_{t+2} - (1 + r_{t+1}) b_{t+1} - k_{t+2}) \right] + k_{t+1}.$$

Now add b_{t+1} to both sides of this equation and use the fact that $b_{t+1} = E_t[m_{t+1}(1 + r_{t+1}) b_{t+1}]$ by the first-order for bond holdings in Equation (10.52) to obtain:

$$q_t + b_{t+1} = E_t \left[m_{t+1}(q_{t+1} + b_{t+2} - k_{t+2}) \right] + k_{t+1}. \qquad (10.70)$$

This is a stochastic difference equation which has the solution:

$$q_t + b_{t+1} = k_{t+1} \quad \forall t. \qquad (10.71)$$

(To verify this statement, substitute this solution into both sides of Equation (10.70).) Hence, we can express the (ex-dividend) value of the firm as the value of the capital stock at the end of the period, or:

$$W_t^e = q_t + b_{t+1} = k_{t+1}. \qquad (10.72)$$

Under the assumptions that (i) the firm finances investment by retained earnings; (ii) there is no borrowing ($b_{t+1} = 0$); (iii) there are no new equity shares issued; and (iv) production displays constant returns to scale, the ex-dividend value of the firm is:

$$W_t^e = q_t = k_{t+1}. \qquad (10.73)$$

The expression for equity prices in Equation (10.69) implies that:

$$q_t = E_t \left\{ m_{t+1} \left[f'(k_{t+1}, \theta_{t+1}) k_{t+1} + (1 - \delta) k_{t+1} \right] \right\}, \qquad (10.74)$$

where we have used $q_{t+1} = k_{t+2}$ together with $b_t = 0$ for all t.

Define the equity return as $1 + r_{t+1}^e \equiv (q_{t+1} + d_{t+1})/q_t$. The equity return satisfies:

$$1 = E_t \left[m_{t+1}(1 + r_{t+1}^e) \right]$$
$$1 = E_t \left\{ m_{t+1} \left[f'(k_{t+1}, \theta_{t+1}) + (1 - \delta) \right] \right\}. \qquad (10.75)$$

Using Equation (10.52), we can show that the risk-free rate of return is given by $1 + r_{t+1}^f = 1/E_t(m_{t+1})$. Thus, the *conditional equity premium*, which shows the expected value of the difference between the equity return and the return on the risk-free bond, is:

$$E_t(r^e_{t+1}) - r^f_{t+1} = -\frac{1}{E_t(m_{t+1})}\text{Cov}_t\left[m_{t+1}, f'(k_{t+1}, \theta_{t+1})\right]. \quad (10.76)$$

Hence, the equity premium depends on the conditional covariance between the intertemporal MRS in consumption and the marginal productivity of capital. Notice that if the restrictions on equilibrium consumption and returns are not imposed, then the model with production has essentially the same predictions as the consumption-based asset-pricing model in terms of defining risk premia as the covariance of the intertemporal MRS and the asset return. However, if we recognize that, unlike the pure exchange model in which consumption is exogenous, the intertemporal MRS or stochastic discount factor depends on factors that affect both consumption and investment, then the asset-pricing model with production acquires content.

10.4.3. Empirical implications

In a fully-specified asset-pricing model with production, a variety of factors affect the magnitude of the equity premium. These include:

- consumers' attitudes toward risk;
- the variability and persistence of productivity shocks;
- the marginal product function for capital.

Using an asset-pricing model with production, Donaldson and Mehra [156] derive a variety of comparative dynamics results for the behavior of the risk-free rate, the equity return, and the equity premium. They first compute the decisions rules for consumption and the capital stock based on a parameterization that is identical to the one that we described in Section 10.3.1. Together with the stationary distribution for the capital stock, they then numerically evaluate the asset-pricing functions to compute unconditional risk premia and returns. First, they show that the unconditional equity premium rises as agents become more risk averse and the risk-free rate declines. They also find that the average or unconditional equity return first rises and then declines with greater risk aversion. The reason for the eventual decline in the equity return is that the reduced variation in consumption due to increased risk aversion is accompanied by the increased variation in output. Since the equity return is the marginal product of capital, the average equity return falls when the economy operates at higher levels of capital. Finally, increases in the discount factor reduce both the risk-free rate and the equity return. The equity return falls because consumers with higher discount factors invest a larger fraction of output. The risk-free rate falls because consumers who value the future more are willing to pay a higher price for a certain payoff in the future. The links among risk aversion, production, and the equity premium are also discussed in Benninga and Protopapadakis [55].

Cochrane [107] uses a version of Equation (10.75) to discuss the asset-pricing implications of the model with production. Unlike our approach, he does not fully specify the consumer's side of the economy. Instead he derives a version of Equation (10.75) using the present-value maximization problem of the firm under the assumption that cash flows in different states of the world or events are discounted using the contingent claims prices for those states. This is equivalent to our framework because in a fully specified equilibrium model, the stochastic discount factor m_{t+1} equals the ratio of the contingent claims prices. Cochrane [107] also assumes the existence of adjustment costs in investment, an issue that we will discuss in the next chapter. However, this feature of his model is not important for our purposes. To understand Cochrane's approach, we note that the quantity

$$f'(k_{t+1}, \theta_{t+1}) + (1 - \delta) \tag{10.77}$$

is the rate of return to:

- buying a unit of capital in period t;
- obtaining the marginal product of capital in period $t + 1$ and;
- selling off the undepreciated part in period $t + 1$.

Cochrane [107] notes that the return to investment is equal to the return on owning a claim to the firm or a stock. In our earlier analysis, we showed that the value of the firm W_t^e is equal to the value of the capital stock k_{t+1}, which under the assumption that the firm finances investment only through retained earnings, also equals to the equity price. (See Equation (10.73).) Cochrane [107] uses these relations to link forecasts of stock returns and investment returns to a set of business-cycle related variables. In his framework, investment returns as defined by (10.77) are computed using actual data on the investment-capital ratio and hence reflect real investment decisions in the economy.

Cochrane [107] reports the following. First, investment returns and stock returns are positively correlated at both quarterly and annual frequencies. Second, in regressions of stock returns and investment returns on variables known to forecast stock returns such as the term premium, the corporate premium, the lagged real stock return, the dividend-price ratio, and the investment-capital stock ratio, the hypothesis that with the exception of the dividend-price ratio the determinants of both stock returns and investment returns are identical cannot be rejected at conventional significance levels. This suggests that with the exception of the dividend-price ratio, all variables used in these forecasting equations have a common "business cycle" component that forecasts both types of returns. Third, regressions of stock returns and investment returns on current, lagged, and future investment-capital stock ratios suggest that forecasts of both types of returns from investment-capital stocks are essentially the same. Finally, the paper examines the forecastability of GDP growth from stock returns and investment returns, and again fails to reject the hypothesis that both sets of forecasts are the same. These results provide some evidence in favor of the production-based asset-pricing model, which suggests that investment returns and stocks returns should be equal. Cochrane's [107] analysis is different from other analyses of the production-based asset-pricing model because it abstracts from factors that jointly determine consumption and capital stock allocations with asset returns. However, it nevertheless helps to illustrate the implications of the model for the association between stock returns and investment returns and their relationship to future economic activity.

Jehrmann [264] considers a fully specified equilibrium model with a production side. He solves the production-based model by first log-linearizing the first-order conditions and then applying the log-linear asset-pricing functions that we derived in Chapters 8 and 9. To provide another example of a solution method, we illustrate the method of log-linearizing the optimality conditions of the growth model considered in section 10.1 around a deterministic steady state. Our procedure follows Uhlig [435].

Example 10.2 Assume that preferences are of the CRRA variety and the production function is Cobb-Douglas. Also assume that the depreciation rate is 100%. Also assume that the logarithm of the technology shock follows a stationary first-order autoregressive process as $\ln(\theta_{t+1}) = (1-\rho) + \rho\ln(\theta_t) + \epsilon_{t+1}$, $0 < \rho < 1$ and $\epsilon_t \sim N(0, \sigma_\epsilon^2)$ and i.i.d. The optimality conditions can be written as

$$\beta\left[\left(\frac{C_{t+1}}{C_t}\right)^{-\gamma} \alpha\theta_{t+1}K_{t+1}^{\alpha-1}\right] = 1, \tag{10.78}$$

$$C_t + K_{t+1} = \theta_t K_t^\alpha \tag{10.79}$$

where $\gamma > 0, \gamma \neq 1$ and $0 < \alpha < 1$. Denote the steady-state values of the variables by $\bar{C}$ and $\bar{K}$. These allocations satisfy:

$$\bar{K} = \beta^{\frac{1}{1-\alpha}}, \tag{10.80}$$

$$\bar{C} = \bar{\theta}\bar{K}^\alpha - \bar{K}. \tag{10.81}$$

Define $\tilde{c}_t \equiv \ln(C_t) - \ln(\bar{C})$ and $\tilde{k}_t \equiv \ln(K_t) - \ln(\bar{K})$ as the percentage deviation of each variable from its steady state. Thus, $\tilde{c}_t = 0.05$ means that consumption in levels is 5% above its steady state. Now write:

$$C_t = \bar{C}\exp(\tilde{c}_t) \approx \bar{C}(1+\tilde{c}_t),$$

$$K_t = \bar{K}\exp(\tilde{k}_t) \approx \bar{K}(1+\tilde{k}_t).$$

First evaluate the left side of the resource constraint under this approximation:

$$
\begin{aligned}
C_t + K_{t+1} &= \bar{C} \exp(\tilde{c}_t) + \bar{K} \exp(\tilde{k}_{t+1}) \\
&\approx \bar{C}(1 + \tilde{c}_t) + \bar{K}(1 + \tilde{k}_{t+1}) \\
&= \bar{C} + \bar{K} + \bar{C}\tilde{c}_t + \bar{K}\tilde{k}_{t+1}.
\end{aligned}
$$

Now evaluate the right side:

$$
\begin{aligned}
\theta_t K_t^\alpha &= \bar{\theta}\bar{K}^\alpha \exp(\tilde{\theta}_t + \alpha\tilde{k}_t) \\
&\approx \bar{\theta}\bar{K}^\alpha(1 + \tilde{\theta}_t + \alpha\tilde{k}_t).
\end{aligned}
$$

Substituting for the steady-state relations, the resource constraint becomes:

$$
\bar{C}\tilde{c}_t + \bar{K}\tilde{k}_{t+1} = \bar{\theta}\bar{K}^\alpha(\tilde{\theta}_t + \alpha\tilde{k}_t).
$$

The consumption Euler equation can be written:

$$
1 = \beta\left[\left(\frac{\bar{C}\exp(\tilde{c}_t - \tilde{c}_{t+1})}{\bar{C}}\right)^\gamma \alpha\bar{\theta}\bar{K}^{\alpha-1}\exp(\tilde{\theta}_t + (\alpha - 1)\tilde{k}_{t+1})\right],
$$

$$
0 \approx \beta\left[\alpha\bar{\theta}\bar{K}^{\alpha-1}(\gamma(\tilde{c}_t - \tilde{c}_{t+1}) + \tilde{\theta}_t + (\alpha - 1)\tilde{k}_{t+1})\right],
$$

$$
0 = \beta\left[(\gamma(\tilde{c}_t - \tilde{c}_{t+1}) + \tilde{\theta}_t + (\alpha - 1)\tilde{k}_{t+1})\right].
$$

Thus, the log-linearized conditions are:

$$
\tilde{c}_t + \frac{\bar{K}}{\bar{C}}\tilde{k}_{t+1} = \frac{\bar{Y}}{\bar{C}}(\tilde{\theta}_t + \alpha\tilde{k}_t), \tag{10.82}
$$

$$
\beta\left[(\gamma(\tilde{c}_t - \tilde{c}_{t+1}) + \tilde{\theta}_t + (\alpha - 1)\tilde{k}_{t+1})\right] = 0, \tag{10.83}
$$

$$
\tilde{\theta}_{t+1} = \rho\tilde{\theta}_t + \epsilon_{t+1}. \tag{10.84}
$$

The resulting system can be further simplified by substituting for $\tilde{\theta}_t$ and also for $\tilde{c}_t$ and $\tilde{c}_{t+1}$ in terms of the current and future capital stocks. This will typically yield a linear second-order difference equation for $\tilde{k}_{t+1}$ which can be solved using methods for solving difference equations.[5] Once we obtain a solution to this difference equation, this solution can be simulated for different histories of the technology shocks and the log-linear asset-pricing equations can be evaluated for those histories.

[5] See, for example, Uhlig [435], Section 4.7.

Jermann [264] follows this approach and presents a calibration of his model to determine the parameter values entering preferences, the production function, and the technology process. He shows that the introduction of production does not necessarily help in resolving the equity premium "puzzle." If households can save through capital accumulation, they can alter their consumption streams to reduce fluctuations in consumption over time. Thus, consumption becomes even smoother as agents become more risk averse. Jermann argues that it is necessary to introduce additional frictions which will prevent such consumption smoothing in equilibrium and which will lead to sufficient variation in the intertemporal MRSs to account for the equity premium. For this purpose, he introduces adjustment costs in investment and habit formation in preferences following Constantinides [118] and others. We discuss his results further in the next chapter.

Akdeniz and Dechert [13] use a version of Brock's asset-pricing model with production to re-examine the "equity premium puzzle." They consider a version of the one-sector optimal growth model with multiple risky technologies. They argue that it is not necessary to change preferences to obtain a higher equity premium but that including production is sufficient. They also argue that the equity premium in a simple model with production is *state-dependent*; that is, if one defines a business cycle in terms of the possible realizations of output, in their framework, the equity premium is higher at the bottom of a business cycle than it is at the top. By contrast, most discussions of the equity premium are based on unconditional moments which average over the business cycle. To obtain these results, they consider both systematic and idiosyncratic shocks to the firm-specific technologies. They use the approach of approximating the policy functions for consumption (or capital) by Chebeychev polynomials as described by Judd [269].

10.4.4. *Taxes and the debt-equity ratio*

The effect of taxation on optimal capital structure has been widely studied in the financial economics literature. In the US tax code, corporations can deduct the interest payments on debt but not dividend payments from taxable corporate income. The "balancing theory" of corporate financial structure states that firms balance the tax advantage of debt against various costs associated with "financial distress."[6] Yet Miller [343] has noted that the usual arguments for the tax advantage of corporate debt relative to corporate equity would be offset by the tax on interest income paid by holders of corporate debt. We now use a version of the model in Brock

[6] See the discussion and references in Kim [275].

and Turnovsky [80] with distortionary taxes to demonstrate Miller's equilibrium with debt and taxes and to describe the effects of distortionary taxes on the firm's cost of capital.

The government assesses a proportional income tax equal to τ_y on households so that a household's budget constraint becomes:

$$c_t + q_t z_{t+1} + b_{t+1} \leq (1 - \tau_y)[w_t l_t + r_t b_t + z_t d_t] + b_t + z_t q_t. \quad (10.85)$$

Notice that only interest income and dividend income are taxed; a capital gains tax is studied by Brock and Turnovsky [80].

The representative household maximizes the objective function in Equation (10.48) subject to the constraint in Equation (10.85) by choosing sequences for c_t, z_{t+1}, and b_{t+1}. The first-order conditions are:

$$U'(c_t) = \lambda_t, \quad (10.86)$$

$$q_t \lambda_t = \beta E_t \left\{ \lambda_{t+1}[(1 - \tau_y)d_{t+1} + q_{t+1}] \right\}, \quad (10.87)$$

$$\lambda_t = \beta E_t \left\{ \lambda_{t+1}[1 + r_{t+1}(1 - \tau_y)] \right\}. \quad (10.88)$$

We will use these conditions later to determine the value of the firm.

The firm pays taxes on its gross profits but is allowed to deduct interest payments on debt. We assume constant returns to scale in production for convenience. Since the household supplies labor inelastically, the firm's gross profits are:

$$\pi_t = f(k_t, \theta_t) - w_t. \quad (10.89)$$

The accounting identity in Equation (10.54) is now modified to include tax payments and deductions; the other accounting identity in Equation (10.55) remains unchanged. The gross profits of a firm are distributed as:

$$(1 - \tau_p)\pi_t = RE_t + d_t z_t + (1 + r_t)b_t - \tau_p r_t b_t. \quad (10.90)$$

In this expression, the term $\tau_p r_t b_t$ reflects the deduction of interest payments on debt and $\tau_p \pi_t$ is the amount of tax paid by the firm. Define the after-tax net cash flow as N_t^τ:

$$N_t^\tau \equiv (1 - \tau_p)\pi_t - [k_{t+1} - (1 - \delta)k_t]. \quad (10.91)$$

Solving Equations (10.90) and (10.55) for retained earnings, equating the results, and using the definition of net cash flows, we have:

$$N_t^\tau = d_t z_t + (1 + r_t)b_t - \tau_p r_t b_t + q_t(z_t - z_{t+1}) - b_{t+1}. \quad (10.92)$$

Note that the net cash flow defined above differs from the one in equation (10.57) only in the deduction of interest payments on debt. Define $m_{t+1} = \beta\lambda_{t+1}/\lambda_t$.

The (ex-dividend) value of the firm, W_t^e, is defined as:

$$W_t^e \equiv q_t z_{t+1} + b_{t+1} \tag{10.93}$$
$$= E_t \left\{ m_{t+1}[((1-\tau_y)d_{t+1} + q_{t+1})\, z_{t+1} + (1 + r_{t+1}(1-\tau_y))b_{t+1}] \right\},$$

where we have substituted for $z_{t+1}q_t$ and b_{t+1} after multiplying Equation (10.87) by z_{t+1} and Equation (10.88) by b_{t+1}. Adding and subtracting $q_{t+1}z_{t+2}$ and b_{t+2} from the right side of Equation (10.93), we have:

$$W_t^e = E_t \left\{ m_{t+1}[((1-\tau_y)d_{t+1} + (1 + r_{t+1}(1-\tau_y))b_{t+1} \right.$$
$$\left. + q_{t+1}(z_{t+1} - z_{t+2}) - b_{t+2} + W_{t+1}^e] \right\}. \tag{10.94}$$

Increasing the time subscripts by 1 in Equation (10.92), solving this expression for $q_{t+1}(z_{t+1} - z_{t+2}) - b_{t+2}$, substituting into Equation (10.94) and simplifying, we obtain:

$$W_t^e = E_t \left\{ m_{t+1}[(\tau_p - \tau_y) r_{t+1} b_{t+1} - \tau_y d_{t+1} z_{t+1} + N_{t+1}^\tau + W_{t+1}^e] \right\}.$$

Define the *debt-equity ratio* and the *dividend-price ratio* by:

$$D_t \equiv b_{t+1}/q_t z_{t+1}$$
$$\Psi_{t+1} \equiv d_{t+1}/q_t,$$

respectively. This implies that $q_t z_{t+1} = W_t^e/(1 + D_t)$. The first-order condition in Equation (10.88) can be expressed as $E_t(m_{t+1} r_{t+1}) = [1 - E_t(m_{t+1})]/(1 - \tau_y)$. Substituting these definitions and the re-written first-order condition into the above expression results in:

$$W_t^e = \frac{(\tau_p - \tau_y)}{1 - \tau_y}[1 - E_t(m_{t+1})]\frac{W_t^e D_t}{1 + D_t}$$
$$+ E_t \left\{ m_{t+1} \left[-\tau_y \frac{W_t^e \Psi_{t+1}}{1 + D_t} + N_{t+1}^\tau + W_{t+1}^e \right] \right\}$$
$$= E_t \left[\Omega_{t+1}(N_{t+1}^\tau + W_{t+1}^e) \right], \tag{10.95}$$

where

$$\Omega_{t+1} \equiv \left[\frac{m_{t+1}}{1 + \frac{D_t}{1 + D_t}\frac{\tau_y - \tau_p}{1 - \tau_y}(1 - E_t m_{t+1}) + \frac{\tau_y}{1 + D_t} E_t(m_{t+1}\Psi_{t+1})} \right].$$

Notice that if $\tau_y = \tau_p = 0$, then $\Omega_{t+1} = m_{t+1}$. Generally, $\Omega_{t+1} < m_{t+1}$ which indicates that the cost of capital to the firm, defined as $\rho = 1/\Omega - 1$ when there is taxation and $\rho = 1/m - 1$ when there is not, increases with distortionary taxation. Notice that the cost of capital now depends on the firm's financial decisions such as the debt-equity ratio and the price-dividend ratio. The cost of capital with distortionary taxation can be expressed as:

$$\rho_{t+1} = \frac{1}{m_{t+1}}\left[1 + \frac{b_{t+1}}{W_t^e}\frac{\tau_y - \tau_p}{1-\tau_y}[1 - E_t(m_{t+1})]\right.$$

$$\left. + \frac{\tau_y q_t z_{t+1}}{W_t^e} E_t\left(m_{t+1}\Psi_{t+1}\right) - m_{t+1}\right], \qquad (10.96)$$

which is a weighted average of the cost of debt capital and the cost of equity capital. So, as long as the costs of debt and equity are not equal, the cost of capital of the firm will depend on how much is financed with debt and equity. The Modigliani-Miller theorem no longer holds because clearly the discount rate now depends on the financing decisions made by firms. We can incorporate the effects of distortionary taxation on the value of the firm and the equity return following the steps in Section 10.4.2 and 10.4.3.

The firm maximizes the present value of future cash flows, $W_t = N_t^\tau + W_t^e$, in two steps. First, it minimizes its cost of capital by choosing the optimal debt-equity ratio D_t and the optimal dividend policy. Second, given the minimum cost of capital, it determines the optimal capital and labor sequences $\{k_{t+s}, n_{t+s}^d\}_{s=0}^\infty$. The optimization can be performed in this way because Ω_{t+1} depends only on the financial variables D_t and Ψ_{t+1} while net cash flow N_t^τ depends on the real production variables, k_t and n_t^d. Brock and Turnovsky [80] study the firm's optimization problem and show that the optimal dividend policy and optimal capital structure will involve a corner solution: either all debt financing or all equity financing. To demonstrate this result, we differentiate the expression for ρ_{t+1} with respect to D_t and Ψ_{t+1}:

$$\text{sgn}\frac{\partial \rho_{t+1}}{\partial D_t} = \text{sgn}\left\{\frac{\tau_y - \tau_p}{1-\tau_y}[1 - E_t(m_{t+1})] - \tau_y E_t\left(m_{t+1}\Psi_{t+1}\right)\right\},$$

$$\text{sgn}\frac{\partial \rho_{t+1}}{\partial \Psi_{t+1}} = \text{sgn}\left\{\tau_y E_t\left(m_{t+1}\right)\right\}.$$

These conditions are similar to those derived by Brock and Turnovsky. Since τ_y is positive, the firm minimizes its cost of capital by minimizing the value of the dividend payout ratio, $E_t(m_{t+1}\Psi_{t+1})$. Brock and Turnovsky note that in the absence of any constraints, this would involve repurchase of shares. However, this is discouraged under the US tax code. Instead of modeling the legal constraints faced by firms, we assume that the firm minimizes the value of its dividend payments by setting $E_t(m_{t+1}\Psi_{t+1}) = E_t(m_{t+1}\tilde{\Psi})$, where $\tilde{\Psi}$ is the minimum payout rate, or the ratio of dividends to the earnings per share, taken to be exogenous. Then, the optimal financial mix is determined as follows:

$$\text{if } \frac{\tau_y - \tau_p}{1 - \tau_y}[1 - E_t(m_{t+1})] < \tau_y E_t\left(m_{t+1}\tilde{\Psi}\right), \text{ set } D_t = \infty, \tag{10.97}$$

$$\text{if } \frac{\tau_y - \tau_p}{1 - \tau_y}[1 - E_t(m_{t+1})] > \tau_y E_t\left(m_{t+1}\tilde{\Psi}\right), \text{ set } D_t = 0. \tag{10.98}$$

Notice that $D_t = \infty$ implies all bond financing while $D_t = 0$ involves all equity financing.

We can also derive versions of Equations (10.97) and (10.98) that allow for a capital gains tax τ_c on equities. In this case, if the net after-tax income on bonds exceeds the net after-tax income from equity, where the latter are taxed twice, first as corporate profits and second as personal income to shareholders, no investor will wish to hold stocks and the firm must engage in all debt financing. Otherwise, the firm will engage in equity financing. A sufficient condition for the former to hold is that the corporate profit tax rate τ_p exceeds the personal income tax rate τ_y.

Other explanations of corporate capital structure that are based on conflicts of interest among shareholders, bondholders, and managers have been provided by Myers [350], Jensen and Meckling [265], and others. Firms' financial structure and dividend policy have also been explained in terms of signaling models. In Ross's [369] signaling model, the debt-equity ratio serves as a signaling mechanism to outsiders about the firm's risk and profitability. Likewise, Bhattacharya [65] uses a signaling model to rationalize why firms pay dividends despite the fact that dividends are taxed at a higher rate than capital gains. Although private information considerations and incentive problems are potentially important ways for explaining corporate capital structure and other observed contractual arrangements, the papers cited above do not derive the form of the proposed arrangements as part of an optimal contract.

10.5. CONCLUSIONS

In this chapter, we have reviewed a variety of results regarding the one-sector optimal growth model. As we have shown, this model constitutes the workhorse for dynamic general equilibrium models. It can be used to analyze growth and capital accumulation, the impact of taxation on capital accumulation, asset pricing with production, investment and the financial structure of a firm, to name a few. The neoclassical growth model also constitutes the basis for "real business cycle" analysis, a topic that we discuss in Chapter 12. In this chapter, we have omitted a discussion of endogenous growth models considered by Romer [368], Lucas [320], and others. In contrast to the neoclassical model, these models allow for sustained growth from the existence of externalities and increasing returns in production (Romer [368]) or from human capital accumulation (Lucas [320]).

APPENDIX: THE INVARIANT DISTRIBUTION

In this appendix, we provide a formal proof of the existence of the stationary distribution of the capital stock. Our discussion is based on Danthine and Donaldson [132] and Stokey and Lucas [418], Chapters 8 and 11.

To study the existence of the stationary distribution for the capital stock, we consider a simple version of the one-sector optimal growth model in which the technology has the multiplicative form:

$$y_t = f(k_t)\theta_t.$$

We assume that the technology shock is i.i.d. with distribution function defined by Assumption 10.6. The solution is a pair of policy functions:

$$c = g(y),$$

$$k' = h(y) = y - g(y).$$

We now use the policy functions, the production function, and the distribution function of the technology shock G to determine the distribution for the output process; we denote this undetermined function as $\bar{G}$.

The basic issue can now be described. We know that output is bounded above, say by B, so that there is some feasible range of the capital stock $[0, B]$. Our goal is to determine whether there is a range $[\underline{y}, \bar{y}]$ where $0 < \underline{y}$ and $\bar{y} < B$ such that $Pr(\underline{y} \leq y_t \leq \bar{y}) = 1$ for $y \in [\underline{y}, \bar{y}]$. Also if $y \notin [\underline{y}, \bar{y}]$, we want to show that the probability that y moves into $[\underline{y}, \bar{y}]$ in a finite number of periods is 1.

The set $[\underline{y}, \bar{y}]$ is called the *ergodic set* and the set of points in $[0, B]$ disjoint from $[\underline{y}, \bar{y}]$ is called the *transient set*. To study the properties of the ergodic set $[\underline{y}, \bar{y}]$, we study the fixed points of the deterministic difference equations:

$$y_{t+1} = f(h(y_t))\underline{\theta}$$

$$y_{t+1} = f(h(y_t))\bar{\theta}.$$

We will show that the *fixed point* of

$$y_{t+1} = f(h(y_t))\theta \quad \text{for } \theta \in [\underline{\theta}, \bar{\theta}], \tag{10.99}$$

or the set of points for which $y = f(h(y))\theta$ for $\theta \in [\underline{\theta}, \bar{\theta}]$, is contained in the interval $[\underline{y}, \bar{y}]$. The basic approach is to rule out certain configurations of fixed points so that the only remaining configurations are ones such that the deterministic difference equations are stable.

We know that

$$\Pr(y_{t+1} \le y' | y_t = y) = \Pr(f(y - g(y))\theta' \le y')$$
$$= \Pr\left(\theta' \le \frac{y'}{f(y - g(y))}\right)$$
$$= G\left(\frac{y'}{f(y - g(y))}\right). \tag{10.100}$$

Define the *stochastic kernel* as:

$$Q(y', y) \equiv G\left(\frac{y'}{f(y - g(y))}\right). \tag{10.101}$$

The stochastic kernel takes $Y \times Y' \to [0, 1]$ where $y \in Y$ and $y' \in Y'$. The transition probability function, $F(y', y)$, that we studied in the context of the Lucas asset-pricing model is a stochastic kernel with $Y = Y'$.

To consider a specific example, suppose that $U(c) = (c^{1-\gamma} - 1)/(1 - \gamma), \gamma \ge 0$ and $y = \theta k^{\alpha}$, θ i.i.d. and $\theta \in [\underline{\theta}, \bar{\theta}]$. Then

$$\Pr(y_{t+1} \le y' | y_t = y) = \Pr((y - g(y))^{\alpha}\theta' \le y')$$
$$= \Pr\left(\theta' \le \frac{y'}{(y - g(y))^{\alpha}}\right)$$
$$= G\left(\frac{y'}{(y - g(y))^{\alpha}}\right).$$

What we would like to find is the unconditional or invariant distribution for y_t denoted $\bar{G}$ such that

$$\bar{G}(y') = \int_{\underline{y}}^{\bar{y}} Q(y', y) d\bar{G}(y) \tag{10.102}$$

such that the probability is one for $y_t \in [\underline{y}, \bar{y}]$ and zero if $y_t \notin [\underline{y}, \bar{y}]$. For this purpose, we define an operator from the relation in Equation (10.102).

Given an initial output equal to y, the probability that output will be less than or equal to y' is equal to the last expression in Equation (10.100). The stochastic kernel defines an operator $\mathcal{T}$ which we use in the following way. If output is distributed at time t according to $\bar{G}(y)$, then output at time $t + 1$ is distributed as:

$$\mathcal{T}\bar{G}(y) = \int_{\underline{y}}^{\bar{y}} G\left(\frac{y'}{f(y - g(y))}\right) d\bar{G}(y) \tag{10.103}$$

where $[\underline{y}, \bar{y}]$ were defined above and are the objects to be determined. We have the following theorem.

Theorem 10.2 *Under Assumptions (10.1), (10.3) and (10.6), the operator T defined by (10.103) has a unique solution $G^\star$ and for any $\bar{G}$, $\lim_{n\to\infty} T^n\bar{G} = G^\star$. Furthermore, $G^\star$ has a unique continuous density function dG which is strictly positive on the closed subset $[\underline{y}, \bar{y}]$ where*

$$\bar{y} \equiv \min_y\{y : dG(y - g(y))\bar{\theta} = y\},$$

$$\underline{y} \equiv \max_y\{y : dG(y - g(y))\underline{\theta} = y\}.$$

First, we prove two properties of the stochastic kernel.

Lemma 10.3 *Under Assumption (10.6), the stochastic kernel Q is regular. This means that Q has a continuous density function, denoted $q(y, y')$, and the family of transforms $\nu_t(\cdot)$, defined by*

$$\nu_t(y') = \int q(y, y')\nu_{t-1}(y)dy$$

where $\nu_0 = \nu$ and ν is continuous and bounded, is equicontinuous whenever ν_0 is uniformly continuous.

PROOF

Let $B^y = \max_{y\in[\underline{y},\bar{y}]} |\nu_0(y)|$. Then by definition of ν_t, $|\nu_t(y)| \le B^y$ so that

$$\begin{aligned}|\nu_t(y) - \nu_t(y')| &= \left|\int q(\alpha, y)\nu_{t-1}(\alpha)d\alpha - \int q(\alpha, y')\nu_{t-1}(\alpha)d\alpha\right| \\ &\le \int |\psi(\alpha, y) - \psi(\alpha, y')| \; |\nu_{t-1}(\alpha)d\alpha| \\ &< \epsilon\end{aligned}$$

for some δ sufficiently small such that $|y - y'| < \delta \Rightarrow |\psi(\alpha, y) - \psi(\alpha, y')| < \epsilon/B^y$ for all ν. There is such a δ if q is uniformly continuous on $[\underline{y}, \bar{y}]$. ∎

This lemma is used to show that there exists a probability measure satisfying $\lim_{n\to\infty} T^n\bar{\Psi} = \Psi$ for any G.

We use some properties of the policy functions in the next lemma.

Lemma 10.4 *Let b,d be such that $f(h(b))\bar{\theta} = b$ and $f(h(d))\underline{\theta} = d$. Then $b \ge d$.*

PROOF

The optimal policy functions satisfy

$$U'(g(b)) = \beta f'(h(b)) \int U'(g(f(h(b))\theta'))\theta' dG(\theta'),$$

$$U'(g(d)) = \beta f'(h(d)) \int U'(g(f(h(d))\theta'))\theta' dG(\theta').$$

For some θ, $b > \beta f'(h(d))\theta$ or $U'(g(b)) < U'(g(f(h(b))\theta))$. Therefore $1 > \beta f'(h(b)) \int \theta' dG(\theta')$ and conversely $1 < \beta f'(h(d)) \int \theta' dG(\theta')$. Hence $f'(h(d)) > f'(h(b))$ or $d < b$. ∎

Lemma 10.5 *The set $[\underline{y}, \bar{y}]$ is the ergodic set of the Markov process with transition probability $Q(y, y')$; the complement of $[\underline{y}, \bar{y}]$ is the transient set of the process.*

PROOF

First, once the process has entered the set $[\underline{y}, \bar{y}]$ there is zero probability of leaving it. This follows from

$$\underline{y} \leq f(h(y))\theta \leq \bar{y}$$

so that for any $A \notin [\underline{y}, \bar{y}]$, and $y \in [\underline{y}, \bar{y}]$,

$$\psi(y, A) = d\Psi(A/f(h(y))) = 0.$$

Second, we show that any subset of $[\underline{y}, \bar{y}]$ has positive measure. Because f, g, dG are continuous and, for all $y \in [\underline{y}, \bar{y}]$, there exists an interval of positive length around y, defined $\ell(y)$, such that $q(y, \ell(y)) > 0$.

We need to show that any interval $[y_1, y_2]$ disjoint from $[\underline{y}, \bar{y}]$ is a transient set so that there is a positive probability of leaving the interval and 0 probability of reentering it. We can use Lemma 10.4 to show that all fixed points of $f(h(y))\underline{\theta}$ are less than the fixed points of $f(h(y))\bar{\theta}$. An interval $[y_1, y_2]$ to the right of and disjoint from $[\underline{y}, \bar{y}]$ that is characterized by $f(h(y))\theta < y$ for all θ and all $y \in [y_1, y_2]$ will generate a y process that will leave the interval in a finite number of steps for all possible realizations. Consider an interval $[y_1, y_2]$ to the right of and disjoint from $[\underline{y}, \bar{y}]$ such that $y_1 = f(h(y_1))\theta$ and $y_2 = f(h(y_2))\theta$. By the continuity of f and h, there exists a $\hat{\theta} > \underline{\theta}$ such that for all $\theta \in [\underline{\theta}, \hat{\theta}]$ and $y \in [y_1, y_2]$ such that $f(h(y))\theta < y$. Hence there exists an $n \geq N$ such that $T^n f(h(y))\theta < y_1$. We can show that the expected number of visits to the interval $[y_1, y_2]$ is strictly less than infinity, hence $[y_1, y_2]$ is a transient set. The same type of argument applies to intervals below $\underline{y}$.

It is straightforward to show that $\bar{y}$ is finite because f is bounded. To show that $\underline{y} > 0$, assume that for some $\epsilon > 0$, $f(h(y))\theta < y$ for all θ and

$y \in [0, \epsilon]$. Suppose that there is a sequence $\{y_t, \ldots, y_{t+n}\}$ such that $y_t < \epsilon$ so that the sequence is tending to 0. The first-order condition is:

$$U'(g(a_{t+n})) = \beta f'(h(a_{t+n})) \int_{\underline{\theta}}^{\bar{\theta}} U'(g(f(y_{t+n})\theta))\theta dG(\theta)$$

But $U'(g(a_{t+n})) < U'(g(f(y_{t+n})\theta))$ because $f(h(y))\theta < y$. This implies that $1 > \beta f'(h(y_{t+n}))$ which cannot hold if y_{t+n} is tending to infinity because by assumption $f'(0) = \infty$. ∎

There are several reasons for studying the properties of this distribution. First, one can ask how differences in discount rates, attitudes toward risk, and technological productivity affect the mean, variance, or range of the stationary distribution of consumption, investment, and output. (See, for example, Danthine and Donaldson [132].) Second, the stationary distribution can be used to compute unconditional moments for these variables, and describe how such moments vary across different economies. This is one of the principal ways in which the performance of real business cycle models has been judged in the recent literature.

10.6. EXERCISES

1. Consumption/Leisure Choices with Distortionary Taxation
Let preferences depend on government consumption so that the representative agent maximizes:

$$E\left[\sum_{t=0}^{\infty} \beta^t U(c_t + \pi g_t, l_t)\right] \tag{10.104}$$

where g_t is real government expenditures and l_t is leisure. Assume that:

$$U(c_t + \pi g_t, l_t) = \ln(c_t + \pi g_t) + \gamma l_t.$$

Households have three sources of income. The first is rental income on capital $r_t k_t$, the second is labor income $w_t n_t$, and the third is a lump-sum transfer from the government ψ_t. The law of motion for the capital stock is:

$$k_{t+1} = (1 - \delta)k_t + i_t, \tag{10.105}$$

where i_t is investment.

Households also pay distortionary taxes. Taxes are assessed on capital income at rate τ so capital income tax paid is $\tau(r_t - \delta)k_t$ and labor income is taxed at rate ϕ so that tax paid is $\phi w_t n_t$. The household's budget constraint is:

$$c_t + i_t \leq r_t k_t + n_t w_t + \psi_t - \phi w_t n_t - \tau(r_t - \delta)k_t. \tag{10.106}$$

Labor-leisure choices are constrained to satisfy:

$$l_t + n_t \leq 1. \tag{10.107}$$

Firms rent capital from households, hire labor and are price takers. The production function is:

$$y_t = \lambda_t k_t^{\theta} n_t^{(1-\theta)}, \tag{10.108}$$

where λ_t is an exogenous productivity shock. The firm maximizes:

$$\Pi_t = \lambda_t k_t^{\theta} n_t^{(1-\theta)} - r_t k_t - w_t n_t \tag{10.109}$$

given w_t and r_t.

Government expenditures g_t are exogenous and stochastic. The government's budget constraint is:

$$g_t + \psi_t = \tau(r_t - \delta)\kappa_t + \phi w_t N_t \tag{10.110}$$

where κ_t is the aggregate capital stock and N_t is aggregate labor.

(a) Derive the first-order conditions for the household assuming that the household takes as given the prices, government expenditures, and transfers. Set up the Bellman equation and be explicit about the state variables.

(b) Derive the first-order conditions for the profit-maximizing firm.

(c) What is the aggregate state vector? What are the feasibility conditions? Write down the equilibrium conditions.

(d) Derive the solution under the assumptions that $\pi = \tau = \phi = 0$.

(e) Set $\pi = 0$ but assume that $\tau = \phi > 0$ and describe the equilibrium.

2. Suppose the firm is all debt-financed, which means that debt-to-equity ratio is $D_t = \infty$, or the share of debt in firm's value $b_{t+1}/W_t^e = 1$.

(a) Show that when there are no taxes or any other frictions, the cost of capital equals the cost of debt.

(b) Assuming that the interest payment on debt is tax deductible, show that when there is corporate tax $\tau_p > 0$ and income tax $\tau_y > 0$, the cost of capital does not equal the cost of debt. The cost of capital when there is the tax payment is lower than without the tax. How would you explain this?

(c) Solve the problem in part b) assuming that the interest payment on debt is NOT tax deductible. Does the cost of capital of the firm equal to cost of debt now? Why? Is the cost of capital higher or lower now?

3. Suppose households maximize

$$\max_{\{c_t, b_{t+1}, z_{t+1}^c, z_{t+1}^p\}_{t=0}^{\infty}} E_0 \left\{ \sum_{t=0}^{\infty} \beta^t U(c_t) \right\}$$

where z^c_{t+1}, z^p_{t+1} denotes the holdings of common and preferred stock, respectively. Households pay a proportional income tax equal to $\tau_y > 0$ so that the budget constraint is given by:

$$c_t + q^c_t z^c_{t+1} + q^p_t z^p_{t+1} + b_{t+1} \leq (1 - \tau_y)[w_t l_t + r_t b_t + z^c_t d^c_t]$$
$$+ b_t + z^c_t q^c_t + z^p_t q^p_t,$$

where we assume that the firm does not make any dividend payments for the preferred stock. The firm's gross profits are given by:

$$\pi_t = f(k_t, \theta_t) - w_t.$$

The firm pays $\tau_p > 0$ on its gross profits and is allowed to deduct its interest payments on debt.

(a) Find the first-order conditions with respect to $c_t, b_{t+1}, z^c_{t+1}, z^p_{t+1}$.
(b) Find the ex-dividend value of the firm.
(c) Find the cost of capital of the firm.
(d) Now suppose the households pay a capital gains tax $\tau_c > 0$ on the preferred equities they hold. Determine the sufficient condition for the firm's cost of capital under the capital gains tax to be higher than it is without it (compare it with the result you found in c).

4. Human Capital Accumulation in a Deterministic Economy
A representative consumer has preferences given by:

$$U = \sum_{t=0}^{\infty} \beta^t \frac{c_t^{1-\sigma} - 1}{1 - \sigma}, \quad \sigma > 0.$$

The production of the single good depends on physical and human capital denoted K_t and H_t, respectively. The resource constraint and the law of motion for human capital are given by:

$$c_t + K_{t+1} - (1 - \delta)K_t = AK_t^{\alpha}((1 - s_t)H_t)^{1-\alpha}, \quad 0 < \alpha < 1,$$

$$H_{t+1} = \theta H_t s_t + (1 - \delta)H_t,$$

where $\theta H_t s_t$, $s_t \in [0, 1]$ and $\theta > 0$, is new investment in human capital.

Show that along a *balanced growth path* the growth rates for consumption, physical and human capital satisfy:

$$\gamma_C = \gamma_K = \gamma_H \theta \bar{s} - \delta.$$

CHAPTER 11

Investment

Investment theory typically distinguishes between the desired capital stock and the actual capital stock. According to the neoclassical model of Jorgenson [266] and Hall and Jorgenson [222], the desired capital stock is determined as a function of output and input prices, technology, and interest rates, and an exogenous partial adjustment model is stipulated to yield the adjustment of the actual capital stock to the desired capital stock. Following Lucas [313], Treadway [433], Gould [211], an alternative approach postulates that firms face costs of adjusting when undertaking investment decisions. Proponents of this view argue that it costs time and resources to put in new machinery, to integrate it into the production process, and to train new workers. Various authors including Abel [1] and Hayashi [243] have shown that the adjustment-cost model under perfect competition and constant returns to scale yields a Q-theory of investment. This states that the firm's demand for new capital goods, as captured by its investment expenditures, should be increasing in the price of existing capital relative to new capital, a relative price that is called "Tobin's Q."

A number of authors have emphasized irreversibility and uncertainty as important factors in the gradual adjustment of the capital stock. The irreversible model of investment under uncertainty leads to an option value of waiting. If the decision to invest in fixed capital today cannot be undone by the firm next period, then the firm may prefer to wait today instead of undertaking an investment that it may wish to reverse in the face of new information received after the fact. The adjustment-cost model and the irreversible-investment model under uncertainty may be viewed as competing rather than complementary theories of investment. As shown by Demers [148], the irreversible-investment model under uncertainty leads to an *endogenous* marginal cost of adjustment that depends on information about the future profitability or costs of investment.

Investment theory has typically been developed from the viewpoint of the individual firm or industry. Lucas and Prescott [322] provide an analysis of industry equilibrium under uncertainty. Yet our analysis up to this point has been based on simple dynamic general equilibrium frameworks. Sargent [383] provides an early example of a general equilibrium model of investment under uncertainty with irreversibility. He uses a version of the one-sector optimal growth model with irreversible investment to study the relationship between Q and investment. Dow and Olson (1992) analyse a two-sector stochastic growth model where aggregate investment is subject to a non-negativity constraint. Coleman (1997) examines the impact of investment irreversibility in a multi-sector, stochastic growth model where there is no exogenous aggregate uncertainty, but where each sector is subject to an idiosyncratic productivity shock and to an irreversibility constraint. Kogan [281], [282] uses an equilibrium model with irreversible investment to study the relationship between stock returns, investment and Q. He considers a two-sector model in which the irreversibility constraint affects only one of the sectors. In this chapter, we describe alternative models of investment and link them to asset-pricing phenomena.

11.1. THE NEOCLASSICAL MODEL OF INVESTMENT

The neoclassical model of investment has formed the mainstay of modern investment theory. The basis for this theory can be found in the concept of the *cost of capital*. To describe the implications of this theory, we return to the optimality condition for the one-sector growth model in Equation (10.15). This is given by:

$$U'(c_t) = \beta E_t \left\{ U'(c_{t+1})[f_1(k_{t+1}, \theta_{t+1}) + (1 - \delta)] \right\}, \tag{11.1}$$

where $c_t = f(k_t, \theta_t) + (1 - \delta)k_t - k_{t+1}$. Now suppose that the gross real interest rate is a constant, that is:

$$1 + r_t^f = \frac{1}{E_t(m_{t+1})} = \frac{1}{\beta E_t[U'(c_{t+1})/U'(c_t)]} = \bar{R}.$$

Some conditions under which this can occur are if $c_t = c_{t+1} = \bar{c}$ or $U'(c)$ is constant. Then $1 + r^f = 1/\beta$, which implies that the net interest rate is given by $r^f = R - 1 = \rho$, the consumer's subjective rate of time preference. Substituting this result into Equation (11.1) yields:

$$1 + r^f = E_t[f_1(k_{t+1}, \theta_{t+1}) + (1 - \delta)],$$

or:

$$r^f + \delta = E_t[f_1(k_{t+1}, \theta_{t+1})]. \tag{11.2}$$

The quantity $r^f + \delta$ is typically called the *user cost of capital*. Recall that k_{t+1} is chosen in period t based on information at time t. Suppose

$$f(k, \theta) = k^\alpha \theta.$$

Then we can use this condition to solve for the desired stock of capital to be carried over into period $t+1$ as:

$$k^d_{t+1} = \left[\frac{\alpha E_t(\theta_{t+1})}{r^f + \delta}\right]^{1/(1-\alpha)}. \tag{11.3}$$

This expression shows that the desired capital stock depends positively on expected productivity, $E_t(\theta_{t+1})$, and the share of capital in production, α, and negatively on the real interest rate, r, and the depreciation rate, δ. Notice that we have not made any assumptions regarding the time series properties of the technology shock. If $\{\theta_t\}$ is i.i.d., then the desired capital stock is a constant; otherwise, k^d_{t+1} varies with current realization of the technology shock.

In the above discussion, no explicit account was made of the impact of various tax provisions on capital accumulation. Suppose, for simplicity, that there is a corporate income tax τ that is collected as a fraction of a firm's output. Also assume that there is an investment tax credit such that the firm gets back γ of the price of the investment good. Then assuming that firms own the capital stock and make all investment decisions, we can write their problem as:

$$\max_{\{n_{t+i},\, k_{t+1+i}\}} E_t \left\{ \sum_{i=0}^{\infty} \left(\frac{1}{1+r^f}\right)^i [(1-\tau)F(k_{t+i}, n_{t+i}, \theta_{t+i}) - w_{t+i}n_{t+i} - (1-\gamma)I_{t+i}] \right\},$$

subject to the law of motion for the capital stock, $k_{t+1} = (1-\delta)k_t + I_t$. The first-order conditions are:

$$(1-\tau)F_2(k_t, n_t, \theta_t) = w_t,$$

$$(1-\tau)E_t[F_1(k_{t+1}, n_{t+1}, \theta_{t+1})] = (1-\gamma)(r^f + \delta).$$

In this case, the cost of capital includes the effect of the investment tax credit, and the corporate income tax affects the future (after-tax) marginal product of capital.

One problem with the neoclassical model of investment is that it does not lead to a determinate level of investment. In this model, firms choose the level of the capital stock. Thus, as the cost of capital changes, firms should instantaneously adjust their capital stock to the "desired" level. For instance, if r increases (or δ increases), the desired capital stock should decrease to ensure that the expected marginal product of capital equals the higher capital cost. The problem is that in this model there is no mechanism which tells us how much the capital stock will decrease. In practice, investment adjusts gradually to changes in the determinants of the cost of capital. To account for this empirical phenomenon, typically a partial adjustment mechanism is added to the theory of the desired capital stock to yield a model of investment.

11.2. THE *Q* THEORY ADJUSTMENT-COST MODEL OF INVESTMENT

An alternative way of obtaining a determinate investment function is to postulate the existence of adjustment costs. Various authors including Abel [1] and Hayashi [243] have shown that the adjustment-cost model under perfect competition and constant returns to scale yield a *Q* theory of investment. We now formulate a model with adjustment costs and relate it to the *Q* theory of investment.

11.2.1. The Q theory of investment

An alternative theory of investment was developed by Tobin [430] that does not rely on the notion of the desired capital stock. Tobin stipulated that investment should be an increasing function of the ratio of the firm's market value to the replacement cost of its capital stock. Recall that the ex-dividend value of the firm is denoted W_t^e and denote the price of new investment goods by p_{It}. *Average Q* can be expressed as:

$$Q^a = \frac{\text{market value of the firm}}{\text{the replacement cost of capital}} = \frac{W_t^e}{p_{It}k_{t+1}}.$$

Tobin's *Q* theory of investment states that firms will invest if Q^a exceeds unity, and will disinvest if Q^a falls below unity. Put differently, the firm will invest as long as the firm's market value is large enough to cover the cost of replacing its existing capital. Unlike the neoclassical model, Tobin's approach uses stock market data to capture firms' expectations with respect to future profitability.

We can also define a measure of *Q* as the ratio of the marginal value of an additional unit of capital (or its shadow value) to its replacement cost. Let p_{kt} denote the price of existing capital. *Marginal Q* is defined as:

$$Q^m = \frac{\text{marginal value of an additional unit of capital}}{\text{its replacement cost}} = \frac{p_{kt}}{p_{It}}.$$

In what follows, we will examine the relationship between average *Q* and marginal *Q*.

11.2.2. Adjustment costs

Adjustment costs in investment arise because installing new capital goods is disruptive, with the installation or adjustment costs increasing in the amount of new capital installed. Holding factor inputs fixed, the adjustment cost model assumes that the cost of the investment good in terms of the consumption good is increasing as the rate of investment increases. Let i_t/K_t be the ratio of investment to the beginning of period capital stock. Assume that the resources or output required to install i_t units of new capital are given by:

$$i_t[1 + h(i_t/K_t)].$$

Let $x \equiv i/K$ be the rate of investment relative to the capital stock. The function $h(\cdot)$ is denoted the *adjustment cost* function. We have the following assumption.

Assumption 11.1 *(i)* $h(0) = 0$*; (ii)* $h'(x) \geq 0$*; (iii)* $2h'(x) + xh''(x) > 0$ *for all* $x > 0$.

The first part of this assumption says that adjustment costs are zero at zero investment. The second and third parts of this assumption show that adjustment costs are increasing and convex.

Output in this economy is produced according to a constant-returns-to-scale production function with a multiplicative technology shock:

$$y_t = f(K_t)\theta_t, \tag{11.4}$$

where the aggregate capital stock K_t is measured as per capita. In equilibrium it turns out that $n_t = 1$. Hence, under constant returns to scale this causes no problems. The production function satisfies $f' > 0$, $f'' < 0$, $f'(0) = \infty$, and $f'(\infty) = 0$. The technology shock is i.i.d. and has a distribution that satisfies Assumption 10.6.

The per capita capital stock evolves according to:

$$K_{t+1} = i_t + (1 - \delta)K_t, \tag{11.5}$$

where $0 < \delta \leq 1$ is the depreciation rate. The resource or feasibility constraint for this economy is given by:

$$c_t + i_t[1 + h(i_t/K_t)] \leq f(K_t)\theta_t. \tag{11.6}$$

Notice that this is a one-sector model so that the output of the single good can be consumed or invested in capital. However, unlike the standard one-sector growth model, the feasibility constraint also accounts for the resources expended due to the adjustment costs. In a later section, we will also consider a two-sector model in which one sector produces investment goods.

11.2.3. The social planner's problem

The social planner's problem allows us to characterize the optimal allocations in the presence of adjustment costs.

The social planner solves:

$$V(K_t, \theta_t) = \max_{c_t, i_t}\{U(c_t) + \beta E_t[V(K_{t+1}, \theta_{t+1})]\} \tag{11.7}$$

subject to the resource constraint in Equation (11.6) and given the law of motion for capital in Equation (11.5) and the fixed initial capital stock, K_t. Let λ_t^p denote the multiplier for the resource constraint in Equation (11.6). Define

$$H(x) \equiv 1 + h(x) + xh'(x) \tag{11.8}$$

as the derivative of the term $i_t[1 + h(x_t)]$ with respect to i_t, or the *marginal cost* of new investment at time t. The existence of a solution to the functional equation in (11.7) can be demonstrated using the approach in Chapter 10.

Substituting for the law of motion for capital, the first-order conditions with respect to c_t and i_t are:

$$U'(c_t) = \lambda_t^p, \tag{11.9}$$

$$\lambda_t^p H(x_t) = \beta E_t[V_1(K_{t+1}, \theta_{t+1})]. \tag{11.10}$$

The envelope condition is:

$$V_1(K_t, \theta_t) = \lambda_t^p[f'(K_t)\theta_t + (x_t)^2 h'(x_t)] + (1 - \delta)\beta E_t[V_1(K_{t+1}, \theta_{t+1})]. \tag{11.11}$$

Using the first-order condition with respect to i_t in Equation (11.11) yields:

$$V_1(K_t, \theta_t) = \lambda_t^p[f'(K_t)\theta_t + (x_t)^2 h'(x_t) + (1 - \delta)H(x_t)]. \tag{11.12}$$

The optimal allocation for the social planner's problem can be determined using the standard methods for solving dynamic programming problems. Define $m_{t+1} = \beta U'(c_{t+1})/U'(c_t)$. Making use of the first-order conditions and the envelope condition, we have that

$$1 = E_t\left[m_{t+1}\frac{f'(K_{t+1})\theta_{t+1} + (x_{t+1})^2 h'(x_{t+1}) + (1 - \delta)H(x_{t+1})}{H(x_t)}\right]. \tag{11.13}$$

subject to $c_t + x_t K_t[1 + h(x_t)] \leq f(K_t)\theta_t$.

The solution for the model with adjustment costs differs from the solution for the frictionless neoclassical model that we analyzed in Chapter 10 in several ways. First, the aggregate feasibility constraint accounts for the resources expended due to the adjustment costs. Second, the return on capital includes the reduction in the opportunity cost of installation made possible by the extra capital available at date $t + 1$ due to new investment at time t, $(x_{t+1})^2 h'(x_{t+1})$, plus the value of the undepreciated part of the capital stock carried over from period t evaluated at the marginal cost of new capital at time $t+1$, $(1-\delta)H(x_{t+1})$. Thus, the condition in Equation (11.13) equates the marginal cost of new investment at time t, $H(x_t)$, to the expected discounted benefit of this new investment at $t+1$, where the discounting is done using the intertemporal MRS.

11.2.4. The market economy

Next, we describe the market economy. We assume that the firm is the owner of the capital stock and is a price-taker. The firm not only participates in the goods market where it sells consumption goods and new capital goods, it also participates in the used capital good market. In the frictionless neoclassical model of investment, new and used capital goods are perfect substitutes. Hence, the price of used capital is equal to the price of new capital, which equals one in a model with a single consumption good. When there are adjustment costs, irreversibilities, and other frictions, however, this price may differ from the price of new capital.

We now assume that used capital sells for a price of $p_{k,t}$. Hence, the value of the capital stock that the firm can sell at the end of the period is $p_{k,t}(1-\delta)k_t$. The firm also purchases used capital with a value of $p_{k,t}k_t^d$. The firm's receipts from selling its output consist of sales of the consumption good, c_t^s, and used capital, $p_{k,t}(1-\delta)k_t$. The firm pays wages w_t, buys used capital $p_{k,t}k_t^d$, and buys new investment goods i_t^d. The law of motion for the firm's capital stock is:

$$k_{t+1} = i_t^d + k_t^d, \tag{11.14}$$

which says that next period's capital stock is equal to purchases of new and used capital. The firm's gross profits are:

$$\pi_t = f(k_t)\theta_t - w_t n_t - i_t^d[1 + h(i_t^d/k_t)], \tag{11.15}$$

where the cost of installing new capital $h(i_t^d/k_t)$ is included. Notice that this is a one-sector model so that the relative price of new investment goods, p_{It}, is normalized as one. Gross profits are disbursed according to

$$\pi_t = RE_t + d_t z_t + (1 + r_t)b_t.$$

Purchases of used capital (net of the receipts from sales of existing capital carried from the previous period) are financed by retained earnings, by new equity issues or by new debt as:

$$p_{k,t}k_t^d - p_{k,t}(1-\delta)k_t = RE_t + q_t(z_{t+1} - z_t) + b_{t+1}.$$

The net cash flow from the firm to the household is defined as:

$$\begin{aligned} N_t &\equiv \pi_t - p_{k,t}k_t^d + p_{k,t}(1-\delta)k_t \\ &= f(k_t)\theta_t - w_t n_t - i_t^d[1 + h(i_t^d/k_t)] - p_{k,t}k_t^d + p_{k,t}(1-\delta)k_t \\ &= RE_t + d_t z_t + (1+r_t)b_t + q_t(z_t - z_{t+1}) - b_{t+1} - RE_t \\ &= d_t z_t + (1+r_t)b_t + q_t(z_t - z_{t+1}) - b_{t+1}. \end{aligned} \tag{11.16}$$

The household's problem is standard and identical to the problem in Section 10.4. It consists of choosing sequences for c_t, z_{t+1}, and b_{t+1} to maximize the objective function in Equation (10.48) subject to the wealth constraint in Equation (10.49) and given the restriction that $0 \leq n_t^s \leq 1$. The first-order conditions are identical to Equations (10.50)–(10.52).

The firm maximizes

$$W(k_t, \theta_t) = N_t + E_t[m_{t+1}W(k_{t+1}, \theta_{t+1})] \tag{11.17}$$

given k_t by choosing n_t, k_t^d, i_t^d, where we have substituted for the constraint (11.14). The first-order conditions are:

$$w_t = f(k_t)\theta_t - f'(k_t)\theta_t, \tag{11.18}$$

$$p_{k,t} = E_t[m_{t+1}W_1(k_{t+1}, \theta_{t+1})], \tag{11.19}$$

$$H(i_t^d/k_t) = E_t[m_{t+1}W_1(k_{t+1}, \theta_{t+1})]. \tag{11.20}$$

The envelope condition is:

$$W_1(k_t, \theta_t) = f'(k_t)\theta_t + \left(i_t^d/k_t\right)^2 h'\left(i_t^d/k_t\right) + (1-\delta)p_{k,t}. \tag{11.21}$$

Recall that marginal Q is defined as the ratio of the marginal value of an additional unit of capital (or its shadow value) to its replacement cost. In this model, the firm invests until the shadow value of capital equals the price of an additional unit of used capital. (See Equation (11.19).) The replacement cost of capital net of the adjustment cost is p_{It}. However, in a one-sector model, p_{It} equals the price of output, which equals one. Hence, we find that marginal Q is given by:

$$Q^m = \frac{p_{kt}}{p_{It}} = p_{kt}. \tag{11.22}$$

Equations (11.19) and (11.20) imply that:

$$H(i_t^d/k_t) = p_{k,t}. \tag{11.23}$$

The left side of this expression equals the marginal cost of investment and the right-side is the shadow price of installed capital, which also equals marginal Q. Since H is strictly increasing, we can solve Equation (11.23) for

i_t/k_t as an increasing function of the shadow price of capital or marginal Q^m, as hypothesized by Tobin:

$$i_t/k_t = H^{-1}(p_{k,t}) = H^{-1}(Q^m). \tag{11.24}$$

An equivalent way of examining the implications of the Q theory-adjustment cost model is through present value relations. Using the first-order condition in Equation (11.19) together with the envelope condition in Equation (11.21), we can obtain an expression for $p_{k,t}$ as:

$$\begin{aligned} p_{k,t} &= E_t\left\{m_{t+1}\left[f'(k_{t+1})\theta_{t+1} + (x_{t+1})^2 h'(x_{t+1}) + (1-\delta)p_{k,t+1}\right]\right\} \\ &= E_t\left\{\sum_{i=0}^{\infty}(1-\delta)^i m_{t+i+1}[f'(k_{t+i+1})\theta_{t+i+1} + (x_{t+i+1})^2 h'(x_{t+i+1})]\right\}, \end{aligned}$$

where we have obtained the expression on the second line by recursively substituting for $p_{k,t+i}$ and using the fact that $\lim_{h\to\infty} E_t[m_{t+h+1}p_{k,t+h+1}] \to 0$. This expression shows that the price of an additional unit of existing capital is equal to the expected discounted value of the future *total* marginal product of capital, where the term $(x_{t+i})^2 h'(x_{t+i})$ represents the reduction in the opportunity cost of installation made possible by the additional unit of capital at time $t+i$. The discount factor is the product of one minus the depreciation rate and the intertemporal MRS for consumption between periods t and $t+i$ to account for the fact a unit of existing capital at time t depreciates at the rate $(1-\delta)^i$ at time $t+i$.

Now consider the value of installed capital at the end of the period, $p_{k,t}k_{t+1}$. To find an expression for this, multiply the expression for $p_{k,t}$ by k_{t+1} to obtain:

$$\begin{aligned} p_{k,t}k_{t+1} &= E_t\left\{m_{t+1}\left[f'(k_{t+1})\theta_{t+1}k_{t+1} + (1-\delta)p_{k,t+1}k_{t+1}\right.\right. \\ &\quad \left.\left. + \left((i^d_{t+1})^2/k_{t+1}\right) h'(i^d_{t+1}/k_{t+1})\right]\right\} \\ &= E_t\left\{m_{t+1}\left[f(k_{t+1})\theta_{t+1} - w_{t+1} + (1-\delta)p_{k,t+1}k_{t+1}\right.\right. \\ &\quad \left.\left. - i^d_{t+1}[1 + h(i^d_{t+1}/k_{t+1})] - i_{t+1}H(i^d_{t+1}/k_{t+1})\right]\right\} \\ &= E_t\left\{m_{t+1}\left[f(k_{t+1})\theta_{t+1} - w_{t+1} + (1-\delta)p_{k,t+1}k_{t+1}\right.\right. \\ &\quad \left.\left. - i^d_{t+1}[1 + h(i^d_{t+1}/k_{t+1})] - p_{k,t+1}k^d_{t+1} + p_{k,t+1}k_{t+2}\right]\right\}, \end{aligned}$$

where the second line follows by the homogeneity of degree one of the production function and the installation cost functions. Thus, by the latter property and using the definition of $H(x)$, we can substitute

$(i^2/k)h'(i/k) = -i[1+h(i/k)] - H(i/k)i$. The third line follows by noting that $H(i_{t+1}/k_{t+1}) = p_{k,t+1}$ and by using the law of motion for capital $k_{t+2} = i^d_{t+1} + k^d_{t+1}$ to substitute for i^d_{t+1}. Iterating the last expression forward and using the definition of net cash flows N_{t+i} yields:

$$
\begin{aligned}
p_{k,t}k_{t+1} &= E_t\Bigg\{\sum_{i=1}^{\infty} m_{t+i}\big[f(k_{t+i})\theta_{t+i} - w_{t+i} + (1-\delta)p_{k,t+i}k_{t+1+i} \\
&\qquad - i_{t+i}[1 + h(x_{t+i})] - p_{k,t+i}k_{t+i}\big]\Bigg\} \\
&= W^e_t,
\end{aligned}
$$

where $n_{t+i} = 1$ for all i. The ratio W^e_t/k_{t+1} is identical to average Q, which shows the ratio of the market value of capital to its replacement cost:

$$
Q^a = \frac{W^e_t}{p_{It}k_{t+1}} = \frac{W^e_t}{k_{t+1}} = p_{k,t}, \tag{11.25}
$$

since $p_{It} = 1$. Recall that marginal Q equals the price of existing capital, that is, $Q^m = p_{kt}$. Hence, we find that average Q is equal to marginal Q, $Q^m = Q^a$. This is just the result that Hayashi [243] derives, that is, for a competitive firm that faces a constant returns to scale production function and a linearly homogeneous installation cost function, average Q and marginal Q are equal.

Abel [1] tests a version of the Q theory using quadratic costs of adjustment in investment. Abel and Blanchard [5] construct a measure of marginal Q that does not rely on stock market data. They find that regressing investment on their measure of marginal Q implies that a large, serially correlated fraction of investment is left unexplained, similar to results from regressions of investment on average Q. This analysis can be extended to other models of investment. Altug [17] derives restrictions between the price of new and used capital goods and the term structure of real interest rates for the time-to-build model of investment. Although the empirical work described above is implemented with aggregate data, the theoretical framework constrains the behavior of individual firms. A few recent papers have employed panel data on firms to exploit both cross-sectional and time series variation in prices and quantities. Hayashi and Inoue [245] and Blundell, Bond, Devereux, and Schiantarelli [70] estimate Q models of investment using panel data on firms from Japan and the UK, respectively. The former find that a tax-adjusted measure of Q is a significant determinant of investment but cash flow variables are also significant in some years while the latter find that the coefficient on Q is significant but small.

11.2.5. *Asset-pricing relations*

We can also derive a relationship involving the return to investing defined as $R_{I,t+1}$. Using the first-order condition in Equation (11.19) together with the envelope condition yields:

$$\begin{aligned} 1 &= E_t\left[m_{t+1}R_{I,t+1}\right] \\ &= E_t\left[m_{t+1}\frac{f'(k_{t+1})\theta_{t+1} + (x_{t+1})^2 h'(x_{t+1}) + (1-\delta)p_{k,t+1}}{p_{k,t}}\right] \\ &= E_t\left[m_{t+1}\frac{f'(k_{t+1})\theta_{t+1} + (x_{t+1})^2 h'(x_{t+1}) + (1-\delta)H(x_{t+1})}{H(x_t)}\right]. \end{aligned}$$

In the absence of adjustment costs, $H(x_t) = 1$ and $h'(x_t) = 0$ which implies that the price of capital goods is equal to the price of output, which equals unity. Hence, we have that $p_{k,t} = 1$ and the return to investment simplifies to the case that we analyzed in Chapter 10 for the one-sector optimal growth model where $R_{I,t+1} = f'(k_{t+1})\theta_{t+1} + (1-\delta)$. When there are adjustment costs, the cost of investing today is $p_{k,t}$. The payoff from this investment is the expected marginal value of capital, which equals the marginal product of the installed capital plus two other terms. In Cochrane's [107] asset-pricing model with production, these additional terms also appear because he assumes the existence of adjustment costs. The first term, $(x_{t+1})^2 h'(x_{t+1})$, represents the reduction in the opportunity cost of installation $i_t[1 + h(i_t/k_t)]$ made by the additional unit of capital at time $t+1$. The second term represents the resale value of the undepreciated part of the period $t+1$ capital stock evaluated at the price of new capital at date $t+1$. In a model with adjustment costs, the price of capital goods, $p_{k,t}$, equals one plus marginal adjustment cost, or $H(x_t)$.

Suppose that adjustment costs are quadratic:

$$h(x) = \frac{\alpha}{2}(x)^2,$$

where $x = i/k$.

Then we can express the investment return as:

$$R_{I,t+1} = \frac{f'(k_{t+1})\theta_{t+1} + \alpha(x_{t+1})^3 + (1-\delta)[1 + (3/2)\alpha x_{t+1}^2]}{1 + (3/2)\alpha x_t^2}.$$

This expression shows that if the investment-capital stock ratio at time t is high, the return is low because investment leads to large adjustment costs. When the investment-capital stock ratio at time $t+1$ is high, the return is high both because the resale value and the reduction in the opportunity cost of installation due to the existence of additional capital at time $t+1$ are high.

Cochrane [107] argues that stock prices may drift away from the relation based on the predicted investment-capital ratios for the Q theory-adjustment cost model. By contrast, stock returns may be better modeled by the investment return. As discussed in Chapter 10, he provides a set of empirical results suggesting that stock returns and investment returns are essentially equal. Jermann [264] models the behavior of stock returns using a model with an internal habit and adjustment costs in investment. He solves the model by log-linearizing the Euler equations and calculates expressions for asset returns under a joint log-normality assumption. Jermann finds that the model with habit formation and capital adjustment costs makes it possible to match the standard business cycle facts. (See, for example, Cooley and Prescott [124].) However, neither model feature *alone* serves to do this. The reason is that habit formation implies a strong aversion to intertemporal substitution. Hence, in the absence of capital adjustment costs, consumers can optimally choose their consumption paths to be very smooth, thereby counteracting the effects of the habit on the equity premium. Capital adjustment costs make it more costly to smooth consumption so that consumers end up taking more consumption risk. However, as Jermann notes, the model with habit formation and adjustment costs also implies that interest rates vary a lot. Ironically, this is also due to aversion to intertemporal substitution together with the capital adjustment costs. Likewise, he finds that the premium for long-term bonds is close to the equity premium in the model whereas long-term bonds display a much smaller premium in the data. One solution that he proposes to this problem is *financial leverage*, which increases the equity premium relative to the premium on long-term bonds by making dividends more risky but at the same much more volatile than observed dividends. These results provide new intuition about the determinants of risk premia on alternative assets and show that much new research is needed to reconcile such asset-market phenomena with models that deal explicitly with the "real" side of the economy.

11.3. IRREVERSIBLE INVESTMENT

An alternative theory of investment is provided by the theory of "irreversible" investment. Irreversibility refers to the fact that the resale value of a firm's capital stocks may not be equal to its initial purchase price. This may occur because the capital stock is highly firm-specific. Alternatively, the capital stock may be industry-specific, but industry-level uncertainty may affect all firms similarly and hence prevent firms from selling their excess capital stocks in response to an adverse demand shock. Even for less firm- or industry-specific capital goods, there may exist a "lemons" problem of adverse selection in the market for used capital that may similarly prevent firms from disinvesting.

Much of the irreversible investment literature has evolved on the notion of determining the timing of a given investment project. See, for example, Cukierman [130], Bernanke [57], or Brennan and Schwartz [75], amongst others. Authors such as Brennan and Schwartz apply financial options pricing to the analysis of irreversible investment decisions, leading this approach to the analysis of corporate investment to be called the "real options" approach. A number of authors have also emphasized irreversibility and uncertainty as important factors underlying the gradual adjustment of the capital stock. In particular, Nickell [352], [353] focuses on delivery lags and timing uncertainty as an explanation of the gradual adjustment of the capital stock and shows that the irreversibility constraint strengthens the need for caution.[1] Demers, Demers, and Altug [149] provide an extensive review and discussion of the investment literature with a particular emphasis on irreversible investment models. In what follows, we present a model with partial irreversibility and expandability.

11.3.1. A model with partial irreversibility and expandability

Expandability refers to the possibility for the firm to put off its investment decision. The cost of delaying its investment decision is the price differential it may have to pay to acquire the same capital stock in the future. The firm also faces irreversibility in the sense that the resale price for its excess capital stock is lower than the price at which the stock was purchased. The lower the resale price, the greater is the degree of irreversibility faced by the firm.

The household's problem is identical to the problem in Section 10.4. It consists of choosing sequences for c_t, z_{t+1}, and b_{t+1} to maximize the objective function in Equation (10.48) subject to the wealth constraint in Equation (10.49) and given the restriction that $0 \leq n_t^s \leq 1$. The first-order conditions are identical to Equations (10.50)–(10.52).

Define:

- p_t^{kH} as the purchase price of new capital goods;
- p_t^{kL} as the resale price of used capital goods.

Also assume that the price of used capital goods is less than the price of new capital goods:

$$p_t^{kH} \geq p_t^{kL}. \tag{11.26}$$

[1] Demers [148] introduces the learning behavior of a firm, and shows how output price uncertainty reduces the investment of a Bayesian firm facing irreversibility, while Pindyck [361], Bertola and Caballero [61], Dixit and Pyndick [154] and others characterize the optimal investment decision with Brownian motions for the relevant stochastic variables.

Perfect expandability occurs when the future purchase price of new capital goods is equal to the current purchase price:

$$p_t^{kH} = p_{t+1}^{kH}.$$

However, the higher the future purchase price of capital, the less the expandability of the firm. An infinite future purchase price for the capital stock implies the total lack of expandability. In this case the firm faces a "now or never" situation vis-a-vis its current investment decision. By contrast, the firm faces *total irreversibility* when resale markets are absent, which is equivalent to assuming that the resale price is zero:

$$p_t^{kL} = 0.$$

In this case, once the firm invests, it cannot get rid of the additional capital stock even if economic conditions warrant a lower desired capital stock. Because it cannot access resale markets, it can only allow its excess capital stock to depreciate through time.

Define the short-run profit function for the firm at time t by $\pi(K_t, \theta_t)$ as:

$$\pi(K_t, \theta_t) = \max_{n_t > 0} \{F(K_t, n_t, \theta_t) - w_t n_t\} = f'(k_t)\theta_t k_t, \tag{11.27}$$

where the second result follows by CRTS. Notice that this problem involves static maximization under certainty. Assume that i_t is the firm's rate of gross investment (measured in physical units) if $i_t > 0$ and its sales of capital goods if $i_t < 0$. The firm's net cash flow at time t, N_t, is defined as:

$$N_t = \pi(K_t, \theta_t) - p_t^{kH} \max\{i_t, 0\} - p_t^{kL} \min\{i_t, 0\}. \tag{11.28}$$

Let primed variables denote future values and unprimed variables denote current values. Define the vector of capital good prices as $h^k \equiv (p^{kH}, p^{kL})'$ and $G^\theta(\theta'|\theta)$ denote the distribution function of θ' conditional on θ. The optimization problem of the firm now becomes:

$$W(k, \theta, h^k) = \max_i \{N + E[m' W(k', \theta', (h^k)')|\theta, h^k]\}$$

subject to $p^{kH} \geq p^{kL}$ and the law of motion for the capital stock $k' = (1 - \delta)k + i$. If resale markets were perfect the model would be identical to the neoclassical model since there are no costs of adjustment. However, when we assume partial irreversibility, the investment decision of the firm becomes dynamic, contrary to the neoclassical model.

The first-order conditions are given by:

$$-p^{kH}+E[m'W_1(k',\theta',(h^k)')|\theta,h^k]=0 \tag{11.29}$$

$$\text{if } E[m'W_1((1-\delta)k,\theta',(h^k)')|\theta,h^k]>p^{kH}$$

$$-p^{kL}+E[m'W_1(k',\theta',(h^k)')|\theta,h^k]=0 \tag{11.30}$$

$$\text{if } E[m'W_1((1-\delta)k,\theta',(h^k)')|\theta,h^k]<p^{kL}$$

$$k'=(1-\delta)k$$

$$\text{if } p^{kL}\leq E[m'W_1((1-\delta)k,\theta',(h^k)')|\theta,h^k]\leq p^{kH}. \tag{11.31}$$

To understand these conditions, notice that the value function is concave in k. First assume that there is no investment in the current period so that next period's capital stock is $k'=(1-\delta)k$. If at this point the expected marginal value of capital exceeds the price of new capital, then the firm should invest until the expected marginal value of capital equals p^{kH}. While the inequalities above determine whether the firm should invest or not, the first-order conditions give the optimum amount of investment. Similarly, if the expected marginal value of existing capital carried over from period t to period $t+1$ is below the resale price, the firm would increase its expected marginal value by decreasing next period's capital stock, $k'<(1-\delta)k$. Finally, the firm should do nothing if the expected marginal value of existing capital at $t+1$ falls in the interval $[p^{kL},p^{kH}]$.

For any given value of the inherited capital stock, k, and for any pair of capital goods prices (p^{kL},p^{kH}), there are critical values of θ^H and θ^L such that the expected marginal value of capital conditional on θ^H is equal to p^{kH} with zero investment and the expected marginal value of capital conditional on θ^L is equal to p^{kL} with zero capital sales. Hence, we can define θ^H and θ^L respectively by:

$$p^{kH}=\int_0^\infty m'W_1[(1-\delta)k,\theta',(h^k)']dG(\theta'|\theta^H) \tag{11.32}$$

$$p^{kL}=\int_0^\infty m'W_1[(1-\delta)k,\theta',(h^k)']dG(\theta'|\theta^L). \tag{11.33}$$

The first-order conditions indicate the following;

- If $p^{kH}<E[m'W_1((1-\delta)k,\theta',(h^k)')|\theta,h^k]$, the firm chooses a positive level of investment, $i^*>0$, and the first-order condition in Equation (11.29) holds with equality. In other words, for high states of productivity $\theta\geq\theta^H$, the firm invests.
- If $p^{kL}>E[m'W_1((1-\delta)k,\theta',(h^k)')|\theta,h^k]$, the firm chooses $i^*<0$, and (11.30) holds with equality. Hence, for low states of productivity $\theta\leq\theta^L$, the firm sells used capital.

- For intermediate states of productivity $\theta^L \leq \theta \leq \theta^H$, the firm finds itself in a zone of inaction where it neither invests nor disposes of its used capital.

Define $C_t(k_{t+1}, p^{kH}_{t+1})$ as the *call option* of investing an additional unit of capital at time $t+1$:

$$C_t(k_{t+1}, p^{kH}_{t+1}) = -\int_{\theta^H_{t+1}}^{\infty} E_{t+1}\{m_{t+2}[W((1-\delta)k_{t+1} + i_{t+1}, \theta_{t+2}, h^k_{t+2}) \\ - W((1-\delta)k_{t+1}, \theta_{t+2}, h^k_{t+2})] - p^{kH}_{t+1} i_{t+1}\} dG(\theta_{t+1}|\theta_t). \tag{11.34}$$

Similarly, define $P_t(k_{t+1}, p^{kL}_{t+1})$ as the *put option* of selling a unit of capital at time $t+1$:

$$P_t(k_{t+1}, p^{kL}_{t+1}) = \int_{0}^{\theta^L_{t+1}} E_{t+1}\{m_{t+2}[W((1-\delta)k_{t+1} + i_{t+1}, \theta_{t+2}, h^k_{t+2}) \\ - W((1-\delta)k_{t+1}, \theta_{t+2}, h^k_{t+2})] - p^{kL}_{t+1} i_{t+1}\} dG(\theta_{t+1}|\theta_t). \tag{11.35}$$

The *call option* is the discounted value of making a positive investment at $t+1$. Recall that a call option gives the right to the owner to purchase an asset at some future date for some pre-specified price denoted the exercise price. The *put option* is the discounted value of selling capital goods at $t+1$. To provide interpretations of the call and put options, notice that in addition to this period's investment decision, the firm should think about next period's investment. After the realization of θ_t, the firm has three possibilities. Either it will make a positive investment today or it will sell some capital or else it will do nothing. Suppose that the purchase price of capital next period is less than the expected value of capital at that date. Then the firm will be making positive investment at $t+1$. Likewise, if the resale price of capital is greater than the expected marginal value of capital, then the firm will sell capital at $t+1$.

First suppose that the firm expects to be investing next period. If the price of new capital at time t is lower than it is expected to be at $t+1$, why would the firm wait to buy capital goods it will need next period? However, if the purchase price is expected to decrease, the firm would prefer to wait. The call option gives the value of waiting to invest or to purchase new capital goods until $t+1$. Of course, this is only valid for values of $\theta_{t+1} > \theta^H_{t+1}$ where $E_{t+1}\{m_{t+2}[W((1-\delta)k_{t+1} + i_{t+1})]\} > E_{t+1}\{m_{t+2}[W((1-\delta)k_{t+1})]\}$. We can therefore interpret the term:

$$E_{t+1}\{m_{t+2}[W((1-\delta)k_{t+1} + i_{t+1})]\} - E_{t+1}\{m_{t+2}[W((1-\delta)k_{t+1})]\}$$

as the benefit of making an investment at $t+1$, given that $\theta_{t+1} > \theta^H_{t+1}$, and $p^H_{t+1} i_{t+1}$ as the total cost of investment. The difference between them is the value of waiting and making the investment at $t+1$. Thus, higher values of p^{kH}_{t+1}, that is, higher values of the future purchase price of capital, lower the value of waiting and, as will be shown, induce the firm to invest at t.

Now suppose that the firm expects to sell capital at time $t+1$. If the firm expects to be disposing of capital next period, and if the resale price of capital at time t is greater than it is expected to be at $t+1$, why would the firm wait to sell capital goods until next period? However, if the resale price is expected to increase, the firm would prefer to wait. The put option gives the value of waiting to sell used capital goods at $t+1$. The firm will choose to exercise this option only if $\theta_{t+1} \leq \theta^L_{t+1}$. Referring to Equation (11.35), the expression on the right side is the value of the option to sell capital at $t+1$ at a price of p^{kL}_{t+1}. Lower values of p^{kL}_{t+1}, that is, lower values of the resale price of capital, decrease the value of the put option and as will be shown, cause the firm to invest less at time t.

The expected valuation function can be expressed as:

$$E_t[m_{t+1}W(k_{t+1}, \theta_{t+1}, h^k_{t+1})]$$

$$= E_t\left\{m_{t+1}\left[N_{t+1} + E_{t+1}\left(m_{t+2}W(k_{t+2}, \theta_{t+2}, h^k_{t+2})\right)\right]\right\}. \qquad (11.36)$$

Remember the definition of net cash flows:

$$N_{t+1} = \pi(K_{t+1}, \theta_{t+1}) - p^{kH}_{t+1}\max\{i_{t+1}, 0\} - p^{kL}_{t+1}\min\{i_{t+1}, 0\}.$$

Making use of the fact that when $\theta^L_{t+1} \leq \theta_{t+1} \leq \theta^H_{t+1}$, there will be no investment or sales of capital and the firm's only cash flow is its profits at time $t+1$, we can re-write this as:

$$N_{t+1} = \pi(K_{t+1}, \theta_{t+1}) - \int_{\theta^H_{t+1}}^{\infty} p^{kH}_{t+1} i_{t+1} dG(\theta_{t+1}|\theta_t)$$

$$- \int_0^{\theta^L_{t+1}} p^{kL}_{t+1} i_{t+1} dG(\theta_{t+1}|\theta_t). \qquad (11.37)$$

Now consider the expected valuation function conditional on $t+1$:

$$E_{t+1}(m_{t+2}W(k_{t+2}, \theta_{t+2}, h^k_{t+2}))$$

$$= \int_0^{\theta^L_{t+1}} E_{t+1}[m_{t+2}W((1-\delta)k_{t+1} + i_{t+1}, \theta_{t+2}, h^k_{t+2})]dG(\theta_{t+1}|\theta_t)$$

$$+ \int_{\theta^L_{t+1}}^{\theta^H_{t+1}} E_{t+1}[m_{t+2}W((1-\delta)k_{t+1}, \theta_{t+2}, h^k_{t+2})]dG(\theta_{t+1}|\theta_t)$$

$$+ \int_{\theta^H_{t+1}}^{\infty} E_{t+1}[m_{t+2}W((1-\delta)k_{t+1} + i_{t+1}, \theta_{t+2}, h^k_{t+2})]dG(\theta_{t+1}|\theta_t).$$

$$(11.38)$$

Notice that when $\theta_{t+1} < \theta^L_{t+1}$, the firm sells capital and when $\theta_{t+1} > \theta^H_{t+1}$, the firm purchases capital. Hence, investment is either negative or positive and the value function takes the form of $W((1-\delta)k_{t+1} + i_{t+1}, \theta_{t+2}, h^k_{t+2})$. By contrast, if the firm expects to be in the zero-investment region, that is, if $\theta^L_{t+1} \leq \theta_{t+1} \leq \theta^H_{t+1}$, then i_{t+1} is zero and the value function becomes $W((1-\delta)k_{t+1}, \theta_{t+2}, h^k_{t+2})$. We will focus on the second term in the right side of Equation (11.38):

$$\int_{\theta^L_{t+1}}^{\theta^H_{t+1}} E_{t+1}m_{t+2}[W((1-\delta)k_{t+1}, \theta_{t+2}, h^k_{t+2})]dG(\theta_{t+1}|\theta_t)$$

$$= E_{t+1}[m_{t+2}W((1-\delta)k_{t+1}, \theta_{t+2}, h^k_{t+2})]$$

$$- \int_0^{\theta^L_{t+1}} E_{t+1}[m_{t+2}W((1-\delta)k_{t+1}, \theta_{t+2}, h^k_{t+2})]dG(\theta_{t+1}|\theta_t)$$

$$- \int_{\theta^H_{t+1}}^{\infty} E_{t+1}[m_{t+2}W((1-\delta)k_{t+1}, \theta_{t+2}, h^k_{t+2})]dG(\theta_{t+1}|\theta_t).$$

Then the second term on the right side of Equation (11.36) becomes:

$$E_{t+1}[m_{t+2}W(k_{t+2}, \theta_{t+2}, h^k_{t+2})] = E_{t+1}[m_{t+2}W((1-\delta)k_{t+1}, \theta_{t+2}, h^k_{t+2})]$$

$$+ \int_0^{\theta^L_{t+1}} E_{t+1}m_{t+2}[W((1-\delta)k_{t+1} + i_{t+1}, \theta_{t+2}, h^k_{t+2})$$

$$- W((1-\delta)k_{t+1}, \theta_{t+2}, h^k_{t+2})]dG(\theta_{t+1}|\theta_t)$$

$$+ \int_{\theta^H_{t+1}}^{\infty} E_{t+1}m_{t+2}[W((1-\delta)k_{t+1} + i_{t+1}, \theta_{t+2}, h^k_{t+2})$$

$$- W((1-\delta)k_{t+1}, \theta_{t+2}, h^k_{t+2})]dG(\theta_{t+1}|\theta_t).$$

Combining the equation above with the equation we have found for the net cash flow in (11.37), taking the expectation conditional on time t, using the definition of the call and put options, and substituting into the expected valuation function in (11.36) yields:

$$\begin{aligned} E_t[m_{t+1}W(k_{t+1}, \theta_{t+1}, h^k_{t+1})] &= E_t\{m_{t+1}[\pi(k_{t+1}, \theta_{t+1}) \\ &+E_{t+1}[m_{t+2}W((1-\delta)k_{t+1}, \theta_{t+2}, h^k_{t+2})]]\} \\ &+ P_t(k_{t+1}, p^{kL}_{t+1}) - C_t(k_{t+1}, p^{kH}_{t+1})\}, \end{aligned} \tag{11.39}$$

Hence, the expected value of the firm is the sum of next period's expected profit, the discounted future value assuming the firm does not invest next period, and a put and call option. From Equation (11.39) after differentiating with respect to k_{t+1} we obtain:

$$E_t[m_{t+1}W_1(k_{t+1},\theta_{t+1},h^k_{t+1})] = E_t\{m_{t+1}\pi_K(k_{t+1},\theta_{t+1}) \quad (11.40)$$

$$+ (1-\delta)E_{t+1}[m_{t+2}W_1((1-\delta)k_{t+1},\theta_{t+2},h^k_{t+2})]\}$$

$$+ P_{Kt}(k_{t+1},p^{kL}_{t+1}) - C_{Kt}(k_{t+1},p^{kH}_{t+1}),$$

where C_{Kt} and P_{Kt} are the marginal call and put options respectively.

$$C_{Kt}(k_{t+1},p^{kH}_{t+1}) = -\int_{\theta^H_{t+1}}^{\infty}(1-\delta)E_{t+1}\{m_{t+2}[W_1((1-\delta)k_{t+1}+i_{t+1},\theta_{t+2},h^k_{t+2})$$

$$- W_1((1-\delta)k_{t+1},\theta_{t+2},h^k_{t+2})]\}dG(\theta_{t+1}|\theta_t)$$

$$= \int_{\theta^H_{t+1}}^{\infty}(1-\delta)[-p^{kH}_{t+1} + E_{t+1}m_{t+2}W_1((1-\delta)k_{t+1},\theta_{t+2},h^k_{t+2})]dG(\theta_{t+1}|\theta_t)$$

$$= (1-\delta)E_t\max\{0, E_{t+1}[m_{t+2}W_1((1-\delta)k_{t+1},\theta_{t+2},h^k_{t+2}) - p^{kH}_{t+1}]\} \geq 0.$$

Using the optimality conditions for optimal purchases and sales of capital equipment at $t+1$, we find that the marginal call option is positive since, for $\theta_{t+1} \geq \theta^H_{t+1}$ it is optimal to invest. That is, $C_{Kt} \geq 0$ provided that $G(\theta^H_{t+1}|\theta_t) < 1$. Furthermore, since

$$\partial C_{Kt}(k_{t+1},p^{kH}_{t+1})/\partial p^{kH}_{t+1} = -(1-\delta)[1 - G(\theta^H_{t+1}|\theta_t)] \leq 0,$$

a higher future purchase price for machinery and equipment which limits the firm's expandability options lowers the marginal call option. In other words, as the purchase price of future capital increases, the firm is less likely to wait to invest at $t+1$, implying that the marginal value of the call option falls with p^{kH}_{t+1}.

We can obtain P_{Kt} similarly as:

$$P_{Kt}(k_{t+1},p^{kL}_{t+1})$$

$$= \int_0^{\theta^L_{t+1}}(1-\delta)E_{t+1}\{m_{t+2}[W_1((1-\delta)k_{t+1}+i_{t+1},\theta_{t+2},h^k_{t+2})$$

$$- W_1((1-\delta)k_{t+1},\theta_{t+2},h^k_{t+2})]\}dG(\theta_{t+1}|\theta_t)$$

$$= \int_0^{\theta^L_{t+1}}(1-\delta)\{p^{kL}_{t+1} - E_{t+1}[m_{t+2}W_1((1-\delta)k_{t+1},\theta_{t+2},h^k_{t+2})]\}dG(\theta_{t+1}|\theta_t)$$

$$= (1-\delta)E_t\max\{0, p^{kL}_{t+1} - E_{t+1}m_{t+2}[W_1((1-\delta)k_{t+1},\theta_{t+2},h^k_{t+2})]\} \geq 0.$$

Using the optimality conditions for optimal sales of capital equipment at $t+1$, we find that the marginal put option is positive since for $\theta_{t+1} \leq \theta^L_{t+1}$ it is optimal to sell capital goods at $t+1$. In addition, noting that

$$\partial P_{Kt}(k_{t+1}, p^{kL}_{t+1})/\partial p^{kL}_{t+1} = (1-\delta)G(\theta^L_{t+1}|\theta_t) \geq 0,$$

a higher future resale price for capital goods raises the marginal put option. Hence, the firm will choose to invest more today as the resale price of capital increases in the future.

Assuming $\theta_t \geq \theta^H_t$ so that it is optimal to invest at time t and substituting for $E_t[m_{t+1}W_1(k_{t+1}, \theta_{t+1}, h^k_{t+1})]$ from (11.40) we can express the optimality condition (11.29) as:

$$p^{kH}_t + C_{Kt}(k_{t+1}, p^{kH}_{t+1}) - P_{Kt}(k_{t+1}, p^{kL}_{t+1}) = E_t\{m_{t+1}\pi(k_{t+1}, \theta_{t+1}) + (1-\delta)E_{t+1}[m_{t+2}W_1((1-\delta)k_{t+1}, \theta_{t+2}, h^k_{t+2})]\}. \quad (11.41)$$

The cost of investing consists of the market price for capital goods and the discounted marginal call option. By investing one additional unit at t, the firm loses the opportunity to invest that unit in the future and incurs a loss of a call option. That is, the firm loses the option to wait and invest that unit at $t+1$. This additional cost tends to discourage investment. On the other hand, the marginal put option lowers the current cost of investing. That is, the marginal put option stimulates investment since an additional unit of investment raises the value of the put option.

Similarly, assume $\theta_t \leq \theta^L_t$ so that it is optimal to sell capital at time t and substituting for $E_t[m_{t+1}W_1(k_{t+1}, h_{t+1}, h^k_{t+1})]$ from (11.40), we can write (11.30) as:

$$p^{kL}_t + C_{Kt}(k_{t+1}, p^{kH}_{t+1}) - P_{Kt}(k_{t+1}, p^{kL}_{t+1}) = E_t\{m_{t+1}\pi(k_{t+1}, \theta_{t+1}) + (1-\delta)E_{t+1}[m_{t+2}W_1((1-\delta)K_{t+1}, \theta_{t+2}, h^k_{t+2})]\} \quad (11.42)$$

Now the left side of this expression shows the benefits of selling capital. By selling capital today, the firm loses the opportunity to sell capital tomorrow. Hence, the marginal put option reduces the benefits from selling capital today. By contrast, the firm gains the marginal value of the call option by selling capital today because it maintains the ability to invest in additional capital at time $t+1$.

We can relate optimal investment to Q theory as follows. On the right-hand side of (11.41) add and subtract $\beta E_t \sum_{j=1}^{\infty} m_{t+j}(1-\delta)^j \pi_K((1-\delta)^j K_{t+1}, \theta_{t+j+1})$. We obtain:

$$p^{kH}_t + C_{Kt}(k_{t+1}, p^{kH}_{t+1}) - P_{Kt}(k_{t+1}, p^{kL}_{t+1}) = Q_t + \Upsilon_t \quad (11.43)$$

where:

$$Q_t = \beta E_t \sum_{j=0}^{\infty} m_{t+j}(1-\delta)^j \pi_K((1-\delta)^j K_{t+1}, \theta_{t+j+1}). \qquad (11.44)$$

$$\Upsilon_t = \beta^2(1-\delta)E_{t+1}[m_{t+1}W_1((1-\delta)K_{t+1}, \theta_{t+2}, h^k_{t+2})]$$

$$- \beta E_t \sum_{j=1}^{\infty} m_{t+j}(1-\delta)^j \pi_K((1-\delta)^j k_{t+1}, \theta_{t+j+1}). \qquad (11.45)$$

The first term on the right-hand side of Equation (11.45) represents the expected marginal value of capital from time $t+2$ onward given that the firm does not invest at time $t+1$, but may invest or disinvest in future periods. The second term represents the expected marginal value of capital if the firm never invests or disinvests from $t+2$ onward. Thus, Υ_t represents the increase in the expected marginal value of capital due to *future* marginal call and put options available to the firm. Q_t in Equation (11.44) is Tobin's Q, and represents the expected marginal value of capital if the firm never invests or disinvests from $t+1$ onward and simply allows its capital stock to depreciate. The first term on the right-hand side of Equation (11.44) thus represents the "naive net present value" of an additional unit of capital. Thus, firms which make their investment decisions according to the naive NPV rule would be behaving sub-optimally since they would be ignoring the availability of the future marginal call and put options that is captured by the term Υ_t.[2]

11.3.2. *A model of irreversible investment*

In the sequel, we will focus on irreversible investment. The short-run profit function for the firm continues to satisfy Equation (11.27). Now, however, the firm's net cash flow described by Equation (11.28) is modified as:

$$N_t = \pi(k_t, \theta_t) - p_t^{kH} i_t, \qquad (11.46)$$

where investment satisfies the irreversibility constraint

$$i_t \geq 0. \qquad (11.47)$$

Another way of understanding the effects of (full) irreversibility is to note that the resale price of capital is zero, $p_t^{kL} = 0$.

[2] It is also possible to derive a modified cost-of-capital for the model with partial irreversibility and expandability. See Abel and Eberly [6] in the context of a continuous time model of the firm which faces a stochastic demand shock that follows a geometric Brownian motion. See also Demers, Demers, and Altug [149] for a similar discussion in a discrete time context.

The optimization problem of the firm now becomes:

$$W(k,\theta,p^{kH}) = \max_{i} \{N + E[m' W(k',\theta',(p^{kH})')|\theta,p^{kH}]\}$$

subject to the law of motion for the capital stock $k' = (1-\delta)k + i$ and the irreversibility constraint $i \geq 0$. Demers [148] uses a dynamic programming approach to show the existence of the unknown value function W for an imperfectly competitive firm that faces a constant returns to scale production technology. Substituting for k' using the law of motion for capital and denoting the Lagrange multiplier on irreversibility constraint by μ, the first-order and envelope conditions are given by:

$$E[m' W_1(k',\theta',(p^{kH})')|\theta,p^{kH}] = p^{kH} - \mu, \tag{11.48}$$

$$W_1(k,\theta,p^{kH}) = \pi_K(k,\theta) + (1-\delta)(p^{kH} - \mu). \tag{11.49}$$

To evaluate the first-order condition in (11.48), consider the version of the envelope condition that holds at time $t+1$:

$$W_1(k_{t+1},\theta_{t+1},p^{kH}_{t+1}) = \pi_K(k_{t+1},\theta_{t+1}) + (1-\delta)(p^{kH}_{t+1} - \mu_{t+1}).$$

There are two cases depending on whether the irreversibility constraint is binding at time $t+1$ or not. Using the first-order condition, these are given by:

$$\mu_{t+1} = 0 \Leftrightarrow E_{t+1}[m_{t+2} W_1(k_{t+2},\theta_{t+2},p^{kH}_{t+2})] = p^{kH}_{t+1}.$$

$$\mu_{t+1} > 0 \Leftrightarrow E_{t+1}[m_{t+2} W_1((1-\delta)k_{t+1},\theta_{t+2},p^{kH}_{t+2})] < p^{kH}_{t+1},$$

where we have obtained the last condition by evaluating the first-order condition at $i^\star_{t+1} = 0$. Hence, following Demers [148] and Altug, Demers, and Demers [20], we can write the envelope condition compactly as:

$$\begin{aligned} W_1(k_{t+1},\theta_{t+1},p^{kH}_{t+1}) &= \pi_K\,(k_{t+1},\theta_{t+1}) \\ &+ (1-\delta)\min[p^{kH}_{t+1}, E_{t+1}(m_{t+2} W_1((1-\delta)k_{t+1},\theta_{t+2},p^{kH}_{t+2}))]. \end{aligned} \tag{11.50}$$

Now, using the definition of μ_t, the optimality conditions characterizing irreversible investment are given by:

$$\begin{aligned} E_t[m_{t+1} W_1(k_{t+1},\theta_{t+1},p^{kH}_{t+1})] = p^{kH}_t \quad &\Leftrightarrow \quad i^\star_t > 0, \\ E_t[m_{t+1} W_1(k_{t+1},\theta_{t+1},p^{kH}_{t+1})] < p^{kH}_t \quad &\Leftrightarrow \quad i^\star_t = 0, \end{aligned} \tag{11.51}$$

where $i^\star_t$ is the optimal level of investment and $W_1(k_{t+1},\theta_{t+1},p^{kH}_{t+1})$ is evaluated using (11.50).

Let us examine the implications of the model under some additional assumptions. First suppose that the stochastic discount factor is constant and equal to the subjective discount factor of consumers, $m_{t+1} = \beta = 1/r$

for all t. Suppose also that the irreversibility condition does not bind at time t. Then the first-order condition can be written as:

$$E_t \pi_K (k_{t+1}, \theta_{t+1}) = c_t + \Phi_t \tag{11.52}$$

where

$$c_t \equiv (r + \delta) p_t^{kH} - (1 - \delta)(E_t p_{t+1}^{kH} - p_t^{kH})$$

is the traditional Jorgensonian cost of capital. The term

$$\Phi_t = (1 - \delta) E_t \left\{ p_{t+1}^{kH} - \min[p_{t+1}^{kH}, \beta E_{t+1} W_1((1 - \delta)k_{t+1}, \theta_{t+2}, p_{t+2}^{kH})] \right\}$$

is an *endogenous risk premium* or *endogenous cost of adjustment*, and it arises due to irreversibility. If investment were reversible, (11.52) would reduce to:

$$p_t^{kH} = \beta E_t \pi_K (k_{t+1}, \theta_{t+1}) + \beta (1 - \delta) E_t p_{t+1}^{kH}, \tag{11.53}$$

just as in the frictionless neoclassical model described in Section 11.1.

We define the firm's desired stock of capital, $k_{t+1}^{\star}$, as follows: If $i_t^{\star} > 0$, $k_{t+1}^{\star}$ solves (11.52) and if $i_t^{\star} = 0$, $k_{t+1}^{\star} = (1 - \delta)k_t$. The existence of the endogenous risk premium or adjustment cost implies that the desired capital stock with irreversibility, $k_{t+1}^{\star}$, is smaller than the desired stock without any frictions, k_{t+1}^{f}, which solves (11.53). Nevertheless, if low values of θ_t are realized the firm may find itself with excess capital because it cannot disinvest. Therefore, the actual capital stock of a firm facing irreversible investment may be larger than when investment is reversible.

11.4. AN ASSET-PRICING MODEL WITH IRREVERSIBLE INVESTMENT

In this section, we develop a two-sector discrete-time general-equilibrium model of a production economy with irreversible investment. Our discussion derives from Kogan [281, 282]. This model allows us to examine the relationship among stock returns, investment, and Q. It also allows us to examine the existence of a solution to the dynamic optimization problem under the assumption of a production technology that is linear in capital.

11.4.1. *The model*

In this two-sector model, there are two representative firms, which produce two different goods, called good 1 and good 2. The only input for the production in the first sector is capital denoted by K_{1t}, which is rented from the households. The production technology of the first sector is constant returns to scale given by $y_{1t} = (\alpha + \theta_t)K_{1t}$, where θ_t denotes the technology shock. Notice that the production function is linear in its parameters. Firms in the first sector use the first capital good to produce the first consumption good and to invest in the production in the second sector. It is assumed that the first capital good depreciates at the constant rate δ, $0 < \delta < 1$.

Firms in the second sector make investment decisions to maximize the present value of their firms. They produce the consumption good 2 and sell their output at the spot market at a price of S_t. The production technology for the second sector is given by $y_{2t} = K_{2t}$, where K_{2t} denotes the second capital good and is supplied by the first sector. The second capital good is also assumed to depreciate at a constant rate of $0 < \delta < 1$. Therefore, between t and $t + 1$, the second capital depreciates by δK_{2t} and since the output of the second sector cannot be converted back into physical capital, the capital stock in the second sector can be increased only by investment from the first sector into the second.

There exists a spot market, where the consumption good 2 is traded against the numeraire good, good 1, at the spot price S_t. Households purchase good 2 for consumption at the spot market and have access to two financial assets. The first asset is the bond, which earns riskless rate of interest r_t^f. The price of the bond is expressed in units of consumption good 1 and it is assumed to be in zero net supply such that $b_t = 0$ (for all t), where b_t denotes the amount of bond holdings at time t. The second asset, the equity issued by firms, is a claim on the total stream of cash flows generated by the second sector. Each period, the stock earns a dividend, $d_t S_t$ in units of good 1. Let q_t denote the stock price at time t and z_t be the amount of share holdings at time t. We assume that there exists single share outstanding, $z_t = 1$ for all t. The feasibility condition for sector 1 requires that consumption of goods in sector 1, c_{1t}, plus investment in capital goods for sectors 1 and 2, I_{it} for $i = 1, 2$, are less than or equal to output produced in sector 1, that is, $c_{1t} + I_{1t} + I_{2t} \leq y_{1t} = (\alpha + \theta_t)K_{1t}$. Likewise, consumption of sector 2 goods exhausts sector 2 output, $c_{2t} \leq y_{2t} = K_{2t}$.

Households own the entire stock of the first capital good and rent it to firms in the first sector at the rental price of r_t. Households obtain utility from the consumption of both goods and maximize the expected discounted value of utility derived from consumption of goods 1 and 2 denoted by c_{1t}, c_{2t}, respectively, and by holdings of new capital, bonds, and shares of the firm in the second sector.

11.4.2. The social planner's problem

We begin by considering a centralized version of this economy. We show the existence of a solution to the social planner's problem and characterize the properties of this solution. We then show how the allocations to the social planner's problem can be supported in a competitive equilibrium.

We have the following assumptions.

Assumption 11.2 *The utility function is given by:*

$$U(c_1, c_2) = \begin{cases} \frac{1}{1-\gamma} c_1^{1-\gamma} + \frac{b}{1-\gamma} c_2^{1-\gamma}, & \gamma > 0, \gamma \neq 1, \\ \ln(c_1) + b \ln(c_2), & \gamma = 1 \end{cases}$$

Assumption 11.3 *The technology shock $\theta \in [0, \infty]$ is i.i.d. with stationary distribution function G. The function G has the properties that $G(\theta) = 0$ for $\theta \leq 0$ and $G(\theta) = 1$ for $\theta \to \infty$. Also $dG > 0$ and dG is continuous.*

The social planner chooses consumption allocations in goods 1 and 2 and decides how much to invest in sector 1 versus sector 2 to maximize the utility of a representative consumer. Recall that the first capital good is not subject to an irreversibility constraint. However, once investment in the second capital good has been made, it cannot be costlessly converted back into output of sector 1. We can write the social planner's problem as follows:

$$\max_{\{c_{1t}, c_{2t}, I_{1t}, I_{2t}\}} E_0 \left\{ \sum_{t=0}^{\infty} \beta^t U(c_{1t}, c_{2t}) \right\}, \quad 0 < \beta < 1, \tag{11.54}$$

subject to the set of constraints:

$$c_{1t} \leq (\alpha + \theta_t) K_{1t} - I_{1t} - I_{2t}, \tag{11.55}$$

$$c_{2t} \leq K_{2t}, \tag{11.56}$$

$$K_{1t+1} = (1 - \delta) K_{1t} + I_{1t}, \tag{11.57}$$

$$K_{2t+1} = (1 - \delta) K_{2t} + I_{2t}, \tag{11.58}$$

$$I_{2t} \geq 0, \tag{11.59}$$

given K_{10} and K_{20}.

To analyze the problem further, note that for $\gamma = 1$, $U(c) = \ln(c)$. When $\gamma \leq 1$, the utility function is unbounded from above on $\Re_{++}$ and unbounded from below when $\gamma \geq 1$. Recall that the production technology in both sectors is linear in capital. Hence, we have an unbounded return function and an unbounded state space. To deal with this problem, we follow the approach in Stokey and Lucas [418] and restrict the growth rate of the capital stocks. Notice that the capital stock in sector 2 depends on output and hence, the capital stock in sector 1. Hence, if we can bound the expected growth rate of capital in sector 1, the consumption-capital ratio, C_{1t}/K_{1t}, and the ratio of the capital stocks, $\kappa_t = K_{2t}/K_{1t}$, will also be stationary variables. Note that $K_{1t} > 0$ because the marginal utility of consumption of the first good is infinite for c_{1t} equal to zero. Likewise, by the irreversibility constraint $K_{2t} \geq (1-\delta)^t K_{20} > 0$ for $K_{20} > 0$. Hence, $\kappa_t > 0$. To further characterize the behavior of capital in sector 1, substitute the laws of motion for the capital stocks into the aggregate feasibility constraint for the first sector to obtain:

$$\frac{c_1}{K_1} + \frac{K_1'}{K_1} + \frac{K_2'}{K_1} \leq (\alpha+\theta) + (1-\delta) + (1-\delta)\frac{K_2}{K_1},$$

or

$$\begin{aligned}\frac{K_1'}{K_1} &\leq (\alpha+\theta) + (1-\delta)(1+\kappa) - \frac{c_1}{K_1} - \frac{K_2'}{K_2}\kappa \\ &\leq (\alpha+\theta) + (1-\delta)(1+\kappa),\end{aligned}$$

where we have made use of the fact that c_1/K_1 and K_2'/K_2 are bounded below by 0 and $(1-\delta)$, respectively. We will seek an equilibrium in which $E[K_1'/K_1] \leq E[\alpha+\theta+1-\delta]$. We restrict the expected growth rate of K_{1t} further as follows:

Assumption 11.4 $\beta E[(\alpha+\theta'+1-\delta)^{1-\gamma}] < 1$ *for* $\gamma \neq 1$ *and* βE [ln $(\alpha+\theta'+1-\delta)] < 1$ *for* $\gamma = 1$

We consider two cases:

- $\gamma \neq 1$. Since θ is i.i.d., we can equivalently replace conditional expectations with unconditional expectations. We can write the absolute value of the supremum function for the social planner's problem as:

$$\begin{aligned}\left|\tilde{V}(K_{10})\right| &\equiv \left|\frac{1}{1-\gamma}E\left\{\sum_{t=0}^{\infty}\beta^t K_{1t}^{1-\gamma}\left[\left(\frac{c_{1t}}{K_{1t}}\right)^{1-\gamma} + b\kappa_t^{1-\gamma}\right]\right\}\right| \\ &\leq \left|\frac{1}{1-\gamma}\right| K_{10}^{1-\gamma}\sum_{t=0}^{\infty}E\left\{\beta^t\Phi_t\left[\left(\frac{c_{1t}}{K_{1t}}\right)^{1-\gamma} + b\kappa_t^{1-\gamma}\right]\right\},\end{aligned}$$

  where

$$\Phi_t = \prod_{i=0}^{t-1}(\alpha+\theta_i+1-\delta)^{1-\gamma}, \quad \Phi_0 = 1.$$

Now consider a term in the infinite sum above. Using an iterated expectations argument, we can write

$$\beta^t E\left\{\Phi_t\left[\left(\frac{c_{1t}}{K_{1t}}\right)^{1-\gamma}+b\kappa_t\right]\right\}$$

$$= \beta E\left\{(\alpha+\theta_0+1-\delta)^{1-\gamma}\beta E_0\left\{(\alpha+\theta_1+1-\delta)^{1-\gamma}\ldots\right.\right.$$

$$\left.\left.\beta E_{t-2}\left\{(\alpha+\theta_{t-1}+1-\delta)^{1-\gamma}\beta E_{t-1}\left[\left(\frac{c_{1t}}{K_{1t}}\right)^{1-\gamma}+b\kappa_t\right]\right\}\right\}\right\}$$

$$\leq \beta E\left\{(\alpha+\theta_0+1-\delta)^{1-\gamma}\beta E_0\left\{(\alpha+\theta_1+1-\delta)^{1-\gamma}\ldots\right.\right.$$

$$\left.\left.\beta E_{t-2}\left\{(\alpha+\theta_{t-1}+1-\delta)^{1-\gamma}B\right\}\right\}\right\} \leq \phi^t B.$$

This result follows because $E_{t-1}\left[(c_{1t}/K_{1t})^{1-\gamma}+b\kappa_t^{1-\gamma}\right]$ is finite and $\beta E[(\alpha+\theta_t-\delta)^{1-\gamma}]=\phi<1$ by Assumption 11.4. Hence,

$$\left|\tilde{V}(K_{10})\right| \leq \left|\frac{1}{1-\gamma}\right| K_{10}^{1-\gamma}\sum_{t=0}^{\infty}\phi^t B.$$

Therefore, $\left|\tilde{V}(K_{10})\right|/K_{10}^{1-\gamma}$ is bounded for $K_{10}\in\Re_{++}$ even though total expected discounted utility is not.

- $\gamma=1$. In this case,

$$\left|\tilde{V}(K_{10})\right| \equiv \left|E\left\{\sum_{t=0}^{\infty}\beta^t\left[\ln(K_{1t})+\ln(c_{1t}/K_{1t})+b\ln(\kappa_t)\right]\right\}\right|$$

$$\leq \left|E\left\{\sum_{t=0}^{\infty}\beta^t\left[\Phi_t+\ln(K_{10})+\ln(c_{1t}/K_{1t})+b\ln(\kappa_t)\right]\right\}\right|,$$

where

$$\Phi_t=\prod_{i=0}^{t-1}\ln(\alpha+\theta_i+1-\delta),\quad \Phi_0=1.$$

As before, $\beta E[\ln(\alpha+\theta_t+1-\delta)]<1$ and $E\left[\ln(c_{1t}/K_{1t})+b\ln(\kappa_t)\right]$ is finite. Hence, using an iterated expectations argument as in the previous case to evaluate $\beta^t E(\Phi_t)$, $|\tilde{V}(K_{10})|-|\ln(K_{10})|/(1-\beta)$ is bounded for any $K_{10}\in\Re_{++}$.

Also notice that the supremum function $\tilde{V}(K_{10})$ is homogeneous of degree $1-\gamma$ in K_{1t} and K_{2t}.

In this application, the value function depends on the levels of the capital stocks in sectors 1 and 2. We can write the value function for the social planner's problem as:

$$V(K_1, K_2) = \max_{c_1, c_2, I_1, I_2} \left\{ U(c_1, c_2) + \beta \int_0^\infty V(K_1', K_2') dG(\theta') \right\} \tag{11.60}$$

subject to the resource constraints in (11.55) and (11.56), the irreversibility constraint in (11.59), given the laws of motion for the capital stocks in (11.57–11.58). Since the capital stocks are growing, we chose the value function to be from the space of functions that are growing no faster than $K_1^{1-\gamma}$, that are homogeneous of degree $1-\gamma$ in K_1 and K_2, and that are jointly continuous in their arguments. Define the space of such functions by $\mathcal{B}$; define the norm of the elements of $\mathcal{B}$ by:

$$\|g\|_\varphi = \sup_{K_1, K_2 \in \Re_{++}} \left| \frac{g(K_1, K_2)}{\varphi(K_1)} \right| < \infty,$$

where $\varphi \in \mathcal{B}$; in our case, $\varphi(K_1) = K_1^{1-\gamma}$. This function is still an element of $\mathcal{B}$ even though it is not an explicit function of K_2. We can show that the space $\mathcal{B}$ is a complete, normed linear space.

Proposition 11.1 *Under Assumptions 11.2, 11.3, and 11.4, there exists a unique solution $V^* \in \mathcal{B}$ to Equation (11.60). The fixed point function V^* is increasing and concave in K_1 and K_2.*

PROOF

Apply the approach for the proof of Proposition 8.3 in Chapter 8. ∎

Let λ_{it} for $i = 1, 2$ and μ_t denote the multipliers for resource constraints and the irreversibility constraint, respectively. The first-order conditions with respect to c_{1t}, c_{2t}, I_{1t} and I_{2t} are given by:

$$U_{1t} = \lambda_{1t}, \tag{11.61}$$

$$U_{2t} = \lambda_{2t}, \tag{11.62}$$

$$\lambda_{1t} = \beta E_t[V_1(K_{1t+1}, K_{2t+1})] \tag{11.63}$$

$$\lambda_{1t} = \beta E_t[V_2(K_{1t+1}, K_{2t+1})] + \mu_t, \tag{11.64}$$

where $V_1(K_{1t+1}, K_{2t+1})$ and $V_2(K_{1t+1}, K_{2t+1})$ denote the derivative of the value function with respect to K_{1t+1} and K_{2t+1}. The envelope conditions are given by:

$$V_1(K_{1t}, K_{2t}) = \lambda_{1t}(1 - \delta + \alpha + \theta_t), \tag{11.65}$$

$$V_2(K_{1t}, K_{2t}) = (\lambda_{1t} - \mu_t)(1 - \delta) + \lambda_{2t}. \tag{11.66}$$

The first-order conditions in Equations (11.61) and (11.63) imply the optimal consumption rule at time t as:

$$U_{1t} = \beta E_t[V_1(K_{1t+1}, K_{2t+1})]. \tag{11.67}$$

Likewise, the first-order conditions in Equations (11.63) and (11.64) imply the following simple rule for optimal investment at time t:

$$E_t[V_2(K_{1t+1}, K_{2t+1})] = E_t[V_1(K_{1t+1}, K_{2t+1})] \Leftrightarrow \quad I^\star_{2t} > 0;$$

$$E_t[V_2(K_{1t+1}, K_{2t+1})] < E_t[V_1(K_{1t+1}, K_{2t+1})] \Leftrightarrow \quad I^\star_{2t} = 0. \tag{11.68}$$

In words, if the expected shadow price of capital in the second sector at time $t + 1$ is greater than or equal to that of capital in the first one, then the second sector should receive a positive level of investment. If, however, the expected shadow price of capital in the second sector falls short of the one in the first sector, it is better for the economy not to make any investments in the second sector. The value function $V(\cdot)$ is increasing and concave in both K_1 and K_2 because it inherits these properties from the utility function. This implies that the investment decision rule given by $E_t[V_2(K_{1,t+1}, K_{2,t+1})] \geq E_t[V_1(K_{1,t+1}, K_{2,t+1})]$ can also be represented by $K_{2,t+1} \leq K_2^\star(K_{1,t+1})$, where $K_2^\star$ denotes the optimal level of the second capital stock written as a function of the first capital stock. We discuss the implications of this statement further below.

Following our earlier discussion, the envelope condition for the shadow value of capital in the second sector can be written as:

$$V_2(K_{1t}, K_{2t}) = U_{2t} + (1 - \delta)\min[U_{1t}, \beta E_t V_2(K_{1t+1}, (1 - \delta)K_{2t})], \tag{11.69}$$

where the term $(1 - \delta)K_{2t}$ in the derivative of the value function with respect to K_{2t} is used to denote that there is no investment into the second sector for the next period. Now, suppose that the firm makes a positive investment decision at time t such that $I^\star_{2t} > 0$. To further characterize the optimal interior choice of investment, define $V_{2t+2} \equiv V_2(K_{1t+2},$

$(1-\delta)K_{2t+1})$. Iterate on the envelope condition and substitute it into the first-order condition given in (11.61) to obtain:

$$U_{1t} = \beta E_t \left[U_{2t+1} + (1-\delta) \min \left[U_{1t+1}, \beta E_{t+1} V_{2t+2} \right] \right]. \tag{11.70}$$

Dividing and multiplying the right side of this equation by U_{1t+1} and simplifying yields:

$$E_t \left\{ m_{1t+1} \left[\frac{U_{2t+1}}{U_{1t+1}} + (1-\delta) \min \left(1, \beta E_{t+1} \frac{V_{2t+2}}{U_{1t+1}} \right) \right] \right\} = 1, \tag{11.71}$$

where $m_{1t+1} = \beta U_{1t+1}/U_{1t}$. The conditions in (11.67), (11.68) and by (11.70) together with feasibility constraint in (11.55) fully characterize the solution for the social planner's problem. We return to these conditions when discussing the competitive equilibrium for this economy.

11.4.3. The competitive equilibrium

Households

Suppose that there exists a representative household. The household solves the problem:

$$\max_{\{c_{1t}, c_{2t}, b_{t+1}, K_{1t+1}, z_{t+1}\}} E_0 \left\{ \sum_{t=0}^{\infty} \beta^t U(c_{1t}, c_{2t}) \right\}, \quad 0 < \beta < 1, \tag{11.72}$$

subject to the budget constraint

$$c_{1t} + S_t c_{2t} + b_{t+1} + K_{1t+1} + q_t z_{t+1} \leq$$
$$+ r_t K_{1t} + (1-\delta)K_{1t} + (q_t + d_t S_t)z + (1 + r_t^f) b_t.$$

The household receives the rental income $r_t K_{1t}$ from firms in the first sector together with the undepreciated part of the capital stock at the end of the period, $(1-\delta)K_{1t}$.[3] Let λ_t denote the Lagrange multiplier on the budget constraint. The first-order conditions with respect to $c_{1t}, c_{2t}, b_{t+1}, K_{t+1}, z_{t+1}$ are given by:

[3] We omit a discussion of the existence of a solution for the household's problem and the problem of firms in sector 2. However, we note that the approach that we followed in the previous section to demonstrating existence must be used in these problems as well.

$$U_{1t} = \lambda_t, \tag{11.73}$$

$$U_{2t} = \lambda_t S_t, \tag{11.74}$$

$$\lambda_t = \beta E_t[\lambda_{t+1}(1 + r_t^f)], \tag{11.75}$$

$$\lambda_t = \beta E_t[\lambda_{t+1}(r_{t+1} + 1 - \delta)], \tag{11.76}$$

$$\lambda_t q_t = \beta E_t[\lambda_{t+1}(q_{t+1} + d_{t+1} S_{t+1})], \tag{11.77}$$

where $U_{it} \equiv \partial U(c_{1t}, c_{2t})/\partial c_{it}$ for $i=1,2$. It follows from the first-order conditions in (11.73) and (11.74) that the spot price for consumption 2 is given by:

$$S_t = \frac{U_{2t}}{U_{1t}}. \tag{11.78}$$

This expression shows that the spot price is determined by the *intratemporal* marginal rate of substitution between the first and the second consumption goods. Define the *intertemporal* MRS for consumption goods 1 and 2 by:

$$m_{it+1} \equiv \beta \frac{U_{it+1}}{U_{it}}, \quad i = 1, 2$$

and use these definitions and the equation for the spot price S_t we have found above to re-write the first-order condition given in (11.77) as follows:

$$\begin{aligned} q_t &= E_t[m_{1t+1}(q_{t+1} + d_{t+1} S_{t+1})] \\ &= E_t\left[m_{1t+1}\left(q_{t+1} + d_{t+1}\frac{U_{2t+1}}{U_{1t+1}}\right)\right]. \end{aligned}$$

Dividing and multiplying the second term on the right-side of the equation above with U_{2t} and re-arranging yields:

$$q_t = E_t\left[m_{1t+1} q_{t+1} + m_{2t+1} d_{t+1} S_t\right]. \tag{11.79}$$

Notice that the current stock price is given by the discounted value of the next period's price plus dividend. While m_{2t+1} discounts d_{t+1} in units of good 2, S_t converts this discounted value into units of good 1.

Define the gross real risk-free rate by R_t^f. Using the first-order condition in Equation (11.75) together with (11.73), it follows that:

$$1 = E_t\left[m_{1t+1}(1 + r_t^f)\right] \equiv E_t\left[m_{1t+1} R_t^f\right] \tag{11.80}$$

which implies that

$$R_t^f = [E_t(m_{1t+1})]^{-1}.$$

Thus, the real risk-free rate is just equal to the inverse of the expected intertemporal MRS for consumption of good 1. Likewise, for the (gross) real return on capital, we have the condition:

$$1 = E_t\left[m_{1t+1}(1 + r_{t+1} - \delta)\right] \equiv E_t\left[m_{1t+1}R_{t+1}\right]. \tag{11.81}$$

Note that in equilibrium, the expected discounted return from capital and the return from the riskless bond are equal. Equation (11.81) says that the household will undertake investment in the first capital good until the expected discounted value of the return from this investment equals unity. We could use a dynamic programming approach to provide an alternative interpretation of this condition. According to this approach, the right-side of this expression is the expected shadow value of additional capital which at the consumer's optimum, equals the price of new capital, defined here as unity.

Firms

Firms in sector 1

The first sector is a perfectly competitive sector, in which all firms are profit maximizing. Firms rent capital from households, paying a rental rate of r_t, and return the undepreciated part of the capital to the households at the end of each period. Since households own the entire stock of the first capital and invest directly into the production of the first sector, firms' problem is to maximize a static one-period profit function. Assume that there is a large number of identical firms in the economy and consider the problem of a typical firm.

Each firm is endowed with a technology that enables the firm to produce a single output according to a production function that is linear in K_{1t}:

$$F(K_{1t}, \theta_t) = (\alpha + \theta_t)K_{1t}.$$

Here, K_{1t} denotes the stock of capital 1, θ_t is a random shock to technology and α is a constant parameter. In this representation, $\{\theta_t\}_{t=0}^{\infty}$ is i.i.d. with cumulative distribution function G that satisfies Assumption 11.3.

Investment in the first sector follows the simple neoclassical assumptions, where one unit of investment in period t, denoted by I_{1t} yields an additional unit of capital in period $t + 1$, without any investment frictions (i.e. irreversibility, adjustment cost, etc.). Therefore, production at time $t + 1$ relies on the stock of capital determined at time t. The capital stock evolves in the classical way:

$$K_{1t+1} = I_{1t} + (1 - \delta)K_{1t}. \tag{11.82}$$

The typical firm in the first sector chooses the capital input to maximize current period profits given by:

$$\pi_t = (\alpha + \theta_t)K_{1t} - r_t K_{1t}.$$

The result of this static maximization problem of the firm is the well-known competitive market equilibrium result, which is to produce at the level where the marginal product of capital equals its marginal cost:

$$r_t = \alpha + \theta_t.$$

Combining the above equation resulting from the profit-maximization problem of the firm with the one in (11.81) yields:

$$E_t[m_{1t+1}R_{t+1}] = E_t[m_{1t+1}(1 + \alpha + \theta_{t+1} - \delta)] = 1.$$

Firms in sector 2

Firms in the second sector have a different production technology. In contrast to firms in the first sector, firms in the second sector own the stock of the second capital and use it to produce consumption good 2. As a simple device for deriving the relationship between average Q and marginal Q, assume that the used capital sells for a price of $p_{k,t}$. Hence, the firm is able to sell the undepreciated part of its used capital and purchase used capital at the end of the period. The firm also buys new capital, denoted by I_t^d. The law of motion for capital is given by:

$$K_{2t+1} = I_{2t}^d + K_{2t}^d,$$

where K_{2t}^d denotes the demand for the used capital at the end of period t. So, the level of capital in period $t + 1$ is determined by the demand for new and used capital. The gross profit of the firm is given by $S_t K_{2t} - I_{2t}^d$ and net cash flow from the firm to households is:

$$N_t = S_t K_{2t} - I_{2t}^d - p_{k,t} K_{2t}^d + p_{k,t}(1 - \delta) K_{2t}. \tag{11.83}$$

Recall that the replacement cost of capital is normalized to one. I_{2t}^d and $p_{k,t}K_{2t}^d$ denote expenditures on new and used capital, respectively and $p_{k,t}(1 - \delta)K_{2t}$ is the receipts from sale of (undepreciated) used capital. Notice that in equilibrium, the net supply of capital is zero, that is, $K_{2t}^d = (1 - \delta)K_{2t}$.

The firm's problem involves maximizing the present value of net cash flows by choosing new investment expenditures and by purchases of used capital. Recall that firms in the first sector rent physical capital from households in an amount that is not bounded by any constraints other than $K_{1t} \geq 0$ for all t. However, in the second sector once firms decide to make a fixed amount of investment (or decide to convert a fixed amount of good 1 into physical capital 2), this amount of capital is stuck within the sector. Because of the irreversibility constraint ($I_{2t} \geq 0$), physical capital can be eliminated only through depreciation over time. Thus, $K_{2t+1} \geq (1 - \delta)K_{2t}$ must hold for all t.

We know that the firm's ex-dividend value is given by:

$$W_t^e = E_t\left[\sum_{t=1}^{\infty} m_{1t+i}N_{t+i}\right]$$

So, the firm chooses how much to invest in new capital and the purchases of used capital to maximize its value. Using a dynamic programming approach, the firm's problem is given by:

$$W(K_{2t}) = \max_{I_{2t}^d, K_{2t}^d} \{N_t + E_t[m_{1t+1}W(K_{2t+1})]\}$$

subject to

$$K_{2t+1} = (1-\delta)K_{2t}^d + I_{2t}^d, \tag{11.84}$$

$$I_{2t}^d \geq 0, \tag{11.85}$$

given K_{2t}. Let μ_t denote the Lagrange multiplier on the irreversibility constraint. Imposing the market-clearing condition that $K_{2t}^d = (1-\delta)K_{2t}$, the first-order and envelope conditions are given by:

$$E_t[m_{1t+1}W'(K_{2t+1})] = 1 - \mu_t \tag{11.86}$$

$$E_t[m_{1t+1}W'(K_{2t+1})] = p_{k,t} \tag{11.87}$$

$$W'(K_{2t}) = S_t + (1-\delta)(1-\mu_t), \tag{11.88}$$

where $W'(\cdot)$ denotes the partial derivative of $W(\cdot)$ with respect to k. Iterating the envelope condition one period further and recalling our discussion of Section 11.3.2, we can write the envelope condition compactly as:

$$W'(K_{2t+1}) = S_{t+1} + (1-\delta)\min[1, E_{t+1}(m_{1t+2}W'((1-\delta)K_{2t+1}))]. \tag{11.89}$$

Returning to the first-order condition in (11.73), the irreversibility condition given by $I_{2t} \geq 0$ imposes two possibilities for μ_t: either the irreversibility condition is not binding for the current period ($\mu_t = 0$) or it is binding ($\mu_t > 0$). If it does not bind, then the optimal level of investment $I_{2t}^\star > 0$ and if it is, then $I_{2t}^\star = 0$. Hence, we can characterize the optimal investment decision as:

$$E_t[m_{1t+1}W'(K_{2t+1})] = 1 \Leftrightarrow \quad I_{2t}^\star > 0$$

$$E_t[m_{1t+1}W'(K_{2t+1})] < 1 \Leftrightarrow \quad I_{2t}^\star = 0. \tag{11.90}$$

As long as the expected discounted marginal effect of capital on firm value in the second sector is less than one, the irreversibility condition is binding. If it is greater or equal to one, then firms in the second sector should invest into physical capital, so that the condition is not binding. Notice that the boundary condition for investment is given by $E_t[m_{1t+1}W'(K_{2t+1})] = 1$, which says that the minimum level of expected marginal benefit should be equal to unity for the firm to make a positive investment.

Suppose that the firm chooses to undertake a positive level of investment today so that $I^*_{2t} > 0$. Using the envelope condition in Equation (11.89), we can write the first-order condition for the optimal interior choice of investment as:

$$E_t\left\{m_{1t+1}(S_{t+1} + (1-\delta)\min[1, E_{t+1}(m_{1t+2}W'((1-\delta)K_{2t+1}))])\right\} = 1. \tag{11.91}$$

Thus, how much investment that will be undertaken today depends on the firm's expectation of whether the irreversibility condition will be binding in the next period. Otherwise, if the firm invests too much today, it will be stuck with excess capital which it cannot costlessly dispose of tomorrow. Thus, the irreversibility constraint induces a gradual adjustment of the capital stock compared to a situation without irreversibility.

11.4.4. *The value of the firm and Q*

Recall that average Q is defined as the ratio of the ex-dividend value of the firm to the replacement cost of the whole existing capital stock while marginal Q is defined as the marginal value of an additional unit of capital to its replacement cost. If the production exhibits constant returns to scale, average Q and marginal Q are expected to be equal.

Returning to the firm's problem in Section 11.4.3, recall that used capital sells for the price p_{kt}. Substitute the first-order condition in (11.87) into the envelope condition and iterate one period further to obtain:

$$p_{k,t} = E_t[m_{1t+1}W'(K_{2t+1})] = E_t[m_{1t+1}(S_{t+1} + (1-\delta)p_{k,t+1})]. \tag{11.94}$$

Iterating on this condition, we can show that the shadow price of existing capital is just equal to the expected discounted marginal product of the second capital good which, given the linear production technology, is the relative price of good 2 in terms of good 1.

$$p_{k,t} = E_t \left\{ \sum_{i=0}^{\infty} (1-\delta)^i m_{t+1+i} S_{t+1+i} \right\}. \tag{11.95}$$

Since the replacement cost of capital is unity in this model, we also have that p_{kt} is equal to marginal Q, that is, $p_{kt} = Q^m$.

We follow the approach in Section 10.2.4 to deriving average Q. Recall that the equity price for firms in sector 2 satisfies the relation:

$$q_t = E_t[m_{1t+1}(q_{t+1} + d_{t+1} S_{t+1})].$$

As in Section 10.2.4, we assume that the purchases of used capital are financed by retained earning or by new equity issues:

$$p_{k,t} K_{2t}^d - p_{k,t}(1-\delta) K_{2t} = RE_t + q_t(z_{t+1} - z_t),$$

and that gross profits are disbursed as dividends or held as retained earnings:

$$S_t K_{2t} - I_{2,t}^d = RE_t + d_t S_t z_t.$$

Thus, using the expression for net cash flows, we have that:

$$\begin{aligned} N_t &= S_t K_{2t} - I_{2,t}^d - p_{k,t} K_{2t}^d + p_{k,t}(1-\delta) K_{2t} \\ &= RE_t + d_t S_t z_t + q_t(z_t - z_{t+1}) - RE_t \\ &= d_t S_t z_t + q_t(z_t - z_{t+1}). \end{aligned}$$

But in equilibrium $z_{t+i} = 1$ for all $i \geq 0$. Therefore, we have that $d_t = N_t / S_t$. Substituting this expression for d_t into the expression for the equity price, we obtain:

$$\begin{aligned} q_t &= E_t \left[m_{1t+1} \left(q_{t+1} + S_{t+1} K_{2t+1} - I_{2,t+1}^d - p_{k,t+1} K_{2,t+1}^d \right.\right. \\ &\quad \left.\left. + p_{k,t+1}(1-\delta) K_{2,t+1} \right) \right] \\ &= p_{k,t} K_{2,t+1} + E_t \left[m_{1t+1} \left(q_{t+1} - I_{2,t+1}^d - p_{k,t+1} K_{2,t+1}^d \right) \right] \\ &= p_{k,t} K_{2,t+1} + E_t \left[m_{1t+1} \left(q_{t+1} - \mu_{t+1} I_{2,t+1}^d - p_{k,t+1} K_{2,t+2} \right) \right], \end{aligned}$$

where we obtained the second line by using the relation in Equation (11.94) and the third line by using the law of motion for capital and the first order-conditions to substitute for $K_{t+1}^d = K_{t+2} - I_{2,t+1}^d$ and $1 - p_{k,t+1} = \mu_{t+1}$. To complete our derivation, we note that $\mu_{t+i} I_{2,t+i}^d = 0$ for $i \geq 0$. This follows from the fact that either the irreversibility constraint is not binding so that $\mu_{t+i} = 0$ or it is, in which case $I^d_{2,t+i} = 0$. Hence, we find that

$$q_t = p_{k,t}K_{2,t+1} + E_t\left[m_{1t+1}\left(q_{t+1} - p_{k,t+1}K_{2,t+2}\right)\right].$$

But this is a stochastic difference that has the solution:

$$q_{t+i} = p_{k,t+i}K_{2,t+1+i}, \quad i \geq 0. \tag{11.96}$$

Recalling that in equilibrium the ex-dividend value of the firm equals the equity price, we find that:

$$q_{t+1} = W^e_t = p_{k,t}K_{2,t+1},$$

which implies that average Q and marginal Q are equal, $Q^m = Q^a$.

11.4.5. *The relation among stock returns, investment, and Q*

One of the reasons for studying this model has been to understand the relationship among stock returns, investment, and Q. The model seeks to capture the idea that stock return variability will be high when the investment is low in the economy. Remember that in equilibrium, the stock price is given by:

$$q_t = E_t[m_{t+1}(q_{t+1} + S_{t+1}K_{2t+1} - I_{2t+1})]$$

for the baseline model. Define the stock return as:

$$R_{t+1} = \frac{q_{t+1} + S_{t+1}K_{2t+1} - I_{2,t+1}}{q_t},$$

and notice that the excess return satisfies:

$$1 = E_t[m_{1t+1}R_{t+1}].$$

We can apply a covariance decomposition to the expression for the excess return as:

$$E_t(R_{t+1}) - R^f_t = -R^f_{t+1}Cov_t\left(m_{1t+1}, \frac{S_{t+1}K_{2t+1} - I_{2t+1}}{q_t} + \frac{q_{t+1}}{q_t}\right) \tag{11.97}$$

where $R^f_t = E_t[m_{1t+1}]^{-1}$. Since $Cov(X+Z, Y) = Cov(X, Y) + Cov(Z, Y)$, we obtain:

$$\frac{E_t(R_{t+1}) - R^f_t}{R^f_{t+1}} = -\frac{1}{q_t}[Cov_t\left(m_{1t+1}, S_{t+1}K_{2t+1} - I_{2t+1}\right) + Cov_t\left(m_{1t+1}, q_{t+1}\right)].$$

Recall that $q_{t+i} = p_{kt+i}K_{2t+1+i}$. Since investment occurs only when $p_{kt+i} = 1$, we can further simplify this equation as:

$$\frac{E_t(R_{t+1}) - R_t^f}{R_{t+1}^f} = -\frac{1}{p_{kt}K_{2t+1}}[Cov_t\,(m_{1t+1}, S_{t+1}K_{2t+1})$$

$$+ Cov_t\left(m_{1t+1}, p_{kt+1}K_{2t+2}\right)]. \quad (11.98)$$

The left side of this equation is the excess return on the stock relative to the risk-free return, which is referred to by Hall [226] as *valuation residual.* For a given level of $p_{k,t}$ Equation (11.98) shows that the valuation residual depends on both the covariance between the gross profits for firms in sector 2 and the MRS, and the covariance between Q and the MRS.

The main implications of the model are summarized in Equation (11.98). The first term shows the impact of variation in profitability for firms on the stock return. Notice that firm profitability is affected by the irreversibility in investment. Since industry demand is typically a downward-sloping function of output which, in turn, depends on the amount of capital accumulation, irreversibility affects the market price of output and hence, firms' profitability. Second, irreversibility has a more direct effect on the stock return through variation in the second term. Suppose there occurs a positive shock to investment demand, in our case, a more favorable shock to productivity. If the shadow price of existing capital, i.e. p_{kt}, is much lower than its replacement cost, firms will not choose to invest and hence, the productivity shock must be absorbed by prices, implying that the stock return will be variable.

Now consider two regimes.

Non-binding irreversibility constraint ($p_{kt} \approx 1$): In this case, the magnitude of the last term in (11.98) is expected to be small since a small increase in marginal Q will cause firms to invest. Hence, variation in profitability will lead to changes mostly in the supply of capital and not in the price of capital. This regime will correspond to low conditional volatility in stock returns.

Binding irreversibility constraint ($p_{kt} < 1$): Firms will not choose to invest in the immediate future and irreversibility will prevent the costless disposal of capital. Hence, the supply of capital will be relatively inelastic, implying instead that the price of existing capital will respond to the shock. In this case, the stock return will be relatively more volatile.

Thus, the model delivers predictions regarding the conditional volatility of stock returns and Q. It also implies that the conditional expected return will respond negatively to Q. Kogan [282] provides a simple test of this hypothesis by proxying Q with the market-to-book ratio, and by regressing the absolute excess returns on various specifications involving the market-to-book ratio for industry portfolios based on the two-digit

SIC code industries. He considers a specification that includes the market-to-book ratio and its square and another specification that is piecewise linear in the market-to-book ratio. He finds that real investment frictions which operate through the variable Q are significant determinants of stock return volatility.

11.5. CONCLUSIONS

In this chapter, we have provided an overview of the modern theory of investment and derived its asset pricing implications. Investment theory has remained one of the most challenging areas in the macroeconomics literature, not only because investment is one of the key determinants of growth but also because accounting for the cross-sectional and time series properties of real investment has proved far from simple or conclusive. (For a further discussion, see the review of Caballero [85].) Among the topics that we have not studied in this chapter are the impact of such factors as changes in tax policy, productivity, market structure or risk, and uncertainty on investment behavior. For a thorough review and discussion of this issue, see Demers, Demers, and Altug [149]. Nevertheless, we have provided a consistent theoretical framework and discussed how it can be analyzed under alternative assumptions.

11.6. EXERCISES

1. The neoclassical growth model assumes that investment can be negative. This implies that existing capital can be costlessly converted into the consumption good. Assume that households maximize:

$$\sum_{t=0}^{\infty} \beta^t U(c_t)$$

subject to

$$y_t = k_t^{\alpha} n_t^{1-\alpha},$$

$$K_{t+1} = (1-\delta)k_t + i_t,$$

$$y_t = c_t + i_t,$$

$$i_t \geq 0.$$

Let $n_t = 1$.

(a) Derive the Bellman equation, the first-order conditions and the envelope condition when investment is constrained to be non-negative.

(b) Derive the solution for this problem under the assumption that investment can be negative. How does the solution differ from the solution in part (a)?

2. Consider the version of the model described in Section 11.2.2 without adjustment costs but with irreversibility. Assume that the firm can purchase used capital goods at the price p_{kt}.
   (a) Derive the firm's net cash flow for this problem and formulate its problem as a stationary dynamic programming problem.
   (b) Derive the first-order conditions and the envelope condition.
   (c) Show that an appropriately defined measure of Tobin's Q satisfies the following relation under irreversibility:

$$\begin{aligned} Q &= 1 \quad \text{if } i_t > 0 \\ Q &< 1 \quad \text{if } i_t = 0. \end{aligned} \tag{11.99}$$

   (d) Sargent [383] derives a similar result between investment expenditures and the ratio of the shadow price of existing capital to its replacement cost. He interprets this as a version of the Q theory of investment although he notes that the implied relationship is an equilibrium relationship between two endogenously determined variables. Interpret Sargent's statement.

3. Time-to-Build
   Suppose there exists a representative firm, and assume that today's investment resources are distributed among J projects, each with a lifetime J. All projects are the same in that they generate one unit of capital when they are completed. However, the time-to-maturity of each project depends on the period in which the project is initiated. Let $s_{j,t}$ denotes the number of projects with j periods to maturity at time t. Each period, investment resources are distributed among J projects with different maturities such that investment demand at time t is given by:

$$I_t^d = \sum_{j=1}^{J} \phi_j s_{j,t}, \quad s_{j,t} \geq 0 \ \forall j,$$

   where $0 < \phi_j < 1$, for $j = 1, \ldots, J$ and $\sum_{j=1}^{J} \phi_j = 1$. The share of each project in investment expenditures is constant for all periods and given by ϕ_j, for a project that will be completed in j periods.
   The law of motion for the existing capital stock is given by:

$$K_{t+1} = (1 - \delta)K_t + I_t, \quad 0 < \delta < 1.$$

   The incomplete capital stocks evolve as:

$$s_{j,t+1} = s_{j+1,t}, \quad j = 1, \ldots, J - 1.$$

The firm chooses the demand for used capital, denoted by K_t^d, and the new projects that will be initiated at time t and that will be finished within J periods, denoted by $s_{J,t}$. There exists a market for used capital, where capital is sold at a price of $p_{k,t}$. Here, we impose the condition that a market for unfinished projects does not exist.

(a) Write down the representative firm's net cash flows and derive present value of the firm.

(b) Re-write the firm's value problem using a dynamic programming approach. Specify the law of motion for capital.

(c) Solve the firm's maximization problem and show that the value of capital is equal to the expected discounted sum of its costs. Specify the first-order and envelope conditions explicitly.

CHAPTER 12

Business cycles

The notion that economies are subject to recurring fluctuations dates back to Kondratiev [283]. In his framework, cyclical fluctuations were modeled as periodic movements or "long waves" in economic variables. Schumpeter [393, 394] advanced the notion that both growth and business cycles could be ascribed to technological innovations. A different line of thought is due to Ragnar Frisch [192], who created the conceptual basis for much thinking regarding business cycles by formulating the notions of impulse and propagation mechanisms. In Frisch's model, business cycles arise through the response of a second-order dynamic system to random shocks. Slutsky's [407] contribution was to note that the sum of a number of uncorrelated shocks is capable of producing smooth movements in the generated series. Concurrent with these developments, the work of Burns and Mitchell [83] laid the groundwork for business cycle methodology at the National Bureau of Economic Research (NBER). This research involves the dating of business cycles and the development of leading indicators for the US economy which continues to this day.[1]

Following the early work of Burns and Mitchell, interest waned in the study of business cycles as the post World War II focus shifted to stabilization policy. Keynes's *General Theory* [274] laid the foundations for the analysis of short-run economic fluctuations. During the post World War II period, the Keynesian framework was interpreted as a model of output determination at a point in time. The oil shocks of the 1970s and the policy experience regarding the failure of stabilization policy during that period led to the revival of interest in examining aggregate economic activity as recurrent phenomena characterizing the functioning of economies with optimizing agents. In his paper "Understanding Business Cycles," Lucas [316] catalogued the remarkable conformity in a set of economic series and set forth an agenda for explaining these facts using an *equilibrium* approach. During this period, monetary models of the business cycle beginning with Phelps [360], Lucas [314, 315], and others focused on the impact of informational frictions as a way of providing a consistent

[1] See also Zarnovitz [451].

theoretical foundation for the impact of changes in money on output. In Lucas' framework, a significant role was assigned to unexpected shocks to money in generating economic fluctuations. (See Lucas [314].) Following Long and Plosser [312] and Kydland and Prescott [297], the more recent "real business cycle"(RBC) approach has emphasized the role of technology shocks in generating cyclical phenomena. The key idea of the RBC theory is that business cycles can arise in frictionless, perfectly competitive and complete markets in which there are real or technology shocks. It is notable because its micro foundations are fully specified and it links the short-run with the neoclassical growth model. More recently, New Keynesian theories have revived interest in business cycle models that are capable of producing short-run economic fluctuations based on the types of forces that Keynes had initially postulated. Focus has also shifted to understanding the factors behind international business cycles (see, for example, Backus and Kehoe [39]) or business cycles in an international historical context (see Basu and Taylor [48]).

In this chapter, we will address the analysis of business cycles from several viewpoints. First, we will catalogue a set of stylized facts regarding business cycles. Second, we will discuss the issue of modeling business cycles. While there are many different models available, there is no single accepted model that can explain all the so-called *stylized facts of business cycles*. Third, we will discuss the empirics of business cycles.

12.1. BUSINESS CYCLE FACTS

The term "business cycle" refers to the joint behavior of a wide range of macroeconomic variables such as output, employment, prices, and investment. A business cycle exhibits two important features:

- When the variable is measured as deviations from trend, the ups and downs in a series display a great deal of persistence. More formally, the correlations of the observations one period apart are large and positive.
- Outputs in different sectors move together.

We will call these two features *persistence* and *comovement*. A business cycle is a recurrent fluctuation of output or employment. The **duration** of a cycle is the number of months from peak to peak (or trough to trough) of the cycle. The **amplitude** of a cycle is the deviation from trend. See Figure 12.1.

Time series are categorized into three categories: procyclical, countercyclical, or acyclical. Variables that move in the same direction over the cycle as real output are *procyclical*. Examples are consumption and investment. Variables that move in the opposite direction (rise during recessions and fall in expansions) are *countercyclical*. An example is unemployment. Variables that display little correlation with output over the cycle are called *acyclical*. An example is agricultural output. Some time series are out of

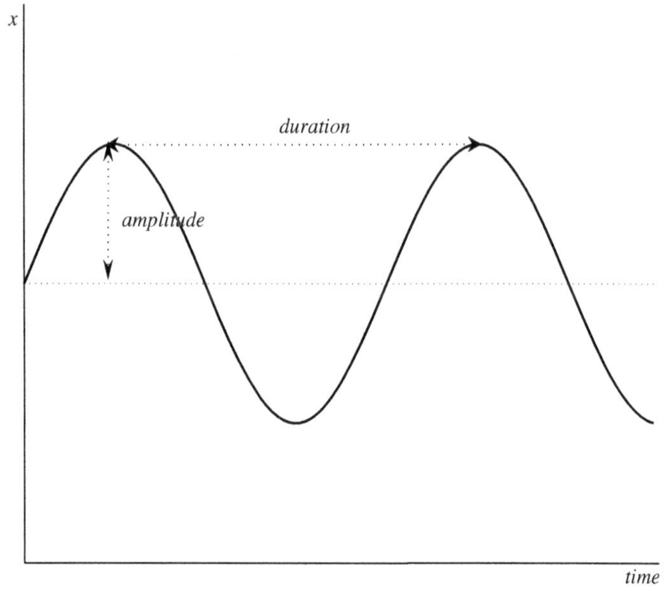

Figure 12.1. Amplitude and duration of a business cycle

phase with real GDP. For example, a **leading indicator** reaches a peak before real GDP reaches its peak and bottoms out (reaches a trough) before real GDP. Leading indicators are useful for predicting subsequent changes in real GDP. **Coincident indicators** reach a peak or a trough at roughly the same time as real GDP. Finally, **lagging indicators** reach a peak or trough after real GDP.

The literature on business cycles has been concerned with generating the stylized facts regarding cyclical fluctuations. The work of Burns and Mitchell [83] provides a convenient reference for describing the main features of business cycles based on the post-war US experience. More recently Stock and Watson [413] have presented a methodology for describing business cycles in terms of the cyclical time series behavior of the main macroeconomic series and their co-movement with cyclical output. One difference between the NBER approach to identifying business cycles and the approach in Stock and Watson is that the former is based on the (absolute) downturn of the level of output whereas the latter considers the decline in the series measured as a deviation from its long-run trend. Following the terminology in Zarnovitz [451], Stock and Watson refer to such cycles as *growth cycles*.[2]

[2] There is an issue of how to identify the cyclical component of a given series. For this purpose, Stock and Watson make use of the so-called *band-pass filter* in Baxter and King [51] which filters out both the long-run trend and the high-frequency movements by making use of spectral techniques.

We can group the stylized facts of business cycles in several areas. The first set of facts refers to the cyclical behavior of the main components of GDP. Real output across virtually all sectors of the economy moves together. Put differently, the contemporaneous correlation of output in different sectors of the economy is large and positive. Exceptions are production of agricultural goods and natural resources, which are not especially procyclical. Consumption, investment, inventories, and imports are all strongly procyclical. Consumption of durables is much more volatile than consumption of non-durable goods and services. Consumption of durable goods fluctuates more than GDP whereas non-durables fluctuate considerably less. Investment in equipment and non-residential structures is procyclical with a lag. Investment in residential structures is procyclical and highly volatile. Government spending tends to be acyclical. The correlation between government expenditures and output is nearly zero. Net exports are countercyclical. The correlation of output is generally negative, but weakly so. Since imports are more strongly procyclical than exports, the trade balance tends to be countercyclical.

Labor market fluctuations emphasize the cyclical behavior of employment, wages, and productivity. Total employment, employee hours, and capacity utilization are all strongly procyclical. The employment series lag the business cycle by a quarter while capacity utilization tends to be coincident. Employment fluctuates almost as much as output and total hours of work while average weekly hours fluctuate much less. The implication is that most fluctuations in total hours result from movements in and out of the work force rather than adjustments in average hours of work. Real wages are procyclical or acyclical. They have not displayed a steady pattern in terms of variability to GDP or in terms of leading/coincident/lagging indicators. Productivity is slightly procyclical but both real wages and productivity vary considerably less than output. This set of facts has proven to be among the most challenging facts to be reconciled with current business cycles models, as we discuss below.

The behavior of asset prices and returns has also received much scrutiny in the business cycle literature. In this regard, profits are highly volatile. Second, nominal interest rates tend to be procyclical. The yield curve which shows the rates of return on bonds of different maturities tends to be upward sloping during an expansion and downward sloping at the onset of a recession. That is, an expansion is characterized by expectations of higher interest rates at longer horizons whereas a recession typically signals a decline in long-term interest rates relative to short, namely, an inverted yield curve. Velocity and the money supply are procyclical. The risk premium for holding private debt, or the yield spread between corporate paper and Treasury bills with six month maturity, tends to shrink during expansions and increase during recessions. The reason for this countercyclical behavior is likely to be changes in default risk. The stock market is positively related to the subsequent growth rate of real GDP. In this sense, changes in stock prices have been taken as providing information about the future course of the real economy. Between 1945 and 1980, the stock market fell in the quarter before each of the eight recessions, although it is important to emphasize that the market has fallen without a subsequent recession.

The behavior of monetary aggregates and their relationship to real output has implications for alternative models of business cycles. Money (M2) is procyclical and tends to be a leading indicator of output. However, the procyclicality of M2 has diminished since the 1980s. The behavior of inflation has appeared to change over time. In the pre-World War I period and interwar period, inflation was procyclical with a very low mean. Since the early 1980s, inflation appears to be countercyclical. The standard deviation of inflation is lower than that of real GDP. Inflation is a coincident indicator. There is also a marked increase in the persistence of inflation after World War II. Finally, contemporaneous correlations between output fluctuations in different countries were highest in the interwar period, reflecting the common experience of the Great Depression, with the exception of Germany and Japan. The correlation is typically larger in the post-war period than in the pre-war period.

The literature on cataloguing business cycle regularities is too vast to be summarized in the current context. Nevertheless we can cite some papers that have extended this literature in alternative ways. The European business cycle has been well studied. See, for example, Artis, Kontolemis, and Osborn [35]. Artis and Zhang [34] investigate the relationship of the European Exchange Rate Mechanism (ERM) to the international business cycle in terms of the linkage and synchronization of cyclical fluctuations between countries. Their findings suggest the emergence of a group-specific European business cycle since the formation of the ERM, which is independent of the US cycle. Stock and Watson [414] find that the volatility of business cycles has moderated in most G7 countries over the past 40 years, and provide further evidence on the emergence of two cyclically coherent groups, the Euro-zone and English-speaking countries including Canada, the UK, and the US, respectively. Köse, Otrok, and Whiteman [286] consider the issue of a *world* business cycle, and use data on 60-odd countries covering seven regions of the world to determine factors underlying cyclical fluctuations that are common to all aggregates across all countries and regions and to countries and aggregates separately.

Basu and Taylor [48] examine business cycles within an international historical perspective. They consider the time series behavior of output, prices, real wages, exchange rates, total consumption, investment and the current account for 15 countries including the US, the UK, and other European countries plus Argentina for the period since 1870. They divide this period into four periods that also reflect the monetary and capital account regimes prevailing in them. The first period from 1870 to 1914 represents the era of the classic gold standard, which featured fixed exchange rates and worldwide capital market integration. In the second period from 1919 to 1939, the world economy went from a globalized regime to one which was nearly autarkic. This is also the period corresponding to the Great Depression. The third regime is the Bretton Woods era from 1945 to 1971, which corresponds to the post-World War II era of reconstruction and a resumption of global trade and capital flows. Finally, the fourth period corresponds to the period since the early 1970s to the present with a floating exchange rate regime. Basu and Taylor [48] argue that considering such a breakdown allows for the analysis of the impact of different regimes on cyclical phenomena, and also provides a way to identify the importance of demand versus supply-side factors or shocks and the role of alternative propagation mechanisms such as price rigidity. For example, most explanations of the Great Depression attribute the source of this massive downturn which simultaneously occurred in a number of countries to monetary phenomena. We return to controversies regarding the source of cyclical fluctuations in a later section.

12.2. SHOCKS AND PROPAGATION MECHANISMS

A business cycle model may be described in terms of impulses and a propagation mechanism. An *impulse* is the event that causes a variable to deviate from its steady state. A *propagation mechanism* is the mechanism causing deviations from the steady state to persist. The impulses may be real or monetary shocks.

Technology shocks alter the economy's production possibilities set. Permanent improvements in technology make it possible to reach higher combinations of outputs for a given level of inputs. Equivalently, new technologies may be viewed as cost-reducing, reducing the cost of attaining a given level of output. The introduction of computer technology is an example of this type of shift, as the costs of producing a myriad set of goods and services have fallen due to the availability of information technology. Historically, we may view the transition to settled agriculture as a form of technological progress as well as the adoption of more advanced agricultural technologies such as irrigation, cross-breeding and so on. Technology shocks may also be transitory such as increases in oil prices.

Political shocks and government expenditures shocks are another source of output fluctuations. Shocks associated with wars may be viewed as a form of temporary shock. Between 1700 and 1920, the British Empire fought eight major wars (treating the wars with France during the period

1793 to 1815 as one war).[3] Changes in political regimes or political parties may also have effects on an economy's production possibility set through the impact of tax policy, regulation policy, market access, rent-seeking and the like.

Natural disasters and weather are often responsible for large declines in output and aggregate economic activity. The hurricane that hit New Orleans and the Gulf states in the US in 2005 was responsible for substantial declines in output. Droughts, frosts, flooding, and other types of natural disasters are other examples of "weather" shocks.

That **monetary shocks** can have real effects is one of the enduring hypotheses in economics. The treatise by Friedman and Schwartz [191] examining the relation between money and output growth remains as an important set of facts to be accounted for by macroeconomists of different persuasions.

Taste shocks may also be responsible for various sorts of fluctuations. The positivist approach to economics advocated by Friedman and others has typically precluded changes in taste based on the idea that allowing for shifts in preferences is a convenient way to "explain anything." Nevertheless, changes in culture may affect the consumption of variety of goods. Coffee culture originated in 16th-century Turkey (or the Ottoman Empire) and spread from there to many other parts of the world. The interest in world culture and goods has led to the growth of stores or chains such as Starbucks that market international coffees and teas and ethnically-inspired stores that sell Asian and African-style housewares, clothing and accessories.

Suppose a shock does occur. How is it transmitted to the rest of the economy?

- Real business cycle models emphasize the role of *intertemporal substitution* motives. Agents typically respond to a temporary negative shock by lowering savings and also by working less. The impact of these changes is to induce fluctuations in labor supply and employment as well as investment. Furthermore, if the economy experiences a period with lower investment, it will have a lower capital stock in the future, implying that the effect of the shock persists. Long and Plosser [312] provide an early example of a real business cycle model. See Exercise 2.
- Keynesian and New Keynesian models stress the role of frictions such as *price stickiness.* In a simple labor market model, if real wages do not adjust downward when there is a negative shock to demand, the result is unemployment and larger declines in output relative to a situation with flexible prices. Prototypical New Keynesian models such as Rotemberg and Woodford [373] allow for imperfect competition and

[3] See Barro [45].

markups to capture alternative propagation mechanisms in response to technology shocks or shocks to government expenditures. Limited participation models also allow alternative mechanisms for the propagation of real and monetary shocks.[4]

- The recent crises in East Asia and the experience of the Great Depression also point to the importance of *credit market frictions*, with shocks originating in various financial markets, leading to a widening circle of bankruptcies and bank failures and large and negative effects on real output. Bernanke and Gertler [58] employ a model with such frictions to try to account for the experience of the Great Depression in the US.

12.3. REAL BUSINESS CYCLE MODELS

The recent analysis of business cycles is notable for the fact that it has wed growth theory with business cycle theory. The proto-typical RBC model has the structure of a standard neoclassical growth model with a labor/leisure choice incorporated. We start with the standard production function:

$$Y_t = A_t K_t^{\alpha} H_t^{1-\alpha}, \quad 0 < \alpha < 1. \tag{12.1}$$

Under constant returns to scale and perfect competition in the product and factor markets, the Solow residual is defined as the difference between the growth of output and the share-weighted growth rates of the inputs. To derive the Solow residual, take the logarithm and then take the first differences:

$$\Delta \ln Y_{t+1} = \Delta \ln A_{t+1} + \alpha \Delta \ln K_{t+1} + (1-\alpha)\Delta \ln H_{t+1},$$

which can be rewritten in growth rates as:

$$\Delta y_{t+1} = \Delta a_{t+1} + \alpha \Delta k_{t+1} + (1-\alpha)\Delta h_{t+1},$$

where Δx denotes log-differences of X. To derive an observable measure of the Solow residual, the parameter α is typically measured as the share of capital in real output defined as $s_{Kt} = r_t K_t / P_t Y_t$, where r_t denotes the competitively determined rental rate on capital and P_t denotes the product price. Under constant returns to scale, $s_{Kt} + s_{Ht} = 1$, where $s_{Ht} = w_t H_t / P_t Y_t$ denotes the share of labor in national income. Under these assumptions, the growth in the total factor productivity (TFP) is measured as a residual:

$$\Delta a_{t+1} = \Delta y_{t+1} - s_{Kt}\Delta k_{t+1} - (1 - s_{Kt})\Delta h_{t+1}.$$

The importance of the Solow residual has been demonstrated in a number of empirical studies. Solow [410] showed that the residual accounts for about one-half of the US GDP growth between 1909–1949. Similarly,

[4] For a review and discussion of these models, see Christiano, Eichenbaum, and Evans [105].

according to Denison [151], 40% of GNP growth in the USA between 1929 and 1957 resulted from technical development. Using this representation, the growth in output per worker is

$$\Delta y_{t+1} - \Delta h_{t+1} = \Delta a_{t+1} + s_{Kt}[\Delta k_{t+1} - \Delta h_{t+1}].$$

The Solow residual is typically treated as *exogenous*. In terms of its statistical properties, it appears to be a random walk with drift.

The empirical behavior of the Solow residual also has implications for the source of cyclical fluctuations. Observed productivity or the Solow residual is *procyclical*. According to the RBC approach, the observed procyclical movements in productivity should merely be a response to exogenous technology shocks. (See Prescott [363].) In a series of papers, Hall [224], [225] has argued persuasively that there may be endogenous components to the cyclical movement of productivity arising from imperfect competition at the firm level and internal increasing returns to scale in production. To see these results, consider a production function for gross output for the ith firm or productive unit Y_{it} as:

$$Y_{it} = F^i(H_{it}, K_{it}, M_{it}, A_{it}), \tag{12.2}$$

where H_{it} denotes man-hours, K_{it} denotes services from capital, M_{it} denotes materials inputs, and A_{it} is a technology shock.[5] The function F^i is assumed to be homogeneous of degree γ_i in H, K, and M, and homogeneous of degree one in A. Suppose that the output price includes a (possibly) time-varying markup over marginal cost as:

$$\frac{P_{it}}{\mathrm{MC}_{it}} = \mu_{it}, \tag{12.3}$$

where $\mu_{it} \geq 1$. Also define the cost shares of the inputs by:

$$c_{it}^J = \frac{P_{it}^J J_{it}}{\sum_J P_{it}^j J_{it}}, \quad J = H, K, M$$

where P_{it}^J denotes the price of the Jth input. The first-order conditions for the firm's cost minimization are given by $P_{it}^J = \lambda_{it} F_J(H_{it}, K_{it}, M_{it}, A_{it})$ for $J = H, K, M$, where λ_{it} is a Lagrange multiplier that has the interpretation of marginal cost and F_J is the derivative of the production function with respect to the Jth input. Making use of the expression for the markup, it follows that

$$\frac{F_J J_{it}}{Y_{it}} = \mu_{it}\left(\frac{P_{it}^J J_{it}}{P_{it} Y_{it}}\right) = \mu_{it} s_{it}^J. \tag{12.4}$$

[5] As is typical of this literature, we differentiate between a production function for gross output and value-added at the firm level of analysis. See, for example, Basu [47].

Using the fact that $\gamma_i = \mu_{it} \sum_J s_{it}^J$ together with the definition of the cost shares c_{Jt}^i yields an expression for the growth rate of output in sector i as:

$$\Delta y_{i,t+1} = \gamma_i \left[c_{it}^H \Delta h_{i,t+1} + c_{it}^K \Delta k_{i,t+1} + c_{it}^M \Delta m_{i,t+1} \right] + \Delta a_{i,t+1}. \tag{12.5}$$

Subtracting the quantity $\Delta x_{i,t+1} \equiv [c_{it}^H \Delta h_{i,t+1} + c_{it}^K \Delta k_{i,t+1} + c_{it}^M \Delta m_{i,t+1}]$ from both sides of this expression yields:

$$\Delta y_{i,t+1} - \Delta x_{i,t+1} = (\gamma_i - 1)\Delta x_{i,t+1} + \Delta a_{i,t+1}. \tag{12.6}$$

Since $\gamma_i \geq 1$, observed productivity (defined from the left side of this expression) can be procyclical even in the absence of positive shocks to technology. For example, a demand shock that stimulates output can be associated with increases in productivity by leading to endogenous increases in efficiency. Similarly, if there is cyclical variation in factor utilization rates, then the conventional Solow residual inappropriately includes a component due to unobserved variation in capital and/or labor utilization rates due to labor hoarding, for example. In what follows, we examine the implications of the standard RBC approach which assumes perfect competition, CRTS in production, and full utilization of all factors. In later sections, we discuss deviations from these assumptions.

12.3.1. An RBC model

The standard RBC model is a one-sector growth with a labor-leisure choice. The representative agent has time-separable preferences over consumption and leisure choices given by:

$$U = E_0 \left\{ \sum_{t=0}^{\infty} \beta^t u(c_t, l_t) \right\}, \tag{12.7}$$

where $0 < \beta < 1$ is the discount factor. The time constraint requires that the sum of leisure and labor hours sum to one:

$$l_t + h_t = 1. \tag{12.8}$$

There is a representative firm with a CRTS production function that is affected by a stochastic technology shock each period:

$$y_t = \exp(z_t) k_t^{\alpha} h_t^{1-\alpha}, \quad 0 < \alpha < 1. \tag{12.9}$$

Assume that the technology shock follows an AR(1) process:

$$z_{t+1} = \mu + \rho z_t + \epsilon_{t+1}, \quad 0 < \rho < 1, \ \epsilon \sim i.i.d. \text{ and } N(0, \sigma_e^2). \tag{12.10}$$

Capital evolves according to

$$k_{t+1} = (1 - \delta)k_t + i_t, \tag{12.11}$$

where i_t denotes economy-wide investment and $0 < \delta < 1$ is the depreciation rate. The aggregate feasibility constraint is defined as:

$$c_t + i_t = y_t. \tag{12.12}$$

We can show the existence of a value function for the social planner's problem for this model using the recursive approach that we introduced earlier. Assuming a solution exists, let λ_t denote the Lagrange multiplier on the resource constraint. The first-order conditions with the envelope conditions substituted in with respect to c_t, k_{t+1} and l_t are as follows:

$$U_1(c_t, l_t) = \lambda_t, \tag{12.13}$$

$$\lambda_t = \beta E_t\{\lambda_{t+1}[\exp(z_{t+1})\alpha k_{t+1}^{\alpha-1} h_{t+1}^{1-\alpha} + (1 - \delta)]\}, \tag{12.14}$$

$$U_2(c_t, l_t) = \lambda_t \exp(z_t)(1 - \alpha)h_t^{-\alpha} k_t^{\alpha}. \tag{12.15}$$

These conditions can be rewritten as

$$\frac{U_{2t}}{U_{1t}} = \exp(z_t)(1 - \alpha)(k_t/h_t)^{\alpha} \tag{12.16}$$

$$\beta E_t\left\{\frac{U_{1,t+1}}{U_{1t}}[\exp(z_{t+1})\alpha(k_{t+1}/h_{t+1})^{\alpha-1} + (1 - \delta)]\right\} = 1. \tag{12.17}$$

The first equation shows that the marginal rate of substitution between consumption and leisure is equal to the marginal product of labor. The second equation is the intertemporal Euler equation. Observe that the ratio U_2/U_1 is a function of the capital-labor ratio, k_t/h_t. There is no unemployment in the model as time not spent working is (optimally) taken as leisure. This means that the capital accumulation process will also be a function of the capital-labor ratio.

To show this more explicitly, suppose that the utility function has the form:

$$U(c_t, l_t) = c_t^{\theta} l_t^{1-\theta}, \quad 0 < \theta < 1.$$

The intratemporal MRS between consumption and leisure can be expressed as:

$$\frac{U_2(c_t, l_t)}{U_1(c_t, l_t)} = \frac{(1 - \theta)c_t^{\theta} l_t^{-\theta}}{\theta c_t^{\theta-1} l_t^{1-\theta}} = \frac{1 - \theta}{\theta}\frac{c_t}{l_t}.$$

Using this result to evaluate the MRS between consumption and leisure in Equation (12.16), we obtain:

$$\frac{(1 - \theta)c_t}{\theta l_t} = \exp(z_t)(1 - \alpha)(k_t/h_t)^{\alpha}. \tag{12.18}$$

Likewise, we can re-write the intertemporal Euler equation by noting that $U_1(c_{t+i}, l_{t+i}) = \theta(c_{t+i}/l_{t+i})^{\theta-1}$ for $i \geq 0$ and using the result in Equation (12.18). This yields:

$$\beta E_t \left\{ \left[\exp(z_{t+1}) \left(\frac{k_{t+1}}{h_{t+1}} \right)^{\alpha} \right]^{\theta-1} \left[\alpha \exp(z_{t+1}) \left(\frac{k_{t+1}}{h_{t+1}} \right)^{\alpha-1} + 1 - \delta \right] \right\}$$

$$= \left[\exp(z_t) \left(\frac{k_t}{h_t} \right)^{\alpha} \right]^{\theta-1}. \tag{12.19}$$

Observe that this is a non-linear stochastic difference equation in k_t/h_t with forcing process given by the technology shock. It can be solved for the optimal $\{k_t/h_t\}_{t=0}^{\infty}$ sequence using methods for solving stochastic difference equations. Given a solution for k_t/h_t, Equation (12.18) can be used together with the feasibility constraint and the time constraint to solve for h_t.[6]

Kydland and Prescott [297] introduced an influential and much-cited version of an RBC model. In their framework, the random technology shock is the sole impulse. The main propagation mechanisms are that:

- risk-averse agents smooth consumption over time using capital;
- lags in investment (time-to-build) cause shocks to propagate;
- agents substitute leisure in response to transitory changes in wages (or changes in the marginal product of labor);
- inventories are used to meet unexpected changes in demand. (See Christiano [103].)

In the "real business cycle" literature, the model is then calibrated with the data. Calibration refers to the practice of the determining the parameters of the models based on its steady state properties and the results of other studies, given particular functional forms for the production function and the utility function. (See Cooley and Prescott [124].) A stochastic process for z_t is also specified and a random number generator is used to simulate the total factor productivity time series. The simulated series are used to generate time series for consumption, output, investment and labor. Trends in the data are removed using a given filter. The means, variances, covariances, and cross correlations for the simulated time series are compared with the comparable statistics in the data. The model is then judged to be close or not based on this comparison, so the approach differs significantly from standard econometrics. One of the problems with the RBC approach is that the model is constructed so that all variability in output is explained by shocks to TFP.

[6] An alternative way to find the solution for the basic RBC model is to log-linearize the optimality conditions around the deterministic steady state following the approach in Uhlig [435]. See Example 10.3 in Chapter 10.

Kydland and Prescott use this approach to analyze the properties of a real business cycle model in which preferences are not separable over time with respect to leisure and there exists a time-to-build feature in investment for new capital goods. The production function displays constant returns to scale with respect to hours worked and a composite capital good. The only exogenous shock to their model is a random technology shock which follows a stationary first-order autoregressive process. They use the quadratic approximation procedure to obtain linear decision rules for a set of aggregate variables and generate time series for the remaining series by drawing realizations of the innovation to the technology shock.

They calculate a small set of moments associated with each series to match the model with the data. When calibrating their model, Kydland and Prescott choose the variance of the innovation to the technology shock to make the variability of the output series generated by their model equal to the variability of observed GNP. As McCallum [336] notes, this feature of their analysis makes it difficult to judge whether *"technology shocks are adequate to generate output ... fluctuations of the magnitude actually observed."* More generally, the RBC approach faces the problem of identifying technology shocks that can generate cyclical fluctuations of magnitudes that are observed in the data (see Summers [424]). Despite these problems, the surprising aspect of RBC modeling, in the first instance, is that it is capable of delivering many of the stylized facts of business cycles. Specifically, the model predicts that consumption fluctuates less than output whereas investment fluctuates more. Consumption, investment, and hours are all strongly procyclical, as they are in the data. In terms of the variation accounted by the technology shocks, the technology shock explains much but not all of the variation in output. We illustrate numerically the behavior of a proto-typical RBC model in Section 12.4. Thus, the RBC model can generate cycles endogenously and clearly has some economic significance even if the calibration method is controversial.

12.3.2. *A model with indivisible labor supply*

One of the main problems with the standard RBC model, as we have outlined above, is that it cannot capture the variation in the aggregate labor input. (See, for example, Kydland [296].) In the data, employment is strongly procyclical and almost as variable as output while real wages are weakly procyclical. In the standard model, a productivity shock shifts the marginal product of labor so that the observed variations in employment can only occur if the labor supply curve is relatively elastic. Yet micro studies find that wage elasticity of labor supply is quite low. In this case, the marginal productivity shock should lead to most of the adjustment in real wages and less in the quantity of labor. Furthermore, in the data, hours of work per worker adjusts very little over the cycle. About two-thirds of the variability in total hours worked comes from movements into and out of the labor force, and the rest is due to adjustment in the number of hours worked per employee.

The indivisible labor, lottery models studied by Gary Hansen [228] and Rogerson [365] were devised to explain the stylized fact that aggregate hours vary more than productivity. Their framework provides a way for reconciling large labor supply elasticities at the aggregate level with low labor supply elasticities at the individual level. This is accomplished by assuming that individuals can work all the time or not at all. To account for the non-convexities introduced by the work/non-work decision, it is assumed that individuals choose the probability of working π_t. A lottery then determines whether an individual actually works. This economy is one in which individuals and a firm trade a contract that commits the household to work h_0 hours with probability π_t. Since what is being traded is the contract, the individual gets paid regardless of whether he works or not. We now describe a version of the RBC model due to Richard Rogerson [365] and Gary Hansen [228] that allows for fixed costs and non-convexities in labor supply.

Suppose that workers are constrained to work either zero or $\hat{h}$ hours where

$$0 < \hat{h} < 1. \tag{12.20}$$

The main idea is that there are non-convexities or fixed costs that make varying the number of employed workers more efficient than varying hours per worker. Let π_t denote the probability that a given agent is employed in period t so that per-capita hours worked is given by:

$$H_t = \pi_t \hat{h}. \tag{12.21}$$

Let $c_{0,t}$ denote the consumption of an unemployed worker and $c_{1,t}$ denote the consumption of an employed agent. Then the expected utility of the representative consumer, taking into account the work versus non-work decision, is given by:

$$E[u(c_t, l_t)] = \pi_t u(c_{1,t}, 1 - \hat{h}) + (1 - \pi_t) u(c_{0,t}, 1).$$

Assume that the individual utility function has the form:

$$u(c, l) = \ln(c) + A \ln(l). \tag{12.22}$$

The social planner solves the problem:

$$\max_{\pi_t, c_{0,t}, c_{1,t}} E[u(c_t, l_t)] \text{ s. t. } \pi_t c_{1,t} + (1 - \pi_t) c_{0,t} = c_t.$$

Notice that the social planner chooses the consumption allocations of each agent plus the probability of their working. When agents do work, they must supply $\hat{h}$ hours of work so that there is no choice over hours of work directly. Let λ_t denote the Lagrange multiplier on the feasibility constraint for consumption. Omitting the work-leisure decision for the moment, the first-order conditions with respect to $(c_{0,t}, c_{1,t})$ are:

$$\frac{\pi_t}{c_{0,t}} = \pi_t \lambda_t, \tag{12.23}$$

$$\frac{1-\pi_t}{c_{1,t}} = (1-\pi_t)\lambda_t. \tag{12.24}$$

It follows that $c_{0,t} = c_{1,t} = c_t$ so that the agent consumes the same amount whether or not he is working. Hence the unemployed worker enjoys higher utility since working causes disutility. In this model, *ex ante* all individuals are alike but *ex post* they differ because some work while others enjoy leisure. With complete insurance and identical preferences that are separable with respect to consumption and leisure, all individuals have the same consumption but the unemployed are better off. This is a feature that is counterfactual to the working of actual labor markets. Nevertheless, as we show below, the model delivers predictions that are more in line with the data than the standard RBC framework.

Notice that the agent will consume c_t whether or not he is working. Hence expected utility (where the expectation is over whether or not you work) is:

$$\ln(c_t) + \pi_t A \ln(1-\hat{h}) + (1-\pi_t) A \ln(1), \tag{12.25}$$

where A is a positive constant. Using the definition of H_t, $\pi_t = H_t/\hat{h}$. Now substitute for π_t in (12.25) and use $\ln(1) = 0$ to obtain:

$$\begin{aligned} E[u(c_t, l_t)] &= \ln(c_t) + \pi_t A \ln(1-\hat{h}) \\ &= \ln(c_t) - BH_t. \end{aligned} \tag{12.26}$$

where

$$B = \frac{-A\ln(1-\hat{h})}{\hat{h}}.$$

Comparing Equation (12.22) with Equation (12.26) shows the effect of the lottery assumption. The former specification for preferences implies a low intertemporal elasticity of substitution in labor supply, which is consistent with assumptions about individual behavior. By contrast, the latter specification – which is linear in total hours H_t – implies a high intertemporal elasticity at the aggregate level.

The preferences can now be written as:

$$U = E_0 \left\{ \sum_{t=0}^{\infty} \beta^t u(c_t, H_t) \right\},$$

where $u(c_t, H_t) = \ln(c_t) - BH_t$. We now solve the model subject to the time constraint, resource constraint, production function and law of motion for the capital stock described in Section 12.3. The problem is:

$$\max_{\{c_t,H_t,k_{t+1}\}} E_0 \left\{ \sum_{t=0}^{\infty} \beta^t \left[\ln(c_t) - BH_t + \lambda_t [\exp(z_t) k_t^{\theta} H_t^{1-\theta} \right.\right.$$

$$\left.\left. + (1-\delta)k_t - c_t - k_{t+1}] \right] \right\}.$$

The first-order conditions are:

$$\frac{1}{c_t} = \lambda_t \tag{12.27}$$

$$B = \lambda_t \exp(z_t)(1-\theta) k_t^{\theta} H_t^{-\theta} \tag{12.28}$$

$$\lambda_t = \beta E_t \lambda_{t+1} [\exp(z_{t+1}) \theta k_{t+1}^{\theta-1} H_{t+1}^{1-\theta} + (1-\delta)] \tag{12.29}$$

Notice that (12.28) can be used to solve for H_t as:

$$H_t = \left(\frac{Bc_t}{\exp(z_t)(1-\theta)} \right)^{-1/\theta} k_t$$

$$= \left(-\frac{A \ln(1-\hat{h}) c_t}{\exp(z_t)(1-\theta)\hat{h}} \right)^{-1/\theta} k_t. \tag{12.30}$$

Equations (12.27) and (12.29) yield the intertemporal Euler equation as:

$$1 = \beta \left\{ \frac{c_t}{c_{t+1}} [\exp(z_{t+1}) \theta k_{t+1}^{\theta-1} H_{t+1}^{1-\theta} + (1-\delta)] \right\}, \tag{12.31}$$

where the term in square brackets shows the rate of return to investing in the aggregate production technology. With H_t determined in (12.30), we can use the resource constraint to solve for c_t and then substitute for c_t into the intertemporal Euler equation to obtain a non-linear stochastic in k_{t+1} with forcing process $\{z_t\}$.

Hansen calibrates this model by specifying values for the unknown parameters θ, δ, β, A, and the stochastic process for the technology shock using the approach in Kydland and Prescott. Hansen argues that the model with indivisibilities can generate a variability of hours relative to productivity around 2.7 compared with the model without indivisibilities which implies a value near unity. The purpose of the framework that Gary Hansen and Rogerson consider is to generate the stylized fact with respect to the relative variability of hours versus productivity and it is not intended to incorporate the microeconomic foundations of the labor market.

12.3.3. Other "puzzles"

Despite its apparent success, the RBC model has produced a variety of "puzzles." These puzzles have constituted the basis of much further research in the area. One of these puzzles is known as the *productivity puzzle* regarding the relationship between productivity and output. The second has to do with the issue of *reverse causality* from output to money.

The productivity puzzle

In the data, we find that the correlation between productivity and hours is near zero or negative, while the correlation between productivity and output is positive and around 0.5. See, for example, Christiano and Eichenbaum [104], who measure hours worked and productivity based on both household and establishment-level surveys conducted by the US Department of Labor. Christiano and Eichenbaum [104] note that as long as there is a single shock that drives the behavior of both hours and productivity, the standard model cannot deliver the strong procyclical response of hours without procyclical behavior in productivity. By contrast, the RBC model, which is driven entirely by productivity shocks, generates correlations that are large and positive in both cases. Another problem that arises in matching the model and the data is that in the data, labor's share of income moves countercyclically whereas in the RBC model labor's share is fixed.

One way of improving the model's ability to match the data is to introduce **home production**. Following Benhabib, Rogerson, and Wright [54], consider a decision-maker who has preferences:

$$\sum_{t=0}^{\infty} \beta^t u(c_{mt}, c_{ht}, h_{mt}, h_{ht}),$$

where $0 < \beta < 1$. In this expression, c_{mt} is the consumption of a market good; c_{ht} is consumption of the home-produced good; h_{mt} is labor time spent in market work; and h_{ht} is labor time spent in home work. Assume that $u_1 > 0$, $u_2 > 0$, $u_3 < 0$, and $u_4 < 0$. The total amount of time available to the household is normalized as unity, and leisure is defined as time not spent working in the market or at home:

$$l_t = 1 - h_{mt} - h_{ht}.$$

At each date, the household can purchase market goods c_{mt}, market capital goods k_{mt} and household capital goods k_{ht}. Household capital goods are used in home production but market capital goods are rented to firms at the competitive rental rate r_t. Letting w_t denote the wage rate and δ_m and δ_h denote the depreciation rates on market and home capital, respectively, the household's budget constraint is:

$$c_{mt} + k_{m,t+1} + k_{h,t+1} \leq w_t h_{mt} + r_t k_{mt} + (1 - \delta_m)k_{mt} + (1 - \delta_h)k_{ht}.$$

Home goods are produced according to the home production function:

$$c_{mt} = g(h_{ht}, k_{ht}, z_{ht}),$$

where z_{ht} is a shock to home production and g is increasing and concave in labor and capital. Alternative measures put home production to be in the range of 20–50% of GDP. In the model, home production is used to produce a non-tradeable consumption good. A rise in market productivity may induce households to substitute away from home production towards market production. This gives us another margin on which to substitute market labor and improves the model's predictions. Unlike the standard model, the labor supply curve also shifts in response to a good productivity shock, thereby leading to greater variability in labor. However, one criticism of the home production theory is that it suggests that all movements out of the labor force (toward home production) are **voluntary**.

A second way to resolve the productivity puzzle is through a **labor hoarding** argument. This says that the effective labor input can be altered even though the total number of workers is fixed. The firm may not alter its work force every time there is a productivity shock (which would occur through a shift in the marginal product of labor curve). However, if there are costs to hiring or laying off workers, firms may retain workers even though they are not exerting much effort. Hence labor effort is likely to be adjusted first in response to a productivity shock. Eventually more workers may be hired or fired, but only after longer periods of time. Labor effort is likely to be procyclical. As a variety of authors have noted, movements in the Solow residual are thus likely to reflect, in part, unmeasured changes in effort. To show these results in the context of a simple example, consider a production function for aggregate output Y_t which depends on an exogenous technology shock A_t, capital K_t, and a labor input that reflects variations in work effort following Burnside, Eichenbaum, and Rebelo [84]. Specifically, let f denote a fixed shift length, N_t the total number of workers, and W_t the work effort of each individual. Thus,

$$Y_t = A_t K_t^{\alpha} [f N_t W_t]^{1-\alpha}, \quad 0 < \alpha < 1.$$

In the standard model, the production function can be written as:

$$Y_t = S_t K_t^{\alpha} [H_t]^{1-\alpha},$$

where H_t denotes the total hours worked. In the absence of variations in work effort, $H_t = fN_t$. Notice that the conventionally measured Solow residual S_t is related to true technology shock A_t as:

$$\begin{aligned}\ln(S_t) &= \ln(A_t) + \alpha \ln(K_t) + (1-\alpha)[\ln(f) + \ln(N_t) + \ln(W_t)] \\ &\quad - \alpha \ln(K_t) - (1-\alpha)[\ln(f) + \ln(N_t)] \\ &= \ln(A_t) + (1-\alpha)\ln(W_t).\end{aligned}$$

Decisions to alter effort levels will be the outcome of a maximizing decision, so that the movements in the Solow residual are not entirely exogenous. If labor hoarding is added into the model, then the productivity/hours correlation is reduced and more closely matches the data. The comments made about fluctuations in the effort level of labor also apply to capital. The measured capital in the Solow residual does not take into account optimal fluctuations in capital utilization rates. This can lead to variation in the Solow residual that is not related to changes in productivity or technology.

Reverse causality

The stylized facts of business cycles state that money, especially M2, appears to be a leading indicator of aggregate output. However, this is inconsistent with the notion that TFP shocks are the driving force behind business cycle activity. The conventional wisdom regarding the money-output correlation, summarized by Friedman and Schwartz [191] in their study of monetary history, is that the causality goes from money to output but with "long and variable lags." One approach to dealing with this criticism is to introduce money and banking into the standard RBC model following King and Plosser [277]. These authors observe that transactions services (as provided by money and the banking sector) can be viewed as an intermediate input that reduces the cost of producing output and hence, can be treated as a direct input into the aggregate production function. To briefly describe their framework, suppose the final good is produced according to the production technology:

$$y_t = f(k_{ft}, n_{ft}, d_{ft})\phi_t, \tag{12.32}$$

where k_{ft} is the amount of capital, n_{ft} is the amount of labor services, and d_{ft} is the amount of transactions services used in the final goods industry. In this expression, ϕ_t is a shock to production of the final good at time t. The financial industry is assumed to provide accounting services that facilitate the exchange of goods by reducing the amount of time that would be devoted to market transactions. The production of the intermediate good is given by:

$$d_t = g(n_{dt}, k_{dt})\lambda_t, \tag{12.33}$$

where n_{dt} and k_{dt} denote the amounts of labor and capital allocated to the financial sector, and λ_t captures technological innovations to the financial services industry. Households maximize the expected discounted value of utility from consumption c_t and leisure l_t as:

$$E_0 \left\{ \sum_{t=0}^{\infty} \beta^t U(c_t, l_t) \right\}, \quad 0 < \beta < 1, \tag{12.34}$$

Households are assumed to own the capital stock and to make investment decisions i_t subject to the resource constraint $c_t + i_t \leq y_t + (1 - \delta)k_t$ where $0 < \delta < 1$ is the depreciation rate on capital. By contrast, firms rent labor, capital, and transactions services to maximize profits on a period-by-period basis. Households are also assumed to combine time and transactions services to accomplish consumption and investment purchases. The time required for this activity is:

$$n_{\tau t} = \tau(d_{ht}/(c_t + i_t))(c_t + i_t), \tag{12.35}$$

where $\tau' < 0, \tau'' < 0$. The household chooses an amount of transactions services d_{ht} so as to minimize the total transactions costs, $w_t n_{\tau t} + \rho_t d_{ht}$, where w_t is the real wage and ρ_t is the rental price of transactions services. This implies a demand for transactions services that can be obtained from the first-order condition

$$\rho_t = w_t \tau'(d_{ht}/(c_t + i_t)) \tag{12.36}$$

as $d^{\star}_{ht} = h(\rho_t/w_t)(c_t + i_t)$ where $h = (\tau')^{-1}$. Likewise, hours allocated to producing transactions services is $n^{\star}_{\tau t} = \tau(h(\rho_t/w_t))(c_t + i_t)$. Finally, we require that the household's time allocated to the different activities sums to one, $n_t = n_{ft} + n_{dt} + n_{\tau t}$.

This framework can be used to rationalize the observations regarding money and output. Specifically, *inside money*, or a broad measure of money that includes commercial credit, is more closely related to output than *outside money*. Suppose a shock to the production of final goods or equivalently, a positive shock to productivity occurs. Then consumption and leisure of the representative consumer will rise but so will investment demand as consumers seek to spread the extra wealth over time. If the substitution effect of an increase in the marginal product of labor outweighs the wealth effect of the productivity shock, then hours of work will also rise. As a consequence, investment demand rises and also output will increase in response to the additional hours worked, so firms will wish to finance a greater volume of goods in process. As a result, commercial credit, or inside money, responds to the positive productivity shock. The increase in output will also stimulate the demand for transactions services by households and firms. Hence, the causality runs from the productivity shock to money even though the increase in money occurs before the increase in output.

Ahmed and Murthy [9] provide a test of this hypothesis using a small open economy such as Canada to evaluate the impact of exogenously given terms of trade and real interest rates versus domestic aggregate demand and supply disturbances. Their results are derived from a structural VAR (vector autoregression) with long-run restrictions to identify the alternative structural shocks. Consistent with the RBC view, they find that an important source of the money-output correlation is output shocks affecting inside money in the short-run. Another possibility is that the central bank uses *accommodative monetary policy*.[7] During an expansion, if interest rates are rising and firms wish to invest more in anticipation of higher expected profits, the central bank may expand the money supply to keep interest rates from rising too rapidly.

The policy implications of the RBC model are simple – the business cycle fluctuations are Pareto optimal and there is no role for the government to try to smooth or mitigate the fluctuations. In fact, such policy efforts are inefficient. The strengths of the RBC model are its strong microeconomic foundations and the link that it provides between the long-run and the short-run. An important criticism of the model is that there is no evidence of large, economy-wide disturbances. The only exception would be the oil price shocks, and it is no coincidence that this model was developed after the price shocks of the 1970s. But what are some other examples of big shocks? If shocks are concentrated in a particular sector, what is the mechanism by which these shocks are transmitted to other sectors? One needs to consider multi-sector models since the one-sector growth model does not allow for a consideration of these issues.[8]

12.4. SOLVING BUSINESS CYCLE MODELS

In Chapter 10, we described the approach of numerical dynamic programming for solving growth models. Another approach is to use a quadratic approximation around the deterministic steady state for the model, as proposed by Kydland and Prescott [297]. A third method is to log-linearize the necessary conditions or Euler equations for the dynamic stochastic optimization problem and to use the method of undetermined coefficients to solve for the optimal decision rules directly. This approach derives from the work of Blanchard and Kahn [68], Campbell [89] and others. Uhlig [435] generalizes this methodology and provides a software toolkit for solving a variety of problems. (See Exercise 5.)

12.4.1. *Quadratic approximation*

One approach to solving growth models is to use quadratic approximation around a deterministic steady state. This method has been used because it facilitates the computation of decision rules for models that have multiple choice variables and a high-dimensional state space. According to

[7] See Sims [402].

[8] Nevertheless, multi-sector models may also suffer from some problems because they typically imply that overall expansions in the economy are associated with contractions in one sector. See, for example, Benhabib and Farmer [53].

this method, we replace the non-linear optimization problem described in Section 12.3.1 by a linear-quadratic dynamic optimization problem. The relationship between the solutions of the original non-linear problem and the linear-quadratic problem is generally not established. Although the decision rules or optimal policy functions for the linear-quadratic dynamic optimization problem are also obtained iteratively, the corresponding value function and the optimal policy functions can be expressed as known functions of coefficient matrices that enter the quadratic objective function and the linear laws of motion for the state variables. However, this approach can be implemented in situations where the deterministic steady state can be obtained directly and there are no non-linear constraints such as borrowing constraints or irreversibility.

We now return to the standard business cycle model described in Section 12.3. We assume that capital depreciates at the rate $0 < \delta < 1$ and the technology shock follows the process in Equation (12.10). Since the utility function is strictly increasing, consumption plus investment equals output at the optimum. Using this fact, we can substitute for consumption in the utility function to obtain $u(c_t) = u(\exp(z_t)k_t^{\alpha} h_t^{1-\alpha} - i_t, 1 - h)$. Let $u(c_t, 1 - h_t) = (1 - \theta)\ln(c_t) + \theta \ln(1 - h_t)$, $0 < \theta < 1$. The problem now becomes:

$$\max_{\{i_t, h_t\}_{t=0}^{\infty}} E_0 \left\{ \sum_{t=0}^{\infty} \left[(1 - \theta) \ln(\exp(z_t) k_t^{\alpha} h_t^{1-\alpha} - i_t) + \theta \ln(1 - h_t) \right] \right\}$$

subject to

$$k_{t+1} = (1 - \delta) + i_t, \tag{12.37}$$

$$z_{t+1} = \mu + \rho z_t + \epsilon_{t+1} \tag{12.38}$$

$$c_t \geq 0, \quad 0 \leq h_t \leq 1. \tag{12.39}$$

The quadratic approximation procedure is implemented as follows.

Step 1 Compute the deterministic steady state for the model. This is obtained by setting the exogenous technology shock equal to its mean value and evaluating the conditions (12.18) and (12.19) together with the feasibility conditions at constant values for c_t, k_t, and h_t. Let $\bar{z} = \mu/(1 - \rho)$ denote the unconditional mean for the (log of) technology process. Using Equation (12.19), we can solve for the steady-state capital-labor ratio as:

$$\frac{\bar{k}}{\bar{h}} = \left(\alpha \frac{\exp(\bar{z})}{r + \delta} \right)^{1/(1-\alpha)}. \tag{12.40}$$

Next, note that in the deterministic steady state, investment is equal to depreciation:

$$\bar{i} = \delta \bar{k}. \tag{12.41}$$

Simplifying the result in Equation (12.18), we obtain:

$$\frac{1-\theta}{\theta}\frac{\bar{h}}{1-\bar{h}} = (1-\alpha)\frac{\bar{y}}{\bar{c}}, \tag{12.42}$$

where the aggregate feasibility constraint $\bar{c} + \delta\bar{k} = \bar{y} \equiv \exp \bar{z}\bar{k}^{\alpha}\bar{h}^{1-\alpha}$ is also assumed to hold. To find an explicit expression for $\bar{h}$ in terms of the underlying parameters, use the relation in Equation (12.42) as:

$$(1-\theta)\bar{h}\bar{c} = (1-\alpha)\theta(1-\bar{h})\bar{y}.$$

Re-arranging, substituting for $\bar{c}$ first and then dividing through by $\bar{y}$, we obtain:

$$(1-\theta)\bar{h}\left[1-\delta\frac{\bar{k}}{\bar{y}}\right] + \theta(1-\alpha)\bar{h} = \theta(1-\alpha).$$

Now note that:

$$\frac{\bar{k}}{\bar{y}} = \frac{\bar{k}}{\exp(\bar{z})\bar{k}^{\alpha}\bar{h}^{1-\alpha}} = \frac{(\bar{k}/\bar{h})^{1-\alpha}}{\exp(\bar{z})} = \frac{\alpha}{r+\delta}.$$

Substituting back into the equation defining $\bar{h}$ and simplifying yields:

$$\bar{h}\left[(1-\theta) + \theta(1-\alpha) - (1-\theta)\delta\frac{\alpha}{r+\delta}\right] = \theta(1-\alpha),$$

or

$$\bar{h} = \frac{\theta(1-\alpha)(r+\delta)}{(r+\delta)(1-\theta\alpha) - (1-\theta)\delta\alpha}. \tag{12.43}$$

Step 2 Approximate the original utility function by a quadratic function around the deterministic steady state. For this purpose, let $s \equiv (1, k, z, i, h)$ and $\bar{s} \equiv (0, \bar{z}, \bar{k}, \bar{i}, \bar{h})$. Approximate $u(s)$ near the deterministic steady state $\bar{s}$ using a second-order Taylor series approximation as:

$$u(s) = u(\bar{s}) + (s-\bar{s})'\frac{\partial u(s)}{\partial s} + \frac{1}{2}(s-\bar{s})'\frac{\partial^2 u(s)}{\partial s \partial s'}(s-\bar{s}).$$

Define e as the 5×1 vector with a 1 in the first row and zeros elsewhere. Notice that the utility function can be written as

$$u(s) = (s-\bar{s})'T(s-\bar{s}),$$

where

$$T = e\left[u(\bar{s}) + \frac{1}{2}\bar{s}'\frac{\partial^2 u(s)}{\partial s \partial s'}\bar{s}\right]e' + \frac{1}{2}\left(\frac{\partial u(s)}{\partial s}e' + e\frac{\partial u(s)'}{\partial s}\right) + \frac{1}{2}\left(\frac{\partial^2 u(s)}{\partial s \partial s'}\right),$$

where all partial derivatives are evaluated at $\bar{s}$.

Define the vector of state variables as $x_t = (1, k_t - \bar{k}, z_t - \bar{z})'$ and the vector of control variables as $u_t = (i_t - \bar{i}, h_t - \bar{h})'$. We can write the law of motion for the state variables as:

$$\begin{bmatrix} 1 \\ k_{t+1} \\ z_{t+1} \end{bmatrix} = \begin{bmatrix} 1 & 0 & 0 \\ 0 & (1-\delta) & 0 \\ \mu & 0 & \rho \end{bmatrix} \begin{bmatrix} 1 \\ k_t \\ z_t \end{bmatrix} + \begin{bmatrix} 0 & 0 & 0 \\ 1 & 0 & 0 \\ 0 & 0 & 0 \end{bmatrix} \begin{bmatrix} 0 \\ i_t \\ 0 \end{bmatrix} + \begin{bmatrix} 0 \\ 0 \\ \epsilon_{t+1} \end{bmatrix}.$$

Notice that $s - \bar{s} = (x, u)'$. Thus, the quadratic form $(s - \bar{s})' T (s - \bar{s})$ can be written as

$$\begin{aligned} (s - \bar{s})' T (s - \bar{s}) &= \begin{bmatrix} x \\ u \end{bmatrix}' \begin{bmatrix} T_{11} & T_{12} \\ T_{21} & T_{22} \end{bmatrix} \begin{bmatrix} x \\ u \end{bmatrix} \\ &= \begin{bmatrix} x \\ u \end{bmatrix}' \begin{bmatrix} R & W \\ W' & Q \end{bmatrix} \begin{bmatrix} x \\ u \end{bmatrix}. \end{aligned}$$

Step 3 Convert the original dynamic optimization problem into a problem with linear constraints and a quadratic objective function. Using the definition of T, x_t and u_t, the dynamic optimization problem can now be written as:

$$\max_{\{u_t\}_{t=0}^{\infty}} E_0 \left\{ \sum_{t=0}^{\infty} \beta^t [x_t' R x_t + u_t' Q u_t + 2 x_t' W u_t] \right\} \tag{12.44}$$

subject to the linear law of motion

$$x_{t+1} = A x_t + B u_t + \varepsilon_{t+1}, \quad t \geq 0, \tag{12.45}$$

where $E(\varepsilon_{t+1}) = 0$ and $E(\varepsilon_t \varepsilon_t') = \Sigma$. This is now an optimal control problem with a quadratic objective and linear constraints. Such problems can be solved using the methods for solving dynamic optimization problems that satisfy a certainty equivalence property, namely, that the solution for the stochastic optimal control problem is identical to the solution for the deterministic version of the problem with the shocks ε_{t+1} replaced by their expectation $E(\varepsilon_{t+1})$. This class of problems is known as *optimal linear regulator problems*. Ljungqvist and Sargent [325] and Anderson, Hansen, McGrattan, and Sargent [30] provide further discussion of the formulation and estimation of linear dynamic economic models.

Bellman's equation for this problem is given by:

$$V(x_t) = \max_{u_t} \left\{ x_t' R x_t + u_t' Q u_t + 2 u_t' W x_t + \beta E[V(x_{t+1})] \right\}$$

subject to $x_{t+1} = A x_t + B u_t + \varepsilon_{t+1}$. Given the structure of the problem, notice that the value function will be a quadratic function in the state variables,

$$V(x) = x' P x + d,$$

where d and P are quantities to be determined. Substituting for next period's state variables and using this expression for the value function, Bellman's equation becomes:

$$x'Px + d = \max_u \left\{x'Rx + u'Qu + 2x'Wu \right.$$
$$\left. +\beta E\left[(Ax + Bu + \varepsilon)'P(Ax + Bu + \varepsilon) + d\right]\right\}. \tag{12.46}$$

The first-order conditions with respect to u are:

$$Qu + W'x + \beta[B'PAx + B'PBu] = 0.^{9} \tag{12.47}$$

Solving for u yields:

$$u = -(Q + \beta B'PB)^{-1}(W'x + \beta B'PAx) = -Fx, \tag{12.48}$$

where

$$F = (Q + \beta B'PB)^{-1}(\beta B'PA + W'). \tag{12.49}$$

Notice that the shocks ε_{t+1} do not affect the optimal choice of u_t. Substituting for u back into the definition of $V(x)$ yields

$$P = R + \beta A'PA - (\beta A'PB + W)(Q + \beta B'PB)^{-1}(\beta B'PA + W')$$

$$d = (1 - \beta)^{-1}[\beta E(\varepsilon'P\varepsilon)].$$

The equation for P is known as the *algebraic matrix Riccati* equation for so-called optimal linear regulator problem.[10] The solution for P can be obtained by iterating on the matrix Riccati difference equation:

$$P_{n+1} = R + \beta A'P_nA - (\beta A'P_nB + W)(Q + \beta B'P_nB)^{-1}(\beta B'P_nA + W'),$$

starting from $P_0 = 0$. The policy function associated with P_n is

$$F_{n+1} = (Q + \beta B'P_nB)^{-1}(\beta B'P_nA + W').$$

We now illustrate this solution method for the standard RBC model with a labor-leisure choice presented at the beginning of this section. Consider the parameter values $\beta = 0.95, \alpha = 1/3, \theta = 0.36, \delta = 0.10, \rho = 0.95$ and $\sigma = 0.028$. The steady values for the variables are given by $\bar{k} = 1.1281$,

[9] To derive this result, we have used the rules for differentiating quadratic forms as:

$$\frac{\partial u'Qu}{\partial u} = [Q + Q']u = 2Q_u, \quad \frac{\partial x'Tu}{\partial u} = T'x \text{ and } \frac{\partial u'Tx}{\partial u} = Tx.$$

[10] Notice that the matrices R, Q, A, and B must be further restricted to ensure the existence of a solution to the matrix difference equation defining P_n. One condition that suffices is that the eigenvalues of A are bounded in modulus below unity.

$\bar{i} = 0.1128$, $\bar{y} = 0.4783$, $\bar{c} = 0.3655$, and $\bar{h} = 0.2952$. The values of the R, Q, and W matrices corresponding to these parameter values are:

$$R = \begin{bmatrix} -0.9522 & 0.2784 & 0.4362 \\ 0.2784 & -0.1371 & -0.0430 \\ 0.4362 & -0.0430 & -0.1346 \end{bmatrix},$$

$$Q = \begin{bmatrix} -2.4955 & 2.5880 \\ 2.5880 & -4.1730 \end{bmatrix},$$

$$W = \begin{bmatrix} -1.8241 & 1.7543 \\ 0.3809 & -0.0932 \\ 1.1936 & -0.2919 \end{bmatrix}.$$

The solution for the value function and optimal policy functions is found by iterating on the matrix Riccati equation. The convergence criterion is 10^{-6} and the number of iterations required to get a solution is 640. The solution for the P matrix is given by:

$$P = \begin{bmatrix} -0.5115 & 1.3157 & 5.3900 \\ 1.3157 & -0.5319 & -0.4836 \\ 5.3900 & -0.4836 & 0.8660 \end{bmatrix},$$

and the optimal decision rule $u_t^\star = Fx_t$ by:

$$\begin{bmatrix} i_t^\star \\ h_t^\star \end{bmatrix} = \begin{bmatrix} 0.3681 & -0.0943 & 0.4127 \\ 0.6487 & -0.0808 & 0.1860 \end{bmatrix} \begin{bmatrix} 1 \\ k_t \\ z_t \end{bmatrix}.$$

To derive linear representations for consumption c_t and output y_t, we linearize the production function as:

$$\begin{aligned} y_t &= \bar{y} + a_k(k_t - \bar{k}) + a_h(h_t^\star - \bar{h}) + a_z(z_t - \bar{z}) \\ &= 0.4783 + 0.1526(k_t - \bar{k}) + 1.0371(h_t^\star - \bar{h}) + 0.4783(z_t - \bar{z}). \end{aligned}$$

Then consumption is given by:

$$\begin{aligned} c_t &= y_t - i_t^\star \\ &= 0.4783 + 0.1526(k_t - \bar{k}) + 1.0371(h_t^\star - \bar{h}) + 0.4783(z_t - \bar{z}) - i_t^\star. \end{aligned}$$

Evaluating the expressions for y_t and c_t at the optimal decision rules for $i_t^\star$ and $h_t^\star$ yields the linearized solution for output and consumption.

We first calculate a set of unconditional moments that have been used in the RBC literature to match the model with the data. These are obtained by simulating the behavior of the different series across a given history of

Table 12.1. *Cyclical properties of key variables*

	Standard deviation (in %)	Correlation with output
Output	8.8616	1
Consumption	8.1134	0.9163
Investment	12.9238	0.9807
Hours	1.6684	0.4934
Productivity	7.7496	0.9840

the shock sequence.[11] Specifically, we draw a sequence of shocks $\{\hat{\epsilon}_{t+1}\}_{t=0}^{2999}$ that are normally distributed with mean zero and standard deviation 0.028, and generate a sequence of technology shocks beginning from some initial value z_0 as $\hat{z}_{t+1} = \rho z_t + \hat{\epsilon}_{t+1}$. We then use the linear decision rules for all variables to simulate for the endogenous variables based on the same history of shocks. Finally, following the approach in Danthine, Donaldson, and Mehra [136], we calculate unconditional moments for the different series after dropping the first one thousand observations. The typical set of unconditional moments used in the RBC literature are displayed in Table 12.1. We find consumption varies slightly less than output and investment significantly more. Likewise, productivity is also almost as variable as output. By contrast, we find that the variation in hours is typically quite low. In terms of the correlation of each series with output, we find that all series are procyclical, with hours showing the least procyclicality. Thus, as discussed earlier, the model delivers some of the salient features of the data.

Finally, Figure 12.2 illustrates the response of all the variables to a 1% shock to technology starting from the steady state capital stock. We note that hours and output both increase and then fall back to a lower level. The percentage change in output exceeds the percentage change in the technology shock because optimal hours also shows a positive response to the technology shock. By contrast, capital and consumption show a humped-shaped response, rising first and then declining back to a lower level. Consumption shows a gradual positive response because investment is initially high. These responses have been widely documented in the RBC literature (see, for example, Uhlig [435]).

12.5. BUSINESS CYCLE EMPIRICS

Business cycle models seek to explain the joint covariation of a set of key aggregate variables. In the modern literature, a variety of approaches have been used for empirically analyzing the implications of business models.

[11] See also Danthine, Donaldson, and Mehra [136] for a similar procedure.

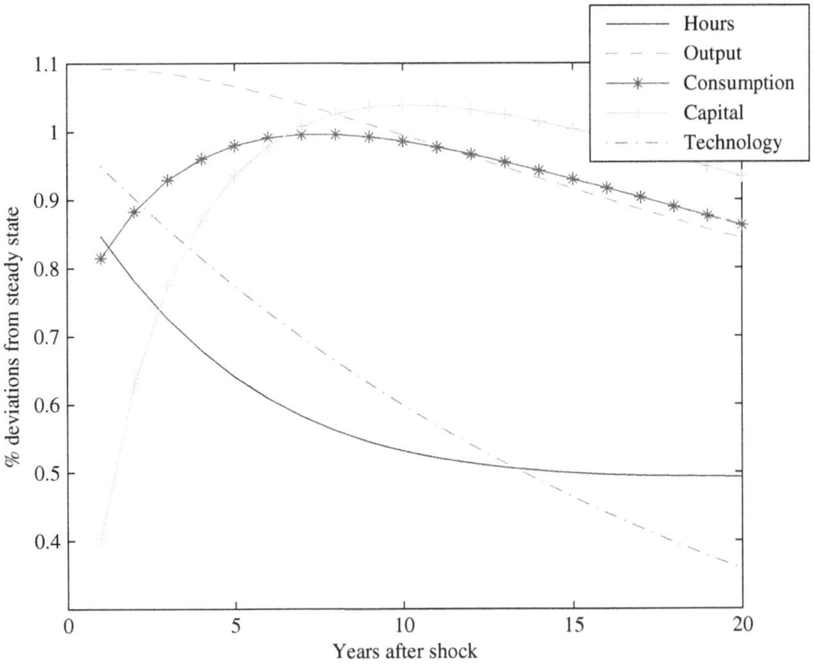

Figure 12.2. Impulse responses to a shock in technology

One approach that has found much favor in the business cycle literature is the method of unobservable index models or dynamic factor analysis due to Geweke [197], Geweke and Singleton [198], and others. Following Sims [403], vector autoregressions (VARs) and structural VARs (SVARs) have also proven to be a favored technique in empirical macroeconomic research. While both models allow for rich dynamic interrelationships among a set of endogenous favorables and an examination of business cycle dynamics based on impulse response functions, structural VARs (SVARs) also permit an identification of shocks. More recently, dynamic stochastic general equilibrium (DSGE) models have been developed for the purpose of identifying shocks and propagation mechanisms of business cycles models. See, for example, Smets and Wouters [408, 409]. Canova [98] is an excellent source on the quantitative and empirical analysis of dynamic stochastic general equilibrium models. In this section, we describe some of the results obtained in the empirical business cycle literature in matching the model with the data using these techniques.

12.5.1. Dynamic factor analysis

Dynamic factor analysis seeks to describe the joint cyclical behavior of a key set of time series in terms of a low-dimensional vector of unobservable factors and a set of idiosyncratic shocks that are mutually uncorrelated and uncorrelated with the factors. To describe how to formulate unobservable index models let $\{\tilde{w}_t\}_{t=0}^{\infty}$ denote an n-dimensional mean zero, covariance stationary stochastic process used to describe observations on the (possibly detrended) values of a set of variables. A k-factor unobservable index model for $\tilde{w}_t$ is given by:

$$\tilde{w}_t = \sum_{s=-\infty}^{\infty} \tilde{H}(s)\tilde{f}_{t-s} + \tilde{v}_t, \tag{12.50}$$

where $\{\tilde{H}(s)\}_{s=-\infty}^{\infty}$ is a sequence of $n \times k$-dimensional matrices, $\tilde{f}_t$ is a $k \times 1$ vector of common factors, and $\tilde{v}_t$ is an $n \times 1$ vector of idiosyncratic shocks that are mutually uncorrelated and uncorrelated with the common factors. More precisely, we require that:

$$E(\tilde{f}_t \tilde{v}_{i,t}) = 0 \quad \text{for } i = 1, \ldots, n \tag{12.51}$$

$$E(\tilde{v}_{i,t} \tilde{v}_{j,t}) = 0 \quad \text{for } i \neq j. \tag{12.52}$$

Both the common factors and the idiosyncratic factors may be serially correlated, that is, $E(\tilde{f}_t \tilde{f}_{t-s}) \neq 0$ for $t \neq s$ and $E(\tilde{v}_{i,t} \tilde{v}_{i,t-s}) \neq 0$ for all i, j and $t \neq s$. According to this model, covariation among the elements of w_t can arise because they are functions of the same common factor or because they are functions of different factors which are themselves correlated at different leads and lags.

Under these assumptions, the variances and autocovariances of the observed series $\{\tilde{w}_t\}$ can be decomposed in terms of the variances and autocovariances of a low-dimensional set of unobserved common factors and the idiosyncratic shocks. Let

$$R_w(r) = E(\tilde{w}_t \tilde{w}_{t+r})', \quad r = \ldots, -1, 0, 1, \ldots$$

be the autocovariance function of $\{w_t\}$. Under the assumptions underlying (12.50),

$$\begin{aligned} R_w(r) &= E\left[\left(\sum_{s=-\infty}^{\infty} \tilde{H}(s)\tilde{f}_{t-s} + \tilde{v}_t\right)\left(\sum_{v=-\infty}^{\infty} \tilde{H}(v)\tilde{f}_{t+r-v} + \tilde{v}_{t+r}\right)'\right] \\ &= E\left[\left(\ldots \tilde{H}(-1)\tilde{f}_{t+1} + \tilde{H}(0)\tilde{f}_t + \tilde{H}(1)\tilde{f}_{t-1} + \ldots\right)\right. \\ &\qquad \left.\left(\ldots \tilde{H}(-1)\tilde{f}_{t+r+1} + \tilde{H}(0)\tilde{f}_{t+r} + \tilde{H}(1)\tilde{f}_{t+r-1} + \ldots\right)'\right] \end{aligned}$$

$$= \sum_{s=-\infty}^{\infty} \tilde{H}(s) \sum_{v=-\infty}^{\infty} E(\tilde{f}_{t-s}\tilde{f}_{t+r-v})\tilde{H}(v)' + E(\tilde{v}_t\tilde{v}_{t+r})$$

$$= \sum_{s=-\infty}^{\infty} \tilde{H}(s) \sum_{v=-\infty}^{\infty} R_f(r+s-v)\tilde{H}(v)' + R_v(r)$$

An alternative representation of the autocovariance function is provided by the spectral density function:

$$S_w(\omega) = \sum_{r=-\infty}^{\infty} R_w(r)e^{-ir\omega}, \quad |\omega| \leq \pi.^{12} \tag{12.53}$$

Assuming that $S_w(\omega)$ is non-singular at each frequency ω, notice that the off-diagonal elements of $S_w(\omega)$ are, in general, complex numbers. However, since $R_{x_l x_h}(r) = R_{x_l x_h}(-r)$, the diagonal elements of $S_w(\omega)$ are real. Substituting for $R_w(r)$ into (12.53) yields:

$$S_w(\omega) = \sum_{r=-\infty}^{\infty} \sum_{s=-\infty}^{\infty} \tilde{H}(s) \sum_{v=-\infty}^{\infty} R_f(r+s-v)(\tilde{H})(v)' \exp(-i\omega r)$$

$$+ \sum_{r=-\infty}^{\infty} R_v(r) \exp(-i\omega r)$$

$$= \sum_{s=-\infty}^{\infty} \tilde{H}(s) \exp(-i\omega s) \sum_{u=-\infty}^{\infty} R_w(u) \exp(-i\omega u)\times$$

$$\sum_{z=-\infty}^{\infty} \tilde{H}(z)' \exp(-i\omega z) + S_v(\omega)$$

$$= \tilde{H}(\omega)S_w(\omega)\tilde{H}(\omega)' + S_v(\omega),$$

where $\tilde{H}(\omega)$ denotes the Fourier transform of $\tilde{H}(s)$. Hence, the dynamic factor model provides decomposition at each frequency that is analogous to the decomposition of variance in the conventional factor model. The dynamic factor model can be estimated and its restrictions tested across alternative frequencies using a frequency domain approach to time series analysis. The unrestricted version of the dynamic factor model does not place restrictions on the matrices $\tilde{H}(s)$, which describe how the common factors affect the behavior of the elements of w_t at all leads and lags. Nor is it possible to identify the common factors with different types of shocks to the economy.

The use of the dynamic factor model in business cycle analysis dates to the work of Sargent and Sims [385]. As these authors observe, dynamic

[12] This function is well defined as long as $\sum_{r=-\infty}^{\infty} R^2_{x_l x_h}(r) < \infty$ for each $l, h = 1, \ldots, n$.

factor analysis may be linked to the notion of a "reference cycle" underlying the methodology of Burns and Mitchell [83] and the empirical business cycle literature they conducted at the National Bureau of Economic Research. Another well-known application of this approach is due to Altug [16], who derives an unobservable index model for a key set of aggregate series by augmenting the approximate linear decision rules for a modified version of the Kydland and Prescott [297] model with i.i.d. error terms. Altug also uses this representation to estimate the model using maximum likelihood (ML) estimation in the frequency domain. The restricted factor model makes use of the cross-equation restrictions across the linear decision rules implied by the original model. The common factor is identified as the innovation to the technology shock and the idiosyncratic shocks are interpreted as i.i.d. measurement errors or idiosyncratic components not captured by the underlying real business cycle model. Unlike the unrestricted factor model which can be estimated frequency by frequency, this model must be estimated jointly across all frequencies because the underlying economic model constrains the dynamic behavior of the different series as well as specifying the nature of the unobserved factor.[13] Altug [16] initially estimates an unrestricted dynamic factor model for the level of per capita hours and the differences of per capita values of durable goods consumption, investment in equipment, investment in structures, and aggregate output. She finds that the hypothesis of a single unobservable factor cannot be rejected at conventional significance levels for describing the joint time-series behavior of the variables. However, when the restrictions of the underlying model are imposed, the model cannot explain the cyclical variation in per capita hours worked.

Watson [443] extends the approach in Altug [16] to show how to derive measures of fit for an underlying economic model which depends on a low-dimensional vector of shocks by adding errors to the stochastic process generated by a theoretical model. Forni and Reichlin [189] use the dynamic factor model to describe business cycle dynamics for large cross sections. They examine the behavior of four-digit industrial output and productivity for the US economy for the period 1958 to 1986 and find evidence in favor of least two economy-wide shocks, both having a long-run effect on sectoral output. However, their results also indicate that sector-specific shocks are needed to explain the variance of the series. Giannone, Reichlin and Sala [201] show how more general classes of equilibrium business cycle models can be cast in terms of the dynamic factor representation. They also describe how to derive impulse response function for time series models which have reduced rank, that is, ones for which the number of exogenous shocks is less than the number of series.

[13] For further discussion of maximum likelihood estimation in the frequency domain, see Hansen and Sargent [235].

12.5.2. ML and GMM estimation approaches

Other papers have employed non-linear estimation and inference techniques to match equilibrium business models with the data. Christiano and Eichenbaum [104] consider the hours-productivity puzzle and use the Generalized Method of Moments approach (see Hansen [229]) to match a selected set of *unconditional* first and second moments implied by their model. Their approach may be viewed as an extension of the standard RBC approach which assesses the adequacy of the model based on the behavior of the relative variability and comovement of a small set of time series. Christiano and Eichenbaum [104] generate the negative correlation between hours worked and real wages or productivity by introducing government consumption shocks. These lead to shifts in the labor supply curve so that even in the absence of technology shocks, hours of work can increase along a downward-sloping labor demand curve. The key assumption in their model is that private and government consumption are not perfect substitutes. Hence, an increase in government consumption leads to a negative wealth effect for consumers through the economy-wide resource constraint. If leisure is a normal good, we observe increases in hours and a decline in average productivity in response to a positive government consumption shock.

Christiano and Eichenbaum [104] consider a proto-typical RBC model with a labor-leisure choice, and utilize the solution of the social planner's problem to derive the competitive equilibrium allocations. Let $\bar{N}$ denote the time endowment of the representative household per period. The social planner ranks alternative consumption-leisure streams according to

$$E_0\left\{\sum_{t=0}^{\infty}\beta^t[\ln(c_t)+\gamma V(\bar{N}-n_t)]\right\}, \tag{12.54}$$

where c_t denote consumption and $\bar{N}-n_t$ denotes leisure of the representative household. Consumption services c_t are related to private and public consumption as follows:

$$c_t = c_t^p + \alpha g_t, \tag{12.55}$$

where c_t^p is private consumption, g_t is public consumption, and α is a parameter that governs the impact of government consumption on the marginal utility of private consumption. They consider two different specifications for the labor/leisure choice, one which is based on a time-separable logarithmic specification with preferences and a second which incorporates the Hansen indivisible labor assumption, namely,

$$V(\bar{N}-n_t) = \left\{\begin{array}{c}\ln(\bar{N}-n_t)\\ \bar{N}-n_t\end{array}\right. \tag{12.56}$$

for all t. Per capita output is produced according to the Cobb-Douglas production function:

$$y_t = (z_t n_t)^{1-\theta} k_t^{\theta}, \quad 0 < \theta < 1, \tag{12.57}$$

where z_t is a technology shock which evolves according to the process

$$z_t = z_{t-1} \exp(\lambda_t). \tag{12.58}$$

In this expression, λ_t is an independent and identically distributed process with mean λ and standard deviation σ_λ. The aggregate resource constraint stipulates that consumption plus investment cannot exceed output in each period:

$$c_t^p + g_t + k_{t+1} - (1-\delta)k_t \leq y_t. \tag{12.59}$$

Following Exercise 1, notice that the technology shock follows a logarithmic random walk. Hence, the solution for the social planner's problem can be more fruitfully expressed in terms of the transformed variables $\bar{k}_{t+1} = k_{t+1}/z_t$, $\bar{y}_t = y_t/z_t$, $\bar{c}_t = c_t/z_t$ and $\bar{g}_t = g_t/z_t$. The specification of the model is completed by assuming a stochastic law of motion for $\bar{g}_t$ as:

$$\ln(\bar{g}_t) = (1-\rho)\ln(\bar{g}) + \rho \ln(\bar{g}_{t-1}) + \mu_t, \tag{12.60}$$

where $\ln(\bar{g})$ is the mean of $\ln(\bar{g}_t)$, $|\rho| < 1$, and μ_t is the innovation to $\ln(\bar{g}_t)$ with standard deviation σ_μ.

Christiano and Eichenbaum derive a solution for the social planner's problem by following the approach that we described in Section 12.4.2, namely, by implementing a quadratic approximation to the original non-linear problem around the deterministic steady states. Since there is a stochastic trend in this economy arising from the nature of technology shock process, the deterministic steady states are derived for the transformed variables. Their estimation strategy is based on a subset of the first and second moments implied by their model. To describe how their approach is implemented, let Ψ_1 denote a vector of parameters determining preferences, technology, and the exogenous stochastic processes. Some of the parameters included in Ψ_1 may be the depreciation rate of capital δ and the share of capital in the neoclassical production function θ. More generally, $\Psi_1 = (\delta, \theta, \gamma, \rho, \bar{g}, \sigma_\mu, \lambda, \sigma_\lambda)'$. As in the standard RBC approach, the parameters in Ψ_1 are estimated using simple first-moment restrictions implied by the model. For example, the depreciation rate δ is set to reproduce the average depreciation on capital as:

$$E\left\{\delta - \left[1 - \frac{i_t}{k_t} - \frac{k_{t+1}}{k_t}\right]\right\} = 0,$$

given data on gross investment i_t and the capital stock k_{t+1}. Likewise, the share of capital satisfies the Euler equation:

$$E\left\{\beta\left[\theta\left(\frac{y_{t+1}}{k_{t+1}}\right)+1-\delta\right]\frac{c_t}{c_{t+1}}-1\right\}=0.$$

(See, for example, Equation (10.24) in Chapter 10.) Proceeding in this way, the elements of Ψ_1 satisfy the unconditional moment restrictions:

$$E\left[H_{1t}(\Psi_1)\right]=0. \tag{12.61}$$

The elements of Ψ_2 consist of the standard RBC second moment restrictions as:

$$E\left[y_t^2(\sigma_x/\sigma_y)^2-x_t^2\right]=0,\quad x=c_t,i_t,g_t, \tag{12.62}$$

$$E\left[n_t^2-\sigma_n^2\right]=0, \tag{12.63}$$

$$E\left\{(y/n)_t^2\left(\sigma_n/\sigma_{y/n}\right)^2-n_t^2\right\}=0, \tag{12.64}$$

$$E\left\{\left[\sigma_n^2/(\sigma_n/\sigma_{y/n})\right]corr(y/n,n)-(y/n)_t n_t\right\}=0, \tag{12.65}$$

where c_t denotes private consumption, g_t public consumption, n_t labor hours and $(y/n)_t$ the average productivity of labor. The unconditional second moments are obtained through simulating the model's solution based on the linear decision rules obtained from the approximate social planner's problem. The restrictions of the model can be summarized as:

$$E\left[H_{2t}(\Psi_2)\right]=0. \tag{12.66}$$

Christiano and Eichenbaum [104] are interested in testing restrictions for the correlation between hours and productivity $corr(y/n,n)$ and the relative variability of hours versus average productivity $\sigma_n/\sigma_{y/n}$. To do this, they use a Wald-type test based on the orthogonality conditions implied by the relevant unconditional moments which we now describe. For any parameter vector Ψ_1 let

$$f(\Psi_1)=[f_1(\Psi_1),f_2(\Psi_1)]' \tag{12.67}$$

represent the model's restrictions for $corr(y/n,n)$ and $\sigma_n/\sigma_{y/n}$. Let $\Psi=[\Psi_1,\Psi_2]'$ denote the $k\times 1$ vector containing the true values of the parameters and second moments for the model. Also let A be a $2\times k$ matrix of zeros and ones such that

$$A\Psi=[corr(y/n,n),\sigma_n/\sigma_{y/n}]', \tag{12.68}$$

and

$$F(\Psi)=f(\Psi_1)-A\Psi. \tag{12.69}$$

Under the null hypothesis that the model is correctly specified,

$$F(\Psi) = 0. \tag{12.70}$$

In practice there is sampling error in estimating Ψ from a finite data set containing T observations. Letting $\hat{\Psi}_T$ denote the estimated value of Ψ, the test statistic for the second moment restrictions is based on the distribution of $F(\hat{\Psi}_T)$ under the null hypothesis. Using this distribution, they show that the statistic

$$J = F(\hat{\Psi}_T)' Var[F(\hat{\Psi}_T)]^{-1} F(\hat{\Psi}_T) \tag{12.71}$$

is asymptotically distributed as a χ^2 random variable with 2 degrees of freedom. Using data on private consumption, government expenditures, investment, aggregate hours, and average productivity, Christiano and Eichenbaum estimate the parameters of the model using GMM and examine the various unconditional second moments implied by the model. Their results indicate an inability to reject the unconditional moment restrictions of the model with government consumption which also incorporates the indivisible labor assumption.

McGrattan, Rogerson, and Wright [337] implement ML (maximum likelihood) estimation of an equilibrium business cycle model with household production and distortionary taxation. They employ a time-domain approach and provide tests of the role of the household production as well as policy experiments regarding the role of tax changes. McGrattan *et al.* employ a quadratic approximation around a non-stochastic steady state to obtain a linear-quadratic dynamic optimization problem. In their application, competitive equilibria do not solve a social planning problem. Hence, they use the linear Euler equations to solve for the time paths of the variables of interest directly. These authors use a state space representation for their model with a law of motion and measurement equation and apply a Kalman filter algorithm to form the likelihood function. Their measurement equation corresponds to the optimal decision rule augmented with idiosyncratic measurement error shocks as in Altug [16]. They use detrended values of the variables and examine the behavior of their model through unconditional moments that are similar to those reported in calibration-type exercises and the implied impulse response functions. On the whole, they find that home production (as argued above) improves the model's fit and generates different predictions for the effects of tax changes than the model without home production.

12.5.3. A New Keynesian critique

The behavior of hours and productivity has continued to remain a point of controversy. The RBC conclusions regarding the response of hours, output, and other variables to a technology shock have been questioned by empirical results obtained along several different lines. On the one hand, Gali [195] has argued that in a suitably restricted vector-autoregression including measures of hours, productivity, output, and other variables, the response of hours to productivity shocks is negative. This is in contrast to the RBC model, which predicts that hours rise on impact to a positive technology. Proceeding in a different manner, Basu, Fernald, and Kimball [49] also present evidence that hours worked and other variables fall in response to technology improvements in the short-run. Their approach involves purging the standard Solow residual of factors that might lead to procyclicality such as variable factor utilization. (See our discussion in Section 12.3.) We first describe a simple New Keynesian framework that can be used to rationalize the observations, then discuss the empirical findings in more detail.

Consider a simple New Keynesian model with monopolistic competition, price rigidities, and variable labor effort due to Gali [195]. Suppose that a representative household chooses consumption C_t, money holdings M_t, hours worked H_t, and effort levels U_t to maximize

$$E_0\left\{\sum_{t=0}^{\infty}\beta^t\left[\ln(C_t)+\lambda_m\ln\left(\frac{M_t}{P_t}\right)-H(N_t,U_t)\right]\right\} \tag{12.72}$$

subject to

$$\int_0^1 P_{it}C_{it}+M_t=W_tN_t+V_tU_t+\Upsilon_t+\Pi_t, \tag{12.73}$$

for $t=0,1,2,\ldots$. In this expression, C_t is a composite consumption good defined as:

$$C_t=\left(\int_0^1 C_{it}^{(\epsilon-1)/\epsilon}di\right)^{\epsilon/(\epsilon-1)} \tag{12.74}$$

where C_{it} is the quantity of good $i\in[0,1]$ consumed in period t, and $\epsilon>1$ is the elasticity of consumption among consumption goods. The price of good i is given by P_{it}, and

$$P_t=\left(\int_0^1 P_{it}^{1-\epsilon}di\right)^{1/(1-\epsilon)} \tag{12.75}$$

is the aggregate price index. The functional form for $H(N_t,U_t)$ is given by:

$$H(N_t,U_t)=\frac{\lambda_n}{1+\sigma_n}N_t^{1+\sigma_n}+\frac{\lambda_u}{1+\sigma_u}U_t^{1+\sigma_u}. \tag{12.76}$$

Υ_t and Π_t denote monetary transfers and profits, W_t and V_t denote the nominal prices of an hour of work and effort, respectively.

The first-order conditions with respect to the household's problem are given by:

$$\mu_t P_{it} = \frac{1}{C_t}\left(\int_0^1 C_{it}^{(\epsilon-1)/\epsilon} di\right)^{1/(\epsilon-1)} C_{it}^{-1/\epsilon}, \quad i \in [0,1], \tag{12.77}$$

$$\lambda_m \frac{1}{M_t} = \mu_t + \beta E_t(\mu_{t+1}), \tag{12.78}$$

$$\lambda_n N_t^{\sigma_n} = \mu_t W_t, \tag{12.79}$$

$$\lambda_u U_t^{\sigma_u} = \mu_t V_t, \tag{12.80}$$

where μ_t denotes the Lagrange multiplier on the period-by-period budget constraint. We can solve for μ_t from the first-order conditions corresponding to the consumption choice as $\mu_t = 1/(P_t C_t)$. Substituting for this variable and simplifying yields:

$$C_{it} = \left(\frac{P_{it}}{P_t}\right)^{-\epsilon} C_t, \quad i \in [0,1], \tag{12.81}$$

$$\frac{1}{C_t} = \lambda_m \frac{P_t}{M_t} + \beta E_t\left(\frac{1}{C_{t+1}}\frac{P_t}{P_{t+1}}\right), \tag{12.82}$$

$$\lambda_n N_t^{\sigma_n} C_t = \frac{W_t}{P_t}, \tag{12.83}$$

$$\lambda_u U_t^{\sigma_u} C_t = \frac{V_t}{P_t}. \tag{12.84}$$

In this economy, good i is produced by firm i using the production function

$$Y_{it} = Z_t L_{it}^{\alpha}, \tag{12.85}$$

where L_{it} is the quantity of effective labor used by firm i:

$$L_{it} = N_{it}^{\theta} U_{it}^{1-\theta}, \quad 0, \theta < 1. \tag{12.86}$$

Z_t is an aggregate technology shock whose growth rate follows an i.i.d. process $\{\eta_t\}$ with $\eta_t \sim N(0, \sigma_\eta^2)$:

$$Z_t = Z_{t-1} \exp(\eta_t). \tag{12.87}$$

Consider first the choice of optimal inputs of hours and effort chosen by the firm to minimize its costs subject to the production technology. Let λ

be the Lagrange multiplier on the technology constraint. The first-order conditions are given by:

$$W_t = \lambda Z_t \theta \alpha N_{it}^{\theta\alpha - 1} U_{it}^{(1-\theta)\alpha} \tag{12.88}$$

$$V_t = \lambda Z_t (1 - \theta) \alpha N_{it}^{\theta\alpha} U_{it}^{(1-\theta)\alpha - 1}. \tag{12.89}$$

Taking the ratio of these conditions yields:

$$\frac{\theta}{1-\theta} \frac{U_{it}}{N_{it}} = \frac{W_t}{V_t}. \tag{12.90}$$

Notice that the firm will be willing to accommodate any changes in demand at the given price P_{it} as long as this price is above marginal cost. Hence, the firm chooses the output level

$$Y_{it} = \left(\frac{P_{it}}{P_t}\right)^{-\epsilon} C_t. \tag{12.91}$$

Thus, when choosing price the firm will solve the problem:

$$\max_{P_{it}} E_{t-1} \{(1/C_t)(P_{it} Y_{it} - W_t N_{it} - V_t U_{it})\} \tag{12.92}$$

subject to (12.90) and (12.91). To find the first-order condition for this problem, we will use the last two constraints to solve for the firm's cost function as:

$$\begin{aligned} W_t N_{it} + V_t U_{it} &= W_t N_{it} + \frac{1-\theta}{\theta} \frac{W_t}{V_t} V_t N_{it} \\ &= \frac{W_t N_{it}}{\theta} = \frac{W_t Y_{it}^{1/\alpha}}{\theta Z_t^{1/\alpha} ((1-\theta) W_t / \theta V_t)^{1-\theta}} \\ &= \frac{W_t (P_{it}/P_t)^{-\epsilon/\alpha} C_t^{1/\alpha}}{\theta Z_t^{1/\alpha} ((1-\theta) W_t / \theta V_t)^{1-\theta}} \end{aligned}$$

Using this result, the first-order condition is:

$$E_{t-1} \left\{ (1/C_t) \left(\alpha\theta P_{it} Y_{it} - \frac{\epsilon}{\epsilon - 1} W_t N_{it} \right) \right\} = 0. \tag{12.93}$$

Finally, the quantity of money is determined as:

$$M_t^s = M_{t-1}^s \exp(\xi_t + \gamma \eta_t), \tag{12.94}$$

where $\{\xi_t\}$ is a white noise that is orthogonal to $\{\eta_t\}$, with $\xi_t \sim N(0, \sigma_m^2)$.

In a *symmetric equilibrium*, all firms charge the same price P_t and choose the same levels of the inputs and output N_t, U_t, and Y_t. Market clearing in the goods market requires that $C_t = C_{it} = Y_{it} = Y_t$, Finally, equilibrium in the money market requires that the growth rate of the money stock evolve exogenously as $M_t/M_{t-1} = \exp(\xi_t + \gamma\eta_t)$.

Next, guess that consumption is proportional to real balances in equilibrium, $C_t = M_t/P_t$. This together with market-clearing conditions implies that $P_t Y_t = M_t$. Using the first-order condition for consumption in (12.81) and the money growth rule in (12.94) yields:

$$\begin{aligned} C_t &= \lambda_m^{-1}\frac{M_t}{P_t}\left[1 - \beta E_t\left(\frac{P_t}{P_{t+1}}\frac{Y_t}{Y_{t+1}}\right)\right] \\ &= \lambda_m^{-1}\frac{M_t}{P_t}\left[1 - \beta\exp(\sigma_m^2 + \gamma^2\sigma_\eta^2)/2\right], \\ &= \Phi\frac{M_t}{P_t}, \end{aligned} \tag{12.95}$$

where $\Phi = \lambda_m^{-1}\left[1 - \beta\exp(\sigma_m^2 + \gamma^2\sigma_\eta^2)/2\right]$. Next use (12.83–12.84) and (12.90). Taking the ratio of the first two conditions yields:

$$\frac{W_t}{V_t} = \frac{\lambda_n}{\lambda_u}\frac{N_t^{\sigma_n}}{U_t^{\sigma_u}}.$$

Equating this with (12.90) yields:

$$\frac{U_t}{N_t} = \frac{1-\theta}{\theta}\frac{\lambda_n}{\lambda_u}\frac{N_t^{\sigma_n}}{U_t^{\sigma_u}}.$$

Solving for U_t yields:

$$U_t = A^{1/\alpha(1-\theta)} N_t^{(1+\sigma_n)/(1+\sigma_u)}, \tag{12.96}$$

where $A = ((1-\theta)/\theta(\lambda_n/\lambda_u))^{\alpha(1-\theta)/(1+\sigma_u)}$. Substituting this result into the expression for the production function yields:

$$Y_t = AZ_t N_t^{\varphi}, \tag{12.97}$$

where $\varphi = \alpha\theta + (1+\sigma_n)\alpha(1-\theta)/(1+\sigma_u)$. Using the price-setting rule in (12.93) together with (12.83) and the expression for equilibrium consumption and output derived above, we can show that:

$$\Delta p_t = \xi_{t-1} - (1-\gamma)\eta_{t-1} \tag{12.98}$$

$$\Delta y_t = \Delta\xi_t + \gamma\eta_t + (1-\gamma)\eta_{t-1} \tag{12.99}$$

$$n_t = \frac{1}{\varphi}\xi_t - \frac{1-\gamma}{\varphi}\eta_t \tag{12.100}$$

$$\Delta x_t = \left(1 - \frac{1}{\varphi}\right)\Delta\xi_t + \left(\frac{1-\gamma}{\varphi} + \gamma\right)\eta_t$$
$$+ (1-\gamma)\left(\frac{1-\gamma}{\varphi} + \gamma\right)\eta_{t-1}, \qquad (12.101)$$

where $x = y - n$ is the log of labor productivity.

The conditions in (12.98–12.101) can be used to describe the impact of monetary versus technology shocks. A positive *monetary shock* defined by $\xi_t > 0$ has a temporary impact on output, employment and productivity. This can be observed by noting that the levels of y_t, n_t, and x_t depend only on the current ξ_t. Hence, an increase in ξ_t causes output and employment to go up for one period and then to revert to their initial values. The impact of ξ_t on labor productivity is also transitory but the sign depends on whether $\varphi < (>) 1$. We note that measured labor productivity responds positively whenever $\varphi > 1$, which corresponds to the situation of short-run increasing returns to labor. Finally, the price level responds one-for-one to an increase in ξ_t, though with a one-period lag.

A positive *technology shock* defined by $\eta_t > 0$ has a permanent positive one-for-one impact on output and productivity and a permanent negative impact on the price level if $\gamma < 1$. More interestingly, a positive technology shock has a *negative* short-run impact on employment. This result can be best understood by considering the case of $\gamma = 0$, that is, when there is no accommodating response in the money supply to real shocks. In that case, given a constant money supply and predetermined prices, real balances remain unchanged in the face of a positive technology shock. Hence, demand remains unchanged so that firms will be able to meet demand by producing an unchanged level of output. However, with a positive shock to technology, producing the same output will require less labor input, and hence a decline in employment will occur.

Gali [195] estimates a structural VAR and identifies technology shocks as the only shocks that are allowed to have a permanent effect on average labor productivity. This is similar to the approach in Blanchard and Quah [69] for identifying demand versus supply shocks using long-run restrictions on estimated VARs. The structural VAR model interprets the behavior of (log) hours n_t and (log) productivity x_t in terms of two types of exogenous disturbances – technology and non-technology shocks – which are orthogonal to each other and whose impact is propagated through time through some unspecified mechanisms as:

$$\begin{bmatrix} \Delta x_t \\ \Delta n_t \end{bmatrix} = \begin{bmatrix} C^{11}(L) & C^{12}(L) \\ C^{21}(L) & C^{22}(L) \end{bmatrix} \begin{bmatrix} \epsilon_t^z \\ \epsilon_t^m \end{bmatrix} = C(L)\epsilon_t,$$

where ϵ_t^z and ϵ_t^m denote, respectively, the sequences of technology and non-technology shocks. The orthogonality assumption together with a normalization implies that $E(\epsilon_t \epsilon_t') = I$. The identifying assumption is that only technology shocks have a permanent effect on productivity, which can be expressed as the restriction $C^{12}(1) = 0$.[14] Gali [195] estimates this model using postwar US data. Surprisingly, he finds that alternative measures of labor input *decline* in response to a positive technology shock while GDP adjusts only gradually to its long-run level. Furthermore, technology shocks explain only a small fraction of employment and output fluctuations. By contrast, Gali [195] finds that variables that have no permanent effects on employment (and which are referred to as demand shocks) explain a substantial fraction of the variation in both employment and output. By contrast, Christiano, Eichenbaum, and Vigfusson [106] suggest that the standard RBC results hold if per capita hours are measured in log-levels as opposed to differences.

Basu, Fernald, and Kimball [49] present evidence that support the SVAR findings by generating a modified Solow residual that accounts for imperfect competition, non-constant returns to scale, variable factor utilization and sectoral re-allocation and aggregation effects. Unlike the SVAR approach, the evidence obtained from this approach is robust to long-run identifying assumptions or to the inclusion of new variables in the estimated dynamic system. They find that purging the standard Solow residual of these effects in ways that we outlined in Section 12.3 eliminates the phenomenon of "procyclical productivity." They also examine the response of a key set of variables such as output, hours worked, utilization, employment, non-residential investment, durables and residential investment, non-durables and services, and various prices and interest rates to changes in the purified Solow residual. They use both standard regression analysis and simple bivariate VARs for this purpose. Their findings corroborate the findings from the SVAR approach regarding the negative response of hours to technology improvements in the short-run. They also uncover further evidence for the negative response of non-residential investment to such shocks. Following Gali [195] and Gali and Rabanal [196], they advance price rigidity as the major reason for these deviations from the RBC predictions in the short-run. These findings have, on the one hand, generated substantial controversy and on the other, cast further doubt on the ability of the RBC model driven by technology shocks to provide a convincing explanation of economic fluctuations for the major developed countries.

12.6. CONCLUSIONS

This chapter has provided a brief overview of some models and methods in modern business cycle analysis. The scope of the business cycle literature

[14] The value of the matrix $C(L)$ evaluated at $L = 1$ gives the long-run multipliers for the model, in other words, the long-run impact of a given shock.

precludes a full discussion of many key issues in modeling and empirically analyzing business cycles. In the next two sections, we introduce monetary models and models with market incompleteness which have further implications for quantities and prices in clearly specified general equilibrium frameworks. In particular, models with individual heterogeneity constitute an important area of future work. Likewise, much new work in business cycle analysis has adopted an open-economy or international perspective. We also discuss this class of models in later chapters. Nevertheless, the tools that we have introduced up to this point can be fruitfully employed in developing further models for the analysis of economy-wide dynamics.

12.7. EXERCISES

1. Consider an economy where the representative consumer has preferences over stochastic consumption c_t and hours worked h_t given by:

$$E_0\left\{\sum_{t=0}^{\infty}\beta^t[\exp(u_t)\ln(c_t)-\gamma h_t]\right\},\quad \gamma>0,$$

where $\{u_t\}_{t=0}^{\infty}$ is a mean zero i.i.d. preference shock with variance σ_u^2 and E_0 is expectation conditional on information available at time 0.

Output in this economy is produced according to the production function:

$$f(\theta_t,h_t,k_t)=(\theta_t h_t)^{1-\alpha}k_t^{\alpha},\quad 0<\alpha<1,$$

where k_t is the per capita capital stock and θ_t is a technology shock that follows a logarithmic random walk, $\theta_{t+1}=\theta_t\exp(\epsilon_{t+1})$, where $\{\epsilon_t\}_{t=0}^{\infty}$ is a mean zero i.i.d. innovation to technology with variance σ_ϵ^2. We assume that $\{u_t\}_{t=0}^{\infty}$ and $\{\epsilon_t\}_{t=0}^{\infty}$ are mutually uncorrelated.

The capital stock evolves as $k_{t+1}=(1-\delta)k_t+i_t$, where $0<\delta<1$ is the depreciation rate and i_t is investment.

Define the following transformed variables:

$$k_t^\star\equiv\ln(k_t/\theta_t),\quad i_t^\star\equiv\ln(i_t/\theta_t)$$

$$c_t^\star\equiv\ln(c_t/\theta_t),\quad h_t^\star\equiv\ln(h_t).$$

(a) Show that utility in each period can be written as:

$$U\equiv\exp(u_t)c_t^\star+\ln(\theta_t)\exp(u_t)-\gamma\exp(h_t^\star),$$

and the feasibility constraint as:

$$\exp(c_t^\star)+\exp(\epsilon_{t+1})\exp(k_{t+1}^\star)-(1-\delta)\exp(k_t^\star)$$
$$\leq\exp(h_t^\star)^{1-\alpha}\exp(k_t^\star)^{\alpha}.$$

(b) Formulate the social planner's problem for this economy in terms of the transformed variables and show that this problem has a stationary solution.

2. Long-Plosser Real Business Cycle Model

Think of a model economy, populated by single infinite-lived individual, Robinson Crusoe. At the beginning of each period, he chooses the level of consumption, c_{1t}, c_{2t}, the amount of leisure time to be consumed for production of goods 1 and 2 during the period, l_{1t}, l_{2t}, and the capital and labor inputs, k_{it}, n_{it} for $i = 1, 2$. Crusoe's objective is to maximize expected lifetime utility:

$$U \equiv \sum_{t=0}^{\infty} \beta^t u(c_{1t}, c_{2t}, l_t), \quad 0 < \beta < 1,$$

subject to the budget constraint:

$$c_{jt} + \sum_{i=1}^{2} k_{ijt} \leq y_{jt}, \quad j = 1, 2,$$

where k_{ijt} denotes the quantity of commodity j allocated to the production of commodity i, and the time constraint:

$$n_{1t} + n_{2t} + l_t = 1$$

The production function exhibits constant returns to scale, given by:

$$y_{i,t+1} = f(n_{1t}, k_{1t}, n_{2t}, k_{2t}; \lambda_{1,t+1}, \lambda_{2,t+1}), \quad i = 1, 2$$

where λ_t is a shock to production which follows a first-order Markov process. The utility and production functions are given by:

$$u(c_{1t}, c_{2t}, l_t) = \theta_1 \ln(c_{1t}) + \theta_2 \ln(c_{2t}) + \theta_3 \ln(l_t)$$

$$y_{i,t+1} = \lambda_{i,t+1} n_{it}^{\alpha_i} k_{i1t}^{\alpha_{i1}} k_{i2t}^{\alpha_{i2}}$$

where $\alpha_i + \alpha_{i1} + \alpha_{i2} = 1$. Both commodities are assumed to be perishable, that is, the depreciation rate is 100%.

(a) Write down Crusoe's problem in a dynamic programming approach, define the state variables and choice variables of the problem explicitly.
(b) Find the first-order conditions and the envelope condition of the problem.
(c) Using a guess-and-verify technique, find the coefficients of the value function.
(d) Solve for equilibrium allocations ($c_{jt}, l_t, n_{jt}, k_{ijt}$ for $i, j = 1, 2$) and equilibrium prices, particularly, price of the consumption good (p_t), wage-rate (ω_t), and one-period interest rate (r_t).

3. Using Uhlig's Toolkit

   Go to http://www2.wiwi.hu-berlin.de/institute/wpol/html/toolkit.htm and download Uhlig's software toolkit for solving dynamic stochastic models.

   Generate a numerical solution for the Hansen model with indivisible labor.

4. Spectra for Stationary Time Series Models

   Consider the following time series models:

$$y_t = a_0 + a_1 y_{t-1} + \epsilon_t, \quad |a_1| < 1, \tag{12.102}$$

$$z_t = b_0 + \epsilon_t + b_1 \epsilon_{t-1}, \tag{12.103}$$

$$w_t = a_0 + a_1 w_{t-1} b_0 + \epsilon_t + b_1 \epsilon_{t-1}, \quad |a_1| < 1. \tag{12.104}$$

   (a) Find the autocovariance function for each of these processes.
   (b) Find and plot the spectrum for each of these processes given the values $a_1 = 0.9$, $b_0 = 1$, and $b_1 = 2$.
   (c) The *coherence* of two series is given by:

$$C_{yz}(\omega) = \sum_{r=-\infty}^{\infty} R_{yz}(r) e^{-ir\omega},$$

   where $R_{yz}(r)$, $r = \ldots, -1, 0, 1, \ldots$ is the cross-covariogram between $\{y_t\}$ and $\{z_t\}$. Find the coherence for each pair of processes given in part (a) and plot them.
   (d) How can these measures be useful for understanding the sources of cyclical fluctuations?

PART III

Monetary and international models

CHAPTER 13

Models with cash-in-advance constraints

The effects of money and nominal variables on the real economy have been studied extensively. The apparent lack of consensus on how money and monetary policy impact the economy reflects the difficulty of the questions that are raised when money is introduced into a model of the economy. A standard introductory discussion of the role of money highlights its importance as a store of value, medium of exchange, and unit of account. In a model of complete Arrow-Debreu contingent claims, there is no role for money because all transactions in the form of trades of physical goods and dated goods can be carried out in the contingent claims market. Indeed all trades can take place at time zero, before any uncertainty is resolved, or sequentially over time, resulting in identical allocations. Since all trading is centralized, there are no problems with a double coincidence of wants or need for a durable asset. Money is a redundant asset and its introduction leaves allocations unaffected.

One approach to incorporating money is to assume that money must be used to carry out transactions. The cash-in-advance model is an example of this sort of model. As we will show below, this model is equivalent to imposing a borrowing constraint on agents: consumption can be carried out only with current wealth and there is no borrowing against future income. But, just as *ad hoc* models of borrowing constraints have been criticized for lacking sound microeconomic foundations, the cash-in-advance model is appropriately criticized for its lack of microeconomic foundations; see Wallace [442] for example. Other models, such as overlapping generations models (see Wallace [440]) or the Townsend turnpike model (see Townsend [431]), are structured so there are trading frictions. Trade is not centralized in that all agents are not present in the same market at the same date. Hence there is a role for money, or some durable and divisible asset, that allows for trade within a period and over time. These models have yielded interesting theoretical insights into the role of money, but have proven to be difficult to implement empirically. A promising line of research is the search models of money pioneered by Kiyotaki and Wright [279]. In this class of models, trade is decentralized and agents are matched bilaterally and randomly. Without money, trade occurs only if there is a double coincidence of wants. The introduction of money, under some circumstances, facilitates trade and production. Models of this type focus on the micro foundations of money and derive an explicit and essential role for money within the model. The difficulty with many models of money built with explicit microeconomic foundations is the paucity of empirical implications, at least at this date; see Kocherlakota [280] for a discussion. We will describe some of the fundamental issues in this debate, but ultimately will discuss several versions of cash-in-advance models because they are, to date, more useful for discussing policy and deriving empirical implications.

A traditional view of money is that it is a mechanism that eliminates difficulties of a double coincidence of wants. Typically this is thought of in terms of physical goods: barter is possible if there is a double coincidence of wants but impossible if there is not. In such a setting, a divisible, durable, and recognizable asset such as money that can serve as a medium of exchange creates opportunities for trade. Search models of money, such as Kiyotaki and Wright [279], are built on the property of money as a medium of exchange. While these models are interesting, we will broaden our focus to a lack of double coincidence of wants in **dated goods**, and follow the simple example in Kiyotaki and Moore [278], for reasons that are provided below.

13.1. "EVIL IS THE ROOT OF ALL MONEY"

The title of this section is from the paper by Kiyotaki and Moore [278]. They focus on the role of *limited commitment* instead of physical trading frictions. Limited commitment enters in two ways. First, a debtor may not be able to borrow fully against future income. There may be limits because of moral hazard, for example. Let θ_1 denote the upper bound on the fraction of future income that a borrower can credibly commit to repay. Second, there may be a limit on the negotiability of a privately issued bond or paper. If an agent lends to another by purchasing a bond, or an IOU, that bond may or may not be resalable. If the bond is resalable, or liquid, then the bond issuer has made a *multilateral* commitment to repay the ultimate bond holder. If the bond is not negotiable, then the borrower has made a *bilateral* commitment to repay only the original purchaser of the bond. Let θ_2 indicate the negotiability of the paper: if $\theta_2 = 0$ then the paper is non-negotiable and cannot be resold and, if $\theta_2 = 1$ then the paper is fully negotiable and the bond-issuer has made a multilateral commitment to repay.

Kiyotaki and Moore [278] describe the following model to illustrate the roles of limited commitment and negotiability. This is a three-period model. There are three types of agents, with a large number of each type.

- Type I agents want to consume in period 1 but are endowed with period 3 goods.
- Type II agents want to consume in period 2 but are endowed with period 1 goods.
- Type III agents want to consume in period 3 but are endowed with period 2 goods.

If $\theta_1 = 1$, then each type of agent can fully commit to repay a loan and we see that, at date 1, all trades can be executed and the first-best outcome can be achieved: Type j consumes all endowment in period j, regardless of the timing of his endowment. Notice that the value of θ_2 is irrelevant in this case. Specifically, a type I borrows from a type II in the first period, while the type II borrows from a type III in the second period, and in the final period the type I pays back type II and type II pays type III. Since borrowing and lending are arranged bilaterally, the negotiability of the paper is irrelevant.

Now suppose that $\theta_1 = 0$ for the type III agents, so a type III agent always defaults, but $\theta_1 = 1$ for type I and type II agents. Suppose also that $\theta_2 = 1$ for type I agents. When markets open in the first period, type I agents can issue paper, which is a form of borrowing, that will be purchased by type II agents in exchange for goods. Type II agents hold the paper until the next period and then sell it to the type III agents in exchange for their period 3 endowment. Type III agents hold the paper originally issued by type I and, in the third period, receive the payment on the bond from type I agents. In this case, the negotiability of type I's bond issue allows the first-best allocation to be achieved, even though type III agents always default and, hence, do not issue any paper.

Continue to assume that $\theta_1 = 0$ for a type III agent and $\theta_1 = 1$ for types I and II, but now suppose that $\theta_2 = 0$ for the type I agent. Then the system reverts to autarky and there is no trading. The reason is that there will be no trade between type II and type III agents and subsequently no trade among any agents. For convenience, they assume that agents receive a small benefit from consuming their own endowment and gift giving is not allowed. Notice that when type I's paper is negotiable, so $\theta_2 = 1$, type II agents purchase the paper for the purpose of selling it before the maturity date. The bond issue of the type I agent acts like inside money and provides liquidity. The ability of the type I agent to make a multilateral commitment can mitigate problems of distrust in other agents.

Notice that fiat money will not be able to substitute for inside money. Suppose that type I agents are endowed with money in the first period. Then they can buy the consumption good from type II agents using the money. Type II agents will accept the money in exchange for goods only if they believe that type III agents will accept the money. If type III agents will accept it, then in period 2, type II agents buy the consumption good from type III agents in exchange for the fiat money. Type III agents then use the money to purchase goods from type I agents, assuming that type I agents will accept it. But type I agents have no use for money in the third period since there are no more future periods. Hence, in a finite horizon model, it is not clear that fiat money will solve the liquidity problems unless there is trust that money will always be accepted in trade.

We can use this approach – the lack of double coincidence in wants of dated goods – to re-examine the overlapping generations model and the Townsend turnpike models. In the overlapping generations model, we have a lack of the double coincidence of wants in dated goods. There is limited commitment in that an old agent today cannot credibly commit to repay a current young agent next period. Moreover, any paper issued by the old agent has no resale value. In the absence of a clearing house, or fiat money, all transactions are bilateral commitments and none of them is credible. Hence, with $\theta_1 = 0$ for all agents, the only outcome is the autarky equilibrium. In a finite horizon overlapping generations model, fiat currency can't overcome the trading friction. Turn now to the Townsend turnpike model, and assume that $\theta_1 > 0$. The key property on whether private IOUs will circulate is the negotiability of the notes. If $\theta_2 = 1$, then the private notes can circulate, acting like money. If θ_1 or θ_2 equal 0, then there is a role for fiat money. We discuss the overlapping generations and Townsend turnpike models in more detail in later chapters.

We will now turn to the basic cash-in-advance model, despite the shortcomings described below. There are several reasons for this: first we can show that this type of model is equivalent to a borrowing constraint model, or in the notation above, a model with $\theta_1 = 0$. Second, our focus is on the empirical implications of inflation on asset pricing, so we require a fully specified model from which empirical implications can be derived. The cash-in-advance model, which can be modified in many ways, can yield rich empirical implications.

The cash-in-advance model has been used to study the relationship among velocity, nominal interest rates, and output by Lucas [318, 319, 321], Svensson [427], and Lucas and Stokey [323], among others. We study some of these models in a later part of this chapter. From an asset-pricing point of view, the cash-in-advance model allows us to price assets denominated in nominal terms and to define such concepts as the inflation premium in asset returns and inflation risk.

13.2. THE BASIC CASH-IN-ADVANCE MODEL

We begin by describing versions of cash-in-advance models. The basic model is the asset-pricing model described in Chapter 8 except that a constraint – the cash-in-advance constraint – is imposed that motivates the use of money.

We begin by describing a version of the cash-in-advance model that incorporates the timing of trades and information in Lucas [319]. There are two key features of the Lucas model: first, that all households observe realizations of endowment and money growth at the beginning of the period before any decisions are made; and second, that the asset market opens before the goods market.

The representative household has preferences over random sequences of the single consumption good given by:

$$E_0 \left\{ \sum_{t=0}^{\infty} \beta^t U(c_t) \right\} \tag{13.1}$$

where $0 < \beta < 1$ is the discount factor. This is a pure endowment economy.

To start, we assume that households hold nominal wealth in the form of currency and government-issued, one-period discount bonds. All consumption purchases must be made with fiat currency brought into the goods market. The cash-in-advance constraint is:

$$p_t c_t \leq M_t^d, \tag{13.2}$$

where p_t is the current price level, c_t consumption and M_t^d is the nominal currency the agent holds when entering the goods market. The key feature is that agents don't consume their own endowment. An agent's endowment is sold in the goods market for nominal value $p_t y_t$ and the nominal receipts are unavailable for spending until the following period. At the end of period $t-1$, an agent is holding the value of nominal receipts $p_{t-1}y_{t-1}$ plus the value of any unspent nominal balances from the goods market in period $t-1$, equal to:

$$M_{t-1}^d - p_{t-1}c_{t-1}.$$

At the beginning of period t, the agent observes the realization of any exogenous shocks (to be specified below), receives the payment on the nominal bond purchased last period B_{t-1}, and receives a lump-sum monetary transfer G_t. The asset market opens before the goods market. The nominal wealth that the agent brings into the asset market is:

$$H_t \equiv B_{t-1} + G_t + p_{t-1}y_{t-1} + [M_{t-1}^d - p_{t-1}c_{t-1}].$$

The asset market constraint is:

$$M_t^d + Q_t B_t \leq H_t. \tag{13.3}$$

Money required to make desired purchases of consumption goods in the goods market must be held at the close of the asset market.

To demonstrate that this cash-in-advance model is equivalent to a strict form of a borrowing constraint model, solve (13.3) for M_t^d and substitute into (13.2), and re-write

$$H_t - Q_t B_t \geq p_t c_t. \tag{13.4}$$

By assumption, $B_t \geq 0$ and if we let $B_t = 0$, notice that the left side is nominal wealth at the beginning of period t. The cash-in-advance constraint states that all consumption purchases must be financed with nominal wealth accumulated by the beginning of period t. Agents are unable to borrow against current and future income and must provide for consumption by saving. In this sense, the cash-in-advance model is a strict form of a borrowing constraint model, albeit the constraint is ad hoc because the reason agents cannot borrow against future income is not made explicit. As in the first section, we can argue that moral hazard creates difficulties so that agents are unable to commit credibly to repay any loan.

We now move to the more general formulation of the model, which introduces equities. Adding this feature will allow us to discuss the impact of inflation on stock market returns. We now assume that agents can hold equity shares in addition to government issued bonds. We assume that there is a stochastic process s, with properties specified below, and the endowment is a function $y : S \to Y$ where $Y = [\underline{y}, \bar{y}]$. Agents own equity shares of the endowment, which are claims to streams of the endowment over time. There is one outstanding equity share. An agent holds equity z_{t-1} entering period t and the nominal price of an equity is Q_t^e. The constraint that applies in the asset market with the addition of the equity is:

$$M_t^d + Q_t^e z_t + Q_t B_t \leq H_t + Q_t^e z_{t-1}, \tag{13.5}$$

where H_t denotes post transfer money balances held at the beginning of the period after payments on one-period bonds have been made:

$$H_t \equiv p_{t-1} y_{t-1} z_{t-1} + B_{t-1} + M_{t-1}^d - p_{t-1} c_{t-1} + G_t.$$

Notice that an equity share purchased in the current period is a claim to the nominal dividend stream, $p_t y_t$, paid at the end of period t so these funds are unavailable for spending in the current period.

Let s_t denote the vector of exogenous shocks to this economy. The consumer observes the current shock before the asset market opens and knows all past values of output and money supply. Since the consumer knows s_t, y_{t-1} and M_{t-1}, he also knows current output and the current money stock. Figure 13.1 shows the timing of trades in the basic cash-in-advance model.

To complete our discussion, we need to describe the stochastic environment. The vector of exogenous shocks $s \in S \subset \Re^m$ follows a first-order Markov process with a stationary transition function $F : S \times S \to [0, 1]$ such that $F(s, s') \equiv \Pr(s_{t+1} \leq s' \mid s_t = s)$. The transition function F satisfies the following assumption.

Assumption 13.1 *The transition function F has the Feller property so that for any bounded, continuous function $h : S \to \Re$, the function*

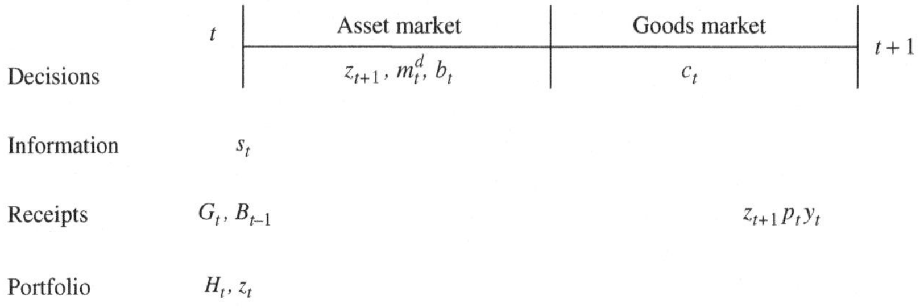

Figure 13.1. Timing of trades in the Lucas model

$Th(s) = \int_S h(s')F(s, ds')$ is continuous. The process defined by F has a stationary distribution Φ.

Notice this is the same assumption we made in Chapter 8. The endowment y_t is exogenous and stationary in levels. Later we discuss some of the issues that arise when endowment and money are growing. The endowment evolves as:

$$y_t = y(s_t). \tag{13.6}$$

The government's budget constraint is described next. The government's outstanding nominal liabilities at the beginning of the period are:

$$B_{t-1} + M_{t-1}.$$

We assume that the government raises funds by issuing new bonds, lump sum transfers (or taxes) and issuing new money. The constraint is:

$$B_{t-1} - Q_tB_t = M_t - M_{t-1} - G_t. \tag{13.7}$$

If the government issues no bonds, so $B = 0$, then money is injected entirely through lump-sum transfers. If we specify a money growth rule $M_t = \omega_t M_{t-1}$, and assume no bonds are issued, then $G_t = [\omega_t - 1]M_{t-1}$. When bonds are issued, money is injected into the economy in two ways: as a lump-sum stochastic transfer or by open market operations. If $G_t = 0$, then any changes in the outstanding money supply occur through open-market operation – the buying and selling of government debt by the central bank. The bond price will be determined in the bond market and B_{t-1}, M_{t-1} are predetermined variables. Hence if we choose a monetary policy

$$M_t^s = \omega(s_t)M_{t-1}^s, \tag{13.8}$$

and a bond supply function $B(s, M)$, then the function G is determined through the budget constraint. Alternatively, we can pick the functions G, ω and then use the constraint and market-clearing conditions to determine the bond supply function.

We begin by formulating the household's problem as a dynamic programming problem. Since the money supply is growing, the household's nominal money holdings are growing in equilibrium. Since there are no natural bounds on the money growth or its level, it will be helpful to transform some of the nominal variables into real variables. We do this by dividing the (nominal) constraints by the current price level. Define $m_t^d \equiv M_t^d/p_t$, $q_t^e \equiv Q_t^e/p_t$, and $h_t \equiv H_t/p_t$.[1] The real constraint in the asset market is:

$$m_t^d + q_t^e z_t + \frac{Q_t B_t}{p_t} \leq h_t + q_t^e z_{t-1}, \tag{13.9}$$

where

$$h_t \equiv \frac{1}{p_t}[p_{t-1}y_{t-1}z_{t-1} + B_{t-1} + p_{t-1}(m_{t-1}^d - c_{t-1}) + G_t].$$

The cash-in-advance constraint is:

$$c_t \leq m_t^d. \tag{13.10}$$

The household takes as given the nominal price of consumption goods and the nominal prices of equities and bonds, which are all assumed to be continuous, strictly positive functions of the current shocks.

The state variables for the consumer's problem consist of the current exogenous state s, and the current holdings of equities z and current real holdings of money h. Given the price functions p, Q^e, and Q, the consumer's value function is defined by:

$$V(s,z,h) = \max_{\{c,m^d,z',B'\}} \left\{ U(c) + \beta \int_S V(s',z',h')F(s,ds') \right\},$$

subject to the constraints in Equations (13.9) and (13.10).

Definition 13.1 *A recursive competitive equilibrium is defined as a set of continuous, strictly positive price functions* $p : S \times \Re_{++} \to \Re_{++}$, $q^e : S \to \Re_{++}$, $Q : S \to \Re_{++}$, *and a value function* $V : S \times Z \times \mathcal{H} \to \Re_+$ *such that (i) given* $p(s,M)$, $q^e(s)$, *and* $Q(s)$, $V(s,z,h)$ *solves the consumer's problem; (ii) markets clear:* $z=1$, $M^d = M$, $B^d = B^s$, $y=c$.

[1] For this transformation of variables to be useful, it requires that all the information be revealed at the beginning of the period. If all information is not revealed so that the price level is unknown until the actual goods market opens, then all nominal variables can be divided by the money stock. We discuss this later in the chapter.

Let $\mu(s)$ denote the multiplier on the cash-in-advance constraint and $\xi(s)$ denote the multiplier on the asset market constraint. The first-order conditions with respect to c, m^d, z', and B' are:

$$U'(c) = \mu(s) + \beta E_s\left[V_h(s', z', h')\frac{p(s, M)}{p(s', M')}\right], \tag{13.11}$$

$$\xi(s) = \mu(s) + \beta E_s\left[V_h(s', z', h',)\frac{p(s, M)}{p(s', M')}\right], \tag{13.12}$$

$$\xi(s)q^e(s) = \beta E_s\left[V_h(s', z', h')\frac{p(s, M)y}{p(s', M')} + V_z(s', z', h')\right], \tag{13.13}$$

$$\xi(s)\frac{Q(s)}{p(s, M)} = \beta E_s\left[V_h(s', z', h')\frac{1}{p(s', M')}\right], \tag{13.14}$$

where $E_s(\cdot) \equiv E(\cdot|s)$. The envelope conditions are:

$$V_h(s, z, h) = \xi(s), \tag{13.15}$$

$$V_z(s, z, h) = \xi(s)q^e(s). \tag{13.16}$$

Incorporate the market clearing conditions and use the envelope conditions to eliminate V_h, V_z. Notice that the first two conditions do not involve the equity or bond price functions. We can solve first for the consumption price function and then solve for the asset prices. Divide both sides of (13.11) by $p(s, M)$ and substitute the envelope condition for V_h. Observe that (13.11) and (13.12) can be rewritten as:

$$\frac{U'(y(s))}{p(s, M)} = \frac{\mu(s)}{p(s, M)} + \beta E_s\left[\frac{U'(y(s'))}{p(s', M')}\right]. \tag{13.17}$$

If $\mu > 0$, then the cash-in-advance constraint is binding and

$$p(s, M) = \frac{M}{y(s)}. \tag{13.18}$$

If $\mu = 0$, then p satisfies:

$$\frac{1}{p(s, M)} = \beta E_s\left[\frac{U'(y(s'))}{U'(y(s))p(s', M')}\right] \tag{13.19}$$

Given a price function, define the function $K(s)$ as the solution to

$$p(s, M)y(s) = \frac{M}{K(s)} \Rightarrow \frac{M}{p(s, M)} = K(s)y(s),$$

where $K(s)$ is the inverse of velocity.

If $\mu > 0$, then $K(s) = 1$, while, if $\mu > 0$, then

$$\frac{1}{p(s,M)} = \frac{K(s)y(s)}{M} = \beta E_s \left[\frac{U'(y(s'))}{U'(y(s))p(s',M')} \right],$$

which can be rewritten as:

$$K(s) = \beta E_s \left[\frac{U'(y(s'))K(s')y(s')M}{U'(y(s))y(s)M'} \right]$$

$$= \beta E_s \left[\frac{U'(y(s'))K(s')y(s')}{U'(y(s))y(s)\omega(s')} \right] > 1.$$

It follows that:

$$K(s) = \max \left[1, \beta E_s \left(\frac{U'(y(s'))K(s')y(s')}{U'(y(s))y(s)\omega(s')} \right) \right]. \tag{13.20}$$

This is a functional equation in the unknown function K. We will discuss the solution of the model, in particular how to solve for the function K later.

Turn now to the first-order condition for the nominal bond (13.14). This equation can be written as:

$$\frac{U'(y(s))Q(s)}{p(s,M)} = \beta E_s \left[U'(y(s')) \frac{1}{p(s',M')} \right]. \tag{13.21}$$

Using the expression for the price function

$$K(s)Q(s) = \beta E_s \left[\frac{U'(y(s'))}{U'(y(s))} \frac{y(s')}{y(s)} \frac{1}{\omega(s')} K(s') \right].$$

We have derived a key property of the standard cash-in-advance model, namely, the close relationship between the binding cash-in-advance constraint and positive nominal interest rates. Notice that if $K(s) = 1$, then $Q(s) < 1$ so that nominal interest rates are positive (recall that Q is the inverse of the nominal interest). If $K(s) > 1$, then $Q(s) = 1$ and nominal rates are equal to zero. The model predicts that if nominal interest rates are positive, then velocity is constant. Velocity varies only if the nominal rate is zero, which is not supported in the data.

The final equation is the first-order condition for the equity price (13.13). This equation can be rewritten as:

$$q^e(s) = \beta E_s \left\{ \frac{U'(y(s'))}{U'(y(s))} \left[\frac{p(s,M)y}{p(s',M')} + q^e(s') \right] \right\} \tag{13.22}$$

and substituting for the price function

$$q^e(s) = \beta E_s \left\{ \frac{U'(y(s'))}{U'(y(s))} \left[\frac{y(s')K(s')}{\omega(s')y(s)K(s)} + q^e(s') \right] \right\}. \tag{13.23}$$

This is a linear functional equation in the unknown function q^e. It can be solved recursively forward. Notice that the inflation tax, in the form of a depreciation of the real value of nominal money balances held between periods, falls on the equity holders when the cash-in-advance constraint is binding. If this constraint is not binding, then the inflation tax falls also on the holder of the unspent nominal balances.

13.2.1. Solution for velocity

We now discuss a contraction mapping argument that can be used to find the solution to the functional equation (13.20) in the unknown function K. We follow Giovannini and Labadie [206].

Define the function

$$\Upsilon(s', s) \equiv \frac{U'(y(s'))}{U'(y(s))} \frac{y(s')}{y(s)} \frac{1}{\omega(s')}.$$

Also define $\mathcal{C}(S)$ as the space of continuous and bounded functions defined on S. The functional equation we are solving is:

$$K(s) = \max\left[1, \beta E_s \Upsilon(s', s) K(s')\right] \tag{13.24}$$

Let $K^{\circ} \in \mathcal{C}(S)$. Define the operator T by:

$$(TK^{\circ})(s) = \max\left[1, \beta E_s \Upsilon(s', s) K^{\circ}(s')\right] \tag{13.25}$$

We now have the following theorem.

Theorem 13.3 *Under Assumption 13.1, there exists exactly one continuous and bounded function K that solves Equation (13.25).*

PROOF

We first show that $T : \mathcal{C}(S) \to \mathcal{C}(S)$. Next, we show that T^n is a contraction. Hence we can conclude that there exists exactly one solution to Equation (13.25).

Under Assumption 13.1, the expectation operator maps continuous, bounded functions into continuous, bounded functions. Under Assumption 13.5 if K° is in the space of bounded, continuous functions, then so is $\beta E_s\left[\Upsilon(s', s) K^{\circ}(s')\right]$. If $f \in \mathcal{C}(S)$, then $\max[1, f(s)]$ is also because the max operator is linear and bounded and, because a linear operator is bounded if and only if it is continuous, it is also continuous. Hence T takes continuous, bounded functions into continuous, bounded functions.

The next step is to verify Blackwell's conditions for a contraction. For any $h, g \in \mathcal{C}(S)$ such that $h(s) > g(s)$ for all $s \in S$, $Th(s) \geq Tg(s)$. Hence, T

is monotone. To determine if T has the discounting property, notice that applying T to an arbitrary function in $C(S)$ will discount because

$$T(g+a)(s) = \max\left[1, \beta \int_S \Upsilon(s', s)(g(s') + a)F(s, ds')\right]$$

$$\leq \max\left[1, \beta \int_S \Upsilon(s', s)g(s')F(s, ds')\right] + \max\left[1, \int_S \Upsilon(s', s)aF(s, ds')\right],$$

where we are using the conditional expectation. Under our assumptions, $\Upsilon(s', s)$ is a stationary process so that there is some $j < \infty$ such that $\beta E_t[\Upsilon(s_{t+j}, s_{t+j-1})] < 1$. Define $N(s_t)$ such that

$$\beta^{N(s_t)} E_t \left(\prod_{i=1}^{N(s_t)} \Upsilon(s_{t+j}, s_{t+j-1}) \right) < 1.$$

Let N denote the maximum over the $N(s_t)$ or $N = \max_{s \in S} N(s)$. Start with an initial guess $\Psi^0 \in C(S)$ and define:

$$\Psi^1(s_t) = (T\Psi^0)(s_t)$$
$$= \max\{1, \beta E_t [\Upsilon(s_{t+1}, s_t)\Psi^0(s_{t+1})]\}.$$

When T is applied M times,

$$T^M \Psi^0(s) = \max\left\{1, \beta E_s \left[\Upsilon(s', s)\Psi^{M-1}(s')\right]\right\}.$$

To determine if T^M has the discounting property, define:

$$T^M(\Psi^0 + a)(s_t) = T^{M-1} \max(1, \beta E_t \{\Upsilon(s_{t+1}, s_t)[\Psi^0(s_{t+1}) + a]\})$$
$$\leq T^{M-1} \max\{1, \beta E_t [\Upsilon(s_{t+1}, s_t)\Psi^0(s_{t+1})]\}$$
$$+ a\beta^M E_t \prod_{i=1}^{M} \Upsilon(s_{t+i}, s_{t+i-1}).$$

If $M > N$, then

$$\beta^M E_t \left(\prod_{i=1}^{M} \Upsilon(s_{t+i}, s_{t+i-1}) \right) a = \delta a$$

where $0 < \delta < 1$. Hence, T^M has the discounting property and is monotone so that T^M is a contraction mapping. By the N-Stage Contraction Mapping Theorem, if T^M is a contraction for some positive integer M, then T has a unique fixed point in $C(S)$, which can be found by the method of successive approximation. ∎

13.2.2. Empirical results

The links among velocity, money growth, output growth, the nominal interest rate, and inflation for the basic cash-in-advance model are studied empirically by Hodrick, Kocherlakota, and Lucas [252] and Giovannini and Labadie [206]. These authors solve explicitly for the equilibrium pricing function and for velocity, and match up the theoretical moments implied by their model with the moments in the data. Since the basic cash-in-advance model implies that velocity is constant when nominal interest rates are positive, the first set of authors consider variations on the basic model due to Svensson [427, 426] and Lucas and Stokey [323] that break the close link between velocity and nominal interest rates.[2] In Svensson's framework, cash balances are chosen before the quantity of output is known. Therefore, agents may choose to carry unspent cash balances across periods, and velocity can in principle vary. In Lucas and Stokey's cash-credit model, only some goods are required to be purchased with currency while other goods can be purchased with credit. Hence, velocity can vary when interest rates are positive. Using quarterly data on consumption and money growth, Hodrick *et al.* estimate a VAR (vector autoregression) and approximate each VAR by a Markov chain using the quadrature method in Tauchen [428] that we described in Chapter 6. They conduct a calibration exercise similar to Mehra and Prescott [341], and examine the unconditional moments of the coefficient of variation of velocity and the correlations of velocity with money growth, output growth, and the interest rate. They also examine the means and standard deviations of real and nominal interest rates, inflation and real balance growth, and the correlations of inflation with money growth, consumption growth, and the nominal interest rate. They find that the cash-in-advance constraint almost always binds and that velocity is constant for the basic cash-in-advance model. They also find that the model is unable to match the sample moments of other endogenous variables for parameter values that result in reasonable values for the variability of velocity. Giovannini and Labadie [206] conduct a complementary study, and consider the basic Lucas model described above and the Svensson model. They focus on a set of unconditional and conditional moments for inflation, velocity, real stock returns, and real interest rates. Consistent with the predictions of the model, they find that the liquidity constraint is binding more frequently in the Lucas model than in the Svensson model. They also examine the relationship between inflation and real stock returns and the behavior of the equity premium, issues which we discuss below.

[2] See Exercises 2 and 7.

13.2.3. Inflation risk and the inflation premium

We now describe the implications of this framework for asset price behavior, including equity prices and the price of real and nominal risk-free assets. Unlike the real models considered earlier, we can use this framework to describe the effects of changes in the nominal price level on equilibrium rates of return for assets that have nominal payoffs.

Returning to Equation (13.23) and reverting to time subscripts, we can derive an expression for the price-dividend ratio as:

$$q_t^e = E_t\left[\sum_{i=1}^{\infty} \beta^i \frac{U'(y_{t+i})y_{t+i}}{U'(y_t)y_t} \frac{K_{t+i}^{\star}}{K_t^{\star}\omega_{t,i}}\right], \tag{13.26}$$

where

$$\omega_{t,i} \equiv \prod_{j=1}^{i} \omega_{t+j}$$

is the sequence of money growth rates between periods $t+1$ and $t+i$. The price-dividend ratio is a claim to the purchasing power of a unit of currency at the end of the period, where the purchasing power of money is defined as the inverse of the price level. Since there is money growth, the purchasing power of money falls by $\omega_{t,i}^{-1}$ between periods t and $t+i$. Unlike the real models of Chapters 8–11, the stochastic discount factor is the ratio of the marginal utility of the purchasing power of money $U'(y(s))/p(s,M)$ at adjacent periods or the *nominal MRS*. The stochastic discount factor converts \$1.00 received tomorrow into utility units today. Specifically, $\beta U'(y(s'))/p(s',M')$ measures the utility value of \$1.00 held one period hence while $U'(y(s))/p(s,M)$ measures the utility value of \$1.00 held today; their ratio measures the intertemporal tradeoff.

The equilibrium price of a one-period nominal bond that pays one unit of currency at the beginning of the next period can be determined from Equations (13.14) and (13.15) as:

$$Q_t = \beta E_t\left[\frac{U'(y_{t+1})p_t}{U'(y_t)p_{t+1}}\right]. \tag{13.27}$$

As we can see, the price of a one-period nominal bond is just equal to the stochastic discount factor. The expected real return to a one-period nominal bond is:

$$E_t(1+r_t^1) = (1+R_t^1)E_t\left(\frac{p_t}{p_{t+1}}\right). \tag{13.28}$$

This is a version of the *Fisher equation*, which divides the nominal interest rate into the expected real interest rate plus the expected rate of inflation.

We can derive similar expressions for the expected real return on all assets denominated in nominal terms, including the nominal equity return.

When agents are risk averse, there is also a risk premium included in the Fisher equation. To derive the inflation risk premium, we consider assets that have real payoffs indexed by inflation. The price of an inflation-indexed bond maturing in one period is given by:

$$q_t = \beta E_t \left[\frac{U'(y_{t+1})}{U'(y_t)} \right]. \tag{13.29}$$

The return to a one-period indexed bond is defined as $(1 + r_t^f) \equiv 1/q_t^1$. The difference between the nominal bond and the inflation-indexed bond is that the stochastic discount factor for the latter is the intertemporal MRS in consumption goods.

We define the *inflation risk premium* as the difference between the expected real return to a one-period nominal bond and the return to a one-period indexed bond, $E(r_t^1) - r_t^f$. Now the nominal interest rate satisfies the relation:

$$1 + R_t^1 = \left\{ \beta E_t \left[\frac{U'(y_{t+1}) p_t}{U'(y_t) p_{t+1}} \right] \right\}^{-1}. \tag{13.30}$$

Using a covariance decomposition, the term in braces can be written as:

$$\beta \mathrm{Cov}_t \left[\frac{U'(y_{t+1})}{U'(y_t)}, \frac{p_t}{p_{t+1}} \right] + \frac{1}{1 + r_t^f} E_t \left[\frac{p_t}{p_{t+1}} \right].$$

The conditional covariance measures the covariation between the intertemporal MRS in consumption with the expected deflation. If we substitute the above expression into Equation (13.28), notice that if the conditional covariance above equals zero, then the expected real return to the nominal bond equals the real interest rate. In this case, we say that the inflation risk premium is zero.

To determine the effects of stochastic inflation on the equity price and the equity premium, notice that we can rewrite Equation (13.22) as:

$$1 = \beta E_t \left[\frac{U'(y_{t+1})}{U'(y_t)} \left(\frac{p_t y_t}{p_{t+1}} + \frac{Q_{t+1}^e}{p_{t+1}} \right) / \frac{Q_t^e}{p_t} \right]$$

$$1 = \beta E_t \left[\frac{U'(y_{t+1})}{U'(y_t)} (1 + r_{t+1}^e) \right],$$

where r_{t+1}^e is the (net) real equity return. The equity premium is defined as the difference between the expected real equity return and the return on a one-period inflation-indexed bond, $E_t(r_{t+1}^e) - r_t^f$. Stochastic inflation affects the real equity premium because dividends are paid in nominal terms. Thus, changes in the nominal price level or, equivalently, changes in the purchasing power of money affect the equity return through current dividends as well as through the future equity price, which depends on the whole future path of nominal price level changes. A second way that stochastic inflation can affect the measured equity premium is that in practice, the real equity premium must be computed as the difference between the expected real equity return and the expected real return on a one-period nominal bond, $E_t(r^e_{t+1}) - E_t(r^1_t)$. As long as $E_t(r^1_t)$ differs from r^f_t due to the inflation risk premium, there arises a second channel by which stochastic inflation affects the equity premium.

Labadie [299] and Giovannini and Labadie [206] study these effects empirically to determine whether they can account for the "equity premium puzzle." The latter authors find that one of the most important predictions of the model is the very high covariation between *ex ante* returns on stocks and nominal bonds, this feature arising from the fact that both returns are driven by the behavior of their common factor, the reciprocal of the marginal rate of substitution in wealth. They also find that stock returns are only occasionally negatively related to inflation, in contrast to the data, and that *ex ante* real interest rates are uncorrelated with expected inflation.

The prices of a variety of other assets can also be determined, assuming that these assets are in zero net supply. Assuming that there is an active secondary market, the price today of a nominal bond paying one unit of currency at time $t + \tau$ is:

$$Q^\tau_t = \beta E_t \left[\frac{U'(y_{t+1}) p_t}{U'(y_t) p_{t+1}} Q^{\tau-1}_{t+1} \right].$$

By repeated substitution for the bond price, notice that this is equivalent to:

$$Q^\tau_t = \beta^\tau E_t \left[\frac{U'(y_{t+\tau}) p_t}{U'(y_t) p_{t+\tau}} \right]. \tag{13.31}$$

Hence, the price of a nominal bond that pays one unit of currency at time $t + \tau$ is just the expected marginal rate of substitution in the purchasing power of money between periods t and $t + \tau$. The return to holding a bond maturing in τ periods for n periods and selling it in the secondary market is defined as $Q^{\tau-1}_{t+1}/Q^\tau_t$. The expected *real* return to a nominal bond maturing in τ periods is defined as:

$$E_t(1 + r^\tau_t) = E_t \left[\frac{Q^{\tau-1}_{t+1}}{Q^\tau_t} \frac{p_t}{p_{t+1}} \right]. \tag{13.32}$$

The expected *real* holding risk premium, defined as the difference between the expected real return to holding for one period a nominal bond maturing in τ periods and the return to a one period indexed bond is:

$$E_t(r_t^\tau) - r_t^f = E_t(r_t^{\mathrm{I}}) - r_t^f + E_t(r_t^\tau - r_t^{\mathrm{I}}). \qquad (13.33)$$

The holding risk premium can be divided into the *inflation risk premium*, defined as $E_t(r_t^{\mathrm{I}}) - r_t^f$ and a *term risk premium*, $E_t(r_t^\tau - r_t^{\mathrm{I}})$. In an early paper, Jaffe and Mandelker [262] study the relationship between inflation and the holding period returns on bonds.

In actual capital markets, we typically observe assets with nominal payoffs being traded. Since the existence of changes in the nominal price level induces another type of risk that risk-averse agents would prefer to avoid, the question arises as to the welfare gains from issuing inflation-indexed bonds and why there are so few instances of this occurring. Fischer [186] studies the welfare gains of issuing inflation-indexed bonds in a multi-good model with price level uncertainty. In his framework, all bonds are in net zero supply.

13.2.4. Velocity shock

The tight relationship between the nominal interest rate and velocity is a weakness of the standard cash-in-advance model. A simple way to remedy this is to add a velocity shock. The model of Alvarez, Lucas, and Weber [26] adds a velocity shock along with differentiated trading opportunities. We will discuss differentiated trading opportunities later and focus on velocity shocks here because it is a simple modification of the model just derived.

Earlier we assumed that none of an agent's current income could be used to finance current consumption expenditures. We now modify this to assume that a random fraction $0 \leq v_t < 1$ can be used so that:

$$p_t y_t v_t$$

of current income can be used to finance consumption expenditures. The cash-in-advance constraint is modified as

$$p_t c_t \leq M_t^d + v_t y_t p_t. \qquad (13.34)$$

For the moment, we drop the assumption that there is an equity market. The asset-market constraint is:

$$M_t^d + Q_t B_t \leq B_{t-1} + G_t + M_{t-1}^d + v_{t-1} p_{t-1} y_{t-1}$$
$$- c_{t-1} p_{t-1} + (1 - v_{t-1}) p_{t-1} y_{t-1}. \qquad (13.35)$$

Assume that the velocity shock satisfies $v : S \to [0, 1)$. Convert the nominal variables to real variables by dividing by the current price level. The Bellman equation is:

$$V(s, h) = \max[U(c) + \beta E_s V(s', h')]$$

subject to the modified cash-in-advance constraint (13.34) and the asset-market constraint (13.35). Since the stochastic velocity shock does not change the basic structure of the model, we forego derivation of the first-order conditions and focus on the differences between the models, specifically the behavior of velocity and prices. Notice that if the cash-in-advance constraint is binding, then the price is:

$$p(s, M) = \frac{M}{(1 - v)y(s)}.$$

If the cash-in-advance constraint is not binding, then define the function K such that:

$$p(s, M) = \frac{M}{(1 - v)y(s)K(s)}.$$

If the constraint is binding, then $K(s) = 1$. The first-order conditions for consumption and real balance are combined to yield:

$$\frac{U'(y(s))}{p(s, M)} = \frac{\mu}{p(s, M)} + \beta E_s \left[\frac{U'(y(s'))}{p(s', M')} \right]. \tag{13.36}$$

Substitute for prices and re-write

$$K(s) = \max \left[1, \beta E_s \frac{U'(y(s'))}{U'(y(s))} \frac{y(s')}{y(s)} \frac{1 - v(s')}{1 - v(s)} \frac{M}{M'} K(s') \right]. \tag{13.37}$$

The first-order condition for nominal bonds can be expressed as:

$$K(s)Q(s) = \beta E_s \left[\frac{U'(y(s'))}{U'(y(s))} \frac{y(s')}{y(s)} \frac{1 - v(s')}{1 - v(s)} \frac{M}{M'} K(s') \right]. \tag{13.38}$$

Notice that the identical conclusion follows: if $K = 1$ then the nominal interest rate is positive, while if $K > 1$, then $Q = 1$. However the difference is that velocity is:

$$(1 - v(s))K(s). \tag{13.39}$$

Hence velocity can vary when interest rates are positive.

13.3. INFLATION AND INTEREST RATES

There are two seemingly contradictory views about the relationship among money supply, interest rates and inflation. The *Fisher-equation view* states that higher money growth leads to higher inflation and higher nominal interest rates. By contrast, the *liquidity effect view* argues that money demand is a downward-sloping function of the nominal interest rate so that an increase in money supply lowers nominal interest rates. These relationships have been studied extensively in the data; see the references of Alvarez, Lucas, and Weber [26] and Monnet and Weber [346], for example. Since there is empirical support for both views, it is important for monetary policy to reconcile these views. The objective is to construct a monetary model that is consistent with both the Fisher equation and the liquidity effect. The Fisher equation is consistent with the quantity theory of money: a higher growth rate in money leads to a proportionately higher inflation rate, raising the nominal interest rate. The model we discuss below can reconcile these two views. Our discussion is based on the articles by Alvarez, Lucas, and Weber [26].

This is exchange economy, where the exogenous and stochastic endowment is stationary in levels and follows (13.6). There are two types of infinitely lived agents with identical preferences and endowments, who differ only in terms of whether they are traders or not. A fraction ρ of agents are traders. This means that they participate in goods markets and asset markets. A fraction $1 - \rho$ are non-traders, who participate only in the goods markets. Agents are endowed with y_t, a stochastic non-storable good. Agents do not consume their own endowment but instead must sell the endowment in the goods market, so current receipts are $p_t y_t$. A fraction v_t of the receipts are available for consumption expenditures in the current period. This is the velocity shock model that we discussed earlier.

For non-traders, the budget constraint is:

$$p_t c_t^n \leq H_t^n + v_t p_t y_t, \tag{13.40}$$

where

$$H_t^n = v_{t-1} p_{t-1} y_{t-1} - p_{t-1} c_{t-1}^n + (1 - v_{t-1}) p_{t-1} y_{t-1},$$

which is the unspent cash carried over from last period.

Traders participate in the asset market and the goods market and are subject to a cash-in-advance constraint in the goods market. The trader's budget constraint in the asset market is:

$$H_t^T \geq Q_t B_t + M_t^T, \tag{13.41}$$

where

$$H_t = B_{t-1} + G_t + M_{t-1}^T + v_{t-1} p_{t-1} y_{t-1} - p_{t-1} c_{t-1}^T$$

is the trader's post-transfer nominal holdings at the beginning of the asset market. Only traders receive the lump-sum transfer in the asset market. Notice that we do not require that the cash-in-advance constraint be binding. In the goods market, the trader faces the cash-in-advance constraint:

$$c_t^T p_t \leq v_t p_t y_t + M_{t-1}^T. \tag{13.42}$$

The objective function for both agents takes the form (13.1). Let μ_t^T denote the multiplier for (13.42) and let ψ_t denote the multiplier for (13.41). Divide all nominal variables by the price level. The Bellman equation is:

$$V^T(s_t, h_t^T) = \max\left[U(c_t^T) + \beta E_t V^T(s_{t+1}, h_{t+1}^T)\right] \tag{13.43}$$

The first-order conditions with respect to c^T, M_t^T, B_t are:

$$U'(c_t^T) = \mu_t^T + \beta E_t\left[V_h^T(s_{t+1}, h_{t+1}^T)\frac{p_t}{p_{t+1}}\right], \tag{13.44}$$

$$\psi_t = \mu_t^T + \beta E_t\left[V_h^T(s_{t+1}, h_{t+1}^T)\frac{p_t}{p_{t+1}}\right], \tag{13.45}$$

$$\psi_t Q_t = \beta E_t\left[V_h^T(s_{t+1}, h_{t+1}^T)\frac{p_t}{p_{t+1}}\right]. \tag{13.46}$$

The first two equations can be combined as:

$$U'(c_t^T) = \mu_t^T + \beta E_t\left[U'(c_{t+1}^T)\frac{p_t}{p_{t+1}}\right]. \tag{13.47}$$

The Bellman equation for non-traders is:

$$V^N(s_t, h_t^N) = \max\left[U(c_t^N) + \beta E_t V^N(s_{t+1}, h_{t+1}^N)\right]. \tag{13.48}$$

The first-order condition with respect to c_t^n is:

$$U'(c_t^N) = \mu_t^N + \beta E_t\left[V_h^N\frac{p_t}{p_{t+1}}\right]. \tag{13.49}$$

The market-clearing conditions are:

$$y_t = \rho c_t^T + (1-\rho)c_t^N \tag{13.50}$$

$$B_t^s = B_t, \tag{13.51}$$

where the money market will clear if the other two markets clear. If the cash-in-advance constraint is always binding for both types of agents, then for traders,

$$p_t c_t^T = v_t p_t y_t + (1 - v_{t-1})p_{t-1}y_{t-1} + \frac{M_t - M_{t-1}}{\rho},$$

where the last term on the right side is the monetary injection (withdrawal if negative) per trader. If the constraint is binding for non-traders, then

$$p_t c_t^N = v_t p_t y_t + (1 - v_{t-1})p_{t-1}y_{t-1},$$

so that, using the goods market clearing condition

$$y_t = \rho \left[v_t y_t + \frac{1}{p_t} \left((1 - v_{t-1}) p_{t-1} y_{t-1} + \frac{M_t - M_{t-1}}{\rho} \right) \right] \tag{13.52}$$

$$+ (1 - \rho) \left[v_t y_t + \frac{(1 - v_{t-1}) p_{t-1} y_{t-1}}{p_t} \right] \tag{13.53}$$

$$= v_t y_t + \frac{(1 - v_{t-1}) p_{t-1} y_{t-1}}{p_t} + \frac{M_t - M_{t-1}}{p_t} \tag{13.54}$$

$$= v_t y_t + \frac{M_t}{p_t} \tag{13.55}$$

because $M_{t-1} = (1 - v_{t-1}) p_{t-1} y_{t-1}$, so that

$$p_t = \frac{M_t}{y_t} \frac{1}{1 - v_t}. \tag{13.56}$$

Will the cash-in-advance constraint always be binding? We need to examine the first-order condition for bonds for traders to answer this question. All information is revealed at the beginning of the period so that the trader knows what the price level will be in the goods market. Any money balances carried over to the goods market from the asset market that are left unspent *after* the goods market closes could have been spent on interest bearing bonds. So the interest rate is the opportunity cost of unspent money balances. Examining the bond condition, observe that

$$Q_t = \beta E_t \left[\frac{U'(c_{t+1}^T)}{U'(c_t^T)} \frac{p_t}{p_{t+1}} \right].$$

If $Q_t > 1$, then the cash-in-advance constraint is binding for the traders. Notice that, although non-traders do not enter the asset market, they do face the same price process as traders in the goods market. For the constraint of non-traders to be binding, it must be the case that nominal prices are not falling too quickly – if the deflation is high enough, then non-traders will hold additional fiat currency between periods to collect the positive return on money. Conditions to rule out this type of deflation are discussed in the appendix of Alvarez, Atkeson, and Kehoe [25]. In the rest of the discussion, we assume the conditions on the money process such that the cash-in-advance constraint is always binding are satisfied for both types of agents.

Under this assumption, then the price process is described by (13.56). Consumption of traders is:

$$c_t^T = y_t \left[\frac{(1 - v_t) M_{t-1}}{M_t} \left(1 - \frac{1}{\rho} \right) + \frac{1}{\rho} + v_t \left(1 - \frac{1}{\rho} \right) \right] \tag{13.57}$$

and consumption of non-traders is:

$$c_t^N = \frac{y_t}{M_t}[v_t M_t + (1 - v_t)M_{t-1}]. \tag{13.58}$$

Notice that if $\rho = 1$, then consumption of traders and non-traders is identical, as we would expect. If $\rho \neq 1$, then consumption of the two types will be different and will depend on the monetary policy. Notice that if there is an open-market purchase of bonds, traders have an increase in their nominal balances, and, for these agents to be content with their portfolio of bonds and fiat money, the price of bonds must increase, driving the nominal interest rate down. The traders take a portion of the monetary injection to the goods market where they purchase the consumption good. Hence the model is consistent with the liquidity effect view, in which an expansion of the money supply leads to a decrease in nominal interest rates.

Suppose that the velocity shock v is constant at $\bar{v}$. Then observe in (13.56) that an increase in money growth leads to a proportional increase in inflation, holding the endowment process stationary in levels. Hence the model, as already mentioned, is consistent with the quantity theory of money. The real interest rate, equal to the inverse of the expected intertemporal marginal rate of substitution in consumption, will vary with the money shock since the consumption of traders will vary with the money shock. In particular, holding expected marginal utility of next period's consumption fixed, an increase in the monetary injection leads to an increase in the consumption of traders, lowering the marginal utility of current consumption of traders and lowering the expected real rate of interest. This is at the heart of the liquidity effect: expansionary monetary policy lowers the expected real rate of interest. Notice that this is a short-run effect. In the long run, the model remains consistent with the Fisher equation effect and the quantity theory.

13.4. TRANSACTIONS SERVICES MODEL

Many other assets besides narrowly defined money play a role in facilitating transactions. US Treasury bonds often back checkable deposits and money market funds and the notion that short-term debt offers transaction services has long been discussed in the literature. If liquid short-term government debt provides transaction services in addition to generating interest income, then the marginal return on this debt should reflect the marginal transaction benefit. This point has been recognized by many, including Bansal and Coleman [44], who examine whether explicitly incorporating the transactions service can help to explain the equity premium puzzle. One way to view that puzzle, discussed in Chapter 8, is that the risk-free rate of return is too low, and this low return explains the size of the premium. Incorporating the transactions services of liquid bonds is one approach to explain why the risk-free rate is so low, although there are other explanations. We develop a simple model in which there are costs to carrying out transactions – in the form of shopping time or search costs, which take away from leisure time. Such a model is discussed in Ljungqvist and Sargent [325]. We combine this transaction cost with the transactions services from holding bonds.

Let τ_t denote the shopping time, a kind of transaction cost, and let l_t denote leisure time. An agent's time constraint is:

$$1 = l_t + \tau_t.$$

Let B_t denote the nominal value of bond holdings. An agent's *liquidity-in-advance constraint* on the purchase of consumption goods is:

$$\frac{M_t}{p_t} + \frac{1}{p_t} f(B_t, \tau_t) \geq c_t. \tag{13.59}$$

The basic intuition is this: consumption purchases must be financed with either cash acquired before entering the goods market or using an account based on the nominal value of liquid bonds held and incurring a transactions cost measured in foregone leisure. The idea is that the consumption good can be purchased with balances from an account other than fiat money, but use of this account requires paying a transaction cost, measured in foregone leisure, and having liquid bonds as a backing. Hence holding liquid bonds provides a transactions service and pays interest in the form of a discount.

The function f has the following properties: $f_b > 0$, $f_\tau > 0$, $f_{bb} < 0$ and $f_\tau \tau < 0$, so the function f is increasing and concave in each argument. Also $f(0, \tau) = 0$ and $f(B, 0) = 0$. An example of a function with these properties is:

$$f(B, \tau) = \tau^\alpha B^\theta,$$

where α, θ are positive and less than one.

To keep the model as simple as possible, we will keep the structure close to the standard cash-in-advance described earlier. Agents receive an endowment $y(s_t)$ that they must sell and are prevented from using the receipts to finance current-period consumption. The representative agent has preferences

$$E_0 \left[\sum_{t=0}^{\infty} \beta^t [U(c_t) + W(l_t)] \right]. \tag{13.60}$$

Let

$$H_t \equiv M_{t-1}^d - p_{t-1}c_{t-1} + p_{t-1}y_{t-1} + B_{t-1}^d + G_t$$

and $h_t = \frac{H_t}{p_t}$. If the liquidity-in-advance constraint is binding, then

$$M^d_{t-1} = p_{t-1}c_{t-1} - f(B^d_{t-1}, \tau_{t-1}),$$

which can be substituted into H_t to show

$$H_t = p_{t-1}y_{t-1} - f(B^d_{t-1}, \tau_{t-1}) + B^d_{t-1} + G_t.$$

Hence any consumption financed out of the liquid bond-backed account affects nominal balances carried over to the next period.

The agent's budget constraint in the asset market is:

$$h_t \geq \frac{M^d_t}{p_t} + \frac{Q_t B^d_t}{p_t}. \tag{13.61}$$

Let ψ_t denote the Lagrange multiplier for the asset market constraint and let μ_t denote the multiplier for the liquidity-in-advance constraint. The Bellman equation is:

$$V(h_t, s_t) = \max[U(c_t) + W(1 - \tau_t) + \beta E_t V(h_{t+1}, s_{t+1})]. \tag{13.62}$$

The first-order conditions and envelope conditions with respect to $c_t, \tau_t, M^d_t, B^d_t$ are:

$$U'(c_t) = \mu_t + \beta E_t \left[V_h(h_{t+1}, s_{t+1}) \frac{p_t}{p_{t+1}} \right], \tag{13.63}$$

$$\frac{\mu_t}{p_t} f_\tau(B^d_t, \tau_t) = W'(1 - \tau_t), \tag{13.64}$$

$$\frac{\psi_t}{p_t} = \frac{\mu_t}{p_t} + \beta E_t \left[V_h(h_{t+1}, s_{t+1}) \frac{1}{p_{t+1}} \right], \tag{13.65}$$

$$\frac{\psi_t Q_t}{p_t} = \frac{\mu_t f_b(B^d_t, \tau_t)}{p_t} + \beta E_t \left[V_h(h_{t+1}, s_{t+1}) \frac{1}{p_{t+1}} \right], \tag{13.66}$$

$$V_h(h_t, s_t) = \psi_t. \tag{13.67}$$

The equilibrium conditions are: $c_t = y_t$, $M^d_t = M_t$ and $B^d_t = B_t$. Use the envelope condition to eliminate V_h, substitute the market clearing conditions, and eliminate ψ in (13.63) and (13.65) to obtain:

$$U'(y_t) = \mu_t + \beta E_t \left[U'(y_{t+1}) \frac{p_t}{p_{t+1}} \right]. \tag{13.68}$$

The liquidity-in-advance constraint is:

$$M_t + f(B_t, \tau_t) \geq p_t y_t.$$

Notice from (13.64) that:

$$\frac{\mu_t}{p_t} = \frac{W'(1-\tau)}{f_\tau(B_t, \tau_t)}.$$

If the liquidity-in-advance constraint is non-binding, then $\mu = 0$ and it follows that $\tau = 0$. Whether $p_t = \frac{M_t}{y_t}$ depends on the nominal interest rate and, at this point, the conditions for the constraint to be binding can be derived using methods discussed earlier. Our focus is on the liquidity of bonds and, for this reason, we assume that the constraint is binding. In this case,

$$p_t = \frac{M_t + f(B_t, \tau_t)}{y_t}.$$

Define

$$\Lambda_t \equiv \beta E_t \left[\frac{U'(y_{t+1})y_{t+1}}{M_{t+1} + f(B_{t+1}, \tau_{t+1})} \right]. \tag{13.69}$$

Use (13.64) to eliminate μ_t in (13.68) and substitute for p_t so that

$$\frac{U'(y_t)y_t}{M_t + f(B_t, \tau_t)} - \frac{W'(1-\tau_t)}{f_\tau(B_t, \tau_t)} = \Lambda_t. \tag{13.70}$$

Let $\Lambda_t = \Lambda > 0$ be given. Observe that the left side is strictly decreasing in τ_t, given y_t, M_t, B_t.[3] Let $\tau^\star(M_t, B_t, y_t, \Lambda)$ denote a solution. It is straightforward to show that $\tau^\star$ is decreasing in Λ. Define

$$G(M, y, B, \Lambda) \equiv y[M + f(B, \tau^\star(M, B, y, \Lambda))]^{-1}$$

Define a mapping

$$T(\Lambda)(y, M, B, s) = \beta E_s \left[U'(y')G(M', y', B', \Lambda(y', M', B', \Lambda')) \right]. \tag{13.71}$$

If $\hat{\Lambda} > \tilde{\Lambda}$, then $T\hat{\Lambda} \geq T\tilde{\Lambda}$ so the operator T is monotone.

Lemma 13.1 *Under our assumptions*

$$G(M, y, B, \Lambda) - \Lambda$$

is weakly decreasing in Λ.

[3] Observe that the derivative is

$$\frac{-U'(y)yf_\tau}{(M+f)^2} + \frac{W''(1-\tau)}{f_\tau} + \frac{W'(1-\tau)f_{\tau\tau}}{f_\tau^2} < 0.$$

PROOF
From (13.69–13.70),

$$G(M, y, B, \Lambda) - \Lambda = \frac{W'(1 - \tau^\star(M, B, y, \Lambda))}{f_\tau(B, \tau^\star(M, B, y, \Lambda))yU'(y)}$$

Differentiate the right side with respect to Λ to show that it is weakly decreasing in Λ, ∎

We can use this lemma to show that the mapping above is a contraction mapping by verifying Blackwell's sufficient conditions for a contraction mapping and the outline of a formal proof is provided here.

We have already demonstrated that the mapping is monotone. From the lemma, we know that $G - \Lambda$ is weakly decreasing in Λ. For any Λ and $a > 0$,

$$G(M, y, B, \Lambda + a) - [\Lambda + a] \leq G(M, y, B, \Lambda) - \Lambda,$$

or

$$G(M, y, B, \Lambda + a) \leq G(M, y, B, \Lambda) + a.$$

It then follows that:

$$\begin{aligned} T(\Lambda + a)(y_t, M_t, B_t, s_t) &= \beta E_t \left[\frac{U'(y_{t+1})}{U'(y_t)} G(M_{t+1}, y_{t+1}, B_{t+1}, \Lambda + a) \right] \\ &\leq \beta E_t \left\{ \frac{U'(y_{t+1})}{U'(y_t)} [G(M_{t+1}, y_{t+1}, B_{t+1}, \Lambda) + a] \right\} \\ &\leq T\Lambda(y_t, M_t, B_t, s_t) + \delta a \end{aligned}$$

where $0 < \delta < 1$.

Let $G^\star(M, y, B)$ denote a solution. We now turn to the reason we are studying the model: the implication of the liquidity-in-advance constraint for the nominal interest rate. Observe (13.66) can be re-written as:

$$Q_t = \frac{W'(1 - \tau_t) f_b(B_t, \tau_t)}{f_\tau(B_t, \tau_t)} + \beta E_t \left[\frac{U'(y_{t+1})}{U'(y_t)} \frac{G^\star(M_{t+1}, y_{t+1}, B_{t+1})}{G^\star(M_t, y_t, B_t)} \right]. \tag{13.72}$$

The bond price now consists of two parts: a liquidity component and the expected return to holding the bond. For any output process and real interest rate process, the bond price will be higher because of the liquidity services, hence the nominal rate will be lower. To see this, suppose that there are two types of bonds: those that can be used to provide transactions services and those that cannot. The bonds that cannot be used will have a bond price equal only to the second term on the right side, all other things equal. Hence the liquid bond will have a higher price, given the same state and maturity date for the bond.

Bansal and Coleman [44] provide some empirical results to support their conclusion that liquid bonds provide transactions services and, once these services are taken into account, the model can explain the equity premium puzzle.

13.5. GROWING ECONOMIES

So far we have assumed that the endowment is stationary in levels so that, even if money is growing, dividing all nominal variables by the price level will convert the transformed variables into stationary real variables. But how should the models be solved if both the endowment and money are growing? We briefly describe a method and discuss some of the technical issues. The reason is more than academic: real output and money are growing in the data and so it is necessary to modify the model to fit the data, rather than the other way around. When endowment is growing, we assume that preferences are of the constant relative risk aversion variety.

The endowment y_t is exogenous and growing over time. The rate of growth is a function of the current shock. The endowment evolves as:

$$y_t = \lambda(s_t)y_{t-1}. \tag{13.73}$$

Money is injected into the economy as a lump-sum stochastic transfer. The law of motion for the money supply process follows (13.8). The following assumption restricts money and endowment growth.

Assumption 13.2 *Define $\mathcal{L} \equiv [\underline{\lambda}, \bar{\lambda}]$ and $\mathcal{W} \equiv [\underline{\omega}, \bar{\omega}]$ where $\underline{\lambda} > 0$, $\underline{\omega} > 0$, $\bar{\lambda} < \infty$, and $\bar{\omega} < \infty$. The functions $\lambda : S \to \mathcal{L}$ and $\omega : S \to \mathcal{W}$ are continuous functions and both are bounded away from zero.*

The following assumption characterizes the utility function.

Assumption 13.3 *The utility function U is given by $(c^{1-\gamma} - 1)/(1-\gamma)$ for $\gamma \geq 0$, and $u(c) = \ln c$ if $\gamma = 1$.*

In equilibrium, consumption equals endowment, $c_t = y_t$, money demand equals money supply, $M_t^d = M_t$, all bonds are held, $B_t = 0$, all shares are held, $z_t = 1$ and the lump-sum money transfer equals the net growth of money, $G_t = (1 - \omega_t)M_{t-1}$. To ensure that the consumer's utility is well defined in equilibrium, we make the following assumption.

Assumption 13.4 $\beta \int_S \lambda(s')^{1-\gamma} d\Phi(s') < 1$, $\gamma \neq 1$.

Define the quantity $\Upsilon(s) \equiv \lambda(s)^{1-\gamma}/\omega(s)$. The existence of a monetary equilibrium is established by making the following assumption.

Assumption 13.5 $0 < \beta \int_S \Upsilon(s') d\Phi(s') < 1,\ \gamma \neq 1.$

For notational convenience, also define $\omega_{t,\tau} \equiv M_{t+\tau}/M_t$ so that $\omega_{t,\tau}$ is the growth of the money supply between periods t and $t+\tau$.

We begin by formulating the household's problem as a dynamic programming problem. Because the money supply is growing, the household's nominal money holdings are growing in equilibrium. To make H_t and M_t stationary, we divide the (nominal) constraints by the current stock of money M_t. With this modification, the problem is now similar to the growing endowment case studied in Chapter 8. Define normalized money and bond holdings by $m_t^d \equiv M_t^d/M_t$, $b_t \equiv B_t/M_t$, and $h_t \equiv H_t/M_t$. The nominal price level and the nominal equity price are normalized by the level of money supply, $p_t \equiv P_t/M_t$ and $q_t^e \equiv Q_t^e/M_t$.[4] The normalized constraint in the asset market is:

$$m_t^d + q_t^e z_t + Q_t b_t \leq h_t + q_t^e z_{t-1}, \tag{13.74}$$

where

$$h_t \equiv \frac{1}{\omega(s_t)}[p_{t-1}y_{t-1}z_{t-1} + b_{t-1} + m_{t-1}^d - p_{t-1}c_{t-1} + (\omega_t - 1)].$$

The cash-in-advance constraint is:

$$p_t c_t \leq m_t^d. \tag{13.75}$$

Notice that as a result of this normalization, the level of the money held drops out of the constraints in equilibrium.

The household takes as given the nominal price of consumption goods and the nominal price of equities and bonds, which are all assumed to be continuous, strictly positive functions of the current shocks. Define an interval $Z = [0, \bar{z}]$ where $\bar{z} < \infty$ such that $z_t \in Z$. Likewise, $b_t \in B$ where $B = [-b, b]$ such that $b > 0$. Let $\mathcal{H} = [0, \bar{h}]$ where $\bar{h} > 1$ such that $h_t \in \mathcal{H}$. Finally, we know that in equilibrium all of the money will be held at the close of the assets market and because we have normalized by the money stock, $m^d = 1$. Hence, define $\mathcal{M} = [0, 1]$.

Notice that endowment y is strictly positive so that y is in $\Re_{++}$. The prices are functions $p(s, y)$, $q^e(s, y)$, and $Q(s)$ and we assume that:

$$p(s, y)y, \quad \frac{q^e(s, y)}{p(s, y)y}$$

are *functions of s only.* Recall that $p(s, y)$ is the nominal price level divided by the money stock (the inverse of real balances) so that the restriction on

[4] In the versions of the cash-in-advance model where all the information is revealed at the beginning of the period, we can also divide the nominal constraints by the price level as we did earlier in the chapter. We use the approach of normalizing by the money stock because it works even when some information is revealed after a market is closed.

$p(s, y)y$ says that real balances divided by endowment is a function of s only. Given the price functions p, q^e, and Q, the consumer's value function is defined by:

$$V(y, s, z, h) = \max_{c, m^d, z', h'} \left\{ U(c) + \beta \int_S V(y', s', z', h') d\Phi(s') \right\},$$

subject to the constraints in Equations (13.74) and (13.75) and $m^d \in \mathcal{M}$, $z' \in Z$, and $h' \in B$.

Under Assumptions 13.4 and 13.5, we can show that V is well defined and finite. Recall that in Chapter 8, we restricted our attention to the space $\mathcal{B}$ of functions $g : \Re_{++} \times S \times Z \times \mathcal{H} \to \Re_+$ that are jointly continuous such that if $g \in \mathcal{B}$, then $\sup_{y,s,z,h} |g(y, s, z, h)|/y^{1-\gamma} < \infty$. We used this norm to verify the Weighted Contraction Mapping Theorem. We will not repeat this because the steps are identical to those proving Proposition 8.3 in Chapter 8 except to note that the modulus of the contraction in the proof is $\delta = \beta \int_S \lambda(s')^{1-\gamma} d\Phi(s')$ which, under Assumption 13.4, is always less than unity. (See Exercise 1.)

13.6. MONEY AND REAL ACTIVITY

In the data, one of the most important stylized facts is the apparent co-movement of monetary aggregates and output. In Chapter 12, we discussed a model of inside money due to King and Plosser [277] where the money-output correlation arises from the role of money as providing transactions services. However, models have also been developed that allow for the real effects of "outside" money. In Lucas [314, 315], informational problems due to agents' misperceptions of relative price changes versus changes in the aggregate price level cause monetary shocks to have real affects. In Chapter 12, we also outlined a new Keynesian framework with imperfect competition and variable factor utilization that allows for a propagation mechanism for monetary shocks based on price rigidity. A third approach to quantifying the impact of monetary shocks on real activity has been in terms of the cash-in-advance model. As we noted earlier, one of the advantages of the cash-in-advance model is its rich empirical implications. Cooley and Hansen [120, 121, 122] study the impact of money shocks in generating business cycle fluctuations as well as the welfare implications of an inflation tax induced by the cash-in-advance model. The role of production and money in explaining the observed behavior of real and nominal interest rates of various maturities has been stressed by den Hann [150], amongst others.

In this section, we first present a model with a consumption-leisure choice that allows for the real effects of money through an inflation tax generated by monetary shocks. This model is also augmented with an income tax. We first present the model and explore its implications for consumption allocations further in Exercise 3. We then extend this model along the lines suggested by Cooley and Hansen [120] to allow for cash and credit goods and an indivisible labor supply. We include technology and monetary shocks and a capital-accumulation process that is endogenous. In this section, we also discuss the efficacy of the model in matching observations and real and monetary variables for the US economy.

13.6.1. Consumption-leisure choices

We now introduce a model that allows for a consumption-leisure choice by agents. Since consumption choices are constrained by cash holdings, a wedge is introduced that allows for the output effects of monetary growth shocks. An explicit government budget constraint is introduced, linking bond supply and the money supply. The government finances an exogenous and stochastic expenditure stream, which is distributed lump-sum to households, by collecting income taxes, seignorage, and borrowing.

Each agent is endowed with one unit of time per period which can be divided between labor n and leisure ℓ. There is an exogenous and stochastic capital stock κ owned by the firm which depreciates 100% each period. The firm issues one equity which is a claim to the return to capital and any profits. The equity is traded each period in a competitive stock market. Output y is produced by a linear homogeneous production function:

$$y_t = A\kappa_t^{1-\theta} n_t^{\theta}, \tag{13.76}$$

where $0 < \theta < 1$. The household owns the labor stock and is a price-taker in the factor market. Each factor is paid the value of its marginal product and these payments exhaust the revenue of the typical firm. The real wage is:

$$w_t = \theta y_t / n_t, \tag{13.77}$$

and the return to the exogenous and stochastic capital stock is:

$$r_t = (1-\theta) y_t / \kappa_t. \tag{13.78}$$

The exogenous and stochastic expenditures G_t are financed by issuing currency $M_t - M_{t-1}$, setting the income tax τ_t, and by borrowing through the issue of one-period nominal bonds B_t^s which are sold at the price Q_t. The government's budget constraint is:

$$B_{t-1}^s + G_t = M_t - M_{t-1} + Q_t B_t^s + \tau_{t-1}(P_{t-1} y_{t-1}), \tag{13.79}$$

where P_{t-1} is the price level in period $t-1$. Define $b^s = B^s/M$, $g = G/M$, and $p = P/M$. The growth of money defined as $M_t/M_{t-1} \equiv \omega(s_t)$ satisfies:

$$g_t = \frac{1}{\omega(s_t)}[\omega(s_t) - 1 - b_{t-1}^s + \tau_{t-1}(p_{t-1} y_{t-1})] + Q_t b_t^s. \tag{13.80}$$

The asset and factor markets open first followed by the goods market. In the factor market, the household decides how to allocate its time between labor n_t and leisure ℓ_t subject to the time constraint:

$$n_t + \ell_t \leq 1. \tag{13.81}$$

In the asset market, the household adjusts its holdings of currency, nominal bonds, and equity shares. We normalize by dividing the nominal constraints by the money stock at the beginning of the period. The agent's beginning-of-period money balances after receiving the lump-sum transfer G_t are denoted H_t. The household's budget constraint in the asset market is:

$$m_t + Q_t b_t + q_t^e z_{t+1} \leq h_t + q_t^e z_t, \tag{13.82}$$

where m_t denotes money balances held at the close of the asset market and $h_t \equiv H_t/M_t$.

After the asset and labor markets close, consumption purchases are made with the currency acquired in the asset market. Because nominal factor payments are received after the goods market is closed, all consumption purchases must be financed with real balances held at the closing of the asset market. The normalized cash-in-advance constraint is:

$$p_t c_t \leq m_t, \tag{13.83}$$

where c_t is consumption and p_t is its price.

After the goods market closes, the household receives the dividend payment $d_t z_{t+1} p_t$ and payment on labor supplied $w_t n_t p_t$, where w_t is the real wage, and pays taxes on this income. The law of motion for the agent's beginning-of-period money holdings is:

$$\begin{aligned} h_{t+1} = g_{t+1} + [b_t + p_t(w_t n_t + z_{t+1} d_t)(1 - \tau_t) \\ + m_t - p_t c_t]/\omega(s_{t+1}). \end{aligned} \tag{13.84}$$

At the time the agent decides on the amount of labor to supply, the real value next period of the factor payment is uncertain because inflation is uncertain. The timing of trades is summarized in Figure 13.2.

The representative household has preferences:

$$E_0 \left\{ \sum_{t=0}^{\infty} \beta^t U(c_t, \ell_t) \right\}, \quad 0 < \beta < 1. \tag{13.85}$$

We have the following assumption.

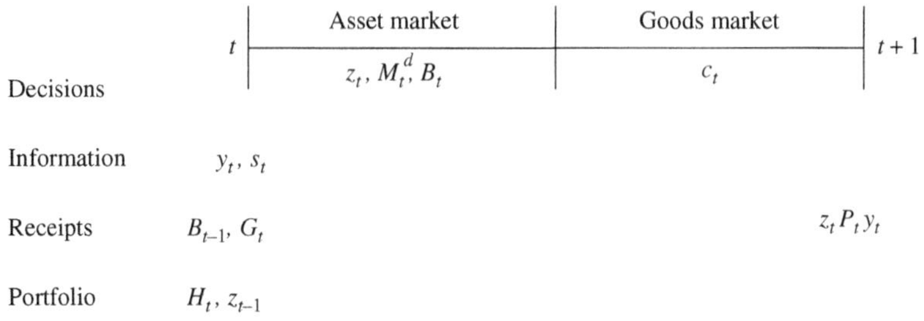

Figure 13.2. Timing of trades in the consumption/leisure model

Assumption 13.6 *(i) The utility function is continuously twice differentiable, strictly increasing, and strictly concave; (ii)* $U_{11} + U_{12} < 0$*,* $U_{22} + U_{21} < 0$*, and* $U_{12} > 0$*;*

$$(iii)\ \lim_{\ell \to 1} \frac{U_1(A\kappa^{1-\theta}(1-\ell)^\theta, \ell)}{U_2(A\kappa^{1-\theta}(1-\ell)^\theta, \ell)} = \infty, \ \lim_{\ell \to 0} \frac{U_2(A\kappa^{1-\theta}(1-\ell)^\theta, \ell)}{U_1(A\kappa^{1-\theta}(1-\ell)^\theta, \ell)} = \infty.$$

Part (ii) of this assumption says that current consumption and leisure are not inferior goods while part (iii) implies both goods will be consumed in equilibrium.

We assume that the shock to the economy s_t satisfies the conditions of Assumption 13.1 and the rate of contraction of the money supply satisfies the conditions of Assumption 13.7. In this model, the capital stock is exogenous. We have the following assumption.

Assumption 13.7 *For all* $s \in S$, $\beta \int_S [1/\omega(s')] F(s, ds') < 1$.

Since the technology for transforming one good into the other is linear if their prices are equal, the agent will be indifferent to the proportion in which they are consumed. To ensure that both types of goods are consumed, we assume that the marginal rate of substitution between cash and credit goods is infinite at zero values for these goods.

Assumption 13.8 *The capital stock* $\kappa : S \to \Re_+$ *is continuous, strictly bounded away from 0, and takes values on* $K \equiv [\underline{\kappa}, \overline{\kappa}]$.

We assume that there is one outstanding equity share traded in a competitive market that is a claim to the nominal return to capital and profits. Because the production function is Cobb-Douglas, the factor payments exhaust all revenue. Hence, there are no profits to be distributed and the firm's maximization problem is straightforward. The following assumption holds for government policy.

Assumption 13.9 *The income tax $\tau : S \to [0, \bar{\tau}]$, with $\bar{\tau} < 1$, is a continuous function. Government expenditure $g : S \to \Re_+$ and the issue of one-period nominal bonds $b^s : S \to \Re_+$ are continuous functions that satisfy Equation (13.80).*

After observing the realization s_t, the government transfers $g(s_t)$ as a lump-sum payment to households and pays $b^s(s_{t-1})$ to bondholders. It finances these expenditures through seignorage revenue and borrowing in the asset market.

The price functions $p : S \to \Re_{++}$, $q^e : S \to \Re_{++}$, $Q : S \to \Re_{++}$, and $w : S \to \Re_{++}$ are assumed to be continuous and strictly positive. The household takes as given the functions describing the government's expenditures, nominal bond supply, income tax rates, and money supply growth. The dynamic programming problem solved by the household is:

$$V(h, z, s) = \max_{\{c,\ell,m,z',b'\}} \left\{ U(c, \ell) + \beta \int_S V(h', z', s') F(s, ds') \right\} \tag{13.86}$$

subject to the time constraint (Equation 13.81), the asset-market constraint (Equation 13.82), the cash-in-advance constraint (Equation 13.83), and the law of motion for money holdings (Equation 13.84). Assume as before that $z \in Z$ and that $h \in \mathcal{H} \equiv [0, \bar{h}]$ where $\bar{h} > 1$.

We can define an equilibrium as before. Define the equilibrium multiplier on the cash-in-advance constraint in Equation (13.83) as $\mu(s)$ and the equilibrium multiplier on the asset market constraint as $\xi(s)$. The first-order conditions with market-clearing for c, ℓ, m, b', z' are:

$$U_1(c, \ell) = \mu(s)p(s) + \beta E_s \left[\frac{U_1(c', \ell')p(s)}{p(s')\omega(s')} \right], \tag{13.87}$$

$$U_2(c, \ell) = \beta E_s \left[\frac{U_1(c', \ell')w(s)p(s)[1 - \tau(s)]}{\omega(s')p(s')} \right], \tag{13.88}$$

$$\xi(s) = \mu(s) + \beta E_s \left[\frac{U_1(c', \ell')}{\omega(s')p(s')} \right], \tag{13.89}$$

$$\xi(s)Q(s) = \beta E_s \left[\frac{U_1(c', \ell')}{\omega(s')p(s')} \right], \tag{13.90}$$

$$\xi(s)q^e(s) = \beta E_s \left\{ \frac{U_1(c', \ell')p(s)d(s)[1 - \tau(s)]}{\omega(s')p(s')} + \frac{U_1(c', \ell')q^e(s')}{p(s')} \right\}. \tag{13.91}$$

This model allows the stochastic inflation tax and the income tax to have real output effects. Notice that if $\mu(s) = 0$, then $U_1(c, \ell)/p = U_2(c, \ell)/wp(1 - \tau)$ so that the cash-in-advance constraint creates a wedge not only in the consumption-leisure choice but also in the intertemporal substitution between leisure today and leisure tomorrow. It also has the feature that the government faces a tradeoff in creating real seignorage revenue. As the government increases the growth of the money supply, it generates real revenue by taxing the stock of real balances held by the private sector but it also decreases the real value of the tax revenue it collected at the end of the previous period.

The wedge introduced by the cash-in-advance constraint implies that we must solve simultaneously for the multiplier on the cash-in-advance constraint $\mu(s)$ and the equilibrium value of leisure $\ell(s)$. Define the functions $\hat{y}$ and $\hat{w}$ as: $\hat{y}(s, \ell) = A[\kappa(s)]^{1-\theta}(1 - \ell)^{\theta}$ and $\hat{w}(s, \ell) = \theta\hat{y}(s, \ell)/(1 - \ell)$. We begin with the following proposition.

Proposition 13.1 *(1) Under Assumption 13.6, $U_1(\hat{y}(s, \ell), \ell)$ is strictly increasing in ℓ.*
(2)

$$\frac{\partial}{\partial \ell}\left[\frac{U_2(\hat{y}(s, \ell), \ell)}{\hat{w}(s, \ell)[1 - \tau(s)]}\right] < 0, \quad \lim_{\ell \to 0}\left[\frac{U_2(\hat{y}(s, \ell), \ell)}{\hat{w}(s, \ell)[1 - \tau(s)]}\right] = \infty.$$

(3) There exists a unique $0 < \ell^\star(s) < 1$ such that

$$U_1(\hat{y}(s, \ell), \ell) - \frac{U_2(\hat{y}(s, \ell), \ell)}{\hat{w}(s, \ell)[1 - \tau(s)]} = 0$$

at $\ell = \ell^\star$. Further, for $\ell > \ell^\star$ the left side is strictly positive.

PROOF
Part (1) follows by differentiating with respect to ℓ and using the strict concavity and $U_{12} > 0$. Part (2) follows also by differentiating and using the concavity and conditions on U specified in the assumption. To prove part (3), we know from part (1) that the first term on the left side is strictly increasing and the second term is strictly decreasing. As $\ell \to 0$, the ratio $U_2/[U_1 w(1 - \tau)]$ tends to ∞, while, as $\ell \to 1$, $y \to 0$ so that the ratio $[U_1 w(1 - \tau)]/U_2$ tends to ∞. Hence, the functions cross at one and only one point, $\ell^\star$ and for $\ell > \ell^\star$, the difference is positive. ∎

Next, define the function $\Lambda : S \to \Re_+$ as:

$$\Lambda(s) \equiv \beta E_s\left[\frac{U_1(\hat{y}(s', \ell'), \ell')}{p(s')\omega(s')}\right].$$

Solve Equation (13.87) for $\mu(s)$ and Equation (13.88) for $p(s)$ and substitute the resulting solution for $p(s)$ into the equation for $\mu(s)$, leading to:

$$\mu(s) = \Lambda(s)\left[\frac{U_1(\hat{y}(s,\ell),\ell),\hat{w}(s,\ell)[1-\tau(s)]}{U_1(\hat{y}(s,\ell),\ell)} - 1\right]. \tag{13.92}$$

The cash-in-advance constraint $p(s)\hat{y}(s,\ell) \leq 1$ and Equation (13.92) form a system of two equations in two unknowns (μ, ℓ).

Choose a fixed value Λ such that $0 < \Lambda < \infty$. Under Assumption 13.6, the function $\hat{\ell}(s,\Lambda)$ satisfying:

$$\frac{U_2\{\hat{y}(s,\hat{\ell}(s,\Lambda)),\hat{\ell}(s,\Lambda)\}}{\hat{w}(s,\hat{\ell}(s,\Lambda))} = \Lambda$$

is well defined. This follows because of the continuous differentiability of U_2 and the continuity of $\hat{y}$ and $\hat{w}$. From the cash-in-advance constraint, we know that the following inequality holds:

$$\hat{y}(s,\ell)\frac{U_2(\hat{y}(s,\ell),\ell)(1-\ell)}{\hat{w}(s,\ell)[1-\tau(s)]} \leq \Lambda, \tag{13.93}$$

and holds with equality when $\mu(s) = 0$. Define the function $\Lambda^\star(s)$ as:

$$\Lambda^\star(s) = \frac{\hat{y}(s,\ell^\star(s))U_2\{\hat{y}(s,\ell^\star(s)),\ell^\star(s)\}}{\hat{w}(s,\ell^\star(s))[1-\tau(s)]}.$$

We have the following proposition.

Proposition 13.2 *Under Assumption 13.6 for any finite $\Lambda \geq 0$, the unique pair ℓ, μ satisfying Equations (13.92) and (13.93) is given by*

$$\ell(s,\Lambda) = \begin{cases} \hat{\ell}(s,\Lambda) & \text{if } 0 \leq \Lambda \leq \Lambda^\star(s) \\ \ell^\star(s) & \text{if } \Lambda > \Lambda^\star(s) \end{cases} \tag{13.94}$$

and μ is given by Equation (13.92).

PROOF

Because $\mu(s) \geq 0$, it follows from Equation (13.92) that $[U_1 w(1-\tau)]/U_2 \geq 1$ which in turn implies that $\ell \geq \ell^\star$. Suppose that $0 \leq \Lambda(s) < \Lambda^\star(s)$. Then $\ell > \ell^\star(s)$ since Equation (13.93) would be violated if $\ell = \ell^\star(s)$ so that $[U_1 w(1-\tau)]/U_2 > 1$. If $[U_1 w(1-\tau)]/U_2 > 1$, then Equation (13.92) implies that $\mu > 0$. Hence, Equation (13.93) must hold with equality so that the solution is $\hat{\ell}(s,\Lambda)$. Suppose next that $\Lambda > \Lambda^\star(s)$. Since $\ell \geq \ell^\star(s)$, Equation (13.93) must hold as an inequality. Therefore $\mu = 0$ and $[U_1 w(1-\tau)]/U_2 = 1$ and $\ell = \ell^\star(s)$. ∎

We make the following assumption.

Assumption 13.10 *For all $s \in S$, $U_1(\hat{y}(s,\ell),\ell)\hat{y}(s,\ell)$ is increasing in ℓ.*

Next define the function $G : S \times \Re_+ \to \Re_+$ by:

$$G(s,\Lambda) = \begin{cases} \hat{y}(s,\hat{\ell}(s,\Lambda))U_1\{\hat{y}(s,\hat{\ell}(s,\Lambda)),\hat{\ell}(s,\Lambda)\} & \text{if } 0 \leq \Lambda \leq \Lambda^*(s) \\ \Lambda^*(s) & \text{if } \Lambda \geq \Lambda^*(s). \end{cases}$$

A solution is a function Λ satisfying

$$\Lambda(s) = \beta \int_S G(s', \Lambda(s'))F(s', ds). \tag{13.95}$$

We have the following proposition.

Proposition 13.3 *For each $s \in S$ and $\Lambda \geq 0$, $G(s,\Lambda) - \Lambda$ is weakly decreasing in Λ.*

PROOF

Under Assumption 13.9, $y(s,\ell)U_1(y(s,\ell),\ell)$ is increasing in ℓ and, from Proposition 13.1, $\hat{\ell}(s,\Lambda)$ is non-increasing in Λ, so that $G_2 \leq 0$. ∎

We then have the following theorem.

Theorem 13.4 *Under Assumptions 13.6, 13.7, and 13.8, Equation (13.95) has a unique solution $\Lambda \in \mathcal{C}$ and for all $\Lambda_0 \in \mathcal{C}$, $\lim_{n\to\infty} \| T^n \Lambda^\circ - \Lambda \| = 0$.*

PROOF

Define the operator T on $\mathcal{C}$ by:

$$(Tf)(s) = \beta \int_S G(s', f(s'))F(s', ds). \tag{13.96}$$

Because f, G are continuous and bounded, Tf is continuous and bounded. Hence $T : \mathcal{C} \to \mathcal{C}$. Finally, T is a continuous operator. Note that:

$$\begin{aligned} \|Tf - Tf_n\| &= \max_{s \in S} |Tf(s) - Tf_n(s)| \\ &\leq \max_{s \in S} \beta \int_S |G(s', f(s')) - G(s', f_n(s'))| F(s, ds') \\ &\leq \beta \max_{s' \in S} |G(s', f(s')) - G(s', f_n(s'))|. \end{aligned}$$

We show that the operator T satisfies Blackwell's conditions. Under the assumptions above and from Proposition 13.1, G is non-decreasing in f, so that T is monotone. We need only verify the discounting property. From Proposition 13.1, $G(s,\Lambda) - \Lambda$ is weakly decreasing in Λ. For any $\Lambda \in \mathcal{C}$

and $a > 0$, $G(s, \Lambda + a) - (\Lambda + a) \leq G(s, \Lambda) - \Lambda$ or $G(s, \Lambda) \leq G(s, \Lambda) + a$. Then:

$$\begin{aligned} T(f + a)(s) &= \beta \int_S G(s', f(s') + a) F(s, ds') \\ &\leq \beta \int_S \{G(s', f(s')) + a\} F(s, ds') \\ &\leq Tf(s) + \beta a, \end{aligned}$$

so that T is a contraction with modulus β. ∎

Let $\ell(s)$ be the solution with the output equal to $y(s)$ when $\ell(s)$ is leisure. Define the stochastic discount factor as the intertemporal marginal rate of substitution in the purchasing power of money:

$$\mathcal{M}(s', s) \equiv \frac{\beta U_1\{y(s'), \ell(s')\} p(s)}{U_1\{y(s), \ell(s)\} \omega(s') p(s')}.$$

All assets denominated in nominal terms in this model are priced using this stochastic discount factor. The income tax and the stochastic inflation tax drive a wedge between consumption and leisure choices and increase the volatility of the stochastic discount factor that is used to price all assets with random payoffs. This wedge is similar to the wedge with cash and credit goods. The role of the income tax and the stochastic inflation tax in affecting consumption and leisure allocations is discussed further in Exercise 3.

Some observations on the term structure of interest rates

The empirical behavior of real and nominal interest rates of various maturities – the term structure, as it is known – has been a topic of wide study in the empirical finance literature. As we discussed in Chapter 8, there are also studies that have examined the implications of the consumption-based asset-pricing model. See, for example, Backus, Gregory, and Zin [41]. However, as a variety of authors have noted, the predictions of the standard consumption-based model are inconsistent with the facts. Specifically, the standard Lucas model with an exogenous endowment process that is calibrated using aggregate consumption growth implies that the term structure of interest rates is downward-sloping, there is little persistence in interest rates, and the standard deviation for long-term interest rates is lower than for short-term interest rates.

den Haan [150] has argued that these findings may be an artifact of omitting such features as capital (or production), variable labor supply, and money from a standard asset-pricing framework. In the data, consumption growth is typically positively autocorrelated, especially if measured at quarterly frequencies, and expected consumption growth possesses little persistence. Yet for the standard consumption-based asset-pricing model to produce an upward-sloping term structure and persistent interest rate movements, consumption growth must be negatively correlated and persistent. den Haan [150] argues that the introduction of production may help to resolve some of these anomalies because agents' attempt to smooth consumption may render growth rates of real variables highly persistent. Likewise, introducing leisure may improve the model because agents typically want to smooth the marginal utility of consumption. In a model with consumption-leisure choices, this will be easier for agents to do because they can also choose leisure. Finally, money must be included to allow for modeling of the behavior of nominal interest rates. Yet, as we discussed above, most monetary models such as cash-in-advance models imply that velocity does not fluctuate very much. For this purpose, den Haan [150] introduces money through a shopping time technology.

As in Exercise 6 in Chapter 8, den Haan [150] considers a trend-stationary and a difference-stationary endowment process. Since the trend-stationary model that is fit according to US quarterly data typically implies better behavior in the absence of production or other features, he compares the behavior of the consumption-based versus production-based model under the assumption that the exogenous endowment (or technology shock) process follows the trend-stationary model. However, to examine the role of production alone, he also compares both models under the assumption of i.i.d. shocks. One of his noteworthy findings is that the model with production delivers greater persistence in interest rates *regardless* of the persistence of the underlying exogenous process driving endowments (or technology shocks). However, adding variable labor supply causes the performance of the model to deteriorate in the sense that the interest rate spreads decline and their variances also fall. This occurs because in the model with a consumption-leisure choice, consumption and leisure become negatively correlated, thereby reducing the variance of the marginal utility of wealth. Finally, introducing money through a shopping-time technology allows for a consideration of various puzzles. For example, in Cooley and Hansen [120] the variance of the nominal interest rate is much lower than the observed variance. den Haan [150] finds that the implications of the shopping-time model are better for the variability of velocity but worse for asset pricing, in particular, the variance of interest rates. These results illustrate the range of observed outcomes that can be generated from existing models that allow for real and monetary interactions.

13.6.2. Business cycle implications

Following the analysis in Cooley and Hansen [120] and related papers, we modify the setup in the previous section by allowing for a stochastic technology that affects output and an endogenous capital accumulation process. Thus, output Y_t is produced by a linear homogeneous production function:

$$Y_t = z_t K_t^{1-\theta} H_t^{\theta}, \tag{13.97}$$

where $0 < \theta < 1$ and

$$\ln(z_{t+1}) = \rho \ln(z_t) + \epsilon_{t+1}, \tag{13.98}$$

where $\epsilon_t \sim N(0, \sigma_\epsilon^2)$.

The portion of output that is not consumed is invested in new capital goods. Hence, the law of motion for the capital stock is:

$$K_{t+1} = (1-\delta)K_t + I_t, \quad 0 < \delta < 1. \tag{13.99}$$

The household owns the capital and makes new investment decisions. Notice that this is different to the model in the previous section, which assumes a constant capital stock. It rents out the existing capital stock to a competitive firm that solves a static profit-maximization problem. The real wage rate and the rental rate of capital are determined similarly as in (13.77) and (13.78). Specifically, we have that:

$$w_t = \theta Y_t / H_t, \tag{13.100}$$

$$r_t = (1-\theta) Y_t / K_t. \tag{13.101}$$

The representative household obtains utility from consumption and leisure. Its preferences are described as follows:

$$E_0 \sum_{t=0}^{\infty} \beta^t [\alpha \ln(c_{1t}) + (1-\alpha) \ln(c_{2t}) - \gamma h_t], \tag{13.102}$$

with $0 < \beta < 1$ and $0 < \alpha < 1$. In this expression, c_1 denotes "cash goods" and c_2 denotes "credit goods."[5] The difference arises from the fact that existing money holdings must be used to acquire cash goods. Also, the utility function displays the indivisible labor assumption used earlier by Hansen [228]. At the beginning of period t, the representative household has money holdings equal to $m_t + (1 + R_{t-1} b_t) + T_t$, where m_t is currency carried over from the previous period and $(1 + R_{t-1}) b_t$ is principal plus interest from government bond holdings, b_t. The term T_t is a nominal lump-sum transfer (or tax) paid at the beginning of period t. The asset market opens first and households acquire bonds b_{t+1}, which they then carry over into the next period. This leaves the household with

[5] See also Exercise 7.

$m_t + (1 + R_{t-1})b_t + T_t - b_{t+1}$ units of currency for purchasing goods. Thus, the cash-in-advance constraint is:

$$P_t c_{1t} \leq m_t + (1 + R_{t-1})b_t + T_t - b_{t+1}, \tag{13.103}$$

where P_t is the price level.

The household's allocations also satisfy the sequence of budget constraints:

$$c_{1t} + c_{2t} + i_t + \frac{m_{t+1}}{P_t} + \frac{b_{t+1}}{P_t} \leq w_t h_t + r_t k_{t-1}$$
$$+ \frac{m_t}{P_t} + \frac{(1 + R_{t-1})b_t}{P_t} + \frac{T_t}{P_t}. \tag{13.104}$$

In modeling the government budget constraint, we assume for simplicity that government purchases are zero, $G_t = 0$, and that government bonds are in net zero supply in the economy as whole, $B_t = 0$. Thus, the government budget constraint has the simple form:

$$T_t = M_{t+1} - M_t. \tag{13.105}$$

The money supply grows exogenously as $M_{t+1} = \omega_t M_t$ so that the gross rate of growth is ω_t. We assume that:

$$\ln(\omega_{t+1}) = \eta \ln(\omega_t) + \epsilon_{t+1}, \tag{13.106}$$

where the random shock to money growth is distributed normally as $\epsilon_t \sim N((1 - \eta)\bar{\mu}, \sigma_\epsilon^2)$. The aggregate resource constraint requires that $c_{1t} + c_{2t} + I_t \leq Y_t$.

Since the money supply is growing, we need to divide through by the aggregate stock of money to induce stationarity in the variables. Define $\tilde{m}_t = m_t/M_t$, $\tilde{b}_t = b_t/M_t$ and $\tilde{P}_t = P_t/M_{t+1}$. Notice that the budget constraint can be written as:

$$c_{1t} + c_{2t} + i_t + \frac{\tilde{m}_{t+1}}{\tilde{P}_t} + \frac{\tilde{b}_{t+1}}{\tilde{P}_t} \leq w_t h_t + r_t k_{t-1}$$
$$+ \frac{\tilde{m}_t + \omega_t - 1}{\tilde{P}_t \omega_t} + (1 + R_{t-1})\frac{\tilde{b}_t}{\tilde{P}_t \omega_t}. \tag{13.107}$$

The cash-in-advance constraint becomes:

$$c_{1t} \leq \frac{\tilde{m}_t + \omega_t - 1}{\tilde{P}_t \omega_t} + (1 + R_{t-1})\frac{\tilde{b}_t}{\tilde{P}_t \omega_t} - \frac{\tilde{b}_{t+1}\omega_t}{\tilde{P}_t}. \tag{13.108}$$

Notice that the rate of growth of money ω_t is always positive in this model. Hence, the nominal interest rate is also positive, which implies that the cash-in-advance constraint holds with equality.

Assume that the law of motion for the household's own capital is given by $k_{t+1} = (1 - \delta)k_t + i_t$. Since bonds are in net zero supply in the aggregate economy, we will impose this condition on the household's problem to eliminate the bond holdings. We will also use the law of motion of the household's capital stock to eliminate the variable i. The state variables for the household's problem consist of the current values of the technology shock z, the money shock ω, the household's own capital stock k, the aggregate capital stock K, and transformed money holdings $\tilde{m}$. Given the price functions $w = w(z, \omega, K)$, $r = r(z, \omega, K)$ and $P = P(z, \omega, K)$, the household's problem can be written as:

$$(P)\ V(z, \omega, K, k, \tilde{m}) = \max_{c_1, c_2, h, k', \tilde{m}'} \{\alpha \ln (c_1) + (1 - \alpha) \ln (c_2) - \gamma h$$
$$+ \beta V(z', \omega', K', k', \tilde{m}')\}$$

subject to the laws of motion for the technology and money shocks (13.98) and (13.106), the constraints

$$c_1 \le \frac{\tilde{m} + \omega - 1}{\tilde{P}\omega}, \tag{13.109}$$

$$c_2 + k' + \frac{\tilde{m}'}{\tilde{P}} \le w(z, \omega, K)h + (r(z, \omega, K) + 1 - \delta)k, \tag{13.110}$$

and also the laws of motion for the aggregate variables

$$K' = K'(z, \omega, K), \quad H = H(z, \omega, K), \quad P = P(z, \omega, K). \tag{13.111}$$

A *recursive competitive equilibrium* for this economy consists of a set of decision rules $c_1(\zeta), c_2(\zeta), h(\zeta), k'(\zeta), \tilde{m}'(\zeta))$, where $\zeta \equiv (z, \omega, k, K, \tilde{m})'$; a set of per capita or economy-wide decision rules $k'(z, \omega, K)$ and $H(\zeta, \omega, K)$; pricing functions $w(z, \omega, K), r(z, \omega, K), P(z, \omega, K)$ and value function $V(\zeta)$ such that (i) given prices, the individual decision rules solve the consumer's problem in (P); (ii) the pricing functions $w(\cdot)$ and $r(\cdot)$ satisfy the condition in (13.101) and (13.101) and (iii) the individual decision rules are consistent with aggregate outcomes so that $k'(z, \omega, K, K, 1) = k'(z, \omega, K)$, $h(z, \omega, K, K, 1) = H(z, \omega, K)$ and $\tilde{m}'(z, \omega, K, K, 1) = 1$ for all values of the aggregate state z, ω, K.

The competitive equilibrium cannot be obtained as the solution to a social planner's problem, which is the approach that we followed in solving the "real" models of Chapters 10–12. The reason is that the inflation tax induces a wedge between the consumption of cash and credit goods and between consumption of cash goods and leisure. Instead we need to solve for the competitive equilibrium directly. Furthermore, given the form of the utility function, we need to employ a numerical solution technique to compute the competitive equilibrium. Hansen and Prescott [233] provide a general algorithm that can be used to transform a variety of recursive equilibrium frameworks into a general linear-quadratic dynamic optimization problem which approximates the original non-linear problem around the deterministic steady state. We already described how this approach could be implemented for competitive equilibria that solve the social planner's problem in Chapter 12. The approach to solving models with monetary distortions can also be mapped into a similar framework. The additional complication is that consistency must be imposed between the individual decision variables and the aggregate state at each stage of the iterative procedure used to generate the optimal value function and decision rules. We briefly describe this approach and discuss some of the empirical findings associated with the model.

The approach to solving the original non-linear model involves finding the deterministic steady state. This can be obtained by considering the first-order conditions for a deterministic version of the problem. Let μ_t denote the multiplier on the cash-in-advance constraint and ξ_t the multiplier on the budget constraint. The first-order conditions with respect to $c_{1t}, c_{2t}, h_t, k_{t+1}, \tilde{m}_{t+1}$ with the envelope conditions substituted are:

$$\frac{\alpha}{c_1} = \mu_t + \xi_t, \tag{13.112}$$

$$\frac{1-\alpha}{c_{2t}} = \xi_t, \tag{13.113}$$

$$\gamma = \xi_t w_t \tag{13.114}$$

$$\xi_t = \beta[\xi_{t+1}(r_{t+1} + 1 - \delta)], \tag{13.115}$$

$$\frac{\xi_t}{\tilde{P}_t} = \beta\left[\frac{\mu_{t+1}}{\tilde{P}_{t+1}\omega_{t+1}} + \frac{\xi_{t+1}}{\tilde{P}_{t+1}\omega_{t+1}}\right]. \tag{13.116}$$

In the deterministic steady state, all dated variables equal a constant. Notice that we can solve the last condition for $\mu + \xi$ as:

$$\mu + \xi = \frac{\xi\omega}{\beta}.$$

Now consider the ratio of the first two conditions as:

$$\frac{\alpha c_2}{(1-\alpha)c_1} = \frac{\mu+\xi}{\xi} = \frac{\omega}{\beta}. \tag{13.117}$$

The expression on the right side is equal to one plus the nominal interest rate, R, for this economy, where the gross rate of growth of the money supply ω is one plus the inflation rate in the steady state and $1/\beta$ is the (gross) real interest rate. Dividing through by α and adding $c_1/(1-\alpha)c_1$ to both sides yields:

$$\frac{c}{c_1} = \frac{1}{\alpha} + \frac{1-\alpha}{\alpha}R, \tag{13.118}$$

where $c = c_1 + c_2$ so that c/c_1 is just equal to consumption velocity for this economy. From the fourth condition we observe that the real interest rate is also equal to the real rate of return on physical capital accumulation:

$$(1-\theta)\frac{y}{k} + 1 - \delta = \frac{1}{\beta}, \tag{13.119}$$

where we have substituted for the rental rate of capital. The second and third conditions show that the marginal rate of substitution between consumption of credit goods and hours worked is equal to the real wage:

$$\frac{\gamma c_2}{1-\alpha} = w = \theta\frac{y}{h}. \tag{13.120}$$

Finally, the aggregate resource constraint implies that:

$$c_1 + c_2 + \delta k = y = zk^{1-\theta}h^{\theta}. \tag{13.121}$$

Notice that we can solve for the steady state values for c_1, c_2, h, k using the conditions in (13.117), (13.119), (13.120), and (13.121). The normalized price level is then determined from the cash-in-advance constraint as:

$$c_1 = \frac{\tilde{m}}{\tilde{P}\omega}, \tag{13.122}$$

where $\tilde{m} = 1$. These conditions can also be used to calibrate the model. For example, we can use the condition in (13.118) to regress a measure of velocity against the nominal interest rate to obtain an estimate of α, which shows the weight of cash versus credit goods in the utility function. The parameters of the technology shock process can be calibrated from a measure of the Solow residual and the remaining parameters of preferences and technology can be obtained from the average values of the capital share in output, the investment-output ratio, the capital-output ratio and the share of time spent working in the market.

The next step is to replace the original non-linear problem with one which a quadratic objective and linear constraints. For the cash-in-advance model, define the return function $R(z, \omega, k, K, H, \tilde{m}, k', \tilde{m}')$ by:

$$R(z, \omega, k, K, H, \tilde{m}, \tilde{p}, k', \tilde{m}') = \alpha \ln (c_1) + (1 - \alpha) \ln (c_2) - \gamma h$$

$$c_1 = \frac{\tilde{m} + \omega - 1}{\tilde{P}\omega},$$

$$c_2 = w(z, \omega, K)h + (r(z, \omega, K) + 1 - \delta)k - k' - \frac{\tilde{m}'}{\tilde{P}}.$$

Now define $y \equiv (z, \omega, k, K, H, \tilde{m}, \tilde{p}, h, k', \tilde{m}')'$. Replacing the return function with a quadratic in y, the original problem can be expressed as:

$$v(z, \omega, k, K, \tilde{m}) = \max\{y^T Qy + \beta v(z', \omega', k', K', \tilde{m}')\}$$

$$K' = K'(z, \omega, K) \; H = H(z, \omega, K) \; \tilde{P} = P(z, \omega, K).$$

In this problem, we have the exogenous state variables (z, ω) and we have substituted for the endogenous state variable k' using the law of motion for the household's capital. Now let $d = (h, k', \tilde{m})$ denote the decision variables. The solution for the problem is found through successive approximation on the mapping generating v starting from some initial negative definite matrix for v^0. The aggregate consistency conditions are imposed by differentiating the value function at the nth stage with respect to d_i and by evaluating the expression for each d_i as $d_i = D_i(z, \omega, K, K, 1)$. Since the objective function is quadratic, the first-order conditions characterizing each d_i are linear. The function P is obtained from the first-order condition for $\tilde{m}'$ after imposing the aggregate consistency conditions that $k = K$ and $\tilde{m} = 1$.

Despite the potential interest in the model, Cooley and Hansen [123] find that monetary shocks do not contribute much to the fluctuation of the real variables relative to the standard neoclassical growth model. However, as discussed earlier, the introduction of money through a cash-in-advance constraint leads to distortions due to the inflation tax. The welfare losses of the inflation tax are studied further by Cooley and Hansen [121, 122]. Braun [72] examines the magnitude of the optimal inflation tax.

13.7. CONCLUSIONS

Providing micro-foundations for money has been a problem that economists of different persuasions have grappled with over the years. The cash-in-advance model that we have studied here provides a simple framework whereby money gets valued in equilibrium and also allows for an analysis of monetary phenomena in empirical and quantitative terms. On the one hand, the cash-in-advance model allows for an asset-theoretic approach to analyzing the impact of monetary shocks on real and nominal asset returns. On the other hand, this class of models has been used to examine the response of real variables to monetary disturbances.

13.8. EXERCISES

1. Consider the basic asset-pricing model in Section 13.1. Define $\mathcal{B}$ as the space of bounded, continuous functions on $\Re_{++} \times S \times Z \times \mathcal{H}$ such that $\sup_{y,s,z,h} |V(y,s,z,h)/y^{1-\gamma}| < \infty$. For $V \in \mathcal{B}$, define the operator T:

$$(TV)(y,s,z,h) = \max_{c,m^d,z',h'} \left\{ U(c) + \beta \int_S V(y',s',z',h')F(s,ds') \right\},$$

subject to the constraints in Equations (13.74) and (13.75) and $m^d \in \mathcal{M}$, $z' \in Z$, and $h' \in B$.

Show that under Assumptions 13.1, 13.2, and 13.4, T has a unique fixed point in $\mathcal{B}$.

2. The Svensson Model

At the beginning of the period, the household observes the realization s_t. The money supply evolves as $M_{t+1} = \omega(s_t)M_t$ and endowment is stationary in levels. The rate of contraction of the money supply satisfies Assumption 13.7. The normalized money balances held at the beginning of the asset market are $m_t^d \equiv p_t y_t z_t + b_t + h_t - p_t c_t + \omega_t - 1$. The normalized budget constraint in the asset market is:

$$h_{t+1}\omega_t + q_t^e z_{t+1} + Q_t b_{t+1}\omega_t \leq m_t^d + q_t^e z_t. \tag{13.123}$$

The normalized cash-in-advance constraint is:

$$p_t c_t \leq h_t, \tag{13.124}$$

and the state vector for the representative household is (s_t, z_t, b_t, h_t).

(a) Formulate the household problem in a stationary equilibrium in which prices $p(s)$, $q^e(s)$, and $Q(s)$ are continuous, strictly positive functions of the economy-wide state variables.

(b) Derive the first-order conditions, envelope conditions, and specify the market-clearing conditions.

(c) Discuss the relationship between a binding cash-in-advance constraint and strictly positive nominal interest rates. Are consumers willing to hold nominal money balances at a positive nominal interest rate?

3. Consumption and Leisure Choices
Use the labor-leisure model in Section 13.6.1 and assume that the utility function takes the form:

$$U(c_t, \ell_t) \equiv \frac{1}{1-\gamma}(c_t^{\alpha}\ell_t^{1-\alpha})^{1-\gamma}.$$

Let $\rho \equiv 1 - \gamma$ for notational simplicity and assume that $\rho > 0$. Also assume that $0 < \alpha < 1$. For the utility function to be concave in both arguments, the following conditions must hold: $\alpha\rho < 1$ and $(1 - \alpha)\rho < 1$. Also notice that, if $\rho > 0$, $U_{c\ell} > 0$ (so leisure and consumption are complements).
   (a) Derive the first-order conditions and the envelope conditions.
   (b) Next, use the basic structure of the consumption-leisure model but drop the cash-in-advance constraint to make it a real model. Construct the equilibrium for two cases: a zero tax rate τ and a positive tax rate. Compare the consumption and leisure streams for the three versions of the model.
4. A Cash-in-Advance Model with Storage[6]
There is a representative competitive firm that produces a non-durable consumption good y_t using an input x_t. The production function is $y_t = \lambda(s_t)x_t^{\alpha}$, where $\lambda : S \to \Re_+$ is a technology shock. The intermediate good x_t depreciates at 100% when used in production. The firm buys the input from consumers in a competitive market at the real price of w_t. The firm solves:

$$\max_{x_t} \lambda(s_t)x_t^{\alpha} - x_t w_t.$$

The intermediate good is storable when held by households. The law of motion for the consumer's holdings of the intermediate good at the beginning of the period is given by:

$$k_{t+1} = \theta(s_{t+1})(k_t - x_t). \tag{13.125}$$

The capital stock is assumed to be non-negative ($k_{t+1} \geq 0$). If we assume that the storage shock θ is positive with probability one, then the non-negativity assumption is equivalent to the constraint $k_t - x_t \geq 0$. The realization of the shock θ_{t+1} is unknown when x_t is chosen in period t.
The timing of trades is identical to the Svensson model. The asset market opens and equity shares are traded and money holdings

[6] This exercise is derived from Eichenbaum and Singleton [170].

adjusted. The normalized law of motion for money holdings at the beginning of the period is

$$h_{t+1} = \frac{1}{\omega(s_t)}[h_t - p_t c_t + b_t + (q_t^e + p_t d_t) z_t$$
$$- q_t^e z_{t+1} + w_t p_t x_t + \omega(s_t) - 1] - Q_t b_{t+1}. \quad (13.126)$$

The cash-in-advance constraint is identical to Equation (13.124).

The agent's preferences are:

$$E_0 \left\{ \sum_{t=0}^{\infty} \beta^t v_t \log(c_t) \right\}, \quad 0 < \beta < 1, \quad (13.127)$$

where $E_0(\cdot)$ denotes expectation conditional on information at time 0. The taste shock is assumed to follow the process $v_{t+1} = v_t^a \epsilon_{t+1}$, where $|a| \leq 1$ and $\log \epsilon$ is normally distributed with mean zero, variance σ_ϵ^2, and is not autocorrelated. We assume that v_{t-1} and ϵ_t are part of s_t.

(a) Derive the equilibrium wage rate and dividends.

(b) The household's state variables are h_t, z_t, b_t, k_t, as well as s_t and the economy-wide capital stock, κ_t which takes values on an interval $\mathcal{K} \equiv [0, \bar{\kappa}]$ and evolves as $\kappa_{t+1} = \theta(s_{t+1})(\kappa_t - x_t)$. Formulate the household's problem as a dynamic program.

(c) Derive the equilibrium first-order conditions and envelope conditions for $\{c, h', z', b', x\}$.

(d) Let $\tilde{x}(s, \kappa)$ be a fixed policy that satisfies the non-negativity constraint and let $\tilde{y}(s, \kappa)$ be the output produced under this policy. Define a function Ψ such that, for all (s, κ), the price level satisfies $p(s, \kappa) = 1/\tilde{y}(s, \kappa)\Psi(s, \kappa)$. Show that Ψ satisfies the functional equation:

$$\Psi(s, \kappa) = \max \left[1, \beta E_s \left(\frac{v'}{v} \frac{\Psi(s', \kappa')}{\omega(s)} \right) \right]. \quad (13.128)$$

(e) Assume that the money supply rule is not a function of κ. Prove that there exists a fixed point for Equation (13.128) that is a function of s only. Denote this fixed point $\Psi^\star$.

(f) Define $\Lambda(s_{t+1}, s_t) \equiv \beta\,[v_{t+1}\Psi^\star(s_{t+1})/\omega_t \Psi^\star(s_t)]$. Use the equilibrium first-order conditions and the fact that $w_t/c_t = \alpha/x_t$ in equilibrium to show that $\Lambda(s_{t+1}, s_t)$ satisfies the equation:

$$\frac{\mu_k(s_t, \kappa_t)}{\beta\alpha} = E_t \left[\frac{\Lambda(s_{t+1}, s_t)}{x(s_t, \kappa_t)} \right] - \beta E_t \left[\frac{\Lambda(s_{t+2}, s_{t+1})\theta(s_{t+1})}{x(s_{t+1}, \kappa_{t+1})} \right].$$

(g) Suppose that $\beta E_t[v_{t+1}/v_t \omega_t] < 1$. Show that the cash-in-advance constraint is always binding and $\Psi_t^\star = 1$ for all t.

(h) Show that the non-negativity constraint on capital is not binding and find a closed-form expression for the intermediate good.

5. Assume that $\zeta_{t+1} = \zeta_t^{\eta} u_{t+1}$ where $|\eta| < 1$ and u_t is lognormally distributed with mean zero and variance σ_u^2. Find a closed-form solution for the one-period nominal bond in the storage model.
6. Construct the factor supply function for the storage model for a *real* version of the model; that is, assume that no money is required for trading to occur. Compare the solutions and provide some intuition for the wedge introduced by the cash-in-advance constraint.
7. A Model with Cash and Credit Goods
   In this model, the representative agent has preferences given by:

$$E\left\{\sum_{t=0}^{\infty} \beta^t U(c_{1,t}, c_{2,t})\right\}, \quad 0 < \beta < 1, \tag{13.129}$$

where $c_{1,t}$ is consumption of the cash good, $c_{2,t}$ is consumption of the credit good, and the expectation is over realizations of the shocks at time zero. To retain the assumption that there is only one type of good produced and yet make the distinction between cash and credit goods, assume that there is a linear technology for transforming cash goods into credit goods on the production or supply side. Let y_t be the exogenous endowment. The linear technology constraint is:

$$x_{1,t} + x_{2,t} = y_t, \tag{13.130}$$

where $x_{1,t}$ is the production of the cash good and $x_{2,t}$ is the production of the credit good.

Assumption 13.1 on the shocks to the economy still holds and the money supply process satisfies Equation (13.8) but we now assume that the endowment process is stationary in levels. We also require that money growth satisfies Assumption 13.7.

Assumption 13.11 *(i) The utility function $U : \Re_+^2 \rightarrow \Re$ is continuously differentiable, strictly increasing, and strictly concave. For all $y > 0$,*

$$\lim_{c \to 0} \frac{U_1(c, y-c)}{U_2(c, y-c)} = \infty, \quad \lim_{y \to c} \frac{U_1(c, y-c)}{U_2(c, y-c)} = 0;$$

(ii) For all $y \geq 0$, $cU_2(c, y-c)$ is strictly increasing in c, with

$$\lim_{c \to 0} cU_2(c, y-c) = 0, \quad \lim_{c \to y} cU_2(c, y-c) = \infty,$$

and for some $A < \infty$, $cU_1(c, y-c) \leq A$ for all $0 \leq c \leq y$ and all $y \geq 0$.

At the beginning of the period, the agent starts with currency accumulated last period M_{t-1}, observes the realization of the current shocks s_t, and receives the lump-sum money transfer G_t. The agent's post transfer money holdings are $H_t = M_{t-1} + G_t$ where $G_t = M_t - M_{t-1}$. To make the nominal variables stationary, we divide the agent's post transfer balances by the money supply in period t so that:

$$h_t \equiv m_{t-1} + [\omega(s_t) - 1]/\omega(s_t).$$

The agent's initial wealth takes the form of money holdings, an equity share z_t which is a claim to a stochastic nominal dividend stream, and one-period nominal bonds B_{t-1}, each of which is a claim to one unit of currency at time t. The goods market opens first and the agent's purchases of cash goods $p_t c_{1,t}$ are subject to the following constraint:

$$p_t c_{1,t} \leq h_t \tag{13.131}$$

where p_t is the price level as a ratio of the money stock. The agent also purchases credit goods in the amount $p_t c_{2,t}$, payment for which can be postponed until the asset market opens.

At the close of the goods market, the agent receives the nominal dividend payment $z_t p_t y(s_t)$ and the payment on one-period nominal bonds B_{t-1} purchased last period. Define $b_t \equiv B_t/M_t^s$. The agent's budget constraint in the asset market after normalization by the money stock is:

$$\begin{aligned} p_t c_{2,t} + m_t + q_t^e z_{t+1} + Q_t b_t \leq (y_t p_t + q_t^e) z_t \\ + h_t - p_t c_{1,t} + b_{t-1}/\omega(s_t), \end{aligned} \tag{13.132}$$

where Q^e is the nominal price of the equity share, $q^e \equiv Q^e/M^s$ and Q is the nominal price of the one-period bond.

(a) Show the existence of a solution to the consumer's problem.
(b) Find the first-order and envelope conditions.
(c) Using the first-order conditions for bonds, comment on the relation between velocity and nominal interest rates.
(d) Find an expression for the equity price. How does it differ from the equity price in an economy without money?

CHAPTER 14

International asset markets

The role of international trade and exchange in leading to welfare gains is one of the most basic topics in the economics literature. In recent years, this issue has been examined from the viewpoint of international risk sharing. There has also been a proliferation of international models of the business cycle, which seek to understand the mechanisms for the transmission of real and monetary shocks. Third, as international asset markets have grown in size and importance, there has been an increase in the variety of assets that are traded. Paralleling the growth of these markets is the increased interest in examining the empirical behavior of assets denominated in alternative currencies.

In this chapter, we begin by describing a real model of international trade and exchange that allows us to illustrate the role of risk sharing and portfolio diversification across countries. This discussion clarifies the ways in which international trade can lead to perfect sharing even in the absence of international capital flows. It also links to the literature on international business cycles. Next, we introduce a monetary model of international trade and exchange. For this purpose, we use a two-country model with cash-in-advance constraints in which purchases of goods must be made with sellers' currencies. We certainly do not mean to suggest that this is the only model or even the most commonly accepted model of exchange rates and asset prices. We choose this model because it allows us to demonstrate the existence of equilibrium based on utility-maximizing behavior of agents and it provides a useful framework for examining a variety of observed relationships. We describe the basic model in Section 14.2 while in Section 14.3, we modify it to incorporate non-traded goods and investment and capital flows.

Earlier models in the exchange rate literature include the Dornbusch model [157] and the Mussa model [348], both of which emphasize differential speeds of adjustment and neither of which is based on utility-maximizing behavior. Obstfeld and Stockman [354] provide a useful survey that includes a description of these alternative models of exchange rate determination. Exchange rate behavior has also been studied in money-in-the-utility-function models (see Calvo [86] and Calvo and Rodriguez [87]) and in overlapping generations models (see Kareken and Wallace [271] and Greenwood and Williamson [215]).

There is a large literature on the empirical behavior of foreign exchange rate markets. It is beyond the scope of this text to describe the issues that arise in this literature. However, the modeling of risk premia that takes into account exchange rate risk together with risks emanating from the real economy provides a useful framework for empirical analysis.

14.1. A TWO-COUNTRY MODEL

Before we incorporate money into a simple two-country, two-good model, it will be useful to discuss some important issues in a non-monetary pure endowment economy. Our discussion is based on Cole [111] and Cole and Obstfeld [112].

We begin our discussion with a two-country real version of the Lucas asset-pricing model (see Lucas [318]). Agents from both countries are identical in terms of preferences and differ only in terms of endowments. There are two goods, Y_1 and Y_2. Country 1 has a random endowment of good Y_1 and country 2 has a random endowment of good Y_2. Neither good is storable. We assume that endowments are stationary in levels. The case with growing endowments can be analyzed using an approach similar to that in Chapter 8.

Let $s_t \in S \subseteq \Re^m_+$ denote a vector of exogenous shocks that follows a first-order Markov process with a stationary transition function F. The transition function F satisfies Assumption 13.1 in Chapter 13.

At the beginning of the period, agents observe the current realization. We assume that endowment is a time-invariant function of the exogenous shock.

Assumption 14.1 *Define* $\mathcal{Y} \equiv [\underline{y}, \bar{y}]$ *where* $\underline{y} > 0$, *and* $\bar{y} < \infty$. *The functions* $y_1 : S \to \mathcal{Y}$ *and* $y_2 : S \to \mathcal{Y}$ *are continuous functions that are bounded away from zero.*

The representative consumer in country j has preferences over random sequences $\{c^j_{1,t}, c^j_{2,t}\}_{t=0}^{\infty}$ defined by:

$$E_0 \left\{ \sum_{t=0}^{\infty} \beta^t U(c^j_{1,t}, c^j_{2,t}) \right\}, \quad 0 < \beta < 1. \tag{14.1}$$

We have the following assumption.

Assumption 14.2 *The utility function* $U : \Re_+^2 \rightarrow \Re$ *is continuously differentiable, strictly increasing, and strictly concave. For all* $c_1, c_2 > 0$,

$$\lim_{c_1 \to 0} \frac{U_1(c_1, c_2)}{U_2(c_1, c_2)} = \infty, \quad \lim_{c_2 \to 0} \frac{U_1(c_1, c_2)}{U_2(c_1, c_2)} = 0.$$

This requirement on the utility function ensures that both goods are consumed in equilibrium.

Central planning problem

We start with the central planning problem. Let ϕ_j denote the Pareto weight for country j. Since preferences are time separable, the endowment is non-storable, and there is no investment process, the problem at time t is just

$$\max \left[\phi_1 U(c_{1,t}^1, c_{2,t}^1) + \phi_2 U(c_{1,t}^2, c_{2,t}^2) \right] \tag{14.2}$$

subject to

$$c_{1,t}^1 + c_{1_t}^2 = y_{1,t},$$

$$c_{2,t}^1 + c_{2_t}^2 = y_{2,t}.$$

It is straightforward to show that the first-order conditions reduce to

$$\frac{U_1(c_{1,t}^1, c_{2,t}^1)}{U_1(c_{1,t}^2, c_{2,t}^2)} = \frac{\phi_2}{\phi_1}, \tag{14.3}$$

$$\frac{U_2(c_{1,t}^1, c_{2,t}^1)}{U_2(c_{1,t}^2, c_{2,t}^2)} = \frac{\phi_2}{\phi_1}. \tag{14.4}$$

It is convenient to assume that preferences are Cobb-Douglas:

$$U(c_1, c_2) = \frac{(c_1^\alpha c_2^{1-\alpha})^{1-\rho}}{1-\rho}, 0 < \rho < 1, 0 < \alpha < 1. \tag{14.5}$$

Under the assumption that preferences are Cobb-Douglas, we can show that $c_1^1 = \delta y_1$, $c_2^1 = \delta y_2$, $c_1^2 = (1-\delta) y_1$, and $c_2^2 = (1-\delta) y_2$, where

$$\delta = \left[1 + \left(\frac{\phi_2}{\phi_1} \right)^\sigma \right]$$

and $\sigma = \frac{1}{\rho}$. Hence the ratio of marginal utilities across agents in different countries is equalized for all states and goods.

No asset trading

In this section, we examine the case in which there is trade in goods but no trade in international assets. Essentially we are forcing the current account to equal zero in each period. Let p_t denote the relative price of good y_2 in terms of the numeraire good y_1. Country 1 and 2's budget constraints are:

$$c^1_{1,t} + p_t c^1_{2,t} = y_{1,t}. \tag{14.6}$$

$$\frac{c^2_{1,t}}{p_t} + c^2_{2,t} = y_{2,t}. \tag{14.7}$$

Once again, this is a static problem because there are no assets for intertemporal consumption smoothing and the endowment is non-storable. If we assume the Cobb-Douglas functional form for preferences, then the consumption allocations are:

$$c^1_1 = \alpha y_1,$$

$$c^1_2 = \frac{(1-\alpha)y_1}{p},$$

$$c^2_1 = \alpha p y_2,$$

$$c^2_2 = (1-\alpha)y_2.$$

Equilibrium in the two goods markets requires that:

$$c^1_1 + c^2_1 = y_1. \tag{14.8}$$

$$c^1_2 + c^2_2 = y_2. \tag{14.9}$$

Substitute the consumption functions into the market clearing conditions and solve for the relative price to show that:

$$p = \frac{(1-\alpha)y_1}{\alpha y_2}.$$

This price can be substituted into the consumption functions above to show that $c^1_2 = \alpha y_2$ and $c^2_1 = (1-\alpha)y_1$.

Notice that the no-asset-trading allocation is identical to the central planning allocation if:

$$\alpha = \delta = \left[1 + \left(\frac{\phi_2}{\phi_1}\right)^{\sigma}\right]$$

or

$$\phi^1 = \left[1 + \left(\frac{1-\alpha}{\alpha}\right)^{\rho}\right]^{-1}$$

and $\phi^2 = 1 - \phi^1$.

This exercise illustrates several points:

- The absence of international capital mobility does not necessarily imply that the allocation is not Pareto optimal. Efficient risk sharing can occur despite the lack of financial assets and insurance.
- The international ratio of marginal utilities across countries is identical across goods and states. A large and positive shock in the amount of good y_1 is positively transmitted to the residents of country 2 by the increase in demand (and hence the relative price) for good y_2. A large negative shock in the amount of a good is similarly transmitted across borders, despite the absence of trade in financial assets. Hence efficient risk sharing occurs through changes in the relative price of goods.
- Notice that we can price financial assets in the model, under the assumption that the current account is zero, and can show that real interest rates and real asset returns will be equal for the two countries, despite the absence of financial capital mobility.
- The total consumption of countries 1 and 2 is:

$$c_1^1 + pc_2^1 = \alpha y_1 + \alpha y_2,$$

$$c_1^2 + pc_2^2 = (1-\alpha)y_1 + (1-\alpha)y_2.$$

  Observe that correlation of the total value of consumption of country 1 and country 2 is positive and equal to one.

As Cole and Obstfeld [112] point out, the positive transmission of shocks occurs because countries *specialize* in the production of goods.

Non-specialization in endowments

To illustrate the impact of non-specialization, Cole and Obstfeld [112] introduce a third good. Call this third good w. Assume that both countries receive an exogenous and stochastic endowment of good w and let $w^j : S \rightarrow W = [\underline{w}, \bar{w}]$ denote the realization of good w in country j. Let $\alpha_1, \alpha_2, \alpha_w$ denote the expenditure shares under the assumption of Cobb-Douglas preferences and let w be the numeraire good, so that p_1 denotes the relative price of good y_1 in terms of w and p_2 denotes the relative price of good y_2 in units of w. Agents in country 1 and 2 have budget constraints:

$$p_{1,t}c_{1,t}^1 + p_{2,t}c_{2,t}^1 + c_{w,t}^1 \leq p_{1,t}y_{1,t} + w_t^a,$$

$$p_{1,t}c_{1,t}^2 + p_{2,t}c_{2,t}^2 + c_{w,t}^2 \leq p_{2,t}y_{2,t} + w_t^b.$$

The equilibrium relative prices satisfy:

$$p_1 = \frac{\alpha_1 [w^1 + w^2]}{\alpha_w y_1},$$

$$p_2 = \frac{\alpha_2 [w^1 + w^2]}{\alpha_w y_2}.$$

The consumption of good 1 by agents in countries 1 and 2, under the assumption of Cobb-Douglas preferences, can be shown to satisfy:

$$c^1_{1,t} = \left[\alpha_w \left(\frac{w^1_t}{w^1_t + w^2_t}\right) + \alpha_1\right] y_1,$$

$$c^2_{1,t} = \left[\alpha_w \left(\frac{w^2_t}{w^1_t + w^2_t}\right) + \alpha_2\right] y_1.$$

Similar expressions can be derived for the consumption of goods, y_2, w. The ratio of marginal utilities of both countries for each good will be equal to a constant across all states, a condition for Pareto optimality, only if the share of the endowment of w, defined as $(\frac{w^1_t}{w^1_t+w^2_t})$ and $(\frac{w^2_t}{w^1_t+w^2_t})$, is constant as the total w varies with s. The shocks to w^1 and w^2 must be perfectly correlated for the allocation with no trade in financial assets to be Pareto optimal. If these shocks are not perfectly correlated, then there will be benefits to trading equity shares or other forms of financial assets.

This creates an important distinction between country-specific shocks, which affect all sectors within a country, and industry-specific shocks. Shocks to y_1 or y_2 are by definition country-specific shocks whereas shocks to w^1, w^2, where w^1, w^2 are not perfectly correlated, are sector-specific shocks. Hence, when there are sector-specific shocks, there are gains to asset trading that improve risk sharing and allow diversification. The intuition is that, in the absence of trade in financial assets, the country with a negative shock to the endowment of w would like to run a current account deficit by importing w and borrowing against future endowment. Since the current account must always be balanced, the country must export more of the good in which it specializes in production to finance the import of good w. Notice that the relative price of w may not adjust much if w^1 and w^2 are negatively correlated but the sum $w^1 + w^2$ fluctuates very little.

Non-traded goods

Suppose now that the third good is a non-traded good. Call this good n and assume that $n^j : S \rightarrow N = [\underline{n}, \bar{n}]$ denote the realization of good n in country j. Let $\alpha_1, \alpha_2, \alpha_n$ denote the expenditure shares under the assumption of Cobb-Douglas preferences and let y_1 be the numeraire good. Under the assumption of balanced trade and Cobb-Douglas preferences, the demands for the goods satisfy:

$$c_1^1 = \frac{\alpha_1}{1-\alpha_n} y_1,$$

$$c_2^1 = \frac{\alpha_1}{1-\alpha_n} y_2,$$

$$c_1^2 = \frac{\alpha_2}{1-\alpha_n} y_1,$$

$$c_2^2 = \frac{\alpha_2}{1-\alpha_n} y_2.$$

Each country consumes its endowment of the non-traded good, n^1, n^2. The ratio of marginal utility across countries for a traded good will now depend on the ratio $\frac{n^1}{n^2}$. Unless n^1, n^2 are perfectly correlated, then the resulting allocations will not be Pareto optimal. There are gains from international risk sharing through asset trade. Notice that the correlation of consumption across countries will now depend on the proportion of a country's consumption that is non-tradeable. If this sector constitutes a large fraction of consumption, then even if consumption of traded goods is perfectly correlated, the correlation of national consumption levels may be close to zero.

Trade in equity shares

We now introduce trade in financial assets. An agent in country 1 holds equity shares that are claims to the endowment stream for goods y_1 (the domestic good) and claims to y_2 (the foreign good). We now discuss the impact of asset trading and relate it to the model without asset trade discussed earlier.

Let $z_{i,t}^j$ for $j=1,2$ and $i=1,2$ denote the shares of good i held by an agent in country j at the beginning of period t. An agent's budget constraint is:

$$z_{1,t}^j[y_{1,t}+q_{1,t}]+z_{2,t}^j[p_{2,t}y_{2,t}+q_{2,t}] \geq c_{1,t}^j+p_{2,t}c_{2,t}^j+q_{1,t}z_{1,t+1}^j+q_{2,t}z_{2,t+1}^j. \tag{14.10}$$

The agent maximizes his objective function subject to the constraint. The first-order conditions are:

$$U_1(c_{1,t}^j, c_{2,t}^j) = U_2(c_{1,t}^j, c_{2,t}^j)p_{2,t}. \tag{14.11}$$

$$U_1(c_{1,t}^j, c_{2,t}^j)q_{1,t} = \beta E_t U_1(c_{1,t+1}^j, c_{2,t+1}^j)[q_{1,t+1} + y_{1,t+1}]. \tag{14.12}$$

$$U_1(c_{1,t}^j, c_{2,t}^j)q_{2,t} = \beta E_t U_1(c_{1,t+1}^j, c_{2,t+1}^j)[q_{2,t+1} + p_{2,t+1}y_{2,t+1}]. \tag{14.13}$$

In equilibrium, all equity shares are held and the endowment of each good is completely consumed. Lucas [318] assumes that agents hold identical portfolios, so that $z^j_{i,t} = 1/2$ for $j = 1, 2$ and $i = 1, 2$ so that $\phi^j = 1/2$ and $\delta = 1/2$. In such a world, national wealth is equal across countries and agents have perfectly diversified portfolios. Agents across countries have identical consumption in this case, unlike the economy in which there is no trade in financial assets. In the initial model described above in which there was no trade in financial assets and specialization in endowments, the allocation was Pareto optimal. We commented that we could price financial assets even if these assets were not traded. What distribution of endowment shares will result in this allocation? In particular, if $z^1_1 = z^1_2 = \alpha$ and $z^2_1 = z^2_2 = 1 - \alpha$, then the equilibrium allocation with no trade in financial assets can be achieved. Hence we have at least two stationary allocations, depending on the initial distribution of the claims. This simple example, when combined with our discussion of the equilibrium with no trade in financial assets, illustrates an important point. International risk sharing can be achieved through fluctuations in relative prices in the current account and by trade in financial assets. The existence of non-traded goods or lack of specialization in production of a good can affect how much consumption insurance can be achieved through relative price fluctuations. If we introduced trade in equity shares when there is a third good w that is produced by both countries, notice that portfolio diversification may require that an agent holds equity shares for w^1 and w^2 if the endowment shocks for w are not perfectly correlated. If these shocks are perfectly correlated, then portfolio diversification may be achieved by specializing in the holding of equity shares of one country only.

There has been a substantial literature on the lack of international portfolio diversification and the degree of international consumption risk sharing. The international portfolio diversification puzzle is the notion that investors hold too little of their wealth in foreign securities to be consistent with the standard theory of portfolio choice. Baxter and Jermann [50] argue that the failure of international diversification is substantial. Their model incorporates human and physical capital and, within the context of their model, optimal behavior would lead to a short position in domestic assets because of a strong positive correlation between the returns to human and physical capital. A more recent paper by Heathcote and Perri [248] extends the Baxter and Jermann model to include more than one traded good. They find, as we have noted above, that consumption insurance is available through relative price fluctuations and these price fluctuations can be sufficient to achieve efficient risk sharing. Clearly the conclusion on whether there is sufficient or insufficient risk sharing is very sensitive to the model specifications.

Empirical evidence on international consumption risk sharing is provided in Backus, Kehoe, and Kydland [40]. Lewis [310] further documents that there is insufficient intertemporal risk sharing in consumption. As we have noted above, the existence of non-traded goods combined with the assumption that utility is non-separable in traded and non-traded goods makes it more difficult to determine the optimal degree of consumption risk sharing. We have also shown above that relative price fluctuations can be a substitute for trade in financial assets in achieving consumption insurance. Lewis documents that the non-separability of utility or the restriction of asset trade alone are not enough to explain the risk sharing that we observe, but that when non-separability and asset trade restrictions are combined, she cannot reject the hypothesis that there is risk sharing. As Obstfeld and Rogoff [355] argue, many of the puzzles in international macroeconomics may just be specific to the models researchers are using. They do find that adding transport costs generally improves a model's predictions for real trade.

14.2. INTERNATIONAL MONETARY MODEL

We continue our discussion with a simple two-country version of the Lucas asset-pricing model with a cash-in-advance constraint (see Lucas [318]). Agents from both countries are identical in terms of preferences so they can differ only in terms of initial endowments. In this model, we study what is typically referred to as a pooled equilibrium – if initial endowments are identical or if somehow the economy converges to an equilibrium with equal forms of wealth (so wealth is the same in all states), then we will show that the economy will stay in this equilibrium.

We assume that endowments are stationary in levels but that money supplies are growing. The case with growing endowments can be analyzed using an approach similar to that in Chapter 13, but for expositional purposes we consider the case when only money supplies are growing. The outstanding stock of money of country i at time t is $M_{i,t}$ and the money supply process is:

$$M_{i,t} = \omega_i(s_t)M_{i,t-1}, \quad i = 1, 2. \tag{14.14}$$

At the beginning of the period, agents observe the current realization of the endowment of each country denoted $y_{i,t}$ for $i = 1, 2$. Endowment in each country and money growth satisfy the counterparts of Assumptions 13.11 and 13.7 in Chapter 13.

At the beginning of the period, the representative agent of country 1 receives one-half of the money transfer from its government denoted T_1^1

and one-half of the money transfer from country 2 denoted T_2^1. The representative agent from country 2 receives a similar set of transfers, T_i^2 for $i = 1, 2$.[1]

Country 1 is defined as the domestic country and good 1 is the numeraire good. The nominal exchange rate e_t converts nominal quantities defined in the currency of country 2 into units of the domestic currency. The nominal wealth of an agent in country j consists of the currency $M_{1,t-1}^j$ of country 1, currency $M_{2,t-1}^j$ of country 2, claims to a nominal dividend for good 1 denoted as $z_{1,t-1}^j$, which can be sold for a price $Q_{1,t}^e$, and claims to nominal dividend for good 2 denoted $z_{2,t-1}^j$, which can be sold for a price $Q_{2,t}^e$ and is denominated in units of country 2's currency. Later on, we introduce nominal bonds of various maturities that are in zero net supply and forward and futures contracts for foreign exchange.

The price of good 1 measured in units of M_1 is $p_{1,t}$ and the price of good 2 measured in units of M_2 is $p_{2,t}$. Thus, the representative agent in country j has posttransfer beginning-of-period nominal balances measured in units of country 1's currency equal to:

$$H_t^j \equiv M_{1,t-1}^j - p_{1,t-1}c_{1,t-1}^j + e_t(M_{2,t-1}^j - p_{2,t-1}c_{2,t-1}^j) \\ + p_{1,t-1}y_{1,t-1}z_{1,t-1}^j + e_t p_{2,t-1}y_{2,t-1}z_{2,t-1}^j + T_{1,t}^j + e_t T_{2,t}^j, \tag{14.15}$$

where the last two terms are the transfers made to the representative agent in country j.

The asset market opens first. Agents trade in securities, bonds, and currency. While in the asset market, agents acquire the currency they need to make consumption purchases. It is assumed that domestic sellers will accept payment only in their domestic currency. This means that the buyer has no access to the foreign exchange market once the asset market has closed. Since there is no new information revealed after the asset market closes and before the goods market opens, this is similar to the cash-in-advance constraint in the one-country version of the model with the Lucas timing in which there is only a transactions demand and no liquidity or store of value demand for money.

The budget constraint in the asset market faced by the representative agent of country j is:

$$Q_{1,t}^e z_{1,t}^j + e_t Q_{2,t}^e z_{2,t}^j + M_{1,t}^j + e_t M_{2,t}^j \le H_t^j + Q_{1,t}^e z_{1,t-1}^j + e_t Q_{2,t}^e z_{2,t-1}^j. \tag{14.16}$$

[1] In Exercise 8, this assumption is dropped and, instead, we assume that claims in the transfers are traded just like any other security. In equilibrium, the representative agent from country 1 will hold one-half of the claims to the transfer of country 1 and one-half of the claims to the transfer from country 2, just as in the money transfers scheme just described.

The demand by agent j for units of currency i, $i \neq j$, is:

$$F^j_{i,t} \equiv M^j_{i,t} - [M^j_{i,t-1} + T^j_{i,t} + p_{i,t-1}(y^j_{i,t-1}z^j_{i,t-1} - c^j_{i,t-1})]. \quad (14.17)$$

In the goods market, the following cash-in-advance constraints apply to the purchases of goods 1 and 2 by the agent from country j:

$$p_{1,t}c^j_{1,t} \leq M^j_{1,t}, \quad (14.18)$$

$$e_t p_{2,t} c^j_{2,t} \leq e_t M^j_{2,t}. \quad (14.19)$$

After the goods market closes, the agent receives the nominal dividend payments on the claims from both countries.

Notice that the consumer's nominal wealth is growing because the money supply is growing. To eliminate the effects of such growth, we divide all nominal variables by the nominal price of good 1. We also define the relative price of good 2 in terms of good 1 as:

$$\zeta_t = \frac{e_t p_{2,t}}{p_{1,t}}. \quad (14.20)$$

This relative price is often called the *terms of trade* or the *real exchange rate*. Later on, we show that this relative price is independent of the money stocks.

Let lower-case letters denote the nominal value divided by the appropriate price; that is, define $h_t \equiv H_t/p_{1,t}$, $q^e_{i,t} \equiv Q^e_{i,t}/p_{i,t}$, $m_{i,t} \equiv M_{i,t}/p_{i,t}$, and $\tau_{i,t} \equiv T_{i,t}/p_{i,t}$ for $i = 1, 2$. For notational convenience, also define the variable $\pi_{i,t} \equiv p_{i,t-1}/p_{i,t}$ for $i = 1, 2$. The normalized budget constraint in the asset market can be written as:

$$q^e_{1,t}z^j_{1,t} + \zeta_t q^e_{2,t}z^j_{2,t} + m^j_{1,t} + \zeta_t m^j_{2,t} \leq h^j_t + q^e_{1,t}z^j_{1,t-1} + \zeta_t q^e_{2,t}z^j_{2,t-1}, \quad (14.21)$$

where

$$h^j_t = \pi_{1,t}(m^j_{1,t-1} - c^j_{1,t-1}) + \zeta_t \pi_{2,t}(m^j_{2,t-1} - c^j_{2,t-1})$$
$$+ \pi_{1,t}y_{1,t-1}z^j_{1,t-1} + \zeta_t \pi_{2,t}y_{2,t-1}z^j_{2,t-1} + \tau^j_{1,t} + \zeta_t \tau^j_{2,t}. \quad (14.22)$$

Likewise, we divide the cash-in-advance constraints in Equations (14.18) and (14.19) by $p_{1,t}$ to obtain:

$$c^j_{1,t} \leq m^j_{1,t}, \quad (14.23)$$

$$\zeta_t c^j_{2,t} \leq \zeta_t m^j_{2,t}. \quad (14.24)$$

Notice that dividing the nominal constraints by the price level has transformed the variables into real quantities or else ratios of prices for the same good at different points in time.

The market-clearing conditions for this economy for $i=1,2$ are:

$$c_{i,t}^{1}+c_{i,t}^{2}=y_{i,t}, \tag{14.25}$$

$$M_{i,t}^{1}+M_{i,t}^{2}=M_{i,t}, \tag{14.26}$$

$$z_{i,t}^{1}+z_{i,t}^{2}=1, \tag{14.27}$$

$$e_tF_{2,t}^{1}+F_{1,t}^{2}=0. \tag{14.28}$$

There are seven markets. Using Walras's Law, if six of them clear, then the seventh market – the foreign exchange market – will also clear.

Let primes denote future values and unprimed variables denote current values. We will seek an equilibrium in which the nominal price levels and the nominal exchange rate depend on the realization of the shock s and the stocks of money, $M\equiv(M_1,M_2)$, but the equity prices and the real exchange rate depend only on s. The price functions q_i^e,ζ are assumed to be continuous and strictly positive functions $q_i^e : S\rightarrow\Re_{++}$, $i=1,2$ and $\zeta : S\rightarrow\Re_{++}$. The nominal exchange rate e and the nominal price levels p_i for $i=1,2$ are assumed to be continuous and strictly positive functions $e : S\times\Re_{+}^{2}\rightarrow\Re_{++}$, $p_i : S\times\Re_{+}^{2}\rightarrow\Re_{++}$ for $i=1,2$. Define the (gross) deflation rate by $\pi_i(s')\equiv p_i(s,M)/p_i(s',M')$. Notice that we assume that deflation is a function of s' and, in particular, does not depend on the stocks of money. This is a property that must be demonstrated.

Because agents are identical in equilibrium, we drop the index j. The consumer's state variables consist of his initial wealth h, his share holdings z_i for $i=1,2$, and the current exogenous shock s. Given the price functions ζ, e and q_i^e and p_i for $i=1,2$, the resident of each country chooses $(c_1,c_2,m_1,m_2,z_1',z_2')$ to solve:

$$V(h,z_1,z_2,s)=\max\left\{U(c_1,c_2)+\beta E_s[V(h',z_1',z_2',s')]\right\} \tag{14.29}$$

subject to the asset market constraint (Equation 14.21), the law of motion for post-transfer real balances (Equation 14.22), and the cash-in-advance constraints (Equations 14.23 and 14.24). We can show the existence of a solution to the consumer's value function as an application of Proposition 8.1 in Chapter 8.

In equilibrium, agents are identical so that $c_i^1=c_i^2=(1/2)y_i$ and $z_i^1=z_i^2=1/2$. When the market-clearing conditions are substituted into the law of motion for the posttransfer money holdings, these holdings become $h=(1/2)\left[(M_1/p_1)+\zeta(M_2/p_2)\right]$, which is just the world supply of real balances measured in units of good 1. Let $\mu_i(s)$ denote the multiplier for the cash-in-advance constraint on good i, and $\xi(s)$ denote the multiplier on the budget constraint in the asset market. Let U_i be the partial derivative of U with respect to its ith argument and define $U_i(s) \equiv U_i(y_1/2, y_2/2)$. Substituting the envelope conditions, the equilibrium first-order conditions with respect to $c_1, c_2, m_1, m_2, z_1', z_2'$ are:[2]

$$U_1(s) = \mu_1(s) + \beta E_s\left[\xi(s')\pi_1(s')\right], \tag{14.30}$$

$$U_2(s) = \zeta(s)\mu_2(s) + \beta E_s\left[\xi(s')\pi_2(s')\zeta(s')\right], \tag{14.31}$$

$$\xi(s) = \mu_1(s) + \beta E_s\left[\xi(s')\pi_1(s')\right], \tag{14.32}$$

$$\zeta(s)\xi(s) = \mu_2(s)\zeta(s) + \beta E_s\left[\xi(s')\pi_2(s')\zeta(s')\right], \tag{14.33}$$

$$q_1^e(s)\xi(s) = \beta E_s\left\{\xi(s')[\pi_1(s')y_1(s) + q_1^e(s')]\right\}, \tag{14.34}$$

$$q_2^e(s)\zeta(s)\xi(s) = \beta E_s\{\xi(s')\zeta(s')[\pi_2(s')y_2(s) + q_2^e(s')]\}. \tag{14.35}$$

We also have the slackness conditions with respect to the multipliers $\xi(s)$ and $\mu_i(s)$ for $i = 1, 2$.

These equilibrium first-order conditions are similar to the first-order conditions that we derived for the basic cash-in-advance model in Chapter 13. The difference arises from the fact that we have to determine the relative price of country 2's good in terms of country 1's good, or the real exchange rate $\zeta(s)$. We also need to determine the nominal exchange rate $e(s, M)$. For this purpose, we need to determine the nominal price level in each country, $p_i(s, M)$ for $i = 1, 2$. We do this following the approach in the previous chapter by deriving the inverse of the velocity functions for each currency.

Adding the cash-in-advance constraints for the two types of agents and imposing market-clearing yields $y_i \leq M_i/p_i$. Define the variables:

$$\Psi_i \equiv M_i/p_i y_i \quad i = 1, 2.$$

Because M, y are exogenous and positive, solving for Ψ_i is equivalent to solving for p_i. Notice that the multipliers $\mu_i(s)$ satisfy the conditions:

$$\mu_i(s) = U_i(s) - \beta E_s[U_i(s')\pi_i(s')], \quad i = 1, 2.$$

But $\pi_i(s') \equiv p_i(s, M)/p_i(s', M')$ by definition. Substituting for $\pi_i(s')$ and recalling that $\mu_i(s) \geq 0$, the functions Ψ_i must satisfy:

$$U_i(s)y_i(s)\Psi_i(s) = \max\left[U_i(s)y_i(s), \beta E_s\left(\frac{U_i(s')y_i(s')\Psi_i(s')}{\omega_i(s')}\right)\right] \tag{14.36}$$

for $i = 1, 2$. Notice that these equations are expressed in terms of the stationary growth rates of money supplies and the stationary endowments so

[2] In Exercise 2, the reader is asked to derive the first-order conditions and envelope conditions for the agent's dynamic programming problem.

that Ψ_i is a function only of the shock s. Furthermore, Equation (14.36) can be solved separately from the other price functions and, in particular, does not depend on the exchange rate. To find a fixed point to these functional equations, define the functions:

$$\Gamma_i(s) \equiv U_i(s) y_i(s) \Psi_i(s), \quad i = 1, 2.$$

Since $y_i(s) > 0$ for all s, studying the properties of the function Γ_i is equivalent to studying the function Ψ_i. This follows as an application of the implicit function theorem. Using the definition of the functions Γ_i, define the operators $T_i\Gamma_i$ for $i = 1, 2$ by:

$$(T_i\Gamma_i)(s) \equiv \max\left[U_i(s)y_i(s), \beta E_s\left(\frac{\Gamma_i(s')}{\omega_i(s')}\right)\right]. \tag{14.37}$$

Notice that, under Assumptions 13.1 and 14.3, T_i maps $C(S)$, the space of bounded and continuous, real-valued functions defined on S, into itself. It is straightforward to verify that T_i is monotone. Under Assumption 14.4, $\beta E_s[\omega_i(s')^{-1}] < 1$ for all s so that T discounts,

$$\beta E_s\left\{\omega_i(s')^{-1}\left[\Gamma_i(s') + a\right]\right\} \leq \beta E_s[\Gamma_i(s')] + \delta a,$$

where $0 < \delta < 1$. Therefore, Contraction Mapping Theorem implies that T_i has a fixed point in $C(S)$. Let $\Psi_i^\star$ denote this fixed point.

We can use these fixed points and the first-order conditions in Equations (14.34) and (14.35) to construct the equity price functions. Define the functions:

$$\phi_i(s) \equiv q_i^e(s) U_i(s), \quad i = 1, 2.$$

Notice that these functions satisfy the following mapping:

$$(T_i\phi_i)(s) = \beta E_s\left[\frac{U_i(s')y_i(s')\Psi_i^\star(s')}{\omega_i(s')\Psi_i^\star(s)} + \phi_i(s')\right], \tag{14.38}$$

where we have substituted for $\pi_i(s') = p_i/p_i'$ and $p_i = M_i/\Psi_i^\star y_i$ for $i = 1, 2$. Under Assumptions 13.1, 14.3, and 14.4, it is straightforward to show that there exist functions $\phi_i^\star \in C(S)$ that are the fixed points of Equation (14.38).

14.2.1. The terms of trade and the exchange rate

We are now in a position to derive expressions for the equilibrium real and nominal exchange rate and to show the implications of the model for their behavior.

We use Equations (14.30) and (14.31) to express the terms of trade or the real exchange rate as:

$$\zeta(s) = \frac{U_2(s)}{U_1(s)}. \tag{14.39}$$

Fluctuations in the endowment of either good affect the real exchange rate while fluctuations in the money supply have no effect on the real exchange rate. This last result is known as *purchasing power parity* and it is the open economy counterpart of the quantity theory of money. It has been widely studied as an empirical phenomenon.

Given the solutions $\Psi_i^\star$, we can use the definition of the real exchange rate to find a solution for the equilibrium nominal exchange rate as a function of M_1/M_2 and y_2/y_1 as:

$$e(s, M) = \frac{U_2(s)}{U_1(s)} \frac{\Psi_2^\star(s)}{\Psi_1^\star(s)} \frac{M_1 y_2(s)}{M_2 y_1(s)}. \tag{14.40}$$

Hence, the equilibrium exchange rate is affected by changes in relative velocity, changes in the MRS in consumption, and changes in the relative supplies of the goods and money stocks. Real disturbances affect both the exchange rate and the terms of trade so that we would expect these variables to be correlated. Notice that some standard results apply. An increase in the money supply of country 1 depreciates the exchange rate for currency 1 (increases e) while an increase in the money supply of country 2 appreciates it (decreases e).

Notice that the change in the nominal exchange rate satisfies:

$$\frac{e(s', M')}{e(s, M)} = \frac{U_2(s')y_2(s')}{U_2(s)y_2(s)} \frac{U_1(s)y_1(s)}{U_1(s')y_1(s')} \frac{\Psi_1^\star(s)}{\Psi_1^\star(s')} \frac{\Psi_2^\star(s')}{\Psi_2^\star(s)} \frac{\omega_1(s')}{\omega_2(s')}.$$

Since the growth rate of money supplies in each country is a stationary random variable, changes in nominal exchange rates are also stationary. We can multiply both sides of the expression in Equation (14.40) by M_2/M_1 to obtain:

$$\frac{M_2}{M_1} e(s, M) = \frac{U_2(s)}{U_1(s)} \frac{\Psi_2^\star(s)}{\Psi_1^\star(s)} \frac{y_2(s)}{y_1(s)} = \zeta(s) \frac{\Psi_2^\star(s)}{\Psi_1^\star(s)} \frac{y_2(s)}{y_1(s)}.$$

Since the right side of this expression is stationary, notice that the nominal exchange rate times the ratio of the money supplies in the two countries is also a stationary random variable. Recall that we did not restrict the relative money supplies to be stationary. Nevertheless, the assumption that the equilibrium real exchange rate is a stationary variable implies restrictions for the time series behavior of the nominal exchange rate and the relative money supplies.

These expressions also allow us to discuss tests of alternative forms of purchasing power parity. The absolute version of purchasing power parity says that the real exchange rate or the relative price of the foreign versus domestic goods is just unity in the long run. Using the expression for the real interest rate, the absolute version of purchasing power parity can be expressed as:

$$\log(\zeta_t) = \log(e_t) - \log(p_{1,t}/p_{2,t}) = 0. \tag{14.41}$$

The relative version of purchasing power parity states that this relation holds in first differences:

$$\Delta \log(\zeta_t) = \Delta \log(e_t) - \Delta \log(p_{1,t}/p_{2,t}) = 0, \tag{14.42}$$

where Δ is the first difference operator.

Notice that if purchasing power parity holds in the long-run, movements in nominal exchange rates should be offset by movements in relative price levels. A number of studies have argued that the real exchange rate follows a random walk (see Adler and Lehman [8]), which implies that deviations from purchasing power parity can be expected to be permanent. Mark [334] reports similar findings using monthly observations from June 1973 through February 1988. He uses consumer price index data taken from the International Monetary Fund publication *International Financial Statistics* to measure commodity prices. Exchange rate data are taken from Harris, Bank's *Foreign Exchange Weekly Review*, which reports Friday closing prices in London. The countries chosen are Belgium, Canada, France, Germany, Italy, Japan, and the United Kingdom. Mark examines three sets of bilateral relationships, with the United States, the United Kingdom, and Germany serving as the home country, and finds that movements in nominal exchange rates and relative price levels are unrelated in the long-run as well as in the short-run.

Mark also suggests a test of purchasing power parity as a long-run relationship by testing whether $\log(e_t)$ and $\log(p_{1,t}/p_{2,t})$ are cointegrated series. According to this methodology, two sequences of random variables $\{x_t\}$ and $\{y_t\}$ are said to be *cointegrated* if (*i*) they are non-stationary in levels; (*ii*) they are stationary in first differences; and (*iii*) there exists a linear combination of the levels, $u_t = x_t + \alpha y_t$, which is stationary. The variable α is referred to as the cointegrating constant. To test for cointegration, we determine whether $\{x_t\}$ and $\{y_t\}$ are non-stationary in levels but stationary in first differences. Next, x_t is regressed on y_t, or vice versa. This is called the cointegrating regression and $\{u_t\}$ is defined as the residual from this regression. The cointegrating constant can be consistently estimated by least squares. Finally, an augmented Dickey-Fuller test is performed on the error sequence, $\{u_t\}$.[3]

[3] To do this test, consider the regression

$$(1 - \theta_1 L - \theta_2 L^2)(1 - \rho L)u_t = v_t,$$

where $\{v_t\}$ is an i.i.d. sequence and L is the lag operator. We wish to test whether $\rho = 1$. We rewrite the above equation as $u_t = -\phi_1 u_{t-1} + \phi_2 \Delta u_{t-1} + \phi_3 \Delta u_{t-2} + v_t$, where $\phi_1 = (1-\rho)(1-\theta_1-\theta_2)$.

Mark first tests for unit roots in $\log(e_t)$ and $\log(p_{1,t}/p_{2,t})$. He finds that the logarithms of the nominal exchange rate are non-stationary in levels but stationary in first differences. For some country pairs, the unit root hypothesis can be rejected for the logarithms of the relative price levels. Excluding these country pairs, he is unable to reject at conventional significance levels the null hypothesis of no cointegration for $\log(e_t)$ and $\log(p_{1,t}/p_{2,t})$ or, equivalently, that the real exchange rate has a unit root. He argues that while small departures from the null hypothesis may be hard to detect with existing data, there is evidence to suggest that shocks to the real exchange rate are persistent enough to prevent a return to purchasing power parity in the long run.

Huizinga [258] studies the long-run behavior of real exchange rates using an alternative set of statistical procedures. He considers the real exchange rates of the US dollar, the British pound, and the Japanese yen against ten major currencies. His sample consists of monthly observations on the logarithm of the real exchange rate for the floating exchange rate period from 1974 to 1986. He finds the long-run behavior of real exchange rates differs from a random walk by having a notable mean-reverting component. In contrast to the serially uncorrelated changes implied by a random walk, there is substantial negative serial correlation of changes in real exchange rates, which he argues is a common feature among the real exchange rates of many countries. Despite the existence of a mean-reverting component, he finds that the permanent component accounts for between 52% and 77% of the variance of the actual change in the real exchange rate of the US dollar against ten currencies. These results are in accord with Campbell and Clarida [91], who develop an empirical model of real exchange rates using Kalman filtering techniques.

A related empirical issue is the behavior of the real exchange rate across different nominal exchange rate regimes. For example, Mussa [349] argues that the behavior of the real exchange rate has become more variable in the floating exchange rate period since the breakdown of the Bretton Woods agreement in 1973. Grilli and Kaminsky [216] examine a variety of nominal exchange rate regimes since 1885, including the gold standard eras in the nineteenth century and in the interwar era, and the fixed and floating exchange rate eras since World War II. They find that transitory disturbances are important for the behavior of the real exchange rate in the pre-World War II era and that the behavior of the real exchange rate varies more by historical episode than by the exchange rate regime. Recall that in our model, the real exchange rate is a stationary random variable so that real shocks or shocks to endowments have only a temporary effect.

Under the null hypothesis of no cointegration, $\phi_1 = 0$. The distribution of the usual t-statistic is not standard. However, critical values tabulated by Engle and Granger [173] may be used.

14.2.2. *Pricing alternative assets*

We can derive the prices of a variety of assets using this framework, including equity prices, the price of pure discount bonds, and the prices of forward and futures contracts for foreign exchange.

We first briefly discuss the determinants of equity prices in the domestic and foreign country. We already described how to construct the equity price functions using the fixed points $\phi_i^\star$ for $i = 1, 2$. Using Equations (14.34) and (14.35), the equity prices satisfy:

$$q_{1,t}^e = \beta E_t \left[\frac{U_{1,t+1}}{U_{1,t}} (\pi_{1,t+1} y_{1,t} + q_{1,t+1}^e) \right]$$

$$q_{2,t}^e = \beta E_t \left[\frac{U_{1,t+1}}{U_{1,t}} \frac{\zeta_{t+1}}{\zeta_t} (\pi_{2,t+1} y_{2,t} + q_{2,t+1}^e) \right],$$

where $U_{1,t+k}$ is the marginal utility of consumption of the first good at date $t+k$ evaluated at equilibrium consumption. Notice that the nominal prices of goods 1 and 2 affect the equity pricing formulas only so far as they affect the term involving the dividend payment. The dividend on the claims to good 1 are paid in the currency of country 1 and likewise for equities issued by country 2. Because the nominal dividend $p_{1,t} y_{1,t}$ is paid at the end of period t, it can only be used to purchase consumption goods in period $t + 1$. Hence, we divide the nominal dividend by the nominal price of 1 in period $t + 1$ to convert it to a real quantity. The same arguments apply to the real price of claims to good 2: in this case, $q_{2,t}$ is the price of equities expressed in units of good 2. We convert the MRS for consumption in good 1 to units of good 2 by multiplying it with the ratio of the relative prices ζ_{t+1}/ζ_t.

We can also derive the price of pure discount bonds denominated in country i's currency. The equilibrium price of a k-period nominal bill for country i is given by:

$$Q_{t,k}^i = \beta^k E_t \left[\frac{U_{i,t+k}}{U_{i,t}} \pi_{i,t+k} \right], \quad i = 1, 2. \tag{14.43}$$

Define $R_{t,k}^i \equiv 1/Q_{t,k}^i$ as the (gross) return on the nominal bond. Notice that the nominal bond price depends on the nominal MRS, which is the MRS in consumption times the ratio of purchasing powers of money between periods t and $t + k$.

There are many other types of assets that can be priced in this economy. A particularly important one is a *forward contract* for foreign exchange, which is an obligation to deliver one unit of foreign exchange at some specified date in the future. It is bought or sold at a current price measured in units of domestic currency. Although a forward contract involves no expenditures in the current period, leaving the current period budget constraint unaffected, the agent's budget constraint is affected in the period in which the delivery occurs.

Assume that the delivery occurs at the beginning of the period. Let the domestic market price at date t of one unit of foreign currency at time $t+k$ be defined as $G_{t,k}$. Suppose that the agent has purchased $z^G_{t,k}$ contracts forward at price $G_{t,k}$. After the delivery, the agent's real balances at the beginning of period $t+k$ evaluated in units of good Y_1 are:

$$h_{t+k} + \frac{z^G_{t,k}}{p_{1,t+k}}(e_{t+k} - G_{t,k}),$$

where h_{t+k} is defined as in Equation (14.22). The total return (or loss) is equal to the difference between the spot exchange rate at the date the contract is delivered and the price at which the contracts are purchased, or $(e_{t+k} - G_{t,k})z^G_{t,k}$. Because no expenditure is required at time t, the first-order condition for the choice of $z^G_{t,k}$ is:

$$0 = \beta^k E_t \left[\frac{U_{1,t+k}}{U_{1,t}} \pi_{1,t+k}(e_{t+k} - G_{t,k}) \right], \tag{14.44}$$

where we have multiplied both sides by $p_{1,t}/U_{1,t}$. As before, the nominal MRS is used to discount the return. Because $G_{t,k}$ is known at time t, we can re-write this as:

$$\beta^k E_t \left[\frac{U_{1,t+k}}{U_{1,t}} \pi_{1,t+k} e_{t+k} \right] = \beta^k E_t \left[\frac{U_{1,t+k}}{U_{1,t}} \pi_{1,t+k} \right] G_{t,k}.$$

Using the expression for the bond price in Equation (14.43), we can write the forward price as:

$$G_{t,k} = \beta^k E_t \left[\frac{U_{1,t+k}}{U_{1,t}} \pi_{1,t+k} e_{t+k} \right] R^1_{t,k}, \tag{14.45}$$

where $R^1_{t,k} \equiv 1/Q^1_{t,k}$.

Using a covariance decomposition, we can re-write Equation (14.45) as:

$$E_t(e_{t+k}) - G_{t,k} = -R^1_{t,k} \mathrm{Cov}_t \left(\frac{\beta^k U_{1,t+k}}{U_{1,t}} \pi_{1,t+k}, e_{t+k} \right). \tag{14.46}$$

The left side is the *expected profit* on a long position in the forward market, which involves a purchase of foreign currency in the forward market, while the right side is the *risk premium*. Notice that there are two sources of time-varying risk premia or expected profits in the forward market: the first derives from movements in the conditional covariance between the future spot rate and the nominal MRS and the second derives from movements in the nominal risk-free rate, $R^1_{t,k}$. Notice also that *if* the nominal MRS and the spot exchange rate were independent, then $G_{t,k} = E_t(e_{t+k})$, or the forward price is an unbiased predictor of the future spot rate. Thus, the forward rate is a biased predictor of the future spot rate as long as the conditional covariance between the future spot rate and the nominal MRS is different from zero.[4] We describe tests of the unbiasedness hypothesis and alternative ways of modeling risk premia in Section 14.3.

We now derive the risk premium in the forward market using interest rate arbitrage. This involves comparing the returns from purchasing foreign currency using an uncovered investment strategy versus a covered investment strategy in the market for foreign exchange. An *uncovered* one-period investment in a foreign-denominated bond is one in which an agent exchanges $e_t Q^2_{t,1}$ units of domestic currency for e_{t+1} units of domestic currency next period. Converting these nominal quantities into current units of good Y_1 and discounting the uncertain payoff next period, the equilibrium condition is:

$$1 = \beta E_t \left[\frac{U_{1,t+1}}{U_{1,t}} \pi_{1,t+1} R^2_{t,1} \frac{e_{t+1}}{e_t} \right]. \tag{14.48}$$

Such an investment strategy is subject to exchange rate risk in the sense that the payoff on the bond at time $t+1$ of one unit of country 2's currency has an uncertain value in units of country 1's currency. To eliminate the exchange rate risk, the investor can sell a forward contract at time t (so that he agrees to supply foreign currency in exchange for domestic currency at time $t+1$). This is a covered position or a *covered* one-period investment and a covered interest arbitrage argument, which eliminates exchange rate risk, satisfies:

$$1 = \beta E_t \left[\frac{U_{1,t+1}}{U_{1,t}} \pi_{1,t+1} R^2_{t,1} \frac{G_{t,1}}{e_t} \right]. \tag{14.49}$$

Using the expression for bond prices in Equation (14.43) and noting that $R^2_{t,1}$, $G_{t,1}$, and e_t are known at time t, Equation (14.49) implies that the

[4] One might conclude that this biasedness is necessarily a result of risk aversion. To show that this conclusion is wrong, suppose that agents are risk neutral. In this case, we have a linear utility function and constant marginal utility of consumption. Thus, Equation (14.45) becomes:

$$\begin{aligned} G_{t,k} &= \beta^k E_t \left(\pi_{1,t+k} e_{t+k} \right) R^1_{t,k} \\ &= E_t(e_{t+k}) + \beta^k \mathrm{Cov}_t \left(\pi_{1,t+k}, e_{t+k} \right) R^1_{t,k}. \end{aligned} \tag{14.47}$$

As long as the covariance between the future spot rate and the ratio of the purchasing powers of money is non-zero, the forward rate is a biased predictor of the future spot rate. This bias does not arise from the risk premium but from the covariance of changes in the nominal price of goods and the future exchange rate.

ratio of current nominal interest rates is equal to the ratio of the forward rate and the spot exchange rate:

$$\frac{R^1_{t,1}}{R^2_{t,1}} = \frac{G_{t,1}}{e_t}. \tag{14.50}$$

This is a statement of *interest rate parity*, which says that an agent is indifferent between investing in a bond denominated in the domestic currency, or investing a unit of the domestic currency in the foreign-denominated bond and selling the foreign-denominated proceeds in the forward market. The return on the former strategy is $R^1_{t,1}$ while the return on the latter strategy is $(G_{t,1}/e_t)R^2_{t,1}$, which are equal by Equation (14.50).

The uncovered and covered investment strategies can be compared by subtracting Equation (14.48) from Equation (14.49):

$$0 = \beta E_t \left[\frac{U_{1,t+1}}{U_{1,t}} \pi_{1,t+1} R^2_{t,1} \left(\frac{e_{t+1} - G_{t,1}}{e_t} \right) \right]. \tag{14.51}$$

Using the covariance decomposition and dividing by $R^2_{t,1}$, this equation can be rewritten in terms of the risk premium as in Equation (14.46).

Another related quantity is the *forward premium*, defined as $G_{t,k} - e_t$. We can derive an alternative expression for the forward premium by subtracting e_t from both sides of Equation (14.46) as:

$$G_{t,k} - e_t = E_t(e_{t+k}) - e_t + R^1_{t,k} \text{Cov}_t \left(\frac{\beta^k U_{1,t+k}}{U_{1,t}} \pi_{1,t+k}, e_{t+k} \right). \tag{14.52}$$

This says that the forward premium is equal to the sum of expected depreciation on the domestic currency and the risk premium.

Now let us consider the pricing of *futures contracts* for foreign exchange. The difference between forward contracts and futures contracts for foreign exchange lies in the institutional features of the futures market. The key feature is the daily resettlement of profit and loss on a contract called "marking to market." The resettlement is accomplished by a clearinghouse in the futures exchange which stands between the buyer and seller of a futures contract. The clearinghouse takes no active position in the market. We assume that the daily resettlement occurs at the beginning of the period so that the agent's initial holdings of real balances are affected if the futures price changes.

Suppose that two parties have contracts at time t with the clearinghouse at the initial futures price $F_{t,k}$. The agent who sells a contract to deliver currency is in a short position and the agent who buys the contract is in a long position. If, in the next time period, the price rises (falls) to $F_{t+1,k-1}$, the amount $F_{t+1,k-1} - F_{t,k}$ is credited to (debited from) the account of the party who bought the contract and debited from (credited to) the account of the short party who sold the contract. The sequence of cash flows between the initial contract date and the date at which the contract is delivered is the major difference between futures contracts and forward contracts.

Let $z^F_{t,k}$ denote the quantity of futures contracts bought (sold) in period t to be delivered at time $t+k$. This decision does not alter the agent's budget constraint at time t but, at time $t+1$, marking to market occurs and the agent's budget constraint at time $t+1$ is affected. Thus, the quantity $(F_{t+1,k-1} - F_{t,k})z^F_{t,k}$ (which can be positive or negative) enters the agent's budget constraint at time $t+1$. The first-order condition with respect to $z^F_{t,k}$ is:

$$0 = \beta E_t \left[\frac{U_{1,t+1}}{U_{1,t}} \pi_{1,t+1} \left(F_{t+1,k-1} - F_{t,k} \right) \right],$$

where we have multiplied both sides by $p_{1,t}/U_{1,t}$, The futures price is given by:

$$F_{t,k} = \beta E_t \left[\frac{U_{1,t+1}}{U_{1,t}} \pi_{1,t+1} R^1_{t,1} F_{t+1,k-1} \right].^5 \tag{14.53}$$

For notational convenience, define the nominal MRS between periods t and $t+k$ as $\mathcal{M}^1_{t,k} \equiv \beta^k (U_{1,t+k}/U_{1,t})\pi_{1,t+k}$. Substituting for $F_{t+i,k-i}$, $i = 1, \cdots, k$ in the above expression and using an iterated expectation argument, we obtain:

$$F_{t,k} = E_t \left[\mathcal{M}^1_{t,k} \left(\prod_{i=t}^{t+k-1} R^1_{i,1} \right) e_{t+k} \right], \tag{14.54}$$

where the last line follows because $F_{t+k,0} = e_{t+k}$.

Using a covariance decomposition, we can write the futures price as:

$$F_{t,k} = E_t(e_{t+k}) + \mathrm{Cov}_t \left[\mathcal{M}^1_{t,k} \left(\prod_{i=t}^{t+k-1} R^1_{i,1} \right), e_{t+k} \right]. \tag{14.55}$$

[5] Since $F_{t,k}$ is known at time t, we can simplify the first-order condition as:

$$\beta E_t \left[\frac{U_{1,t+1}}{U_{1,t}} \pi_{1,t+1} F_{t+1,k-1} \right] = Q_{t,1} F_{t,k},$$

and use the definition of $R^1_{t,1}$.

We are now in a position to compare the futures price and the forward price. Let us consider the difference:

$$F_{t,k} - G_{t,k} = E_t \left[\mathcal{M}^1_{t,k} e_{t+k} \left(\prod_{i=t}^{t+k-1} R^1_{i,1} - R^1_{t,k} \right) \right].$$

The forward price $G_{t,k}$ differs from the futures price $F_{t,k}$ because the product of the one-period nominal rates of return (which are random as of time t) does not necessarily equal the k-period risk-free rate between t and $t+k$, which is $R^1_{t,k}$. This difference can be attributed to the sequence of cash flows that is generated by the futures contract but not by the forward contract.

14.3. VARIANTS OF THE BASIC MODEL

In this section, we consider two variants of the basic two-country model with cash-in-advance constraints that we developed in the previous section. We first study the effects of non-traded goods on equilibrium exchange rates and asset prices. In the second variant of the basic model, we introduce capital flows and study a model with the Stockman-Svensson timing of trades.

14.3.1. Non-traded goods

In this section, we introduce non-traded goods in such a way that agents are no longer identical in terms of their wealth or asset holdings. Modifying the model in this way results in a richer velocity function and more interesting dynamics for asset prices. Our discussion is derived from the paper by Stockman and Dellas [416].

The setup is identical to the model just described aside from the fact that households living in country 1 receive not only an endowment of y_1 units of a traded good but also n_1 units of a non-traded good while households residing in country 2 receive an endowment of y_2 of a traded good and n_2 of a non-traded good. Goods Y_1 and Y_2 are traded costlessly while goods n_1 and n_2 are only traded domestically. All goods are perishable. The endowments of the non-traded goods are assumed to be stationary in levels. They are determined as $n_{i,t} = \eta_i(s_t)$. Let $\mathcal{N} \equiv [\underline{\eta}, \bar{\eta}]$ with $\underline{\eta} > 0$ and $\bar{\eta} < \infty$. Similar to Assumption 14.3, we assume that $\eta_i : S \to \mathcal{N}$ is a continuous function that is bounded away from zero.

The representative household in country j chooses consumption and end-of-period assets to maximize:

$$E_0 \left\{ \sum_{t=0}^{\infty} \beta^t [U(c^j_{1,t}, c^j_{2,t}) + W(c^j_{n,t})] \right\}, \tag{14.56}$$

where U satisfies Assumption 14.2 and W is strictly increasing, strictly concave, continuously differentiable with $\lim_{c\to 0} W'(c) = \infty$ and $W(0) = 0$.

At the outset, we allow agents to hold claims to the endowment of the non-traded good of either country. The asset market opens first followed by the goods market. Let $q^n_{i,t}$ denote the real price of a claim to the non-traded good dividend in country i, denominated in units of Y_i, and let $x^i_{j,t}$ denote the beginning-of-period shares of the non-traded endowment in country j held by an agent from country i. Let the nominal price of n_1 in units of country 1's currency be p^n_1, the nominal price of n_2 in units of country 2's currency be p^n_2, and define $\zeta^n_{i,t} = p^n_{i,t}/p_{i,t}$ to be the relative price of the non-traded good measured in units of Y_i. The representative agent in country 1 has post-transfer beginning-of-period real balances, measured in units of good Y_1, equal to:

$$\begin{aligned} h^1_t \equiv{}& \pi_{1,t}[m^1_{1,t-1} - c^1_{1,t-1} - \zeta^n_{1,t-1} c^1_{n,t-1}] + \zeta_t \pi_{2,t}[m^1_{2,t-1} - c^1_{2,t-1}] \\ &+ \pi_{1,t}[y_{1,t-1} z^1_{1,t} + \zeta^n_{1,t-1} n_{1,t-1} x^1_{1,t}] + \\ &\zeta_t \pi_{2,t}[y_{2,t-1} z^1_{2,t} + \zeta^n_{2,t-1} n_{2,t-1} x^1_{2,t}] + \tau^1_{1,t} + \zeta_t \tau^1_{2,t}, \end{aligned} \tag{14.57}$$

where the last two terms are the transfers made to the representative agent in country 1. The representative agent in country 2 has post-transfer beginning-of-period real balances, measured in units of good Y_1, equal to:

$$\begin{aligned} h^2_t \equiv{}& \pi_{1,t}[m^2_{1,t-1} - c^2_{1,t-1}] + \zeta_t \pi_{2,t}[m^2_{2,t-1} - c^2_{2,t-1} - \zeta^n_{2,t-1} c^2_{n,t-1}] \\ &+ \pi_{1,t}[y_{1,t-1} z^2_{1,t} + \zeta^n_{1,t-1} n_{1,t-1} x^2_{1,t}] \\ &+ \zeta_t \pi_{2,t}[y_{2,t-1} z^2_{2,t} + \zeta^n_{2,t-1} n_{2,t-1} x^2_{2,t}] + \tau^2_{1,t} + \zeta_t \tau^2_{2,t}. \end{aligned} \tag{14.58}$$

The asset market opens first and agents trade in securities and currency. While in the asset market, agents acquire the currency they need to make consumption purchases in the subsequent goods market. It is assumed that domestic sellers will accept payment only in their domestic currency. The budget constraint in the asset market faced by the representative agent of country j is:

$$\begin{aligned} & q^e_{1,t} z^j_{1,t+1} + q^n_{1,t} x^j_{1,t+1} + \zeta_t [q^e_{2,t} z^j_{2,t+1} + q^n_{2,t} x^j_{2,t+1}] + m^j_{1,t} + \zeta_t m^j_{2,t} \\ &\quad \le h^j_t + q^e_{1,t} z^j_{1,t} + q^n_{1,t} x^j_{1,t} + \zeta_t [q^e_{2,t} z^j_{2,t} + q^n_{2,t} x^j_{2,t}], \end{aligned} \tag{14.59}$$

where $q^n_{i,t}$ is the real price at time t of an equity share of the non-traded good in country i measured in units of good Y_i.

In the goods market, the following cash-in-advance constraints apply to the purchases of goods Y_1 and Y_2 by the agent from country 1:

$$c^1_{1,t} + c^1_{n,t} \zeta^n_{1,t} \le m^1_{1,t}, \tag{14.60}$$

$$\zeta_t c^1_{2,t} \le \zeta_t m^1_{2,t}, \tag{14.61}$$

and for the agent from country 2:

$$c_{1,t}^2 \leq m_{1,t}^2, \tag{14.62}$$

$$\zeta_t[c_{2,t}^2 + c_{n,t}^2 \zeta_{2,t}^n] \leq \zeta_t m_{2,t}^2. \tag{14.63}$$

After the goods market closes, the agent receives the nominal dividend payments on the claims from both countries.

Define $\zeta : S \rightarrow R_{++}$, $\zeta^n : S \rightarrow R_{++}$, and $q_i^e : S \rightarrow R_{++}$ for $i = 1, 2$ to be strictly positive, continuous functions. Also define the nominal price of traded and non-traded goods $p_i : S \times R_+^2 \rightarrow R_{++}$ and $p_i^n : S \times R_+^2 \rightarrow R_{++}$ for $i = 1, 2$, and the nominal exchange rate $e : S \times R_+^2 \rightarrow R_{++}$ to be strictly positive, continuous functions. For notational convenience, define the vector $\alpha^j \equiv (z_1^j, z_2^j, x_1^j, x_2^j)$. The consumer's state consists of h^j, α^j and the current shock s. Given the price functions ζ, ζ_i^n, e, q_i^e, p_i and p_i^n for $i = 1, 2$, the resident of country j chooses $(c_1^j, c_2^j, c_n^j, m_1^j, m_2^j, \alpha^{j\prime})$ to solve:

$$V(h^j, \alpha^j, s) = \max \left\{ U(c_1^j, c_2^j) + W(c_n^j) + \beta E_s[V(h^{j\prime}, \alpha^{j\prime}, s')] \right\}$$

subject to the asset market constraint (Equation 14.59), the law of motion for post-transfer real balances (Equation 14.57 or 14.58), and the cash-in-advance constraints (Equations 14.60 and 14.61 or 14.62 and 14.63). The market-clearing conditions require that $c_i^1 + c_i^2 = y_i$, $c_n^i = n_i$, $M_i^1 + M_i^2 = M_i$, $z_i^1 + z_i^2 = 1$, $x_i^1 + x_i^2 = 1$ for $i = 1, 2$.

In the first section, we assumed that agents are identical in equilibrium. In the presence of non-traded goods, we continue to assume that each consumer consumes half the endowment of each country and holds half the shares of the traded goods. To determine the holdings of equity shares of the non-traded endowments, substitute these conditions into the agents' holdings of money balances at the beginning of the period. For $i = 1$,

$$h_t^1 = \pi_{1,t}[m_{t-1}^1 + \zeta_{1,t-1}^n n_{1,t-1}(x_{1,t}^1 - 1)] + \zeta_t \pi_{2,t}[m_{2,t-1}^1 + n_{2,t-1} x_{2,t}^1] + \tau_{1,t}^1 + \zeta_t \tau_{2,t}^1.$$

We have a similar expression for h_t^2. Under the assumption that agents are identical in their consumption of traded goods and holdings of equity shares on traded goods, a stationary equilibrium requires that agents do not hold claims on the non-traded goods of the foreign country, $\hat{x}_2^1 = \hat{x}_1^2 = 0$ and $\hat{x}_1^1 = \hat{x}_2^2 = 1$. Under this allocation, $\hat{h}^1 = \hat{h}^2$, which equal world real balances $.5\left[(M_{1,t}/p_{1,t}) + \zeta_t(M_{2,t}/p_{2,t})\right]$.[6] Notice that in equilibrium, asset holdings are given by $\hat{\alpha}^1 = (.5, .5, 1, 0)$ for residents of country 1 and $\hat{\alpha}^2 = (.5, .5, 0, 1)$ for residents of country 2 while equilibrium consumption satisfies $\hat{c}_1^j = .5y_1$, $\hat{c}_2^j = .5y_2$, and $\hat{c}_n^j = n_j$ for $j = 1, 2$.

[6] If we set $x_j^i = .5$ for $i, j = 1, 2$, the real balances held by the two agents would no longer be equal ($h^1 \neq h^2$). In that case, we would be unable to sustain a perfectly pooled equilibrium in the traded goods and assets markets because the endowment processes for the non-traded goods are not identical while agents have the same utility function for consumption of the non-traded good.

Let $\mu_i(s)$ denote the multiplier for the cash-in-advance constraint on good i, and $\xi(s)$ denote the multiplier on the budget constraint in the asset market. Define $U_i(s)$ as before and let $W_i(s)$ denote the marginal utility with respect to the ith non-traded good. The equilibrium first-order conditions with respect to c_1, c_2, c_n, m_1, m_2, z_1, z_2, x_1, and x_2 for the representative consumer from country 1 are:

$$U_1(s) = \mu_1(s) + \beta E_s\left[\xi(s')\pi_1(s')\right], \tag{14.64}$$

$$U_2(s) = \zeta(s)\mu_2(s) + \beta E_s\left[\xi(s')\pi_2(s')\zeta(s')\right], \tag{14.65}$$

$$W_1(s) = \zeta_1^n(s)\mu_1(s) + \beta E_s\left[\xi(s')\pi_1(s')\zeta_1^n(s')\right], \tag{14.66}$$

$$\xi(s) = \mu_1(s) + \beta E_s\left[\xi(s')\pi_1(s')\right], \tag{14.67}$$

$$\zeta(s)\xi(s) = \zeta(s)\mu_2(s) + \beta E_s\left[\xi(s')\pi_2(s')\zeta(s')\right], \tag{14.68}$$

$$q_1^e(s)\xi(s) = \beta E_s\left\{\xi(s')[\pi_1(s')y_1(s) + q_1^e(s')]\right\}, \tag{14.69}$$

$$q_2^e(s)\zeta(s)\xi(s) = \beta E_s\left\{\xi(s')\zeta(s')[\pi_2(s')y_2(s) + q_2^e(s)]\right\}, \tag{14.70}$$

$$q_1^n(s)\xi(s) = \beta E_s\left\{\xi(s')[\pi_1(s')\zeta_1^n(s)n_1(s) + q_1^n(s')]\right\}, \tag{14.71}$$

$$q_2^n(s)\zeta(s)\xi(s) = \beta E_s\left\{\xi(s')\zeta(s')[\pi_2(s')\zeta_2^n(s)n_2(s) + q_2^n(s')]\right\}. \tag{14.72}$$

The slackness conditions can be derived in a straightforward manner.

A similar set of conditions characterizes the problem of a representative consumer from country 2. The only different condition involves the non-traded good from country 2:

$$W_2(s) = \zeta(s)\zeta_2^n(s)\mu_2(s) + \beta E_s\left[\xi(s')\pi_2(s')\zeta(s')\zeta_2^n(s')\right]. \tag{14.73}$$

We now derive the implications of this model for equilibrium prices. The right side of Equation (14.64) equals the right side of Equation (14.67) so that $U_1(s) = \xi(s)$. Similarly, the right side of Equation (14.65) equals the right side of Equation (14.68) so that $U_2(s) = \zeta(s)\xi(s)$. Finally, using Equations (14.64) and (14.66) together yields a solution for $\zeta_1^n(s)$ as:

$$\zeta_1^n(s) = \frac{W_1(s)}{U_1(s)}. \tag{14.74}$$

This says that the relative price of the non-traded good in country 1 is defined in terms of the MRS in consumption between the traded and non-traded good. We can derive a similar expression for $\zeta_2^n(s)$.

It is straightforward to demonstrate that the inverse of the velocity function for country i satisfies:

$$U_i(s)[y_i(s) + \zeta_i^n(s)n_i(s)]\Psi_i(s) = \max\Big\{U_i(s)[y_i(s) + \zeta_i^n(s)n_i(s)],$$
$$\beta E_s\left(\frac{U_i(s')[y_i(s') + \zeta_i^n(s')n_i(s')]\Psi_i(s')}{\omega_i(s')}\right)\Big\}. \tag{14.75}$$

Introducing non-traded goods into this setup creates another way for velocity to fluctuate because it depends on the relative price of the traded to the non-traded good.

The nominal exchange rate is determined from Equations (14.65) and (14.68), from which it follows that $U_2(s) = \zeta(s)U_1(s)$. Hence,

$$e(s, M) = \frac{U_2(s)}{U_1(s)}\frac{M_1}{M_2}\frac{[y_2(s) + \zeta_2^n(s)n_2(s)]}{[y_1(s) + \zeta_1^n(s)n_1(s)]}\frac{\Psi_2^\star(s)}{\Psi_1^\star(s)}, \tag{14.76}$$

where $\Psi_i^\star$ denotes the solution to Equation (14.75). Notice that the terms of trade ($\zeta = U_2/U_1$) and the relative price of non-traded goods affect the nominal exchange rate. The effect of an increase in the supply of the non-traded good on the exchange rate will depend on the sign of $W''n + W'$. If the supply of n_1 increases and if $W''n + W' < 0$, then the exchange rate increases (or depreciates).

The price of a one-period nominal bond that pays one unit of currency i next period with certainty satisfies:

$$Q_1^i(s) = \beta E_s\left[\frac{U_i(s')\Psi_i(s')[y_i(s') + \zeta_i^n(s')n_i(s')]}{U_i(s)\Psi_i(s)[y_i(s) + \zeta_i^n(s)n_1(s)]\omega_i(s')}\right]. \tag{14.77}$$

Notice that changes in the supply of the non-traded good affect the nominal interest rate. In this model, velocity is constant whenever interest rates are positive. The bond price can be substituted into the functional equation for Ψ and clearly if nominal interest rates are positive, then the cash-in-advance constraint is binding.

14.3.2. Exchange rates and international capital flows

We now introduce a model with investment and international capital flows. Our discussion derives from the paper by Stockman and Svensson [417]. This model has the Stockman-Svensson timing convention which assumes that the goods market opens first and the consumer makes goods purchases using the sellers' currencies and then the asset market opens.

In this model, countries are completely specialized in production. Output of the domestic good denoted $x_{1,t}$ depends on the domestic capital stock denoted k_t and a random disturbance θ_t as:

$$x_{1,t} = f(k_t, \theta_t), \tag{14.78}$$

where $f(\cdot, \theta)$ is strictly increasing, strictly concave, and differentiable. The capital stock depreciates 100% each period. Output of the foreign good denoted $x_{2,t}$ is exogenous. Only the foreign good can be used for domestic investment. Investment at time t transforms the foreign goods into domestic capital at time $t + 1$ so that the quantity of foreign goods available for world consumption at time t is $x_{2,t} - k_{t+1}$.

The shocks to the economy s_t follow a first-order Markov process with a transition function F that satisfies the conditions of Assumption 13.1. The money supplies in each country evolve according to Equation (14.14) and satisfy Assumption 14.4. The endowment of country 2 at time t is a time-invariant function of the exogenous shock, $x_{2,t} \equiv x_2(s_t)$ and so is the disturbance to the production function of country 1 which we denote by $\theta_t \equiv \theta(s_t)$. Define $\mathcal{X} \equiv [\underline{x}_2, \bar{x}_2]$ and $\Theta \equiv [\underline{\theta}, \bar{\theta}]$, where $\underline{x}_2 > 0$, $\bar{x}_2 < \infty$, $\underline{\theta} > 0$ and $\bar{\theta} < \infty$. We assume that $x_2 : S \to \mathcal{X}$ and $\theta : S \to \Theta$ are continuous functions that are bounded away from zero. Since output takes values in a compact set and there is 100% depreciation, notice that k_{t+1} takes values in the compact set $\mathcal{K} \equiv [\underline{k}, \bar{k}]$ where $\underline{k} > 0$ and $\bar{k} < \infty$.

The household in country j begins the period with holdings of domestic and foreign currency denoted $M^j_{1,t}$ and $M^j_{2,t}$ and claims to dividends $z^j_{1,t}$ and $z^j_{2,t}$ for the production processes in each country. There is one outstanding equity share in each production process. The household is assumed to be the owner of the capital stock and, at the beginning of the period, it rents out the capital accumulated the previous period k^j_t in exchange for rental income paid by the firm after the goods market closes. We assume that there is a competitive rental market so that households and firms are price-takers.[7] Essentially the firm receives the nominal revenue from selling output in the goods market and, after the close of the market, it pays rent and dividends to households so that the firm holds no money between periods.

After the goods markets close, the asset markets open and all interest and dividend payments are made, factor payments are made to the owners of capital, and assets are traded. The consumer in country j also receives the lump-sum money transfers $T^j_{i,t}$ from the government of country i which equal the net growth of money, $T^j_{i,t} = [\omega_i(s_t) - 1]\bar{M}_{i,t}$. The constraint in the asset market for the representative consumer in country j at time t denominated in units of the domestic currency is:

[7] The assumption that households own the capital stock and rent it to the firm differs from the setup in Stockman and Svensson who assume that, when the consumer holds a share in the domestic firm, it receives the dividends $d_{1,t}$ from the firm but in addition, it agrees to deliver investment goods to the firm in each period equal to k_{t+1}.

$$p_t c^j_{1,t} + e_t p_{2,t}(c^j_{2,t} + k^j_{t+1}) + M^j_{1,t+1} + e_t M^j_{2,t+1} + Q^e_{1,t} z^j_{1,t+1}$$
$$+ e_t Q^e_{2,t} z^j_{2,t+1} \leq (Q^e_{1,t} + p_{1,t} d_{1,t}) z^j_{1,t} + e_t (Q^e_{2,t} + p_{2,t} d_{2,t}) z^j_{2,t}$$
$$+ M^j_{1,t} + T^j_{1,t} + e_t (M^j_{2,t} + T^j_{2,t}) + R_t k^j_t,$$

where R_t is the nominal rent paid to owners of the capital stock. The cash-in-advance constraints are:

$$p_{1,t} c^j_{1,t} \leq M^j_{1,t},$$
$$e_t p_{2,t}(c^j_{2,t} + k^j_{t+1}) \leq e_t M^j_{2,t}.$$

Since the money supplies are growing, we divide the nominal constraints by the domestic currency price of country 1's goods to convert nominal quantities into units of good 1. The asset market constraint becomes:

$$c^j_{1,t} + \zeta_t (c^j_{2,t} + k^j_{t+1}) + \frac{M^j_{1,t+1}}{p_{1,t}} + \zeta_t \frac{M^j_{2,t+1}}{p_{2,t}} + q^e_{1,t} z^j_{1,t+1}$$
$$+ \zeta_t q^e_{2,t} z^j_{2,t+1} \leq (q^e_{1,t} + d_{1,t}) z^j_{1,t} + \zeta_t (q^e_{2,t} + d_{2,t}) z^j_{2,t}$$
$$+ \frac{M^j_{1,t}}{p_{1,t}} + \tau^j_{1,t} + \zeta_t \left(\frac{M^j_{2,t}}{p_{2,t}} + \tau^j_{2,t} \right) + r_t k^j_t, \tag{14.79}$$

where $\zeta_t \equiv e_t p_{2,t}/p_{1,t}$, $r_t \equiv R_t/p_{1,t}$, $q^e_{i,t} \equiv Q^e_{i,t}/p_{i,t}$, and $\tau_{i,t} \equiv T_{i,t}/p_{i,t}$ for $i = 1, 2$. Likewise, the cash-in-advance constraints become:

$$c^j_{1,t} \leq M^j_{1,t}/p_{1,t}, \tag{14.80}$$
$$\zeta_t (c^j_{2,t} + k^j_{1,t+1}) \leq \zeta_t M^j_{2,t}/p_{2,t}. \tag{14.81}$$

Consumers in both countries have identical information and portfolios and their preferences are defined as in Equation (14.1), where the utility function satisfies Assumption 14.2. The household observes the current exogenous shock s and so observes the current disturbance to domestic production, the endowment of country 2, and the money growth rates. The consumer's state at time t is summarized by its money holdings M^j_1, M^j_2, equity holdings z^j_1, z^j_2, and its stock of capital k^j. The aggregate state consists of the aggregate capital stock k and the current shock s.

We will seek an equilibrium in which the terms of trade, the rental rate, and the equity prices are time-invariant functions of k and s, and the nominal exchange rate and nominal prices levels are time-invariant functions of s, k, and $M \equiv (\bar{M}_1, \bar{M}_2)$. Define $\mathcal{S} \equiv S \times \mathcal{K}$. Define $\zeta : \mathcal{S} \to \mathrm{R}_{++}$, $r : \mathcal{S} \to \mathrm{R}_{++}$, and $q^e_i : \mathcal{S} \to \mathrm{R}_{++}$ for $i = 1, 2$ to be positive, continuous functions and $p_i : \mathcal{S} \times \mathrm{R}^2_+ \to \mathrm{R}_{++}$ for $i = 1, 2$ and $e : \mathcal{S} \times \mathrm{R}^2_+ \to \mathrm{R}_{++}$ to be positive, continuous functions. For notational convenience, define

$\alpha^j \equiv (M_1^j, M_2^j, z_1^j, z_2^j, k^j)$. Given the price functions ζ, e, r and q_i^e and p_i for $i = 1, 2$, the representative agent's problem in country j is to solve:

$$V(\alpha^j, k, s) = \max_{c_1^j, c_2^j, \alpha^{j'}} \left\{ U(c_1^j, c_2^j) + \beta E_s[V(\alpha^{j'}, k, s')] \right\}$$

subject to the asset market constraint (Equation 14.79) and the cash-in-advance constraints (Equations 14.80 and 14.81). We can show the existence of the consumer's value function using the methods defined earlier.

The market-clearing conditions are:

$$c_{1,t}^1 + c_{1,t}^2 = x_{1,t}, \tag{14.82}$$

$$c_{2,t}^1 + c_{2,t}^2 + k_{t+1}^1 + k_{t+1}^2 = x_{2,t}, \tag{14.83}$$

$$z_{i,t+1}^1 + z_{i,t+1}^2 = 1, \tag{14.84}$$

$$M_{i,t+1}^1 + M_{i,t+1}^2 = \omega_i(s_t)\bar{M}_{i,t}, \tag{14.85}$$

for $i = 1, 2$.

We assume that the optimal consumption and capital holdings by the representative consumer in country j can be expressed as time-invariant functions of the aggregate state, $c_1(k, s)$, $c_2(k, s)$, and $K(k, s)$. Define $U_i(k, s)$ as the partial derivative of U with respect to its ith argument evaluated at $c_i(k, s)$ for $i = 1, 2$. Let $\xi(k, s)$ denote the Lagrange multiplier on the asset market constraint and $\mu_i(k, s)$ denote the Lagrange multiplier on the cash-in-advance constraints. Substituting the envelope conditions, the first-order conditions with respect to c_i, M_i', z_i' for $i = 1, 2$ and k' are:

$$U_1(k, s) = \xi(k, s) + \mu_1(k, s), \tag{14.86}$$

$$U_2(k, s) = \zeta(k, s)[\xi(k, s) + \mu_2(k, s)], \tag{14.87}$$

$$\begin{aligned} \xi(k, s) = \beta E_s\{\pi_1(k', s')[\xi(k', s') \\ + \mu_1(k', s')]\}, \end{aligned} \tag{14.88}$$

$$\begin{aligned} \zeta(k, s)\xi(k, s) = \beta E_s\{\pi_2(k', s')\zeta(k', s')[\xi(k', s') \\ + \mu_2(k', s')]\}, \end{aligned} \tag{14.89}$$

$$q_1^e(k, s)\xi(k, s) = \beta E_s\{\xi(k', s')[d_1' + q_1^e(k', s')]\}, \tag{14.90}$$

$$\begin{aligned} \zeta(k, s)q_2^e(k, s)\xi(k, s) = \beta Es\{\zeta(k', s')\xi(k', s')[d_2' \\ + q_2^e(k', s')]\}, \end{aligned} \tag{14.91}$$

$$\zeta(k, s)[\xi(s) + \mu_2(k, s)] = \beta E_s[\xi(s')r(k', s')]. \tag{14.92}$$

In these expressions, $\pi_i(k', s') \equiv p_i(k, s, M)/p_i(k', s', M')$ for $i = 1, 2$. We also have the slackness conditions with respect to the multipliers $\xi(k, s)$ and $\mu_i(k, s)$ for $i = 1, 2$.

For country 2, where the output of good 2 is determined exogenously, the dividend is equal to the amount of good 2 produced so that $d_2 = x_2(s)$. Now turn to the problem solved by a firm which produces good 1. The firm chooses the amount of capital k_t to rent that maximizes its profits; it solves:

$$d_{1,t} \equiv \max_{k_t}[f(k_t, \theta_t) - r_t k_t]. \tag{14.93}$$

The firm rents capital up to the point where its marginal product equals the rental rate. When capital markets clear, the amount hired by firms just equals the amount held by the representative household. The profits of the firm are paid out as dividends to shareholders.

The first-order condition for investment, with the equilibrium condition $r_t = f_k(k_t, \theta_t)$ substituted in, is:

$$\beta E_t[\xi_{t+1} f_k(k_{t+1}, \theta_{t+1})] = (\xi_t + \mu_{2,t})\zeta_t = U_{2,t}, \tag{14.94}$$

where f_k denotes the partial derivative of $f(k, \theta)$ with respect to k. The right side is just the marginal cost of investment at time t. The left side shows the expected marginal benefit at time $t + 1$: a higher value of capital at time $t + 1$ produces additional output at $t + 1$ and ξ_{t+1} is the marginal utility of this income.

We study the pooled equilibrium for this model. The pooled equilibrium requires that:

$$c_1 = x_1/2, \quad c_2 = [x_2 - K(k, s)]/2,$$

$$z_i' = 1/2, \quad M_i' = \omega_i(s)\bar{M}_i/2, \quad i = 1, 2.$$

We assume that the utility function in each country U is separable with respect to c_1 and c_2. In this case, we can use the conditions in Equations (14.86), (14.88), and (14.94) to solve for the function K and the inverse of the velocity function in country 1. Since U is separable, we can write U_1 and U_2 as functions of the equilibrium consumption of domestic and foreign goods only, $U_1(x_1/2)$ and $U_2[(x_2 - k')/2]$.

We add the cash-in-advance constraints for members of country 1 and 2 in the domestic and the foreign currency and define the functions:

$$\Psi_1 \equiv \bar{M}_1/p_1 x_1, \tag{14.95}$$

$$\Psi_2 \equiv \bar{M}_2/(p_2 x_2 + k'). \tag{14.96}$$

Notice that we can derive an expression for the multiplier on the cash-in-advance constraint for country 1 as:

$$U_1(k,s)\Psi_1(k,s)x_1 = \mu_1(k,s) + \beta E_s\left[\frac{U_1(k',s')\Psi_1(k',s')x_1'}{\omega_1(s')}\right].$$

In equilibrium, $x_1(k,s) = f(k,s)$ is given. It will be more convenient to derive a mapping for the function:

$$\Gamma(k,s) \equiv U_1(k,s)\Psi_1(k,s)x_1(k,s)$$

from the above expression by considering the cases when $\mu_1 = 0$ and $\mu_1 > 0$ as:

$$\Gamma(k,s) = \max\left[U_1(k,s)x_1(k,s), \beta E_s\left(\frac{\Gamma(k',s')}{\omega(s')}\right)\right]. \tag{14.97}$$

Notice that k' is a decision variable. If the capital process were given exogenously, then we could define an operator with a fixed point Γ^* that satisfies Equation (14.97). Instead, we need to solve also for the equilibrium capital path. Here we will outline the steps that are necessary to solve this model.

Recall that the first-order condition for investment can be expressed as:

$$U_2[x_2(s) - k'] = \beta E_s[\xi(k',s')f_k(k',\theta')] \tag{14.98}$$

Notice that U_2 is increasing in k' given s so that we can define k' from $\phi(k,s) = U_2[x_2(s) - k']$ for $\phi_1 > 0$ as:

$$k' = H(\phi,s) = x_2(s) - U_2^{-1}(\phi).$$

Notice also that H is increasing in its first argument. Let $K(k,s)$ be a feasible solution and define $\phi(k,s) \equiv U_2[x_2(s) - K(k,s)]$. We can then write Equation (14.98) as:

$$\phi(k,s) = \beta E_s\{\xi(H[\phi(k,s),s],s')f_k(H[\phi(k,s),s],\theta')\}. \tag{14.99}$$

Notice that we evaluate ϕ at (k,s) on both sides of the equation. By assumption f_k is strictly decreasing in its first argument. For fixed (k,s), consider the solution scalar $\phi > 0$, that is, the solution to:

$$\phi = \beta E_s\{\xi[H(\phi,s),s']f_k[H(\phi,s),\theta']\}. \tag{14.100}$$

If we assume that ξ is decreasing in its first argument, then for fixed (k,s) the left side is clearly increasing in ϕ and the right side is strictly decreasing so there exists a unique solution ϕ for each (k,s) pair. Let $(S\xi)(k,s)$ denote the solution ϕ to Equation (14.100).

Given the function Γ, we can define the multiplier function ξ using the following argument. Let $K(k,s)$ be given. When $\mu_1 = 0$, $\xi(k,s) = U_1(s)$ and $\Gamma(k,s) = \beta E_s[\Gamma(k',s')/\omega(s')]$. When $\mu_1 > 0$, then $\Gamma(k,s) = U_1(s)x_1(s)$ and

$\xi(k,s) = \beta E_s[\Gamma(k',s')/(x_1(s)\omega(s'))]$. From the definition of the function Γ, it follows that:

$$\xi(k,s) \equiv \min\left[U_1(k,s), \beta E_s\left(\frac{\Gamma(k',s')}{x_1(s)\omega(s')}\right)\right]. \tag{14.101}$$

Let T_2 be the operator that yields ξ from Γ or $\xi(k,s) = (T_2\Gamma)(k,s)$. Given $\xi(k,s) = (T_2\Gamma)(k,s)$, we can find the solution ϕ to Equation (14.100). Define the operator T_1 by:

$$\begin{aligned}\phi(k,s) &\equiv (T_1\Gamma)(k,s)\\ &= \beta E_s\left\{(T_2\Gamma)(H[\phi(k,s),s],s')f_k(H[\phi(k,s),s],\theta')\right\}.\end{aligned} \tag{14.102}$$

We can now define the operator T_∞ as follows:

$$\begin{aligned}\Gamma^{n+1}(k,s) &= (T_\infty\Gamma^n)(k,s)\\ &= \max\left[U_1(k,s)x_1(k,s), \beta E_s\left(\frac{\Gamma^n\{H[\phi(k,s)],s'\}}{\omega(s')}\right)\right],\end{aligned} \tag{14.103}$$

where $\phi(k,s) = (T_1\Gamma)(k,s)$ is the solution to the previous mapping. The form of this mapping is different from the other mappings that we studied earlier. A proof can be constructed using the approach in Deaton and Laroque [139] but it is beyond the scope of our analysis to provide the entire derivation. Assuming a solution has been found, let $\xi^\star(k,s)$ denote a fixed point and let $K^\star(k,s)$ be the optimal investment function. Given the solution for $\Psi_1^\star(k,s)$ and $K^\star(k,s)$, we can use Equations (14.87) and (14.89) to solve for $\Psi_2(k,s)$ and Equations (14.90) and (14.91) to solve for the equity prices $q_1^e(k,s)$ and $q_2^e(k,s)$.

Since there is one equity share outstanding, the value of the firm is just $q_{1,t}^e$. We can derive an expression for firm value by solving Equation (14.90) forward:

$$q_{1,t}^e = \frac{1}{\xi_t}E_t\left(\sum_{\tau=t+1}^{\infty}\beta^{t-\tau}\{\xi^\star(k_\tau^\star,s_\tau)[x_1(k_\tau^\star,s_\tau) - f_k(k_\tau^\star,\theta_\tau)k_\tau^\star]\}\right),$$

where we have made use of the fact that equilibrium dividends at each date τ are equal to domestic profits at that date.

We now use this framework to define a number of accounting identities involving international capital flows. The domestic country's *current account surplus* is defined as the change in its net holdings of foreign assets, which is also the *capital account deficit*. We denote the capital account deficit (current account surplus) in period t, measured in units of the domestic good, by C_t. The total world values of foreign assets $V_{2,t}$ and domestic assets $V_{1,t}$ are:

$$V_{1,t} = q^e_{1,t} + \omega_1(s_t)m_{1,t}, \tag{14.104}$$

$$V_{2,t} = \zeta_t[q^e_{2,t} + \omega_2(s_t)m_{2,t}], \tag{14.105}$$

where $m_{i,t} \equiv \bar{M}_{i,t}/p_{i,t}$ for $i = 1, 2$ denote the world real balances of the domestic and foreign currencies. Foreign assets consist of shares in the foreign firm and the real balances of foreign money. Domestic assets are the shares in the home firm and real balances of domestic money.

Households in the domestic country have a net foreign account asset position at the end of period t, denoted F_t, which is given by:

$$F_t = V_{2,t}/2 - V_{1,t}/2. \tag{14.106}$$

The current account surplus in period t is:

$$C_t = \Delta F_t = (V_{2,t} - V_{2,t-1} - V_{1,t} + V_{1,t-1})/2, \tag{14.107}$$

where Δ denotes the first difference operator. Define domestic saving S_t as the change in domestic wealth, $S_t = \Delta(V_{2,t}/2 + V_{1,t}/2)$, and domestic investment I_t as the change in the value of domestic assets, $I_t = \Delta V_{1,t}$. The current account surplus C_t can be written as:

$$C_t = S_t - I_t. \tag{14.108}$$

We now define the balance-of-trade surplus and the service account surplus. The *trade account surplus* measured in domestic goods is defined as:

$$TA_t = c^2_{1,t} - \zeta_t(c^1_{2,t} + k_{t+1}) = x_{1,t}/2 - \zeta_t[x_{2,t} + K(k_t, s_t)]/2.$$

The first term shows exports, which equal half of domestic output. The second term shows imports of consumption goods and the third term shows imports of goods for investment.

The *service account surplus* consists of net dividends or interest payments and capital gains on all assets:

$$SA_t = [\zeta_t x_{2,t} - x_{1,t} + K(k_t, s_t) + \Delta(\zeta_t q^e_{2,t} - q^e_{1,t}) + \zeta_t(\omega_{2,t} - 1)m_{2,t}$$
$$- (\omega_{1,t} - 1)m_{1,t} + (\Delta\zeta_t p^{-1}_{2,t})\bar{M}_{2,t} - (\Delta p^{-1}_{1,t})\bar{M}_{1,t}]/2.$$

The first three terms are the net dividends from the foreign and domestic production processes received by the domestic country. The fourth and fifth terms show the capital gains on foreign equity minus foreigners' capital gains on domestic equity. The sixth and seventh terms show the receipt of foreign monetary transfers minus the payment of domestic monetary transfers. The last two terms show domestic capital gains on holdings of foreign currency minus foreign capital gains on holdings of domestic currency. Notice that $C_t = TA_t + SA_t$.

One difference between these measures and reported current-account data is that capital gains are arbitrarily excluded from the latter so that the sum of SA_t and TA_t does not equal the change in the net foreign asset position. Also, the definitions of saving and investment given above do not correspond to national-income-accounting (NIA) definitions. The NIA definition of gross domestic savings is the difference between "income" defined as $[x_{1,t} + \zeta_t(x_{2,t} + k_{t+1})]/2$ and consumption:

$$[x_{1,t} + \zeta_t(x_{2,t} + k_{t+1})]/2 - c^1_{1,t} - \zeta_t c^1_{2,t} = k_{t+1}.$$

The NIA definition of gross domestic investment is k_{t+1} so savings minus investment is zero according to the NIA definitions and it is not equal to the change in the net foreign asset position.

Stockman and Svensson use the solution to the model to analyze the determinants of the current account surplus (the capital account deficit) and the covariation between capital flows C_t and such variables as investment (defined as $k_{t+1} - k_t$), national outputs, $x_{1,t}$ and $x_{2,t}$, the terms of trade ζ_t, and the rate of change in the exchange rate. For example, we can ask under what conditions real appreciation of the domestic currency is associated with a current account surplus versus a deficit. Stockman and Svensson find that these covariances depend on the degree of risk aversion (or the degree of intertemporal substitution in consumption), the size and magnitude of net foreign assets, the marginal product of capital, and the stochastic properties of the disturbances to productivity and money growth. To derive such results, we need to use the properties of the optimal investment policy $K^\star(k, s)$, the inverse velocity functions $\Psi^\star_i(k, s)$, and the equity price functions $q^e_i(k, s)$ for $i = 1, 2$.

14.4. CONCLUSIONS

In this chapter, we have provided both real and nominal models of international trade and exchange. The real models allow us to analyze risk sharing and portfolio diversification across countries and to analyze the sources of international business cycles. By contrast, the nominal models provide a useful framework for examining exchange risk, the determination of forward and future prices of foreign exchange and similar issues. Incorporating capital into international models also allows an analysis of capital international flows.

14.5. EXERCISES

1. Consider the dynamic programming problem defined in Equation (14.29). Define $\phi(s) \equiv V(h(s), 0.5, 0.5, s)$ and let $\phi_h = V_h$, $\phi_1 = V_{z_1}$,

and $\phi_2 = V_{z_2}$ denote the first partial derivative of the consumer's valuation function with respect to h, z_1 and z_2, respectively, evaluated at equilibrium money and asset holdings, and the current state.

Derive the equilibrium first-order conditions and envelope conditions for the consumer's problem and show that they yield the conditions described by Equations (14.30) through (14.35).

2. Siegel's Paradox

   Siegel [401] has argued that the proposition that the level of the forward rate is equal to the expected value of the level of the future spot rate would lead to a contradiction. If this were true for exchange rates quoted as the British pound per US dollar, then it could not be true for the exchange rate quoted as US dollar per British pound.

   (a) Using Jensen's inequality, state the nature of Siegel's paradox.
   (b) Comment on Siegel's paradox in an equilibrium model with risk-neutral consumers.

3. Derive the forward rate and the risk premium, the futures price, and the stock prices for the two-country model with the Stockman-Svensson timing.

4. [8] Modify the two-country model with the Stockman-Svensson timing in the previous exercise by assuming that the government does not consume any endowment and that money is injected by way of a lump-sum transfer at the beginning of the asset market. Assume, however, that agents can trade the two currencies taken to the goods market. For a representative agent who enters the good market with holdings $H_{1,t}$ and $H_{2,t}$, the following budget constraint holds:

$$H_{1,t} + \bar{e}_t H_{2,t} \geq \ell_{i,t}\bar{H}_{1,t} + \bar{e}_t \ell_{2,t}\bar{H}_{2,t}$$

   where $\bar{e}_t$ is the equilibrium exchange rate in the exchange market that meets at the same time as the goods market, ℓ_i is the nominal price of acquiring one more unit of currency i, and $\bar{H}_{1,t}$ and $\bar{H}_{2,t}$ are the adjusted money holdings. The agent now has two additional decision variables, $\bar{H}_{1,t}$ and $\bar{H}_{2,t}$.

   (a) Derive the first-order conditions for the new decision variables and determine the equilibrium price ℓ and the exchange rate.
   (b) Derive the equilibrium prices $\bar{p}_1$ and $\bar{p}_2$. Derive the forward exchange rate.

5. [9] Variations in the roles of national currencies in the international economy are studied. Assume that there is only one endowment good which is received by both countries. Let p_h denote the price of the good in units of the home country currency and let p_f denote the price of the

[8] This exercise derived from Engel [172].
[9] This exercise derived from Helpman and Razin [251].

good in units of the foreign country currency. Assume that the timing corresponds to that of the Lucas version of the model. If the endowment good of both countries is to be bought and consumed, then the law of one price must hold: $p_h = ep_f$.

Consider two monetary mechanisms. Under the first, the seller will accept only domestic currency. This is the mechanism that we have used throughout our discussion of international cash-in-advance models. Under the second mechanism, we assume that all transactions are constrained to take place with the buyer's domestic currency.

(a) Derive the first-order conditions and equilibrium prices, real and nominal exchange rates, and equilibrium nominal interest rates under the first mechanism. Derive the forward rate.

(b) Derive the first-order conditions and equilibrium prices, real and nominal exchange rates, and equilibrium nominal interest rates under the second mechanism. Derive the forward rate.

6. [10] Consider the Lucas two-country model and assume that preferences are given by:

$$U(c_1, c_2) = [\theta c_1^{1-\gamma} + (1-\theta) c_2^{1-\gamma}]/(1-\gamma), \quad \gamma \geq 0, \; 0 < \theta < 1.$$

(a) Find expressions for the changes in the logs of the nominal and real exchange rates.

(b) To be broadly consistent with actual experience, the model must produce real and nominal exchange rates that are of roughly equal variance and that are highly correlated. Using your answer to (a), show that the Lucas model generally requires monetary variability to be more important than real variability for these results to obtain.

7. Assume that shares to the monetary transfers are traded in the Lucas version of the two-country model. Determine the equilibrium price of the shares under the assumption that there is a pooled equilibrium.

[10] This exercise is derived from Mark [334].

PART IV

Models with market incompleteness

CHAPTER 15

Asset pricing with frictions

Up to this point, our discussion has been based on frictionless trading in a representative consumer context. In Chapter 2, we argued that trading frictions such as short sales constraints or transactions costs can alter the implications of a variety of asset-pricing relations. As an example, we showed that in the presence of such frictions, a strict form of the Law of One Price may fail to hold. In this chapter, we will introduce such frictions into asset-pricing models and discuss some of the empirical implications. We will also consider some of the empirical implications of allowing for market incompleteness for asset-pricing phenomena. Various authors have noted that such models have the potential to account for a variety of economic phenomena that cannot be explained easily using the simple representative consumer economies that we have studied so far.

As our earlier discussion indicates, resolution of such asset-pricing anomalies as the "equity premium puzzle," the "real risk-free rate puzzle," and the behavior of the term premiums may lie in the relaxation of the representative consumer, complete markets assumption. In a representative agent model, all asset returns are driven by a common stochastic discount factor which suggests that, to some extent, stocks and bonds should tend to move together. Yet the empirical evidence appears to be at odds with this requirement.[1] By introducing market incompleteness, borrowing constraints, and other sorts of frictions, some have suggested that this close link can be broken. In this chapter, we will study the asset-pricing implications of uninsurable idiosyncratic risk. It turns out that the results hinge on the nature of uninsurable idiosyncratic risk. As Constantinides and Duffie [119] demonstrate, a resolution of asset-pricing anomalies requires that volatility of idiosyncratic income risk vary with the aggregate state of the economy. We will also introduce a model with bid-ask spreads and review some of the empirical implications regarding the impact of transactions costs.

The final topic in this chapter is the construction of volatility bounds with frictions. Following Luttmer [327] and He and Modest [246], we

[1] See, for example, Barsky [46].

show how to derive volatility bounds for intertemporal MRSs when there exist short sales constraints, and other frictions.

15.1. THE ROLE OF IDIOSYNCRATIC RISK FOR ASSET PRICING

In Chapter 7, we examined the implications of the full risk-sharing hypothesis in intertemporal environments where there is both idiosyncratic and aggregate risk. We showed that in a situation where there is only idiosyncratic risk, consumers can insure away all fluctuations in their consumption stream. By contrast, when there is aggregate risk, the full risk-sharing hypothesis implies that some risk must be borne by consumers. We also showed that the common intertemporal MRS across consumers in the full risk-sharing equilibrium is equal to the pricing function or pricing kernel used to price any asset in this equilibrium.

To understand the role of idiosyncratic risk, consider the basic asset-pricing equation:

$$1 = E_t\left[M_{i,t+1}R_{jt}\right], \tag{15.1}$$

where R_{jt} denotes the (gross) return on any asset and $M_{i,t+1}$ is the intertemporal MRS for each consumer i. Under the complete markets assumption, consumers set their intertemporal MRSs equal to the common ratio of the contingent claims prices, p_{t+1}/p_t, as discussed in Chapter 7. Typically, this ratio depends on the history of the shocks and hence varies in a random fashion so that the common intertemporal MRS is the stochastic discount factor. In the representative consumer pure exchange economy of Chapter 8, the stochastic discount factor is equal to the random intertemporal MRS of the representative consumer and can be evaluated using a parametric specification of preferences and aggregate or per capita consumption data. With incomplete markets, asset-pricing relations based on an intertemporal MRS evaluated with aggregate or per capita consumption data are not valid. Likewise, market frictions such as short sales constraints and bid-ask spreads will alter the relationship between individual intertemporal MRSs and the common stochastic discount factor used to value random payoffs.

One approach to characterizing the stochastic discount factor in incomplete market settings is to solve directly for the asset-pricing function. An early example of this approach is provided by Scheinkman and Weiss [391], who consider an economy with heterogeneous agents and borrowing constraints. In their framework, idiosyncratic shocks are perfectly negatively correlated across agents, implying that the complete contingent claims allocations are constant across consumers. However, in the presence of uninsurable idiosyncratic risk and borrowing constraints, they show that the allocations and the asset price depend on the average holdings of the asset that agents use to smooth consumption over time. Put differently, the cross-sectional distribution of wealth varies over time and helps to determine economic outcomes. We analyze more formally models with borrowing or short sales constraints in Chapter 16.

A variety of papers have used versions of this type of model to examine the role of idiosyncratic risk on allocations and asset prices. In a model with no aggregate uncertainty and with i.i.d. shocks for individuals, Aiyagari and Gertler [11] have found in simulations that the borrowing constraints did not generate enough volatility of asset returns. To improve their results, they also included transactions costs. This is similar to the results of the papers by Heaton and Lucas [249, 250], who work with a three-period model and incorporate transactions costs, short sales constraints, and borrowing constraints. Telmer [429] develops a model in which there is both aggregate and individual uncertainty. He finds that introducing a risk-free asset allows the agents to do a great deal of consumption smoothing.[2] Constantinides and Duffie [119] have pointed out that in most of these models, the idiosyncratic labor income shocks are i.i.d. and hence transient so that the permanent income of agents is almost equal across agents despite imperfect risk sharing. Hence, the consumption-smoothing opportunities afforded by a risk-free bond are almost enough to allow risk sharing and that this is the reason transactions costs and short sales constraints are needed. See also Krusell and Smith [293] and Storesletten, Telmer, and Yaron [422], amongst others.

To illustrate the impact of idiosyncratic risk using a simple example, suppose that the intertemporal MRS and asset returns are jointly log-normally distributed. Under these assumptions we showed in Chapter 8 that the excess return on the risky asset relative to the risk-free asset, or the risk premium, can be expressed as:

$$E_t(r_{t+1}) - r_t^f + \frac{1}{2} Var_t(r_{t+1}) = -Cov_t(m_{i,t+1}, r_{t+1}), \tag{15.2}$$

where $r_{t+1} = \ln(R_{t+1})$, $m_{it+1} = \ln(M_{i,t+1})$, and r_t^f is the real risk-free rate. This expression says that the expected excess return plus the variance of returns (due to the Jensen effect) equals the risk premium. Suppose also that preferences are of the CRRA variety. This implies that:

$$\ln(m_{i,t+1}) = \ln(\beta) - \gamma \Delta c_{i,t+1},$$

where $\Delta c_{i,t+1} = \ln(C_{i,t+1}/C_{it})$. Thus, the expression for the risk premium becomes:

$$E_t(r_{t+1}) - r_t^f + \frac{1}{2} Var_t(r_{t+1}) = \gamma Cov_t(\Delta c_{i,t+1}, r_{t+1}). \tag{15.3}$$

[2] Other related papers are by Brown [81] and Danthine, Donaldson, and Mehra [137].

Now suppose that individual consumption growth has an aggregate and an idiosyncratic component as:

$$\Delta c_{i,t+1} = A_{t+1} + \epsilon_{i,t+1}. \tag{15.4}$$

Notice that only the aggregate risk will get priced in equilibrium. Equivalently, the conditional covariance of any return that is traded with the idiosyncratic part of consumption growth will be zero. (Recall also our discussion in Chapter 8.) Hence, idiosyncratic risk that enters linearly in a log SDF will not affect asset-pricing relations.[3]

As various authors have noted, idiosyncratic shocks can affect asset prices in equilibrium only if their variance depends on the aggregate state. Mankiw [331] shows that the concentration of uninsurable idiosyncratic shocks throughout the population affects the equity premium. In his model, idiosyncratic income risk in an incomplete markets setting affects the equity premium because the volatility of idiosyncratic shocks depends negatively on aggregate consumption. Similarly, Constantinides and Duffie [119] assume that uninsurable idiosyncratic shocks are both persistent and heteroscedastic and that the conditional volatility of the idiosyncratic shocks is a function the aggregate state of the economy. These authors employ the device of postulating an idiosyncratic income process under which the no-trade allocation for each consumer is an equilibrium. Specifically consider a pure exchange economy populated with a large number of agents such that each agent has the exogenous income process:

$$y_{it} = \delta_{it} C_t - D_t, \tag{15.5}$$

where C_t is aggregate consumption, D_t is the aggregate dividend and δ_{it} is defined as:

$$\delta_{it} = \exp\left[\sum_{s=1}^{t}\left(\eta_{is} y_s - \frac{y_s^2}{2}\right)\right], \tag{15.6}$$

$$y_t = \sqrt{\frac{2}{\gamma^2 + \gamma}}\left[\ln\left(\frac{M_t}{M_{t-1}}\right) + \rho + \gamma \ln\left(\frac{C_t}{C_{t-1}}\right)\right]^{\frac{1}{2}}, \tag{15.7}$$

where M_t has the interpretation of the equilibrium pricing kernel, $\{\eta_{it}\}$ are independent across i and t, and η_{it} is standard normal and independent of the information set at time $t-1$, I_{t-1}, and of y_t.[4]

[3] The risk-free rate may fall, however, due to precautionary savings effects.

[4] We omit a discussion of the technical details required to render this problem well defined. In particular, notice that for the postulated income process to be consistent with equilibrium, it must be the case that $\sum_{i\in A} \delta_{it} = 1$ for the entire set of agents A.

Consider the intertemporal Euler equation for any consumer i:

$$\beta E_t \left[R_{j,t+1} \left(\frac{C_{i,t+1}}{C_{it}} \right)^{-\gamma} \right] = 1. \tag{15.8}$$

To simplify this expression, suppose that the no-trade allocation is an equilibrium. Then $C_{it} = y_{it} + D_t = \delta_{it} C_t$. Substituting this for the ratios of consumption and simplifying yields:

$$\begin{aligned}
\left(\frac{C_{i,t+1}}{C_{it}} \right)^{-\gamma} &= \left(\frac{C_{t+1}}{C_t} \frac{\delta_{i,t+1}}{\delta_{it}} \right)^{-\gamma} \\
&= \left(\frac{C_{t+1}}{C_t} \right)^{-\gamma} \exp\left[-\gamma \left(\eta_{i,t+1} y_{t+1} - \frac{y_{t+1}^2}{2} \right) \right].
\end{aligned}$$

where we have used the definition of δ_{it} for each t. Now evaluate

$$\begin{aligned}
&\beta E_t \left[R_{j,t+1} \left(\frac{C_{i,t+1}}{C_{it}} \right)^{-\gamma} \right] \\
&= \beta E_t \left\{ R_{j,t+1} \left(\frac{C_{t+1}}{C_t} \right)^{-\gamma} \exp\left[-\gamma \left(\eta_{i,t+1} y_{t+1} - \frac{y_{t+1}^2}{2} \right) \right] \right\} \\
&= \beta E_t \left\{ R_{j,t+1} \left(\frac{C_{t+1}}{C_t} \right)^{-\gamma} \Upsilon_{it} \right\},
\end{aligned}$$

whereby an iterated expectations argument,

$$\begin{aligned}
\Upsilon_{it} &= E \left\{ \exp\left[-\gamma \left(\eta_{i,t+1} y_{t+1} - \frac{y_{t+1}^2}{2} \right) \right] | I_t \cup y_{t+1} \right\} \\
&= \exp\left[\frac{\gamma(\gamma + 1)}{2} y_{t+1}^2 \right].
\end{aligned}$$

Hence, the intertemporal Euler equation can be written as:[5]

$$\beta E_t \left\{ R_{j,t+1} \left(\frac{C_{t+1}}{C_t} \right)^{-\gamma} \exp\left[\frac{\gamma(\gamma + 1)}{2} y_{t+1}^2 \right] \right\} = 1. \tag{15.9}$$

[5] It takes one more step to establish the existence of the no-trade equilibrium. Specifically, this is shown by noting that $\Upsilon_{it} = \beta (C_{t+1}/C_t)^{\gamma} (M_{t+1}/M_t)$, implying that M_{t+1} is indeed the pricing kernel in any asset-pricing relationship.

To complete the argument, we note that y_{t+1}^2 denotes the variance of the cross-sectional distribution of consumption:

$$\begin{aligned} \ln\left(\frac{C_{i,t+1}/C_{t+1}}{C_{it}/C_t}\right) &= \ln\left(\frac{\delta_{it+1}}{\delta_{it}}\right) \\ &= \eta_{i,t+1}y_{t+1} - y_{t+1}^2/2 \\ &\sim N\left(-\frac{y_{t+1}^2}{2}, y_{t+1}^2\right) \end{aligned}$$

since η_{it} is standard normal and independent of y_{t+1}.

To illustrate the implications, we consider some special cases:

- If $y_{t+1}^2 = 0$, then the model reduces to the representative agent model evaluated using aggregate consumption data.
- If

$$y_{t+1}^2 = a + b\ln\left(\frac{C_{t+1}}{C_t}\right),$$

then the Euler equation in (15.9) is evaluated in the same way but with the parameters

$$\tilde{\beta} = \beta\exp\left[\frac{\gamma(\gamma+1)}{2}a\right],$$

$$\tilde{\gamma} = \gamma - \frac{\gamma(\gamma+1)}{2}b.$$

- In general, we replace the stochastic discount factor evaluated using only aggregate consumption growth with one in which the term y_{t+1}^2 also enters:

$$\Gamma_{t+1} \equiv \left(\frac{C_{t+1}}{C_t}\right)^{-\gamma}\exp\left[\frac{\gamma(\gamma+1)}{2}y_{t+1}^2\right].$$

In this case, we can write the risk premium as:

$$E_t(R_{j,t+1}) - r_t^f = -r_t^f\, Cov_t(R_{j,t+1}, \Gamma_{t+1}). \tag{15.10}$$

Now there is an additional source of variation arising from the presence of the y_{t+1}^2 in the conditional covariance. Thus, we say that asset j has a positive (negative) risk premium if the conditional covariance of its return with Γ_{t+1} is negative (positive).

Lettau [307] provides a simple diagnostic regarding the role of idiosyncratic shocks in resolving asset-pricing anomalies. In contrast to many models of idiosyncratic risk that allow agents to trade in a small number of assets, Lettau [307] assumes agents consume their income and examines the Sharpe ratio for risky assets computed using individual income data. In other words, he considers the volatility bound:

$$\frac{|E_t(R_{j,t+1} - r_t^f)|}{SD_t(R_{j,t+1})} \leq \frac{SD_t(m_{i,t+1})}{E_t(m_{i,t+1})},$$

where $m_{i,t+1}$ is evaluated using individual income data. If it is the case that individual income growth is negatively correlated, then consumption is smoother than income because income shocks will have a less than one-to-one effect on permanent income, and conversely if income growth is positively autocorrelated. Hence, volatility bounds evaluated under individual income data will provide a useful lower bound for actual asset market data. As we discussed in Chapters 8 and 9, the Sharpe ratio estimated from postwar data using S&P 500 excess returns is around 0.50 on an annual basis. Lettau [307] considers the *maximal* bound on the Sharpe ratio computed using individual income data. Surprisingly, he finds that none of the estimated income processes in models that assume incomplete markets and uninsurable income risk is capable of matching the Sharpe ratio in the data. For example, the idiosyncratic income process estimated by Heaton and Lucas [250] from the Panel Study of Income Dynamics (PSID) data set implies a Sharpe ratio of around 0.18. A similar finding emerges for Krusell and Smith's [293] model of idiosyncratic risk in which unemployed agents face a higher probability of becoming unemployed when aggregate times are bad. Based on a calibration for quarterly data, the highest Sharpe ratio implied by the model (for employed agents in good times) is only capable of matching the observed quarterly Sharpe ratio. Finally, in Storesletten, Telmer, and Yaron [422] the calculated Sharpe ratios are only one-fifth of their observed values even after allowing for the variance of idiosyncratic shocks to vary depending on whether the aggregate economy is above or below trend.

15.2. TRANSACTIONS COSTS

Up to this point, we have considered the implications of borrowing constraints and other restrictions on securities trades. In actual securities markets, another important friction has to do with **transactions costs**. In this section, we briefly review this literature and present an example of a model with transactions costs.

During the process of buying or selling most assets, some kind of transactions cost is incurred. Often, these costs take the form of a difference between the price at which the asset is sold and the price at which it can be purchased, commonly known as the "bid-ask" spread. Transactions costs can take other forms such as up-front fees on load mutual funds and brokerage commission costs. Aiyagari and Gertler [11] report that the ratio of the bid-ask spread to the price is 0.52% for actively traded stocks and that this ratio increases as firm size declines, reaching 6.55% for the average firm with assets under ten million dollars. For the buyer or seller, there are additional costs associated with managing a portfolio such as information costs and bookkeeping costs. For the financial intermediary, which may take the form of an exchange or an organized market, the fees, commissions, and the bid-ask spread paid by the buyer and seller of assets are charges for the services provided by the intermediary. Three kinds of costs faced by an intermediary have been emphasized in the literature: order-processing costs, which can include research and information-gathering costs and costs of providing financial counseling; inventory-holding costs, which take the form of price risk because there may be a time lag between the time the dealer buys an asset and the time he sells it; and adverse-information costs. Adverse-information costs may be incurred when there is asymmetric information. Current prices may signal negative information about the value of the asset which changes its equilibrium price. If the dealer is the asset holder, he may suffer a loss from the price change. A general discussion on the components of the bid-ask spread is by Stoll [420] and Glosten and Harris [207]. The inventory risk has been studied by Amihud and Mendelson [27] and Stoll [419], among others, while the adverse information costs have been studied by Copeland and Galai [126], Glosten and Milgrom [208], and Easley and O'Hara [167].

If the liquidity of an asset is measured by the cost of immediate execution of a transaction, then the quoted ask price can include a premium for immediate purchase and the bid price can include a discount for immediate sale. The bid-ask spread can be interpreted as a measure of liquidity; the spread is smaller for more liquid assets. Several empirical studies, such as that by Amihud and Mendelson [28], have concluded that average risk-adjusted returns increase with their bid-ask spread. An empirical study of liquidity and yields is by Amihud and Mendelson [29].

Another type of cost affecting trading volume is a securities transactions tax. This type of tax has been considered in the US and exists in many other countries; see the survey by Schwert and Seguin [396] and the article by Umlauf [436] for examples. Proponents argue that the tax would reduce excess price volatility caused by excessive speculation, generate tax revenues, and increase the planning horizons of managers; arguments for this sort of tax are contained in the articles by Stiglitz [411] and Summers and Summers [425]. The notion that there is excess volatility in financial markets because of destabilizing speculation is discussed by DeLong, Shleifer, Summers, and Waldman [145]. Critics of the tax proposal argue that it would increase the costs of capital, distort optimal portfolio decisions, reduce market efficiency and drive markets to lower tax countries; see the papers by Grundfest and Shoven [220], and Kupiec [294] [295],

Roll [366], Ross [372], Schwert [395], and the article by Grundfest [221] for examples.

While there is an extensive literature studying transactions costs in asset markets, there has not been a great deal of work on the effects of these costs on equilibrium interest rates. One approach is to assume price processes and then derive the effect of transactions costs on optimal consumption and portfolio decisions. This is the approach taken by Constantinides [117], Duffee and Sun [162], Dumas and Luciano [163], among others. Grossman and Laroque [217] study optimal portfolio and consumption choices in the presence of an illiquid durable consumption good such as housing. In their model, optimal consumption is not a smooth function of wealth. It is optimal for a consumer to wait until a large change in wealth occurs before changing his consumption. A rise in transactions cost increases the average time between the sale of durable goods. They conclude that the standard consumption CAPM does not hold.

Aiyagari and Gertler [11], Heaton and Lucas [249], and Vayanos and Vila [438] are examples of general equilibrium models with transactions costs. The papers by Aiyagari and Gertler and Vayanos and Vila have no aggregate uncertainty although there is individual-specific risk. The Heaton and Lucas model has aggregate uncertainty but is a three-period model. They find that, if trading in some assets is costless, then agents substitute almost entirely away from assets that are costly to trade. Agents would prefer to alter the composition of their portfolio rather than pay transactions costs or tolerate more volatile consumption. Because agents tend to specialize in holdings of assets that are costless to trade, they conclude that small changes in transactions costs do not have significant price effects.

In this section, we provide two further results on models with transactions costs. To study the effect of transactions costs on trading volume and equilibrium asset prices requires the use of a model with heterogeneous agents, which has proven to be analytically difficult.[6] Instead, we provide a basic description of the dynamic programming problem faced by an agent in a model with bid-ask spreads. Second we discuss the issue of volatility bounds for intertemporal MRSs with frictions.

15.2.1. A model with bid-ask spreads

Suppose that there is a financial intermediary, such as an organized exchange which facilitates trade but charges a proportional fee in an amount depending on whether the client is buying or selling an asset. The fees may reflect the costs of processing the order, price risks associated with

[6] It is possible to incorporate transactions costs in the production technology. For example, Marshall [335] incorporates money into a general equilibrium model assuming that holding real balances lowers the resource costs of consuming.

the transactions, and informational asymmetries. For simplicity, we assume that the profits of the intermediary are distributed lump-sum to the agents of the economy. At time t, agent i has random income y_t^i and holds a portfolio comprised of an equity share z_t^i, which pays a fixed dividend d_t, and risk-free bonds issued by the government which sell at discount at price $1/(1+r_t)$. If agent i sells an equity share, he receives the price $q_t(1-\alpha_s)$ and if he buys an equity share, he pays the price $q_t(1+\alpha_b)$. The difference in the prices at which the equity is sold and bought is the "bid-ask" spread, which equals:

$$q_t(\alpha_b - \alpha_s).$$

Notice that we make no attempt to explain the origins of the spread and instead treat α_b and α_s as parameters. We can view this spread times the number of transaction as the profit of the financial intermediary; let π_f denote the per capita profit of the intermediary. This is described more fully below. Let s_t denote the vector of exogenous state variables that agent i needs to make a forecast of returns, dividends, income and consumption next period. The budget constraint of agent i at time t takes the form:

$$y_{i,t} + b_{i,t} + z_{i,t}d_t - \tau_t - q_t \max\{\alpha_b(z_{i,t+1} - z_{i,t}), \alpha_s(z_{i,t} - z_{i,t+1})\}$$
$$+ \pi_{f,t} \geq c_{i,t} + q_t(z_{i,t+1} - z_{i,t}) + \frac{b_{i,t+1}}{1+r_t}. \tag{15.11}$$

We set this up as a dynamic programming problem. The representative type i agent solves:

$$V(y_i, z_i, b_i, s) = \max[U(c_i) + \beta E_s V(y_i', z_i', b_i', s')] \tag{15.12}$$

subject to constraints described below. Notice that the first-order conditions depend on whether the agent decides to buy, sell or hold the equity share $z_{i,t}$.

To study the properties of the dynamic programming problem under transactions costs, we split the problem into three sub-problems. Define V_s as the value of selling equity shares. The problem is:

$$V_s(y, z, b, s) = \max_{\{c,b',z'\}} [U(c) + \beta E_s V(y', z', b', s')] \tag{15.13}$$

subject to (15.11) and the constraint

$$z \geq z'. \tag{15.14}$$

Next, define the value function if the agent decides to buy, V_b. The problem is:

$$V_b(y, z, b, s) = \max_{\{c,b',z'\}} [U(c) + \beta E_s V(y', z', b', s')] \tag{15.15}$$

subject to (15.11) and the constraint

$$z \leq z'. \tag{15.16}$$

Finally, the value of holding onto the existing equity shares,

$$V_h(y, z, b, s) = \max_{\{c, b'\}}[U(c) + \beta E_s V(y', z, b', s')] \tag{15.17}$$

subject to

$$c + \frac{b'}{1+r} \leq y + zd - \tau + \pi_f. \tag{15.18}$$

We can then write the dynamic programming problem as:

$$V(y, z, b, s) = \max[V_s(y, z, b, s), V_h(y, z, b, s), V_b(y, z, b, s)] \tag{15.19}$$

Under this formulation, we have retained the recursive structure of the problem. As an example, we solve one of the sub-problems. Consider the solution to V_s. The first-order conditions are:

$$U'(c) = \xi_s \tag{15.20}$$

$$\frac{\xi_s}{1+r} = \beta E_s V_3(y_i', z_i', b_i', s'), \tag{15.21}$$

$$\xi_s q(1 - \alpha_s) = \beta E_s V_2(y_i', z_i', b_i', s') + \mu_s, \tag{15.22}$$

where μ_s is the multiplier attached to the constraint (15.14), and ξ_s the multiplier on the budget constraint. If $\mu_s = 0$, then the constraint is non-binding and

$$\xi_s q(1 - \alpha_s) = \beta E_s V_2(y_i', z_i', b_i', s'),$$

otherwise,

$$\xi_s q(1 - \alpha_s) \geq \beta E_s V_2(y_i', z_i', b_i', s').$$

We can derive a similar equation for the sub-problem of buying the equity share with the result that:

$$\xi_b q(1 + \alpha_b) \leq \beta E_s V_2(y_i', z_i', b_i', s'),$$

which holds with equality if the constraint (15.16) is non-binding. Notice that under this formulation, the function V denotes the value function assuming that the agent behaves optimally at all future dates. The slope of the value function with respect to equity shares is given, and the agent must choose the optimal course of action – buy, sell, or hold – in the current period.

We can define an operator T by:

$$TV^n(y, z, b, s) = \max[V_s^n(y, z, b, s), V_h^n(y, z, b, s), V_b^n(y, z, b, s)] \tag{15.23}$$

where V_i^n is defined for $i = s, b, h$. Notice that T is monotonic. If $W > V$ for all (y, z, b, s), then notice that $TW \geq TV$. Furthermore, T discounts. Each of the V_i is concave and the maximization operator preserves concavity so that V is concave.

Our discussion is incomplete in the sense that the agent takes as given the equity price function q and the return on the risk-free asset r. As we mentioned earlier, constructing an equilibrium with heterogeneous agents is analytically difficult.

15.3. VOLATILITY BOUNDS WITH FRICTIONS

In Chapter 8, we described how to derive the mean-standard deviation region for intertemporal MRSs that are used to price random payoffs in dynamic asset-pricing models. We now extend this discussion to account for short sales constraints, transaction costs, and borrowing constraints. As in our earlier discussion, the volatility bounds we derive here can be used as a diagnostic tool for determining the class of asset-pricing models that is consistent with asset market data. The approach in this section involves deriving restrictions for intertemporal MRSs with various forms of frictions under a complete markets interpretation. This precludes analyzing the interaction of market incompleteness together with the existence of short sales or solvency constraints. As an example of this latter approach, Scheinkman and Weiss [391] restrict the set of underlying securities at the same time as they impose a short sales constraint on the existing securities. However, the approach in Luttmer yields representations for volatility bounds that can be evaluated using aggregate consumption data as stressed by Cochrane and Hansen [110].

Consider the sequential interpretation of the complete contingent claims equilibrium that we described in Chapter 7. Define $z(s_{t+1})$ as the quantity of securities purchased at time t which pay off $x(s_{t+1})$ conditional on the state s_{t+1} at time $t+1$. We assume consumers can purchase securities that pay off for each possible realization of the economy. Portfolios with such payoffs can be purchased at the price $q(s_{t+1}, s_t)$ period t. Using this notation, agent i faces a sequence of one-period constraints of the form:

$$c_i(s_t) + \sum_{s=1}^{S} q(s_{t+1}, s_t)x(s_{t+1})z_i(s_{t+1}) \leq \omega_i(s_t) + x(s_t)z_i(s_t), \tag{15.24}$$

for $t \geq 0$. We can obtain a single budget constraint for the consumer by solving (15.24) forward, where we implicitly impose a condition that the value of limiting portfolio payoff goes to zero.

Volatility bounds with frictions have been derived by Luttmer [327] and He and Modest [246] who consider different types of constraints. Luttmer considers a *solvency* constraint of the form:

$$x(s_{t+1})z_i(s_{t+1}) \geq 0 \quad \text{for all } s_{t+1} \in S. \tag{15.25}$$

According to this constraint, any contingent contract that allows debt in some state of the world is prohibited. A weaker version of the constraint is employed by He and Modest who require that:

$$\sum_{s=1}^{S} q(s_{t+1}, s_t)x(s_{t+1})z_i(s_{t+1}) \geq 0. \tag{15.26}$$

This states that the value of the portfolio today must be non-negative. It does not preclude $q(s_{t+1})z_i(s_{t+1})$ from being negative in some states of the world. We refer to it as the *market-wealth* constraint.

Now we analyze the implications of these constraints for individual intertemporal MRSs with complete markets. Consider the problem of consumer i in such an equilibrium. The value function can be expressed as:

$$V(z_{it}, s_t) = \max_{c_{it}, z_{i,t+1}} \left\{ U(c_{it}) + \beta \sum_{s_{t+1} \in S} \pi(s_{t+1}|s_t) V(z_{i,t+1}, s_{t+1}) \right\}$$

subject to (15.24) and the solvency constraint (15.25). Let $\xi_i(s_t)$ denote the multiplier on the single-period budget constraints (15.24) and $\mu_i(s_{t+1})$ the multiplier on the solvency constraint, where we have indexed this multiplier with s_{t+1} to take into account the fact there is a solvency constraint for each possible future state $s_{t+1} \in S$. Assume that consumers' preferences are given by Eq. (7.62). The first-order and envelope conditions are given by:

$$U(c_i(s_t)) = \xi_i(s_t),$$

$$V_z(z_i(s_t), s_t) = \xi_i(s_t)x(s_t),$$

$$\xi_i(s_t)q(s_{t+1}, s_t)x(s_{t+1}) = \beta\pi(s_{t+1}|s_t)V_z(z_i(s_{t+1}), s_{t+1}) + \mu_i(s_{t+1})x(s_{t+1}).$$

The first-order condition with respect to the portfolio weights $z_i(s_{t+1})$ imply that:

$$q(s_{t+1}, s_t)x(s_{t+1})\xi_i(s_t) - \beta\pi(s_{t+1}|s_t)x(s_{t+1})\xi_i(s_{t+1}) - \mu_i(s_{t+1})x(s_{t+1}) = 0,$$

where the elements of the vector $\mu_i(s_{t+1})$ equal zero if and only if the corresponding elements of $z_i(s_{t+1})$ are strictly positive. Substituting for $\xi_i(s_t)$:

$$\beta\pi(s_{t+1}|s_t)\frac{U'(c_i(s_{t+1}))}{U'(c_i(s_t))}x(s_{t+1}) \leq q(s_{t+1}, s_t)x(s_{t+1}). \tag{15.27}$$

Let $\mathcal{M}_i \equiv \beta U'(c_i(s_{t+1}))/U'(c_i(s_t))$ denote the individual intertemporal MRS, and $\wp \equiv q(s_{t+1}, s_t)/\pi(s_{t+1}|s_t)$ be the probability-weighted contingent claims prices between dates $t+1$ and t. Summing over s_{t+1} and also taking expectations with respect to the conditioning variable s_t, we can write the condition in (15.27) as:

$$E(\mathcal{M}^i x) \leq E(\wp x). \tag{15.28}$$

Since we assumed complete markets in the construction of the payoffs of the traded securities so that $x > 0$, and given that both $\mathcal{M}^i$ and $\wp$ are non-negative, we also have that:

$$\mathcal{M}^i \leq \wp. \tag{15.29}$$

Thus, with solvency constraints, the individual intertemporal MRS is downward biased relative to the market-determined stochastic discount factor that is used to value payoffs on one-period securities. For certain classes of utility functions (including exponential and power utility functions), we can show that the intertemporal MRS evaluated with per capita consumption data also inherits this downward bias:

$$\mathcal{M}^a \leq \wp \tag{15.30}$$

where $\mathcal{M}^a \equiv \beta U'(\bar{c}(s_{t+1}))/U'(\bar{c}(s_t))$, and U is a function of the average subsistence levels, $\bar{\gamma}$, and per capita consumption, $\bar{c}_t$. (See Exercise 3.)

Now let us consider the implications of the less restrictive market-wealth constraint in Equation (15.26). In contrast to the earlier case, there is now a single multiplier on the market wealth constraint denoted by $\mu_i(s_t)$, and the relevant condition characterizing consumer's optimal portfolio choice problem is:

$$q(s_{t+1}, s_t)x(s_{t+1})\xi_i(s_t) = \beta\pi(s_{t+1}|s_t)x(s_{t+1})\xi_i(s_{t+1}) + \mu_i(s_t)q(s_{t+1}, s_t)x(s_{t+1}). \tag{15.31}$$

Define the return of the security that pays off conditional on $s_{t+1} \in S$ next period by $R(s_{t+1}, s_t) = x(s_{t+1})/q(s_{t+1}, s_t)$. Substituting for $\xi_i(s_t)$ and $\xi_i(s_{t+1})$, dividing both sides by $q(s_{t+1}, s_t)$ and summing over the future states s_{t+1} yields:

$$\beta \sum_{s_{t+1}\in S} \pi(s_{t+1}|s_t)\frac{U'(c_i(s_{t+1}))}{U'(c_i(s_t))}R(s_{t+1}, s_t) = \sum_{s_{t+1}\in S} x(s_{t+1})\left[1 - \frac{\mu_i(s_t)}{U'(c_i(s_t))}\right].$$

Consider two securities with returns $R(s_{t+1} = s_j, s_t)$ and $R(s_{t+1} = s_k, s_t)$. Notice that we can write the above condition in terms of the excess return on securities j and k as:

$$\sum_{s_{t+1}\in S} \pi(s_{t+1}|s_t)\frac{\beta U'(c_i(s_{t+1}))}{U'(c_i(s_t))}[R_j(s_{t+1}, s_t) - R_k(s_{t+1}, s_t)] = 0. \tag{15.32}$$

Assume that consumers can form portfolios in addition to those described above. Let $\mathcal{X}$ denote the set of one-period security payoffs with zero market prices, or equivalently, the set of excess returns. Using the results in (15.31) and (15.32), any payoff in $\mathcal{X}$ satisfies the market-wealth constraint:

$$E_t[\mathcal{M}^i x] = E_t[\wp x] = 0 \quad \text{for } x \in \mathcal{X}. \tag{15.33}$$

The payoff $\mathcal{M}^i - \wp E_t(\wp \mathcal{M}^i)/E_t(\wp^2)$ has a zero market price, that is, $E_t[\wp(\mathcal{M}^i - \wp E_t(\wp \mathcal{M}^i)/E_t(\wp^2))] = 0$. Using this payoff for x in relation (15.33), we have

$$\mathcal{M}^i = \psi^i \wp \text{ for } \psi^i = E_t(\wp \mathcal{M}^i)/E_t(\wp^2). \tag{15.34}$$

Furthermore, (15.28) implies that $0 < \psi^i \leq 1$. For the power utility function, we can show that

$$\mathcal{M}^a = \psi^a \wp, \tag{15.35}$$

where $0 < \psi^a \leq 1$. (See Exercise 3.) Recall that the market-wealth constraint is less restrictive than the solvency constraint. As the above results demonstrate, the less restrictive constraint imposes the more stringent proportionality requirement on the aggregate intertemporal MRS.

The construction of volatility bounds using actual asset market data are described by Hansen and Jagannathan [232], Cochrane and Hansen [110], Luttmer [327], and He and Modest [246] for economies with and without frictions. The approach followed is to assume that there is a finite set of payoffs and to obtain an expression for the intertemporal MRS through simple projection arguments. In Chapter 2, we already derived an expression for the intertemporal MRS by imposing the absence of arbitrage implied by the Law of One Price. (See Section 2.1.1.) The idea is to choose the stochastic discount factor or intertemporal MRS to be a linear combination of the N basis payoffs. However, as Hansen and Jagannathan show, this representation for the intertemporal MRS does not impose strict positivity. To do that, one considers random variables that can be interpreted as either European call or put options on the payoffs traded by consumers. When there are short sales or solvency constraints and other frictions, the Euler equalities characterizing the intertemporal MRS are supplanted by Euler inequalities of the form in Eq. (15.28). Luttmer [327] and He and Modest [246] present evidence showing that the introduction of market frictions of the type discussed in this section can go some way in helping to reconcile asset-pricing behavior based on a simple representative consumer asset pricing with CRRA utility.

15.4. CONCLUSIONS

In this chapter, we have explored some asset-pricing implications of trading frictions. In the next chapter on borrowing constraints, we will examine the role of market incompleteness under a variety of assumptions on the nature of markets and the types of trades that agents can enter into. There we will characterize the equilibrium explicitly and demonstrate the conditions under market incompleteness of various forms matters. We also consider models in which there exist endogenous solvency constraints due to a participation constraint on agents.

15.5. EXERCISES

1. There are two types of consumers, and three states of the world. Each agent is endowed with one unit of labor in each state and each period. The following table relates output per unit of labor of consumer $i = 1, 2$ in state of the world $j = 1, 2, 3$:

i,j	1	2	3
1	4	3	2
2	2	3	4

Output might be stored by individual consumers at no cost and the utility function of consumer i is given by:

$$E_0 \sum_{t=1}^{2} (\ln (c_{it}) - \ell_{it}),$$

where $E_0(.)$ denotes expectation conditional on information at time 0 and ℓ_{it} denotes the amount of labor used in the production of the consumption good. States are i.i.d. and $\pi_1 = \pi_3 = 0.25$ and $\pi_2 = 0.5$, where π_i denotes the probability of state i in any period.

(a) Find the consumption and labor supply allocations of type $i = 1, 2$ if there exists a full set of contingent claims markets. Characterize the behavior of aggregate consumption in equilibrium.

(b) Find the autarkic allocations.

(c) Using your answers to parts (a) and (b), discuss whether an econometrician can use aggregate consumption data in order to determine whether markets are complete or not, if s/he does not know the form of the production technology.

2. [7] Suppose that agents live two periods and that per capita consumption takes one of two values, μ or $(1 - \phi)\mu$ where $0 < \phi < 1$, with each state occurring with probability $1/2$. At time zero, agents choose their portfolio. At time 1, the uncertain endowment is realized, the payoff on the portfolio is made and then agents consume. The portfolio pays -1 in the bad state and $1 + \pi$ in the good state where π is a risk premium.

[7] This problem is based on Mankiw [331].

(a) Assume that all agents are identical. The representative consumer maximizes $E[U(c)]$. Let R denote the payoff on the portfolio so that the budget constraint at time 1 is $c \leq \theta R$, where θ denotes the quantity held of the asset.
Let $U = c^{1-\gamma}/(1-\gamma)$. Solve for the risk premium π under this assumption.

(b) We now introduce heterogeneity and incomplete markets. Agents are identical *ex ante* but not *ex post.* In the bad state assume that the fall in aggregate consumption equal to $\phi\mu$ is concentrated among a fraction λ of the population.
   i. Derive the first-order condition and the premium π.
   ii. Show that the premium depends not only on the size of the aggregate shock ϕ but also on its distribution within the population.
   iii. Assume that utility is constant relative to risk aversion and show that a decrease in λ increases π (so the more concentrated the shock, the larger the premium).

3. a) Show that the volatility bound in (15.30) holds for the following utility functions:

$$(i)\ \ U(c_i) = ((c_i - \gamma^i)^{1-\sigma} - 1)/(1-\sigma), \quad \sigma > 0, \qquad (15.36)$$

$$(ii)\ \ U(c_i) = -\exp(-\alpha(c_i - \gamma^i)) \quad \alpha > 0. \qquad (15.37)$$

b) Let $\gamma^i = 0$ in (15.36), and show that (15.35) holds with

$$\psi^a = \left[\sum_i \psi^{1/\sigma}(c_{i,t}/\bar{c}_t)\right]^{-\sigma}.$$

CHAPTER 16

Borrowing constraints

In this chapter, we will discuss economies in which there may exist restrictions of various forms on trading by agents. One of the most common forms of market friction is the presence of a borrowing constraint. However, there may also exist economies in which only a small number of assets is traded. Typically we refer to economies in which the number of assets traded is less than the set of random states as economies with market incompleteness. Such market incompleteness may arise from private information considerations or intergenerational restrictions. We consider the role of intergenerational frictions in Chapter 17. In contrast to environments where individual heterogeneity does not matter in a fundamental way, an important implication of models with market incompleteness is that the cross-sectional distribution of non-human wealth will vary over time and help to determine economic outcomes.

In this chapter, we start with a model of idiosyncratic endowment risk, in which aggregate output is constant and there is a countable infinity of agents. This setup was introduced by Bewley [64] as a way of providing general equilibrium foundations for the permanent income hypothesis. In such an environment, agents can trade a variety of assets to eliminate the impact of idiosyncratic income or endowment risk on their consumption profiles. Using this framework, we distinguish between the impact of closing down contingent claims markets and the impact of closing down credit markets. We consider three different market arrangements – complete contingent claims, pure insurance markets, and pure credit markets. When complete contingent claims markets are available, agents are unrestricted in the quantity or type of trades that they can enter into across alternative dates and states of the world. By contrast, in a pure insurance economy, there are restrictions on short sales of contingent claims. Equivalently, there are borrowing constraints. Finally, in a pure credit economy (of the type studied by Huggett [257], for example), agents trade private IOUs at a constant interest rate. In this latter setup, they can be demanders or issuers of such IOUs, leading to a potential interpretation of the traded claims as "inside money."[1] It turns out that when the idiosyncratic shocks are distributed as i.i.d., the three different trading arrangements are equivalent: agents can obtain the same consumption allocations regardless of the set of asset trades permitted. This result no longer holds for environments in which the shocks follow a Markov process. Models with ad hoc borrowing constraints, idiosyncratic risk, and no aggregate uncertainty typically rule out contingent claims markets and impose arbitrary constraints on borrowing. Our analysis indicates that the Markov structure of the model is critical.

We then turn to the topic of market frictions when there is aggregate uncertainty. Our discussion is based on the Townsend [431] turnpike model, which incorporates a physical trading friction, namely, that agents trade with only a small subset of agents over their lifetime and that trade takes place at distinct locations and is bilateral. This creates a role for a financial intermediary to maintain records of transactions and debt. Market incompleteness is incorporated by assuming that the clearing house has limited record keeping which creates natural limits on borrowing. We examine allocations when there are standard borrowing constraints, short-sale constraints, and debt constraints. Our discussion is based on the models of Kehoe and Levine [272, 273], Kocherlakota [280], and Alvarez and Jermann [24].

16.1. IDIOSYNCRATIC RISK AND BORROWING CONSTRAINTS

The complete markets version of this model was discussed in Chapter 7 and in this section we just review the model so that the chapter is self-contained. It is helpful to review the complete markets allocations discussed in that chapter because it is a natural starting point to understand how borrowing constraints impact consumption allocations.

We start with a pure endowment model in which all agents are *ex ante* identical. Agents face idiosyncratic endowment risk and aggregate endowment is deterministic. The focus is on the role of *ex post* heterogeneity among individuals under alternative trading arrangements.

Typically models with borrowing constraints impose joint assumptions: (i) the non-existence of contingent claims markets and (ii) restrictions on credit markets. The goal in this section is to separate the impact of these two assumptions. We start with a pure insurance market: contingent claims can be purchased but the value of the end-of-period portfolio must be non-negative. Next we examine a pure credit market in which agents can

[1] For a further discussion of the implications of the pure credit model, see Ljungqvist and Sargent [325].

borrow and lend at a risk free rate, but contingent claims contracts are unavailable.

16.1.1. The basic model

Each period, an agent draws a random endowment that is assumed to follow a first-order Markov chain. Let $\theta \in \Theta$, with $\Theta \equiv \{\underline{\theta}, \ldots, \bar{\theta}\}$, be a discrete random variable such that $\underline{\theta} \geq 0$ and $\bar{\theta}$ is finite. Let $g(\theta'|\theta)$ denote the probability of moving from state θ to θ' in one period. Define $\phi(\theta)$ as the unconditional probability of θ, let θ_m denote the unconditional mean, and let $\theta_m(\theta)$ denote the conditional mean. Also define $g^j(\theta_j \mid \theta_0)$ as the *j-step ahead probability*, specifically the probability of $\theta = \theta_j$ in j periods when the current θ is θ_0. Finally, define $\theta_m^j(\theta)$ as the *j-step ahead conditional mean.*

There is a countable infinity of agents $i \in \mathcal{I}$, where $\mathcal{I}$ is the set of integers. Each period t, agent i receives an endowment $\theta_{t,i}$ drawn from Θ. The history for agent i is denoted $\theta_i^t = \{\theta_{1,i}, \ldots, \theta_{t,i}\}$. An agent is characterized by his history $\theta_i^t \in \Theta^t$. The fraction of agents with history θ^t is identical to the probability of observing the history of the endowment shocks θ^t, and this is equal to $g_t(\theta^t)$, given θ_0. The unconditional probability of observing θ_t in the general population is $\phi(\theta_t)$ and, with a countable infinity of agents, the fraction of agents with θ is $\phi(\theta)$. The total endowment per capita of the economy each period is:

$$\theta_m = \sum_{\theta \in \Theta} \phi(\theta)\theta = \sum_{\theta \in \Theta} \sum_{\theta_j \in \Theta} g(\theta \mid \theta_j)\phi(\theta_j)\theta, \tag{16.1}$$

so there is no aggregate uncertainty.

The *commodity space* for this economy consists of history-dependent sequences $\{c_t(\theta^t)\}_{t=0}^{\infty}$, where each element of the sequence denoted $c_t(\theta^t) \in \Re_+$ is indexed by the history of endowment shocks up to that date, $\theta^t \in \Theta^t$. The representative agent has lifetime preferences:

$$\sum_{t=0}^{\infty} \sum_{\theta^t \in \Theta^t} \beta^t g_t(\theta^t) U(c_{i,t}(\theta^t)). \tag{16.2}$$

Agents are identical at the beginning of time and become differentiated over time because of different endowment realizations.

16.1.2. Restrictions on markets

We start with the pure insurance case in which a full array of contingent claims is available but there is a restriction on the value of the portfolio held at the end of the period that prevents any borrowing. We then turn to the pure borrowing economy.

16.1.3. Pure insurance economy

We rule out any borrowing or lending but allow insurance in the form of purchases of contingent claims. This means there is no borrowing or lending and the value of the contingent claims portfolio held at the end of the period must be non-negative.

Let $q(\theta', \theta)$ denote the price of a contingent claim that pays off next period conditional on state θ' occurring. Also let $z(\theta', \theta)$ be the shares purchased of these claims conditional on state θ occurring today. There is a borrowing constraint which precludes the total value of shares purchased today from being negative. We can formulate the dynamic programming problem for this example. The Bellman equation is:

$$V(z, \theta) = \max_{\{c, z'\}} [U(c) + \beta \sum_{\theta' \in \Theta} g(\theta' \mid \theta) V(z', \theta')]$$

subject to

$$c + \sum_{\theta' \in \Theta} q(\theta', \theta) z(\theta', \theta) \leq \theta + z, \tag{16.3}$$

$$\sum_{\theta' \in \Theta} q(\theta', \theta) z(\theta', \theta) \geq 0. \tag{16.4}$$

Let $\lambda(\theta)$ denote the Lagrange multiplier for the budget constraint and $\mu(\theta)$ the multiplier for the borrowing constraint. The first-order conditions and envelope condition are:

$$U'(c_t) = \lambda(\theta), \tag{16.5}$$

$$q(\theta', \theta)[\lambda(\theta) + \mu(\theta)] = \beta g(\theta' \mid \theta) V_z(z', \theta'), \tag{16.6}$$

$$V_z(z, \theta) = \lambda(\theta). \tag{16.7}$$

The conditions can be re-written as:

$$[U'(c) + \mu(\theta)] q(\theta', \theta) = \beta g(\theta' \mid \theta) U'(c'). \tag{16.8}$$

Since there are no lending opportunities, because there is no borrowing, consumption is determined by the current endowment θ and claims purchased in the previous period so that:

$$c = z + \theta,$$

regardless of the value of μ. Hence we can solve for the equilibrium price

$$q(\theta', \theta) = \frac{\beta g(\theta' \mid \theta) U'(z(\theta') + \theta')}{U'(z + \theta) + \mu(\theta)}. \tag{16.9}$$

We study two cases for the distribution of the endowment shock.

IID endowment

Assume that the endowment process is i.i.d. over time for every agent. This implies that the optimal portfolio choices $z(\theta')$ do not depend on the current value of the state variables $\theta, z(\theta)$. Hence, if the portfolio choices are invariant with respect to the current state, then the implication is that the multiplier μ is either always zero or always positive. A positive μ in all states means the agent always wishes to borrow against future income. But if Ponzi schemes are ruled out, then this cannot occur, so that $\mu = 0$ for all states. In that case,

$$q(\theta', \theta) = \frac{\beta g(\theta') U'(z(\theta') + \theta')}{U'(z + \theta)}.$$

A natural conjecture is that:

$$c = \theta_m,$$

which requires that consumption is constant and equal to the average value of the endowment. Under this conjecture, the first best allocation is achieved. To verify this conjecture, observe that, if the conjecture is correct, then the price is:

$$q(\theta', \theta) = \beta g(\theta')$$

and the portfolio constraint (16.4) is:

$$\sum_{\theta'} \beta g(\theta')[\theta_m - \theta] = 0.$$

By definition of the mean, the equation holds. Hence, the first-order condition, the budget constraint, portfolio constraint, and market-clearing conditions are satisfied, so that the guess $c = \theta_m$ has been verified and is a solution.

The value function is:

$$V(z, \theta) = U(\theta_m)[1 + \beta + \beta^2 \ldots] = \frac{U(\theta_m)}{1 - \beta}.$$

Hence, when the endowment is i.i.d., a pure insurance economy which disallows borrowing or lending results in a Pareto optimal allocation and the borrowing constraint has no impact on the ability of agents to smooth consumption.

Markov endowment

We have just shown in the i.i.d. case that the borrowing constraint has no impact on the allocations and the first best outcome is achieved. Does this still hold when the endowment process is first-order Markov?

Recall that the dynamic programming version of the complete contingent claims solution results in a first-order condition given by:

$$q(\theta', \theta) U'(c(\theta)) = \beta g(\theta'|\theta) U'(c(\theta')),$$

and the budget constraint is:

$$c + \sum_{\theta' \in \Theta} q(\theta', \theta) z(\theta', \theta) \leq \theta + z.$$

To check if borrowing and lending are necessary to achieve the complete contingent claims solution, set $c = \theta_m$ and $q(\theta', \theta) = \beta g(\theta' \mid \theta)$ as before and then check if the first-order condition, budget constraints, and market-clearing conditions are satisfied. If $c = \theta_m$, then the agent's budget constraint is:

$$\theta + z = \theta_m + \beta \sum_{\theta' \in \Theta} g(\theta' | \theta) z(\theta', \theta).$$

If $z = \theta_m - \theta$ then the portfolio constraint for each θ must satisfy:

$$0 = \sum_{\theta' \in \Theta} g(\theta' | \theta)[\theta_m - \theta'].$$

But notice this equation does not hold since

$$\sum_{\theta' \in \Theta} g(\theta' | \theta) \theta' = \theta_m(\theta),$$

which is the conditional mean. Hence, if no borrowing is allowed but pure insurance is available through contingent claims markets, setting consumption equal to:

$$c(\theta_t, \theta_{t-1}) = \theta_m(\theta_{t-1}), \tag{16.10}$$

will satisfy the portfolio constraint. The first-order condition under this policy is:

$$[U'(\theta_m(\theta_{t-1})) + \mu(\theta_t, \theta_{t-1})] q(\theta_{t+1}, \theta_t) = \beta g(\theta_{t+1} \mid \theta_t) U'(\theta_m(\theta_t)). \tag{16.11}$$

Since this equation must hold for any $\theta_{t-1} \in \Theta$, it follows that:

$$q(\theta_{t+1}, \theta_t) = \frac{\beta g(\theta_{t+1} \mid \theta_t) U(\theta_m(\theta_t))}{U'(\theta_m(\theta_{t-1})) + \mu(\theta_t, \theta_{t-1})} \tag{16.12}$$

so that $\mu > 0$ for some agents. The goods market-clearing condition can be expressed as:

$$\sum_{\theta^t} g_t(\theta^t)[\theta_t - \theta_m(\theta_{t-1})] = \sum_{\theta_{t-1}} \sum_{\theta_t} g(\theta_t \mid \theta_{t-1})[\theta_t - \theta_m(\theta_{t-1})] = 0 \tag{16.13}$$

so the goods market clearing condition is satisfied. Hence the guess that $c = \theta_m(\theta_{t-1})$ has been verified.

The distribution of wealth is described next. The agent's net claim or wealth is equal to:

$$z(\theta_t, \theta_{t-1}) = \theta_m(\theta_{t-1}) - \theta_t.$$

Conditional on the past realization of the endowment shock θ_{t-1}, observe that the sequence for net wealth over time, $\{z(\theta_t, \theta_{t-1}), z(\theta_{t+1}, \theta_t), \ldots\}$ is uncorrelated. Moreover, notice that:

$$z(\theta_t, \theta_{t-1}) = \theta_m(\theta_{t-1}) - \theta_t = \theta_m(\theta_{t-1}) - \theta_m + [\theta_m - \theta_t],$$

where the first term after the second equality is the deviation of the conditional mean from the unconditional mean and the second term in brackets is the deviation of the endowment from the unconditional mean.

Hence the consumer can insure against risk conditional on the endowment θ_{t-1} but cannot achieve smooth consumption without borrowing or lending to smooth out fluctuations in the conditional mean. Hence imposing a borrowing constraint in a Markov model with contingent claims markets for insurance limits agents' ability to smooth consumption because of fluctuations in the conditional mean of the endowment. Fluctuations around the conditional mean can be smoothed through state-contingent insurance but fluctuations in the conditional mean over time cannot be smoothed without borrowing and lending.

16.1.4. Pure credit model

We now turn to another extreme model – one in which borrowing and lending are allowed but there are no state-contingent markets. Notice that this is similar to the borrowing-lending model that we studied in Chapter 5. However, in that case our focus was on describing the consumer's optimal consumption and saving (dissaving) plan whereas here we are concerned with the characterization of equilibrium prices and allocations in a pure credit economy.

To describe this economy, let r denote the (non-random) return to lending, and let a_t denote an agent's asset holdings (possibly negative) at the beginning of period t. The agent's problem is to choose sequences of consumption and asset holdings to maximize (16.2) subject to the set of budget constraints

$$c_t + a_t \leq a_{t-1} r + \theta_t, \quad t \geq 0. \tag{16.14}$$

Assume that $a_0 = 0$ for all agents.

At time t, an agent has a history of endowment realizations $\hat{\theta}^t$. Conditional on this history, an agent's expected discounted present value of lifetime income from period t forward is:

$$A_t(\hat{\theta}^t) = \sum_{\tau=t}^{\infty} \sum_{\theta^\tau | \hat{\theta}^t} \left(\frac{1}{r}\right)^{\tau-t} g_\tau(\theta^\tau \mid \hat{\theta}^t)\theta_\tau.$$

At any time t conditional on $\hat{\theta}^t$, the maximum amount that an agent can borrow is $A_t(\hat{\theta}_t)$, which is a natural debt limit. Imposing the constraint that

$$a_t(\hat{\theta}^t) \geq -A_t(\hat{\theta}_t) \tag{16.15}$$

rules out the possibility of a Ponzi scheme.

The pure credit economy can be studied as a dynamic programming problem with Bellman equation

$$V(a_{t-1}, \theta_t) = \max_{a_t}[U(a_{t-1}r + \theta_t - a_t)$$
$$+ \beta \sum_{\theta_{t+1} \in \Theta} g(\theta_{t+1} \mid \theta_t) V(a_t, \theta_{t+1})] \tag{16.16}$$

subject to the initial condition $a_0 = 0$. The first-order condition with the envelope condition incorporated is:

$$U'(a_{t-1}r + \theta_t - a_t) = \beta r \sum_{\theta_{t+1} \in \Theta} g(\theta_{t+1} \mid \theta_t) U'(a_t r + \theta_{t+1} - a_{t+1}). \tag{16.17}$$

Notice that if $\beta r = 1$, then the first-order condition states that an agent sets his end-of-period assets such that current marginal utility just equals the expected marginal utility. If $\beta r > 1$, marginal utility would need to fall over time for the first-order condition to hold. This would mean that consumption must rise over time. But if the endowment process is stationary then it is impossible for consumption to rise for all agents over time. If $\beta r < 1$, then the opposite argument can be made. Hence, the only stationary solution for consumption is $\beta r = 1$, which we assume holds for the rest of the discussion.

Before we describe the market-clearing conditions, it will be useful to discuss the distribution of assets a_{t-1} at the beginning of period t. The actual time path of debt depends on the sample path of endowment and the consumption function. Suppose the agent picks a consumption function $\hat{c}_t : \Theta^t \rightarrow \Re_+$ that is feasible. Then, in the first period under this consumption policy, his asset holdings at the end of period 1 with endowment $\hat{\theta}_1$ are:

$$a_1(\hat{\theta}_1) = \hat{\theta}_1 - \hat{c}_1(\hat{\theta}_1),$$

where the assumption $a_0 = 0$ is incorporated. In the second period with endowment $\hat{\theta}_2$, his end-of-period holdings are:

$$\begin{aligned} a_2(\hat{\theta}^2) &= ra_1(\hat{\theta}_1) + \hat{\theta}_2 - \hat{c}_2(\hat{\theta}^2) \\ &= r[\hat{\theta}_1 - \hat{c}_1(\hat{\theta}_1)] + \hat{\theta}_2 - \hat{c}_2(\hat{\theta}^2). \end{aligned}$$

More generally,

$$a_t(\hat{\theta}^t) = \sum_{h=1}^{t} r^{t-h}[\hat{\theta}_h - \hat{c}_h(\hat{\theta}^h)]. \tag{16.18}$$

Hence the history of borrowing and saving is summarized by $a_t = a_t(\hat{\theta}^t)$. At time t, a fraction $g_t(\hat{\theta}^t)$ of agents will have asset holdings $a_t(\hat{\theta}^t)$ at the end of the period. Hence at time t, there will be a wealth distribution. Summing over consumption, endowment, and asset-holding allocations using the fraction of individuals with histories of the shocks θ^t, $g_t(\theta^t)$, the market-clearing conditions are:

$$\sum_{\theta^t \in \Theta^t} g_t(\theta^t)[\theta_t - c_t(\theta^t)] = 0, \tag{16.19}$$

$$\sum_{\theta^t \in \Theta^t} g_t(\theta^t)a_t(\theta^t) = 0 \tag{16.20}$$

where the first condition is goods market clearing and the second is that borrowing equals lending. The equilibrium has the property that the first-order conditions are satisfied for all agents $\theta^t \in \Theta^t$ and the market-clearing conditions are satisfied. If we had assumed that agents differed in terms of a_0, then the initial debt would also be an argument of the function $a_t(\cdot)$.

An agent's asset position at the beginning of period t is summarized by $ra_{t-1}(\theta^{t-1})$ in current value. Conditional on the endowment realization $\hat{\theta}_t$, the agent's expected *future* net claims under consumption policy c_t are:

$$\Lambda_t(\hat{\theta}_t) = \sum_{j=1}^{\infty} \sum_{\theta^{t+j}|\hat{\theta}_t} r^{-j} g_{t+j}(\theta^{t+j} \mid \hat{\theta}_t)[c_{t+j}(\theta^{t+j}) - \theta_{t+j}].$$

We now relate the state variable $a_{t-1}(\theta^{t-1})$ to the expected future net claims through the budget constraint. Solve the budget constraint for a_{t-1} as:

$$a_{t-1}(\theta^{t-1}) = \frac{1}{r}[c_t(\theta^t) + a_t - \theta_t].$$

Update the time subscript by one in the equation above and compute the expectation conditional on θ_t:

$$ra_t(\theta^t) = \sum_{\theta_{t+1}|\theta_t} g(\theta_{t+1} \mid \theta_t)[c_{t+1}(\theta^{t+1}) + a_{t+1} - \theta_{t+1}].$$

Solving this equation recursively forward results in:

$$ra_t(\theta^t) = \sum_{j=1}^{\infty} \sum_{\theta_{t+j}|\theta_t} \left(\frac{1}{r}\right)^{j-1} g^j(\theta_{t+j} \mid \theta_t)[c_{t+j}(\theta^{t+j}) - \theta_{t+j}] \quad (16.21)$$

where we have imposed the no-Ponzi condition that the value of debt at some future date $t + n$ tends to zero in expected value as $n \to \infty$:

$$\lim_{n\to\infty} \frac{1}{r} \sum_{j=1}^{n} \sum_{\theta_{t+j}|\theta_t} \left(\frac{1}{r}\right)^{j-1} g^j(\theta_{t+j}|\theta_t) a_{t+n}(\theta^{t+n}) \to 0.$$

Substitute this expression into ra_{t-1} to obtain:

$$ra_{t-1}(\theta^{t-1}) = c_t(\theta^t) - \theta_t + \Lambda_t(\theta_t) \quad (16.22)$$

Hence the link between the history of debt/asset position, summarized by $a_{t-1}(\theta^{t-1})$, and the expected present value of future net claims is the end-of-period asset position a_t.

This provides us with a convenient way to understand borrowing constraints. A borrowing constraint places restrictions on the value of the sequence Λ_t, the expected present value of future claims. In the pure insurance economy, this value was restricted to equal zero. In general, the borrowing constraint impedes an agent's ability to borrow against future income, which means that the value of Λ is restricted.

Notice that this rules out a situation in which the consumer can obtain unlimited consumption by infinitely rolling over his/her existing debt. The endowment history $\hat{\theta}^t$ generates a credit history summarized by:

$$ra_{t-1}(\hat{\theta}^{t-1}) - c_t(\hat{\theta}^t) + \hat{\theta}_t.$$

This is the current value of actual net claims under the consumption policy. The current value of net claims and the expected discounted present value of future net claims are related as

$$\Lambda_t(\hat{\theta}_t) = ra_{t-1}(\hat{\theta}^{t-1}) + \hat{\theta}_t - c_t(\hat{\theta}_t).$$

We now study some special cases of this environment.

IID endowment

Assume that the endowment shock is i.i.d. We concluded in the complete contingent claims model that $c = \theta_m$ was the equilibrium solution. Is the consumption policy $c = \theta_m$ a solution in our pure credit economy assuming i.i.d. endowment shocks? Suppose that $c = \theta_m$. Then the agent's saving behavior is:

$$a_t = a_{t-1}r + \theta_t - \theta_m,$$

or

$$\theta_t - \theta_m = a_t - a_{t-1}r,$$

so the changes in an agent's debt position are i.i.d. and have zero mean.

Will this satisfy the individual agent's first-order conditions and the market-clearing conditions assuming $\beta r = 1$? Substitute $c = \theta_m$ into the first-order condition to show that:

$$U'(\theta_m) = \beta r \sum_{\theta'} g(\theta')U'(\theta_m), \tag{16.23}$$

which holds identically since $\sum_{\theta'} g(\theta') = 1$ and $\beta r = 1$. Hence, the first-order condition is satisfied under this consumption policy.

Market clearing in the goods market requires that:

$$\sum_{\theta^t} g_t(\theta^t)[\theta_t - \theta_m] = \sum_{\theta_t} g(\theta_t)[\theta_t - \theta_m] = 0$$

which holds by definition of the mean. The market-clearing condition in the credit market is:

$$0 = \sum_{\theta^t \in \Theta^t} g_t(\theta^t)a_t(\theta^t) \tag{16.24}$$

Hence the first-order condition and market-clearing conditions are satisfied so that $c = \theta_m$ is a solution to the model. Hence the pure credit economy can achieve the first best outcome when endowment shocks are i.i.d.

How does the wealth distribution evolve over time? Starting at $a_0 = 0$, at time 1,

$$a_1 = \theta_1 - \theta_m,$$

at time 2,

$$a_2 = ra_1 + \theta_2 - \theta_m$$

and so on until

$$a_t = \sum_{j=1}^{t} r^{t-j}[\theta_j - \theta_m].$$

At time 0, $E_0 a_t = 0$ and the value of Λ is:

$$\Lambda_t(\hat{\theta}_t) = \sum_{i=1}^{\infty} \sum_{\theta_{t+i}|\hat{\theta}_t} \left(\frac{1}{r}\right)^i g(\theta_{t+i})[\theta_m - \theta_{t+i}] = 0.$$

Hence an agent's changes in assets are uncorrelated over time.

The price of a claim that pays off one unit for sure in each state is given by:

$$q = \sum_{\theta \in \Theta} q(\theta),$$

where $q(\theta)$ is the contingent claims price in the pure insurance economy. From this it follows that the real interest rate is equal to:

$$r = \frac{1}{\beta} = \frac{1}{q} = \frac{1}{\sum_{\theta \in \Theta} q(\theta)}.\text{[2]} \tag{16.25}$$

Then the first-order condition for the pure credit model is equivalent to the first-order conditions for the first-best and pure-insurance models evaluated under the constant consumption policy $c = \theta_m$. Hence, if the endowment is i.i.d., then the pure-insurance and pure-credit allocations are identical and equal to the allocations in the complete contingent claims solution. By contrast, we showed that the prices in an economy with a full set of contingent claims or in the pure insurance economy depend on the past realization of the endowment shock when this shock follows a Markov process. As a consequence, we might expect this equivalence to break down when we consider the equilibrium for a pure credit economy for the Markov case.

Markov endowment

Assume now that the endowment process is first-order Markov so that the first-order condition is (16.17). Let $c(\theta)$ denote a solution. The conjecture that consumption depends only on the current θ is based on the intuition that in a world with borrowing and lending, an agent is able to smooth consumption intertemporally so that the endowment last period, which affected his savings at the end of the period, need not impact consumption in the current period.

The first-order condition is:

$$U'(c(\theta_t)) = \beta r \sum_{\theta_{t+1} \in \Theta} g(\theta_{t+1} \mid \theta_t) U'(c(\theta_{t+1})).$$

Is the optimal consumption $c = \theta_m$ a solution? The first-order condition will be satisfied because $\beta r = 1$.

[2] Recall that we showed this result in Chapter 2 based on the absence of arbitrage arguments.

The remaining question is whether such consumption behavior is market-clearing. To determine if the goods market clears, observe that at time t, a fraction $\phi(\theta)$ have endowment θ, regardless of the individual agent's history up to time $t-1$. Hence,

$$\sum_{\theta_t} \phi(\theta_t)[\theta_t - \theta_m] = 0$$

under the policy $c = \theta_m$. Hence the goods market clears.

To examine whether the asset market clears, recall that the expected discounted present value of future net claims under consumption policy $c = \theta_m$ is:

$$\begin{aligned}
\Lambda_t(\hat{\theta}_t) &= \sum_{j=1}^{\infty} \sum_{\theta^{t+j}|\hat{\theta}_t} r^{-j} g(\theta^{t+j} \mid \hat{\theta}_t)[\theta_m - \theta_{t+j}] \\
&= \sum_{j=1}^{\infty} r^{-j}[\theta_m - \theta_m^j(\theta_t)], \qquad (16.26)
\end{aligned}$$

where $\theta_m^j(\theta)$ is the j-step ahead conditional mean, conditional on θ_t. Notice that the term on the right side is generally not equal to 0. As in the complete contingent claims model with Markov endowment, the size of Λ depends on the speed of mean reversion. The market-clearing condition is:

$$\begin{aligned}
0 = \sum_{\theta^t} g_t(\theta^t) a_t(\theta^t) &= \frac{1}{r} \sum_{\theta^t} g_t(\theta^t)[\theta_m - \theta_t + \Lambda_t(\theta_t)] \\
&= \sum_{\theta^t} g_t(\theta^t) \Lambda(\theta_t).
\end{aligned}$$

Notice that:

$$\begin{aligned}
\sum_{\theta^t} g_t(\theta^t)\Lambda(\theta_t) &= \sum_{\theta_t} \phi(\theta_t)\Lambda(\theta_t) \\
&= \sum_{\theta_t} \phi(\theta_t) \left[\sum_{j=1}^{\infty} \left(\frac{1}{r}\right)^j [\theta_m - \theta_m^j(\theta_t)] \right] \\
&= 0.
\end{aligned}$$

While, for an individual agent, $\theta_m - \theta_m^j(\theta_t) \neq 0$, the average over all agents will equal zero because the average of the conditional means is just equal to the unconditional mean. The last equality follows by using an iterated expectations argument as:

$$\sum_{\theta_t} \phi(\theta_t)[\theta_m - \theta_m^j(\theta_t)] = \theta_m - \sum_{\theta_t} \phi(\theta_t)\theta_m^j(\theta_t) = 0$$

for all horizons $j \geq 1$.

Hence, if the endowment risk is Markov but borrowing and lending are restricted only to rule out Ponzi schemes, then the allocations are identical to those of the complete contingent claims equilibrium.

16.1.5. Asset span

We have shown that in the pure credit economy in which prices are not state contingent, the consumption allocations are identical to the first-best allocations regardless of whether the endowment is i.i.d. or first-order Markov. However, this conclusion does not hold if we consider the pure-insurance economy with Markov shocks. To understand these results, notice that in an economy with idiosyncratic risk only – regardless of whether these shocks are i.i.d. or Markov – agents can smooth their consumption merely by borrowing and lending. By contrast, if only insurance contracts are available and the shocks are Markov, conditional on the current state, agents would like to borrow to smooth their consumption streams. When they face borrowing constraints, however, even if they can purchase claims that pay off in any possible state next period conditional on the state, they cannot perfectly smooth their consumption over time. For this reason, most models, such as Huggett [257], Aiyagari [10], or Ljungqvist and Sargent [325], impose joint restrictions limiting contingent claims trading and self-insurance.

We generally do not see state-contingent prices and claims of the sort that we study in the Arrow-Debreu equilibrium. So does that imply that the markets in which we actually trade are incomplete? The analysis above indicates that allocations achieved in a complete contingent claims market structure can also be achieved within a restricted asset space. In the pure-credit model with a single short-term and fixed-rate asset, an individual could take a long (saving) or short (borrowing) position and the full insurance allocation could be achieved. In the pure-insurance model, the restriction on borrowing had an impact on the allocations only in the case of a Markov endowment process. The notion that market incompleteness may not matter is explored in the paper by Levine and Zame [309]. They show market incompleteness may not matter when agents have a long time horizon and can self-insure through borrowing and lending. The conclusion may not hold if there are multiple consumption goods or the wrong types of assets are traded. We can interpret our pure insurance economy with Markov endowment as an example of an economy with the wrong type of assets being traded. The examples in this section have examined only idiosyncratic risk.

When there is aggregate uncertainty, the impact of market incompleteness may be important. Levine and Zame [309] show that market incompleteness may not matter when there is aggregate risk provided agents have the same constant relative risk-aversion utility and the right set of assets is traded. This point is also explored by Krueger and Lustig [292]. Krueger and Lustig [292] show that if aggregate risk is incorporated into a model with idiosyncratic risk, and if the distributions of the aggregate shocks and idiosyncratic shocks are independent, then the risk premium is unaffected.

We have established that, under some circumstances, market incompleteness has no impact on consumption allocations or risk premiums. The conclusion is that restrictions on the asset span may not have a significant impact. Yet empirical studies indicate that market incompleteness and frictions are important and so the task is to incorporate frictions into trading that result in changes in equilibrium allocations and prices. We next turn to a model that incorporates a trading friction – trading is bilateral and takes place at decentralized locations each time period. The model can be related to our pure-credit and pure-insurance models just discussed.

16.2. TOWNSEND TURNPIKE MODEL

The discussion above focused on models of idiosyncratic risk in which aggregate output is deterministic. We shift now to the impact of market incompleteness when there is aggregate uncertainty. While aggregate uncertainty cannot be diversified away, it can be shared efficiently when markets are complete.

This section is based on the Townsend [431] turnpike model. The model has a specific trading friction, namely, trade is bilateral and location-specific. The decentralization of trade and the feature that an agent will interact with only a small subset of agents creates a role for a financial intermediary. The standard contingent claims model does not specify a site or location for delivery of goods, implicitly assuming that all agents are located at the same site or that goods can be costlessly and instantaneously moved across sites at a point in time. Models of incomplete markets sometimes assume that the incompleteness arises because of spatial separation, although many other models of market incompleteness are studied, such as private information or lack of enforcement mechanisms, for example. In this model we assume that at a point in time agents are characterized not only by the aggregate state and their type but also by their location. The stochastic endowment is received by an agent at a particular site, and this non-storable consumption good cannot be transported across sites within a time period.

Transactions across agents at different sites will depend on the communication across sites and the restrictions on the delivery of the contract, which in turn are related to enforcement and limited commitment. Full communication means that agents can enter into contingent contracts with agents at other sites. Unrestricted delivery means that delivery can be guaranteed even if the counter parties are at different sites on the delivery date. Full communication with restricted delivery leads to partial insurance against aggregate risk, even though an agent can enter into a countable infinity of contracts. A model in which there is full communication but partially restricted delivery because of record-keeping constraints or limited netting of transactions is equivalent to a model with borrowing constraints. We also show that the Alvarez-Jermann model of endogenous solvency constraints is related to a particular netting scheme in which there is no default in equilibrium.

In this setting, the Arrow-Debreu complete markets allocation can be achieved if contingent claims are pooled across all sites and agents. All contracts must specify the delivery site. If trade is decentralized among agents at different sites, there must be full communication across locations. Specifically, agents located at different sites at time t must be able to communicate and to enter into contingent claims contracts. Second, there must be unrestricted delivery on the contracts. This means that the two counter parties in the contract can be located at different sites at the delivery date. We examine several versions of the model under different assumptions about communication across sites and restrictions on delivery.

16.2.1. *Description of the model*

An agent is indexed by his type, his location, the date, and the history of the system. There are two types of agents: type E (east-moving) and type W (west-moving). There is a countable infinity of each type of agent.

At time t, the type E or W agent is at a location $i \in I$, where I is the set of integers. In period $t+1$, an E-type will move to site $i+1$ while the W-type agent will move to site $i-1$. If, at time t a type E agent is located at site i and a type W agent is located at site j, then the following set of potential interactions are possible. If $j < i$, then the two agents never meet in the future. If $i = j$, then the agents are present at the same site at the same point of time, but never meet again. If $j > i$, then the two agents may potentially be at the same site at the same time. If $j - i$ is an even (and positive) number, then the agents are at the same site at time $t + \frac{j-i}{2}$. If $j - i$ is odd, then the two agents are never at the same site at the same point in time. All agents at all locations act as price-takers.

At each site and in each time period, each type of agent receives a stochastic and exogenous endowment. The exogenous endowments follow a stationary, first-order Markov chain. Let $s_t \in S = \{\epsilon_1, \ldots, \epsilon_n\}$. A type E

agent at site i has a non-storable endowment $y_e^i : S \rightarrow Y = [\underline{y}, \bar{y}]$, where $\underline{y} \geq 0$. Type W agent at site i has non-storable endowment $y_w^i : S \rightarrow Y$. Denote $\bar{y}^i(s) = y_e^i(s) + y_w^i(s)$ as total endowment in state s at site i. The endowment is non-storable and cannot be moved across sites during the time period it is received. Moreover, let $y_e^i = y_e$ and $y_w^i = y_w$ for all i, so that type E agents are identical across sites, as are type W. In much of the discussion, the location index will be dropped when there is no ambiguity.

Define $\pi_{i,j} = prob(s_{t+1} = \epsilon_j \mid s_t = \epsilon_i)$ for $i, j = 1, \ldots, n$. Define Π as the $n \times n$ matrix of transition probabilities with (i,j)-element $\pi(s_j \mid s_i)$, where summation across a row equals one. Finally, let $\hat{\pi}(s)$ denote the unconditional probability of being in state s, and $\hat{\Pi}$ denote the vector of unconditional probabilities. Let $s^t = (s_1, \ldots, s_t)$ be the history of realizations up to time t and let $\pi_t(s^t)$ denote the probability of s^t, where $s^t \in S^t = \underbrace{S \times \cdots \times S}_{t}$. Hence, at time t an agent is characterized by his type, location i where $i \in I$, and the common history s^t.

There are some important differences between the model with idiosyncratic risk discussed in the first part of this chapter and the current model in terms of the underlying uncertainty. In the first with idiosyncratic risk, there was a countable infinity of agents so that the sample realization generated a sample mean equal to the underlying population mean, using the Law of Large Numbers. Under certain conditions on trading, agents could achieve full risk sharing and constant consumption over time. In the current model there is both aggregate and idiosyncratic risk. The total endowment at a particular site is:

$$y^i(s) \equiv y_e^i(s) + y_w^i(s),$$

which varies with the state s so that there is aggregate uncertainty. Aggregate uncertainty, by definition, cannot be diversified away. The issue is whether that aggregate risk is optimally shared across agents. We also see heterogeneity among agents: as total endowment $y^i(s)$ fluctuates, the share of the total endowment for a type E may vary. But notice that there are no risk sharing arrangements among agents of the same type, because agents of the same type are identical. We could also incorporate a location-specific shock that is i.i.d. across sites to generate more variability in endowment and create risk-sharing arrangements among agents of the same type.

A type E agent has preferences over consumption bundles described by:

$$\sum_{t=0}^{\infty} \sum_{s^t} \beta^t \pi_t(s^t) U(c_t), \tag{16.27}$$

where $0 < \beta < 1$. Let $c_t^i(s^t)$ denote the consumption of a type E agent at time t, location i when the history is s^t. The type W agent has preferences over consumption bundles described by:

$$\sum_{t=0}^{\infty} \sum_{s^t} \beta^t \pi_t(s^t) W(\eta_t). \tag{16.28}$$

Let $\eta_t^i(s^t)$ denote the consumption of a type W agent in location i at time t when history is s^t. The functions U, W are assumed to be strictly increasing, strictly concave, and twice continuously differentiable. Let U_1, W_1 denote the first derivatives and assume the Inada conditions hold: $\lim_{c \to 0} \mathcal{U}_1(c) = \infty$ and $\lim_{c \to \infty} \mathcal{U}_1(c) = 0$ for $\mathcal{U} = U, W$.

Before proceeding with a borrowing-constrained model, it is useful to discuss the role of the financial intermediary or clearing house. If there were no accounting system or agency to keep track of and enforce the delivery of contingent claims contracts, then no agent would enter into these contracts and the only outcome is autarky, where each agent just consumes his endowment. The reason is clear: each agent meets a particular agent of different type at most once. Hence if the east agent wishes to borrow from a particular west agent, the west agent will lend only if the debt instrument issued by the east agent is enforceable and negotiable. Enforceability means that the east agent cannot default on the contract and negotiability means that the west agent can sell the contract to another agent and still have the contract honored by the issuer. Hence the Townsend turnpike model creates a role for a durable asset, such as money, or a clearing house that facilitates borrowing and lending. In the discussion below, we emphasize the clearing house interpretation. The clearing house facilitates the delivery on a contract.

The complete markets competitive equilibrium is solved first. In this case, the clearing house intermediates borrowing and lending and enforces contracts. The type E agent who is located at site i at $t = 0$ has a budget constraint:

$$0 = \sum_{t=0}^{\infty} \sum_{s^t} q_t^{i+t}(s^t)[y_e^{i+t}(s_t) - c_t^{i+t}(s^t)] \tag{16.29}$$

Let λ^i denote the Lagrange multiplier, and assume that $\lambda_i = \lambda$ for all $i \in I$. The first-order condition is:

$$\beta^t \pi_t(s^t) U_1(c_t^{i+t}(s^t)) = \lambda q_t^{i+t}(s^t). \tag{16.30}$$

The budget constraint for a type W agent who starts at location i at $t = 0$ is:

$$0 = \sum_{t=0}^{\infty} \sum_{s^t} q_t^{i-t}(s^t)[y_w^{i-t}(s_t) - \eta_t^{i-t}(s^t)]. \tag{16.31}$$

Let ϕ denote the Lagrange multiplier. The first-order condition is:

$$\beta^t \pi_t(s^t) W_1(\eta_t^{i-t}(s^t)) = \phi q_t^{i-t}(s^t) \tag{16.32}$$

At site i, the market-clearing condition is:

$$\bar{y}^i(s_t) - c_t^i(s^t) - \eta_t^i(s^t) = 0 \tag{16.33}$$

The first-order conditions for the two agents located at site i at time t can be solved for the price to obtain:

$$\frac{W_1(\eta_t^i(s^t))}{\phi} = \frac{q_t^i(s^t)}{\beta^t \pi_t(s^t)} = \frac{U_1(c_t^i(s^t))}{\lambda} \tag{16.34}$$

Consider stationary solutions of the form $c^i : S \to Y$ for $i \in I$. With market clearing at each site, (16.34) can be re-written with market clearing as:

$$\frac{U_1(c^i(s_t))}{W_1(\bar{y}^i(s_t) - c^i(s_t))} = \frac{\lambda}{\phi}. \tag{16.35}$$

Observe that the left side is strictly decreasing in c. The stationary solution is:

$$c(s_t) = g\left(s_t, \frac{\lambda}{\phi}\right).$$

To determine the value of $\frac{\lambda}{\phi}$, substitute for the equilibrium price into the type E's budget constraint:

$$0 = \sum_{t=0}^{\infty} \sum_{s^t} \beta^t \pi_t(s^t) U_1\left(g(s_t, \frac{\lambda}{\phi})\right) \left[y_e(s_t) - g\left(s_t, \frac{\lambda}{\phi}\right)\right]. \tag{16.36}$$

The right side is strictly increasing in $\frac{\lambda}{\phi}$, hence there exists a unique solution $(\lambda/\phi)^\star$.

With the benchmark case established, we turn now to borrowing-constrained households.

16.2.2. Borrowing-constrained households

To examine the impact of the borrowing constraint when there are contingent claims and aggregate risk, the borrowing constraint is modeled as a lower bound on the value of the portfolio at the end of the period. The constraint is best understood in a sequential model using dynamic programming.

Let $V_e(s_t, z^e)$ denote the value function of a type E agent at location i in state s_t who holds contingent claims z^e at the beginning of the period. The type E agent solves:

$$V_e(s_t, z^e) = \max[U(c_t) + \beta \sum_{s_{t+1}} \pi(s_{t+1} \mid s_t) V_e(s_{t+1}, z^e(s_{t+1}))], \tag{16.37}$$

subject to

$$y_e(s_t) + z^e = c_t + \sum_{s_{t+1}} \hat{q}(s_{t+1}, s_t) z^e(s_{t+1}), \tag{16.38}$$

and

$$D \leq \sum_{s_{t+1}} \hat{q}(s_{t+1}, s_t) z^e(s_{t+1}), \tag{16.39}$$

where $D \leq 0$, places a restriction net indebtedness since the constraint implies

$$0 \leq c_t \leq y_e(s_t) + z^e(s_t) - D.$$

Notice the non-negativity constraint on consumption implies that:

$$z^e(s_t) \geq D - y_e(s_t),$$

which places a lower (negative) bound on contingent claims holdings (a short sale constraint).

Let $\mu_e(s_t)$ denote the Lagrange multiplier for the budget constraint (16.38) and let $\lambda_e(s_t)$ denote the multiplier for the borrowing constraint (16.39) for a type E agent. The first-order conditions and envelope condition are

$$U_1(c_t) = \mu_e(s_t), \tag{16.40}$$

$$\mu_e(s_t)\hat{q}(s_{t+1}, s_t) - \lambda_e(s_t) = \beta\pi(s_{t+1} \mid s_t) V_{2,e}(s_{t+1}, z^e(s_{t+1})), \tag{16.41}$$

$$V_{2,e}(s_t, z^e(s_t)) = \mu_e(s_t). \tag{16.42}$$

These conditions simplify as:

$$U_1(c_t)\hat{q}(s_{t+1}, s_t) - \lambda_e(s_t) = \beta\pi(s_{t+1} \mid s_t) U_1(c_{t+1}). \tag{16.43}$$

Market clearing requires that:

$$z^e(s_{t+1}) + z^w(s_{t+1}) = 0.$$

At first glance, it might seem that our pure-insurance economy described at the beginning of the chapter is an example of this model in which $D = 0$. This is not the case because of the aggregate risk. Will the borrowing constraint ever be binding when there is aggregate risk that is i.i.d.? Suppose that $D=0$ so that no borrowing is allowed. Optimal risk sharing in this model is an allocation such that:

$$\frac{U'(c(s_{t+1}))}{W'(\eta(s_{t+1}))} = K,$$

where K is a positive constant and the consumption of a type E is a function $c(s_t, K)$. The agent's portfolio constraint can be expressed as:

$$0 = \sum_{s_{t+1}} \beta\pi(s_{t+1} \mid s_t)U_1(c(s_{t+1}, K))[y^e(s_{t+1}) - c(s_{t+1}, K)],$$

where both sides have been multiplied by $U'(c_t)$. Notice that the right side is a function of the unknown K. This model can be solved by using the first-order condition for the type W agent to show that, when the aggregate shock is i.i.d., the first-best allocation can be achieved when $D=0$. For this reason we will assume that the endowment is Markov for the rest of the discussion.

Under the assumption of Markov endowment, one outcome is that the constraint is non-binding for both types of agents. A second case is that the constraint binds for one of the agents. Notice that it can bind for only one type of agent in each time period. If the constraint is binding for a type E agent, then consumption is $c(s_t) = y_e(s_t) + z^e(s_t) - D$ so that:

$$\lambda_e(s_t) = \max[0, U_1(y_e(s_t) + z^e(s_t) - D)\hat{q}^i(s_{t+1}, s_t) - \beta\pi(s_{t+1} \mid s_t)U_1(c_{t+1})].$$

If $\lambda_e(s_t) > 0$, then observe that the equilibrium consumption of a type W agent is $\eta(s_t) = y_w(s_t) + z^w + D$. Hence, in this simple model with two types of agents, it is clear that the consumption allocations of the unconstrained agent are affected by the borrowing constraint through the limits on his transactions with the constrained agent.

Before examining the asset-pricing implications of the model, we will interpret the borrowing constraint as a specific netting scheme or record-keeping technology used by the clearing house.

16.2.3. Borrowing constraints as netting schemes

In this section, we exploit the physical frictions in trading by interpreting these frictions as a type of netting scheme. For intermediation to occur, the clearing house must facilitate delivery on contracts between counter parties located at different sites on the delivery date. To prevent Ponzi schemes from occurring, the clearing house will need to maintain records all of the contingent claims contracts entered into by agents $W(i)$ or $E(i)$, $i \in I$. As discussed earlier, there is a countable infinity of such contracts. In this section, the clearing house maintains records but is technologically constrained from maintaining records and deliveries on all contracts at all sites over time. In particular, an agent at site i at time t will be allowed to borrow from agents that are no more than n sites away from site i. There is an upper bound on how much the agent can borrow, equal to the expected discounted present value of his income for the next n periods. Agents are allowed limited opportunities to roll this debt over and, over his lifetime, the expected discounted present value of expenditures cannot exceed the expected discounted present value of income.

Suppose that the clearing house nets deliveries at site $i+1$ at time $t+1$ with deliveries at site $i-1$. If $E(i)$ borrows from $W(i+2)$ at time t, resources are shifted from $W(i)$ to $E(i)$ for the loan to take place. Agent $W(i)$ will be repaid at site $i-1$ from payments made by $E(i-2)$ and $W(i+2)$ will be repaid at site $i+2$ by $E(i)$ for resources that $W(i+2)$ shifted to $E(i+2)$. Although multiple agents are involved in the transaction, the initial loan takes place at two sites $(i, i+2)$ and the repayment takes place at two sites $(i-1, i+1)$. Rolling the debt over will expand the number of agents and sites involved in the transaction.

Define

$$A_{n,t}(s^t) = q_t(s^t)y_e(s_t) + \sum_{s_{t+1}} \pi_{t+1}(s_{t+1})A_{n-1,t+1}(s^{t+1}),$$

where $A_{0,t}(s^t) \equiv 0$, which equals the discounted present value of endowment for n periods in the future, including the current period, measured in time 0 prices. Similarly for the type W agent define

$$B_{1,t}(s^t) \equiv q_t(s^t)y_w(s_t)$$

and

$$B_{n,t}(s^t) = q_t(s^t)y_w(s_t) + \sum_{s_{t+1}} \pi_{t+1}(s^{t+1})B_{n-1,t+1}(s^{t+1}).$$

For general netting schemes, the problem solved by a type E is to maximize (16.27) subject to:

$$0 \le \sum_t \sum_{s^t} q_t^{i+t}(s^t)[y_e^{i+t}(s_t) - c_t^{i+t}(s^t)], \tag{16.44}$$

$$0 \le A_{n,t}^{i+t}(s^t) - q_t^{i+t}(s^t)c_t^{i+t}(s^t). \tag{16.45}$$

The first constraint is the standard lifetime budget constraint, while the second constraint states that the agent's borrowing is capped by the expected discount present value of income for the next n periods. This places a limit on the amount of debt that an agent can acquire. It also has the following interpretation: that claims against an agent at time t in state s^t, site i, when netted against agents at sites $i, \dots, i+n$ are bounded above by the agent's ability to repay in the next n periods. Suppose that (16.45) binds in period t. Then next period, the agent faces (16.45) updated one time period and can borrow, as long as (16.44) is satisfied over his lifetime. This formulation allows a more general and flexible borrowing constraint than is typically used.

Let μ_e denote the multiplier for the lifetime constraint for a type E agent and let $\lambda^n_{e,t}(s^t)$ denote the multiplier for the borrowing constraint (16.45). The first-order condition is:

$$\beta^t \pi_t(s^t) U'(c_t^{i+t}(s^t)) = [\mu_e + \lambda^n_{e,t}(s^t)] q_t^{i+t}(s^t) \tag{16.46}$$

If $n = 1$, then the clearing house will not intermediate any loans between the agents at site i at time t and the equilibrium allocation is autarky. If $n = 2$, then the clearing house will intermediate loans but only for agents that are no more than two sites apart at time $t+1$. Clearly, as n grows large, the constraint is less likely to bind because the lifetime budget constraint must be satisfied. As $n \to \infty$, the constraint is equivalent to the no-Ponzi scheme condition.

16.2.4. Liquidity-constrained households

Kehoe and Levine [273] define liquidity constraints as a restriction on short-sales of an asset. A short-sale constraint in this model takes the form

$$y_e(s_t) - c(s_t) \geq D(s_t).$$

The implications of this constraint are discussed next and then related to the Alvarez and Jermann model [24] of endogenous debt constraints.

The east and west traveling agents maximize their objective functions subject to their lifetime budget constraints (16.31) and the short-sale constraint of the form

$$y_i(s_t) - c_i(s_t) \geq D(s_t) \tag{16.47}$$

where $i = e, w$ and $D(s_t) < 0$. Notice that the constraint is generally state-dependent, and is stronger than the borrowing constraint model above since it limits not only the end-of-period portfolio

$$\sum_{s_{t+1}} q_{t+1}(s^{t+1})[y_i(s_{t+1}) - c_i(s_{t+1})] \geq \sum_{s_{t+1}} q_{t+1}(s^{t+1}) D(s_{t+1})$$

but also indebtedness in each state. Observe also that the short-sale constraint can be binding even if the aggregate shock is i.i.d., unlike the pure-insurance models or the borrowing constraint model.

Let $\phi_i(s_t)$ denote the Lagrange multiplier for the short-sale constraint and let μ_i denote the multiplier for the lifetime budget constraint (16.31). The first-order condition for a type E agent is:

$$\pi_t(s^t)\beta^t U_1(c_t(s^t)) = \mu_e q_t(s^t) + \phi_e(s_t). \tag{16.48}$$

If $\phi_e > 0$ then $c(s_t) = y_e(s_t) - D(s_t)$. From market clearing, it follows that $\eta(s_t) = y_w(s_t) + D(s_t)$. If the east-type agent has $\phi_e(s_t) > 0$, then $\phi_w(s_t) = 0$ and conversely. The short-sale constraint can be binding for only one type of agent in equilibrium. If $\phi_e > 0$ then the equilibrium price will satisfy:

$$\frac{q_t(s^t)}{\pi_t(s^t)\beta^t} = \frac{U_1(y_e(s_t) - D(s_t)) - \phi_e(s_t)}{\mu_e} = \frac{W_1(y_w(s_t) + D(s_t))}{\mu_w}. \tag{16.49}$$

Hence the allocation either satisfies:

$$\frac{U'(c(s_t))}{W'(\eta(s_t))} = \frac{\mu^e}{\mu_w}$$

and the price is proportional to $\beta\pi(s_t|s_{t-1})$ or else the constraint is binding and the equilibrium satisfies the equation above.

16.2.5. Debt-constrained economies

Alvarez and Jermann [24] derive a constrained efficient equilibrium based on endogenous solvency constraints. Their work builds on earlier work by Kocherlakota [280] and Kehoe and Levine [272, 273], who construct equilibria in endowment economies where there are participation constraints. Agents can always opt to revert to the autarky solution and so any efficient allocation with market participation must take this into account. Alvarez and Jermann [24] show that the participation constraints can be interpreted as endogenous solvency constraints. Agents can choose to default and revert to the autarky solution. They derive endogenous borrowing constraints such that the agent, while having the option of default, will in equilibrium never choose default.

Define $V_e^a(s_t)$ as:

$$V_e^a(s_t) = U(y_e(s_t)) + \beta \sum_{s_{t+1}} \pi(s_{t+1} \mid s_t) V_e^a(s_{t+1}) \tag{16.50}$$

so that V^a is the value of the endowment under autarky. The agent will choose to default whenever his current value function is less than V^a. The problem can be directly solved by requiring $V_e(s_t, z_t) \geq V^a(s_t)$. An alternative approach taken by Alvarez and Jermann [24] is to show that the solution to the following model is identical to the model with the participation constraint. They study the following debt-constrained economy:

$$V_e(s_t, z^e) = \max[U(c_t) + \beta \sum_{s_{t+1}} \pi(s_{t+1} \mid s) V_e(s_{t+1}, z^e(s_{t+1}))] \tag{16.51}$$

subject to

$$y_e(s_t) + z^e = c_t + \sum_{s_{t+1}} \hat{q}(s_{t+1}, s) z^e(s_{t+1})$$

and

$$z^e(s_{t+1}) \geq D(s_{t+1}),$$

which is the dynamic programming version of the short-sale constrained model in the previous section. Let $\mu_e(s_t)$ denote the multiplier on the budget constraint and let $\lambda_e(s_{t+1})$ denote the multiplier on the borrowing constraint. The first-order conditions and the envelope condition are:

$$U_1(c_t) = \mu_e(s_t) \tag{16.52}$$

$$\mu_e(s_t)\hat{q}(s_{t+1}, s_t) = \lambda_e(s_{t+1}) + \beta\pi(s_{t+1} \mid s_t) V_{2,e}(s_{t+1}, z^e(s_{t+1})) \tag{16.53}$$

$$V_{2,e} = \mu_e(s_{t+1}) \tag{16.54}$$

They show that the solvency constraint is not too tight if

$$V_e(s_t, D(s_t)) = V_e^a(s_t). \tag{16.55}$$

As long as the short-sale constraint is not too tight, the agent will never choose to default on debt. This implies that there is a netting scheme such that no agent will default in equilibrium.

16.3. CONCLUSIONS

In this chapter, we have examined the role of restrictions on markets and on trades. We have considered economies in which there is only idiosyncratic risk and also ones for which there is also aggregate uncertainty. In the former case, we have examined the nature of equilibria in pure credit and pure insurance economies under alternative assumptions for the shocks. We have also analyzed the Townsend turnpike model in which there are locational trading frictions. These models show the impact of market incompleteness and trading frictions and allow us to understand how individual allocations and asset prices differ from the pure frictionless Arrow-Debreu complete contingent claims economy. In the next chapter, we employ similar techniques to analyze the overlapping generations model under pure exchange and with production.

16.4. EXERCISES

1. Consider an economy in which there are two types of agents, where $\alpha \in (0, 1)$ denotes the fraction of agents of type a. Also assume that there are two states of the world, $s \in S = \{1, 2\}$ and suppose that

the sequence of shocks $\{s_t\}$ are i.i.d. where $\pi = Prob(s_t = 1)$. Let $\theta_i(s_t)$ denote the productivity of each agent i in state s_t. The production function for an agent of type i is:

$$y_{i,t} = \theta_i(s_t)\ell_{i,t}, \tag{16.56}$$

where $\ell_{i,t}$ is the labor supply of agent i in period t. If $s = 1$, $\theta_1(1) = 1$ and $\theta_2(1) = 0$ while if $s = 2$, $\theta_2(2) = 0$ and $\theta_1(2) = 1$. Hence, productivity shocks are perfectly negatively correlated across agents.

A typical type i consumer has preferences over stochastic sequences $\{c_{i,t}, \ell_{i,t}\}$ of the form:

$$U^i = \sum_{t=0}^{\infty} \sum_{s_t \in S} \{\beta^t [U(c_{i,t}) - \ell_{i,t}]\}. \tag{16.57}$$

At time zero, agent of type i maximizes (16.57) subject to the lifetime constraint

$$0 = \sum_{t=0}^{\infty} \sum_{s_t} p_t(s_t)[\theta_i(s_t) l_{i,t}(s^t) - c_i(s_t)], \tag{16.58}$$

where p_t denotes the contingent claims prices at time zero.

The market-clearing condition is:

$$\alpha c_{1,t} + (1 - \alpha) c_{2,t} = \alpha \theta_1(s_t)\ell_{1,t} + (1 - \alpha)\theta_2(s_t)\ell_{2,t}.$$

(a) Find the first-order conditions and market-clearing conditions for the complete contingent claims equilibrium.
(b) Find the expected present value of lifetime earnings for agents of type 1 and 2.
(c) Find the complete contingent claims allocations and prices under the assumption that (i) $\alpha = 1/2$ and $\pi = 1/2$; (ii) $\pi = 2/3$ and $\alpha = 1/2$.

2. Now consider an economy in which a complete set of contingent claims do not exist but where borrowing and lending are permitted. Assume that there is a durable and non-depletable asset that is fixed in per capita supply at one unit. The asset is bought and sold at a real price q_t at time t. Let $z_{i,t}$, denote the asset holdings of a type i agent at time t.
   (a) Formulate each household's problem as a dynamic programming problem and show that it has a solution.
   (b) Show that the allocations and prices in the borrowing and lending equilibrium are identical to those in the complete contingent claims equilibrium.

CHAPTER 17

Overlapping generations models

In this chapter, we study the overlapping generations model of Samuelson [381]. The main feature of this model is that an agent "lives" for two periods: in the first period, he has a non-trivial decision on how much to save and how much to consume, and in the second and final period, he consumes all of his wealth so that the second-period decision is trivial. Each time period, a new generation enters into trading so that there are always two types of agents – young and old. The overlapping generations model has a special type of friction – because of the physical environment, agents are unable to commit to certain transactions over time. Bilateral borrowing and lending arrangements are not available because of incomplete participation. We have other models in which the physical environment precludes bilateral transactions over time, namely the Townsend turnpike model with east and west traveling agents (see Townsend [431]). In the terminology of Kocherlakota [280], these environments are characterized by agents that are "... unable to commit themselves to a particular allocation of resources" (p. 233). The overlapping generations model also has the property that allocations can be **dynamically inefficient**, implying that a reallocation of resources would make some agents better off and no agent worse off. The dynamic inefficiency arises because there is a double infinity of agents and time periods, according to Shell [397]. We explore the implications of dynamic efficiency in the overlapping generations model.

In the overlapping generations framework with stochastic endowment, there are two concepts of Pareto optimality: equal-treatment Pareto optimality and conditional Pareto optimality. In the first case, young agents born in period t are viewed as identical regardless of the current state, whereas in the second case, young agents born in different states but in the same time period are viewed as different agents. In either case, an allocation can be dynamically inefficient. In a deterministic pure endowment model, the dynamic inefficiency arises because of the double infinity of agents and time periods. Transfers can be made such that the initial old generation is strictly better off while no other agent is worse off. The introduction of a clearing house or a durable asset, such that the transfer can be implemented through the market system, will eliminate the inefficiency. When the endowment is stochastic, the dynamic inefficiency can arise when there is inefficient risk sharing. There is a recent literature which discusses these issues in the context of the overlapping generations model. (See, for example, Demange and Laroque [147] and Demange [146].)

In a deterministic model of capital accumulation, Diamond [152] showed that there may be an over-accumulation of capital in an intergenerational economy, leading to a dynamic inefficiency. By decreasing the capital stock and redistributing the good, the dynamic inefficiency can be eliminated. Diamond [152] shows that the presence of the dynamic efficiency can be determined from a simple relationship between the rate of growth of the population and the marginal productivity of capital, or equivalently, the real interest rate. Recent research has shown that when the environment is stochastic, determining whether an economy is dynamically inefficient is more subtle. Our discussion in this section follows Abel *et al.* [7], Bertocchi [59] and Bertocchi and Kehagias [60].

The issue of dynamic inefficiency and different concepts of Pareto optimality are of more importance than just academic interest. Social security schemes can be justified if an economy is dynamically inefficient. As we have argued, dynamic inefficiency is intimately related to lack of risk sharing in a stochastic environment. As an example, Krueger and Kubler [291] analyze the social security debate from the viewpoint of aggregate risk sharing in an incomplete markets economy. If an economy is dynamically inefficient, the introduction of a safe asset such as outside money or risk-free government bonds may also eliminate the inefficiency, as will income insurance and various types of state-contingent transfers. The form of the optimal policy will depend on the concept of Pareto optimality also. We discuss some of these issues later in this chapter.

17.1. THE ENVIRONMENT

The overlapping generations model is a simple framework for capturing the effects of what we will term "incomplete participation." The Arrow-Debreu framework has infinite-lived agents who meet at time 0 and sign state-contingent contracts. The overlapping generations model has a fundamentally different setup, as we will see later when we study an OLG model using Arrow-Debreu pricing.

17.1.1. Primitives

It is useful to start out with a description of the environment underlying the overlapping generations model.

Demographics There are n agents in each cohort. Agents born in period t live two periods and expire in period $t+1$, with no bequest motive.

Hence each period there are $2n$ agents: n young and n old. The model was initially designed as a demographic model. As we will discuss below, this is too narrow an interpretation.

Consumption The time t consumption of an agent born in period t is denoted c_t^t. The time $t+1$ consumption of an agent born in period t is denoted c_{t+1}^t. Hence the superscript denotes the period of birth and the subscript denotes the current time period.

Endowment Let w_t^t denote the time t endowment of an agent born in period t and let w_{t+1}^t denote the time $t+1$ endowment of an agent born in period t. Let $W = [0, \bar{w}]$ where $w_{t+1}^t \in W$.

Feasible Allocations Feasible allocations satisfy:

$$w_t^{t-1} + w_t^t \geq c_t^t + c_t^{t-1} \tag{17.1}$$

Preferences An agent born in period $t \in T$, $T = \{1, 2, \ldots\}$, has additive preferences:

$$U(c_t^t) + V(c_{t+1}^t) \tag{17.2}$$

Initial Old Generation There is always an issue of how to treat the initial old at time 1 – the standard is to assume that they never experienced the joys of youth and have preferences:

$$V_0(c_1^0)$$

and have endowment w_1^0.

17.1.2. *Autarky in the absence of an outside asset*

The implications of the overlapping generations model under different trading arrangements lie at the heart of many debates in the literature. Hence, it is important to understand the structure of the trading arrangements in this model. Suppose, in particular, that there is no government or clearing house or other agency that facilitates trade between agents of different cohorts. Then, as we argue below, there is no trade.

Consider the possible kinds of trades.

Trade with agents within a cohort: If agents within a cohort (from the same generation) are heterogeneous, then these agents can trade privately issued IOUs. They essentially can borrow and lend among themselves since they share the same lifetimes. Hence within a generation, the marginal rates of substitution across agents will be equalized, as will the intertemporal marginal rate of substitution. Hence we can work with a representative member of generation t.

Trade between agents of different cohorts: At time t, there are two types of agents present in the economy: old agents born in period $t-1$ and young agents t. A young agent at period t will never lend to an old agent at time t because the old agent will expire by period $t+1$ when the loan is to be repaid. Similarly the old agent at time t will never lend to a young agent at time t because the old agent will be dead next period and unable to use the repayment. A young agent generally would like to shift some consumption from youth to old age, but to do so would require entering into an agreement with a young agent born at time $t + 1$. Such trades are not allowed if we consider sequential trading because the time $t + 1$ young agent is not available to negotiate trades at time t. But suppose for the moment that such trades could be negotiated. Suppose that a young agent at time t could sign a contract with a young agent at time $t+1$. Would there be an incentive for the agents to enter into a contract? If the young agent would like to shift some of his wealth forward to time $t + 1$, that would require that the young agent at time $t + 1$ transfer some resources to the old generation at time t. But what can the young agent at time t offer to a young agent at time $t + 1$? The young agent at time t is unable to transfer resources to period $t + 2$, which is the time period that young agents born in period $t+1$ would like to receive the resources. Hence, even if contingent claims among young agents at time t and $t + 1$ could be negotiated, no one would enter into these contracts. Hence, the OLG model is not a model of incomplete markets, because these markets exist, it is just that no one wishes to participate in them. Hence for there to be any trading among different cohorts, there must be an outside asset or some institution that clears the trades. A convenient outside asset is nominal money.

Dynamic inefficiency: For an allocation to be Pareto optimal the expected discounted present value of the wealth of the society must be finite. In an overlapping generations model, this measure of society's wealth may not be finite, indicating that the economy is dynamically inefficient. The dynamic inefficiency can arise because of the double infinity of types of agents and time periods in the model. Each time period there are two types of agents, those born at time $t+i$ and $t+i+1$. As $i = 1, \ldots, \infty$, there is an infinite number of types of agents and an infinite number of time periods for the economy. In an economy with this type of double infinity in which the expected discounted present value of the society's wealth is not finite, the infinite value of wealth signifies that the current price of a unit of endowment in the distant future is large. If the current generation could consume more today and borrow from future generations, welfare might be improved. Essentially an old agent today can borrow from a current young agent who, in turn, borrows from a young agent next period and so on into the infinite future. It is always possible to borrow from a future young generation because there is an infinite number of time periods and infinite number of types, or generations, of agents. The debt is rolled over indefinitely and essentially is a Ponzi scheme. The introduction of an outside asset, such as fiat money which is intrinsically worthless, is an example of a mechanism that can eliminate the dynamic inefficiency. The introduction of an intermediary which allows this borrowing from the future can also eliminate the dynamic inefficiency.

In the absence of an outside asset, agents would consume their own endowment; this is called *autarky*. In this case, $c_t^t = w_t^t$. The marginal rate of substitution between old and young agents is:

$$\frac{V'(w_t^{t-1})}{U'(w_t^t)}.$$

We will discuss the stochastic case later. Notice that if the endowment is fluctuating, the marginal rate of substitution is fluctuating over time. Compare this with our infinite-lived Arrow-Debreu allocation in the absence of aggregate risk. In that case, the MRS was constant over time. Hence the model fails to achieve *static efficiency* (using Azariadis's [38] terminology).

The types of financial mechanisms that can be used to support the Pareto optimal allocations in the deterministic and stochastic versions of the overlapping generations model have been the topic of much study. As we discuss below, the implementation of the Pareto optimal allocations typically requires some transfer scheme. There exist all sorts of institutional arrangements that can be used for this purpose. The role of fiat money, both constant and stochastically growing, and also other government policies such as risk-free bonds, state-contingent taxes, social security, and insurance have also received attention in the literature. (See, for example, Chamley and Polemarcharkis [101], Weiss [447], and Wallace [441].) The various policies are equivalent in the sense that the consumption allocations and the underlying state-contingent prices are unaffected by the policy changes.

17.2. THE STOCHASTIC OVERLAPPING GENERATIONS MODEL

Now consider the stochastic overlapping model. Here we will illustrate the source of the dynamic inefficiency, which does not arise from incomplete markets but rather from what Shell [397] refers to as the "double infinity of agents and time periods." We make this point by demonstrating that the overlapping generations model can be mapped directly into the standard Arrow-Debreu framework. Our discussion is based on the articles by Shell [397] and Labadie [301], [302].

There are overlapping generations and an agent born in period t lives for two periods. There is no population growth. The endowment is exogenous, stochastic and non-storable. There is an exogenous stochastic process $s_t \in S = \{s_1, \ldots, s_n\}$ that is a stationary, first-order Markov chain. A young agent has a non-storable endowment $w^1 : S \to W = [\underline{w}, \bar{w}]$, where $\underline{w} > 0$ and $\bar{w} < \infty$. Old agents at time t have an endowment $w^2 : S \to [0, \bar{w}]$. The total endowment in state s_t is:

$$w(s_t) = w^1(s_t) + w^2(s_t).$$

The one-step transition probability is $\pi(s_j \mid s_i) = Prob(s_{t+1} = s_j \mid s_t = s_i)$ for $i, j = 1, \ldots, n$. The history of realizations up to time t is $s^t = (s_0, s_1, \ldots, s_t)$. Define $\pi_t(s^t)$ as the probability of s^t. The $n \times n$ matrix of transition probabilities is Π, with (i, j)-element $\pi(s_j \mid s_i)$ such that summation over the elements of a row equals one. Let $\hat{\pi}(s)$ denote the unconditional probability of being in state s. The vector of unconditional probabilities satisfies the relation $\Pi' \hat{\pi} = \hat{\pi}$. By assumption, the Markov chain is stationary, so that $\hat{\pi}$ is the eigenvector of the transition matrix and the eigenvalue is 1.

The preferences of a young agent born in period t are:

$$U(c_t^t) + \sum_{s_{t+1}} \pi(s_{t+1} \mid s_t) V(c_{t+1}^t), \tag{17.3}$$

where c_t^t is the time t consumption of a young agent born in period t and c_{t+1}^t is the time $t+1$ consumption of an agent born in period t. Hence, agents' preferences satisfy the *expected utility* hypothesis.

Assumption 17.1 *The functions U, V satisfy $U'(c) > 0$, $V'(c) > 0$, $U''(c) < 0$, $V''(c) < 0$; U and V are thrice continuously differentiable; and $\lim_{c \to 0} U'(c) = \infty$, $\lim_{c \to 0} V'(c) = \infty$, $\lim_{c \to \infty} U'(c) = 0$, and $\lim_{c \to \infty} V'(c) = 0$.*

To ensure that a transfer of a unit of consumption from youth to old age is always welfare improving, the following assumption is made.

Assumption 17.2 *Let $a > 0$ such that $\underline{w} > a \geq 0$. As $a \to 0$,*

$$-U'(w^1(s) - a) + \sum_j \pi(s_j \mid s) V'(w^2(s_j) + a) > 0. \tag{17.4}$$

Denote $\bar{w}^j = \sum_{i=1}^n \hat{\pi}(s_i) w^j(s_i)$ for $j = 1, 2$. The unconditional means of the endowment processes satisfy

$$U'(\bar{w}^1) = V'(\bar{w}^2). \tag{17.5}$$

Let the marginal utility of second period consumption V' be convex, so that $V'(\bar{w}^2) < \sum_j \hat{\pi}_j V'(w^2(s_j))$.

The restriction on the marginal utilities ensures that young agents wish to save in the stochastic environment. The restriction on the unconditional means of the endowment process ensures that the deterministic competitive equilibrium is Pareto optimal. The convexity of V' is assumed so that the assumptions on endowment processes in the deterministic and stochastic environments are consistent. This point is discussed below.

A feasible solution for the consumption of the young agent is a function of the form $c : S \to W$. Using the resource allocation constraint (and assuming non-satiation), the consumption of the old is $w(s) - c(s)$. The marginal utility of consumption for a young agent in state s is $U'(c(s))$ and the marginal utility for an old agent is $V'(w(s) - c(s))$. The intertemporal marginal rate of substitution between states s_i and s_j for a young agent born in state s_i is:

$$m(s_j, s_i) \equiv \frac{V'(w(s_j) - c(s_j))}{U'(c(s_i))}.$$

This intertemporal marginal rate of substitution (IMRS) will play an important role in dynamic efficiency developed below.

There are basically two matrices of interest in studying dynamic efficiency: first, the contingent claims pricing matrix which depends on the IMRS for a single agent over time and the transition probabilities, and second, the matrix associated with the central planner's problem, which depends on the transition probabilities and the marginal rate of substitution (MRS) across agents within a period. To highlight the relationship between the matrices, we start with a discussion of the central planning problem.

17.2.1. *Central planning problem*

Let $\phi_t(s^t) > 0$ for each $s^t \in S^t$ denote the Pareto weight associated with a young agent born at time t in state s^t, and let ϕ_0 be the Pareto weight associated with the initial old at time period 1.[1] Denote c_i^t as the period i consumption of an agent born in period t, where $i = t, t+1$. The central planning problem is:

$$\max_{\{c_1^0, c_t^t, c_{t+1}^t\}} \Bigg\{ \sum_{s_1} \phi_0 \pi(s_1 \mid s_0) V(c_1^0) \\
+ \sum_{t=1}^{\infty} \sum_{s^t \in S^t} \Bigg[\phi_t(s^t) \Bigg(U(c_t^t) + \sum_{s_{t+1}} \pi(s_{t+1} | s_t) V(c_{t+1}^t) \Bigg) \\
+ \lambda_t(s^t)[w(s_t) - c_t^t - c_t^{t-1}] \Bigg] \Bigg\}, \tag{17.6}$$

[1] There is no loss of generality in making ϕ_0 state contingent and letting the initial weight be $\sum_{s_0} \phi_0(s_0) \pi(s_1 \mid s_0) \hat{\pi}(s_0)$.

where $\lambda_t(s^t)$ is the Lagrange multiplier for the resource constraint at time t. The first-order conditions with respect to $\{c_1^0, c_t^t, c_{t+1}^t\}$ are:

$$\phi_0 \pi(s_1|s_0) V'(c_1^0) = \lambda_1(s^1), \tag{17.7}$$

$$\phi_t(s^t) U'(c_t^t) = \lambda_t(s^t), \tag{17.8}$$

$$\phi_t(s^t)\pi(s_{t+1}|s_t) V'(c_{t+1}^t) = \lambda_{t+1}(s^{t+1}). \tag{17.9}$$

We will study a stationary solution such that the social planning weights and the allocations of the young and old agents are time-invariant functions of a finite set of realizations of the underlying state. Specifically, define the functions $\phi : S \to \Re_+$, $c : S \to \Re_+$ and $c_2 : S \times S \to \Re_+$, such that:

$$\phi_t(s^t) = \beta^t \phi(s_t), \quad 0 < \beta \leq 1,$$

$$c_t^t = c(s_t),$$

$$c_{t+1}^t = c_2(s_{t+1}, s_t).$$

With these restrictions on the functions ϕ, c, c_2, observe that the resource constraint, $w(s_t) = c(s_t) + c_2(s_t, s_{t-1})$ is a function of s_t, s_{t-1} and not the entire history s^t. Hence define the current period Lagrange multiplier as:

$$\lambda(s_t, s_{t-1}) \equiv \beta^{-t} \sum_{s^{t-2}} \lambda_t(s^t).$$

The first-order conditions (17.7)–(17.9) are modified as:

$$\phi_0 \pi(s_1 \mid s_0) V'(c_1^0) = \beta\lambda(s_1, s_0), \tag{17.10}$$

$$\phi(s_t) U'(c(s_t)) = \lambda(s_t, s_{t-1}), \tag{17.11}$$

$$\phi(s_t)\pi(s_{t+1}|s_t) V'(c_2(s_{t+1}, s_t)) = \beta\lambda(s_{t+1}, s_t). \tag{17.12}$$

Decrease the time subscript in (17.12) by one unit, divide both sides by β, sum over s_{t-1}, equate the right side of (17.12) to the right side of (17.11), and re-write to obtain:

$$\phi(s_t) U'(c(s_t)) = \frac{1}{\beta} \sum_{s_{t-1}} \phi(s_{t-1})\pi(s_t \mid s_{t-1}) V'(c_2(s_t, s_{t-1})), \tag{17.13}$$

where summing the left side of (17.11) over s_{t-1} yields the expression itself. Incorporate the resource constraint into (17.13):

$$\phi(s_t) U'(c(s_t)) = \frac{1}{\beta} V'(w(s_t) - c(s_t)) \sum_{s_{t-1}} \phi(s_{t-1})\pi(s_t \mid s_{t-1}). \tag{17.14}$$

This corresponds to equation (3) in Peled [358] or equations (4) and (5) in Aiyagari and Peled [12]. Let $B = \max[U'(\underline{w}), V'(\underline{w})] > 0$. Given the weighting function ϕ, the solution to (17.14) is a function $c^*(s_i, \phi)$,

$s_i \in S$. Such a solution exists because the left side is strictly decreasing in c while the right side is strictly increasing. Moreover, as $c \to 0$, $U' \to \infty$ while $V' \to B > 0$ since the first-period endowment is strictly positive and bounded below. As $c \to w$, $U' \to B$ while $V' \to \infty$. In equilibrium, the consumption of the old is invariant with respect to last period's aggregate shock.

Given a solution $c^\star(s_i, \phi)$, define the $n \times n$ diagonal matrix $\mathcal{U}(c^\star)$ with $(i,i)^{th}$ element $U'(c^\star(s_i, \phi))$ along the diagonal. Next define the $n \times n$ matrix $\mathcal{V}(c^\star)$ with (i,j) element $\pi(s_j \mid s_i)V'(w(s_j) - c^\star(s_j, \phi))$. Define $\underline{0}$ as an $n \times 1$ vector of zeroes and let ϕ be the $n \times 1$ vector of Pareto weights. The first-order condition is expressed in matrix notation as:

$$\underline{0} = [\beta\mathcal{U}(c^\star(\phi)) - \mathcal{V}(c^\star(\phi))]\phi, \tag{17.15}$$

which is a homogeneous system of equations. Notice that this is a vector representation of (17.14). Given the allocation $c^\star$ and the matrices $\mathcal{V}, \mathcal{U}$, the solution ϕ is not unique. This becomes apparent by dividing each of the n equations by $\phi(s_i)$ and solving for the $n - 1$ values $\phi(s_j)/\phi(s_i)$. The functional dependence of the matrices will be suppressed for convenience in the discussion below. Multiply both sides of (17.15) by $(\beta\mathcal{U})^{-1}$ (the inverse of $\beta\mathcal{U}$) to obtain:

$$\underline{0} = [I - (\beta\mathcal{U})^{-1}\mathcal{V}]\phi. \tag{17.16}$$

Observe that the matrix $\mathcal{M} \equiv (\beta\mathcal{U})^{-1}\mathcal{V}$ has all positive elements. The Perron-Frobenius Theorem (see Strang [423], p. 271 for example) can be applied to determine whether the inverse $[I - \mathcal{M}]^{-1}$ exists. Let η_m denote the dominant root of $\mathcal{M}$. If $\eta_m > 1$ then the inverse fails to be non-negative, which cannot be a solution since all elements of ϕ must be positive. If $\eta_m = 1$, then the inverse fails to exist. If $\eta_m < 1$, then

$$(I - \mathcal{M})^{-1} = I + \mathcal{M} + \mathcal{M}^2 + \cdots$$

is a convergent sequence. The important point here is that any arbitrary but feasible set of weights may not result in a dominant root less than unity, implying that there is an additional condition that must be satisfied for the allocation $c^\star$ to be Pareto-optimal. This additional condition is closely related to the size of the dominant root and is discussed next.

Recall that the function λ measures the marginal value of the endowment. The solution must also satisfy the **transversality condition**

$$\lim_{j\to\infty} \sum_{s^{t+j}} \lambda(s_{t+j+1}, s_{t+j}) w(s_{t+j+1}) \pi(s_{t+j+1}|s_{t+j}) = 0, \tag{17.17}$$

which is a requirement that the expected discounted present value of the economy's endowment is finite. This condition must hold for the allocation to be **dynamically efficient**. If (17.17) fails to hold, the economy is **dynamically inefficient**.

To determine whether the proposed solution satisfies the transversality condition, observe (17.11) can be written as:

$$\phi(s_{t-1}) = \frac{\lambda(s_{t-1}, s_{t-2})}{U'(c^\star(s_{t-1}))},$$

where the time subscript has been decreased by one unit. Substitute for $\phi(s_{t-1})$ in (17.14) and re-write:

$$\sum_{s_{t-1}} \lambda(s_t, s_{t-1}) = \frac{1}{\beta} \sum_{s_{t-1}} \pi(s_t \mid s_{t-1}) \left[\lambda(s_{t-1}, s_{t-2})\right] \frac{V'(w(s_t) - c^\star(s_t))}{U'(c^\star(s_{t-1}))}. \tag{17.18}$$

From the first-order condition for the first time period, we have:

$$\sum_{s_0} \lambda(s_1, s_0) = \frac{1}{\beta} \phi_0 \pi(s_1 | s_0) V'(w(s_1) - c^\star(s_1)).$$

Solving (17.18) recursively we have:

$$\sum_{s_t} \lambda(s_{t+1}, s_t) = \left(\frac{1}{\beta}\right) \sum_{s_t} \lambda(s_t, s_{t-1}) \pi(s_{t+1}|s_t) \left[\frac{V'(w(s_{t+1}) - c^\star(s_{t+1}))}{U'(c^\star(s_t))}\right]$$

$$= \left(\frac{1}{\beta}\right)^t \sum_{s^t} \pi_t(s^{t+1}) \left[\prod_{j=1}^{t} \frac{V'(w(s_{j+1}) - c^\star(s_{j+1}))}{U'(c^\star(s_j))}\right] \sum_{s_0} \lambda(s_1, s_0).$$

The transversality condition is satisfied when the IMRS satisfies $V'(w(s_{t+1}) - c(s_{t+1}))/U'(c(s_t)) < 1$ on average, or

$$\sum_{i=1}^{n} \sum_{j=1}^{n} \pi(s_j|s_i) \frac{V'(w(s_j) - c^\star(s_j))}{U'(c^\star(s_i))} \leq 1.$$

The transversality condition ensures that the expected discounted present value of the endowment of the infinite-lived economy is finite.

Satisfying the transversality condition above is equivalent to finding the stationary solution in Aiyagari and Peled [12]. They define a $n \times n$ matrix Q with $(i,j)^{th}$ element:

$$q(s_i, s_j) = \frac{\pi(s_i \mid s_j) V'(w(s_i) - c^\star(s_i))}{U'(c^\star(s_j))} = \frac{\beta \lambda(s_i, s_j)}{\lambda(s_j, s_k)}.$$

They show that an allocation $c^\star$ is Pareto optimal if and only if the matrix Q, which has all positive elements, has a dominant root that is less than or equal to unity. If the dominant root is less than unity, then $(I - Q)^{-1} > 0$ where $I_{n \times n}$ is the identity matrix, and, by the Perron-Frobenius Theorem:

$$(I - Q)^{-1} = I + Q + Q^2 + Q^3 + \cdots,$$

which converges to a fixed matrix. The infinite series of matrices corresponds to the sum in (17.17). In this case, the expected discounted present value of wealth of the economy

$$\Pi^T[I + Q + Q^2 + \cdots]W$$

is finite, where $W^T = [w(s_1), \ldots, w(s_n)]$. It will be shown below that the elements of the matrix Q are the contingent claims prices that support the allocation. Hence, the transversality condition, or equivalently, the properties of the matrix Q ensure that the expected discounted present value of wealth is finite, as required for the allocation to be Pareto optimal.

The matrix Q is related to the matrix $\mathcal{M} = \beta \mathcal{U}^{-1}\mathcal{V}$ discussed above by noting that the matrix Q is:

$$Q = (\mathcal{U})^{-1}(\mathcal{V})^T,$$

where $\mathcal{V}^T$ is the transpose of the matrix $\mathcal{V}$.

17.2.2. *Equal-treatment Pareto-optimal solution*

The Pareto-optimal allocation derived as the solution to the central planning problem above results in a MRS across agents at a point in time equal to

$$\frac{V'(w(s_t) - c^\star(s_t))}{U'(c^\star(s_t))} = \frac{\beta\phi(s_t)}{\sum_{s_{t-1}} \pi(s_t \mid s_{t-1})\phi(s_{t-1})}, \tag{17.19}$$

which, in general, varies across states s_t. This solution is said to be *conditionally Pareto optimal (CPO)*, in which agents born in different states but in the same time period are treated differently. In a static setting, a property of full risk sharing is a constant marginal rate of substitution across states for all agents. The *equal-treatment Pareto-optimal solution (ET-PO)* exhibits constant MRS across states for agents, or

$$\frac{V'(w(s) - c(s))}{U'(c(s))} = \beta \quad \text{for all } s, \tag{17.20}$$

so the ratio of marginal utilities is equal across all states, a property of *full insurance*. In this case, the Pareto weights must satisfy:

$$\hat{\phi}(s_j) = \sum_{s_i} \pi(s_j \mid s_i)\hat{\phi}(s_i),$$

so each Pareto weight $\phi(s_t)$ is proportional to its unconditional probability $\hat{\pi}(s_t)$. Denote c^f as the solution to (17.20), which will be referred to as the ET-PO allocation. Recalling the definition of the matrix $\mathcal{V}$ (see page 512), observe that:

$$(\mathcal{U}(c^f))^{-1}\mathcal{V}(c^f) = \beta\Pi,$$

where Π is the matrix of probabilities with (i, j) element $\pi(s_j \mid s_i)$.

For an agent born in state s_t, the expected IMRS under the ET-PO allocation is:

$$\frac{\sum_{s_{t+1}} \pi(s_{t+1}|s_t) V'(w(s_{t+1}) - c^f(s_{t+1}))}{U'(c^f(s_t))} = \frac{\beta \sum_{s_{t+1}} \lambda(s_{t+1}, s_t)}{\lambda(s_t, s_{t-1})}, \tag{17.21}$$

which varies over s_t.

It is important to examine the implications for risk sharing of the two notions of Pareto optimality. Under conditional Pareto optimality, an agent is characterized by (t, s^t), the time period and state history, including the current state s_t. Two agents $[t, (\hat{s}_t \mid s^{t-1})]$ and $[t, (\bar{s}_t \mid s^{t-1})]$ such that (t, s^{t-1}) are identical, are treated as distinct agents. Hence, all first-period endowment risk is uninsurable by construction. Under equal treatment Pareto optimality, agents born at t with state history s^{t-1} are treated as identical agents, so that first period endowment risk is insurable.

17.3. COMPETITIVE EQUILIBRIUM

Shell [397] demonstrated that the Arrow-Debreu contingent claims framework is versatile enough to study the overlapping generations model. In this section, we construct the Arrow-Debreu prices for the competitive equilibrium and then examine the allocations under two assumptions about the market structure. The key insight is that a complete set of contingent claims can be offered, but without some intervention, such as a clearing house or a financial intermediary, agents will not purchase the claims. This point is illustrated below. In our discussion below, all prices are expressed as time 0 prices for convenience.

17.3.1. Deterministic economy

To clarify the role of uncertainty and to understand the role of a clearing house in the model, we start with a discussion of the model in which the endowment is deterministic, so that w^1, w^2 are constant. Let $\phi_t = \beta\phi_{t-1}$ and $\phi_0 > 0$. The central planning problem becomes:

$$\max_{\{c_1^0, c_t^t, c_{t+1}^t\}} \left\{ \phi_0 V(c_1^0) + \sum_{t=1}^{\infty} \left[\phi_t \left(U(c_t^t) + V(c_{t+1}^t) \right) + \lambda_t (w - c_t^t - c_t^{t-1}) \right] \right\}. \tag{17.22}$$

The first-order conditions are:

$$\phi_0 V'(c_1^0) = \lambda_1, \tag{17.23}$$

$$\phi_t U'(c_t^t) = \lambda_t, \tag{17.24}$$

$$\phi_t V'(c_{t+1}^t) = \lambda_{t+1}. \tag{17.25}$$

As in Section 14.1.1, we assume that $\lambda_{t+1} = \beta^{-1}\lambda_t$. Since the endowment is constant, the first-order conditions (17.24)–(17.25) reduce to:

$$U_1(c) = \beta V_1(w - c). \tag{17.26}$$

We now examine whether a competitive equilibrium can achieve the Pareto optimal allocation.

Let q_t denote the price of a one-period privately issued bond z_{t+1}. Specifically, at time t an agent purchases $q_t z_{t+1}$, which entitles him to payment z_{t+1} at time $t+1$ from the issuer of the bond. All prices are expressed at time 0. In the competitive equilibrium, the young agent born at time t solves:

$$\max_{\{c_t^t, c_{t+1}^t\}} \left[U(c_t^t) + V(c_{t+1}^t)\right] \tag{17.27}$$

subject to

$$0 = q_t[w^1 - c_t^t] + q_{t+1}[w^2 - c_{t+1}^t],$$

where the constraint states that the total value of consumption equals the total value of income, or wealth. Let μ_t denote the Lagrange multiplier for the budget constraint. The first-order conditions are:

$$U'(c_t^t) = \mu_t q_t, \tag{17.28}$$

$$V'(c_{t+1}^t) = \mu_t q_{t+1}. \tag{17.29}$$

Eliminate μ_t, substitute in the resource constraint, and solve for q_{t+1}:

$$q_{t+1} = \frac{V'(w - c_{t+1}^{t+1})}{U'(c_t^t)} q_t. \tag{17.30}$$

The question now is whether privately issued bonds will be traded. The potential buyer of a bond z_{t+1} is a young agent at time t, who wishes to shift some consumption to period $t+1$. The issuer of a bond at time t, the borrower, is the old agent. Since these are privately issued bonds, the bond is the liability of the issuer and, since the issuer has a finite time horizon, the bonds are not a durable asset. Since the issuer (old agents) at time t is unable to make the payment at time $t+1$, a young agent will not purchase the bonds. Hence, equilibrium in the bond market requires that $z_t = 0$ for all t so that consumption is $c_t^t = w^1$ when young and $c_{t+1}^t = w^2$ when old. Before we discuss the role of a clearing house or financial intermediary, we discuss the conditions of Assumption (17.2).

For the moment, suppose Assumption (17.2) does not hold and the allocation of the endowment is such that $V'(w^2) > U'(w^1)$. Then the autarky solution $c = w^1$ results in $q_{t+1} \rightarrow \infty$ as $t \rightarrow \infty$ in (17.30). Hence, the deterministic economy in autarky is dynamically inefficient, implying that the time-0 Arrow-Debreu price for delivery of a unit of consumption in the infinite future is infinity.

As observed by Shell [397], the dynamic inefficiency in the infinite horizon model is a result of the double infinity of agents and time periods. The inefficiency is eliminated by transferring resources from the current young to the current old. The initial old experience a clear welfare gain from such a transfer and the current young are compensated by receiving a transfer in their old age. Since the economy has an infinite time horizon and an infinite number of agents, there is always a future young generation from which such a transfer can be implemented, unlike a finite horizon version of the model. In a finite horizon version of the economy, the autarky solution is Pareto efficient. Young agents will not transfer resources to the current old because the terminal young are always worse off under such a transfer scheme.

Now impose Assumption (17.2). Under this assumption, because $U'(\bar{w}^1) = V'(\bar{w}^2)$, it follows that:

$$q_{t+1} = \frac{V'(\bar{w}^2)}{U'(\bar{w}^1)} q_t = q_t,$$

so that prices are constant and the competitive equilibrium is dynamically efficient in autarky.

17.3.2. *Fiat money*

The introduction of fiat money, currency that is intrinsically worthless, is a mechanism that can be used to eliminate the dynamic inefficiency. Suppose that the initial generation is given worthless pieces of money, in the amount M, which is constant. The initial old generation has a budget constraint

$$c_1^0 = \frac{M}{p_1},$$

where p_1 is the nominal price of a unit of endowment in period 1. The young agent in the first period has a budget constraint

$$w_1^1 \geq c_1^1 + \frac{M^d}{p_1}.$$

In equilibrium $M^d = M$, and the young consumer's first-order condition is:

$$U'(c_1^1)\frac{1}{p_1} = V'\left(w_2^1 + \frac{M}{p_2}\right)\frac{1}{p_2}. \tag{17.31}$$

If $w_t^1 = w^1$ and $w_t^2 = w^2$ so that the endowment of the young and old agents is constant over time, then the stationary solution is $p_t = p$, a constant and

$$U'\left(w^1 - \frac{M}{p}\right) = V'\left(w^2 + \frac{M}{p}\right).$$

We can illustrate the efficiency gain using this model. In the absence of money or any sort of clearing house, young agents consume w^1 and old consume w^2. By assumption, the availability of money is welfare improving because

$$U\left(w^1 - \frac{M}{p}\right) + V\left(w^2 + \frac{M}{p}\right) > U(w^1) + V(w^2).$$

Hence the initial young give up $\frac{M}{p}$ and receive $\frac{M}{p}$ in period 2, as do all future generations. The initial old are now able to consume $w^2 + \frac{M}{p}$ and hence are strictly better off while all other agents are at least as well off so there is a welfare gain. Such a reallocation could not occur if the time horizon were finite. Suppose there are T periods. In period T, the young agents will be unwilling to hold fiat currency because it is the final period so there is no use for it. But if the last young generation has no value for it, then neither will the young at time $T - 1$ because they know it will not have value in the last period. It follows recursively that money will have no value in the first period. This illustrates the importance of an infinity of time periods. If the time horizon is infinite but there is only a finite number of agents with which to trade, then at some point, if an agent makes a loan, the loan will have to be paid back. There is no way to keep rolling over the loan when there is only a finite number of agents.

17.3.3. The stochastic economy

We have just seen that, under Assumption (17.2), the deterministic version of the model is dynamically efficient. We maintain this assumption and now examine the source of dynamic inefficiency when the endowment is stochastic. We will show that inefficient risk sharing can serve as a source of dynamic inefficiency.

Autarky

Let $z(s_t, s_{t+1})$ denote the contingent claim purchased by a young agent in state s_t, conditional on s_{t+1} being realized. Let $q(s_{t+1}, s_t)$ denote the price of a claim. The young agent has lifetime budget constraints

$$w^1(s_t) = c_t^t + \sum_{s_{t+1}} q(s_{t+1}, s_t) z(s_{t+1}, s_t), \tag{17.32}$$

$$c_{t+1}^t = z(s_{t+1}, s_t) + w_2(s_{t+1}), \tag{17.33}$$

for all s_t. Besides the young agents in the market the only other agents are the old agents born at $t-1$ in state s^{t-1}. In the absence of a financial intermediary or clearing house, there will be no buyers of these claims and no contingent claims trading in general in this economy, for the reasons already discussed. Young agents want to trade with young agents next period and not with the current old generation. Hence, as in the deterministic case, $c_t^t = w^1(s_t)$ and $c_t^{t\ 1} = w^2(s_t)$. Notice that contingent claims can be priced under the autarkic allocation, specifically:

$$q_a(s_{t+1}, s_t) = \frac{\pi(s_{t+1}|s_t)V'(w^2(s_{t+1}))}{U'(w^1(s_t))}.$$

The matrix Q^a of contingent claims prices under autarky may have a dominant root that is greater than unity, so that the autarky solution is dynamically inefficient. This would be the case if $w^2(s) = 0$ for any $s \in S$, for example.

Let Q_a denote the matrix $(\mathcal{U})^{-1}\mathcal{V}$ under autarky. Suppose that $w^2(s_j) = 0$ for some s_j. Then

$$[I - (\mathcal{U}(w^1)^{-1}\mathcal{V}(w^2)]^{-1}$$

will fail to exist and the competitive equilibrium in autarky is dynamically inefficient, even though the deterministic version of this economy is dynamically efficient. It is not necessary that $w^2(s_j) = 0$ for some s_j, only that the dominant root of the matrix Q_a be greater than unity. Hence, the issue of inefficient risk sharing in a model of incomplete participation is an issue of the **distribution** of income over agents at a point of time, and is not just a matter of the double infinity in the economy, as was the case in the deterministic setting.

Role of a clearing house

As we have seen, privately issued bonds that are the liability of the issuer are not durable in that the issuer is not in the market at the time payment is made to the bondholder. We now discuss a simple mechanism that allows privately issued bonds to be traded. Suppose, in particular, that there is a "clearing house" that posts prices at time 0 and at those prices compiles aggregate demand and aggregate supply for goods in different periods. The introduction of a clearing house potentially provides a mechanism for the elimination of the dynamic inefficiency, depending on how the clearing house is operated. A contingent claims market can be supported if the clearing house compiles the net supply and demand of assets across all agents present in the economy at a point in time, and sets prices at time 0 so that net demand is zero in each state s^t and time period t.

In a contingent claims equilibrium, the old generation at time t holds claims $z(s_t, s_{t-1})$ purchased last period and the payments from the clearing house to the holder of the claims due this period equal

$$z(s_t, s_{t-1}).$$

The clearing house's receipts from selling contingent claims equal

$$\sum_{s_{t+1}} q(s_{t+1}, s_t) z(s_{t+1}, s_t).$$

If the clearing house adds the payments and receipts, so that

$$z(s_t, s_{t-1}) + \sum_{s_{t+1}} q(s_{t+1}, s_t) z(s_{t+1}, s_t) = 0,$$

then the transactions are feasible for the clearing house. Notice that in the first period,

$$\sum_{s_1} q(s_1) z(s_1, s_0) > 0$$

and this amount is transferred to the initial old generation, which is the beneficiary of the creation of the clearing house. The initial old generation issues liabilities which are covered by purchases of the initial young generation, and so on into the future. The initial old generation is never required to repay this liability, which is the source of increased welfare in the model because no subsequent generation is worse off.

Notice that the clearing house creates transfers that would not occur if all trades were bilateral. Specifically, an agent characterized by $(t, \hat{s}^t)$ would like to trade with agents of type $(t+1, \{\hat{s}^t, s'\}_{s' \in S})$. But any agent born in period $t+1$ is uninterested in the trade because real goods available in period t have no value to the agent *unless* they can be converted into goods in period $t+1$ or $t+2$. This is the role of the clearing house: to intermediate trades between agents of different generations. In the absence of a clearing house, or some durable asset such as money, there will be no trades arranged bilaterally between agents of different generations. In our discussion, we assume the existence of a clearing house but the transactions can be supported by other financial arrangements, a point developed in the problems at the end of the chapter.

In the next two sections, we examine a clearing house that uses two types of netting schemes:

- The first requires net trades between an agent born $(t, \hat{s}^t)$ to balance (sum of the trades net to zero) with trades of agents born in $t+1$ with $(\hat{s}^t, s')$ where $s' \in S$. This is the *conditional futures market.*
- In the second case, the sum of trades of any agent born in period t, so agents $t, \{\hat{s}^{t-1}, s_t\}$ where $s_t \in S$ must balance with the sum of trades of

agents $t+1, \{\hat{s}^{t-1}, s_t, s_{t+1}\}$ for $s_t, s_{t+1} \in S^2$. This is the *equal-treatment futures market*, where agents can purchase insurance against first-period endowment risk.

In the first setting, young agents are able to purchase state-contingent claims that insure against endowment risk in old age, but are unable to diversify away endowment risk when young. This corresponds to the case in Wright [450] where an agent is characterized not only by the time period t in which he is born but also by the history of the system, including the current realization s^t. In the second formulation, the clearing house allows trades that enable young agents to insure against endowment risk when young and old. Essentially any agent born at time t is treated as a single agent and is not differentiated by the state in which he is born. The two formulations will result in different budget constraints for the agent born in time t and different netting schemes for the clearing house.

Conditional futures market

Under this formulation, an agent is characterized by the date in which he is born in addition to the state s^t at time t. The timing is as follows: the aggregate shock is realized and then young agents are born. Hence any trading between young and old agents will be conditional on the history s^t. A young agent can insure against old-age endowment risk but has no opportunity to insure against first-period endowment risk.

Let $q_t(s^t)$ denote the time-0 contingent claim price of a unit of consumption delivered at time t in the event s^t occurs. The lifetime budget constraint of agent (t, s^t) is:

$$0 = q_t(s^t)[w^1(s_t) - c_t^t] + \sum_{s_{t+1}} q_{t+1}(s^{t+1})[w^2(s_{t+1}) - c_{t+1}^t], \qquad (17.34)$$

which holds for each history s^t. Agent (t, s^t) solves:

$$\max_{\{c_t^t, c_{t+1}^t\}} \left[U(c_t^t) + \sum_{s_{t+1}} \pi(s_{t+1} \mid s_t) V(c_{t+1}^t) \right]$$
$$+ \mu_t(s^t) \left[q_t(s^t)[w^1(s_t) - c_t^t] + \sum_{s_{t+1}} q_{t+1}(s^{t+1})[w^2(s_{t+1}) - c_{t+1}^t] \right],$$

where $\mu_t(s^t)$ is the Lagrange multiplier. The first-order conditions are:

$$U'(c_t^t) = \mu_t(s^t) q_t(s^t), \qquad (17.35)$$

$$\pi(s_{t+1} | s_t) V'(c_{t+1}^t) = \mu_t(s^t) q_{t+1}(s^{t+1}). \qquad (17.36)$$

Solve (17.35) and (17.36) for $\mu_t(s^t)$ and re-write

$$\frac{\pi(s_{t+1}|s_t)V'(c^t_{t+1})}{U'(c^t_t)} = \frac{q_{t+1}(s^{t+1})}{q_t(s^t)}. \tag{17.37}$$

A *stationary competitive equilibrium* is a pair of functions $c : S \to \Re^+$ and $c_2 : S \times S \to \Re^+$ such that $c^t_t = c(s_t)$ and $c^t_{t+1} = c_2(s_{t+1}, s_t)$, and a price function, described below. Under the assumption of stationarity in allocations, the budget constraint (17.34) can be summed over all histories s^{t-1}:

$$0 = [w^1(s_t) - c(s_t)] \sum_{s^{t-1}} q_t(s^t) + \sum_{s_{t+1}} [w^2(s_{t+1}) - c_2(s_{t+1}, s_t)] \sum_{s^{t-1}} q_{t+1}(s^{t+1}), \tag{17.38}$$

where the first term on the right side is a function of s_t only and the second term on the right side is a function of (s_{t+1}, s_t), regardless of s^{t-1}. Hence, the Lagrange multiplier $\mu_t(s^t)$ is now a function $\mu(s_t)$ of the current state only. Define

$$q(s_{t+1}, s_t) \equiv \frac{\sum_{s^{t-1}} q_{t+1}(s^{t+1})}{\sum_{s^{t-1}} q_t(s^t)}. \tag{17.39}$$

In this case, (17.37) can be expressed as:

$$\frac{\pi(s_{t+1}|s_t)V'(w(s_{t+1}) - c(s_{t+1}))}{U'(c(s_t))} = q(s_{t+1}, s_t), \tag{17.40}$$

where the goods market clearing condition

$$w(s_t) = c(s_t) + c_2(s_t, s_{t-1})$$

has been incorporated. Using the market-clearing conditions, note that $w^2(s_t) - c_2(s_t, s_{t-1}) = -(w^1(s_t) - c(s_t))$. Substitute this result and the expression for q into the budget constraint and re-write

$$U'(c(s_t))[w^1(s_t) - c(s_t)] = \sum_{s_{t+1}} \pi(s_{t+1}|s_t)V'(w(s_{t+1}) - c(s_{t+1}))[w^1(s_{t+1}) - c(s_{t+1})]. \tag{17.41}$$

This forms a system of n equations for each state s_j in n unknowns $c^e(s_j)$. Let c^e denote a solution. A proof of the existence and uniqueness is now sketched. Let $\mathcal{Q}$ denote the space of matrices $Q : S \times S \to \Re^{n\times n}_+$, with element Q an $n \times n$ matrix of strictly positive elements such that Q has a dominant root strictly less than one. Let $Q^0 \in \mathcal{Q}$ and define

$x(s) \equiv w^1(s) - c(s)$, which shows the amount saved by the young agent. Given Q°, find the solution x to:

$$x(s) = \sum_{s'} Q^{\circ}(s', s)x(s').$$

Let $x^1(s)$ denote the solution and define $q^1(s', s)$ as:

$$q^1(s', s) = \frac{\pi(s' \mid s)V'(w^2(s') + x^1(s'))}{U'(w^1(s) - x^1(s))}. \tag{17.42}$$

This new matrix Q^1 can be shown to be an element of $\mathcal{Q}$ and this establishes a mapping to determine the solution c^e.

Hence, a young agent picks current consumption and state-contingent old-age consumption such that the weighted marginal utilities are equal. The system above can be defined in matrix notation as:

$$\underline{0} = \left[\mathcal{U}(c^e) - \mathcal{V}^T(c^e)\right]x \tag{17.43}$$

where x is an $n \times 1$ matrix with i^{th} element $w^1(s_i) - c^e(s_i)$. Multiply both sides by $(\mathcal{U}(c^e))^{-1}$ and re-write to obtain:

$$\underline{0} = \left[I - Q(c^e)\right]x,$$

where $Q = (\mathcal{U}(c^e))^{-1}\mathcal{V}^T(c^e)$.

Observe that for the two type of agents alive at time t, the marginal rate of substitution between agents is:

$$\frac{V'(w(s_t) - c^e(s_t))}{U'(c^e(s_t))} = \frac{\mu(s_{t-1})}{\mu(s_t)}.^{2} \tag{17.44}$$

This fluctuates across states s_t, reflecting an agent's inability to insure against endowment risk when young. Observe that at time t, in state (s_t, s_{t-1}), the old generation has excess demand $q(s_t, s_{t-1})[c^2(s_t, s_{t-1}) - w^2(s_t)]$ and the young generation has excess supply $q(s_t, s_{t-1})[w^1(s_t) - c(s_t)]$. The two terms must sum to 0 and do when the goods market clears.

To show that this solution is Pareto optimal, observe the Pareto weight vector ϕ solves

$$\underline{0} = [I - (\mathcal{U})^{-1}(c^e)\mathcal{V}(c^e)]\phi,$$

which is identical to Equation (17.16) when $\beta = 1$.

[2] Notice that we pick the first-order conditions at time t for a young agent born at t and old agent born at $t-1$.

Equal-treatment futures market

In this section, the timing of the model is modified: at the beginning of period t, young agents are born and both young and old agents submit excess supplies and demands to the clearing house. Then the realization of the aggregate shock is observed by all agents. Let $\rho_t(s^t)$ denote the time 0 price of a unit of consumption at time t contingent on state s^t.

Muench [347] studies a futures market at time $t-1$ that allows agents born at time t to enter into contingent contracts to insure against endowment risk when young. The clearing house treats an agent born at time t with history s^{t-1}as a single agent, regardless of what the state s_t is at time t.

The budget constraint of an agent born at time t is now no longer balanced state by state but balanced when averaged across states, or:

$$0 = \sum_{s_t} \left[\rho_t(s_t, s^{t-1})[w^1(s_t) - c_t^t] + \sum_{s_{t+1}} \rho_{t+1}(s_{t+1}, s^t)[w^2(s_{t+1}) - c_{t+1}^t] \right] \tag{17.45}$$

for any history $s^{t-1} \in S^{t-1}$. A young agent born at time t solves:

$$\max_{\{c_t^t, c_{t+1}^t\}} \sum_{s_t \in S} \pi_t(s_t \mid s^{t-1}) \left[U(c_t^t) + \sum_{s_{t+1}} \pi(s_{t+1} \mid s_t) V(c_{t+1}^t) \right]$$
$$+ \mu_t(s^{t-1}) \sum_{s_t} \left[[w^1(s_t) - c_t^t]\rho_t(s^t) + \sum_{s_{t+1}} \rho_{t+1}(s^{t+1})[w^2(s_{t+1}) - c_{t+1}^t] \right]. \tag{17.46}$$

The first-order conditions are:

$$\pi_t(s_t|s^{t-1})U'(c_t^t) = \mu_t(s^{t-1})\rho_t(s^t), \tag{17.47}$$

$$\pi(s_{t+1}|s_t)\pi(s_t|s_{t-1})V'(c_{t+1}^t) = \mu_t(s^{t-1})\rho_{t+1}(s^{t+1}). \tag{17.48}$$

Solve for $\mu_t(s^{t-1})$ and rearrange:

$$\frac{\pi(s_{t+1}|s_t)V'(c_{t+1}^t)}{U'(c_t^t)} = \frac{\rho_{t+1}(s^{t+1})}{\rho_t(s^t)}. \tag{17.49}$$

To find the stationary solution in which a young agent buys full insurance against endowment risk when young and old, observe that the budget constraint can be expressed as:

$$0 = \sum_{s_t} \left\{ \sum_{s^{t-1}} \rho_t(s^t)[w^1(s_t) - c(s_t)] \right.$$

$$\left. + \sum_{s_{t+1}} \left[\sum_{s^{t-1}} \rho_{t+1}(s^{t+1})[w^2(s_{t+1}) - c_2(s_{t+1}, s_t)] \right] \right\} \tag{17.50}$$

so that $\mu_t = \mu_t(s^t)$ is constant across states s_t. Solve the first-order conditions for μ_t:

$$\mu_t = \frac{U'(c(s_t))\pi(s_t|s_{t-1})}{\sum_{s^{t-1}} \rho_t(s^t)}$$

$$= \frac{V'(c_2(s_{t+1}, s_t))\pi(s_{t+1}|s_t)\pi(s_t|s_{t-1})}{\sum_{s^{t-1}} \rho_{t+1}(s^{t+1})} \tag{17.51}$$

so that the weighted marginal utility of consumption is equalized for all states. Define

$$\rho(s_{t+1}, s_t) = \frac{\sum_{s^{t-1}} \rho_{t+1}(s^{t+1})}{\sum_{s^{t-1}} \rho_t(s^t)}.$$

Then (17.51) can be expressed as:

$$\frac{\pi(s_{t+1}|s_t)V'(w(s_{t+1}) - c(s_{t+1}))}{U'(c(s_t))} = \rho(s_{t+1}, s_t), \tag{17.52}$$

where the market-clearing condition has been incorporated.

For old and young agents in the market at time t, decrease the time subscript in (17.48) by one unit, substitute in the conditions for a stationary solution, solve for the price and use (17.47) to obtain:

$$\sum_{s^{t-1}} \rho_t(s^t) = \frac{U'(c(s_t)) \sum_{s^{t-1}} \pi_t(s^t)}{\mu_t}$$

$$= \frac{\sum_{s^{t-1}} \pi_t(s^t)V'(w(s_t) - c(s_t))}{\mu_{t-1}}, \tag{17.53}$$

which can be re-written as:

$$\frac{V'(w(s_t)) - c(s_t))}{U'(c(s_t))} = \frac{\mu_{t-1}}{\mu_t} = \beta, \tag{17.54}$$

since $\mu_{t-1} = \beta^{-1}\mu_t$ for all t. Let $c^f(s)$ denote the solution. Such a solution exists because the numerator is continuously increasing in c while the denominator is decreasing. As $c \rightarrow 0$ the left side tends to 0 while, as $c \rightarrow w$ the left side tends to ∞; hence a solution exists and is unique.

When $\beta = 1$, c^f is the *golden rule allocation*. As total endowment increases, c^f rises but by proportionately less.[3] The lifetime budget constraint is:

$$
\begin{aligned}
0 &= \sum_s \hat{\pi}(s)\Big[U'(c^f(s))[w^1(s) - c^f(s)] \\
&\quad - \sum_{s'} \pi(s', s) V'(w(s') - c^f(s'))[w^1(s') - c^f(s')]\Big] \\
&= \sum_s \hat{\pi}(s)\Big[U'(c^f(s))[w^1(s) - c^f(s)] \\
&\quad - \beta \sum_{s'} \pi(s', s) U'(c^f(s'))[w^1(s') - c^f(s')]\Big].
\end{aligned} \tag{17.55}
$$

In matrix notation, the solution is

$$
\begin{aligned}
0 &= \hat{\pi}^T \left[(\mathcal{U}(c^f) - \mathcal{V}(c^f))x^f\right] \\
&= \hat{\pi}^T \mathcal{U}(c^f)[I - (\mathcal{U}(c^f)^{-1}\mathcal{V}(c^f)]x^f,
\end{aligned} \tag{17.56}
$$

where $\hat{\pi}$ is an n dimensional vector of the unconditional probabilities and $\hat{\pi}^T$ is its transpose, $x^f(s_i) = w^1(s_i) - c^f(s_i)$ and x^f is the n dimensional vector. In state (s_t, s_{t-1}), the excess supply of the current young is $\rho(s_t)[w^1(s_t) - c^f(s_t)]$ and the excess demand from the current old generation is $\rho(s_t)[c^2(s_t, s_{t-1}) - w^2(s_t)]$. The two terms sum to zero when the goods market clears.

17.4. EQUITY PRICING IN A GROWING ECONOMY

While the contingent claims prices constructed in the previous section can be used to price any payment stream, it is instructive to derive an explicit equity pricing model with growth and a related capital asset-pricing model (CAPM). This model shares many of the features of the Lucas asset-pricing model that we studied in Chapter 8, and thus allows us to relate the results that we derive in this section to our earlier results.

As in the Lucas model, we assume the single consumption good is nonstorable, and there is no capital accumulation. Unlike the Lucas model, however, we assume that the consumption good is produced by combining

[3] Observe that

$$
\frac{\partial c}{\partial w} = \frac{V''}{\beta U'' + V''}
$$

which lies in the interval $(0, 1)$.

labor L and a fixed factor K according to a linearly homogeneous production function. There is a constant population of $2N$: N young and N old. Each young agent is endowed with one unit of labor which he supplies inelastically for a real wage. Let y_t denote output per unit of labor. Because labor is inelastically supplied, the labor force is fixed, and the capital stock is fixed, the capital-labor ratio is constant at $y_t = k$. More precisely,

$$y_t = L^{-1}A_tF(K,L) = A_tf(KL^{-1}) = A_tf(k), \qquad (17.57)$$

where $k \equiv K/L$ and A_t is a stochastic technology shifter. The production function f is assumed to be twice continuously differentiable, with $f'(\cdot) > 0, f''(\cdot) < 0, f(0) = 0$, and $f'(k) + f''(k)k > 0$.

We assume that there is neutral growth in technology; thus,

$$A_t = \theta_t A_{t-1},$$

where θ_t is the random growth in technology. We make the following assumption.

Assumption 17.3 *Assume that θ_t is a real-valued first-order Markov chain and let θ_t take values on $\Theta \equiv \{\underline{\theta}, \ldots, \bar{\theta}\}$ such that each $\theta \in \Theta$ is finite and strictly positive. Let $\pi(\theta'|\theta)$ be the transition function.*

The assumptions on the production technology imply that output per unit of labor evolves as

$$y_t = \theta_t y_{t-1}, \qquad (17.58)$$

where we have used the fact that

$$A_tf(k) = \theta_t A_{t-1}f(k) = \theta_t y_{t-1}.$$

Hence, θ_t, y_{t-1} summarize the state at time t. With a constant population, there is unbounded growth in output per worker. Define $\bar{y}_t = y_t(\bar{\theta})^{-t}$ for all t. The commodity space is the space of sequences with growth rates that are uniformly bounded. The sequence $\{\bar{y}_t\}$ is assumed to lie in the space of bounded sequences of real numbers normed by:

$$\|\{\bar{y}_t\}\| = \|\{y_t(\bar{\theta})^{-t}\}\| = \sup_t |y_t(\bar{\theta})^{-t}|.$$

Let the state space be $S = \Re^+ \times \Theta$.

The endowed factor has an outstanding equity share that is priced competitively each period in a stock market. An equity is a claim to a share of the income stream of the endowed factor. In the initial period, each member of the old generation holds one equity share. Under the assumptions that production is linearly homogeneous, labor is supplied inelastically, and firms are competitive, the production decision is straightforward. Also, using Euler's theorem on homogeneous functions, we have that:

$$A_t f(k) = A_t \left[k \frac{\partial F(K,L)}{\partial K} + \frac{\partial F(K,L)}{\partial L} \right]$$

$$\equiv w(\theta_t, y_{t-1}) + d(\theta_t, y_{t-1}),$$

where $w_t = w(\theta_t, y_{t-1})$ denotes the real wage, and $d_t = d(\theta_t, y_{t-1})$ dividend payments to owners of capital. The assumption that $f'(k) + f''(k)k > 0$ is made to ensure that payments to both capital and labor increase as output increases.

At the beginning of the period, θ_t is realized and observed by all agents. The young consumer at time t maximizes the expected value of a two-period, time-additive utility function (17.3) by deciding how much to consume and to save from his current wages.

Saving takes the form of buying z_t shares of the security from the current old generation at a price of q_t, so that the young consumer's consumption is:

$$c_t^t = w(\theta_t, y_{t-1}) - q_t^e z_t,$$

assuming that the constraint is binding. Consumption in the second period will depend on the dividends paid next period and the price at which the agent can sell his share in the stock market, namely,

$$c_t^{t-1} = [d(\theta_t, y_{t-1}) + q_t^e] z_{t-1}.$$

Substituting for c_t^t and c_t^{t+1}, the young agent chooses z_t to maximize:

$$U(w(\theta_t, y_{t-1}) - q_t^e z_t) + \beta \sum_{\theta_{t+1} \in \Theta} V(z_t[d(\theta_{t+1}, y_t) + q_{t+1}^e]) \pi(\theta_{t+1} | \theta_t).$$

The first-order condition is:

$$U'(w(\theta_t, y_{t-1}) - q_t^e z_t) q_t^e =$$

$$\beta \sum_{\Theta} \pi(\theta_{t+1} | \theta_t) V'(z_t[d(\theta_{t+1}, y_t) + q_{t+1}^e])[d(\theta_{t+1}, y_t) + q_{t+1}^e]. \qquad (17.59)$$

All agents observe θ_t, y_{t-1} and q_t^e and know the law of motion for y_t described in (17.58) and the distribution of the technology shock. There are two market-clearing conditions:

$$z_t = 1, \qquad (17.60)$$

$$c_t^t + c_t^{t-1} = y_t. \qquad (17.61)$$

Only equilibria that are stationary in the state variables will be considered so that the equilibrium price can be written as a fixed function $q_t^e = q^e(\theta_t, y_{t-1})$. All agents within a cohort are identical and this assumption, in addition to the assumed concavity of the utility function, implies that all young consumers will hold equal amounts of the security. In equilibrium, the security price just equals the saving of young consumers; this follows from the equilibrium conditions and the agent's first-period budget constraint. Hence, given the price function $q^e(\theta_t, y_{t-1})$, use the market-clearing conditions to define

$$c(\theta_t, y_{t-1}) = w(\theta_t, y_{t-1}) - q^e(\theta_t, y_{t-1}) \tag{17.62}$$

as the first-period consumption of a typical young agent at time t. Because $w(\theta_t, y_{t-1})$ is exogenous and always positive, notice that finding the function c is equivalent to finding the function for the equilibrium price of shares q^e. If a solution exists, it satisfies the equilibrium first-order condition:

$$U'(c(\theta_t, y_{t-1}))[w(\theta_t, y_{t-1}) - c(\theta_t, y_{t-1})] =$$

$$\beta \sum_{\Theta} \pi(\theta_{t+1}|\theta_t) V'(y(\theta_{t+1}, y_t) - c(\theta_{t+1}, y_t))[y(\theta_{t+1}, y_t) - c(\theta_{t+1}, y_t)].$$

We briefly describe an approach to construct the equilibrium. Let Q^0 denote an $n \times n$ matrix of strictly positive elements with a dominant root strictly less than one. Let $q_e(s)$ denote a feasible equity price function, specifically strictly positive such that consumption in (17.62) is strictly positive. A mapping can be established as:

$$q_e^1(\theta_t, y_{t-1}) = \beta \sum_{\theta'} \pi(\theta', \theta) Q^0(\theta', \theta)[d(\theta', y_t) + q_e^0(\theta_{t+1}, y_t)],$$

where $Q^0 = (U')^{-1} V'$. Notice that the law of motion for y_t is already determined ($y_t = \theta_t y_{t-1}$) and the dividend function is given. Define a new matrix Q^1 with element

$$\frac{\pi(\theta'|\theta) V'(d(\theta', y) + q_e^1(\theta', y))}{U'(w(\theta, y_{-1}) - q_e^1(\theta, y_{-1}))}. \tag{17.63}$$

This sets up a recursive structure that can be used to find a solution $q_e^1(\theta, y_{-1})$.

Next, we discuss the behavior of asset prices in an OLG model and contrast their behavior with the infinite-lived representative agent model.

17.4.1. Risk premia

We now study some of the model's implications for the asset-pricing relations. The risk premium is defined as the difference between rates of return on the risky security and a one-period bond which delivers a certain unit of the consumption good next period. Denote the return on the equity by:

$$R(\theta', \theta) \equiv \frac{q^e(\theta', y') + d(\theta', y')}{q(\theta, y)},$$

when the current state is θ, y and tomorrow's state is θ', y'. The dependence on y', y is suppressed for convenience below. Observe that $y' = \theta y$ so that there is no ambiguity by not making the functional dependence explicit.

Using this definition, the equilibrium first-order condition can be rewritten as:

$$\sum_{\Theta} R(\theta', \theta) \frac{\beta' V' \left(y(\theta', y) - c(\theta', y)\right)}{U' \left(c(\theta, y)\right)} \pi(\theta', \theta) = 1. \tag{17.64}$$

Recall:

$$m(\theta', \theta) \equiv \frac{\beta' V' \left(y(\theta', y') - c(\theta', y')\right)}{U'(c(\theta, y))}$$

is the IMRS for a young consumer when the current state is θ, y and tomorrow's state is θ', y'. A risk-free bond that is in zero net supply in this economy will have the price $E_\theta[m(\theta', \theta)]$ where E_θ denotes expectation conditional on the state θ. Let $r^f(\theta)$ be the return on the riskless bond, which is defined as:

$$r^f(\theta) \equiv \frac{1}{E_\theta[m(\theta', \theta)]}.$$

The conditional risk premium in the simple OLG model is:

$$E_\theta[R(\theta', \theta)] - r^f(\theta) = -r^f(\theta)\mathrm{Cov}_\theta[R(\theta', \theta), m(\theta', \theta)], \tag{17.65}$$

where we have re-written the expression for the risk premium using the equilibrium condition in equation (17.64) and noting that:

$$E_\theta\left[R(\theta', \theta) m(\theta', \theta)\right] =$$
$$E_\theta[R(\theta', \theta)] E_\theta[m(\theta', \theta)] + \mathrm{Cov}_\theta[R(\theta', \theta), m(\theta', \theta)].$$

The expression in (17.65) is very similar to our expression for the risk premium in the infinite-lived representative agent framework. The variability of the MRS in the OLG model depends on the curvature of the utility function, the variability of the output, and on the variability of the consumption of the young generation. It is the addition of this third feature – the changing proportion of output consumed by the young generation – that distinguishes the OLG model from the infinite-lived representative agent framework. Although output may be growing relatively smoothly over time, fluctuations in the proportion of output consumed by the young, which occur because young agents can save, permit greater fluctuations in the MRS. Although output is perishable, young agents can substitute away from random consumption tomorrow towards certain consumption today because they can vary their savings and hence the proportion of output they consume. The risk premium may be large in an

OLG model even with low values of relative risk aversion because young agents may demand a higher return on the risky asset to hold it willingly.

The equity-price behavior can be compared for the two models. When the state is (θ_t, y_{t-1}), the equity price in the OLG model can be expressed as:

$$q(\theta_t, y_{t-1}) = E_t[m(\theta_{t+1}, y_t, \theta_t, y_{t-1})(q(\theta_{t+1}, y_t) + d(\theta_{t+1}, y_t))]$$

$$= E_t\left[\sum_{j=1}^{\infty} d(\theta_{t+j}, y_{t+j-1}) \prod_{\tau=1}^{j} m(\theta_{t+\tau}, y_{t+\tau-1}, \theta_{t+\tau-1}, y_{t+\tau-2})\right]$$

by repeatedly substituting for $q(\theta_{t+1}, y_t)$. Notice that the discount rate depends on more than per capita consumption since it also depends on how output is divided between the young and old at two adjacent points in time over the entire horizon.

Now compare the equity price for the overlapping generations model with the equity price for the Lucas asset-pricing model. Let $y(\theta_t) = \theta_t y_{t-1}$ denote the exogenous and stochastic endowment process and assume that it is identical to the output process, per worker, of the overlapping generations model. Define $s_t = (\theta_t, y_{t-1})$. In a representative consumer model, the equity price is:

$$q(s_t) = E_t\left[\sum_{j=1}^{J} y(s_{t+j}) \prod_{\tau=1}^{j} \frac{\beta U'(y(s_{t+\tau}))}{U'(y(s_{t+\tau-1}))} + q(s_{t+J}) \prod_{\tau=1}^{J} \frac{\beta U'(y(s_{t+\tau}))}{U'(y(s_{t+\tau-1}))}\right]$$

$$= E_t\left[\sum_{j=1}^{\infty} y(s_{t+j}) \beta^j \frac{U'(y(s_{t+j}))}{U'(y(s_t))}\right].$$

In a Lucas model, current consumption always equals current output so that $\beta U'(y')/U'(y)$ changes only because $U'(y')$ changes as y' changes. But this involves only the curvature of the utility function, which also measures risk aversion. In this type of model, we can simply use aggregate consumption or per capita consumption to discount future values of dividends. The discount rate applied to a dividend received in period $t + j$ is just the intertemporal marginal rate of substitution between periods t and $t + j$. While the one-period discount rates for periods $t + 1$ through $t + j - 1$ cancel in the representative agent model, they do not cancel in the OLG model.

As we have discussed earlier, the behavior of the stochastic discount rate is the key to the behavior of the equity premium. The bounds on the equity premium for the OLG model are:

$$\left|\frac{r^f(\theta) - E_\theta[R(\theta', \theta)]}{S_\theta[R(\theta', \theta)]}\right| \leq \frac{S_\theta[m(\theta', \theta)]}{E_\theta[m(\theta', \theta)]} \tag{17.66}$$

where S_θ is the conditional standard deviation. We will determine these bounds for a parametric example.

Example 17.1 Let two-period preferences be defined as:

$$U(c_t^t) + E(V(c_{t+1}^t)) = \ln(b + c_t^t) + \beta E[\ln(b + c_{t+1}^t)],$$

where $0 < \beta < 1$. Notice that $b + c > 0$ must hold for preferences to be well defined. These preferences allow decreasing, increasing, or constant relative risk aversion, depending on the value of b. Define the coefficient of relative risk aversion as $\ell(c) = -U''(c)c/U'(c)$, and notice that:

- $\ell'(c) > 0$ and $\ell(c) < 1$ if $b > 0$,
- $\ell'(c) = 0$ and $\ell(c) = 1$ if $b = 0$, and
- $\ell'(c) < 0$ and $\ell(c) > 1$ if $b < 0$.

Also, $\lim_{c\to\infty}[\ln(b+c) - \ln c] = 0$, so in a growing economy, we approach the case of constant and unitary relative risk aversion.

Recall that the state of the economy is summarized by $s_t = (\theta_t, y_{t-1})$. The equilibrium first-order conditions are:

$$\frac{q^e(\theta_t, y_{t-1})}{b + c(\theta_t, y_{t-1})} = \beta E_t\left[\frac{\theta_{t+1}y_t - c(\theta_{t+1}, y_t)}{b + \theta_{t+1}y_t - c(\theta_{t+1}, y_t)}\right]. \tag{17.67}$$

Define the function J as

$$J(\theta, y) = \frac{\theta y - c(\theta, y)}{b + \theta y - c(\theta, y)}.$$

The equity price is then written as:

$$q^e(\theta_t, y_{t-1}) = \beta E_t[J(\theta_{t+1}, y_t)(b + c(\theta_t, y_{t-1}))].$$

Substituting for $c(\theta_t, y_{t-1}) = w(\theta_t, y_{t-1}) - q^e(\theta_t, y_{t-1})$, we have:

$$q^e(\theta_t, y_{t-1}) = \beta E_t[J(\theta_{t+1}, y_t)(b + w(\theta_t, y_{t-1}) - q^e(\theta_t, y_{t-1}))],$$

and solving for q^e, we have

$$q^e(\theta_t, y_{t-1}) = \frac{(b + w(\theta_t, y_{t-1}))\beta E_t[J(\theta_{t+1}, y_t)]}{1 + \beta E_t[J(\theta_{t+1}, y_t)]}. \tag{17.68}$$

Suppose the production function is Cobb-Douglas with share of labor defined by $1-\alpha$ and share of capital defined by α. Then, $w(\theta_t, y_{t-1}) = (1-\alpha)\theta_t y_{t-1}$ and $d(\theta_t, y_{t-1}) = \alpha\theta_t y_{t-1}$. Also assume that the technology shock θ_t is i.i.d. and define $y_t = y$ where $y_t = \theta_t y_{t-1}$. Then the price becomes:

$$q^e(y) = \frac{(b + (1-\alpha)y)\beta E[J(y')]}{1 + \beta E[J(y')]}. \tag{17.69}$$

Notice that θ_t is no longer a state variable although $y_t = \theta_t y_{t-1}$ is. Some other properties for the i.i.d. case follow.

(i) For $b = 0$,

$$q(y) = \beta \frac{(1-\alpha)y}{(1+\beta)} = w(y) - c(y), \tag{17.70}$$

which equals the savings of the young.

(ii) For $b \neq 0$,

$$E[J(y')] = E\left[\frac{y' - c(y')}{b + y' - c(y')}\right], \tag{17.71}$$

where y' is next period's output.

Notice that $E[J(y')]$ is equal to a constant which is less than or greater than one depending on the value of b.

What is the conditional risk premium in this model when $b = 0$ and the technology shock is i.i.d.? Evaluating the expressions for $R(y', y)$ and $r^f(y)$, and substituting for current and future consumption, dividends and the equity price, we have:

$$E[R(y', y)] - r^f(y) = E\left[\frac{d(y') + q(y')}{q(y)}\right] - \left[E\left(\frac{\beta c(y)}{y' - c(y')}\right)\right]^{-1}$$

$$= E\left[\frac{\alpha y' + \beta(1-\alpha)y'/(1+\beta)}{\beta \alpha y/(1+\beta)}\right] - \frac{1}{\beta} E\left[\frac{(1-\alpha)y/(1+\beta)}{y' - (1-\alpha)y'/(1+\beta)}\right]^{-1}$$

$$= \frac{\alpha + \beta}{\beta(1-\alpha)}\left[E(y'/y) - E(y/y')^{-1}\right] \tag{17.72}$$

which is positive using Jensen's inequality. Notice that the conditional risk premium falls as $(1-\alpha)$, β, or y increase.

17.5. CAPITAL ACCUMULATION AND SOCIAL SECURITY

Dynamic efficiency is an important issue in capital asset pricing, capital accumulation, and economic growth. We end this chapter with a discussion of a model of capital accumulation and social security. As noted earlier, dynamic inefficiency is the result of a double infinity of agents and time periods. In a pure endowment model with no uncertainty, dynamic inefficiency can arise if there is no durable asset or clearing house to intermediate borrowing and lending between different generations. In a stochastic pure endowment economy, the dynamic inefficiency can arise because of insufficient risk sharing and is the result of the distribution of the stochastic income across heterogeneous agents at a point in time.

In this final section, we allow young agents to save by accumulating capital. Dynamic inefficiency in a model of capital accumulation can occur if there is an overaccumulation of capital, which occurs when an economy has a population growth that exceeds the steady state marginal product of capital or equivalently the economy is consistently investing more than it is earning in profit. The question of whether an economy is dynamically inefficient is important in answering questions about the appropriate fiscal policy, in particular social security. Important references in this are the papers by Diamond [152], Bertocchi [59], Bertocchi and Kehagias [60], and Abel *et al.* [7].

The assessment of the dynamic efficiency of the economy is typically based on estimates of the marginal productivity of capital based on observed accounting profit rates. Since the population rate of growth appears to be less than the steady-state marginal product of capital, it would seem that the US economy is dynamically efficient. As Abel *et al.* [7] comment, an alternative and equally plausible way to judge dynamic efficiency is to look at the safe real interest rate, such as the return to Treasury bills. This return can be measured accurately and the data suggests that the real interest rate on safe assets is less than economic growth rates. By this measure, the US economy might be judged as dynamically inefficient. To reconcile these two approaches, it is necessary to introduce uncertainty and use explicit models in which profitability, the value of capital and the growth rates are uncertain. This implies that there is a distinction between the marginal productivity of capital and the interest rate on safe government securities. In such models, an economy is said to be dynamically efficient if it invests less than the return to capital. In a competitive economy, the issue of dynamic efficiency can be solved by comparing the level of investment with the cash flows generated by production after the payments of wages. This is referred to as the "net cash flow" criterion.

In this section we discuss simple models of social security and standard dynamic inefficiency. Our discussion is based on Abel *et al.* [7] and Bertocchi [59], which are stochastic versions of Diamond [152]. The model is similar in structure to the model with a fixed resource but differs in two important ways. First the population is growing at rate n so that

$$N_{t+1} = (1 + n)N_t.$$

Second, the level of the capital stock depends on the level of investment in the previous period. Capital is assumed to depreciate 100% each period so that the capital accumulation equation is

$$K_{t+1} = I_t,$$

where I_t is investment.

Young households supply labor inelastically so that the labor supply at time t is N_t, the number of young agents. We continue to assume that the production function displays constant returns to scale so that

$$Y_t = A_t F(K_t, N_t) = A_t K_t^{\alpha} N_t^{1-\alpha},$$

where $0 < \alpha < 1$. Output can be expressed as per worker

$$y_t = A_t k_t^{\alpha}$$

where $y_t = Y_t/N_t$ and $k_t = K_t/N_t$. The resource constraint is

$$Y_t = N_{t-1}c_t^{t-1} + N_t c_t^t + K_{t+1}, \tag{17.73}$$

which is converted to per worker as

$$y_t = \frac{c_t^{t-1}}{1+n} + c_t^t + k_{t+1}(1+n).$$

For simplicity, we make the following assumption on technology shocks.

Assumption 17.4 *The technology shock A_t is a first-order Markov chain that is stationary in levels. Let $A_t \in A \equiv \{\underline{a}_1, \ldots, \underline{a}_n\}$ with transition probabilities $\pi(a'|a)$. Let $a^t = \{a_1, \ldots, a_t\}$ denote the history of technology shocks up to time t and let K_0 denote the initial capital endowment.*

Young households own one unit of labor, which they supply inelastically. The wage in the competitive labor market is equal to labor's marginal product:

$$w_t = (1-\alpha)a_t k_t^{\alpha},$$

which is expressed per worker.

Households own stocks in competitive firms and firms own the capital stock. Let Q_t^e denote the time t price of an equity share. Each period their equity shares satisfy

$$1 = N_t z_t. \tag{17.74}$$

A young agent has a unit labor endowment when young and provides for second period consumption by purchasing equity shares in firms. His budget constraints are

$$w_t n_t^s = c_t^t + Q_t^e z_t \quad (1^{st} \textit{ period}) \tag{17.75}$$

$$c_{t+1}^t = z_t[Q_{t+1}^e + D_{t+1}] \quad (2^{nd} \textit{ period}), \tag{17.76}$$

where D_{t+1} denotes the dividend paid in period $t+1$. Since labor causes no disutility, observe that $n_t^s = 1$ for all t.

Solve the first period budget constraint for c_t^t and multiply by N_t to show that

$$N_t c_t^t = N_t w_t - N_t z_t Q_t^e = N_t w_t - Q_t^e,$$

using (17.74). Decrease the time subscripts in (17.76) by one and multiply by N_{t-1} to obtain

$$N_{t-1}c_t^{t-1} = N_{t-1}z_{t-1}[Q_t^e + D_t] = Q_t^e + D_t,$$

again using (17.74). Substitute these equations into the resource constraint:

$$\begin{aligned} Y_t &= N_{t-1}c_t^{t-1} + N_t c_t^t + I_t \\ &= Q_t^e + D_t + N_t w_t - Q_t^e + I_t \quad (17.77) \\ &= D_t + N_t w_t + K_{t+1}, \quad (17.78) \end{aligned}$$

or re-writing

$$Y_t - N_t w_t = \alpha Y_t = D_t + K_{t+1}, \quad (17.79)$$

so that the dividend is

$$D_t = \alpha Y_t - K_{t+1}.$$

The dividend measures the flow of funds from firms to households, net of labor income. Notice that the dividend is defined as the return to capital minus the investment. A *repurchase of shares* by firms is a dividend payment while a *new equity issue* is a negative dividend.

Let μ_t^t denote the Lagrange multiplier for the first-period budget constraint. The first-order conditions with respect to c_t^t, z_t are

$$U'(c_t^t) = \mu_t^t, \quad (17.80)$$

$$\mu_t^t Q_t^e = E_t \left\{ V'(c_{t+1}^t)[Q_{t+1}^e + D_{t+1}] \right\}. \quad (17.81)$$

Observe that

$$\begin{aligned} N_t c_{t+1}^t &= N_t z_t [Q_{t+1}^e + D_{t+1}] \\ &= Y_{t+1} - N_{t+1} c_{t+1}^{t+1} - K_{t+2}. \end{aligned}$$

Use the first-order conditions to eliminate μ_t^t, multiply both sides of the equation by $z_t = 1/N_t$, and re-write to obtain

$$U'(c_t^t)\frac{Q_t^e}{N_t} = E_t \left\{ V'(c_{t+1}^t)\frac{N_{t+1}}{N_t}\left[\frac{Q_{t+1}^e}{N_{t+1}} + \frac{D_{t+1}}{N_{t+1}}\right]\right\}. \quad (17.82)$$

Let $q_t^e \equiv Q_t^e/N_t$ and $d_t \equiv D_t/N_t$ so that this equation can be written as

$$\begin{aligned} q_t^e &= E_t \left\{ (1+n)\frac{V'(c_{t+1}^t)}{U'(c_t^t)}[q_{t+1}^e + d_{t+1}] \right\} \\ &= E_t \left\{ \sum_{j=1}^{\infty} (1+n)^j \prod_{i=1}^{j} \mathcal{M}_{t+i} d_{t+j} \right\}, \quad (17.83) \end{aligned}$$

where

$$\mathcal{M}_{t+i} \equiv \frac{V'(c_{t+i+1}^t)}{U'(c_{t+i}^t)} \quad \text{for all } i.$$

Thus, the ex-dividend stock price or equivalently, the ex-dividend value of the firm, per worker, is equal to the expected discounted present value of the future dividend stream per worker. Clearly the conditions for an allocation to be dynamically efficient are linked with the conditions for convergence of the right-side of this equation. This point is discussed further below.

The financial structure of a firm has already been studied in Chapter 10. In this application, since capital depreciates completely each period and we assume only equities are issued, the firm's maximization problem is to choose next period's capital stock to maximize net present value. Following the approach in Section 10.4 of Chapter 10, define the net cash flow (NCF) of the firm as gross profits minus investment:

$$NCF_t = Y_t - N_t w_t - K_{t+1}.$$

Since the firm issues only new equity, this quantity must also equal dividend payments plus new share issues:

$$NCF_t = D_t z_t + Q_t^e(z_t - z_{t+1}).$$

Now the ex-dividend value of the firm is:

$$\begin{aligned} W_t^e &= Q_t^e z_{t+1} \\ &= E_t\left\{\mathcal{M}_{t+1}(Q_{t+1}^e + D_{t+1})z_{t+1}\right\} \\ &= E_t\left\{\mathcal{M}_{t+1}[(Q_{t+1}^e + D_{t+1})z_{t+1} + Q_{t+1}^e z_{t+2} - Q_{t+1}^e z_{t+2}]\right\} \\ &= E_t\left\{\mathcal{M}_{t+1}[W_{t+1}^e + NCF_{t+1}]\right\}, \end{aligned}$$

where we have obtained the second line from the consumer's first-order condition, and the last line from the definitions of ex-dividend value and NCF. We can iterate this equation forward and solve for the ex-dividend value of the firm as the expected, discounted sum of future net cash flows. The firm's value is the sum of current net cash flow and the ex-dividend value:

$$W_t = NCF_t + E_t\left\{\sum_{i=1}^{\infty}\prod_{j=1}^{i}\mathcal{M}_{t+j}W_{t+i}^e\right\}. \tag{17.84}$$

We can set up a recursive formulation of this problem and maximizing the resulting Bellman equation with respect to investment or the future capital stock K_{t+1}. The first-order condition for this problem with the envelope condition substituted in is:

$$\begin{aligned} 1 &= E_t\left\{\mathcal{M}_{t+1}\alpha a_{t+1}K_{t+1}^{\alpha-1}N_{t+1}^{1-\alpha}\right\} \\ &= E_t\left\{\mathcal{M}_{t+1}\alpha a_{t+1}k_{t+1}^{\alpha-1}\right\}. \end{aligned}$$

The consumer's first-period budget constraint implies that $q_t^e = w_t - c_t^t$ while the second-period budget constraint and resource constraint imply that $q^e_{t+1} + d_{t+1} = y_{t+1} - c^{t+1}_{t+1} - (1+n)k_{t+2}$. Making these substitutions, the equilibrium first-order conditions are

$$U_1(c^t_t)[w_t - c^t_t] = E_t\left\{(1+n)V_1(c^t_{t+1})[y_{t+1} - c^{t+1}_{t+1} - (1+n)k_{t+2}]\right\}$$

$$U_1(c^t_t) = E_t\left\{V_1(c^t_{t+1})\alpha a_{t+1}k^{\alpha-1}_{t+1}\right\}.$$

Define the functions $d : A \times Y \to \Re$, $c : A \times Y \to \Re_+$, and $k : A \times Y \to \Re_+$ such that $d_t \equiv d(a_t, y_t) = \alpha y_t - k_{t+1}(1+n)$, $c^t_t \equiv c(a_t, y_t)$, and $k_{t+1} \equiv k(a_t, y_t)$, where $y_t = a_t k^\alpha_t$. Notice that the possibility that $d < 0$ is incorporated. Also if d is given then, given y, the capital stock per worker is also determined. Then in equilibrium

$$U'(c(a,y))[(1-\alpha)y - c(a,y)] =$$

$$E_a\left\{(1+n)V'(y' - c(a',y') + d(a',y'))[(1-\alpha)y' - c(a',y') + d(a',y')]\right\}, \tag{17.85}$$

$$U'(c(a,y)) = E_a\left\{V'(y' - c(a',y') + d(a',y'))\alpha a'(k(a,y))^{\alpha-1}\right\}, \tag{17.86}$$

$$y' = a'(k(a,y))^\alpha. \tag{17.87}$$

Given a dividend function d, (17.85) is a functional equation in the unknown function c, which can be solved using the methods described in the first section (since given d this is an endowment economy from the point of view of the young household). Given the consumption function, the function k solving (17.87) can be determined. This establishes a new dividend function to be used in the functional equation (17.85).

Abel *et al.* [7] do not focus on the existence and uniqueness of the competitive equilibrium, which require the techniques discussed in Chapter 17 of Stokey, Lucas with Prescott [418]. Instead, they write down the central planning problem and derive restrictions on the planning weights and the allocation to determine if an allocation is dynamically efficient. Let ϕ_0 and $\phi_t(a^t)$ denote Pareto weights, whose dependence on the initial capital stock is suppressed. The central planning problem is to choose $\{c^0_1, c^t_t, c^t_{t+1}, K_{t+1}\}$ to maximize

$$\sum_{a_1} \phi_0 \pi(a_1 \mid a_0) V(c^0_1)$$

$$+\sum_{t=1}^{\infty}\sum_{a^t \in A^t}\left[\phi_t(a^t)\left(U(c^t_t) + \sum_{s_{t+1}} \pi(a_{t+1}, a_t)V(c^t_{t+1})\right)\right.$$

$$\left. + \lambda_t(a^t)[a_t(K_t)^\alpha(N_t)^{1-\alpha} - N_t c^t_t - N_{t-1}c^{t-1}_t - K_{t+1}]\right], \tag{17.88}$$

where $\lambda_t(a^t)$ is the Lagrange multiplier on the resource constraint at time t.

The first-order conditions with respect to $\{c_1^0, c_t^t, c_{t+1}^t, K_{t+1}\}$ are

$$\phi_0 \pi(a_1 \mid a_0) V'(c_1^0); = \lambda_1(a^1, K_0) N_0, \tag{17.89}$$

$$\phi_t(a^t) U'(c_t^t) = \lambda_t(a^t) N_t, \tag{17.90}$$

$$\phi_t(a^t) \pi(a_{t+1} \mid a_t) V'(c_{t+1}^t) = \lambda_{t+1}(a^{t+1}) N_t, \tag{17.91}$$

$$\lambda_t(a^t) = \sum_{a_{t+1}} \lambda_{t+1}(a^{t+1}) a_{t+1} \alpha K_{t+1}^{\alpha-1} N_{t+1}^{1-\alpha}. \tag{17.92}$$

The first-order conditions can be simplified as

$$U'(c_t^t) = \sum_{a_{t+1}} \pi(a_{t+1} \mid a^t) V'(c_{t+1}^t) \alpha a_{t+1} \left(\frac{K_{t+1}}{N_{t+1}}\right)^{\alpha-1}. \tag{17.93}$$

The transversality condition is

$$\lim_{t\to\infty} \sum_{a^t} \lambda_t(a^{t+1}) a_{t+1} \alpha K_{t+1}^{\alpha-1} N_{t+1}^{1-\alpha} K_{t+1} = 0. \tag{17.94}$$

They show that, for a given allocation satisfying feasibility, a set of Pareto weights and Lagrange multipliers can be found that satisfy the first-order conditions and the resource constraint. The principal result of their paper, and the result on which we wish to focus, is the following.

Proposition 17.1 *If $\frac{d_t}{q_t} \geq \epsilon > 0$ in all periods and all states of nature, then the equilibrium is dynamically efficient. If $\frac{d_t}{q_t} \leq -\epsilon < 0$ in all periods and all states of nature, then the equilibrium is dynamically inefficient.*

The proof of the proposition is contained in the appendix of their paper. We outline only some of the critical aspects of the argument here. To establish efficiency, they show that the Lagrange multiplier for the resource constraint must satisfy a transversality condition, just as we saw in our discussion of the pure endowment economy of optimal risk sharing. To determine if a particular competitive equilibrium is dynamically efficient, the allocation is taken as given and the issue is whether Pareto weights and Lagrange multipliers that satisfy the first-order conditions and the transversality condition can be found. If there is a set of weights and Lagrange multipliers satisfying the conditions of the proposition, then the competitive equilibrium allocation is dynamically efficient. They then show that if the conditions of the proposition are not satisfied, a transfer of resources such that some agent is better off while no one else is worse off can be found. If the dividend/price process satisfies $\frac{d_t}{q_t} \leq -\epsilon < 0$, then such a transfer can be made, establishing dynamic inefficiency.

Abel *et al.* define

$$G_{t+1} = \frac{Q_{t+1}}{Q_t}$$

as the growth rate of the value of the portfolio. The market rate of return is

$$R_t^M = \frac{Q_{t+1} + D_{t+1}}{Q_t}.$$

Their second proposition is stated next.

Proposition 17.2 *If there is some asset with rate of return R_t such that $\frac{R_t}{G_t} \geq 1 + \epsilon > 1$ in all periods and all states of nature, then the equilibrium is dynamically efficient. If there is some asset with rate of return R_t such that $\frac{R_t}{G_t} \leq 1 - \epsilon < 1$ in all periods and all states, then the equilibrium is dynamically inefficient.*

The result is applied to the risk-free rate: if the risk-free rate is always greater than the growth rate of the market value of the capital stock, then the economy is dynamically efficient. The implication is that comparisons of the risk-free rate with the average growth rate are not sufficient to establish dynamic efficiency.

17.5.1. Social security

The issue of dynamic efficiency is of more importance than just academic interest. It helps us put into context discussions about optimal fiscal policy, in particular social security. Whether social security is welfare-improving depends on whether or not the economy is dynamically efficient. If it is dynamically inefficient then transfers in the form of social security may be welfare-improving. Another important issue is whether the government needs to play a role in eliminating dynamic inefficiency and, if the answer is yes, what that role should be. We have seen in the case of dynamic inefficiency because of inefficient risk sharing that the creation of a clearing house, or equivalently a durable asset such as money or bonds, will remove the inefficiency. While conditional Pareto-optimal allocations can be achieved through the creation of the durable asset, equal-treatment Pareto-optimal allocations cannot if trading occurs after the current state is realized.

These issues have been considered by a variety of authors. Demange and Laroque [147] characterize the sufficient conditions for interim optimality in the equilibrium of an overlapping generations economy under productivity and demographic shocks. They define *interim optimality* of an allocation as a situation where there does not exist another feasible allocation that gives larger expected utility at birth to current living young and old generations and to all the agents who will be born in the future. They then show the relation between *interim optimality* and *conditional Pareto optimality*. Following that they study the rational expectations equilibrium with and without financial assets to characterize the optimality properties of the equilibria. As a result, regarding the rational expectations equilibrium they confirm the two Welfare Theorems.

Demange [146] studies the optimality properties of an economy with finitely lived agents under interim optimality and ex-ante optimality. Actually she gives a common optimality definition that includes both interim and ex-ante optimality. Interim optimality is as defined above. *Ex-ante optimality* differs from interim optimality in the sense that the date at which the expected utility of agents is calculated is no longer the date of birth but the initial date that the economy starts. The key necessary condition is short-run optimality for the optimality of the economy. Hence, *short-run interim (ex-ante) optimality* is a necessary condition for interim (ex-ante) optimality of the economy. *Short-run optimality* is defined as a condition in which it is not possible to make some agents born before a given date t better off without making others worse off. After giving some characterizations for the optimality of this economy, Demange continues with optimality properties of rational expectations equilibrium under sequentially complete and incomplete markets. Under incomplete markets she studies the optimality of rational expectations equilibrium with productive land and with social security. With productive land she concludes that any equilibrium allocation is interim optimal and with social security there may still be room for Pareto improvement. Krueger and Kubler [291] give an example of an economy with incomplete markets where introduction of a social security system is Pareto-improving in the interim optimality sense.

A literature has also developed that uses in the overlapping generations in computational experiments. A survey of computational social security models is provided by İmrohoroğlu, İmrohoroğlu, and Joines [260]. In this study, they develop a general framework for modeling an unfunded (pay-as-you-go) social security system and describe several of the more important computational models of social security. Another venue of research regarding social security involves the relation of social security models with political economy considerations. In a recent survey, Galasso and Profeta [193] establish the reasons for the existence of social security programs and the interaction between social security systems and other redistributive programs under different multi-dimensional voting models. Moreover, they review the literature studying the relation between political sustainability and social security.

17.6. CONCLUSIONS

In this chapter, we have analyzed issues of dynamic inefficiency and discussed alternative arrangements for implementing Pareto-optimal allocations in the stochastic overlapping generations model. We have also discussed the impact of capital accumulation on the issue of dynamic inefficiency. Finally, we have explored some of the implications of the model for asset pricing. The literature that uses the overlapping generations model as a framework of analysis for optimal monetary and fiscal policy, social security, intergenerational risk sharing, models with human capital, and education, to name a few, is too vast to be summarized here. Nevertheless, the framework that we developed here can be adapted to study such other substantive problems of interest.

17.7. EXERCISES

1. This problem uses the stochastic pure endowment economy that is stationary in levels and has a constant population. Assume that instead of contingent claims, the government gives a fixed amount of fiat currency M_0 to each initial old agent. The nominal price of the consumption good is $p(s)$ where s is the state.
   (a) Derive the budget constraints for a young agent and then solve the agent's maximization problem.
   (b) Derive the equilibrium conditions. What is the equation for the equilibrium price process, assuming that prices are stationary?
   (c) Compare the allocation with that of the asset-pricing model in the first section. Can the monetary equilibrium achieve the conditional Pareto-optimal allocation? Can the fixed money supply obtain the equal-treatment Pareto-optimal allocation?
   (d) Use the same setup as the first part of this question but now assume that the money supply process is stochastic. Specifically, assume that money is a function $M : S \to \Re^+$. For an arbitrary money supply rule, determine the equilibrium price process. Will the allocations be conditional Pareto optimal?
2. In the section on capital accumulation, we assumed that firms owned capital and that households own equity shares in the firm. Now assume that households directly own the capital stock and rent the capital to firms which combine labor and capital to produce the consumption good. If holding capital is the only way for young agents to save, then the budget constraints facing a young agent are

$$w_t = c_t^t + \frac{I_t}{N_t} \tag{17.95}$$

$$c_{t+1}^t = R_{t+1}\frac{I_t}{N_t} \tag{17.96}$$

where R_{t+1} is the rental rate paid to capital in period $t+1$. The rental rate on capital is its marginal product

$$R_{t+1} = a_{t+1}\alpha K_{t+1}^{\alpha-1} N_{t+1}^{1-\alpha}$$

Observe that $K_{t+1} = I_t$.

(a) Derive the first-order conditions.

(b) Observe that there are no direct exchanges between young and old households, unlike the equity model where young households buy equity shares from old households. Will the consumption allocations and capital accumulation be identical in the two versions of the model?

3. Social Security

Assume there is no growth in population or technology. Also assume that there is no depreciation. Young agents born at time t are endowed with one unit of labor that they supply for a wage rate w_t. Factors are paid their marginal product. The production function displays constant returns to scale.

Young households care about leisure. Old agents receive no endowment and must save to provide for old-age consumption. Agents born at time t solve the following problem:

$$\max_{\{c_{1,t}, c_{2,t+1}, n_t\}} \left[a \ln c_{1,t} + b \ln(1 - n_t) + \beta a \ln c_{2,t+1}\right] \tag{17.97}$$

subject to

$$c_{1,t} + \frac{1}{r_{t+1}}[c_{2,t+1} - S_{t+1}] = w_t n_t (1 - \tau) \tag{17.98}$$

where $0 < \tau < 1$ is a labor income tax that is constant over time, w_t is wage rate, and S_{t+1} is a social security payment to old agents at time $t+1$. All savings is invested in capital and r_t denotes the return to capital k_t, equal to the marginal product of capital. Also $0 < \beta < 1$ and a and b are fixed preference parameters.

(a) Derive the first-order conditions. Use the first-order conditions to express $c_{2,t+1}$ as a function of $c_{1,t}$ and r_{t+1}. Use the same conditions to express n_t as a function of w_t and $c_{1,t}$.

(b) Substitute your answers from part (a) into the budget constraint. Use the result to explain how savings is determined.

(c) Consider two systems:

- Pay-as-you-go system: under this system,

  $$S_t = \tau w_t n_t$$

  so that the tax revenue is not invested in next period's capital stock. Determine the steady state capital stock.
- Fully funded system: under this system, $\tau w_t n_t$ is invested in the capital stock. Determine the steady state capital stock.

(d) Discuss how the distortionary income tax affects the steady state capital stock under the two payment schemes.

4. Brouwer Fixed Point Theorem
Assume that output is stationary in levels and that it is i.i.d. over time. Then the equilibrium consumption of the young satisfies

$$U'(c(y))(w(y) - c(y)) = \beta \int_Y V'(g(y') - c(y'))(g(y') - c(y'))dF(y').$$

Define $h(y, c) = U'(c)(w(y) - c)$. Notice that

$$h_c(y, c) = U''(c)(w(y) - c) - U'(c) < 0.$$

Assume that U is twice continuously differentiable. Given a solution $\tilde{c}(y')$, notice that the right side of the first-order condition does not depend on the current realization y, or

$$K = \beta \int_Y V'(g(y') - \tilde{c}(y'))(g(y') - \tilde{c}(y'))dF(y').$$

Given a value $0 \leq H \leq \infty$, define $c(y, H)$ as the consumption satisfying

$$U'(c(y, H))[w(y) - c(y, H)] = H.$$

The properties described in Assumption 17.1 are assumed to hold. Notice that $c(y, H) = w(y)$ and that as $H \to \infty$, $c(y, H)$ tends to 0. Hence, $c : Y \times H \to [0, w(y)]$. Let $\mathcal{C}(Y)$ denote the set of functions c such that $\{c : Y \times \Re^+ \to [0, w(y)]\}$. Consider the following mapping.

$$K = TK = \beta \int_Y V'(g(y') - c(y', K))(g(y') - c(y', K))dF(y'). \quad (17.99)$$

Use the Brouwer Fixed Point Theorem to show that there exists a unique solution K.

5. This problem is taken from Cooley and Salyer [125].
Consider an economy in which two goods, housing services and a consumption good, are produced by constant return technologies. The output of each industry is a function of a fixed specific factor and shiftable capital. The aggregate quantity of capital is fixed at K. Let x and h denote the quantity of consumption goods and housing services produced in the two sectors. Given the production technologies, we can solve for the capital requirement functions in the two sectors as

$$K^x = f(x), \quad \text{and} \quad K^h = g(h),$$

where $f_x, g_h > 0$, and $f_{xx}, g_{hh} > 0$.

In this model, we assume that corporate assets are taxed, but not housing assets. Suppose there two tax states, $s = 0, \tau$, and let $T(s)$ denote the tax rate in those states.

Firms' problems

Firms in each industry maximize

$$\pi^x(s) = \max_x \left\{ x(s) - [1 + T(s)]r(s)f(x(s)) \right\},$$

and

$$\pi^h(s) = \max_h \left\{ R(s)h(s) - r(s)g(h(s)) \right\},$$

where r is the capital rental rate and R is the price of housing services, or its rental rate.

The consumer's problem

The representative consumer derives utility from both housing services and consumption goods, and has preferences given by

$$E_0 \left\{ \sum_{t=0}^{\infty} \beta^t U(x_t, h_t) \right\},$$

where $0 < \beta < 1$, U is a strictly increasing, concave, twice differentiable function, and x and h are both normal goods. In each period, the individual chooses consumption of the background good, housing services, and the purchase of securities. The consumer's budget constraints can be written as

$$x(s) + R(s)h(s) + p^x(s)z^x(s) + p^h(s)z^h(s) \leq w(s),$$

where $w(s)$ denotes the agent's wealth at the beginning of the period, p^x and p^h are the prices to claims of output of the consumption good and housing services, and z^x and z^h are the quantity of such claims purchased. As a result of choices made at t, the wealth at $t+1$ when the state is s' is given by

$$w(s') = z^x(s)[\pi^x(s') + p^x(s')] + z^h(s)[\pi^h(s') + p^h(s')] + r(s')K + \Gamma(s'),$$

where rK is the rental income from the agent's capital endowment, and Γ is the lump-sum transfer of revenues to the individual.

a) Using the first-order conditions for the consumer's optimum, derive an expression for the rental rate on housing, $R(s)$.
b) Using a diagram, describe the production possibilities frontier for this economy, and show that, in equilibrium, the consumer will choose more housing services in the high-tax state, and less consumption of the background good, namely,

$$h(\tau) > h(0), \quad \text{and} \quad x(0) > x(\tau).$$

c) Using this result and the monotonicity of the capital requirements functions K^x and K^h, show that the rental rate on capital will be lower in the high-tax state, namely, $r(0) > r(\tau)$, and that profits in the consumption goods sector will also be lower in that state, namely, $\pi^x(0) > \pi^x(\tau)$.

d) Let the probability of each tax state be such that $P_{i,j} = P$ for $i, j = 0, \tau$. Show that

$$p^x(0) = \frac{\beta\pi^x(0)[P - \beta(2P - 1)] + \beta\pi^x(\tau)\lambda(1 - P)}{(1 - \beta)(1 + \beta - 2P\beta)},$$

$$p^x(\tau) = \frac{\beta\lambda^{-1}\pi^x(0)(1 - P) + \beta\pi^x(\tau)[P - \beta(2P - 1)]}{(1 - \beta)(1 + \beta - 2P\beta)},$$

where $\lambda = U_x(\tau)/U_x(0)$. We also have that

$$p^h(0) = \frac{\beta R(0)[P - \beta(2P - 1)] + \beta R(\tau)\lambda(1 - P)}{(1 - \beta)(1 + \beta - 2P\beta)},$$

$$p^h(\tau) = \frac{\beta\lambda^{-1}R(0)(1 - P) + \beta R(\tau)[P - \beta(2P - 1)]}{(1 - \beta)(1 + \beta - 2P\beta)}.$$

e) Show that

$$p^h(0) > p^h(\tau) \quad \text{and} \quad p^x(0) > p^x(\tau).$$

PART V

Supplementary material

CHAPTER A

Mathematical appendix

The notation conventions that we follow are standard. For example, we let $\Re$ denote the real line. For any positive integer n, $\Re^n$ denotes the set of n-tuples of the form $(x_1, \ldots, x_n)$ with x_i in $\Re$ for all i. For any n-tuple $(x_1, \ldots, x_n)$ with x_i in X for all i, the conventions for inequalities are: (i) $x \geq 0$ means that x is non-negative; for x in $\Re^n$, this is equivalent to $x \in \Re^n_+$; (ii) $x > 0$ means that x is non-negative and not zero but not necessarily strictly positive in all coordinates; (iii) $x \gg 0$ means that X is strictly positive in all coordinates. For x in $\Re^n$, this is equivalent to $x \in \Re^n_{++}$. With these conventions, a function f defined on $\Re^n$ is increasing if $f(x) \geq f(y)$ whenever $x \geq y$ and strictly increasing if $f(x) > f(y)$ whenever $x > y$.

A.1 STOCHASTIC PROCESSES

The basic building block of our analysis is the notion of a stochastic process. A *stochastic procees* is a collecton of random variables $\{X(t), t \in \mathcal{T}\}$. The set $\mathcal{T}$ is known as the *index set* of the process. An important case is when $\mathcal{T} = \{0, \pm 1, \pm 2, \ldots\}$ or $\mathcal{T} = \{0, 1, 2, \ldots\}$. For these cases, we obtain what is known as *discrete time* stochastic processes.

When studying stochastic processes, we introduce the notions of a sample space, events, and a probability function. The *sample space* Ω is the space of all possible outcomes for the random phenomena described by the stochastic process. An *event* is a set of sample observations. For technical reasons, we consider the set of events that belong to the set $\mathcal{F}$, where $\mathcal{F}$ has the following properties:

A. $\Omega \in \mathcal{F}$.

B. If $E \in \mathcal{F}$, then the complement of E denoted $E^c \in \mathcal{F}$.

C. IF $E_1, E_2, \ldots$ belongs to $\mathcal{F}$, then their union also belongs to $\mathcal{F}$, $\cup_{i=1}^{\infty} E_i \in \mathcal{F}$.

To complete the description of random phenomena, we define a probability function $P[\cdot]$ on the family $\mathcal{F}$ of random events. More precisely, for each $E \in \mathcal{F}$, one can define a number $P[E]$ which is called the probability that the event E will occur. Put differently, $P[E]$ represents the probability that an observed outcome of the random phenomena is an element of E.

The function $P[\cdot]$ satisfies the following properties:

(i) $P[E] \geq 0$ for every event E.

(ii) $P[\Omega] = 1$ for the certain event Ω.

(iii) For any sequence of events $E_1, E_2, \ldots$ which are mutually exclusive, that is, $E_j E_K = \emptyset$ where $\emptyset$ denotes the impossible event, we have

$$P\left[\cup_{i=1}^{\infty} E_i\right] = \sum_{i=1}^{\infty} P[E_i]. \tag{A.1.1}$$

In many applications, it often suffices to take the *smallest* family of subsets of the sample space Ω that satisfies properties A.–C. above. For example, if Ω denotes the real line, one adopts as the family of events the family $\mathcal{B}$ of Borel sets, where $\mathcal{B}$ is defined as the smallest family of sets of real numbers that possess properties A.–C. and in addition, contains as members all intervals. (An *interval* is a set of real numbers of the form $\{x : a < x < b\}$, $\{x : a < x \leq b\}$, $\{x : a \leq x < b\}$, $\{x : a \leq x \leq b\}$, where a and b may be finite or infinite numbers.)

An object X is said to be a *random variable* if (i) it is a real finite-valued function on sample Ω on whose family $\mathcal{F}$ of events a probability function $P[\cdot]$ has been defined; (ii) for every Borel set B of real numbers the set $\{\omega : X(\omega) \text{ is in } B\}$ is an event in $\mathcal{F}$.

The *probability function* of a random variable X denoted $P_X[\cdot]$ is a function defined for every Borel set B of real numbers by

$$P_X[B] = P\left[\omega : X(\omega) \text{ is in } B\right] = P[X \text{ is in } B]. \tag{A.1.2}$$

In words, $P_X[B]$ is the probability that an observed value of X is in B.

Two random variables X and Y are said to be *identically distributed* if their probability functions are equal; that is, $P_X[B] = P_Y[B]$ for all Borel sets B.

We can derive the distribution function $F_X(\cdot)$ for any random variable X for any number x as

$$F_X(x) = P[X \leq x]. \tag{A.1.3}$$

A random variable X is said to be *discrete* if there exists a function called the *probability mass function* of X and denoted by $p_X(\cdot)$ which satisfies

$$P_X[B] = P[X \text{ is in } B] = \sum_{x \in B \text{ s.t. } p_X(x) > 0} p_X(x). \tag{A.1.4}$$

Thus, for any real number x, we have that $p_X(x) = P[X = x]$.

A random variable X is said to be *continuous* if there exists a function called the *probability density function* of X and denoted by $f_X(\cdot)$ such that

$$P_X[B] = P[X \text{ is in } B] = \int_B f_X(x)dx. \tag{A.1.5}$$

Since

$$F_X(x) = \int_{-\infty}^{x} f_X(x')dx', \quad -\infty < x < \infty, \tag{A.1.6}$$

it follows that

$$f_X(x) = \frac{d}{dx}F_X(x) \tag{A.1.7}$$

for all real numbers x at which the derivative exists.

We return to the issue of describing the probability law for a stochastic process. One plausible way of describing a stochastic process $\{X(t), t \in \mathcal{T}\}$ defined on an infinite index set $\mathcal{T}$ is to specify the joint probability law of the n random variables $X(t_1), X(t_1), \ldots, X(t_n)$ for all integers n and n points $t_1, t_2, \ldots, t_n \in \mathcal{T}$. To specify the joint probability law of the n random variables $X(t_1), X(t_1), \ldots, X(t_n)$ we can specify the joint distribution function for all real numbers $x_1, \ldots, x_n$ as

$$F_{X(t_1),X(t_2),\ldots,X(t_n)}(x_1, x_2, \ldots, x_n)$$
$$= P[X(t_1) \leq x_1, X(t_2) \leq x_2, \ldots, X(t_n) \leq x_n]. \tag{A.1.8}$$

Let $\{X(t), t \in \mathcal{T}\}$ be a stochastic process with finite second moments. The *mean value function*, denoted $m(t)$, is defined for $t \in \mathcal{T}$ by

$$m(t) = E[X(t)], \tag{A.1.9}$$

and its *covariance kernel* denoted by $K(s, t)$ is defined for all s and t in $\mathcal{T}$ by

$$K(s, t) = Cov[X(s), X(t)]. \tag{A.1.10}$$

Recall that for random variables obeying the normal distribution, knowledge about the mean and variance yields complete knowledge about all the probabilities describing the random variable. In the general case when the functional form of the probability law of the random variable is unknown, the mean and variance still serve to summarize partially the underlying probability law.

We now turn to the issue of *stationary* versus *non-stationary (or evolutionary)* stochastic processes. Intuitively, a stationary stochastic process is one whose distribution remains the same throughout time because the underlying random mechanism generating the process does not change over time.

A stochastic process $\{X(t), t \in \mathcal{T}\}$ whose index set $\mathcal{T}$ is linear is said to be

1. (i) *strictly stationary of order k* where k is a given positive integer if for any k points $t_1, t_2, \ldots, t_k \in \mathcal{T}$ and for any $h \in \mathcal{T}$, the k-dimensional random vectors

$$(X(t_1), \ldots, X(t_k)) \quad \text{and} \quad (X(t_1 + h), \ldots, X(t_k + h))$$

are identically distributed;
2. (ii) *strictly stationary* if for any integer k it is strictly stationary of order k.

There is another concept of stationarity called covariance stationarity, which is much easier to develop theoretically and which suffices for many applications. This is stated as follows.

A stochastic process $\{X(t), t \in \mathcal{T}\}$ is said to be *covariance stationary* if it possesses finite second moments, if its index set $\mathcal{T}$ is linear, and if its covariance kernel $K(s, t)$ is a function only of the absolute difference $|s-t|$ in the sense that there exists a function $R(\cdot)$ such that for all s and t in $\mathcal{T}$

$$K(s, t) = R(s - t), \tag{A.1.11}$$

or more generally, $R(\nu)$ has the property that for t and $t + \nu$ in $\mathcal{T}$

$$Cov[X(t), X(t + \nu)] = R(\nu). \tag{A.1.12}$$

We call $R(\nu)$ the covariance function of the covariance stationary time series $\{X(t), t \in \mathcal{T}\}$.

We say that $\{X(t)\}$ is a *Gaussian* process if the set of random variables $(X(t_1), \ldots, X(t_n))'$ has a multivariate normal distribution. Since the multivariate normal distribution is completely specified by its mean and variance-covariance matrix, if $\{X(t)\}$ is covariance stationary, then it is strictly stationary. When $X(t)$ is a p-dimensional vector of random variables, $\{X(t)\}$ is called a *multivariate stochastic process.* Such multivariate processes allow us to examine relationships among different series. In addition to requiring each series to be stationary, we require that the collection of p series are *jointly stationary*; that is, for each i, j, $\text{Cov}(X_i(t), X_j(s))$ is a function of only the absolute difference $|t - s|$.

A process that has found uses in the applications that we consider here is the *log-normal* process. We say that that the random variable X is log-normally distributed, denoted $X \sim LN(\mu, \sigma^2)$, if

$$f(x) = \frac{1}{\sqrt{2\pi}\sigma x} \exp\left(-\frac{(\ln(x) - \mu)^2}{2\sigma^2}\right), \quad x > 0. \tag{A.1.13}$$

We have that $E[X] = \exp(\mu + \sigma^2/2)$ and $Var[X] = \exp(2\mu + \sigma^2)(\exp(\sigma^2) - 1)$. A useful result is as follows. Since the normal distribution is preserved under linear transformations,

$$\text{if } Y \sim LN[\mu, \sigma^2], \text{ then } \ln(Y^r) \sim N[r\mu, r^2\sigma^2], \tag{A.1.14}$$

for r integer.

A.2 SOME USEFUL THEOREMS

Many applications in economics make use of the properties of continuity and differentiability of the functions characterizing utility, production, etc. In this section, we provide a set of theorems that makes use of these properties.

Theorem A.1 *(Intermediate Value Theorem) Let $A = [a, b]$ be an interval in $\Re$ and let $f : A \to \Re$ be a continuous function. If $f(a) < f(b)$ and if c is a real number such that $f(a) < c < f(b)$, then there exists an $x \in (a, b)$ such that $f(x) = c$. A similar statement holds if $f(a) > f(b)$.*

In general, a function that is differentiable everywhere need not be continuously differentiable. Nevertheless, the derivative still possesses some minimal continuity properties.

Theorem A.2 *(Intermediate Value Theorem for the Derivative) Let $A = [a, b]$ be an interval in $\Re$ and let $f : A \to \Re$ be a function that is differentiable everywhere on A. If $f'(a) < f'(b)$ and c is a real number such that $f'(a), c < f'(b)$, then there is a point $x \in (a, b)$ such that $f'(x) = c$. A similar statement holds if $f'(a) > f'(b)$.*

We also have the following theorem regarding the derivative of an everywhere differentiable function.

Theorem A.3 *(Mean Value Theorem) Let $A = [a, b]$ and let $f : A \to \Re$ be a continuous function. Suppose is f is differentiable on (a, b). Then there exists $x \in (a, b)$ such that*

$$f(b) - f(a) = (b - a)f'(x).$$

Suppose that a function f is at least k-times differentiable, and denote the kth derivative of f evaluated at the point z as $f^{(k)}(z)$. The following theorem which is a generalization of the Mean Value Theorem states that a many-times differentiable function can be approximated by a polynomial.

Theorem A.4 *(Taylor's Theorem) Let $f : A \to \Re$ be a continuously differentiable function of order m, where A is an open interval in $\Re$, and $m \geq 0$ is* *a non-negative integer. Suppose also that $f^{m+1}(z)$ exists for every point $z \in A$. Then for any $z, y \in A$, there is a $z \in (x, y)$ such that*

$$f(y) = \sum_{k=0}^{m} \left(\frac{f^{(k)}(x)(y-x)^k}{k!} \right) + \frac{f^{m+1}(z)(y-x)^{m+1}}{(m+1)!}.$$

In many applications, we are interested in finding the solution to a system of equations that are defined implicitly in terms of a set of variables x and parameters θ. The following is useful for this purpose.

Theorem A.5 *(Implicit Function Theorem)*

Let $x = (x_1, \ldots, x_N)'$ and $\theta = (\theta_1, \ldots, \theta_M)'$, and suppose that there are N equations of the form

$$f_i(x_1, \ldots, x_N; \theta_1, \ldots, \theta_M) = 0, \quad i = 1, \ldots, N.$$

Suppose that every equation $f_i(\cdot)$ is continuously differentiable with respect to its $N + M$ arguments and we consider a solution $\bar{x} = (\bar{x}_1, \ldots, \bar{x}_N)'$ at the parameters $\bar{\theta} = (\bar{\theta}_1, \ldots, \bar{\theta}_M)'$ satisfying $f_i(\bar{x}; \bar{\theta}) = 0$ for all i. Define the Jacobian matrix of the system of equations with respect to the variables x as:

$$D_x f(x, \theta) = \begin{bmatrix} \frac{\partial f_1(\bar{x};\bar{\theta})}{\partial x_1} & \frac{\partial f_1(\bar{x};\bar{\theta})}{\partial x_2} & \cdots & \frac{\partial f_1(\bar{x};\bar{\theta})}{\partial x_N} \\ \frac{\partial f_2(\bar{x};\bar{\theta})}{\partial x_1} & \frac{\partial f_2(\bar{x};\bar{\theta})}{\partial x_2} & \cdots & \frac{\partial f_2(\bar{x};\bar{\theta})}{\partial x_N} \\ \vdots & \vdots & \vdots & \vdots \\ \frac{\partial f_N(\bar{x};\bar{\theta})}{\partial x_1} & \frac{\partial f_N(\bar{x};\bar{\theta})}{\partial x_2} & \cdots & \frac{\partial f_N(\bar{x};\bar{\theta})}{\partial x_N} \end{bmatrix}.$$

If the Jacobean matrix evaluated at $(\bar{x}, \bar{\theta})$ is non-singular, then the system can be solved locally at $(\bar{x}, \bar{\theta})$ by implicitly defined functions $g_i : \Re^M \to \Re^N$ that are continuously differentiable. Furthermore, the first-order effects of θ on x at $(\bar{x}, \bar{\theta})$ can be obtained as:

$$D_\theta g(\bar{\theta}) = -[D_x f(\bar{x}; \bar{\theta})]^{-1} D_\theta f(\bar{x}; \bar{\theta}).$$

The special case of the implicit function theorem occurs where $M = N$ and every equation has the form

$$f_n(x, \theta) = g_n(x) - \theta_n = 0.$$

This is known as the *inverse function theorem.*

In many applications, we are often interested in the properties of a maximized function and the feasible set characterizing optimal intertemporal choices. The following results are useful for this purpose.

We begin by defining the idea of a *correspondence* from some X into a set Y. This is a relation which assigns a set $\Gamma(x) \subseteq Y$ to each $x \in X$. There are several notions of continuity for correspondences.

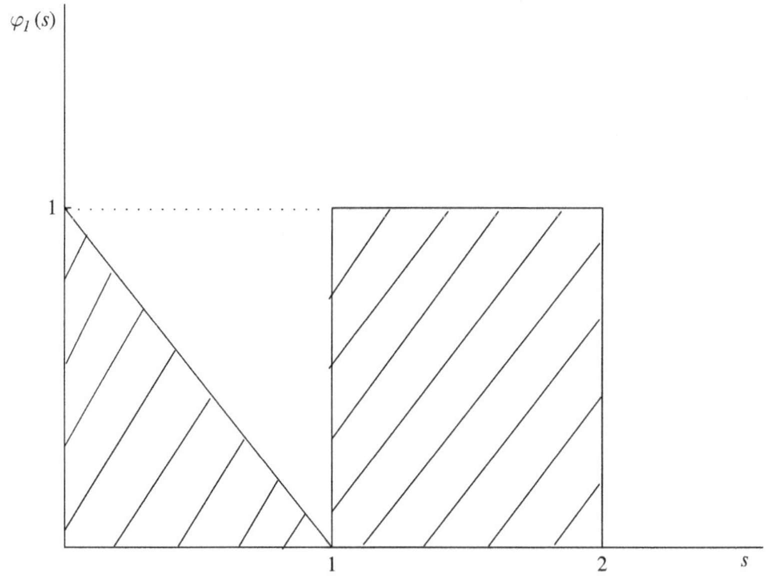

Figure A.1. An upper hemi-continuous correspondence

Definition A.1 *A correspondence $\Gamma : X \to Y$ is upper hemi-continuous (u.h.c) at x if $\Gamma(x)$ is non-empty and if, for every sequence $x_n \to x$ and every sequence $\{y_n\}$ such that $y_n \in \Gamma(x_n)$, for all n, there exists a convergent subsequence of $\{y_n\}$ whose limit point is in $\Gamma(x)$.*

To consider an example, let $S = [0, 2]$ and define the correspondence $\varphi_1 : S \to 2^{[0,1]}$ where $2^{[0,1]}$ denotes all the subsets of $[0, 1]$.

$$\varphi_1(s) = \begin{cases} [0, 1 - s] & \textit{if} \;\; s \in [0, 1) \\ [0, 1] & \textit{if} \;\; s \in [1, 2]. \end{cases}$$

Then $\varphi_1(s)$ is upper hemi-continuous but it is not lower hemi-continuous.

Definition A.2 *A correspondence $\Gamma : X \to Y$ is lower hemi-continuous (l.h.c) at x if $\Gamma(x)$ is non-empty and if, for every $y \in \Gamma(x)$ and every sequence $x_n \to x$, there exists $N \geq 1$ and a sequence $\{y_n\}_{n=N}^{\infty}$ such that $y_n \to y$ and $y_n \in \Gamma(x_n)$, for all $n \geq N$.*

Now define $\varphi_2 : S \to 2^{[0,1]}$ by

$$\varphi_2(s) = \begin{cases} [0, 1 - s] & \textit{if} \;\; s \in [0, 1] \\ [0, 1] & \textit{if} \;\; s \in (1, 2]. \end{cases}$$

Then $\varphi_2(s)$ is lower hemi-continuous but it is not upper hemi-continuous.

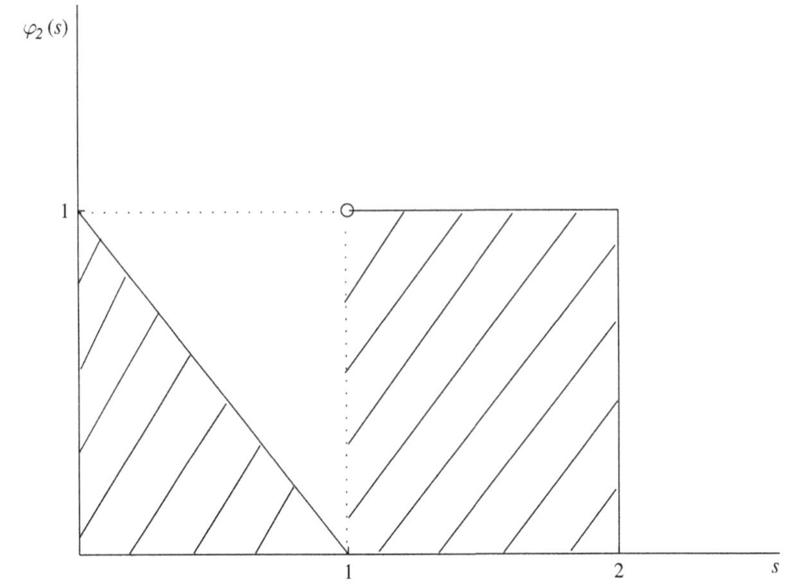

Figure A.2. A lower hemi-continuous correspondence

Definition A.3 *A correspondence $\Gamma : X \to Y$ is called continuous at $x \in X$ if it is both u.h.c. and l.h.c. at x.*

Let $X \subseteq \Re^l$, let $Y \subseteq \Re^m$, let $f : X \times Y \to \Re$ be a single-valued function, and let $\Gamma : X \to Y$ be a non-empty, possibly multivalued correspondence. In many applications that we will consider in this book, we are interested in analyzing the properties of a problem of the following sort: $\sup_{y \in \Gamma(x)} f(x, y)$. If, as we typically assume, $f(x, \cdot)$ is continuous in y and the set $\Gamma(x)$ is non-empty and compact, then for each x the maximum will be attained. In this case, the function

$$h(x) = \max_{y \in \Gamma(x)} f(x, y) \tag{A.2.15}$$

is well defined, as is the non-empty set

$$G(x) = \{y \in \Gamma(x) : f(x, y) = h(x)\} \tag{A.2.16}$$

which denotes the set of values y that attains the maximum.

The following theorem allows us to analyze the conditions under which the function $h(x)$ and the set $G(x)$ vary continuously with x.

Theorem A.6 *(Theorem of the Maximum) Let $X \subseteq \Re^l$, let $Y \subseteq \Re^m$, let $f : X \times Y \to \Re$ be a continuous function, and let $\Gamma : X \to Y$ be a compact-valued and continuous correspondence. Then the function $h : X \to \Re$ is* *continuous and the correspondence $G : X \rightarrow Y$ is non-empty, compact-valued, and u.h.c.*

We can also use the concepts of continuity of functions and correspondences to provide examples of two fixed theorems that are used in many applications in economics.

Theorem A.7 *(Brouwer's Fixed Point Theorem)*
Suppose $X \in \Re^N$ is a non-empty, closed and bounded (compact), convex set, and that $f : X \rightarrow X$ is a continuous function from X onto itself. Then $f(\cdot)$ has a fixed point; that is, there is an $x \in X$ such that $f(x) = x$.

As an example, consider the case with $N = 1$ and $X = [0, 1]$. In this case, the theorem says that the graph of any continuous function from the interval $[0, 1]$ into itself must cross the 45-degree line at least once. This result can be obtained as an application of the *intermediate value theorem* as follows. For this purpose, define the continuous function $\psi(x) = f(x) - x$. Then $\psi(0) \geq 0$ and $\psi(1) \leq 0$ and so $\psi(x) = 0$ for some $x \in [0, 1]$, which implies that $f(x) = x$ for some $x \in [0, 1]$.

A generalization of the Brouwer's Fixed Point Theorem is provided next.

Theorem A.8 *(Kakutani Fixed Point Theorem)*
Suppose $X \in \Re^N$ is a non-empty, compact, convex set, and $\varphi(x)$ is a correspondence relating points in X to closed, convex subsets of X. Then assuming $\varphi(x)$ is upper semi-continuous, there exists at least one point $x^\star \in X$ which belongs to the set into which it is mapped by φ:

$$x^\star \in \varphi(x^\star),$$

and $x^\star$ is a fixed point of φ.

Bibliography

[1] Abel, A. (1980). "Empirical Investment Equations." *Carnegie-Rochester Conference Series on Public Policy* **12**, 39–91.

[2] Abel, A. (1988). "Stock Prices Under Time-Varying Dividend Risk: An Exact Solution in an Infinite-Horizon General Equilibrium Model." *Journal of Monetary Economics* **22**, 375–393.

[3] Abel, A. (1990). "Asset Prices under Habit Formation and Catching Up with the Joneses." *A.E.R. Papers and Proceedings* **80**, 38–42.

[4] Abel, A. and O. Blanchard (1983). "An Intertemporal Model of Saving and Investment." *Econometrica* **51**, 675–692.

[5] Abel, A. and O. Blanchard (1986). "The Present Value of Profits and Cyclical Movements in Investment." *Econometrica* **54**, 249–273.

[6] Abel, A. and J. Eberly (1996). "Optimal Investment with Costly Reversibility." *Review of Economic Studies* **63**, 581–593.

[7] Abel, A., N. G. Mankiw, L. H. Summers, and R. J. Zeckhauser (1989). "Assessing Dynamic Efficiency." *Review of Economic Studies* **56**, 1–20.

[8] Adler, M. and B. Lehman (1983). "Deviations from Purchasing Power Parity in the Long Run." *Journal of Finance* **38**, 1471–1487.

[9] Ahmed, S. and R. Murthy (1994). "Money, Output, and Real Business Cycles in a Small Open Economy." *Canadian Journal of Economics* **27**, 982–993.

[10] Aiyagari, R. (1994). "Uninsured Idiosyncratic Risk and Aggregate Saving." *Quarterly Journal of Economics* **109**, 659–684.

[11] Aiyagari, R. and M. Gertler (1991). "Asset Returns with Transactions Costs and Uninsured Individual Risk." *Journal of Monetary Economics* **27**, 311–331.

[12] Aiyagari, R. and D. Peled (1991). "Dominant Root Characterization of Pareto Optimality and the Existence of Optimal Equilibria in Stochastic Overlapping Generations Models." *Journal of Economic Theory* **54**, 69–83.

[13] Akdeniz, L. and D. Dechert (2007). "The Equity Premium in Brock's Asset Pricing Model." *Journal of Economic Dynamics and Control* **31**, 2263–2292.

[14] Allais, M. (1953). "Le Comportement de L'Homme Rational devant le Risque, Critique des Postulates et Axiomes de l'Ecole Americaine." *Econometrica* **21**, 503–546.

[15] Altonji, J., F. Hayashi, and L. Kotlikoff (1997). *Understanding Saving: Evidence from the United States and Japan*. Cambridge and London: MIT Press, 241–285.

[16] Altug, S. (1989). "Time-to-Build and Aggregate Fluctuations: Some New Evidence." *International Economic Review* **30**, 889–920.

[17] Altug, S. (1993). "Time-to-Build, Delivery Lags, and the Equilibrium Pricing of Capital Goods." *Journal of Money, Credit, and Banking* **25**, 301–319.

[18] Altug, S. and R. Miller (1990). "Household Choices in Equilibrium." *Econometrica* **58**, 543–570.

[19] Altug, S. and R. Miller (1998). "The Effect of Work Experience on Female Wages and Labour Supply." *Review of Economic Studies* **65**, 45–85.

[20] Altug, S., F. S. Demers, and M. Demers (1999). "Cost Uncertainty, Taxation, and Irreversible Investment." In A. Alkan, C. Aliprantis, and N. Yannelis (eds.), *Current Trends in Economics: Theory and Applications.* Springer-Verlag *Studies in Economic Theory*, **8**, 41–72.

[21] Altug, S., F. S. Demers, and M. Demers (2004). "Tax Policy and Irreversible Investment." Centre for Dynamic Macroeconomic Analysis (CDMA) Working Paper 2004/4.

[22] Altug, S., F. S. Demers, and M. Demers (2007). "Political Risk and Irreversible Investment." *CESifo Economic Studies* **53**, 430–465.

[23] Altug, S. and I. Demirci (2007). "A Two Sector Model of Irreversible Investment," Manuscript.

[24] Alvarez, F. and U. Jermann (2000). "Efficiency, Equilibrium, and Asset Pricing with Risk of Default." *Econometrica* **68**, 775–797.

[25] Alvarez, F., A. Atkeson, and Kehoe, P. (2002). "Money, Interest Rates, and Exchange Rates with Endogenously Segmented Asset Markets." *Journal of Political Economy* **110**, 73–112.

[26] Alvarez. F., R. Lucas, and W. Weber (2001)."Interest Rates and Inflation." *American Economic Review* **91**, 219–225.

[27] Amihud, Y. and H. Mendelson (1986). "Asset Pricing and the Bid–Ask Spread." *Journal of Financial Economics* **17**, 223–249.

[28] Amihud, Y. and H. Mendelson (1990). "Dealership Market: Market-Making with Inventory." *Journal of Financial Economics* **8**, 31–53.

[29] Amihud, Y. and H. Mendelson (1991). "Liquidity, Maturity, and the Yields on U.S. Treasury Securities." *Journal of Finance* **46**, 1411–1425.

[30] Anderson, E., L. Hansen, E. McGrattan, and T. Sargent (1996). "Mechanics of Forming and Estimating Dynamic Linear Economies," In H. Amman, D. Kendrick, and J. Rust (eds.) *Handbook of Computational Economics Vol. 1.* Amsterdam: Elsevier Science, North-Holland, 171–252.

[31] Arrow, K. (1953). "Le Rôle des Valeurs Boursières pour la Répartition la Meilleure des Risques." *Económétrie*, pp. 41–48, Centre National de la Recherche Scientifique, Paris. Translated as: (1964) "The Role of Securities in the Optimal Allocation of Risk-Bearing." *Review of Economic Studies* **31**, 91–96.

[32] Arrow, K. (1964). "Comment on 'The Portfolio Approach to the Demand for Money and Other Assets' " by J. Duesenberry, *Review of Economics and Statistics* **45**, 24–27.

[33] Arrow, K. and G. Debreu (1954). "Existence of an Equilibrium for a Competitive Economy." *Econometrica* **22**, 265–290.

[34] Artis, M. and W. Zhang (1999). "Further Evidence on the International Business Cycle and the ERM: Is There a European Business Cycle?" *Oxford Economic Papers* **51**, 120–132.

[35] Artis, M., Z. Kontolemis, and D. Osborn (1997). "Business Cycles for G7 and European Countries." *Journal of Business* **70**, 249–279.

[36] Atkeson, A. and R. Lucas (1992). "On Efficient Distribution with Private Information." *Review of Economic Studies* **59**, 427–454.

[37] Atkinson, K. (1989). *An Introduction to Numerical Analysis,* 2nd ed. New York, NY: John Wiley and Sons.

[38] Azariadis, C. (1993). *Intertemporal Macroeconomics.* Cambridge, MA: Blackwell Press.

[39] Backus, D. and P. Kehoe (1992). "International Evidence on the Historical Perspective of Business Cycles." *American Economic Review* **82**, 864–888.

[40] Backus, D., P. Kehoe, and F. Kydland (1992). "International Real Business Cycles." *Journal of Political Economy* **100**, 745–775.

[41] Backus, D., A. Gregory, and S. Zin (1989). "Risk Premiums in the Term Structure: Evidence from Artificial Economies." *Journal of Monetary Economics* **24**, 371–399.

[42] Backus, D., B. Routledge, and S. Zin (2004). "Exotic Preferences for Macroeconomists." NBER Working Paper 10597.

[43] Baillie, R. and T. Bollerslev (1989). "The Message in Daily Exchange Rates: A Conditional Variance Tale." *Journal of Business and Economic Statistics* **7**, 297–305.

[44] Bansal, R. and W. Coleman (1996). "A Monetary Explanation of the Equity Premium, Term Premium, and Risk-Free Rate Puzzles." *Journal of Political Economy* **104**, 1135–1171.

[45] Barro, R. (1987). "Government Spending, Interest Rates, Prices and Budget Deficits in the United Kingdom, 1701–1918." *Journal of Monetary Economics* **20**, 221–247.

[46] Barsky, R. (1989). "Why Don't Prices of Stocks and Bonds Move Together?" *American Economic Review* **79**, 1132–1145.

[47] Basu, S. (1996). "Procyclical Productivity: Increasing Returns or Cyclical Utilization?" *Quarterly Journal of Economics* **111**, 719–751.

[48] Basu, S. and A. Taylor (1999). "Business Cycles in International Historical Perspective." *Journal of Economic Perspectives* **13**, 45–68.

[49] Basu, S., J. Fernald, and M. Kimball (2006). "Are Technology Improvements Contractionary?" *American Economic Review* **96**, 1418–1448.

[50] Baxter, M. and U. Jermann (1997). "The International Diversification Puzzle is Worse Than You Think." *American Economic Review* **87**, 170–180.

[51] Baxter, M. and R. King (1994). "Measuring Business Cycles: Approximate Band-pass Filters for Economic Time Series." *The Review of Economics and Statistics* **81**, 575–593.

[52] Becker, R. (1985). "Capital Income Taxation and Perfect Foresight." *Journal of Public Economics* **26**, 147–167.

[53] Benhabib, J. and R. Farmer (1996). "Indeterminacy and Sector-Specific Externalities." *Journal of Monetary Economics* **37**, 421–443.

[54] Benhabib, J., R. Rogerson, and R. Wright (1991). "Homework in Macroeconomics: Household Production and Aggregate Fluctuations." *Journal of Political Economy* **99**, 1166–1187.

[55] Benninga, S. and A. Protopapadakis (1991). "The Stock Market Premium, Production, and Relative Risk Aversion." *American Economic Review* **81**, 591–599.

[56] Benveniste, L. and J. Scheinkman (1979). "On the Differentiability of the Value Function in Dynamic Models of Economics." *Econometrica* **47**, 727–732.

[57] Bernanke, B. (1983). "Irreversibility, Uncertainty and Cyclical Investment." *Quarterly Journal of Economics* **98**, 85–106.

[58] Bernanke, B. and M. Gertler (1989). "Agency Costs, Net Worth and Business Fluctuations." *American Economic Review* **79**, 14–31.

[59] Bertocchi, G. (1994). "Safe Debt, Risky Capital." *Economica* **61**, 493–508.

[60] Bertocchi, G. and A. Kehagias (1995). "Efficiency and Optimality in Stochastic Models with Production." *Journal of Economic Dynamics and Control* **19**, 303–326.

[61] Bertola, G. and R. Caballero (1994). "Irreversibility and Aggregate Investment." *Review of Economic Studies* **61**, 223–246.

[62] Bertsekas, D. (1976). *Dynamic Programming and Stochastic Control.* New York, NY: Academic Press.

[63] Bertsekas, D. and S. Shreve (1978). *Stochastic Optimal Control: The Discrete Time Case.* New York, NY: Academic Press.

[64] Bewley, T. (1977). "The Permanent Income Hypothesis: A Theoretical Formulation." *Journal of Economic Theory* **16**, 252–292.

[65] Bhattacharya, S. (1979). "Imperfect Information, Dividend Policy, and 'The Bird in the Hand' Fallacy." *Bell Journal of Economics* **10**, 259–270.

[66] Bizer, D. and K. Judd (1989). "Taxation and Uncertainty." *American Economic Review* **79**, 331–336.

[67] Blackwell, D. (1965). "Discounted Dynamic Programming." *Annals of Mathematical Statistics* **36**, 226–235.

[68] Blanchard, O. and C. Kahn (1980). "The Solution of Linear Difference Models under Rational Expectations." *Econometrica* **48**, 1305–1311.

[69] Blanchard, O. and D. Quah (1989). "The Dynamic Effects of Demand versus Supply Disturbances." *American Economic Review* **79**, 654–673.

[70] Blundell, R., S. Bond, M. Devereux, and F. Schiantarelli (1992). "Investment and Tobin's *Q*: Evidence from Company Panel Data." *Journal of Econometrics* **51**, 233–257.

[71] Boyd, John H. III (1990). "Recursive Utility and the Ramsey Problem." *Journal of Economic Theory* **50**, 326–345.

[72] Braun, R. A. (1994). "How Large is the Optimal Inflation Tax?" *Journal of Monetary Economics* **34**, 201–214.

[73] Braun, P. A., G. M. Constantinides, and W. E. Ferson (1993). "Time Nonseparability in Aggregate Consumption: International Evidence." *European Economic Review* **37**, 897–920.

[74] Breeden, D. (1979). "An Intertemporal Asset Pricing Model with Stochastic Consumption and Investment Opportunities." *Journal of Financial Economics* **7**, 265–296.

[75] Brennan, M. J. and E. Schwartz (1985). "Evaluating Natural Resource Investments." *Journal of Business* **58**, 135–157.

[76] Brock, W. (1979). "An Integration of Stochastic Growth Theory and the Theory of Finance, Part I: The Growth Model." In J. Green and J. Scheinkman (eds.), *General Equilibrium, Growth, and Trade*. New York, NY: Academic Press, 165–192.

[77] Brock, W. (1982). "Asset Prices in a Production Economy." In J. McCall (ed.), *The Economics of Information and Uncertainty*. Chicago, IL: University of Chicago Press, 1–43.

[78] Brock, W. and L. Mirman (1972). "Optimal Economic Growth and Uncertainty: The Discounted Case." *Journal of Economic Theory* **4**, 479–513.

[79] Brock, W. and L. Mirman (1973). "Optimal Economic Growth and Uncertainty: The No Discounting Case." *International Economic Review* **14**, 560–573.

[80] Brock, W. and S. Turnovsky (1981). "The Analysis of Macroeconomic Policies in Perfect Foresight Equilibrium." *International Economic Review* **22**, 179–209.

[81] Brown, D. (1988). "Implications of Nonmarketable Income for Consumption-Based Models of Asset Pricing." *Journal of Finance* **43**, 867–880.

[82] Brown, D. and M. Gibbons (1985). "A Simple Econometric Approach for Utility-Based Asset Pricing Models." *Journal of Finance* **40**, 359–381.

[83] Burns, A. and W. Mitchell (1946). *Measuring Business Cycles*. New York: NBER.

[84] Burnside, C., M. Eichenbaum, and S. Rebelo (1993). "Labor Hoarding and the Business Cycle." *Journal of Political Economy* **101**, 245–274.

[85] Caballero, R. (1999). "Aggregate Investment." In J. Taylor and M. Woodford (eds.), *Handbook of Macroeconomics* **1B**, North Holland: Elsevier Science, chapter 12.

[86] Calvo, G. (1983). "Staggered Contracts and Exchange Rate Policy." In J. Frenkel (ed.), *Exchange Rates and International Macroeconomics*. Chicago, IL: University of Chicago Press, 235–252.

[87] Calvo, G. and C. Rodriguez (1977). "A Model of Exchange Rate Determination Under Currency Substitution and Rational Expectations." *Journal of Political Economy* **85**, 617–625.

[88] Campbell, J. (1986). "Bond and Stock Returns in a Simple Exchange Model." *Quarterly Journal of Economics* **101**, 785–803.

[89] Campbell, J. (1994). "Inspecting the Mechanism: An Analytical Approach to the Stochastic Growth Model." *Journal of Monetary Economics* **33**, 463–506.

[90] Campbell, J. (1999). "Asset Prices, Consumption, and the Business Cycle." In J. Taylor and M. Woodford (eds.), *Handbook of Macroeconomics* 1. Amsterdam: Elsevier.

[91] Campbell, J. and R. Clarida (1987a). "The Dollar and Real Interest Rates." *Carnegie-Rochester Conference Series on Public Policy* **27**, 103–139.

[92] Campbell, J. and R. Clarida (1987b). "The Term Structure of Euromarket Interest Rates: An Empirical Investigation." *Journal of Monetary Economics* **19**, 25–44.

[93] Campbell, J. and J. Cochrane (1999). "By Force of Habit: A Consumption-based Explanation of Aggregate Stock Market Behavior." *Journal of Political Economy* **107**, 205–251.

[94] Campbell, J. and N. Mankiw (1987). "Are Output Fluctuations Transitory?" *Quarterly Journal of Economics* **102**, 857–880.

[95] Campbell, J. and R. Shiller (1987). "Cointegration and Tests of Present Value Models." *Journal of Political Economy* **95**, 1062–1088.

[96] Campbell, J. and R. Shiller (1988). "The Dividend-Price Ratio and Expectations of Future Dividends and Discount Factors." *Review of Financial Studies* **1**, 175–228.

[97] Campbell, J. and R. Shiller (1991). "Yield Spreads and Interest Rate Movements: A Bird's Eye View." *Review of Economic Studies* **58**, 495–514.

[98] Canova, F. (2006). *Methods for Applied Macroeconomic Analysis*. Princeton, NJ: Princeton University Press.

[99] Cass, D. (1965). "Optimum Growth in an Aggregative Model of Capital Accumulation." *Review of Economic Studies* **32**, 233–240.

[100] Chamberlain, G. and M. Rothschild (1983). "Arbitrage, Factor Structure, and Mean-Variance Analysis on Large Asset Markets." *Econometrica* **51**, 1281–1304.

[101] Chamley, C. and H. Polemarcharkis (1984). "Assets, General Equilibrium, and the Neutrality of Money." *Review of Economic Studies* **51**, 129–138.

[102] Chew, S. (1983). "A Generalization of the Quasi-Linear Mean with Applications to the Measurement of Inequality and Decision Theory Resolving the Allais Paradox." *Econometrica* **51**, 1065–1092.

[103] Christiano, L. (1988). "Why Does Inventory Investment Fluctuate So Much?" *Journal of Monetary Economics* **21**, 247–280.

[104] Christiano, L. and M. Eichenbaum (1992). "Current Real-Business Cycle Theories and Aggregate Labor Market Fluctuations." *American Economic Review* **82**, 430–450.

[105] Christiano, L., M. Eichenbaum and C. Evans (1997). "Sticky Price and Limited Participation Models of Money: A Comparison." *European Economic Review* **41**, 1201–1249.

[106] Christiano, L., M. Eichenbaum, and R. Vigfusson (2003). "What Happens After a Technology Shock?" NBER Working Paper 9819.

[107] Cochrane, J. (1991). "Production-based Asset Pricing and the Link between Stock Returns and Economic Fluctuations." *Journal of Finance* **46**, 209–237.

[108] Cochrane, J. (1991). "A Simple Test of Consumption Insurance." *Journal of Political Economy* **99**, 957–976.

[109] Cochrane, J. (2000). *Asset Pricing*. Princeton, NJ: Princeton University press.

[110] Cochrane, J. and L. Hansen (1992). "Asset Pricing Explorations in Macroeconomics." *NBER Macroeconomics Annual 1992*, 115–165.

[111] Cole, H. (1998). "Financial Structure and International Trade." *International Economic Review* **29**, 237–259.

[112] Cole, H. and M. Obstfeld (1991). "Commodity Trade and International Risk Sharing." *Journal of Monetary Economics* **28**, 3–24.

[113] Coleman, W. (1991). "Equilibrium in a Production Economy with an Income Tax." *Econometrica* **59**, 1091–1104.
[114] Coleman, W., C. Gilles, and P. Labadie (1992). "The Liquidity Premium in Average Interest Rates." *Journal of Monetary Economics* **30**, 449–465.
[115] Connor, G. (1984). "A Unified Beta Pricing Theory." *Journal of Economic Theory* **34**, 13–31.
[116] Constantinides, G. (1982). "Intertemporal Asset Pricing with Heterogeneous Consumers and Without Demand Aggregation." *Journal of Business* **55**, 253–267.
[117] Constantinides, G. (1986). "Capital Market Equilibrium with Transaction Costs." *Journal of Political Economy* **94**, 842–862.
[118] Constantinides, G. (1990). "Habit Formation: A Resolution of the Equity Premium Puzzle." *Journal of Political Economy* **98**, 519–543.
[119] Constantinides, G. and D. Duffie (1996). "Asset Pricing with Heterogeneous Consumers." *Journal of Political Economy* **104**, 219–240.
[120] Cooley, T. and G. Hansen (1989). "The Inflation Tax in a Real Business Cycle Model." *American Economic Review* **79**, 733–748.
[121] Cooley, T. and G. Hansen (1991). "The Welfare Costs of Moderate Inflations." *Journal of Money, Credit, and Banking* **23**, 483–503.
[122] Cooley, T. and G. Hansen (1992). "Tax Distortions in a Neoclassical Monetary Model." *Journal of Economic Theory* **58**, 290–316.
[123] Cooley, T. and G. Hansen (1994). "Money and the Business Cycle." In T. Cooley (ed.), *Frontiers of Business Cycle Analysis*. Princeton, NJ: Princeton University Press.
[124] Cooley, T. and E. Prescott (1994). "Economic Growth and Business Cycles," In T. Cooley (ed.), *Frontiers of Business Cycle Analysis*. Princeton, NJ: Princeton University Press.
[125] Cooley, T. and K. Salyer (1987). "The Effects of Inflation-Induced Tax Increases on Stock and Housing Prices." *Scandinavian Journal of Economics* **89**, 421–434.
[126] Copeland, T. and D. Galai (1983). "Information Effects on the Bid–Ask Spread." *Journal of Finance* **38**, 1457–1469.
[127] Copeland, T. and F. Weston (1992). *Financial Theory and Corporate Policy*, (3rd edition), Reading, MA: Addison-Wesley.
[128] Cox, J., J. Ingersoll, and S. Ross (1985). "A Theory of the Term Structure of Interest Rates." *Econometrica* **53**, 385–407.
[129] Cox, J., S. Ross, and M. Rubinstein (1979). "Options Pricing." *Journal of Financial Economics* **7**, 229–263.
[130] Cukierman, A. (1980). "The Effects of Uncertainty on Investment under Risk Neutrality with Endogenous Information." *Journal of Political Economy* **88**, 462–475.
[131] Cumby, R. and M. Obstfeld (1984). "International Interest-Rate and Price-Level Linkages Under Flexible Exchange Rates: A Review of Recent Evidence." In J. Bilson and R. Marston (eds.), *Exchange Rate Theory and Practice*. Chicago, IL: University of Chicago Press for the National Bureau of Economic Research.
[132] Danthine, J.-P. and J. Donaldson (1981). "Stochastic Properties of Fast vs. Slow Growing Economies." *Econometrica* **49**, 1007–1033.

[133] Danthine, J.-P. and J. Donaldson (1985). "A Note on the Effects of Capital Income Taxation on the Dynamics of a Recursive Economy." *Journal of Public Economics* **28**, 255–265.

[134] Danthine, J.-P. and J. Donaldson (1995). "Computing Equilibria in Nonoptimal Economies." In Thomas F. Cooley (ed.), *The Frontiers of Business Cycle Research*. Princeton, NJ: Princeton University Press.

[135] Danthine, J.-P., J. Donaldson, and R. Mehra (1983). "On the Impact of Shock Persistence on the Dynamics of a Recursive Economy." *European Economic Review* **21**, 147–166.

[136] Danthine, J.-P., J. Donaldson, and R. Mehra (1989). "On Some Computational Aspects of Equilibrium Business Cycle Theory." *Journal of Economic Dynamics and Control* **13**, 449–470.

[137] Danthine, J.-P., J. Donaldson, and R. Mehra (1992). "The Equity Premium and the Allocation of Income Risk." *Journal of Economic Dynamics and Control* **16**, 509–532.

[138] Deaton, A. (1992). "Saving and Liquidity Constraints." *Econometrica* **59**, 1221–1248.

[139] Deaton, A. and G. Laroque (1992). "On the Behavior of Commodity Prices." *Review of Economic Studies* **59**, 1–24.

[140] Deaton, A. and C. Paxson (1994). "Intertemporal Choice and Inequality." *Journal of Political Economy* **102**, 437–467.

[141] Debreu, G. (1954). "Valuation Equilibrium and Pareto Optimum." *Proceedings of the National Academy of Sciences*, **40**, 588–592.

[142] Debreu, G. (1959). *Theory of Value*. New Haven, CT: Yale University Press.

[143] DeGroot, M. (1970). *Optimal Statistical Decisions*. New York: McGraw-Hill.

[144] Dekel, E. (1986). "An Axiomatic Characterization of Preferences Under Uncertainty: Weakening the Independence Axiom." *Journal of Economic Theory* **40**, 304–318.

[145] De Long, J., A. Schleifer, L. Summers, and R. Waldman (1989). "The Size and Incidence of the Losses From Noise Trading." *Journal of Finance* **44**, 681–696.

[146] Demange, G. (2002). "On Optimality of Intergenerational Risk Sharing." *Economic Theory* **20**, 1–27.

[147] Demange, G. and G. Laroque (1999). "Social Security and Demographic Shocks." *Econometrica* **67**, 527–542.

[148] Demers, M. (1991). "Investment Under Uncertainty: Irreversibility and the Arrival of Information Over Time." *Review of Economic Studies* **58**, 333–350.

[149] Demers, F. S., M. Demers, and S. Altug (2003). "Investment Dynamics." In S. Altug, J. Chadha, and C. Nolan (eds.), *Dynamic Macroeconomic Analysis: Theory and Policy in General Equilibrium*. Cambridge, UK: Cambridge University Press.

[150] den Haan, W. J. (1995). "The Term Structure of Interest Rates in Real and Monetary Economies." *Journal of Economic Dynamics and Control* **19**, 909–940.

[151] Denison, E. (1985). *Trends in American Economic Growth, 1929–1982*, Washington DC: Brookings.

[152] Diamond, P. (1965). "National Debt in the Neoclassical Growth Model." *American Economic Review* **55**, 1126–1150.

[153] Diamond, P. and J. Stiglitz (1974). "Increases in Risk and in Risk Aversion." *Journal of Economic Theory* **8**, 337–360.

[154] Dixit, A. K. and R. S. Pindyck (1994). *Investment Under Uncertainty.* Princeton, NJ: Princeton University Press.

[155] Donaldson, J. and R. Mehra (1983). "Stochastic Growth with Correlated Production Shocks." *Journal of Economic Theory* **29**, 282–312.

[156] Donaldson, J. and R. Mehra (1984). "Comparative Dynamics of an Equilibrium Intertemporal Asset-Pricing Model." *Review of Economic Studies* **51**, 491–508.

[157] Dornbusch, R. (1976). "Expectations and Exchange Rate Dynamics." *Journal of Political Economy* **84**, 1161–1176.

[158] Dotsey, M. (1990). "The Economic Effects of Production Taxes in a Stochastic Growth Model." *American Economic Review* **80**, 1168–1182.

[159] Duffie, D. (1988). *Security Markets: Stochastic Models.* Boston, MA: Academic Press.

[160] Duffie, D. (1989). *Futures Markets.* Englewood Cliffs, NJ: Prentice-Hall.

[161] Duffie, D. (1992). *Dynamic Asset Pricing Theory.* Princeton, NJ: Princeton University Press.

[162] Duffie, D. and T. Sun (1990). "Transactions Costs and Portfolio Choice in a Discrete-Continuous-Time Setting." *Journal of Economic Dynamics and Control* **14**, 35–51.

[163] Dumas, B. and E. Luciano (1991). "An Exact Solution to a Dynamic Portfolio Choice Problem Under Transactions Costs." *Journal of Finance* **46**, 577–595.

[164] Dunn, K. and K. Singleton (1986). "Modeling the Term Structure of Interest Rates Under Non-Separable Utility and Durability of Goods." *Journal of Financial Economics* **17**, 27–55.

[165] Dybvig, P. and J. Ingersoll (1982). "Mean-Variance Theory in Complete Markets." *Journal of Business* **55**, 233–251.

[166] Dybvig, P. and S. Ross (1985). "Yes, the APT is Testable." *Journal of Finance* **40**, 1173–1188.

[167] Easley, D. and M. O'Hara (1987). "Price, Trade Size and Information in Securities Markets." *Journal of Financial Economics* **19**, 69–90.

[168] Eichenbaum, M. and L. Christiano (1990). "Unit Roots in Real GNP: Do We Know and Do We Care?" *Carnegie-Rochester Conference Series on Public Policy* **32**, 7–62.

[169] Eichenbaum, M. and L. Hansen (1990). "Estimating Models with Intertemporal Substitution Using Aggregate Time Series Data." *Journal of Business and Economic Statistics* **8**, 53–69.

[170] Eichenbaum, M. and K. Singleton (1986). "Do Equilibrium Real Business Cycle Theories Explain Postwar U.S. Business Cycles?" *NBER Macroeconomics Annual 1986*, 91–135.

[171] Eichenbaum, M., L. Hansen, and K. Singleton (1988). "A Time Series Analysis of Representative Agent Models of Consumption and Leisure Choice Under Uncertainty." *Quarterly Journal of Economics* **103**, 51–78.

[172] Engel, C. (1992). "The Risk Premium and the Liquidity Premium in Foreign Exchange Markets." *International Economic Review* **33**, 871–879.

[173] Engle, R. and C. Granger (1987). "Co-integration and Error Correction: Representation, Estimation and Testing." *Econometrica* **55**, 251–276.

[174] Epps, T. and M. Epps (1976). "The Stochastic Dependence of Security Price Changes and Transaction Volumes: Implications for the Mixture-of-Distributions Hypothesis." *Econometrica* **44**, 305–321.

[175] Epstein, L. and S. Zin (1989). "Substitution, Risk Aversion, and the Temporal Behavior of Consumption and Asset Returns: A Theoretical Framework." *Econometrica* **57**, 937–969.

[176] Epstein, L. and S. Zin (1990). "First-Order Risk Aversion and the Equity Premium Puzzle." *Journal of Monetary Economics* **26**, 387–407.

[177] Epstein, L. and S. Zin (1991). "Substitution, Risk Aversion, and the Temporal Behavior of Consumption and Asset Returns: An Empirical Analysis." *Journal of Political Economy* **99**, 263–286.

[178] Fama, E. (1965). "The Behavior of Stock Market Prices." *Journal of Business* **38**, 34–105.

[179] Fama, E. and R. Bliss (1987). "The Information in Long-Maturity Forward Rates." *American Economic Review* **77**, 680–692.

[180] Fama, E. and K. French (1988). "Permanent and Temporary Components of Stock Prices." *Journal of Political Economy* **96**, 246–273.

[181] Fama, E. and G. Schwert (1977). "Asset Returns and Inflation." *Journal of Financial Economics* **5**, 115–146.

[182] Feldman, M. and C. Gilles (1985). "An Expository Note on Individual Risk without Aggregate Uncertainty." *Journal of Economic Theory* **35**, 26–32.

[183] Ferson, W. and G. Constantinides (1991). "Habit Persistence and Durability in Aggregate Consumption." *Journal of Financial Economics* **29**, 199–240.

[184] Ferson, W. and C. Harvey (1992). "Seasonality and Consumption-Based Asset Pricing." *Journal of Finance* **47**, 511–552.

[185] Finn, M., D. Hoffman, and D. Schlagenhauf (1990). "Intertemporal Asset-Pricing Relationships in Barter and Monetary Economies: An Empirical Analysis." *Journal of Monetary Economics* **25**, 431–451.

[186] Fischer, S. (1975). "The Demand for Index Bonds." *Journal of Political Economy* **83**, 509–534.

[187] Flavin, M. (1981). "The Adjustment of Consumption to Changing Expectations About Future Income." *Journal of Political Economy* **89**, 974–1009.

[188] Flavin, M. (1983). "Excess Volatility in the Financial Markets: A Reassessment of the Empirical Evidence." *Journal of Political Economy* **91**, 929–956.

[189] Forni, M. and L. Reichlin (1998). "Let's Get Real: A Factor Analytical Approach to Disaggregated Business Cycle Dynamics." *Review of Economic Studies* **65**, 453–473.

[190] Friedman, M. (1956). *A Theory of the Consumption Function*. Princeton, NJ: Princeton University Press.

[191] Friedman, M. and A. Schwartz (1963). *A Monetary History of the United States, 1867–1960*. Princeton, NJ: Princeton University Press.

[192] Frisch, R. (1933). "Propagation Problems and Impulse Problems in Dynamic Economies." *Economic Essays in Honor of Gustav Cassel*. London: George Allen and Unwin.
[193] Galasso, V. and P. Profeta (2002). "The Political Economy of Social Security: A Survey." *European Journal of Political Economy* **18**, 1–29.
[194] Gale, D. (1995)."The Efficient Design of Public Debt." In F. Allen and D. Gale (eds.), *Financial Innovation and Risk Sharing*. Cambridge, MA: MIT Press.
[195] Gali, J. (1999). "Technology, Employment, and the Business Cycle: Do Technology Shocks Explain Aggregate Fluctuations?" *American Economic Review* **89**, 249–271.
[196] Gali, J. and P. Rabanal (2005). "Technology Shocks and Aggregate Fluctuations: How Well Does the RBC Model Fit Postwar US Data?" In M. Gertler and K. Rogoff (eds.), *NBER Macroeconomics Annual 2004*. Cambridge, MA: MIT Press.
[197] Geweke, J. (1977). "The Dynamic Factor Analysis of Economic Time Series Models." In D. Aigner and A. Goldberger (eds.), *Latent Variables in Socioeconomic Models*. Amsterdam: North-Holland, 365–383.
[198] Geweke, J. and K. Singleton (1981). "Maximum Likelihood 'Confirmatory' Analysis of Economic Time Series." *International Economic Review* **22**, 37–54.
[199] Ghysels, E. and A. Hall (1990). "Are Consumption-Based Intertemporal Asset-Pricing Models Structural?" *Journal of Econometrics* **45**, 121–139.
[200] Ghysels, E. and A. Hall (1990). "A Test for Structural Stability of Euler Conditions Parameters Estimated via the Generalized Method of Moments Estimator." *International Economic Review* **31**, 355–364.
[201] Giannone, D., L. Reichlin, and L. Sala (2006). "VAR's, Common Factors and the Empirical Validation of Equilibrium Business Cycle Models." *Journal of Econometrics* **132**, 257–279.
[202] Gilboa, I. and D. Schmeidler (1989). "Maxmin Expected Utility with Non-unique Priors." *Journal of Mathematical Economics* **18**, 141–153.
[203] Gilles, C. and S. LeRoy (1991). "Econometric Aspects of the Variance-Bounds Tests: A Survey." *Review of Financial Studies* **4**, 753–791.
[204] Giovannini, A. and P. Jorion (1987). "Interest Rates and Risk Premia in the Stock Market and in the Foreign Exchange Market." *Journal of International Money and Finance* **6**, 107–123.
[205] Giovannini, A. and P. Jorion (1989). "The Time Variation of Risk and Return in the Foreign Exchange and Stock Markets." *Journal of Finance* **44**, 307–325.
[206] Giovannini, A. and P. Labadie (1991). "Asset Prices and Interest Rates in Cash-in-Advance Models." *Journal of Political Economy* **99**, 1215–1251.
[207] Glosten, L. and L. Harris (1988). "Estimating the Components of the Bid/Ask Spread." *Journal of Financial Economics* **21**, 123–142.
[208] Glosten, L. and P. Milgrom (1985). "Bid, Ask and Transaction Prices in a Specialist Market with Heterogeneously Informed Traders." *Journal of Financial Economics* **14**, 71–100.
[209] Gorman, T. (1953). "Community Preference Fields." *Econometrica* **21**, 63–80.

[210] Gorman, T. (1980). "A Possible Procedure for Analyzing Quality Differentials in the Egg Market." *Review of Economic Studies* **47**, 843–846.

[211] Gould, J. (1968). "Adjustment Costs in the Theory of the Investment of the Firm." *Review of Economic Studies* **35**, 47–55.

[212] Granger, C. and P. Newbold (1986). *Forecasting Economic Time Series*, 2nd ed. San Diego, CA: Academic Press.

[213] Gregory, A. and G. Voss (1991). "The Term Structure of Interest Rates: Departures from Time-Separable Expected Utility." *Canadian Journal of Economics* **24**, 923–939.

[214] Greene, W. (1993). *Econometric Analysis*, 2nd ed. New York, NY: Macmillan.

[215] Greenwood, J. and S. Williamson (1989). "International Financial Intermediation and Aggregate Fluctuations Under Alternative Exchange Rate Regimes." *Journal of Monetary Economics* **23**, 401–431.

[216] Grilli, V. and G. Kaminsky (1991). "Nominal Exchange Rate Regimes and the Real Exchange Rate: Evidence from the United States and Great Britain, 1885–1986." *Journal of Monetary Economics* **27**, 191–212.

[217] Grossman, S. and G. Laroque (1990). "Asset Pricing and Optimal Portfolio Choice in the Presence of Illiquid Durable Consumption Goods." *Econometrica* **58**, 25–51.

[218] Grossman, S. and R. Shiller (1981). "The Determinants of the Variability of Stock Market Prices." *American Economic Review Proceedings* **71**, 222–227.

[219] Grossman, S. and J. Stiglitz (1980). "On the Impossibility of Informationally-Efficient Markets." *American Economic Review* **70**, 393–408.

[220] Grundfest, J. (1990). "The Damning Facts of a New Stocks Tax." *Wall Street Journal*, July 23.

[221] Grundfest, J. and J. Shoven (1991). "Adverse Implications of a Securities Transactions Excise Tax." *Journal of Accounting, Auditing and Finance* **6**, 409–442.

[222] Hall, R E. and D. W. Jorgenson (1967). "Tax Policy and Investment Behavior." *American Economic Review* **57**, 391–414.

[223] Hall, R. (1978). "Stochastic Implications of the Life Cycle–Permanent Income Hypothesis: Theory and Evidence." *Journal of Political Economy* **86**, 971–987.

[224] Hall, R. (1988). "The Relation Between Price and Marginal Cost in U.S. Industry." *Journal of Political Economy* **96**, 921–947.

[225] Hall, R. (1990). "Invariance Properties of Solow's Productivity Residual." In P. Diamond (ed.), *Growth/Productivity/Employment*. Cambridge, MA: MIT Press.

[226] Hall, Robert E. (2001). "The Stock Market and Capital Accumulation." *American Economic Review* **91**, 1185–1202.

[227] Hamilton, J. (1994). *Time Series Analysis*. Princeton, NJ: Princeton University Press.

[228] Hansen, G. (1985). "Indivisible Labor and the Business Cycle." *Journal of Monetary Economics* **16**, 309–327.

[229] Hansen, L. (1982). "Large Sample Properties of Generalized Method of Moments Estimators." *Econometrica* **50**, 1029–1054.

[230] Hansen, L. and R. Hodrick (1980). "Forward Exchange Rates as Optimal Predictors of Future Spot Rates: An Econometric Analysis." *Journal of Political Economy* **88**, 829–853.

[231] Hansen, L. and R. Hodrick (1983). "Risk Averse Speculation in the Forward Foreign Exchange Market: An Econometric Analysis of Linear Models." In J. Frenkel (ed.), *Exchange Rates and International Macroeconomics*. Chicago, IL: University of Chicago Press for the National Bureau of Economic Research, 113–152.

[232] Hansen, L. and R. Jagannathan (1991). "Implications of Security Market Data for Models of Dynamic Economies." *Journal of Political Economy* **99**, 225–262.

[233] Hansen, G. and E. Prescott (1995). "Recursive Methods for Computing Equilibria of Business Cycle Models." In T. Coooley (ed.), *Frontiers of Business Cycle Research*, Princeton, NJ: Princeton University Press.

[234] Hansen, L. and S. Richard (1987). "The Role of Conditioning Information in Deducing Testable Restrictions Implied by Dynamic Asset Pricing Models." *Econometrica* **55**, 587–614.

[235] Hansen, L. and T. Sargent (1980). "Formulating and Estimating Dynamic Linear Rational Expectations Models." *Journal of Economic Dynamics and Control* **2**, 7–46.

[236] Hansen, L. and T. Sargent (2005). *Recursive Linear Models for Dynamic Economies*, Princeton, NJ: Princeton University Press.

[237] Hansen, L. and K. Singleton (1982). "Generalized Instrumental Variables Estimation of Nonlinear Rational Expectations Models." *Econometrica* **50**, 1269–1286.

[238] Hansen, L. and K. Singleton (1983). "Stochastic Consumption, Risk Aversion and the Temporal Behavior of Asset Returns." *Journal of Political Economy* **91**, 249–265.

[239] Harris, M. (1987). *Dynamic Economic Analysis*. New York: Oxford University Press.

[240] Harrison, J. and D. Kreps (1979). "Martingales and Arbitrage in Multiperiod Securities Markets." *Journal of Economic Theory* **20**, 381–408.

[241] Hart, O. (1979). "On Shareholder Unanimity in Large Stock Market Economies." *Econometrica* **47**, 1057–1083.

[242] Harvey, A. (1981). *Time Series Models*. New York, NY: John Wiley and Sons.

[243] Hayashi, F. (1982). "Tobin's Marginal q and Average q: A Neoclassical Interpretation." *Econometrica* **50**, 213–224.

[244] Hayashi, F. (1985). "Tests for Liquidity Constraints: A Critical Survey and Some New Observations." In T. Bewley (ed.), *Advances in Econometrics: Fifth World Congress, Vol. 2*. Cambridge, UK: Cambridge University Press.

[245] Hayashi, F. and T. Inoue (1991). "The Relation Between Firm Growth and Q with Multiple Capital Goods: Theory and Evidence from Panel Data on Japanese Firms." *Econometrica* **59**, 731–753.

[246] He, H. and D. Modest (1995). "Market Frictions and Consumption-Based Asset Pricing." *Journal of Political Economy* **103**, 94–117.

[247] Heathcote, J. and F. Perri (2002). "Financial Autarky and International Business Cycles." *Journal of Monetary Economics* **49**, 601–627.

[248] Heathcote, J. and F. Perri (2004). "The International Diversification Puzzle is Not as Bad as You Think." Manuscript, August, Georgetown University.

[249] Heaton, J. and D. Lucas (1992). "The Effects of Incomplete Insurance Markets and Trading Costs in a Consumption-Based Asset Pricing Model." *Journal of Economic Dynamics and Control* **16**, 601–620.

[250] Heaton, J. and D. Lucas (1996). "Evaluating the Effects of Incomplete Markets on Risk Sharing and Asset Pricing." *Journal of Political Economy* **104**, 443–487.

[251] Helpman, E. and A. Razin (1984). "The Role of Saving and Investment in Exchange Rate Determination Under Alternative Monetary Mechanisms." *Journal of Monetary Economics* **13**, 307–325.

[252] Hodrick, R., N. Kocherlakota, and D. Lucas (1991). "The Variability of Velocity in Cash-in-Advance Models." *Journal of Political Economy* **99**, 358–384.

[253] Hotz, V., F. Kydland, and G. Sedlacek (1988). "Intertemporal Preferences and Labor Supply." *Econometrica* **56**, 335–360.

[254] Hsieh, D. (1984). "Tests of Rational Expectations and No Risk Premium in Forward Exchange Markets." *Journal of International Economics* **17**, 173–184.

[255] Hsieh, D. (1988). "The Statistical Properties of Daily Foreign Exchange Rates: 1974–1983." *Journal of International Economics* **24**, 129–145.

[256] Huang, C. and R. Litzenberger (1988). *Foundations of Financial Economics*. Amsterdam: North-Holland.

[257] Huggett, M. (1993). "The Risk-free Rate in Heterogeneous, Incomplete-Insurance Economies." *Journal of Economic Dynamics and Control* **17**, 953–969.

[258] Huizinga, J. (1987). "An Empirical Investigation of the Long-run Behavior of Real Exchange Rates." *Carnegie-Rochester Conference Series on Public Policy* **27**, 149–214.

[259] Hull, J. (1993). *Options, Futures, and Other Derivative Securities*, 2nd ed. Englewood Cliffs, NJ: Prentice-Hall.

[260] İmrohoroğlu, A., S. İmrohoroğlu, and D.H. Joines (2000). "Computational Models of Social Security: A Survey." *Cuadernos Economicos* **64**, 109–131.

[261] Ingersoll, J. (1987). *Theory of Financial Decision Making*. Totowa, NJ: Rowman & Littlefield Publishers.

[262] Jaffe, J. and G. Mandelker (1979). "Inflation and the Holding Period Returns on Bonds." *Journal of Financial and Quantitative Analysis* **14**, 959–979.

[263] Jarrow, R. (1988). *Finance Theory*. Englewood Cliffs, NJ: Prentice-Hall.

[264] Jermann, U. J. (1997). "Asset Pricing in Production Economies." *Journal of Monetary Economics* **41**, 257–275.

[265] Jensen, M. and W. Meckling (1976). "Theory of the Firm: Managerial Behavior, Agency Costs and Ownership Structure." *Journal of Financial Economics* **3**, 305–360.

[266] Jorgenson, D. W. (1963). "Capital Theory and Investment Behavior." *American Economic Review* **53**, 47–56.

[267] Judd, K. (1985). "Short-Run Analysis of Fiscal Policy in a Simple Perfect Foresight Model." *Journal of Political Economy* **93**, 298–319.

[268] Judd, K. (1987). "The Welfare Cost of Factor Taxation in a Simple Perfect-Foresight Model." *Journal of Political Economy* **95**, 675–709.

[269] Judd, K. (1998). *Numerical Methods in Economics.* Cambridge, MA: MIT Press.

[270] Kalemli-Ozcan, S., B. Sorensen, and O. Yosha (2002). "Risk Sharing and Industrial Specialization: Regional and International Evidence." *American Economic Review* **93**, 903–918.

[271] Kareken, J. and N. Wallace (1981). "On the Indeterminacy of Equilibrium Exchange Rates." *Quarterly Journal of Economics* **96**, 207–222.

[272] Kehoe, T. and D. Levine (1993). "Debt Constrained Asset Markets." *Review of Economic Studies* **60**, 865–888.

[273] Kehoe, T. and D. Levine (2001). "Liquidity Constrained Markets Versus Debt-Constrained Markets." *Econometrica* **69**, 575–598.

[274] Keynes, J. M. (1936). *The General Theory of Employment, Interest, and Money.* London: Macmillan.

[275] Kim, E. (1989). "Discussion: Optimal Capital Structure in Miller's Equilibrium." In S. Bhattacharya and G. Constantinides (eds.), *Financial Markets and Incomplete Information.* Totowa, NJ: Rowman and Littlefield Publishers.

[276] Kimball, M. S. (1990). "Precautionary Saving in the Small and in the Large." *Econometrica* **58**, 53–73.

[277] King, R. and C. Plosser (1984). "Money, Credit, and Prices in a Real Business Cycle Model." *American Economic Review* **74**, 363–380.

[278] Kiyotaki, N. and J. Moore (2002). "Evil is the Root of All Money." *American Economic Review* **92**, 62–66.

[279] Kiyotaki, N. and R. Wright (1989). "On Money as a Medium of Exchange." *Journal of Political Economy* **97**, 927–954.

[280] Kocherlakota, N. (1999). "Money is Memory." *Journal of Economic Theory* **81**, 232–251.

[281] Kogan, L. (2001). "An Equilibrium Model of Irreversible Investment." *Journal of Financial Economics* **62**, 201–245.

[282] Kogan, L. (2004). "Asset Prices and Real Investment." *Journal of Financial Economics* **73**, 411–431.

[283] Kondratiev, N. (1926). "Die Langen Wellen der Konjunktur [The Long Waves of the Business Cycle]." *Archiv fur Sozialwissenschaft und Socialpolitik* **56**, 573–606.

[284] Koopmans, T. (1960). "Stationary Ordinal Utility and Impatience." *Econometrica* **28**, 287–309.

[285] Koopmans, T. (1965). "On the Concept of Optimal Economic Growth." In Semaine d'Étude sur le rôle de l'analysis écono-métrique dans la formulation de plans de développement, 225–300, Pontificau Academiae Scientiarum Scropta Varia, No. 28, Vatican.

[286] Köse, A., C. Otrok, and C. Whiteman (2003). "International Business Cycles: World, Region, and Country-specific." *American Economic Review* **93**, 1216–1239.

[287] Kreps, D. (1981). "Arbitrage and Equilibrium in Economies with Infinitely Many Commodities." *Journal of Mathematical Economics* **8**, 15–35.

[288] Kreps, D. and E. Porteus (1978). "Temporal Resolution of Uncertainty and Dynamic Choice Theory." *Econometrica* **46**, 185–200.

[289] Kreps, D. and E. Porteus (1979). "Temporal von Neumann-Morgenstern and Induced Preferences." *Journal of Economic Theory* **20**, 81–109.

[290] Kreyszig, E. (1978). *Introductory Functional Analysis with Applications.* New York, NY: John Wiley and Sons.

[291] Krueger, D. and F. Kubler (2002). "Intergenerational Risk Sharing via Social Security when Markets are Incomplete." *American Economic Review* **92**, 407–410.

[292] Krueger, D. and H. Lustig (2006). "The Irrelevance of Market Incompleteness for the Price of Aggregate Risk." Manuscript.

[293] Krusell, P. and T. Smith (1997). "Income and Wealth Heterogeneity, Portfolio Selection, and Equilibrium Asset Returns." *Macroeconomic Dynamics* **1**, 387–422.

[294] Kupiec, P. (1991). "Noise Traders, Excess Volatility, and a Securities Transactions Tax." Unpublished. Fed. Working Paper No. 166, Board of Governors of the Federal Reserve System.

[295] Kupiec, P. (1995). "A Securities Transactions Tax and Capital Market Efficiency." *Contemporary Economic Policy* **13**, 101–112.

[296] Kydland, F. (1995). "Business Cycles and Aggregate Labor Market Fluctuations." In T. Cooley (ed.), *Frontiers of Business Cycle Research.* Princeton, NJ: Princeton University Press.

[297] Kydland, F. and E. Prescott (1982). "Time-to-Build and Aggregate Fluctuations." *Econometrica* **50**, 1345–1370.

[298] Labadie, P. (1986). "Comparative Dynamics and Risk Premia in an Overlapping Generations Model." *Review of Economic Studies* **53**, 139–152.

[299] Labadie, P. (1989). "Stochastic Inflation and the Equity Premium." *Journal of Monetary Economics* **24**, 277–298.

[300] Labadie, P. (1998). "Aggregate Fluctuations, Financial Constraints, and Risk Sharing." *Economic Theory* **12**, 621–648.

[301] Labadie, P. (2004). "Aggregate Risk Sharing and Equivalent Financial Mechanisms in an Endowment Economy of Incomplete Participation." *Economic Theory* **24**, 789–809.

[302] Labadie, P. (2006). "Aggregate Risk Sharing and Equivalent Financial Mechanisms in an Endowment Economy of Incomplete Participation." In Gabriel Camera (ed.), *Recent Developments on Money and Finance.* Berlin: Springer-Verlag, 127–148.

[303] Lancaster, K. (1966). "A New Approach to Consumer Theory." *Journal of Political Economy* **47**, 132–157.

[304] Leland, H. (1968). "Saving and Uncertainty: The Precautionary Demand for Saving." *Quarterly Journal of Economics* **82**, 465–473.

[305] LeRoy, S. and R. Porter (1981). "The Present-Value Relation: Tests Based on Implied Variance Bounds." *Econometrica* **49**, 555–574.

[306] LeRoy, S. and J. Werner (2001). *Principles of Financial Economics.* Cambridge, UK: Cambridge University Press.

[307] Lettau, M. (2002). "Idiosyncratic Risk and Volatility Bounds, or Can Models with Idiosyncratic Risk Solve the Equity Premium Puzzle?" *Review of Economics and Statistics* **84**, 376–380.

[308] Lettau, M. and H. Uhlig (2000). "Can Habit Persistence be Reconciled with Business Cycles Facts?" *Review of Economic Dynamics* **3**, 79–99.

[309] Levine, D. K. and W. R. Zame (2002). "Does Market Incompleteness Matter?" *Econometrica* **70**, 1805–1839.

[310] Lewis, K. (1996). "What Can Explain the Apparent Lack of International Consumption Risk Sharing?" *Journal of Political Economy* **104**, 267–297.

[311] Lintner, J. (1965). "The Valuation of Risky Assets and the Selection of Risky Investment in Stock Portfolios and Capital Budgets." *Review of Economics and Statistics* **47**, 13–37.

[312] Ljungqvist, L. and T. Sargent (2000). *Recursive Macroeconomic Theory.* Cambridge, MA: MIT Press.

[313] Ljungqvist, L. and H. Uhlig (2000). "Tax Policy and Aggregate Demand Management under Catching Up with the Joneses." *American Economic Review* **90**, 356–366.

[314] Long, J. and C. Plosser (1983). "Real Business Cycles." *Journal of Political Economy* **91**, 39–69.

[315] Lucas, R. (1967). "Adjustment Costs and the Theory of Supply." *Journal of Political Economy* **75**, 321–334.

[316] Lucas, R. (1972). "Expectations and the Neutrality of Money." *Journal of Economic Theory* **4**, 103–123.

[317] Lucas, R. (1975). "An Equilibrium Model of the Business Cycle." *Journal of Political Economy* **83**, 1113–1144.

[318] Lucas, R. (1977). "Understanding Business Cycles." In K. Brunner and A. Meltzer (eds.), *Stabilization of the Domestic and International Economy.* Amsterdam: North-Holland Publishing Company, 7–29.

[319] Lucas, R. (1978). "Asset Prices in an Exchange Economy." *Econometrica* **46**, 1429–1445.

[320] Lucas, R. (1982). "Interest Rates and Currency Prices in a Two-Country World." *Journal of Monetary Economics* **10**, 335–359.

[321] Lucas, R. (1984). "Money in a Theory of Finance." *Carnegie-Rochester Conference Series on Public Policy* **21**, 9–45.

[322] Lucas, R. (1988). "On the Mechanics of Economic Development." *Journal of Monetary Economics* **22**, 3–42.

[323] Lucas, R. (1990). "Liquidity and Interest Rates." *Journal of Economic Theory* **50**, 237–264.

[324] Lucas, R. and E. Prescott (1971). "Investment under Uncertainty." *Econometrica* **39**, 659–681.

[325] Lucas, R. and N. Stokey (1987). "Money and Interest in a Cash-in-Advance Economy." *Econometrica* **55**, 491–513.

[326] Luenberger, D. (1969). *Optimization by Vector Space Methods.* New York, NY: John Wiley and Sons.

[327] Luttmer, E. (1996). "Asset Pricing in Economies with Frictions." *Econometrica* **64**, 1439–1467.

[328] Mace, B. (1991). "Full Insurance in the Presence of Aggregate Uncertainty." *Journal of Political Economy* **99**, 928–956.

[329] Machina, M. (1987). "Choice under Uncertainty: Problems Solved and Unsolved." *Journal of Economic Perspectives* **1**, 121–154.

[330] Macklem, T. (1991). "Forward Exchange Rates and Risk Premiums in Artificial Economies." *Journal of International Money and Finance* **10**, 365–391.

[331] Mankiw, N. (1986). "The Equity Premium and the Concentration of Aggregate Shocks." *Journal of Financial Economics* **17**, 211–219.

[332] Mankiw, N., J. Rotemberg, and L. Summers (1985). "Intertemporal Substitution in Macroeconomics." *Quarterly Journal of Economics* **100**, 225–252.

[333] Manuelli, R. (1990). "Existence and Optimality of Currency Equilibrium in Stochastic Overlapping Generations Models: The Pure Endowment Case." *Journal of Economic Theory* **51**, 268–294.

[334] Mark, N. (1990). "Real and Nominal Exchange Rates in the Long Run: An Empirical Investigation." *Journal of International Economics* **28**, 115–136.

[335] Marshall, D. (1992). "Inflation and Asset Returns in a Monetary Economy." *Journal of Finance* **47**, 1315–1342.

[336] McCallum, B. (1986). "On 'Real' and 'Sticky-Price' Theories of the Business Cycle." *Journal of Money, Credit, and Banking* **18**, 397–414.

[337] McGrattan, E., R. Rogerson and R. Wright (1997). "An Equilibrium Model of the Business Cycle with Household Production and Fiscal Policy." *International Economic Review* **38**, 267–290.

[338] McKenzie, L. (1959). "On the Existence of General Equilibrium for a Competitive Economy." *Econometrica* **27**, 54–71.

[339] Mehra, R. (1988). "On the Existence and Representation of Equilibrium in an Economy with Growth and Nonstationary Consumption." *International Economic Review* **29**, 131–135.

[340] Mehra, R. and E. Prescott (1980). "Recursive Competitive Equilibrium: The Case of Homogeneous Households." *Econometrica* **48**, 1365–1379.

[341] Mehra, R. and E. Prescott (1985). "The Equity Premium: A Puzzle." *Journal of Monetary Economics* **15**, 145–161.

[342] Merton, R. (1973). "An Intertemporal Capital Asset-Pricing Model." *Econometrica* **41**, 867–887.

[343] Miller, M. (1977). "Debt and Taxes." *Journal of Finance* **32**, 261–275.

[344] Mirman, L. and I. Zilcha (1975). "On Optimal Growth Under Uncertainty." *Journal of Economic Theory* **11**, 329–339.

[345] Modigliani, F. and M. Miller (1958)."The Cost of Capital, Corporation Finance, and the Theory of Investment." *American Economic Review* **48**, 261–297.

[346] Monnet, C. and W. Weber (2001). "Money and Interest Rates." *Federal Reserve Bank of Minneapolis Quarterly Review*, Fall, **52**, 2–13.

[347] Muench, T. J. (1977)."Efficiency in a Monetary Economy." *Journal of Economic Theory* **15**, 325–344.

[348] Mussa, M. (1982). "A Model of Exchange Rate Dynamics." *Journal of Political Economy* **90**, 74–104.

[349] Mussa, M. (1986). "Nominal Exchange Rate Regimes and the Behavior of Real Exchange Rates: Evidence and Implications." *Carnegie-Rochester Conference Series on Public Policy* **25**, 117–213.

[350] Myers, S. (1977). "Determinants of Corporate Borrowing." *Journal of Financial Economics* **5**, 147–175.

[351] Naylor, A. and G. Sell (1982). *Linear Operator Theory in Engineering and Science*. New York, NY: Springer-Verlag.

[352] Nickell, S. J. (1977). "Uncertainty and Lags in the Investment Decisions of Firms." *Review of Economic Studies* **44**, 249–263.

[353] Nickell, S. J. (1978). *The Investment Decisions of Firms*. Cambridge, UK: Cambridge University Press.

[354] Obstfeld, M. and A. Stockman (1985). "Exchange-Rate Dynamics." In R. Jones and P. Kenen (eds.), *Handbook of International Economics, Vol. 2*. Amsterdam: North-Holland, 917–977.

[355] Obstfeld, M. and K. Rogoff (2000). "The Six Major Puzzles in International Macroeconomics: Is There a Common Cause?" *NBER Macroeconomics Annual* **15**, 339–390.

[356] Papoulis, A. (1984). *Probability, Random Variables, and Stochastic Processes*. New York, NY: McGraw-Hill.

[357] Peled, D. (1982). "Informational Diversity over Time and the Optimality of Monetary Equilibria." *Journal of Economic Theory* **28**, 255–274.

[358] Peled, D. (1984). "Stationary Pareto Optimality of Stochastic Asset Equilibria with Overlapping Generations." *Journal of Economic Theory* **34**, 396–403.

[359] Pemberton, J. (2003). "The Application of Stochastic Dynamic Programming Methods to Household Consumption and Savings Decisions: A Critical Survey." In S. Altug, J. Chadha, and C. Nolan (eds.), *Dynamic Macroeconomic Analysis: Theory and Policy in General Equilibrium*. Cambridge, UK: Cambridge University Press.

[360] Phelps, E. (1970). *Microeconomics Foundations of Employment and Inflation Theory*. New York, NY: W. W. Norton and Company.

[361] Pindyck, R. S. (1988). "Irreversible Investment, Capacity Choice and the Value of the Firm." *American Economic Review* **78**, 969–985.

[362] Pratt, J. (1964). "Risk Aversion in the Small and in the Large." *Econometrica* **32**, 122–136.

[363] Prescott, E. (1986). "Theory Ahead of Business Cycle Measurement." *Carnegie-Rochester Conference Series on Public Policy* **25**, 11–44.

[364] Radner, R. (1974). "A Note on Unanimity of Stockholders' Preferences Among Alternative Production Plans: A Reformulation of the Ekern-Wilson Model." *Bell Journal of Economics* **5**, 181–184.

[365] Rogerson, R. (1988). "Indivisible Labor, Lotteries and Equilibrium." *Journal of Monetary Economics* **21**, 3–16.

[366] Roll, R. (1977). "A Critique of the Asset-Pricing Theory's Tests. Part 1. On Past and Potential Testability of the Theory." *Journal of Financial Economics* **5**, 129–176.

[367] Roll, R. (1989). "Price Volatility, International Market Links, and Their Implications for Regulatory Policies." *Journal of Financial Services Research* **3**, 211–246.

[368] Romer, P. (1986). "Increasing Returns and Long-Run Growth." *Journal of Political Economy* **94**, 1002–1037.

[369] Ross, S. (1976). "The Arbitrage Theory of Capital Asset Pricing." *Journal of Economic Theory* **13**, 341–360.

[370] Ross, S. (1977). "The Determination of Financial Structure: The Incentive-Signalling Approach." *Bell Journal of Economics* **8**, 23–40.
[371] Ross, S. (1978). "A Simple Approach to the Valuation of Risky Streams." *Journal of Business* **51**, 453–475.
[372] Ross, S. (1989). "Using Tax Policy to Curb Speculative Short-Term Trading: Commentary." *Journal of Financial Services Research* **3**, 117–120.
[373] Rotemberg, J. and M. Woodford (1994). "Dynamic General Equilibrium Models of Imperfectly Competitive Product Markets." In T. Cooley (ed.), *Frontiers of Business Cycle Research*, Princeton, NJ: Princeton University Press.
[374] Rothschild, M. and J. Stiglitz (1970). "Increasing Risk I: A Definition." *Journal of Economic Theory* **2**, 225–243.
[375] Rothschild, M. and J. Stiglitz (1971). "Increasing Risk II: Its Economic Consequences." *Journal of Economic Theory* **3**, 66–84.
[376] Rothschild, M. and J. Stiglitz (1976). "Equilibrium in Competitive Insurance Markets: An Essay on the Economics of Imperfect Information." *Quarterly Journal of Economics* **90**, 630–649.
[377] Rubinstein, M. (1974). "An Aggregation Theorem for Securities Markets." *Journal of Financial Economics* **1**, 225–244.
[378] Rubinstein, M. (1976). "The Valuation of Uncertain Streams and the Price of Options." *Bell Journal of Economics* **7**, 407–425.
[379] Rubinstein, M. (1981). "A Discrete-Time Synthesis of Financial Theory." *Research in Finance* **3**, 53–102.
[380] Rubinstein, M. and J. Cox (1985). *Options Markets*. Englewood Cliffs, NJ: Prentice-Hall.
[381] Samuelson, P. (1958). "An Exact Consumption-Loan Model of Interest With or Without the Social Contrivance of Money." *Journal of Political Economy* **66**, 467–482.
[382] Sandmo, A. (1969). "Capital Risk, Consumption and Portfolio Choice." *Econometrica* **37**, 586–599.
[383] Sargent, T. (1980). "'Tobin's *q*' and the Rate of Investment in General Equilibrium." *Journal of Monetary Economics* **12** (Supplement), 107–154.
[384] Sargent, T. (1987). *Dynamic Macroeconomic Theory*. Cambridge, MA: Harvard University Press.
[385] Sargent, T. and C. Sims (1977). "Business Cycle Modeling Without Pretending to Have Too Much A Priori Economic Theory." In *New Methods in Business Cycle Research: Proceedings from a Conference*. Minneapolis, MN: Federal Reserve Bank of Minneapolis, 45–109.
[386] Savage, L. (1954). *The Foundations of Statistics*. New York, NY: Wiley.
[387] Shanken, J. (1982). "The Arbitrage Pricing Theory: Is It Testable?" *Journal of Finance* **37**, 1129–1140.
[388] Shanken, J. (1985). "Multi-Beta CAPM or Equilibrium APT? A Reply." *Journal of Finance* **40**, 1189–1196.
[389] Sharpe, W. F. (1964). "Capital Asset Prices: A Theory of Market Equilibrium Under Conditions of Risk." *Journal of Finance* **19**, 425–442.
[390] Shavell, S. (1979). "On Moral Hazard and Insurance." *Quarterly Journal of Economics* **93**, 541–562.

[391] Scheinkman, J. and L. Weiss (1986). "Borrowing Constraints and Aggregate Economic Activity." *Econometrica* **54**, 23–45.

[392] Shiller, R. (1981). "Do Stock Prices Move Too Much to be Justified by Subsequent Changes in Dividends?" *American Economic Review* **71**, 421–436.

[393] Schumpeter, J. (1934). *The Theory of Economic Growth*. Cambridge, MA: Harvard University Press.

[394] Schumpeter, J. (1939). *Business Cycles*. New York, NY: McGraw-Hill.

[395] Schwert, G. (1990). "Stock Market Volatility." *Financial Analysts Journal* **46**, 23–34.

[396] Schwert, G. and Seguin, R. (1993). "Securities Transaction Taxes: An Overview of Costs, Benefits and Unresolved Questions." Midamerica Institute Research Project, 175 W. Jackson Boulevard, Suite 1801, Chicago, Il. 60604.

[397] Shell, K. (1971). "Notes on the Economics of Infinity." *Journal of Political Economy* **79**, 1002–1011.

[398] Shiller, R. (1979). "The Volatility of Long-Term Interest Rates and Expectations Models of the Term Structure." *Journal of Political Economy* **87**, 1190–1219.

[399] Shiller, R. (1990). "The Term Structure of Interest Rates." In B. Friedman and F. Hahn (eds.), *Handbook of Monetary Economics, Vol. 1*. Amsterdam: Elsevier Science Publishers.

[400] Shiller, R., J. Campbell, and K. Schoenholtz (1983). "Forward Rates and Future Policy: Interpreting the Term Structure of Interest Rates." *Brookings Papers on Economic Activity* **1**, 173–217.

[401] Siegel, J. (1972). "Risk, Information, and Forward Exchange." *Quarterly Journal of Economics* **86**, 303–309.

[402] Sims, C. (1972). "Money, Income and Causality." *American Economic Review* **62**, 540–553.

[403] Sims, C. (1980). "Macroeconomics and Reality." *Econometrica* **48**, 1–48.

[404] Singleton, K. (1980). "Expectations Models of the Term Structure and Implied Variance Bounds." *Journal of Political Economy* **88**, 1159–1176.

[405] Singleton, K. (1985). "Testing Specifications of Economic Agents' Intertemporal Optimum Problems in the Presence of Alternative Models." *Journal of Econometrics* **30**, 391–413.

[406] Skinner, D. J. (1989). "Options Markets and Stock Return Volatility." *Journal of Financial Economics* **23**, 61–78.

[407] Slutsky, E. (1937). "The Summation of Random Causes as the Source of Cyclic Processes." *Econometrica* **5**, 105–146.

[408] Smets, F. and R. Wouters (2003). "An Estimated Dynamic Stochastic General Equilibrium Model of the Euro Area." *Journal of the European Economic Association* **1**, 1123–1175.

[409] Smets, F. and R. Wouters (2005). "Comparing Shocks and Frictions in US and Euro Area Business Cycles: A Bayesian DSGE Approach." *Journal of Applied Econometrics* **20**, 161–183.

[410] Solow, R. (1957). "Technical Change and the Aggregate Production Function." *Review of Economics and Statistics* **39**, 312–320.

[411] Stiglitz, J. (1989). "Using Tax Policy to Curb Speculative Short-Term Trading." *Journal of Financial Services Research* **3**, 101–115.

[412] Stock, J. (1990). "A Comment on 'Unit Roots in Real GNP: Do We Know and Do We Care?' " *Carnegie-Rochester Conference Series on Public Policy* **32**, 63–82.

[413] Stock, J. and M. Watson (2000). "Business Cycle Fluctuations in U.S. Macroeconomic Time Series." *Handbook of Macroeconomics* **1**, Amsterdam: Elsevier Science, North-Holland 1, 3–64.

[414] Stock, J. and M. Watson (2005). "Understanding Changes in International Business Cycle Dynamics." *Journal of European Economic Association* **5**, 968–1006.

[415] Stockman, A. (1980). "A Theory of Exchange Rate Determination." *Journal of Political Economy* **88**, 673–698.

[416] Stockman, A. and H. Dellas (1989). "International Portfolio Nondiversification and Exchange Rate Variability." *Journal of International Economics* **26**, 271–289.

[417] Stockman, A. and L. Svensson (1987). "Capital Flows, Investment, and Exchange Rates." *Journal of Monetary Economics* **19**, 171–201.

[418] Stokey, N. and R. Lucas, with E. Prescott (1989). *Recursive Methods in Economic Dynamics*. Cambridge, MA: Harvard University Press.

[419] Stoll, H. R. (1978). "The Supply of Dealer Services in Securities Markets." *Journal of Finance* **33**, 1133–1151.

[420] Stoll, H. R. (1989). "Inferring the Components of the Bid-Ask Spread: Theory and Empirical Tests." *Journal of Finance* **44**, 115–134.

[421] Stoll, H. and R. Whaley (1993). *Futures and Options: Theory and Applications*. Cincinnati, OH: South-Western Publishing.

[422] Storesletten, K., C. I. Telmer, and A. Yaron (1997). "The Welfare Cost of Business Cycles Revisited: Finite Lives and Cyclical Variation in Idiosyncratic Risk." *European Economic Review* **45**, 1311–1339.

[423] Strang, G. (1988). *Linear Algebra and Its Applications*. San Diego, CA: Harcourt, Brace and Jovanovich, Inc.

[424] Summers, L. (1986). "Some Skeptical Observations on Real Business Cycle Theory." *Federal Reserve Bank of Minneapolis Quarterly Review* **10**, 23–27.

[425] Summers, L. H. and V. P. Summers (1986). "When Financial Markets Work Too Well: A Cautious Case For a Securities Transactions Tax." *Journal of Financial Services Research* **3**, 261–286.

[426] Svensson, L. (1985a). "Currency Prices, Terms of Trade, and Interest Rates: A General Equilibrium Asset-Pricing, Cash-in-Advance Approach." *Journal of International Economics* **18**, 17–42.

[427] Svensson, L. (1985b). "Money and Asset Prices in a Cash-in-Advance Economy." *Journal of Political Economy* **93**, 919–944.

[428] Tauchen, G. (1986). "Finite State Markov-Chain Approximations to Univariate and Vector Autoregressions." *Economics Letters* **20**, 177–181.

[429] Telmer, C. (1993). "Asset Pricing Puzzles and Incomplete Markets." *Journal of Finance* **48**, 1803–1832.

[430] Tobin, J. (1969). "A General Equilibrium Approach to Monetary Policy." *Journal of Money, Credit, and Banking* **1**, 15–29.

[431] Townsend, R. (1980). "Models of Money with Spatially Separated Agents." In J. Kareken and N. Wallace (eds.), *Models of Monetary Economics*. Federal Reserve Bank of Minneapolis.

[432] Townsend. R. (1994). "Risk and Insurance in Village India." *Econometrica* **62**, 539–591.

[433] Treadway, A. (1969). "On Rational Entrepreneurial Behavior and the Demand for Investment." *Review of Economic Studies* **36**, 227–239.

[434] Turnbull, S. and F. Milne (1991). "A Simple Approach to Interest-Rate Option Pricing." *Review of Financial Studies* **4**, 87–120.

[435] Uhlig, H. (1997). "A Toolkit for Analyzing Non-linear Dynamic Stochastic Model Easily." http://www2.wiwi.hu-berlin.de/institute/wpol/html/toolkit.htm

[436] Umlauf, S. (1993). "Transactions Taxes and Stock Market Behavior: The Swedish Experience." *Journal of Financial Economics* **33**, 227–240.

[437] Vasicek, O. (1977). "An Equilibrium Characterization of the Term Structure." *Journal of Financial Economics* **5**, 177–188.

[438] Vayanos, D. and J. Vila (1993). "Equilibrium Interest Rate and Liquidity Premium Under Proportional Transactions Costs." Unpublished. Working Paper, MIT.

[439] von Neumann, J. and O. Morgenstern (1947). *Theory of Games and Economic Behavior*. Princeton, NJ: Princeton University Press.

[440] Wallace, N. (1980). "The Overlapping Generations Model of Fiat Money." In J. Kareken and N. Wallace (eds.), *Models of Monetary Economics*. Federal Reserve Bank of Minneapolis.

[441] Wallace, N. (1981). "A Modigliani-Miller Theory for Open-Market Operations." *American Economic Review* **71**, 267–274.

[442] Wallace, N. (1998) "Introduction to Modeling Money and Studying Monetary Policy." *Journal of Economic Theory* **81**, 223–231.

[443] Watson, M. (1993). "Measures of Fit for Calibrated Models." *Journal of Political Economy* **101**, 1011–1041.

[444] Weil, P. (1989). "The Equity Premium Puzzle and the Riskfree Rate Puzzle." *Journal of Monetary Economics* **24**, 401–421.

[445] Weil, P. (1990). "Nonexpected Utility in Macroeconomics." *Quarterly Journal of Economics* **105**, 29–42.

[446] Weil, P. (1992). "Equilibrium Asset Prices with Undiversifiable Labor Income Risk." *Journal of Economic Dynamics and Control* **16**, 769–790.

[447] Weiss, L. (1980). "The Effects of Money Supply on Economic Welfare in the Steady State." *Econometrica* **48**, 565–576.

[448] West, K. (1988). "Dividend Innovations and Stock Price Volatility." *Econometrica* **56**, 37–61.

[449] Wilson, R. (1968). "The Theory of Syndicates." *Econometrica* **36**, 119–132.

[450] Wright, R. (1987). "Market Structure and Competitive Equilibrium in Dynamic Economic Models." *Journal of Economic Theory* **41**, 189–201.

[451] Zarnowitz, V. (1992). *Business Cycles: Theory, History, Indicators, and Forecasting*. Chicago, IL: The University of Chicago Press.

[452] Zeldes, S. (1989). "Consumption and Liquidity Constraints: An Empirical Investigation." *Journal of Political Economy* **97**, 305–346.

Index

Printed in the United States
By Bookmasters